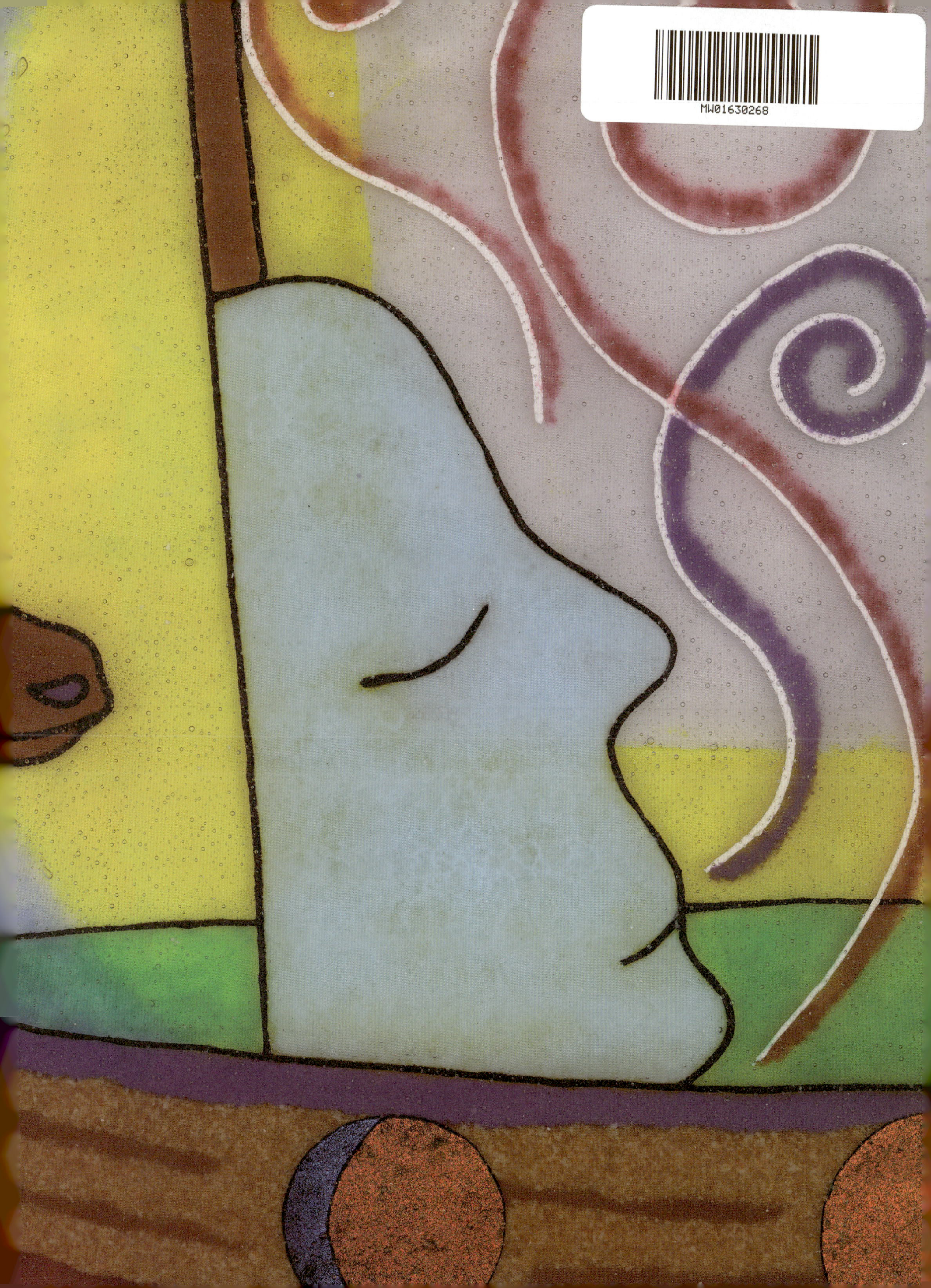

MW01630268

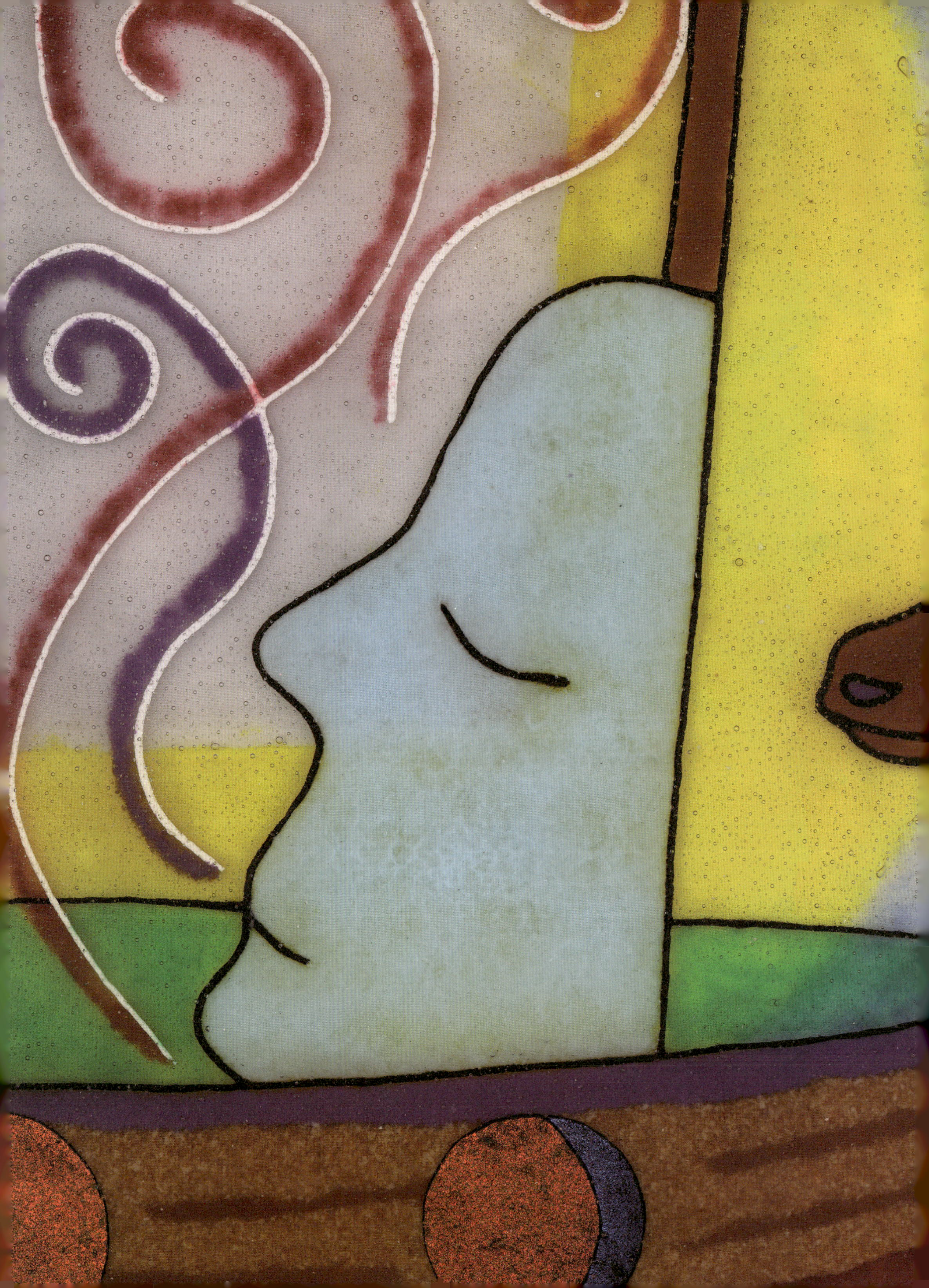

Richard La Londe

Fused Glass Art and Technique

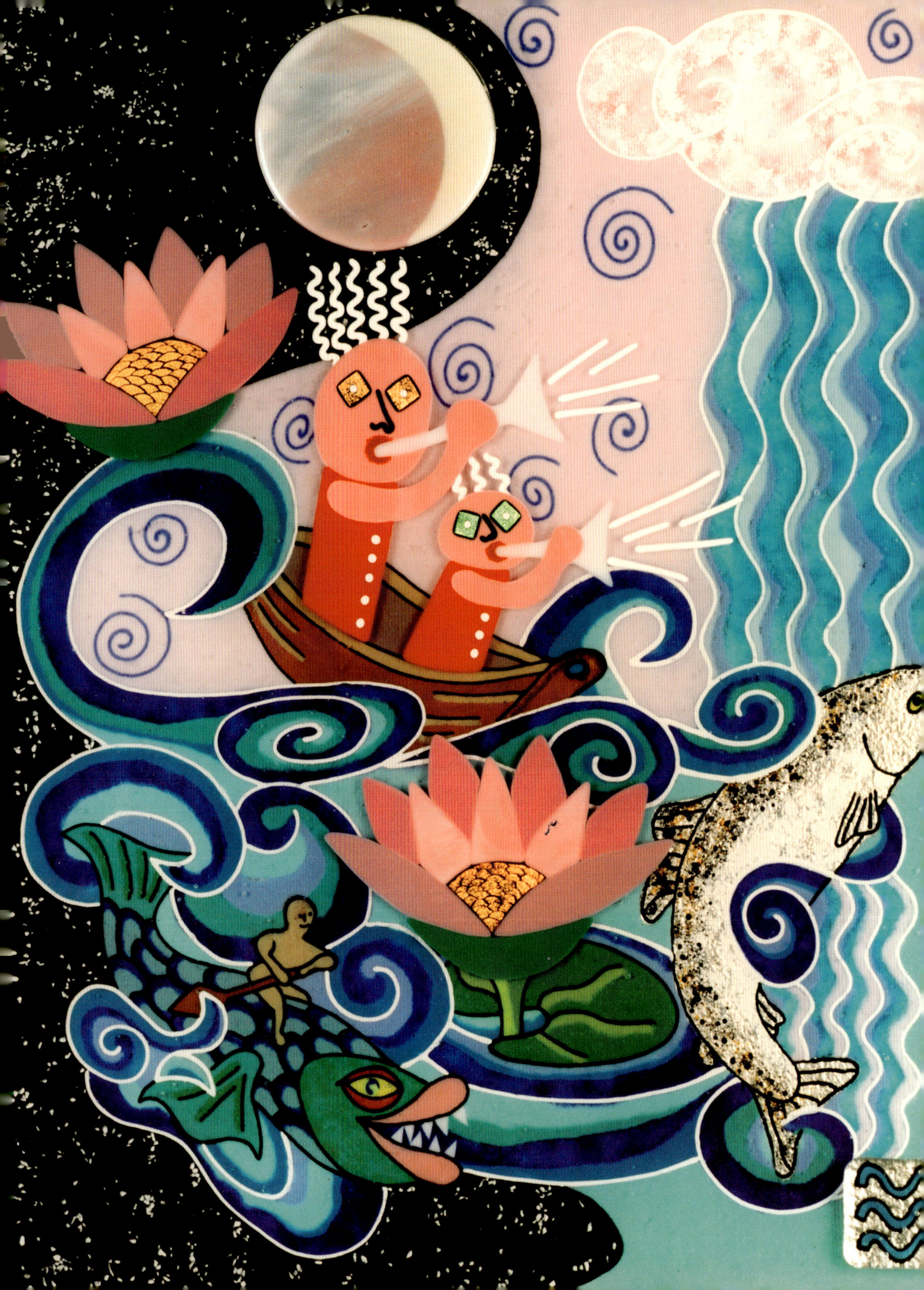

Richard La Londe

Fused Glass Art and Technique

by Richard Parker La Londe

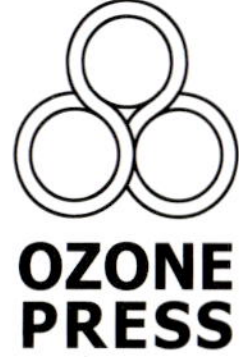

OZONE PRESS

Freeland, Washington

Richard La Londe: Fused Glass Art and Technique

by Richard Parker La Londe

Published by

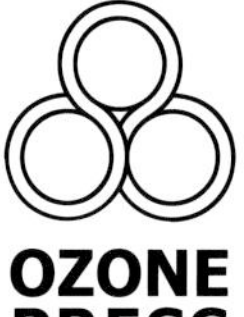

OZONE PRESS

4651 Melody Lane
Freeland, Washington 98249

First Edition

Library of Congress Control Number: 2006902622

ISBN-10 Number: 0-9779126-0-4
ISBN-13 Number: 978-09779126-0-5

Printed in China

www.richardlalonde.com

contents

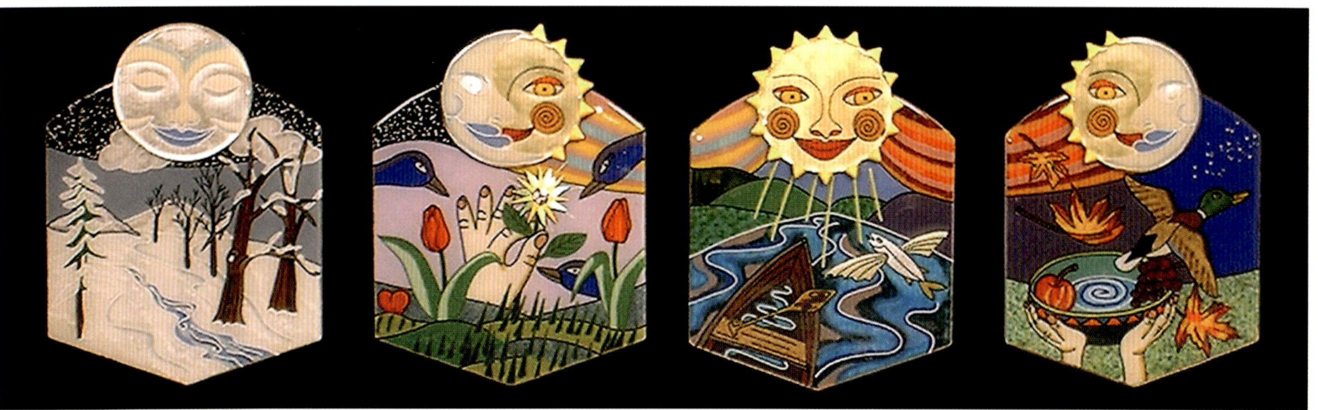

dedication

To the seventh generation!

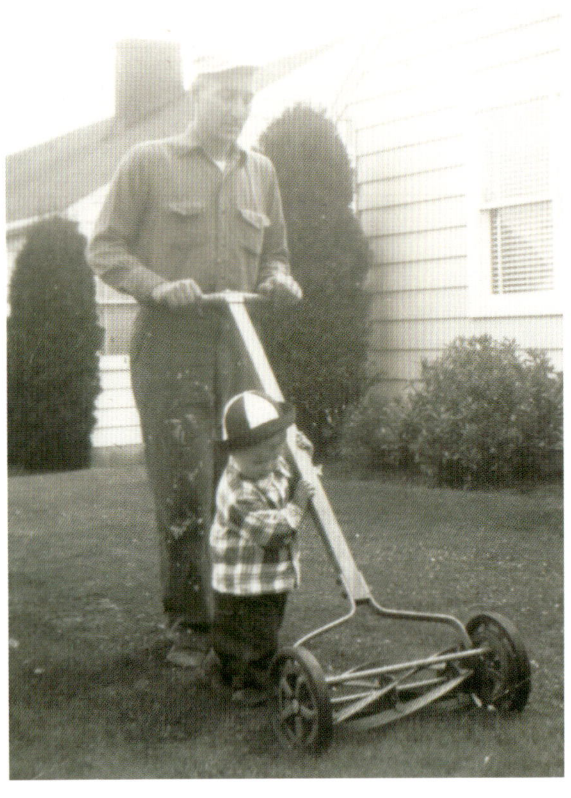

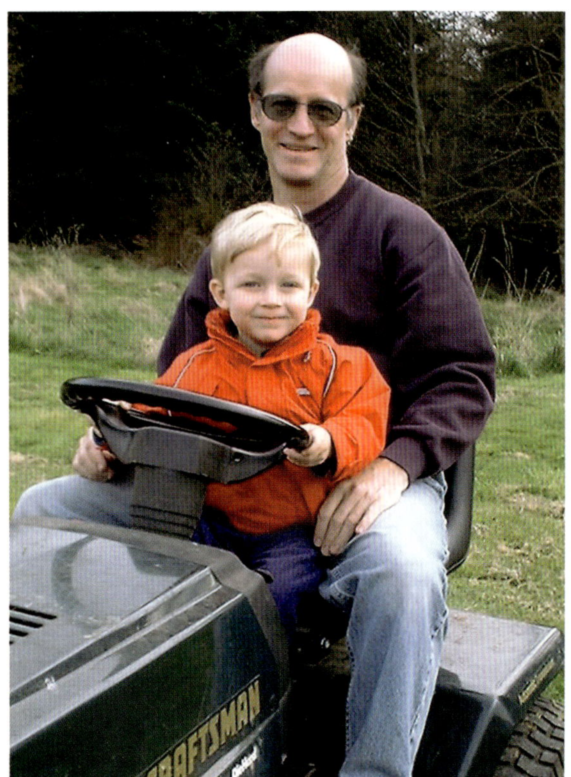

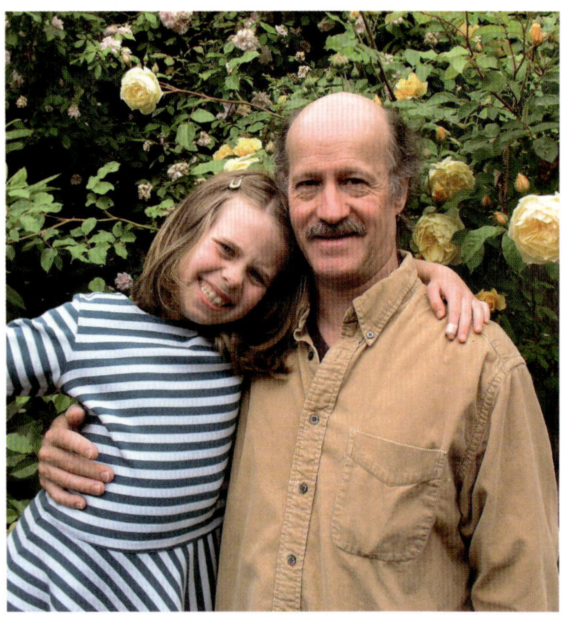

The seventh generation is beyond living memory. My son and daughter can talk to their grandparents, who can remember stories that their grandparents told them. This is six generations of direct living memory. The seventh generation is beyond living memory. In a past time some of the native people of America embraced this philosophy and would always leave a legacy of goodness for the seventh generation.

May we learn from our past and leave a better world for the future!

Richard La Londe June 30, 2006

left: My dad and me, 1952.
upper right: My son Antoine and me, 2002.
lower right: My daughter Amanda and me, 2006.

acknowledgements

I wish to express my gratitude to my family - Angie, Amanda and Antoine - for putting up with me during the process of writing this book and to my parents - Maxine and William La Londe - for believing in me all of these years.

A big thank you to Fritz Dreisbach for encouraging me to pay attention to details in the history and technology section and for writing the foreword.

My gratitude to Vicki Grayson Liden of www.graysondesign.net for her graphic expertise in tweaking the final layout of my book; to Marian Blue, copy editor; to Barry White, software support; and to iocolor, Seattle, WA and C & C Offset Printing Co., Ltd., Portland, OR/Hong Kong.

Thanks to all of the artists for their photographs and helpful suggestions and to both Boyce Lundstrom (who pushed fusing into reality) and Daniel Schwoerer (for making such great fusible glass), for reviewing the Bullseye section.

More grateful thanks to Jill Thomas-Clark (rights and reproductions manager of the Corning Museum of Glass) for providing the wonderful images of ancient and other glass; Elizabeth Hylen, Rakow Library, Corning Museum of Glass; Sharon Dean (executive director of the Cleveland Artists Foundation) for rounding up Edris Eckhardt images; to Malissa Ryder and Ashley Callahan (Georgia Museum of Art) and Mary McCutchen for images of Earl McCutchen's glass pieces; and thanks to Nelson Morgan of the Hargrett Rare Book and Manuscript Library for the great picture of Earl McCutchen.

Thank you to Frances and Michael Higgins who, in 1992 and 1995, graciously allowed me to photograph them and their artwork in their studio.

Thanks to all of the wonderful people who have purchased and commissioned my artwork over the years. This really can't be underestimated; it has allowed me to continue to be an artist.

Thanks to Bev Watt and Alice Taylor of the Washington State Arts Commission. Thanks to Klaus Moje and to the Pilchuck Glass School.

A big thank you to Barbara Mack, Mike Peterson, and JoAnn Overfield of the Gallery Mack in Seattle, WA; to Sally Hanson of the Glass Gallery in Bethesda, MD; and to Bonnie Marx of the Marx/Saunders Gallery in Chicago, IL. Many thanks to Gina Jones, Erika Wise, Susan O'Brien, and Natalie Hahn, who worked with me.

I have tried my best to get the story right and to provide accurate information. Thanks to all who have helped me with this project and over the many years that I have pursued being an artist.

—Richard La Londe

Photo Credits: U = upper, L = lower, M = middle
l = left, r = right

Bill Ayers: p. 188 Ll, 207 U Ll, 208-210.
Ruth Brockmann: p. 63 Ul Ll, 70 Ll, 72 M, 174 Ul L.
Henry P. Boynton: p. 31 Ul.
Collection of the Corning Museum of Glass, Corning, NY: p. 14, 16-22 U, 152 L.
   bequest of Jerome Strauss p. 19 Ll.
   Clara S. Peck Endowment p. 161 U.
Brock Craig: P. 163 Ul M L.
Angie Dixon: p. 6 L.
Michael Dupille: p. 76 Mr, 77 Ml, 130 Ur L, 131.
Jerome Hart: 59 U Ml Mr.
Richard La Londe: p. 8 L, 12 U, Ll, 24, 26 Lr, 27-29, 35, 40, 50, 51, 54 Ul L, 60, 72 U L, 73 M, 76 all but Mr, 77 all but Ml Ll, 81, 83 LM L, 87 U, 91, 94 U, 95, 96 Lr, 97 U, 100, 102-104 U, 106-108, 112-121, 123-129, 130 Ul, 132-135, 138-151, 153, 155-160, 161 L, 162 Ul, 163 Ur, 164-171, 174 Ur, 175-177, 181, 183-187, 202-206, 207 Lr, 211, U M.
Courtesy of Mary McCutchen: p. 34.
Phil Sayer: p. 22 Ll.
Roger Schreiber: p. 2, 5, 10, 48 U, 54 Ur, 62, 64, 66-67, 68 M Lr, 69, 70 U Lr, 73 U L, 75, 78-80, 82, 83 U UM, 84-86, 87 L, 88-90, 92-93, 94 L, 98-99, 122, 136-137, 152 U, 154 Ur Ll Lr, 162 Ur M L, 172, 188 Lr, 201, 211 Lr, 212.
Michael Stadler: p. 8 U, 22 Lr, 154 Ul.
Sherry Yost: p. 46 L.
Constance Wiseman: p. 6.

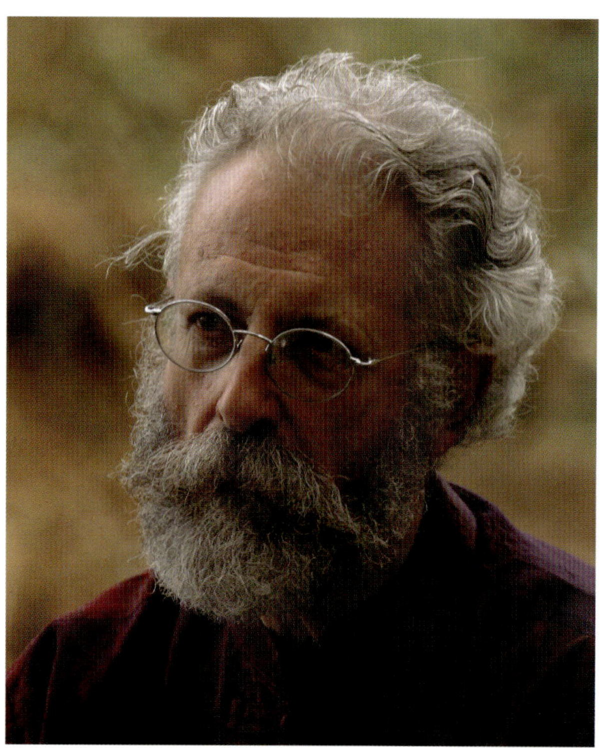

Fritz Dreisbach (b. 1941)
Fritz received his MFA at the University of Wisconsin, Madison and after graduation he set up the glass studio at the Toledo Museum of Art in 1967.

In March of 1971, he was a founder of GAS, (Glass Art Society). Fritz was the third President of the GAS 1976-78, and then president again in 1982-84. In 2002 he received the GAS Lifetime Achievement Award.

His friendship with Dominick Labino led him to add glass technology to his artistic career; he has advised Spectrum Glass Company in Woodinville, WA, the Glass Eye Studio in Seattle, WA, and Kugler Color in Germany.

Fritz is considered "the teacher's teacher" and has given over 300 lectures, workshops, & hot glass demonstrations in 40+ years. He now resides in the Southwest United States and travels around the world making art, teaching, and spreading his wisdom. When I asked him why he had not written a book yet, he replied, "I want to continue working and making art as long as I can, first." Happy Trails.

above: Fritz Dreisbach, 2005
lower: "This is how ya do a lip wrap," Fritz, 1990.

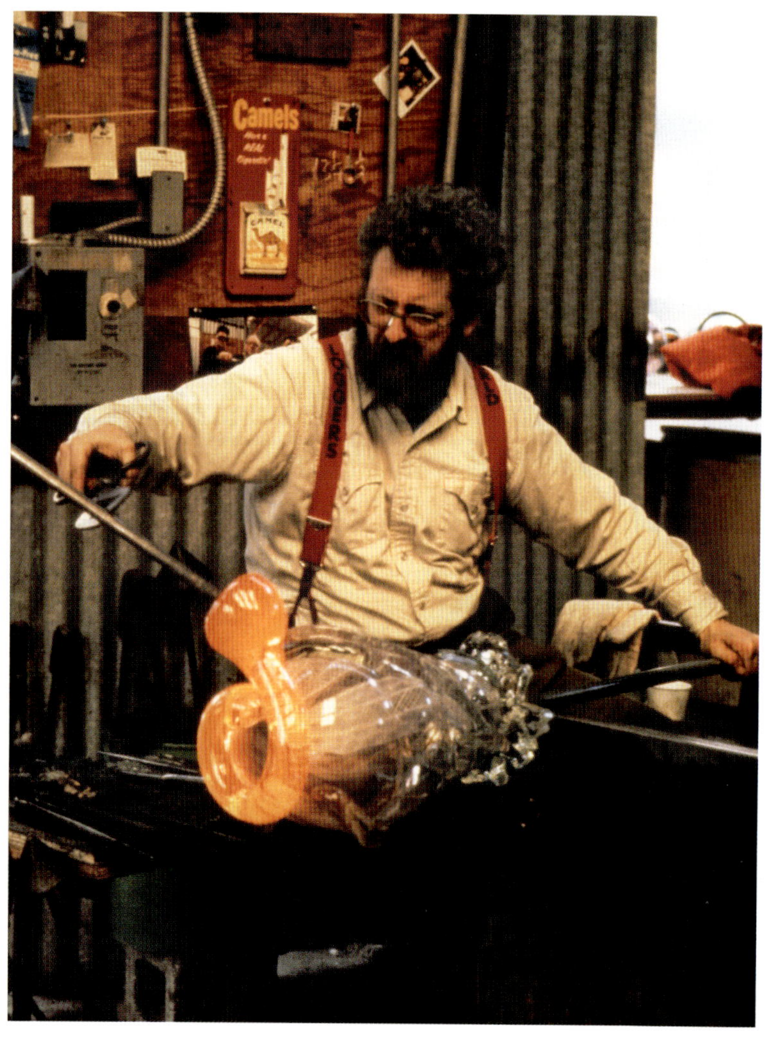

<h1 style="color:#c0392b;text-align:right">foreword</h1>

Three millennia of glasswork – including bead production, small cast figures, intricate patterned canes, fused and slumped bowls, and core vessels – predated the invention of the blowpipe, about 50 B.C. Once glassblowing comes on the scene, it dominates the vast majority of glass production. If we fast-forward to the 1960's we find artists experimenting with glassblowing: a lively show. Blowing is king in the 60's and 70's.

Then in the 1980's a renaissance of fusing and slumping begins, and Richard La Londe is an important part of these renewed explorations in glass. He is present when fusing and slumping are expanding out into the "glass scene" and he brings these moments to life in this book, reliving the stories for us all. Richard discusses the development of fusible glass and chronicles the artists and teachers from the early days of glass fusing through the "Bullseye Fusing Movement." It pleases me to follow the contributions those early artists made to the development of glass artwork and to recognize them for their important achievements.

This book also includes a technical section, in which Richard discusses annealing and compatibility. He has included a chapter about small glory holes and how to build a kiln; which should interest fusers and glass blowers alike. His detailed section about precious metal leaf and foil has never before appeared in a book like this. Also unique is his liquid glass line technique.

Students working with glass today will benefit from this detailed presentation. Collectors who wish to grow their collections will expand their insight and knowledge of fused glass and of the artists who developed this aspect of contemporary glass.

In compiling the book, Richard La Londe successfully combines spectacular photographs with detailed and specific how-to-do-it information. Best of all, he has included a few history lessons along with his personal insights and memories of contacts with artists working with glass. As the "Studio Glass Movement" matures, artists working with glass are combining many different techniques; consequently, slumping, fusing, casting, enameling, carving, and engraving have all joined the blown techniques. It was inevitable that this would happen.

I look forward to a future where glass art becomes art made with glass.

Fritz Dreisbach
May, 2006

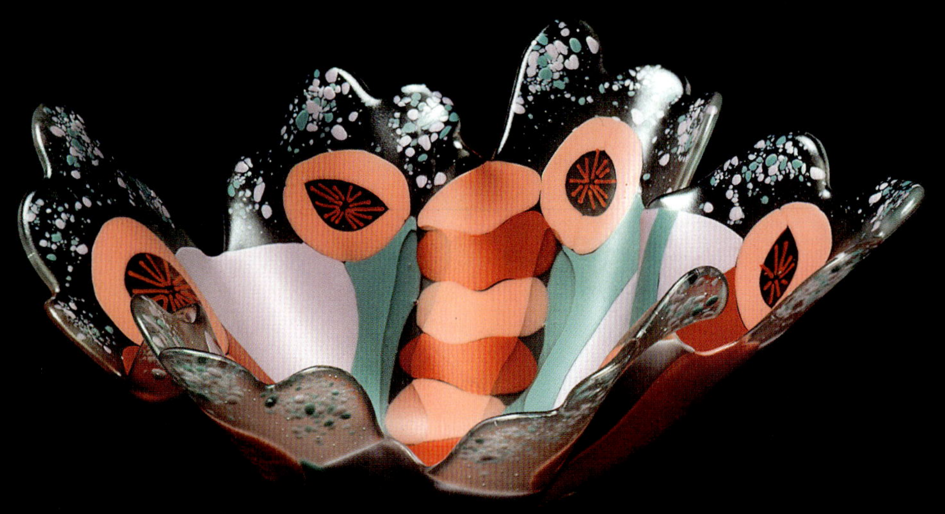
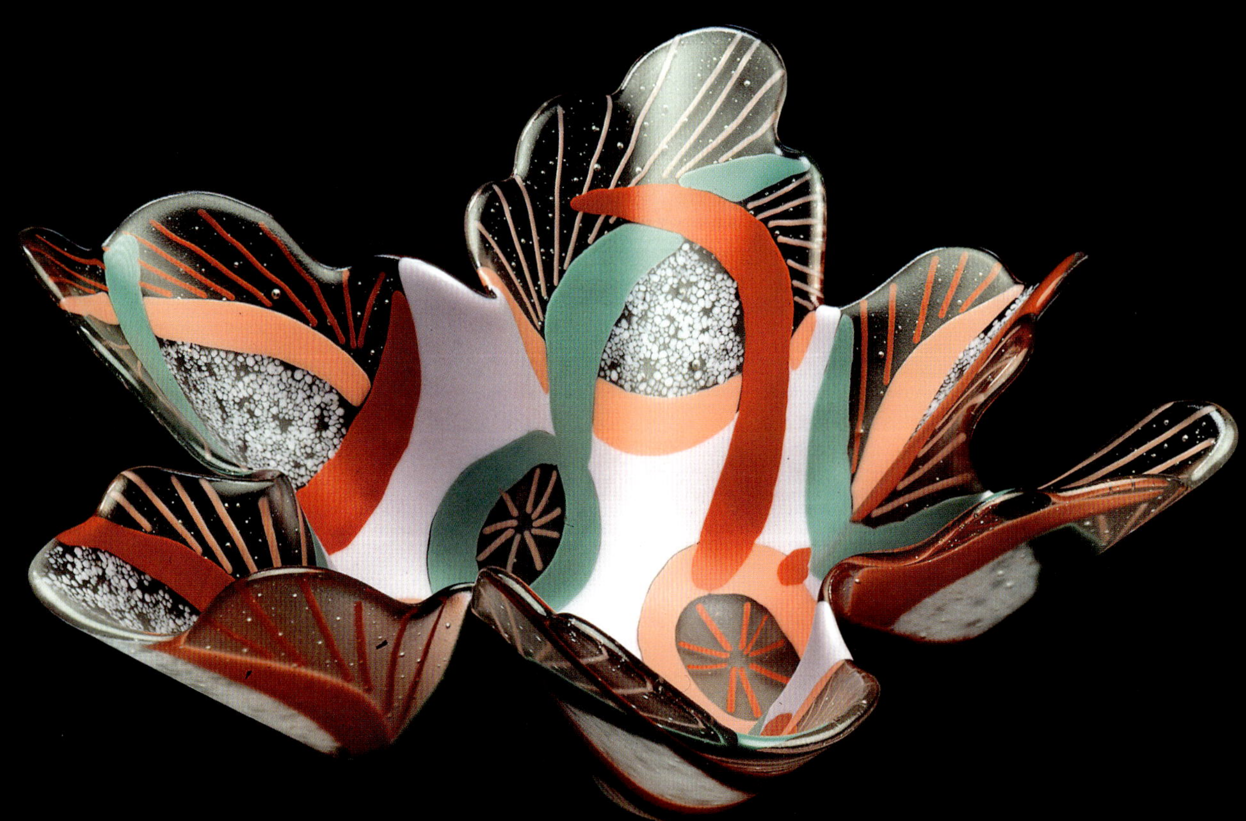

introduction

In recent years, many people have urged me to write about glass history and my techniques – especially about the "liquid glass line" – and also my skills including glory holes, how to build kilns and mounting systems. In this book, I've endeavored to capture all these elements of my own creative and technological progress and also the glass history that made my own development possible. The book is in six sections: History, Richard La Londe, Fusing Concepts, Techniques, Equipment, and the Appendix.

The process of writing this book has been an exciting journey for me; for instance, I became very interested in kiln glass created in the 1950's before the process became popular. By the time the mythic 1962 Littleton/Labino, Toledo Museum Glass Workshops "launched the studio glass movement," the early fusers had already been experimenting and exhibiting for many years. As I wrote about the early days of the "Bullseye Fusing Movement," I realized that developments weren't just about technique, but about the artists, many of whom have become my friends.

Those friendships and my experiences frequently grew out of lucky circumstances that placed me in the right place at the right time. For instance, such good fortune contributed to my becoming, in 1983, one of the first fusing instructors for Bullseye Glass Company in Portland, Oregon; all of my glass pieces shown in this book are made from their glass.

Over the years, these connections with other artists – along with these opportunities, discoveries and accidents – contributed to the development of my glasswork. In reality most our new techniques are rediscoveries and variations on what has come before – "there is nothing new under the sun." I received an email the other day from someone telling me how excited he had been to develop the idea of a squirt bottle with powdered glass in a medium – until he found on the internet that I had been doing it for years. If this sort of thing happens to you, don't let that diminish your excitement! You discovered it on your own, and it's this thrill that keeps us going. I recently found out that artists have used enamels mixed with a medium and dispensed from a squeeze bottle before I did. It's not the technique – it's what you do with it.

If you are unfamiliar with glass fusing, I suggest that you take a basic fusing class, sometimes available through stained glass shops. You can also read a book, and I recommend two introductory books available today: <u>Kiln Firing Glass: Glass Fusing Book One</u> by Boyce Lundstrom, 1994, and <u>Contemporary Warm Glass</u> by Brad Walker. Also www.warmglass.com is a site to visit.

I feel that it is important to say this in the introduction: Wear a Respirator! Breathing powdered and fibrous glass can cause silicosis – which can kill you! – and dust from refractory materials like "Thin Fire" shelf paper is extremely bad for you. Work safely, live long and prosper!!!

Finally, I would like to say that any mistakes and omissions in this book are somebody else's fault and so don't blame me...but, kidding aside, I apologize if I left something or someone out or otherwise screwed up. I hope that you have fun with my book and enjoy this adventure as much as I have.

Richard La Londe June 30, 2006

facing: Post Contemporary Vessels, 1983, H. 7 in. (18 cm) x W. 17 in. (43 cm) x D. 16 in. (41 cm).

Exhibited in: Americans in Glass, The Leigh Yawkey Woodson Art Museum, Wausau, Wisconsin 1984

The 1984 Catalog description: "I like to call my work Futuristic Nostalgia. I use glass to reflect my imagination. To fuse glass, I fire an assemblage of various pieces of glass in an electric kiln until they melt together. This flat shape is then suspended in a stainless steel mold and slumped into the final shape during a second firing. The unique matte surface is achieved by sandblasting and heat polishing. Art from my Post Contemporary Mind!" Richard La Londe

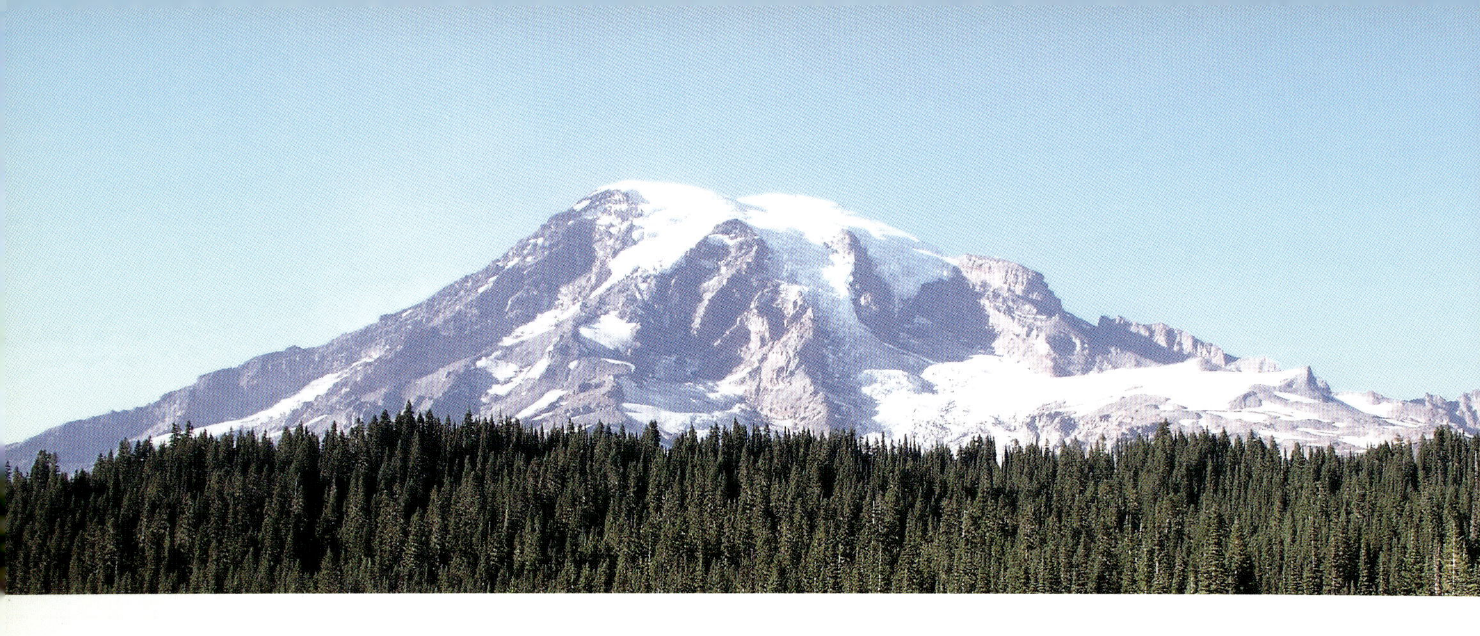

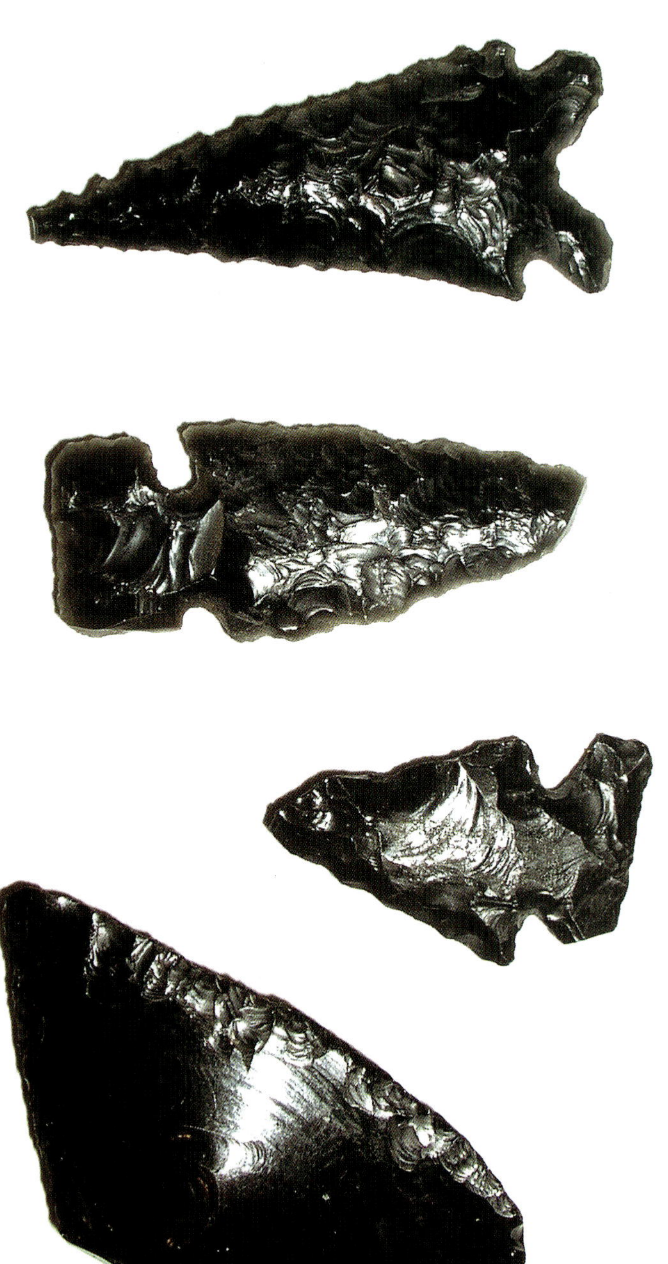

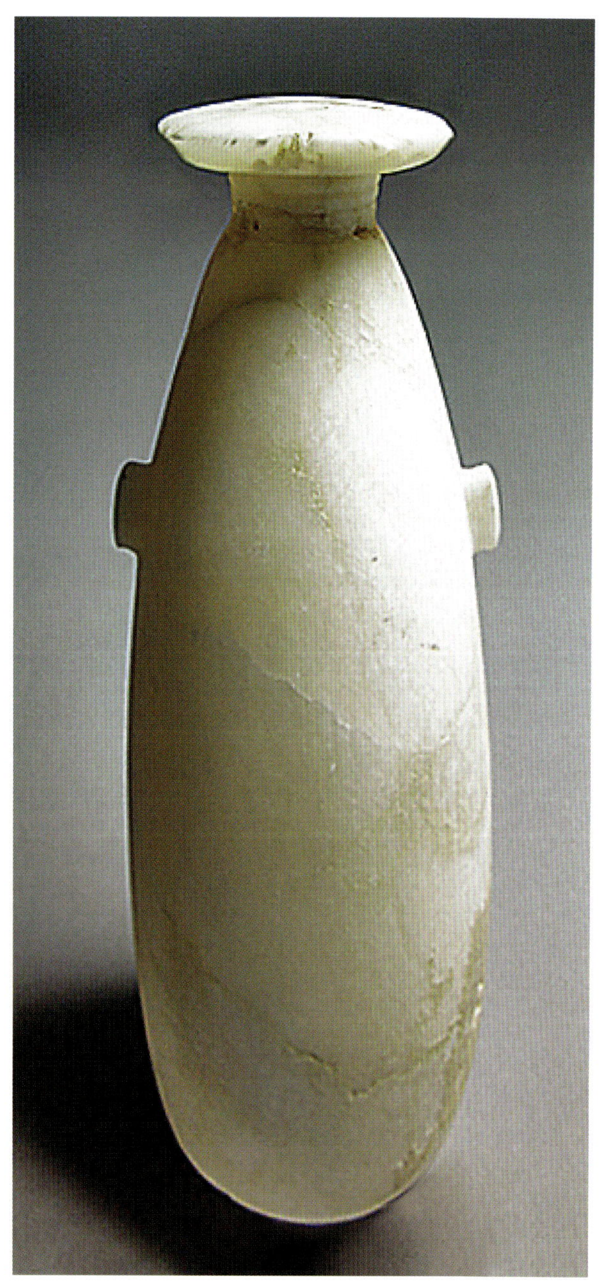

Part 1: History
natural & man-made glass

Genesis: In the beginning nature created glass!
Obsidian is volcanic glass; pumice is a glassy froth, so full of air, that it can float on water. Occasionally lightning strikes sand and makes a glassy tube called a fulgurite, and sometimes a meteorite impact can create glassy tecktites, or they may come all the way from outer space.

Glass is found all around us in everyday life!
We use glass bottles, light bulbs, "glasses" to drink from and "eyeglasses" to see with, fiberglass for strength, glass fiber insulation for our homes, and fiber optic cables for communication. Glass towers define our cities. We are so accustomed to glass that we hardly notice it anymore, but it wasn't always this way. As early as five thousand years ago man-made glass was used for precious objects that only the rich could afford.

Glass is a non-crystalline rigid material that for practical purposes acts like a solid. Glass is an amazing material!
As a viscous material, glass cools before its atoms can organize into a crystalline structure and so ends up in an amorphous state. Molten glass conducts electricity, but solid glass is a good insulator. Tempered glass is strong, yet a small surface scratch can cause it to disintegrate into tiny pieces. Glass can be pulled into very thin threads; be made optically clear or opaque; be thrust into a hot cooking oven; may shatter when dropped; and can be made into wonderful art!

Glass is made by melting mined and processed rocks!
Mining and powdering quartz sand gives us the main ingredient for common glass, silica (SiO_2 – silicon dioxide). A temperature of 3500° F is needed to melt pure silica, which can form a glass all by itself, but building a furnace to do this is difficult and expensive to run. By "fluxing" the sand with soda ash (Na_2CO_3 – sodium carbonate – which is also mined), we can lower the melting point of the silica. If enough soda ash is added, when cooled the mixture can produce sodium silicate (Na_2SiO_4); this result, called "waterglass," is not durable and dissolves in water. Adding lime (CaO – calcium oxide – made by mining and heating limestone), we can produce a durable "soda-lime" glass that won't dissolve. A classic stable formulation contains about 70% silica, 20% soda, and 10% lime. A few early studio artists who formulated their own glass found out about stability the hard way. There was a piece on display at the Corning Museum of Glass that started to decay through a process called "weeping." Also by substituting boron (B_2O_3 – boric oxide) for much of the soda ash we get thermal shock resistant glasses, know as "borosilicates" (some are sold under the name Pyrex). Other chemicals added to glass include metal oxides, carbonates and sulfides for color, fluorides to make the glass opaque, antimony for decolorizing, lead for brilliance and easier cold working.

facing upper: The 14,419 foot (4395 m) tall volcano Mt. Rainier near Seattle, Washington, 2005. Photographed from the 5000 foot (1524 m) level.

bottom left: paleolithic obsidian arrowheads and scraper which is 2 in. (5 cm) long. From the Columbia River area near Portland, Oregon.

bottom right: an example of a carved stone "Alabastron." They are dated from about 3500 B.C. to about 100 B.C. and were made in Egypt, the Mediterranean, and the surrounding area.

Alabastrons ranged in size from about 3 in. (7.5 cm) to 9 in. (23 cm) in height and a few are even larger. The were shaped on a lathe from a stone like Alabaster marble and imitated by the Egyptians and Romans in glass.

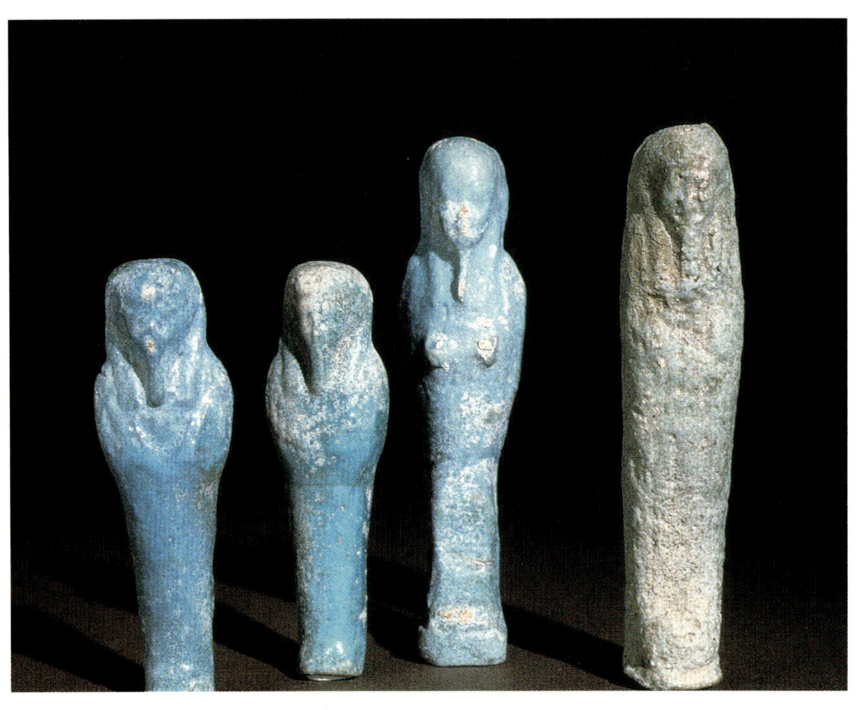

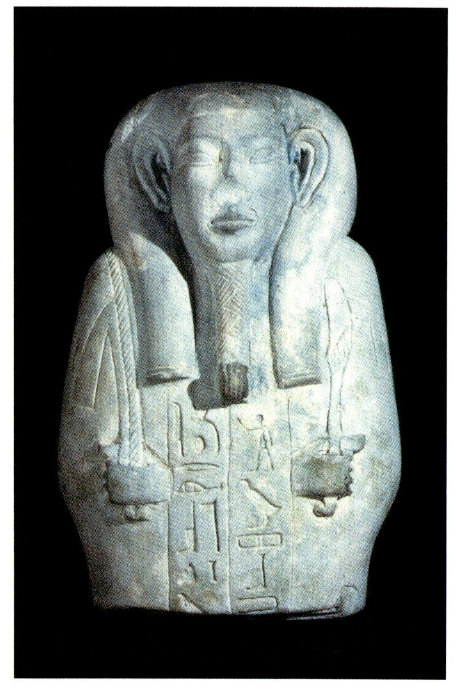

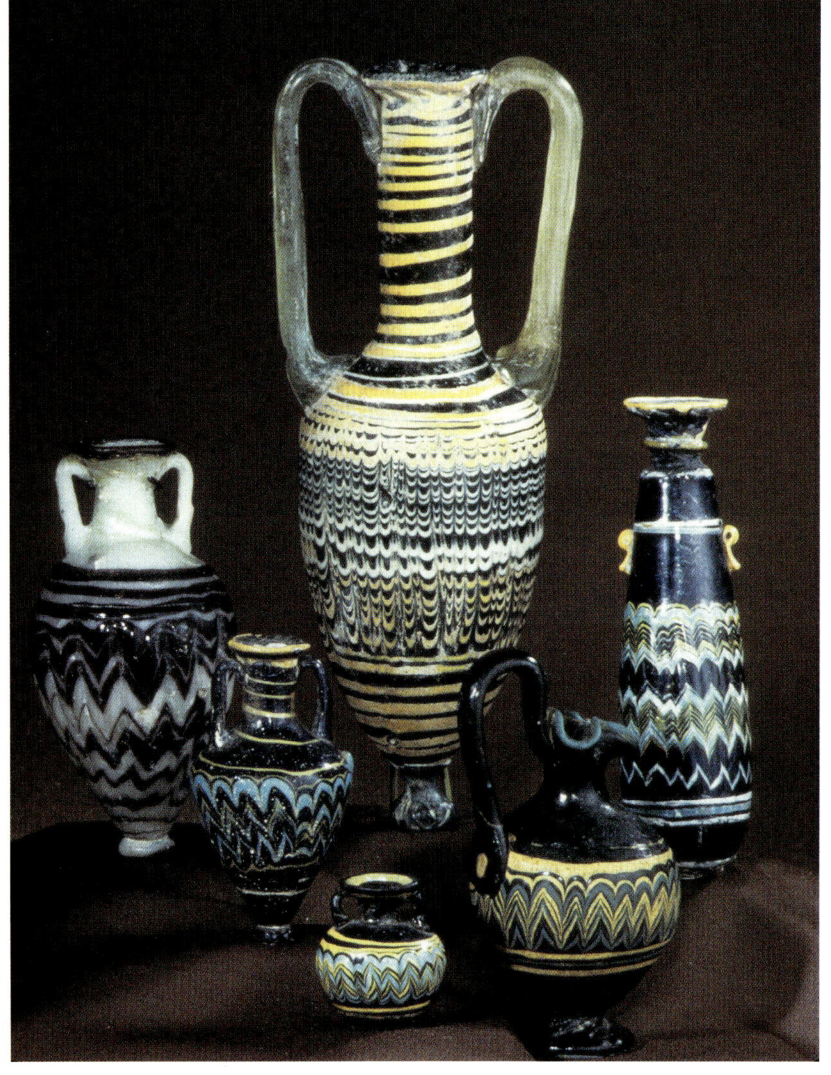

ancient glass: 3000 BC - 500 AD

Ancient History

Discoveries at Nineveh, (modern-day Mosul, Iraq), include cuneiform clay tablets dating from the 7th century BC; these may be copies of texts dating back to 1000 B.C. and contain directions for making glass.

The historical story of how glass making was discovered most often relies on the Roman historian Pliny the Elder. He said that ancient Phoenician sailors built a fire on the sand during a windy storm and propped their cooking pots on blocks of natron (soda ash) from their cargo. The soda ash melted, "fluxed" the sand, and produced bits of glass. Nice story, but we know the campfire would probably not have been hot enough to melt the sand sufficiently to make a recognizable glass.

The genesis of man-made glass is usually attributed to the Mesopotamian (Iran - Iraq) area during the 3rd millennium BC. Evidence for how ancient glass was manufactured was found in 2003, when archeologists unearthed a 1250 B.C. glass factory at Qantir-Piramesses in the eastern Nile Delta of Egypt and *"researchers described a two-step process in which factories melted crushed quartz to form semi-finished glass, then re-melted and colored it to make glass ingots for shipment to artisans elsewhere. They melted the glass again and shaped it into inlays, ornaments and other objects."* see *Washington Post* article in the appendix.

Man-made glass dates back to nearly 3000 B.C.

Glass vessel production (core vessels) dates to about 1500 B.C. and a few glass beads that have been found may date to around 3000 B.C. The invention of man-made glass may have developed from glassy slag associated with bronze foundry operations, or glass may have evolved from the development of "faience" jewelry and beads. Faience is a siliceous ceramic, coated with alkali glazes. Early Egyptians powdered quartz rock and mixed it with "natron," a natural mixture of sodium carbonate and sodium bicarbonate that is found in the Wadi Natrun near Alexandria. This was mixed with water into a paste and pressed into a mold to shape the object. After removal, the sodium salts migrate to the surface, "effloresces," as the paste dries. This self-glazing mixture was then heated in a furnace until the "natron" began to flux the surface of the mixture. When cooled, this thin siliceous shell hardens into what is called faience. The addition of copper and impurities give the paste its typical green to turquoise color, but other colors were also made. *"Chemical analysis reveals that the body of faience usually consist simply of silica with a small admixture of soda and impurities. The study of several specimens by the technique of X-ray diffraction show that the grains of silica uniformly have the crystal structure known as alpha quartz. This indicates that the material was heated to a temperature no higher than 1600° (870° C)"* (*Scientific American* Nov., 1963).

facing upper left: group of Egyptian faience figures, 1100 B.C., tallest 3" in. (8 cm). Courtesy of the Corning Museum of Glass.

facing upper right: Shawabti of Kheb-it, Egyptian glassy faience, 730 – 656 B.C., 3 in. (8 cm). Courtesy of the Corning Museum of Glass.

facing bottom: Core Vessels, tallest 9.5 in. (24 cm), 5th – 1st century B.C. Courtesy of the Corning Museum of Glass.

These glass core vessels were made to look like stone vessels that are called "Alabastrons." The feathered trails of glass are reminiscent to the patterns found in alabaster marble.

I believe that accidents and experiments might have produced glass. Heating faience to a higher temperature would flux more of the silica and could create a glass, but without adding calcium, it would be unstable; maybe that is what happened and why it took many years until true glass showed up.

Ancient Fused Glass

Glass fascinated the ancient Mesopotamians and Egyptians who used it as inlays in burial objects, jewelry, and vessels. The first glass was probably melted in beehive type furnaces that had been developed for bronze casting, which used a bellows to deliver extra air, increasing the oxygen and creating higher temperatures. Examples of early glass include "core vessels," where powdered and trailed glass was applied around a core of sand, clay, and animal dung; this was reheated numerous times, combed, and worked with tools. Sometimes handles and decorative rims were added. After cooling, the core was picked out to leave the vessel hollow. Early "core vessels" originally mimicked the "alabastron" carved from stone; later, glass popularity eclipsed the use of stone. Much ancient glass was cold worked with techniques originally developed for stone.

Core vessels date from about 1500 B.C. Most were made in the Middle Eastern area and later produced by the Romans until about 200 A.D. Also during this time period, techniques were developed to make glass rods with intricate patterns (canes). Fused, molded, and slumped glass objects were made, often in the shape of bowls. Glass and cane making found its way to the Italian island of Murano where, the story has it, glassblowers under the threat of death, hid and guarded the skills for milifiori, lattichino, and other secret techniques from the world.

In ancient times fused glass objects were rare and only affordable by the wealthiest members of society. Kiln-formed glass is found in tombs and graves, wrapped in mummies, and decorating sarcophagi.

The Invention of Glass Blowing & the Demise of Fused Glass

The birth of glass blowing occurred around 50 B.C. Someone might have been using a hollow rod on a core vessel and plugged the outer end. Heating the piece would have expanded the air in the tube and could have blown the core vessel all out of shape. This probably was one of those "Eureka" moments, where a mistake turned into the technique of glass blowing. If something like this hadn't happened, we might have all still been fusing.

This "how" glass blowing started comes from my imagination; the results of the discovery comes from history. Artisans were able to produce blown vessels easier and more quickly than the labor-intensive core vessels. Blown glass became more affordable; many Romans drank from glasses, used glass bowls, and even purchased tourist glass cups celebrating sporting events. This is evidenced by the volume of Roman and other ancient glass found in archaeological sites all over Europe and the Middle East.

The majority of ancient fusing and kiln-forming of glass tapered off around 300 - 500 A.D. It remained a minor technique for the next 1500 years.

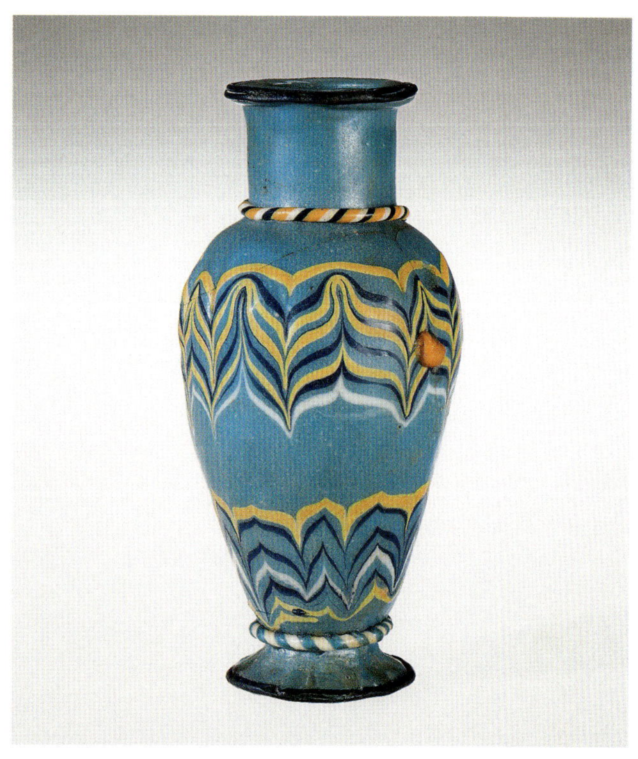

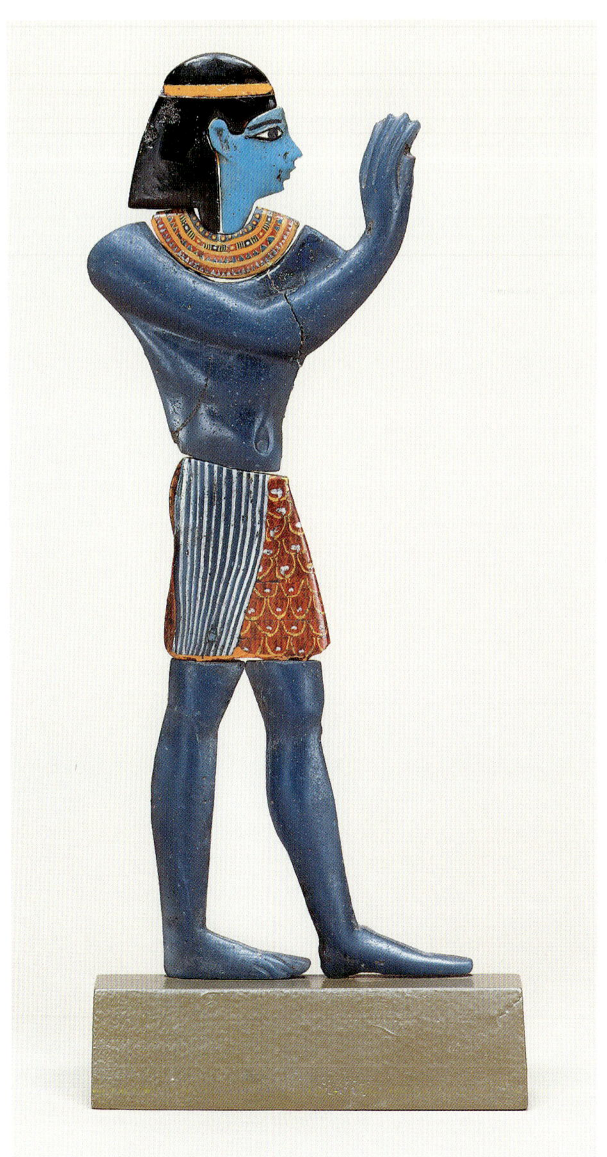

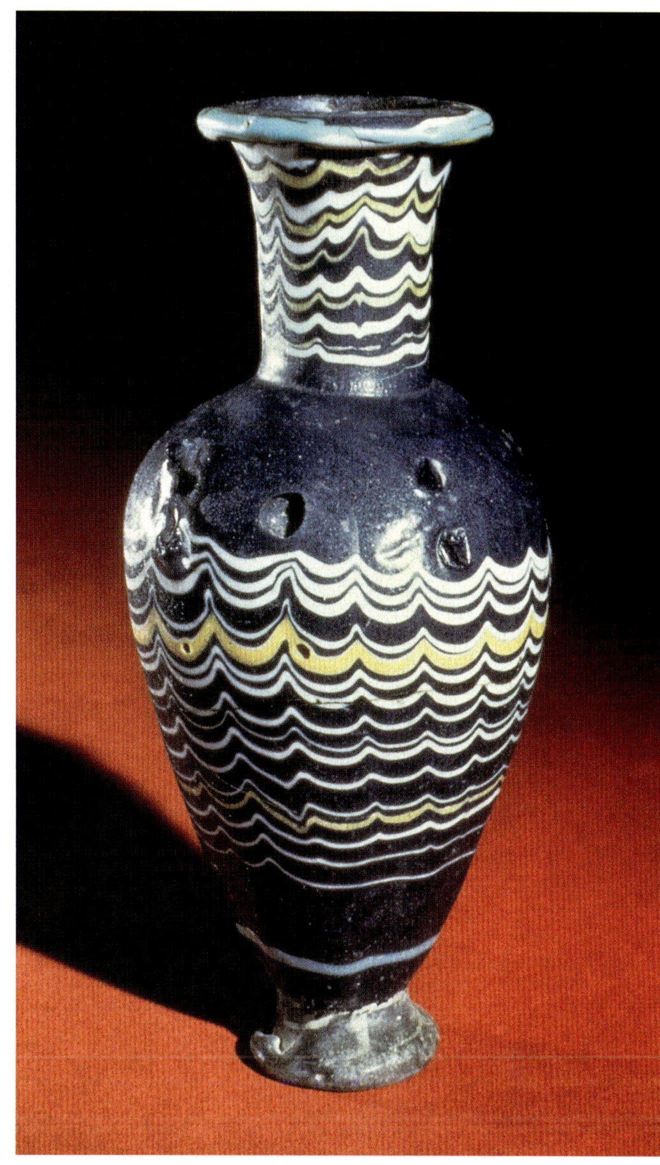

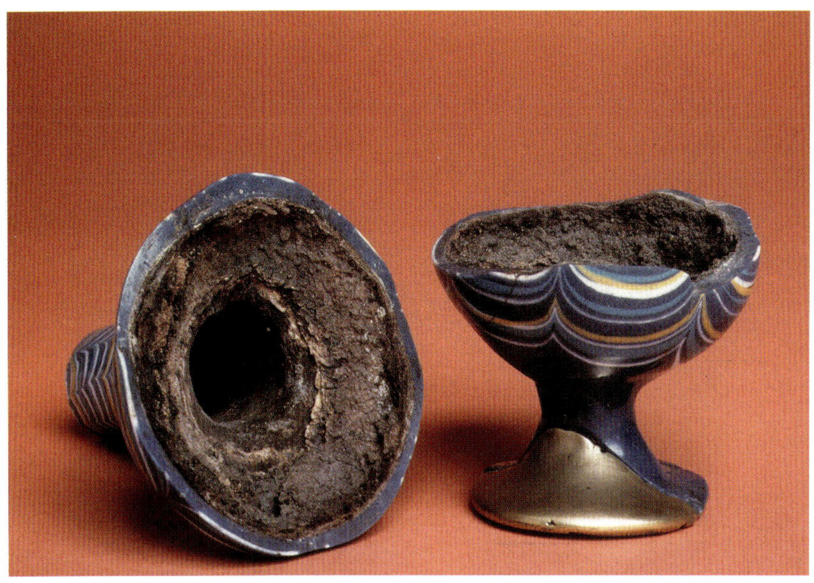

facing: Turquoise Core Vessel, 1400 – 1300 B.C. Egypt, H. 4 ¼ in. (10.7 cm). Decorated with combed and feathered trails of glass. Courtesy of the Corning Museum of Glass.

upper left: Egyptian inlay figure 300 B.C., 8 in. (21 cm) tall. Fused in sections, ground and polished. Courtesy of the Corning Museum of Glass.

Upper right: Egyptian core vessel 1450- 1350 B.C., 4 ½ in. (11 cm) tall. Courtesy of the Corning Museum of Glass.

bottom left: broken Egyptian core vessel showing the residual sand and clay core. Courtesy of the Corning Museum of Glass.

right:
Satyr face, Roman Empire, 100 B.C. – 100 A.D. 1 ⅛ in. (2.7 cm). square. This face cane is created by assembling prefused sections of glass surrounding them with powdered glass, which is then fused in a large mold. For example, I would assemble one half of a face in a 2.5 in. (6 cm) x 5 in. (12 cm) x 5 in. (12 cm) deep mold. The glass would be fused, removed from the mold when hot, and stretched, which creates a long bar with a smaller very detailed face. This can then be cut into many pieces. You can see pattern bar making in the glory hole section of this book. By placing two halves together, you get a whole face for half of the work.

facing upper left:
Satyr Face, Roman Empire, 100 B.C. – 100 A.D. 1 ⅛ in. (2.7 cm). square. Fused preformed canes. The right half of this cane is in the Corning museum and the left half was photographed, flipped, and added to show what the full plaque would look like. Courtesy of The Corning Museum of Glass.

facing upper right:
Female Face With Wreath, Roman Empire, 100 B.C. – 100 A.D. 1 ¼ in. (3.3 cm). square. Fused preformed canes. Digitally manipulated to show what the whole cane would look like. Courtesy of The Corning Museum of Glass.

facing lower left:
Face with Maenad, Roman Empire, 100 B.C. – 100 A.D. 1 ¼ in. (3.3 cm). square. Fused preformed canes. The left half of this cane is in the Corning museum and the right half was digitally manipulated to illustrate the full plaque. Courtesy of The Corning Museum of Glass.

facing lower right:
Masked Face, Roman Empire, 100 B.C. – 100 A.D. 1 ⅛ in. (2.8 cm). square. Fused preformed canes. This plaque consists of two halves put together and are held by a twisted gold wire added later by a collector.

bottom:
Four Face Plaques, 300 B.C. – 100 B.C. Egypt. They are made by placing two half face canes together; cut from the same rod possibly using a turning copper wheel with abrasive grit and water.

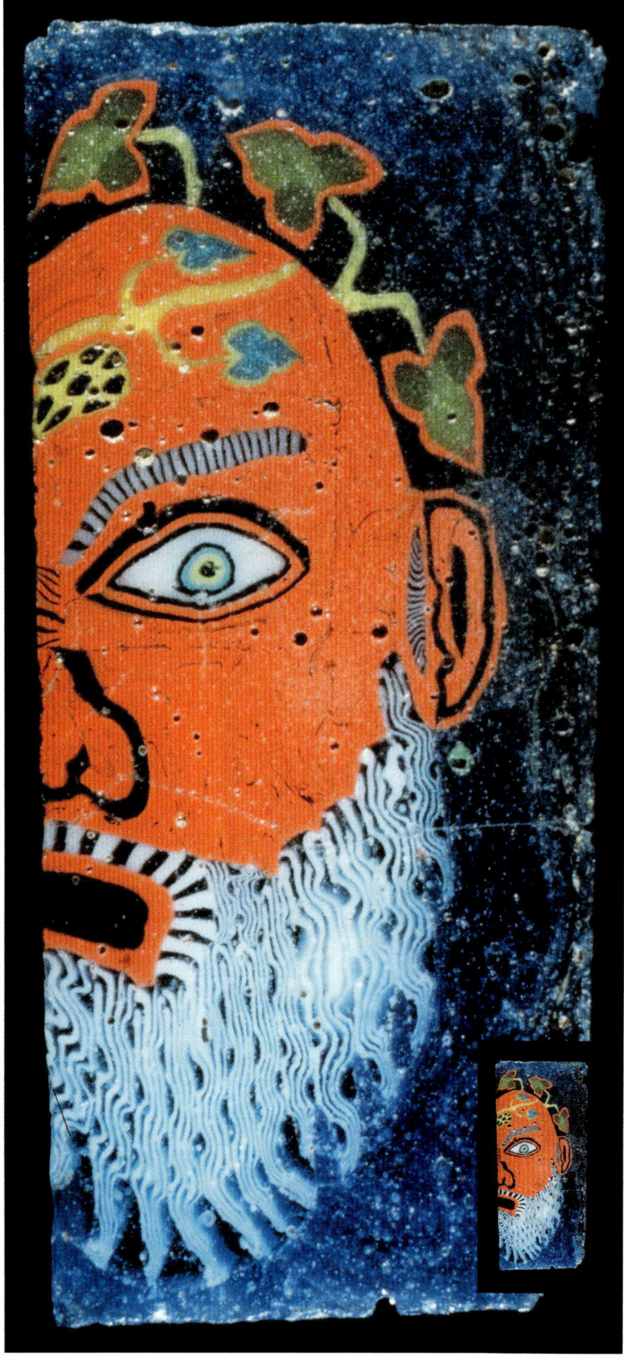

inset above: Satyr face cane shown actual size, 1 ⅛ in. (2.7 cm) x ½ in. (1.25 cm).

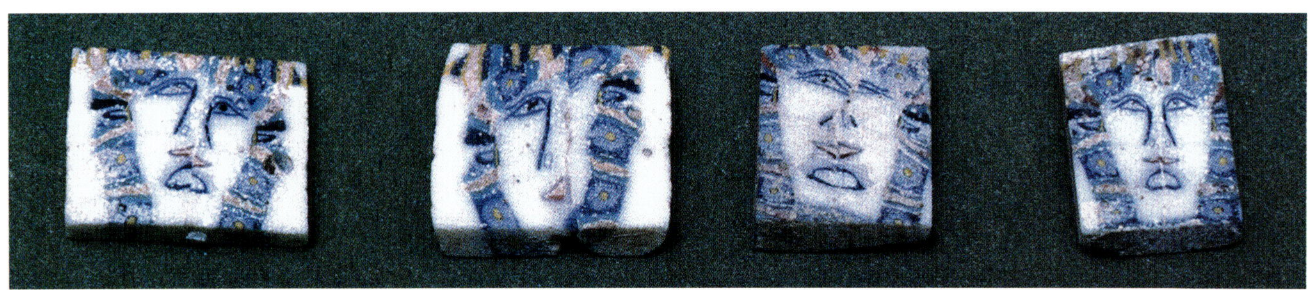

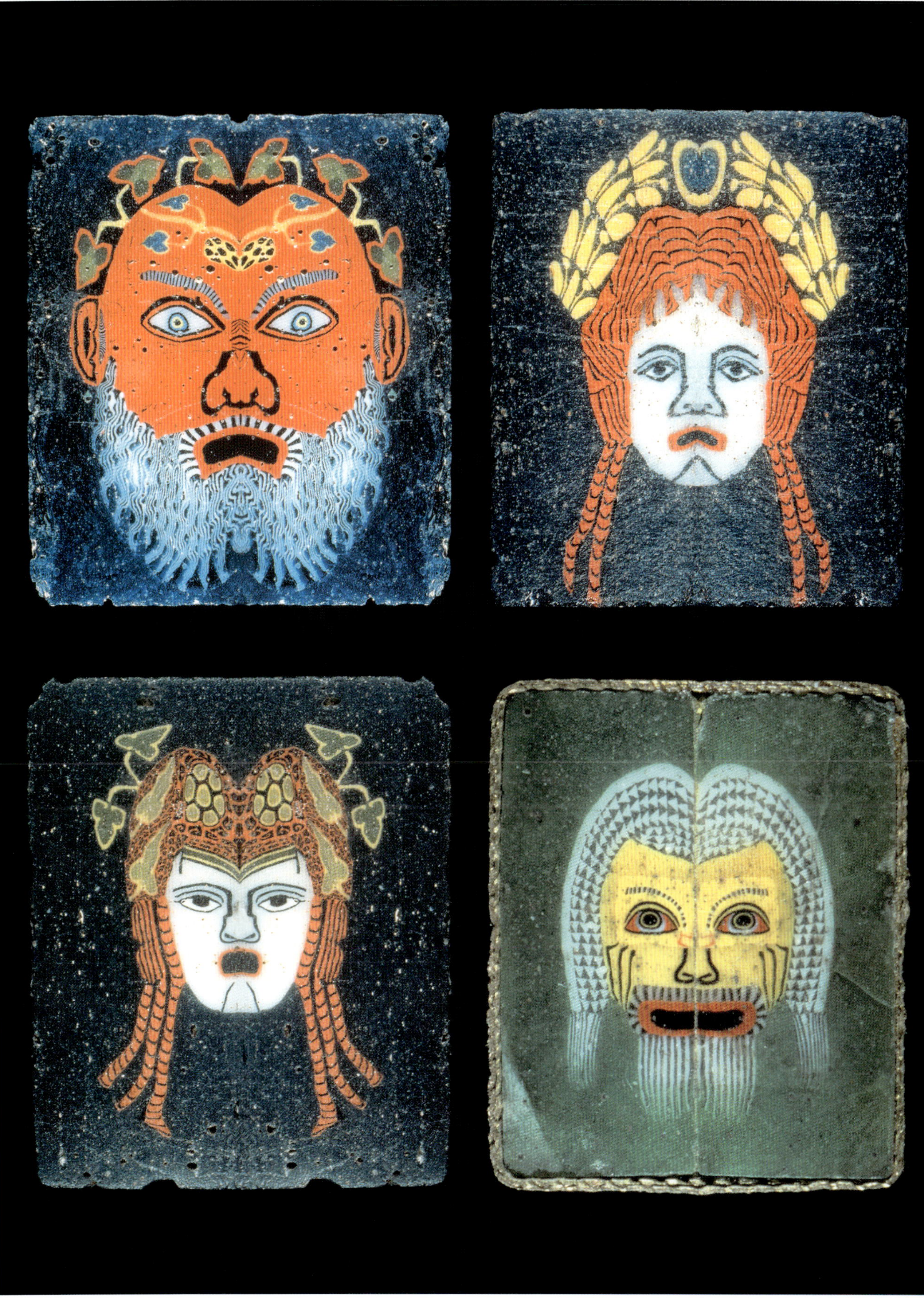

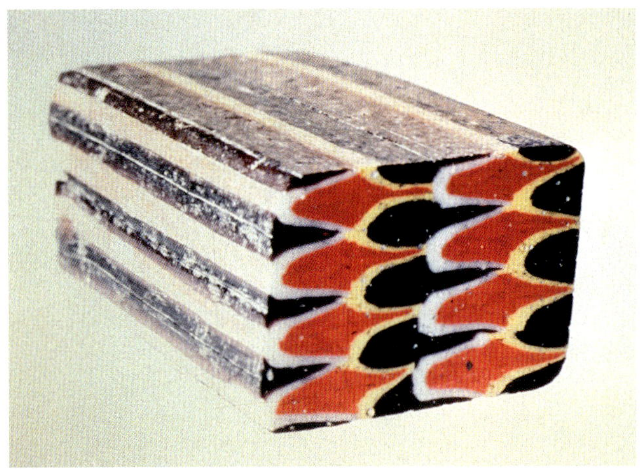

Pieces from millefiori pattern rods might have been placed into a mold and fused with a weighted inner mold holding the shape. It was finished by grinding and smoothing. Courtesy of the Corning Museum of Glass.

facing upper left: Detail of one of the face canes in the Patella Cup below. Courtesy of the Corning Museum of Glass.

facing upper right: Bead, Roman Empire, 100 B.C. – 100 A.D. ½ in. (1.45 cm) square. Face cane with surrounding pattern canes. Pieces like this, without the hole, were assembled to create the cup below. Courtesy of the Corning Museum.

above:
Roman feather or scale patterned bar, mosaic technique, 100 B.C. – 100 A.D. 1 in. (2.5 cm). Courtesy of The Corning Museum of Glass.

below: Roman fused millefiori bowl 100 B.C. - 100 A.D. 3 in. (7.5 cm). The stretched millefiori may give us a clue as to how this vessel was possibly created.

facing bottom:
Patella Cup, Roman Empire, East Mediterranean, 100 B.C. – 100 A.D. H. 1.5 in. (4 cm) x W. 3.75 in. (9.5 cm). This is my favorite ancient fused piece in the Corning Museum, constructed from sliced pattern bar sections and face canes that are possibly fused between two molds and then ground and smoothed. Courtesy of The Corning Museum of Glass.

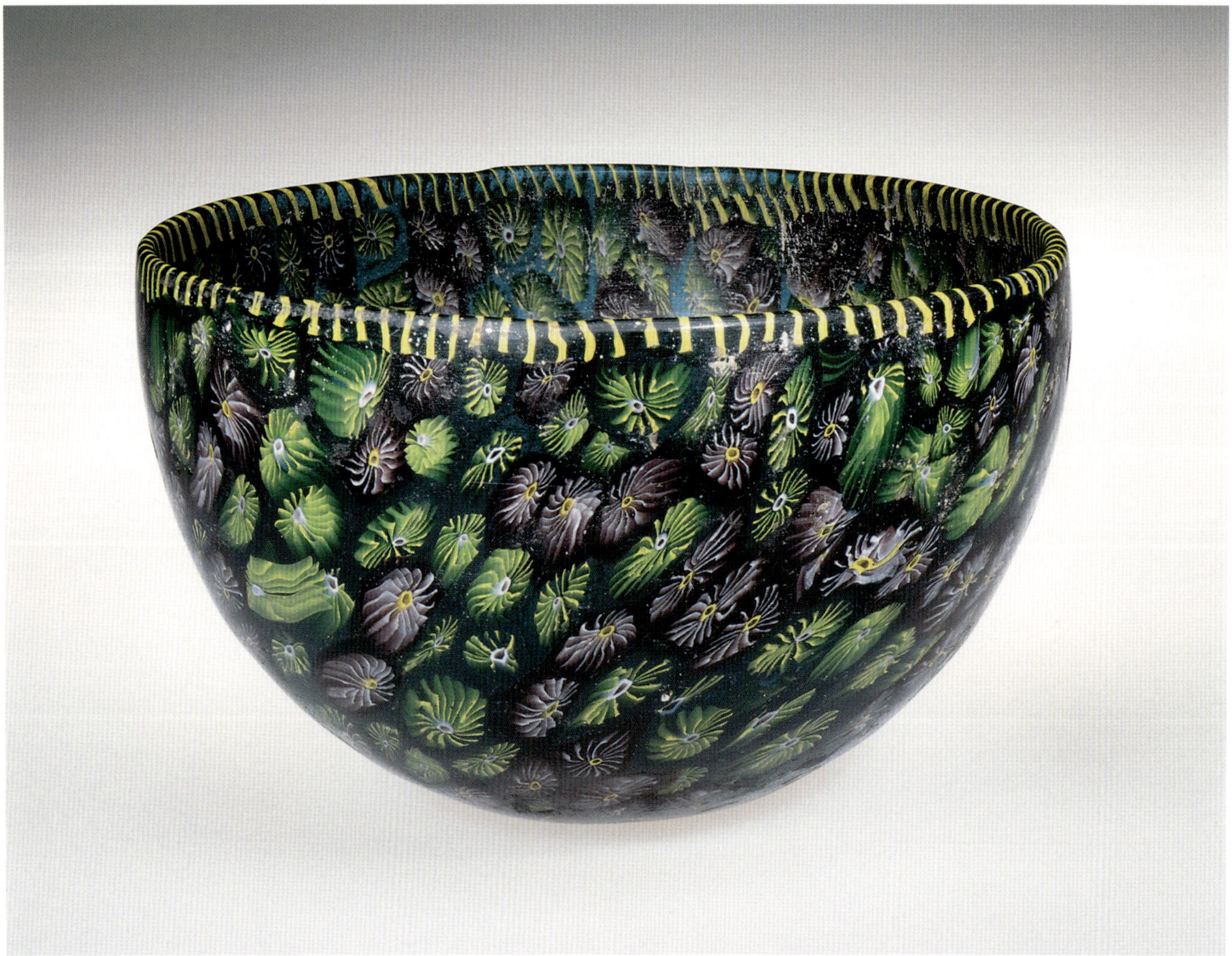

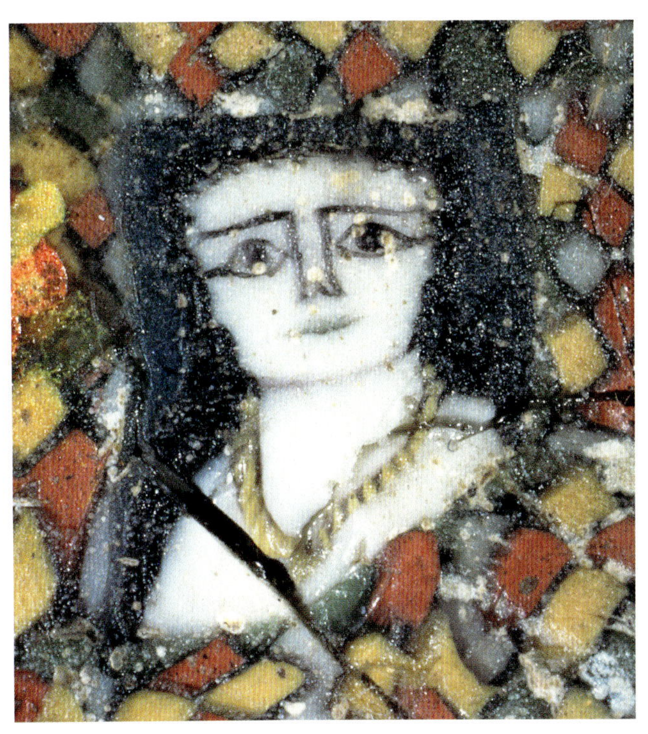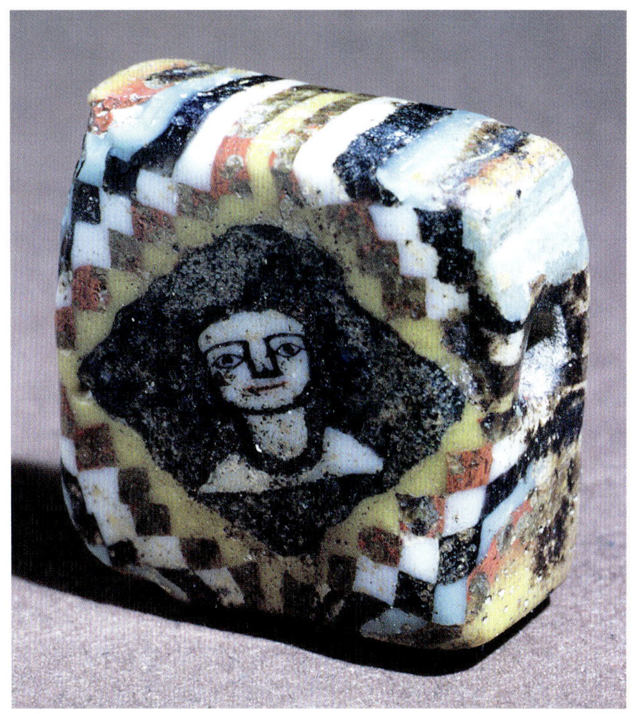

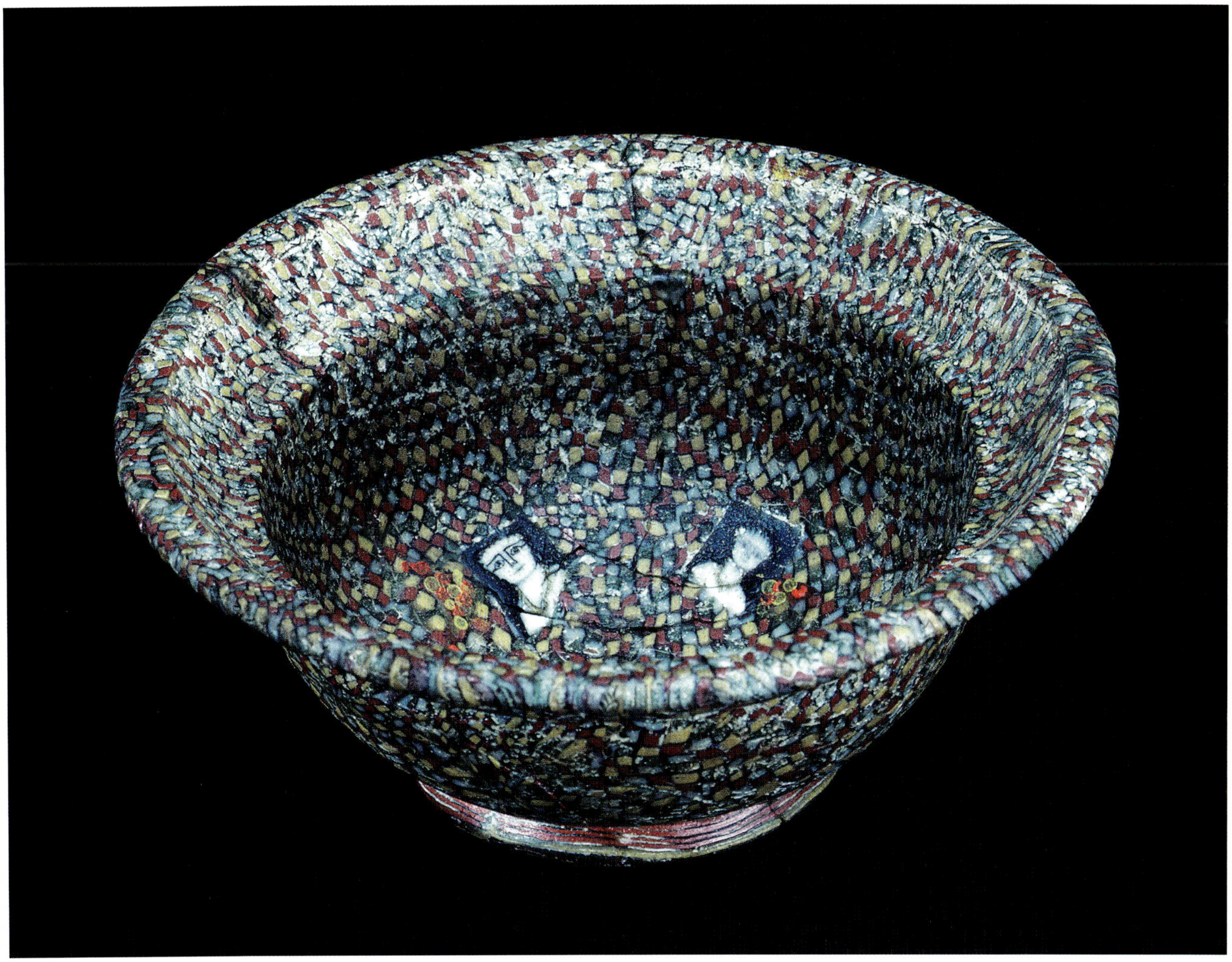

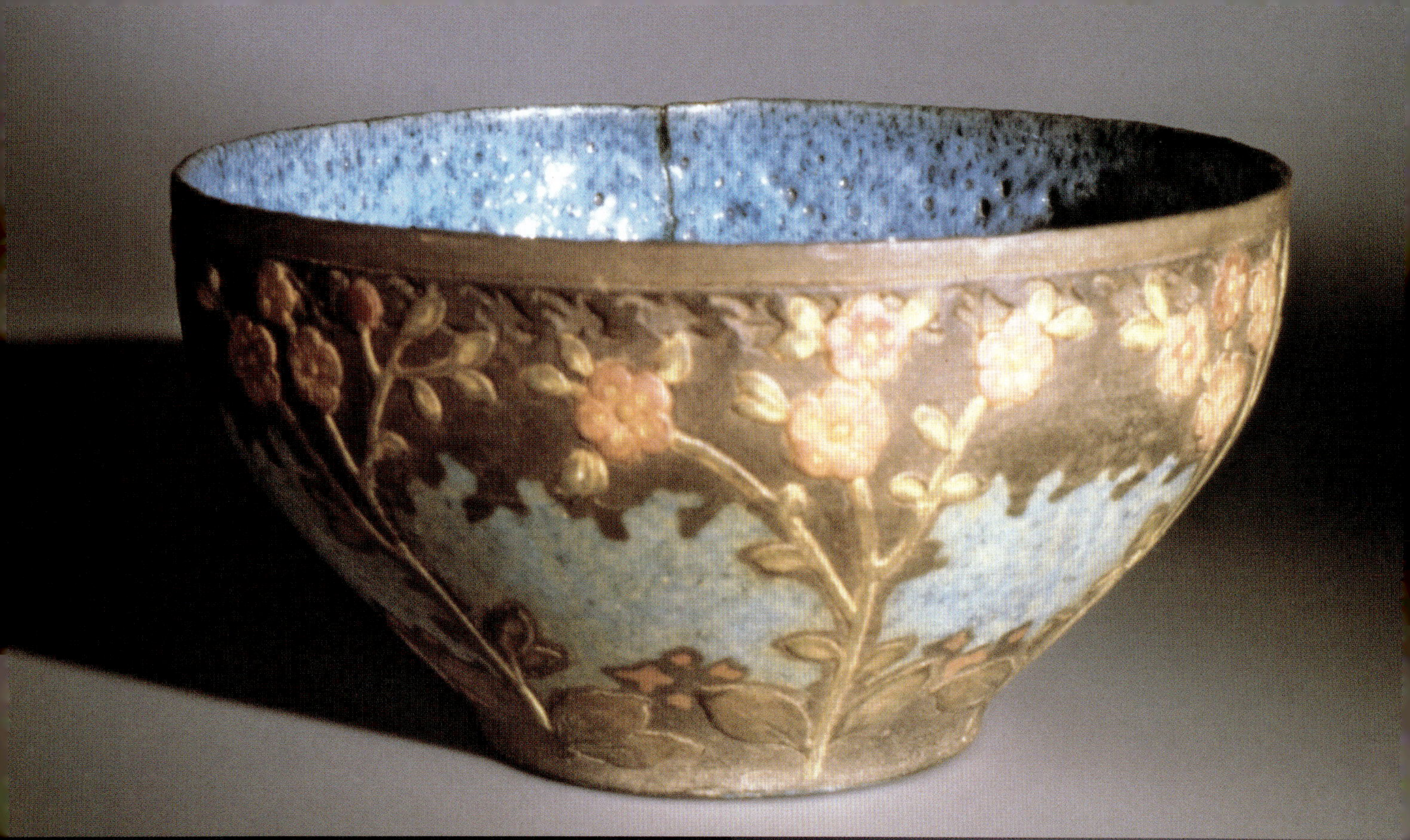

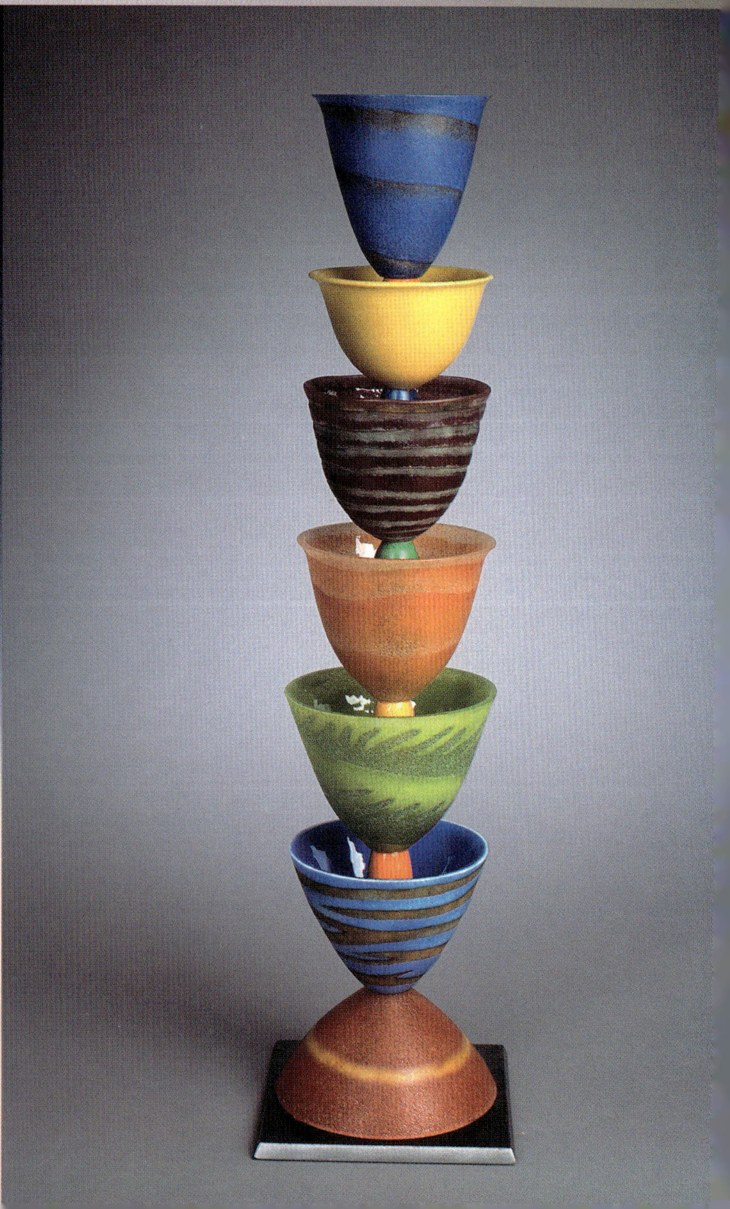

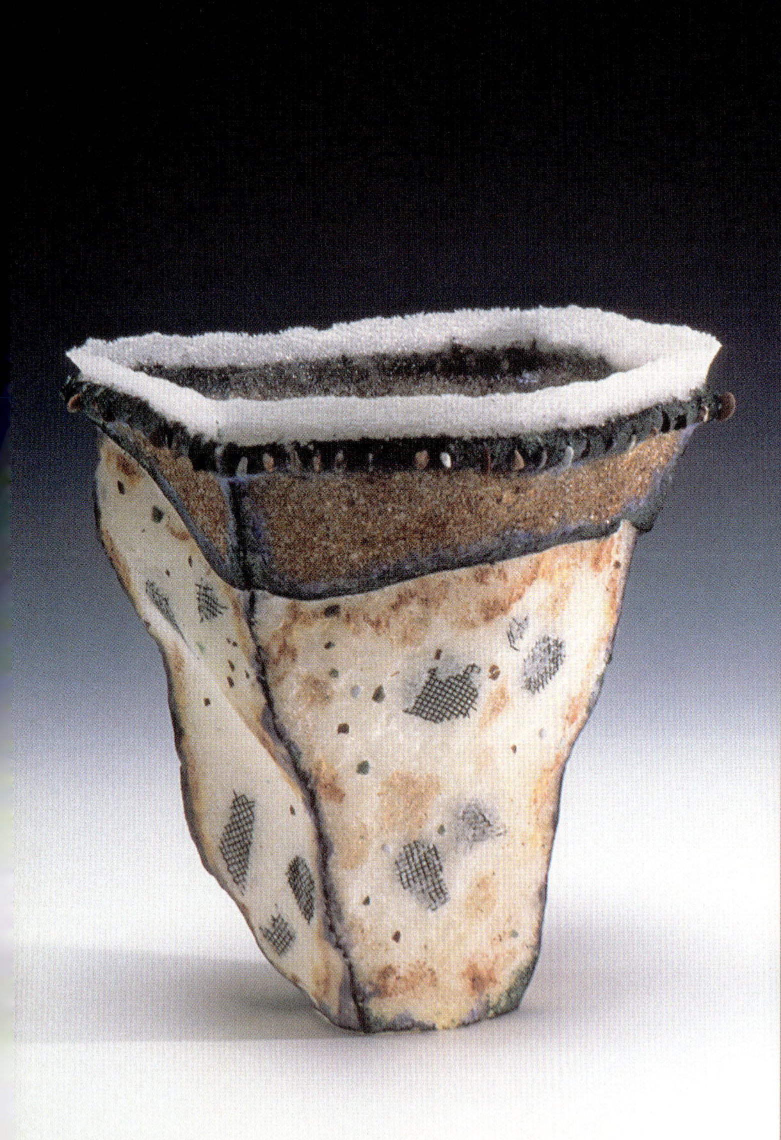
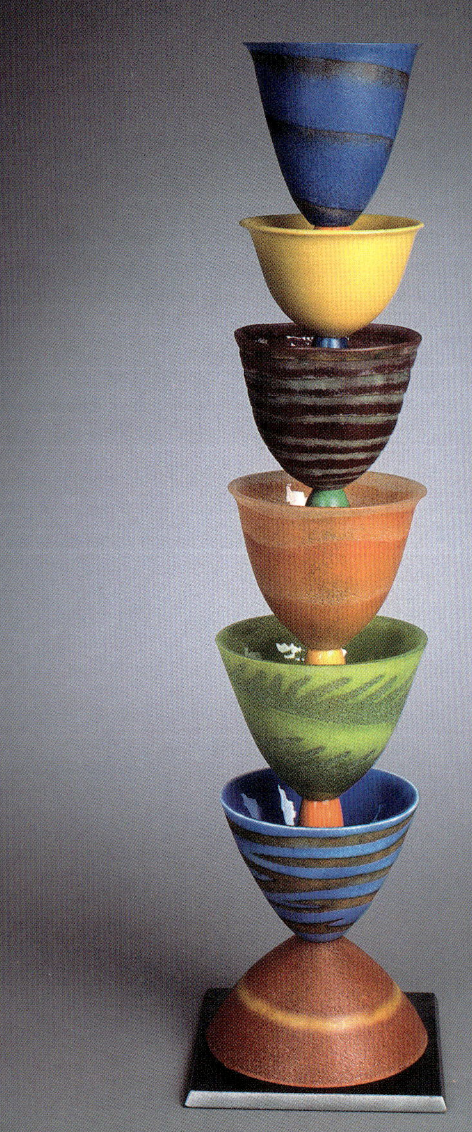

pâte de verre: 1880 - present

Kiln forming of glass entered a dark age from about 500 A.D. until our story continues again in France in the early 1880's.
At that time, a few French artists in the Art Nouveau style – Henri Cros, Albert Dammouse, Amalric Walter, George Despret, Francois Decorchement, Gabriel Argy-Rousseau, and others – experimented with "pâte de verre" – paste of glass, "cire perdue" – lost wax, and fused powdered colored glass in plaster molds, creating small medallions, sculptures, and bowls. After visiting French glass studios in the 1930's, the Japanese Iwata Glass Company also produced "pâte de verre."

Frederick Carder (1863 – 1963), co-founder of Stuben Glass Company in Corning, New York, experimented with lost wax and "pâte de verre" pieces. I met his assistant, Paul Vickers Gardner, who worked with Carder for many years and later became professor emeritus for the Smithsonian Glass collection. He came to my 1988 exhibition at the Glass Gallery in Bethesda, Maryland and was very interested in the new way that I was working with fused glass. We talked about his experiments with "pâte de verre," and he told me that he had made a few kiln-formed pieces for Frederick Carder.

From 1880 to 1950, only a small amount of fused glass in molds was created.
 I consider the thin-walled "paste of glass" vessels to be true "pâte de verre" and the mold pieces, for which glass grains are dry stacked without being made into a paste, to be "kiln cast." For lost wax technique, a mold is made around a wax positive; the wax is melted out and replaced with glass that flows from a reservoir in the same manner as casting bronze.

In England in the early 1980's, Diana Hobson recreated "pâte de verre" in her own style, using lead crystal glass, green colored glass, beach sand, black volcanic sand, red brick, copper mesh, and beach stones at the rim. She pushed glass paste into crevices of a plaster mold and built up a thin vessel wall. Some of the French artists filled their thin-walled vessels with asbestos before firing, to help support the walls, but Hobson fired her vessels open – without a center support – until the glass grains stuck together. She stopped the kiln firing after the glass grains had "fused to stick" just before the wall of her vessel began to collapse.

In the 1990's, Alicia Lomné, began making thin-walled, open-fired "pâte de verre" vessels using Bullseye glass. We happen to live on the same island in Washington State, where she creates "pâte de verre" in her unique comtemporary sculptural style.

I find the thin-walled "pâte de verre" vessels to be the most technically challenging of the mold fired glass work.

facing upper:
"Pâte de Verre Bowl," artist Albert Louis Dammouse, Sevres, France circa 1910, diameter 4 ½ in. (11.2 cm). Courtesy of the Corning Museum of Glass.

facing lower left:
"Freeform Series #7," artist Dianna Hobson, 1984, H. 5.5 in. (14 cm),

facing lower right:
"Stacking #11," artist Alicia Lomné, 2005, H. 23 in. (58 cm) x W. 6 in. (15 cm) x D. 6 in. (15 cm).

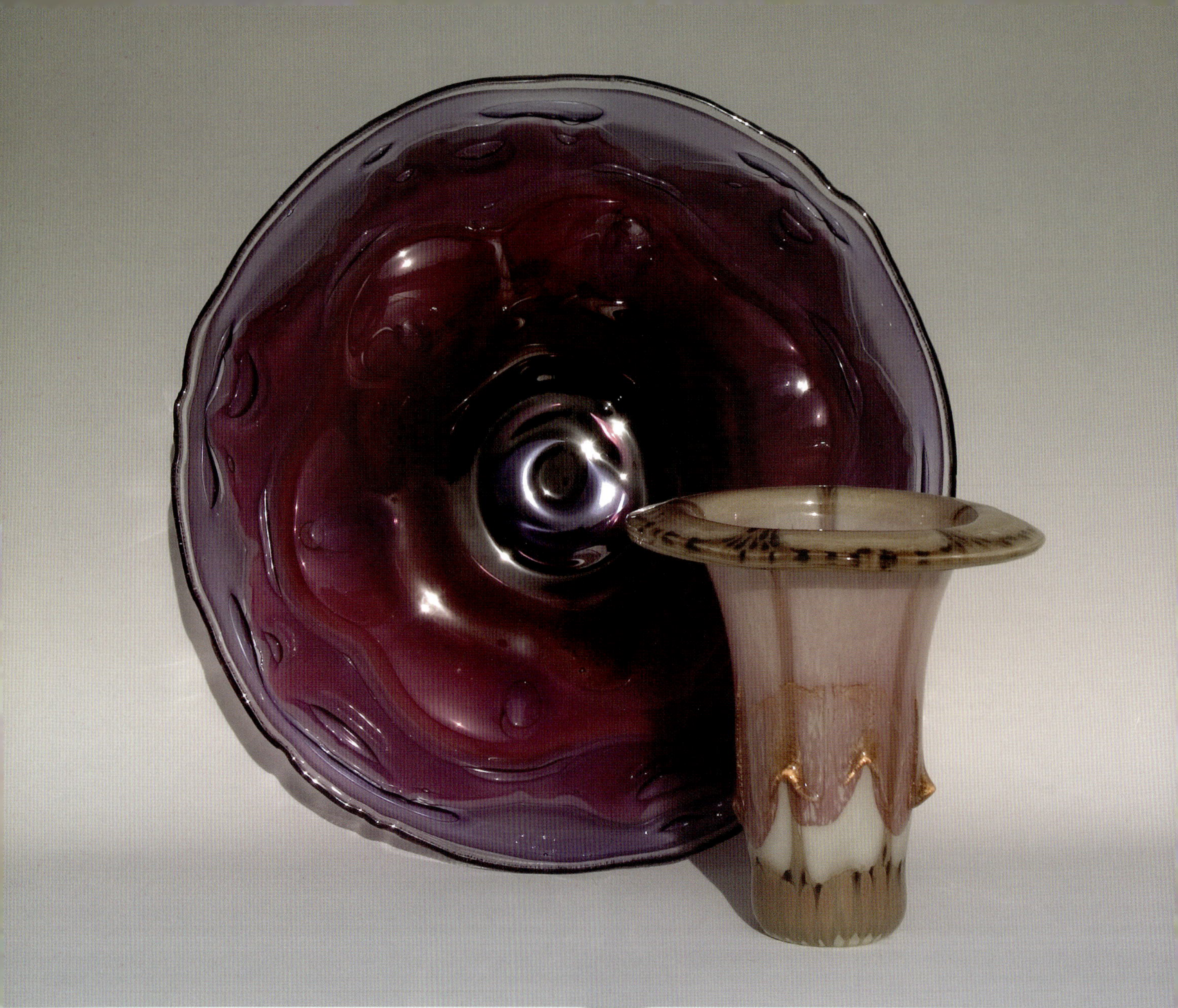

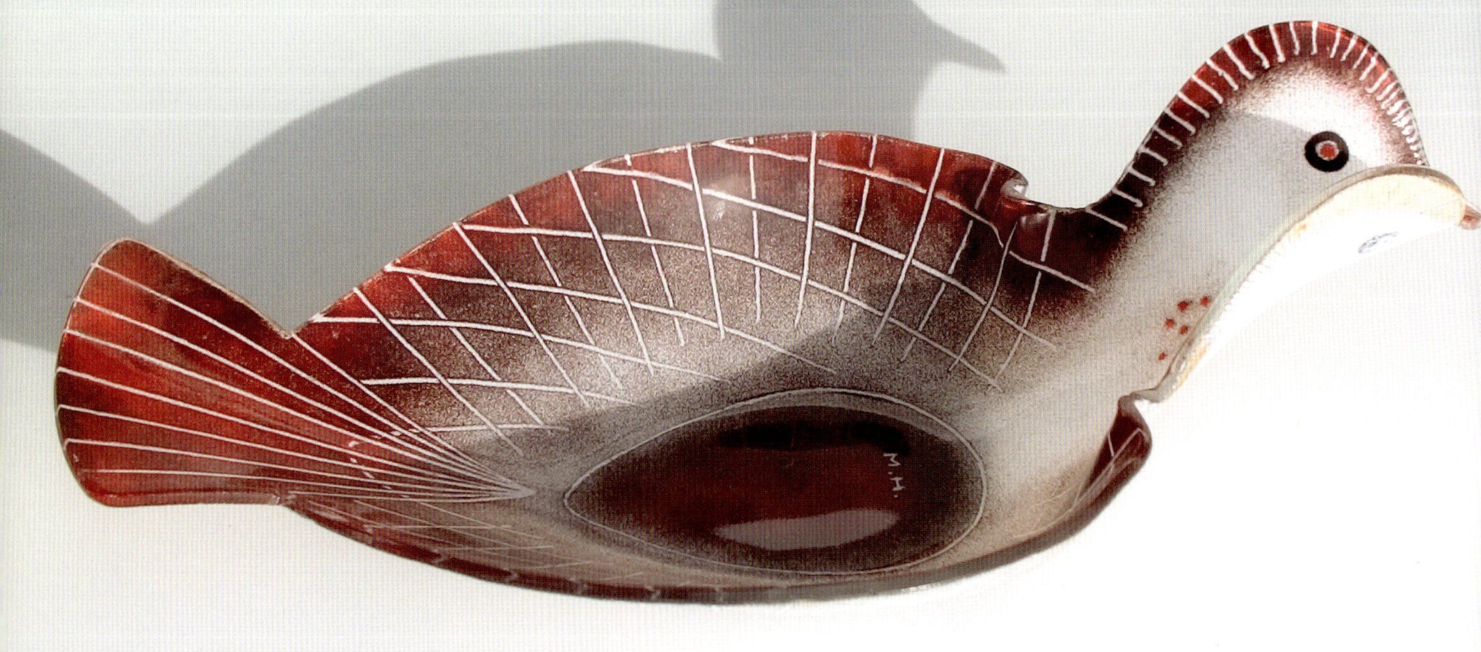

fusing in the USA: 1950's

Window Glass and Enamels

A group of craftsmen working in the late 1940's and 50's fused glass enamels (for copper and steel enameling) on and in between pieces of window glass, in electric soft-brick kilns used for ceramics. They mostly made utilitarian objects: lamp shades, plates, bowls, serving trays, jewelry, and the occasional arty piece. Galleries for art/craft were in their infancy, and these artists sold through department stores and out of their store fronts.

Maurice Heaton (1900 - 1990)

I heard Heaton lecture in the early 1980's. I remember him as a very spry and jaunty man. He described an impressive device that he made, operated like a small human-powered forklift to load his front opening kilns. He called it his "iron horse." Heaton was born in Switzerland and came to America in 1914 to work on stained glass church windows with his father, Clement Heaton. In 1937, Maurice began experimenting with fusing enamels on top of window glass, sometimes utilizing stencils. In 1947 he was fusing coarse enamels underneath glass and, by 1961, enamels between glass. Heaton created lighting fixtures, bowls, and dishes that he formed in steel molds. A 1980's studio pamphlet stated, "The kilns are still housed in the 200-year old grist mill on Old Mill Road, long a dirt road bordering the pond that supplied the power for the firing. The adjoining barn, also a landmark, which contained the atelier, workshop and display room, burned to the ground in April 1974. The entire contents were destroyed. A small new studio has been erected on the ruins of the historic old one." Maurice lived and worked in rural Rockland County, New York and actively pursued his art until 1990. He signed his work simply with his initials M.H.

facing upper left piece:
shallow bowl made by Michael Higgins, H. 3 ¼ in. (8 cm) x 14 in. (35 cm) in diameter, 1992. Created from cut pieces of sheet glass coated with transparent enamels that were prefired, with intentionally trapped air bubbles in some places, signed Higgins 92.

facing upper right piece:
dropout vase made by Frances Higgins, H. 7 in. (18 cm) x 6 ¾ in. (17 cm) in diameter at the rim, with gold veiling, circa 1992, signed Higgins.

facing bottom:
red bird made by Maurice Heaton, fused enamels on the underside of ⅛ in. (3 mm) window glass then slumped into a metal mold. H. 4 ½ in. (11 cm) x W. 7 in. (18 cm) x L. 15 in. (38 cm), circa 1950.

bottom left:
photo of Maurice Heaton sifting enamels onto glass, in his studio, from the cover of a pre-1974 studio brochure.

bottom right:
Maurice Heaton plate with enamels fused on the underside of ⅛ in. (3 mm) window glass, 8 in. (20 cm) in diameter x 1 in. (2.5 cm), circa 1950.

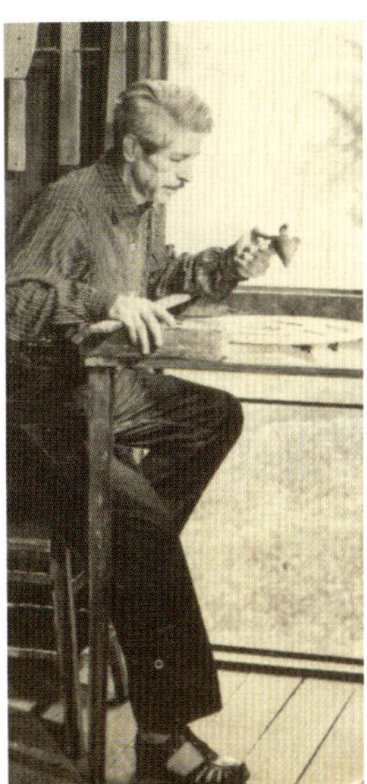

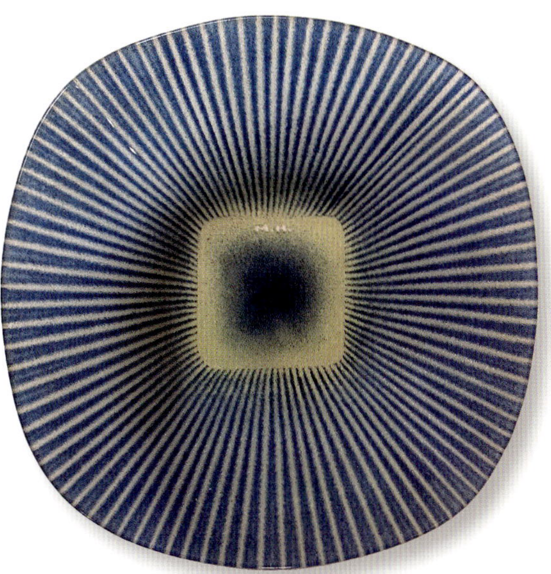

**Frances Higgins (1912 - 2004) and
Michael Higgins (1908 - 1999)**

They called their work, *"modern miracles in everyday glass"* and said in one of their shop handouts, *"we were both University teachers, we left the field of education, joined forces in art and marriage, and began to develop our creativity in fused enameled sheet glass."* Beginning in 1948, Frances and Michael Higgins performed their miracles for over fifty years in the Chicago, Illinois area. In another pamphlet they said, *"We make bowls (4" to 24"), vases, plates, platters, various pendants and other jewelry, plaques for windows & walls, framed and unframed, mobiles, a wide range of decorative pieces, windows, panels and view-blockers made to order and all in fused enameled glass!"* They produced these by the thousands in their "modern" style of the 1950's and 1960's. In the political world of art, this emphasis on craft delayed their acknowledgement as artistic pioneers in the studio glass movement. The books, <u>Higgins: Adventures in Glass</u> and <u>Higgins: Poetry in Glass</u> by Johnson and Piña, have many color pictures of their work.

Beginning in their own studio they fused enamels between window glass in pottery kilns and sold their decorative pieces in department stores including Marshall Field, Bloomingdale's, and Gump's. From 1957 – 1964 they designed pieces and worked at the Dearborn Glass Company in Bedford Park, Illinois creating thousands of pieces and flooding the market with "Higginsware" and other pieces. In 1965 they briefly made glass items at the Haeger factory in southern Illinois. Today you can find these pieces in "collectible malls" and on eBay for as little as $20.

Pieces were placed on one end of a conveyer belt leading into a decorating lehr (kiln) in which they were fused and annealed, coming out the other end as a finished product. Michael lost much of his hearing standing for hours next to the noisy lehr. They were very happy to leave the factory scene, and in 1966 they set up their building in Riverside where they sold their items in their front shop, produced utilitarian ware and created unique "one of a kind" art in the back studio, all while living in an apartment on the second floor. The big event of the year was their Christmas sale where people lined up to get in the door. Frances and Michael Higgins both worked and lived here until they passed away. Louise Wimmer, who had worked for the Higgins' studio since 1978, and her son Jonathan Wimmer took over the studio and continue to produce "Higgins-style" glass today. The studio is located at 33 East Quincy Street, Riverside, Illinois, www.higginsglass.com.

The Higgins invented the dropout!

They placed glass on top of a clay ring and heated it until it sagged through the hole, making a vase. Many glass fusers utilize their technique today. Frances sifted, stenciled, and trapped enamels between window glass to create her pieces, and her dropout tree vases are stunning. She also made patterned frames for her glass, using a plaster cement-like material.

Michael solved the problem of compatible sheet glass by running pieces of window glass coated with enamels through the factory lehr. They amassed a large stock of colored sheets including special gold luster sheets for their projects. Michael would cut pieces from these sheets and create designs and layers that he fused and slumped into platters and dropouts. Michael designed and patented the "Rondelay," a fused glass circle that had metal tabs fused into them for linking to other rondelays to create screens and room dividers. They didn't sign their glass individually but with a joint, "Higgins."

The Higgins were truly innovative!

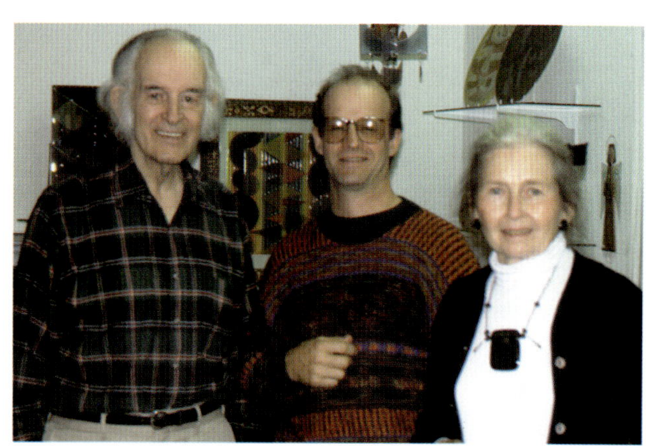

The Higgins' Studio

I was fortunate to have visited the Higgins at
their studio in Riverside, Illinois in 1992 and
1995 and thrilled that they came to my 1992 solo
exhibition at the Marx Gallery in Chicago.

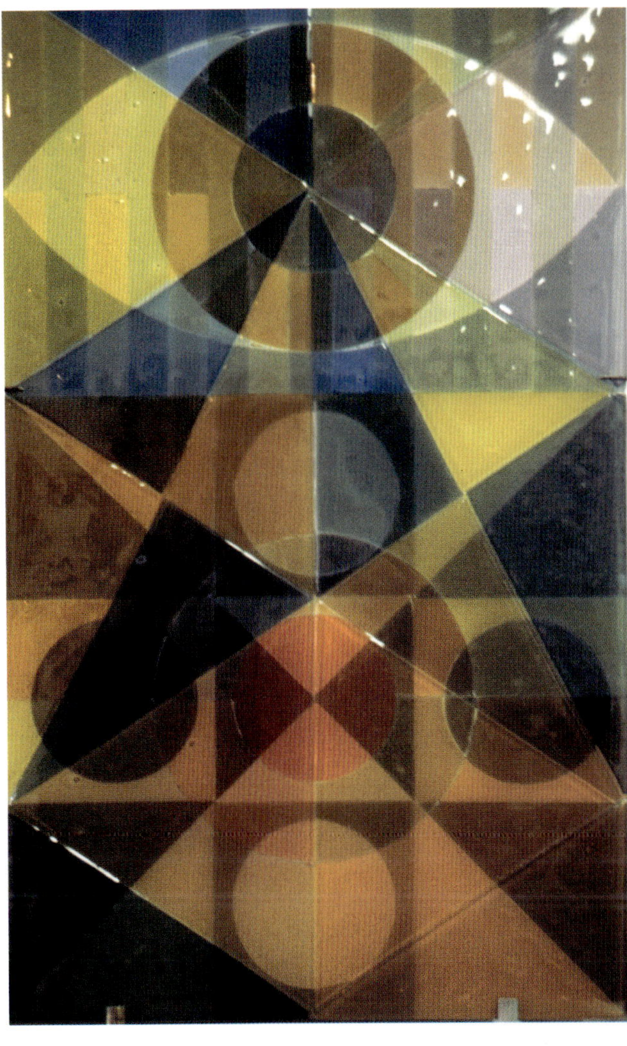

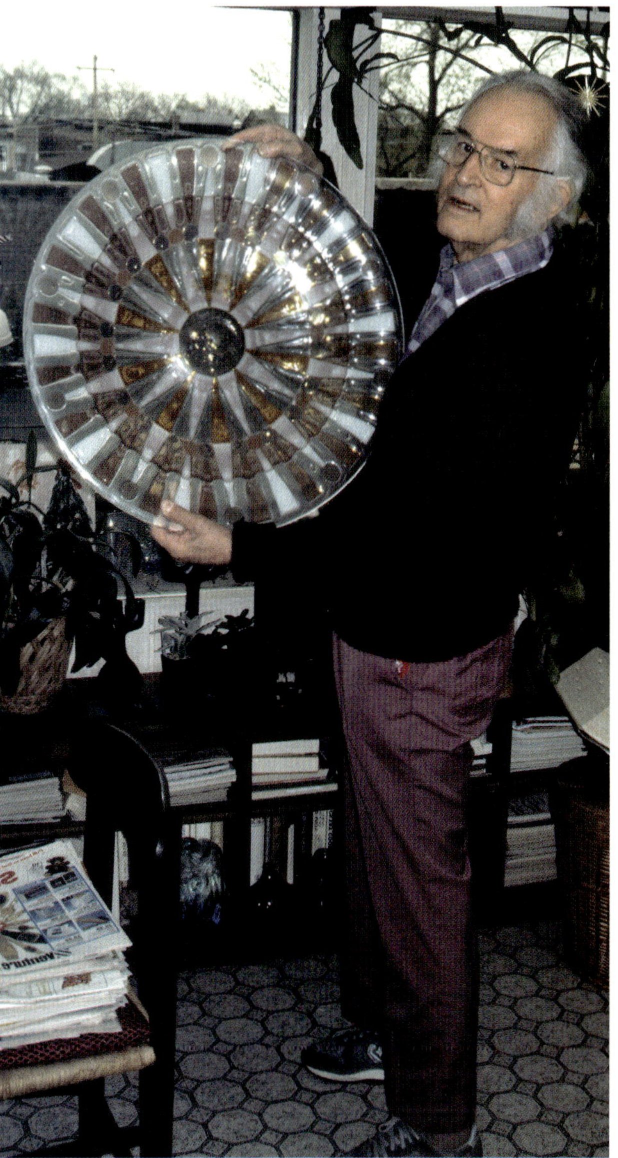

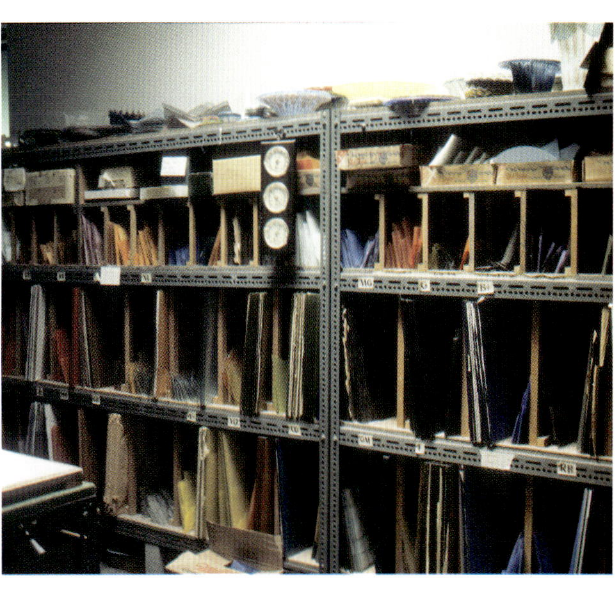

facing: Richard La Londe with Frances and Michael
Higgins in their Riverside gallery, 1995.

bottom right: The glass rack. A Higgins pamphlet
says, "We coat flat sheets of clear glass with micro-
layers of color enamels in about 30 different hues."

top left: Michael Higgins fused glass panel
approximately H. 20 in. (50 cm) x W. 12 in. (30 cm),
photographed in 1992, made from cut and fused
enameled sheets of window glass.

top right: Michael holding his 24 in. (61 cm) fused platter that he made from cut gold lustered and enameled
glass sheets, 1992. This was one of two that Michael
made at Dearborn, in the early 1960s. The one Michael
is holding sold at auction in 2004 for nearly $13,000!

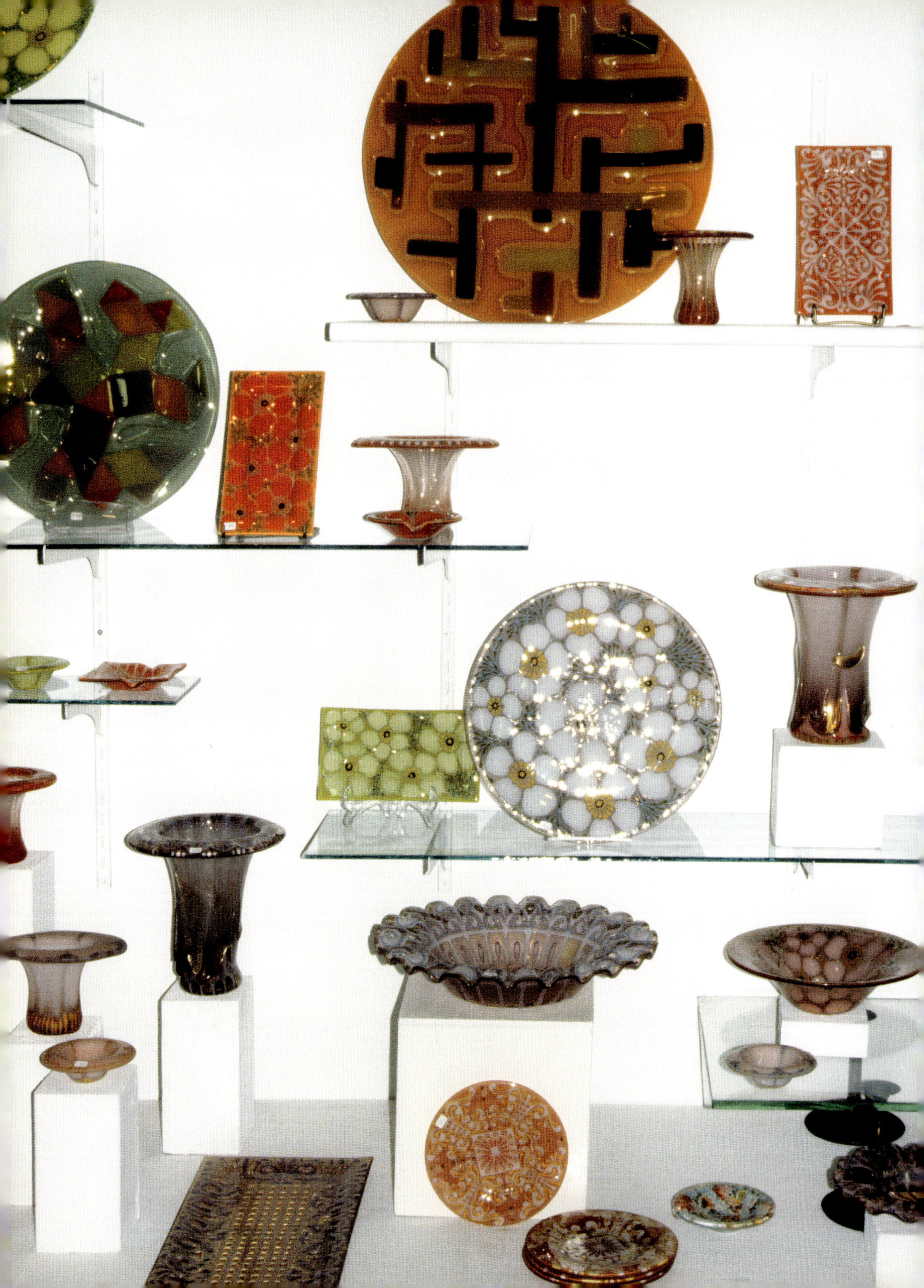

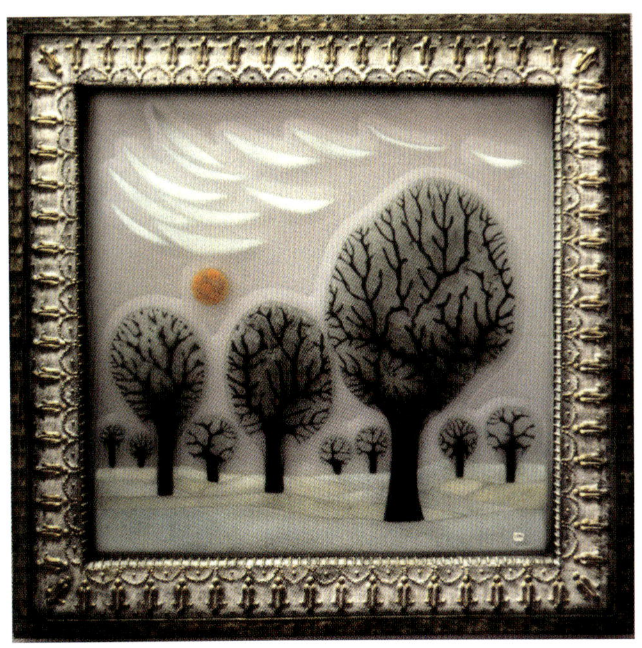

How We Create It
By Frances and Michael Higgins
(Excerpted from a studio pamphlet circa 1995)

"We take large sheets of clear glass, and apply micro-layers of different colored glasses (or enamels - much the same thing). Then we fire these enamels on to the sheets of glass, so that they can be handled and cut safely.

To form an object, we cut two pieces (or more) of the same shape from two different-colored pre-fired enameled sheets. On the bottom one (enamel up) we apply a decorative design, usually by either drawing in powdered glass with a stylus or with brushes, stencils, etc., or by laying on pieces cut from other colored sheets.

Then we lay on the top sheet (color down), and set the assembly on a mold of clay or stainless steel. We subject it to a second firing which fuses it into a single object, shapes it to the mold (or to a flat form), and 'melts' the edges to roundness with the design sealed inside."

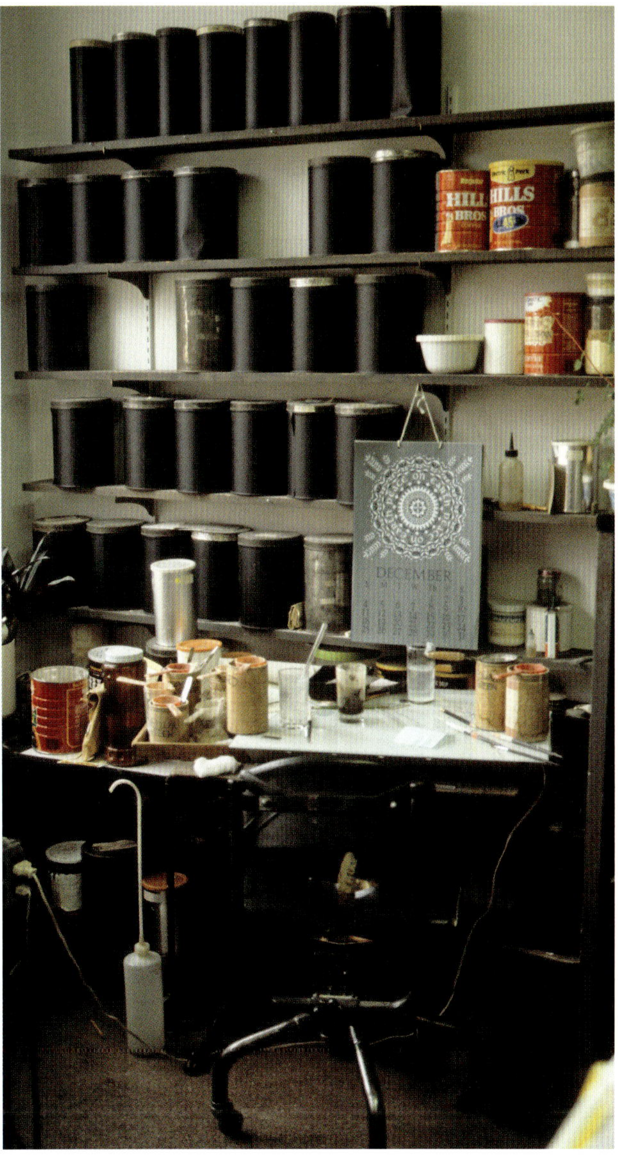

facing: display shelves in their Riverside gallery, 1995. You can see the intricate patterned enamel plates and bowls that Frances made. Michael did the cut sheet glass platter on the upper shelf. They both created the dropout pieces.

upper left: Trees, about H. 16 in. (40 cm) x W. 16 in. (40 cm), photographed in 1992. A fused enamel piece with a patterned cement-like frame that Frances made.

upper right: Frances' workbench with canisters of enamels. The calendar was an inspiration for designs that she was working on, 1992.

Frances and Michael Higgins were nice, generous, and very creative artists. I am honored to have known them.

Edris Eckhart (1905 - 1998)

In 1953, Edris Eckhart who was nationally recognized in the ceramic art world, started experimenting with glass to try to rediscover the ancient Roman technique to produce the gold glass that she had seen in New York City.

Her experiments involved fusing gold between sheets of window glass, which wasn't as successful as she had hoped, so she made her own clear glass in an electric kiln and rolled out small sheets with a wet wooden rolling pin. Edris is believed to be the first American artist to mix and melt her own glass batch.

Her efforts produced a number of artworks with designs cut in gold and silver foil, sandwiched between sheets of transparent glass that were decorated with enamels and pieces of colored glass and then fused in an electric kiln. Edris usually mounted these in a frame, and they were sometimes backlit.

In 1954 she traveled to Corning, New York, where she showed her gold glass to Tom Buechner, director of the Corning Museum of Glass; she also visited with Frederick Carder, the founder of Stuben Glass Works. Her sandwiched gold glass caused quite a stir in the art community and led to two

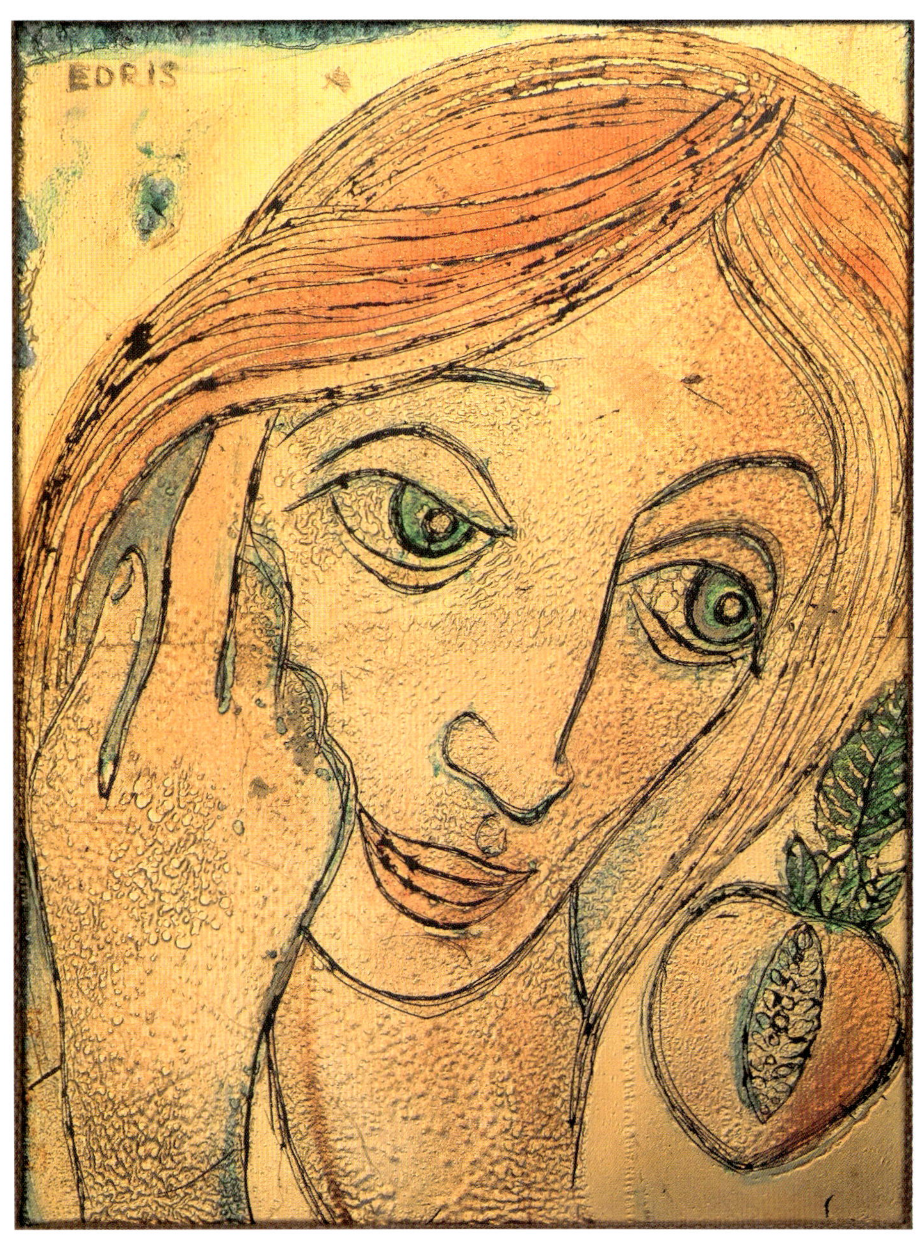

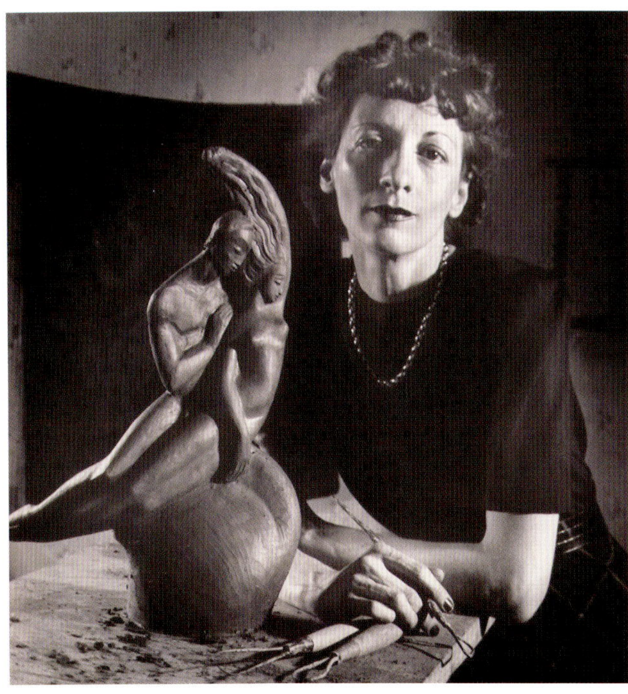

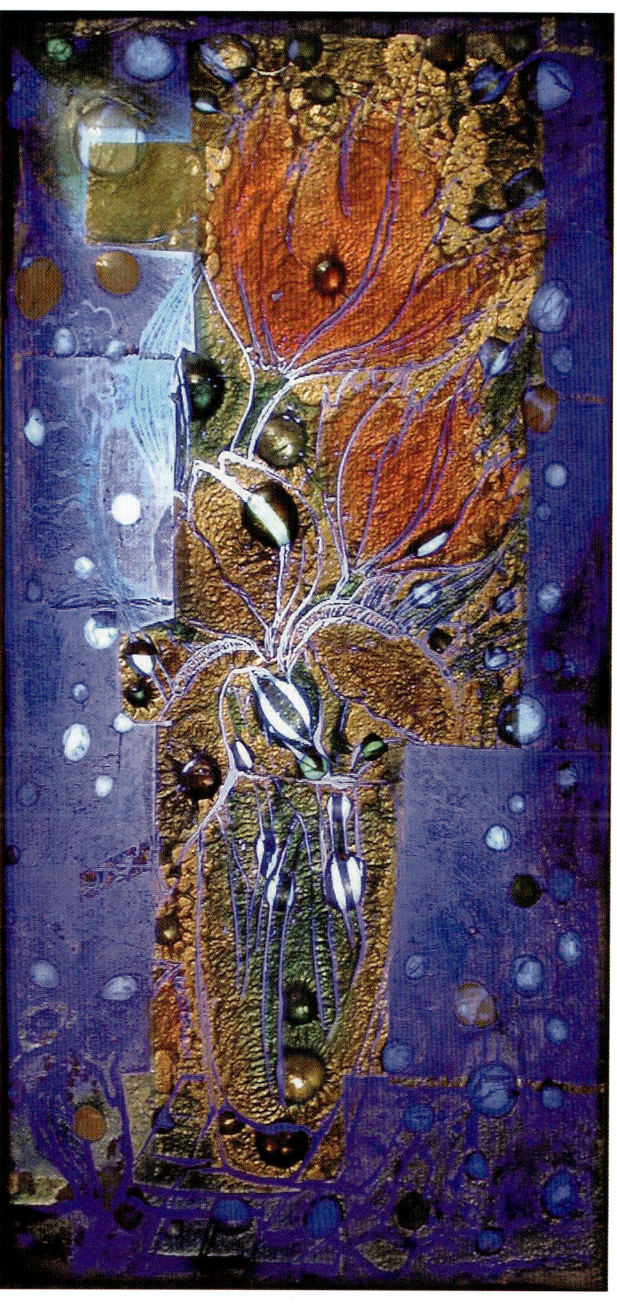

Guggenheim Fellowship awards (1956 & 1959) and a Louis Tiffany Foundation Award (1959).

Edris also discussed lost wax casting of glass – "cire perdue" – with Frederick Carder, the American master of this genre. Her ceramics background and mold making led her to create many lost wax glass sculptures, for which she is mainly recognized today. She carved a wax model, which was cast – "invested" – in a mold that she devised from gypsum and clay. The wax was melted out and replaced with powdered glass, which, upon firing, melted to fill the hollow mold. After the glass was annealed and cooled, the mold was broken away, leaving the glass sculpture.

In 1961, Edris was invited to teach for a year at University of California in Berkeley; she introduced glassmaking to the art department where she developed her technique for casting bronze around pieces of glass.

In 1968 the Corning Museum of Glass honored Edris Eckhart with a retrospective show, the museum's first exhibition of a single contemporary artist. Before her glass career Edris had already had a full artist's life. She graduated from the Cleveland School of Art in 1931. About that time, she changed her name from Edythe Eckhart to Edris, possibly to avoid prejudice toward women in art. In 1932 she worked for Alexander Archipenko in New York and helped make his

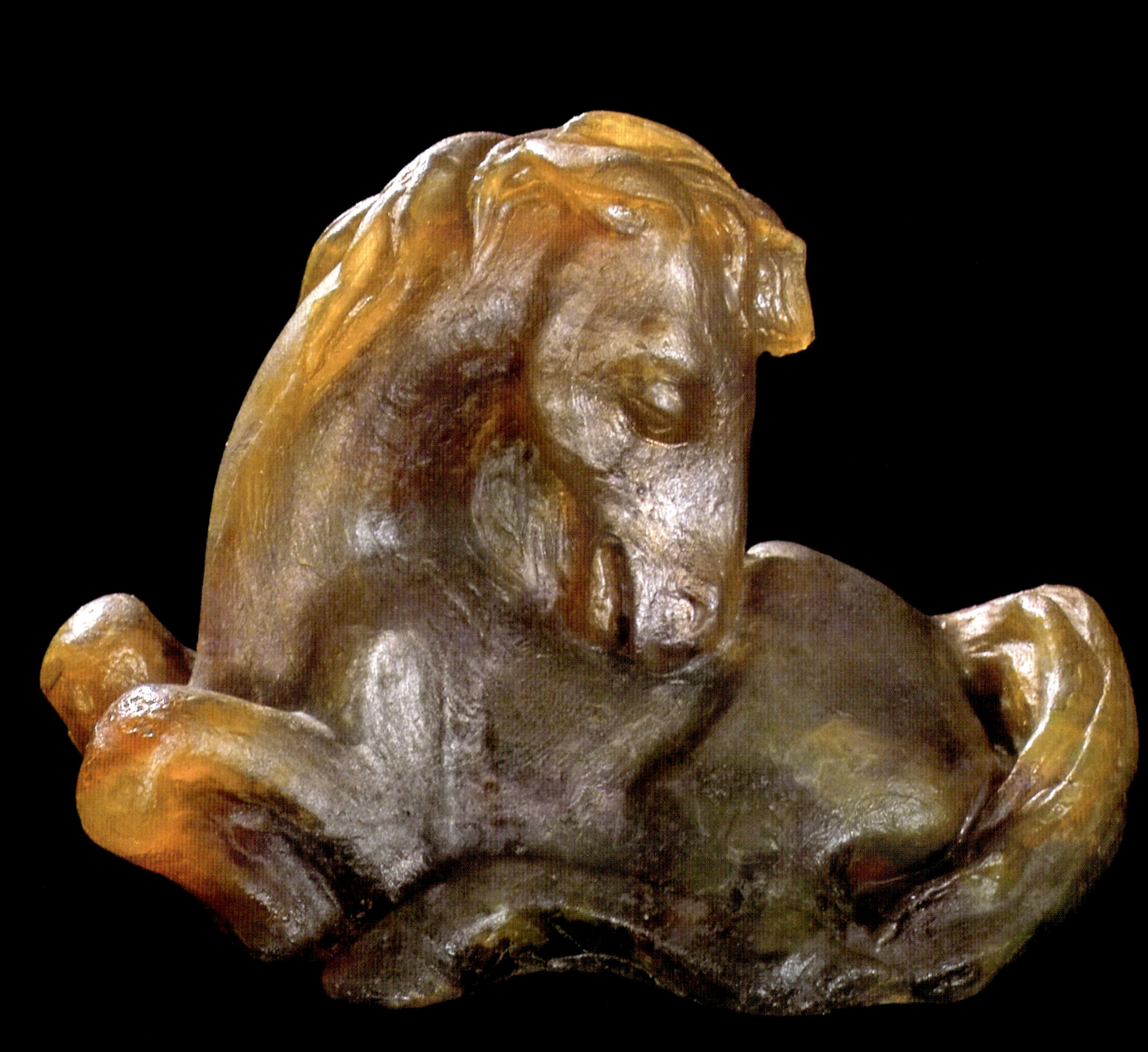

ceramic sculptures. The next year she returned to Cleveland and began designing clay figurines, modeled from children's books, for public libraries through the Public Works of Art Project (PWAP). She became head of the Federal Arts Project/Works Progress Administration Ceramics and Sculpture Division in the Cleveland area, 1935 to 1941. Edris was nationally recognized in the ceramic art world.

Edris was also an arts educator. From 1933 – 1971, she taught ceramics, craft, enamels, and glass at the Cleveland Institute of Art and other universities. Her pieces evoked the ideas of her time and included religious subjects, circus clowns, knights in armor, characters from children's books, and Greek mythology.

She had numerous exhibitions throughout her career, including thirty-two solo shows; she is included in many museum collections. During the 1950's, Edris spoke at the major craft conferences about glass. This was years before Harvey Littleton hosted his 1962 Toledo workshops, supposedly launching the "Studio Glass Movement" – which, by the way, had already been going on for at least a decade!

facing: Dawn, 1977, H. 7 in. (18 cm) x W. 12 in. (30 cm) x D. 8 in. (20 cm). Lost wax cast glass, collection of Craig Bara.

left: Three Fates, 1972, H. 12.5 in. (32 cm) x W. 6 in. (15 cm). Lost wax cast glass, collection of The New Bedford Museum of Glass, New Bedford, MA.

right: Strange Blossom, 1979, H. 20 in. (51 cm) x W. 5.5 in. (14 cm) x D. 5 in. (13 cm). Bronze cast around glass, collection of Charles and Fran Debordeau.

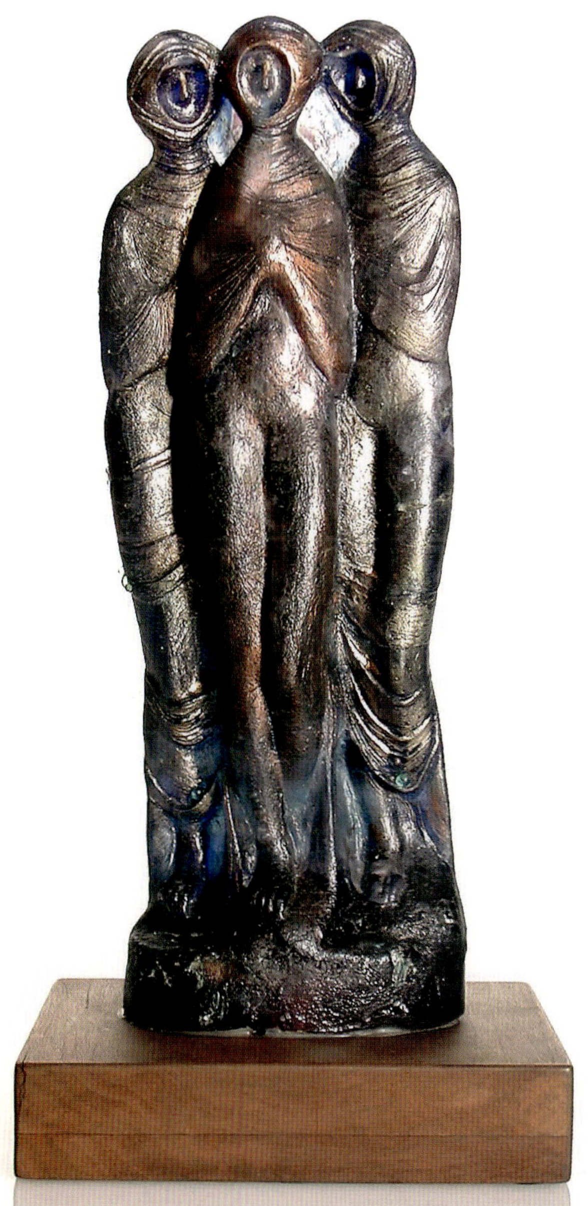

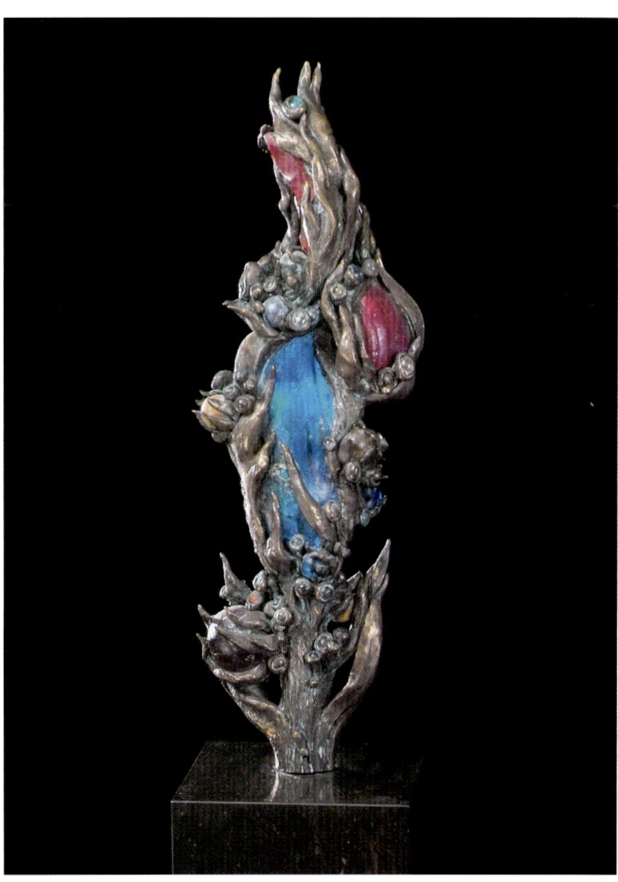

Earl McCutchen (1918 – 1985)
Earl taught ceramics at the University of Georgia 1941 – 1942 and 1945 – 1983. Beginning in the early 1950's, he experimented with glass. He laminated aluminum foil, chicken wire, paper, ceramic glazes, iron filings, copper screen and gold leaf between sheets of old window glass, in part because he was intrigued with their chemical interactions. Earl created plates and bowls by slumping this fused glass into clay molds that he made. Around 1965 he blew glass and set up hot glass classes at the University of Georgia.

An interesting connection from the 1940's is that Frances Higgins was friends with Earl McCutchen and his wife Mary at the University of Georgia.

upper right: "Earl McCutchen holding a slumped bowl." Photo from a digital reproduction courtesy of the Hargrett Rare Book and Manuscript Library/University of Georgia Libraries - Original photograph in possession of Mary McCutchen."

lower left: "Butterfly Plate" ¾ in. (2 cm) x 10 in. diameter (25 cm). Collection of Mary McCutchen.

lower right: "Round Plate" ½ in. (1.25 cm) x 10 in. diameter (25 cm). Collection of Mary McCutchen.

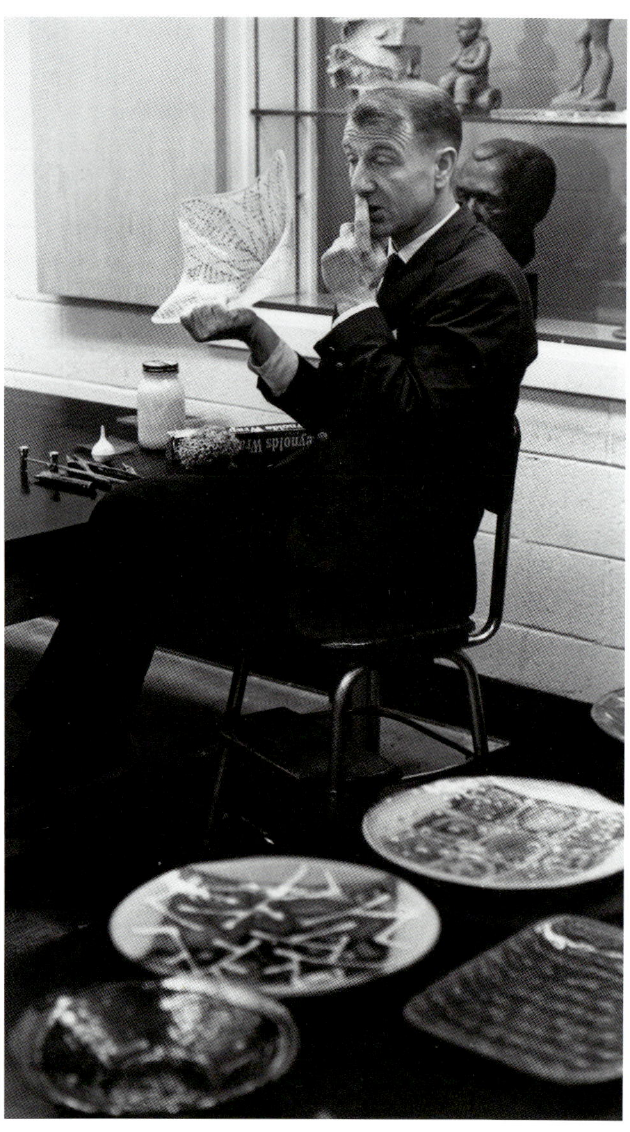

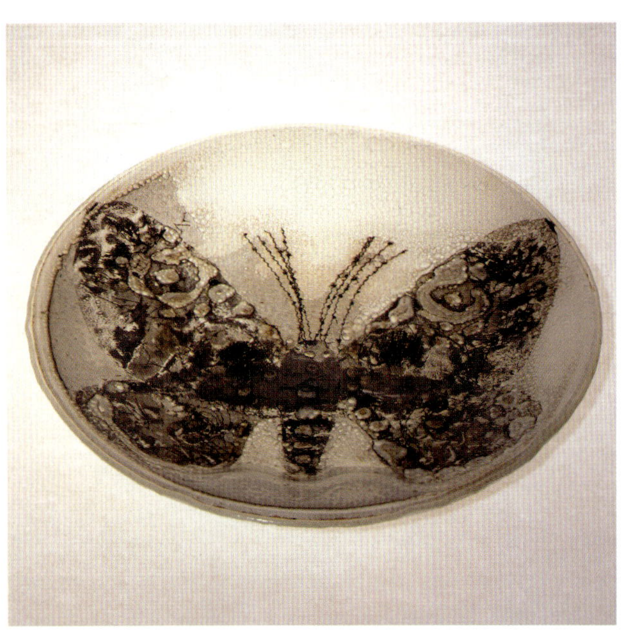

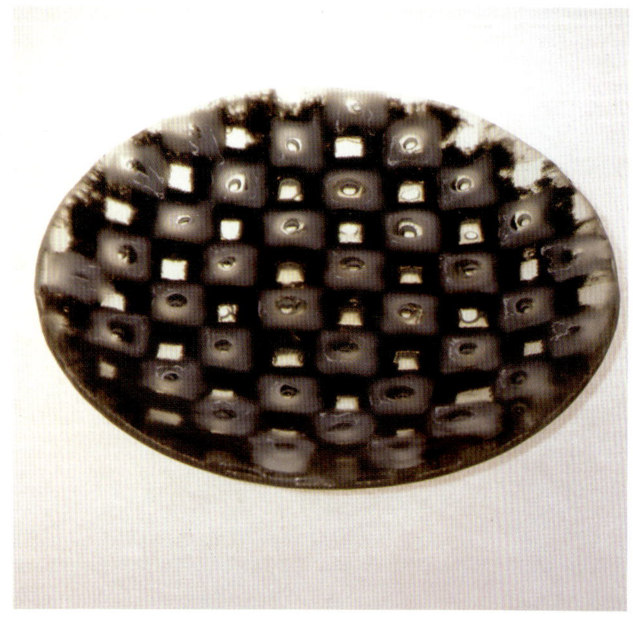

Glen Lukens (1887 – 1967)

As a ceramic artist and teacher, Glen Lukens developed many new glazes and glaze techniques. He taught courses in ceramics, metalwork, and jewelry, at the University of Southern California in Los Angeles during the 1930's. His emphasis was on form and surface treatment; he helped train the next generation of artist teachers who would go on to establish the Studio Pottery movement in the 1950's – 1960's. Two of his students were F. Carlton Ball and Beatrice Wood.

Glen probably began exploring the use of glass in his work during the mid - 1930's, and by the early 1950's, after retiring from USC, he was creating glass vessels and dinnerware that had a smooth interior surface with a tactile bubbly effect on the back. Glen gave his glass a subtle hint of color by airbrushing a light colored glaze onto the surface of the glass before it was fired. On the plate below, it looks like he put a fine mint color onto window glass, and there is also minor surface devitrification. He fused and slumped the glass, in one firing, into a rough clay mold that he made.

below: "Pale Green Bowl" circa 1950 – 1960, 1 in. (2.5 cm) deep x 7 ½ in. (19 cm) in diameter. It is signed Glen Lukens on the back.

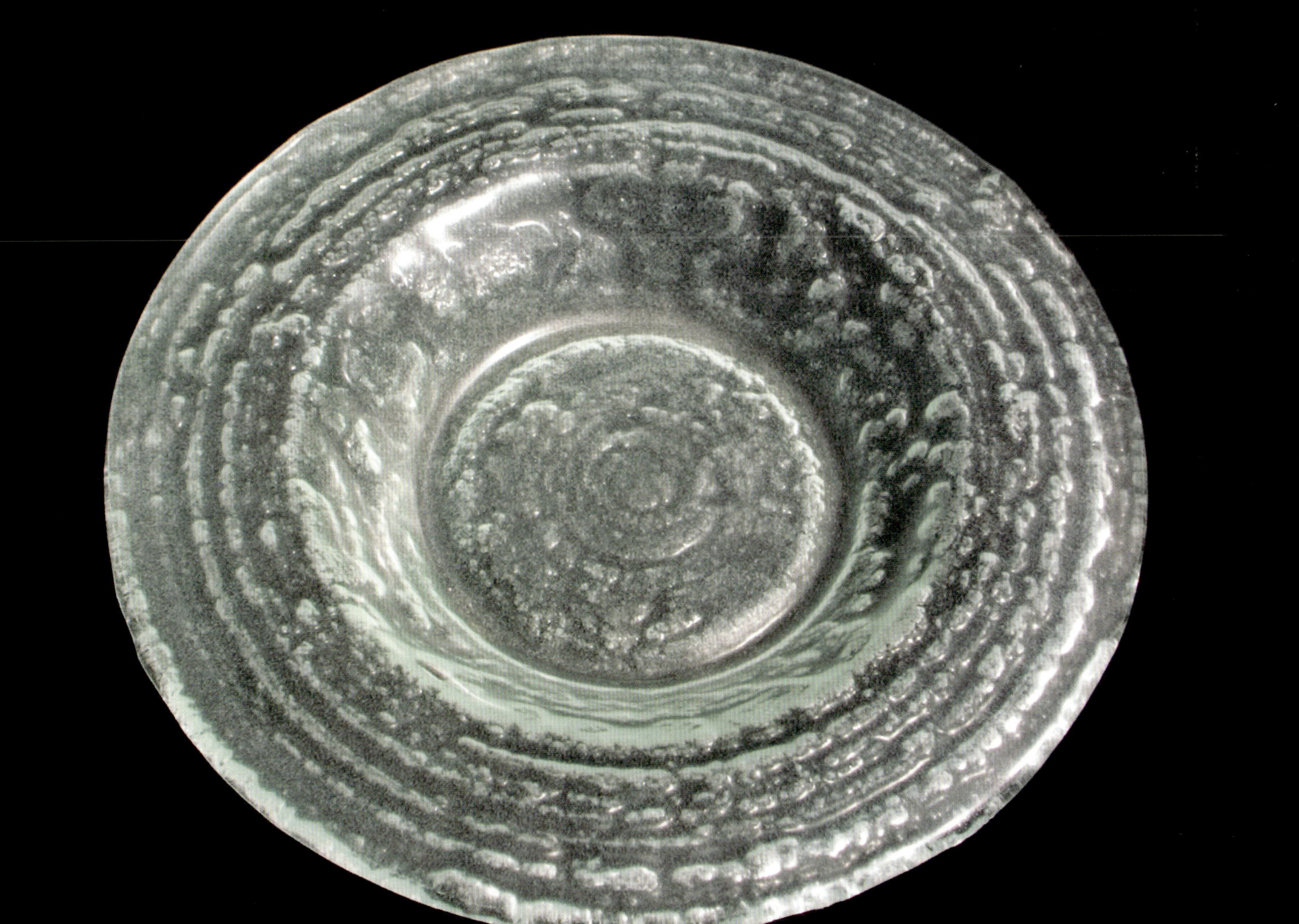

Russell Day (b. 1912)

Russell is recognized as the first artist in the Northwest to experiment with fused glass. In 1957 he did his Master Thesis titled, <u>Experiments in Glass and Colored Light</u>, for the University of Washington, and the art that he created was so unusual that he was asked to show it at the University's Henry Gallery, the first exhibition ever for a Masters candidate. He presented different types of glass fabrication, which included fusing, and showed how glass transmitted, reflected, and projected color.

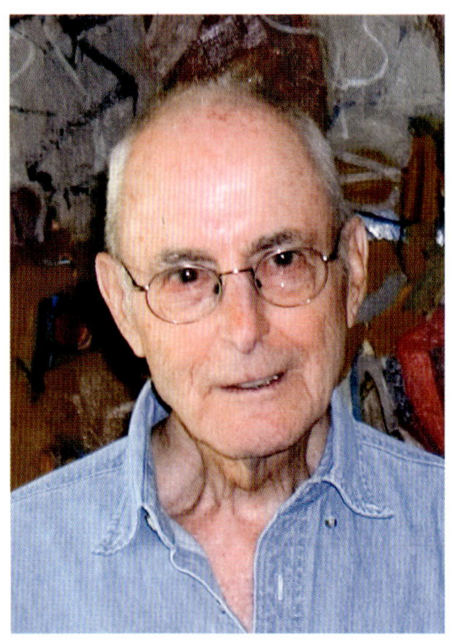

From 1948 to 1976 he led an innovative art department at Everett Community College near Seattle, Washington, which included glass, jewelry, painting, sculpture and design. Russell discussed his glass art at the 1961 Fourth National Conference of the American Craftsmen's Council at the University of Washington in Seattle and was on a panel with Michael Higgins, Edris Eckhart and lampworker John Burton. He attended Harvey Littleton's four-week, 1964 glass blowing seminar at the University of Wisconsin, Madison. Russell Day influenced Bill Boysen, Michael Whitley, Dale Chihuly and Chuck Close.

For the window piece below in his thesis he said, "I made one light by using copper fences one-quarter inch high in a design on a piece of plate glass. Into the various section as outlined by the copper fences was poured crushed glass which, when fired, fused to the under layer of plate glass. Because of the varying melting

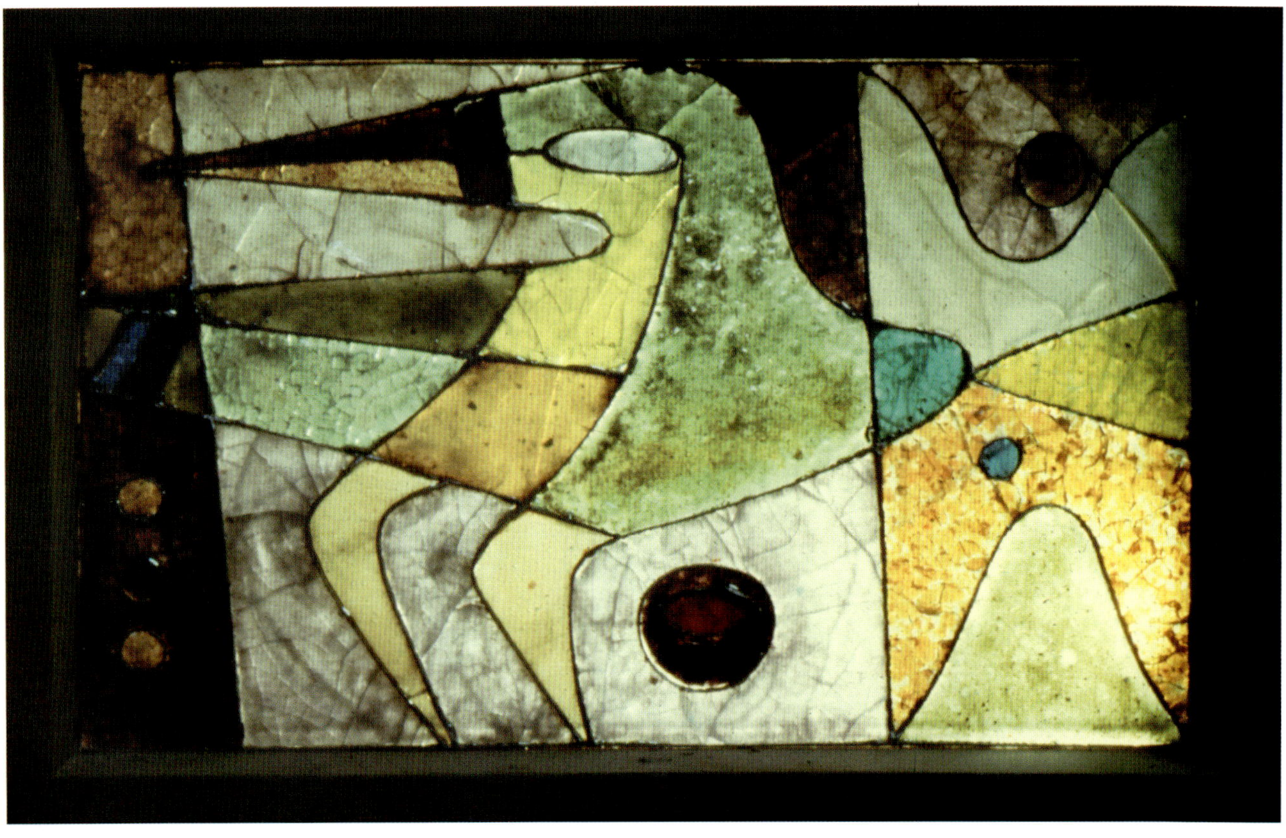

temperatures of the different glasses used, the result was a variety of textural surfaces ranging from sharp little facets piled one upon another to smooth well-flowed liquid areas of color." Russell continues, "I learned also that glass pieces can be fused to other pieces, as many as five or six thicknesses, in a kiln at approximately 1350 degrees Fahrenheit (cone 016). It is possible to insert metal, such as hardware cloth, screening, shavings, etc., between the layers or just lay it on top." "It was discovered also that if the shelf wash were applied roughly rather that smoothly, it added textural surface to the glass, increasing its refractory qualities."

"I fused several pieces of colored glass in a variety of thicknesses. The results were, I thought, quite stunning. Later, using a sheet of fractured glass as large as the kiln shelf would support, I laboriously laid out a fantasy of colored glass shapes, crushed glass, and glass rocks, and fired it. Because of the inner plastic layer used in safety glass, which burned out at the high temperature of firing, the room was filled with a heavy, sooty, black smoke, very acrid and penetrating. Hardly able to wait for the kiln to cool so that I could look at my masterpiece, I was somewhat shocked to find that numerous small explosions had taken place and that, instead of one piece of fused glass, I had thousands of fragments of glass scattered all over the kiln."

"Determined to make it work, I continued to experiment with this type of glass. It is entirely possible, I think, to take a fresh piece of safety glass and with some practice control the fractures into a consistent pattern of light-re-fracting lines in order to strengthen the composition. I have to admit I did not get this far. I did, however, succeed in obtaining a large piece in its entirety by first layering the safety glass over a piece of plate glass as a means of reinforcing. It was found also in this experiment that all glass to be used in firing must be tested, as most of the glass obtainable tends to turn opaque in the firing process, thus shutting out much of the refractory light. Some glass, particularly the reds, tends to alter in

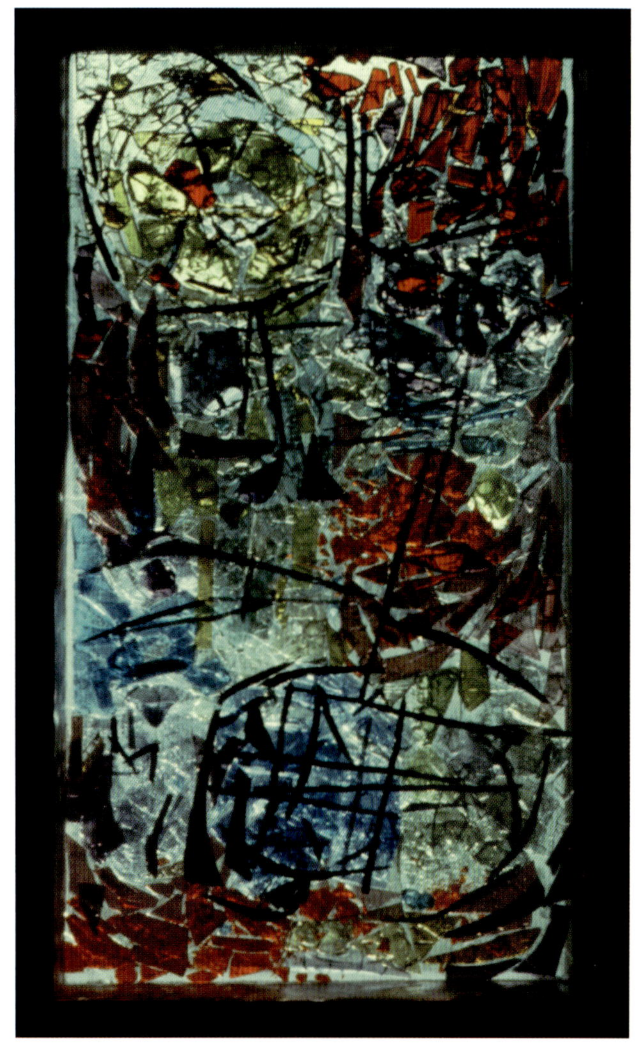

facing upper:
Portrait of Russell Day.

facing lower:
Glass Cloisonné, H. 11 in. (28 cm) x W. 18 in. (46 cm)., 1957, crushed glass surounded by ¼ in. (6 mm) copper fences, fused onto plate glass.

upper:
Fused Laminations, H. 26 in. (66 cm) x W. 13 in. (33 cm), 1957, fused stained glass layers on plate glass.

The fractures on these two pieces are due to the incompatibility of the different glasses, but they hold together.

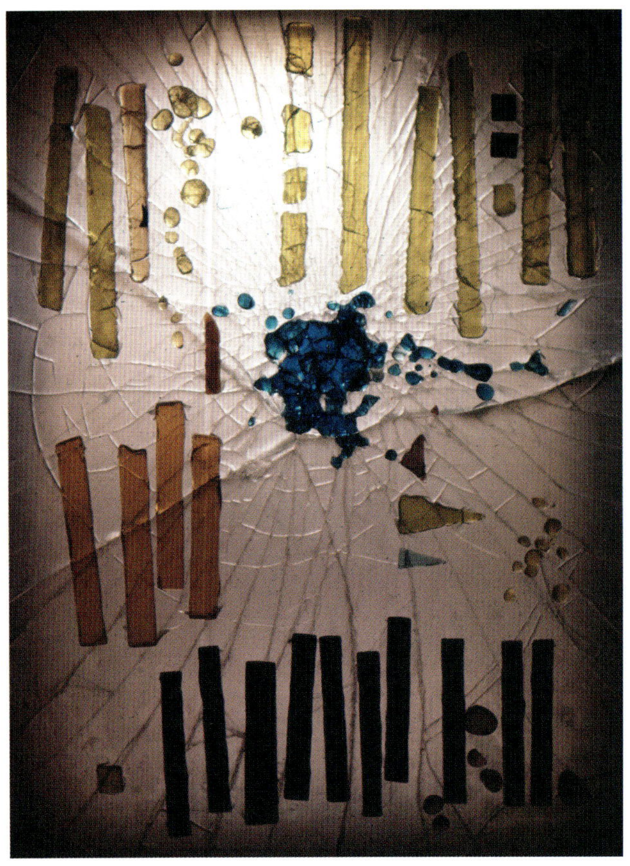

color. Many types of glass have thin coatings of colored glass and were found generally not to be good. Thick pieces of plate glass, some of which can be obtained in color, were especially exciting. Because of its higher melting point, plate glass retains its sharp refractory edges, whereas some glass with low melting points fire into highly polished globules."

Russell also experimented with leaded glass and developed a method for casting stacked colored glass in a concrete mixture so that the light passed through the edges; for this he received recognition by the American Institure of Architects (Northwest) for "Superior Design and Execution in Stained Glass."

In May of 2006, at 93 years old, when I spoke to Russell, he was sharp as a tack. One thing that he told me about his glass experimentation has become a mantra for me:

"You can really accomplish a lot when you don't know what you are doing."

upper left: Fractured Safety Glass, H. 24 in. (61 cm) x W. 20 in. (51 cm), 1957, fused stained glass on pre-fractured saftey glass, fused to plate glass. Notice the different viscosities of the various colored glass.

middle right: Lamination, H. 8 in. (20 cm) x W. 10 in. (26 cm), 1957, part of Russell Day's master's thesis, installed as one of 6 various sized panels in a door. The black lines are fired black glass paint.

lower: fused glass with fired black glass paint lines. These tiles show different viscosities of glass (hard vs. soft) and also incompatibility cracks.

The softness and color shift of these photos are due to age of the color transparency.

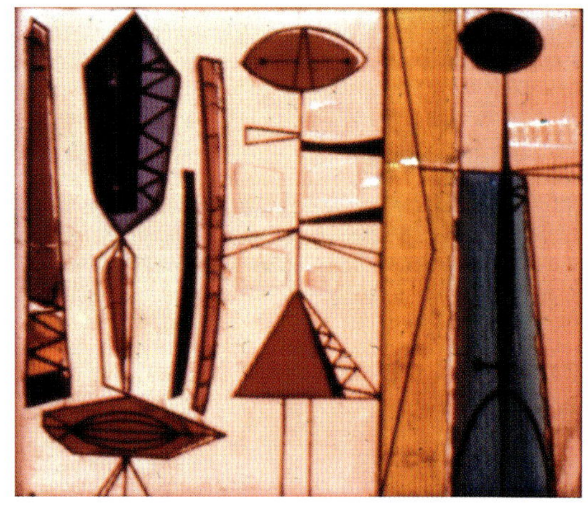

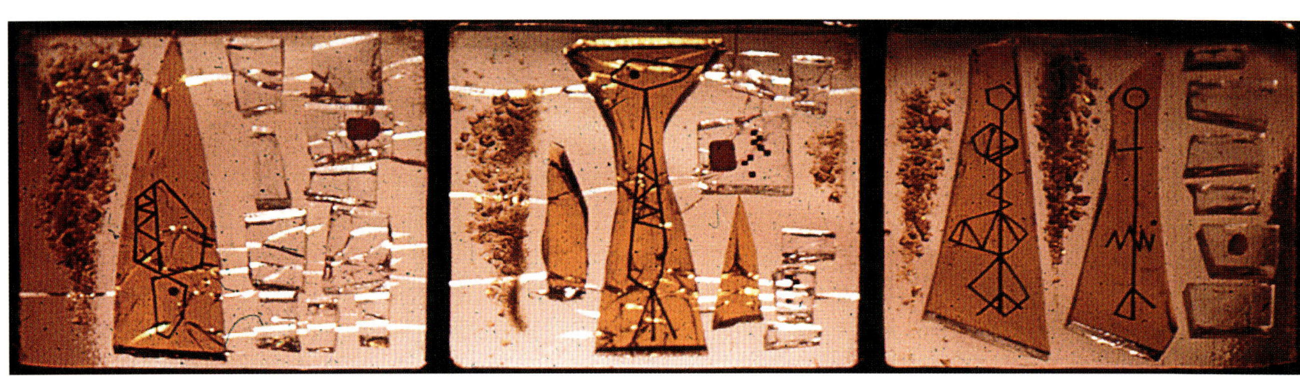

Ruth Dahlberg, from Stone Mountain, Georgia, created fused window pieces and bowls using copper & aluminum foils, enamels, lusters, and fusing between window glass.

After a slide talk that I gave in Atlanta, Georgia in the early 1980's, I was handed a couple slides of Ruth's artwork. I wish that I had met her, as her artwork was quite incredible for the time.

upper right:
"Sea Scene," pre-1980, window glass, enamels, and copper leaf.

below:
"bowl" pre-1980, float plate, hand cut, hand painted 3 ½ in. (9 cm) deep x 10 in. (25 cm) in diameter. Sagged with surface lusters.

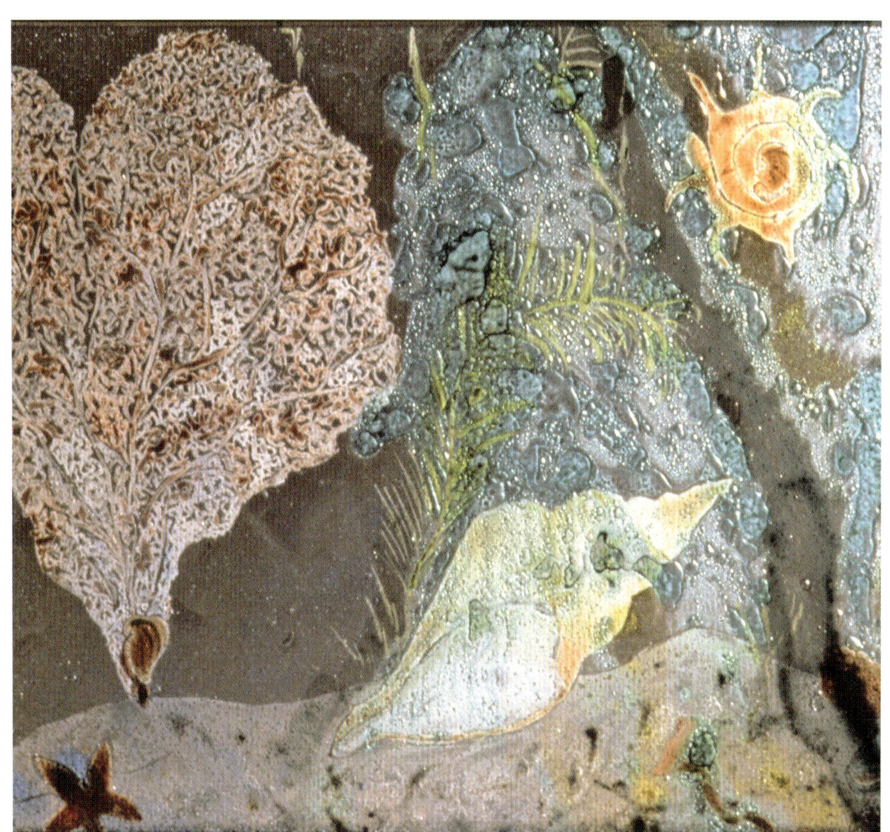

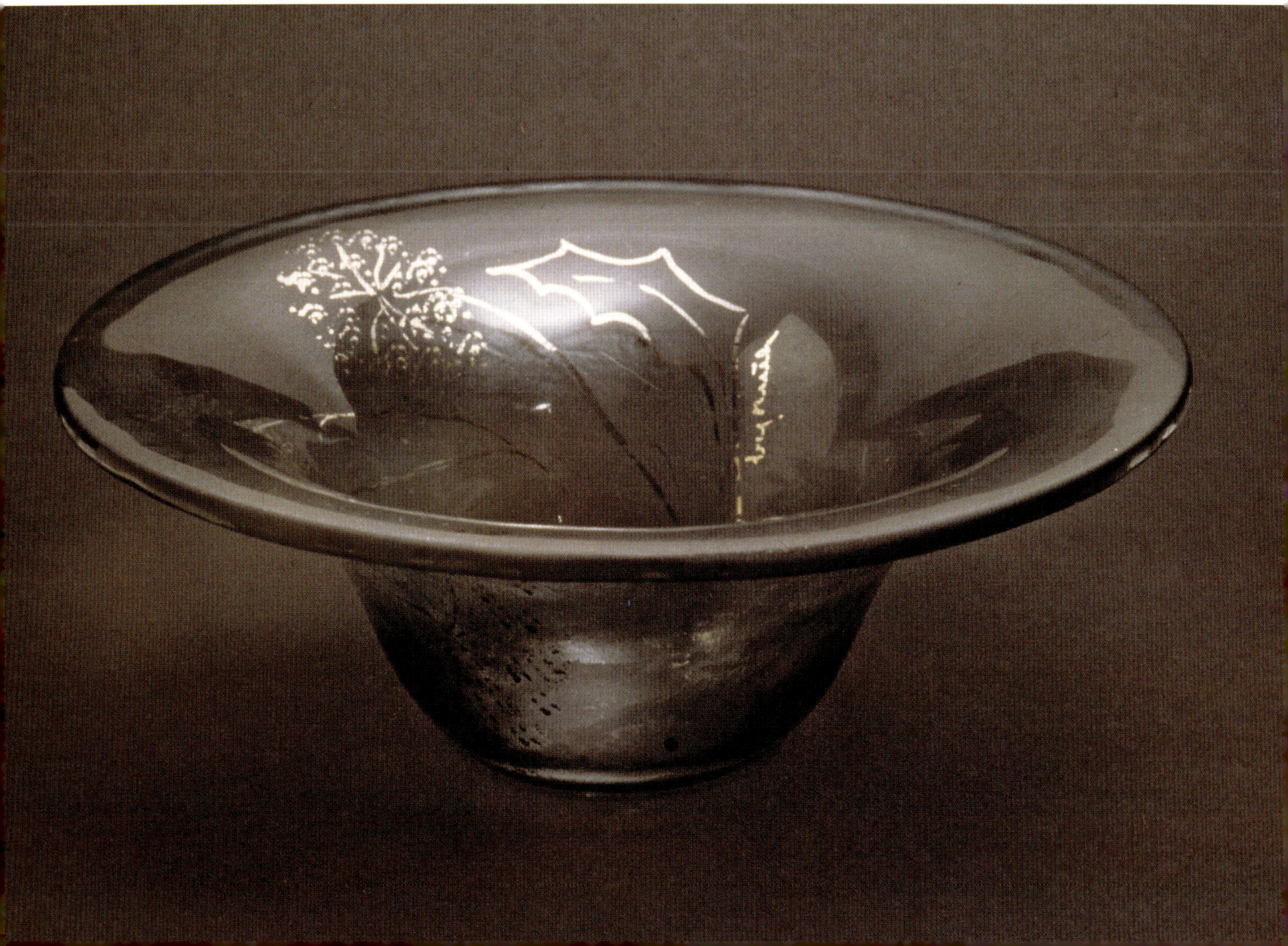

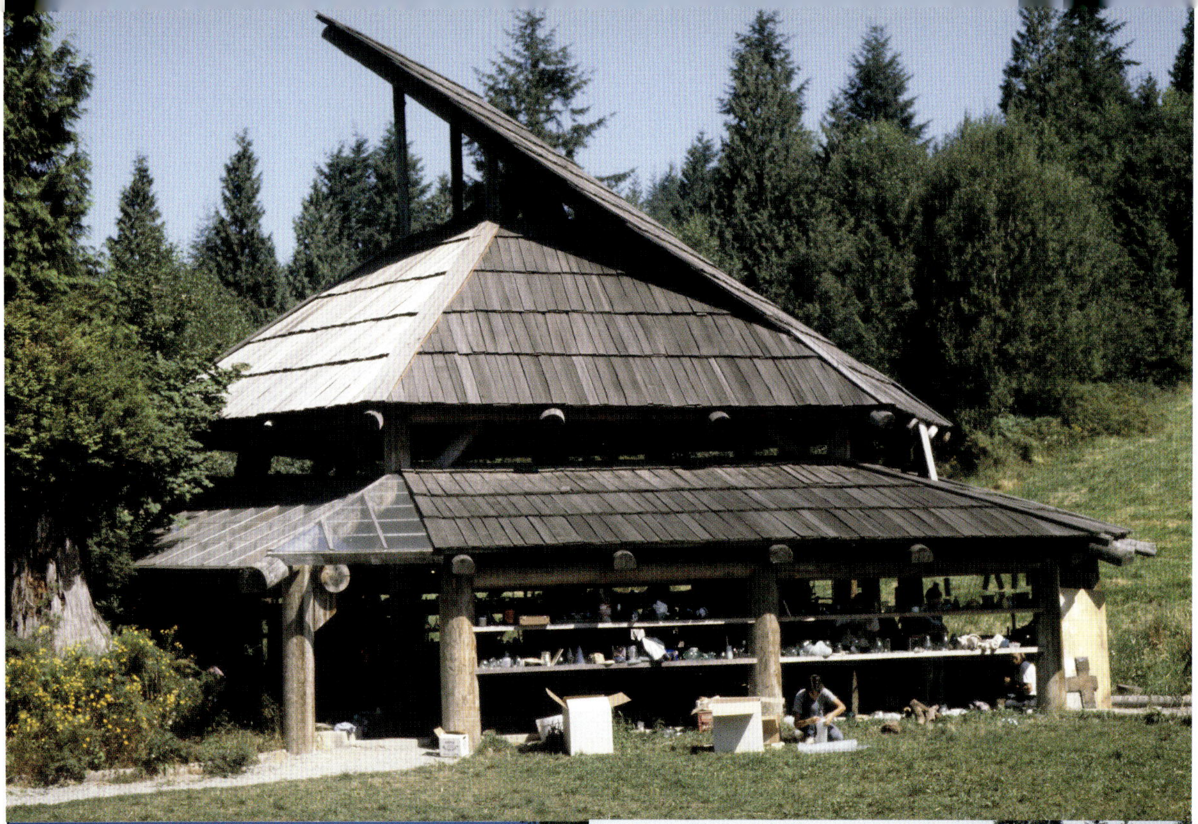

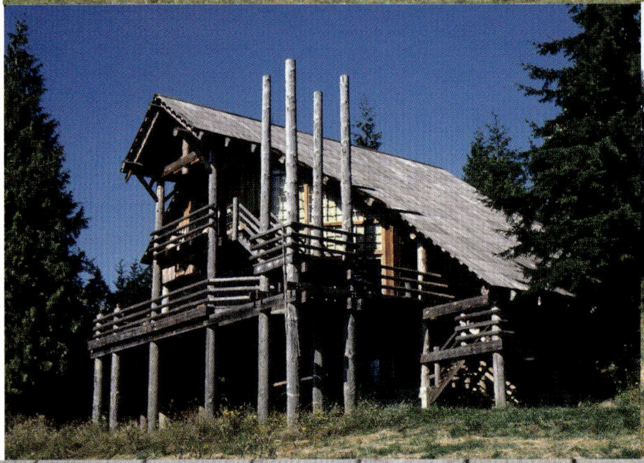

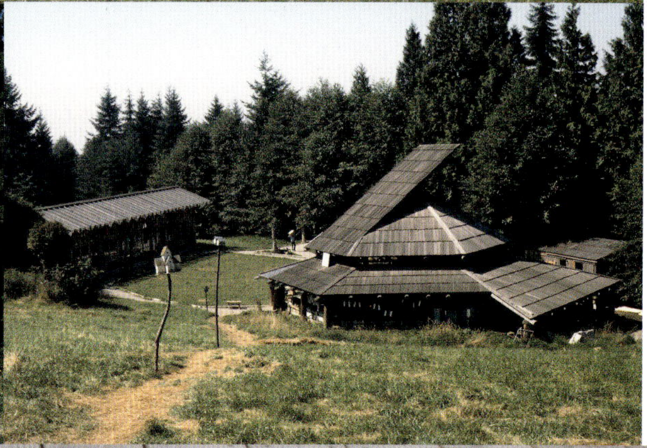

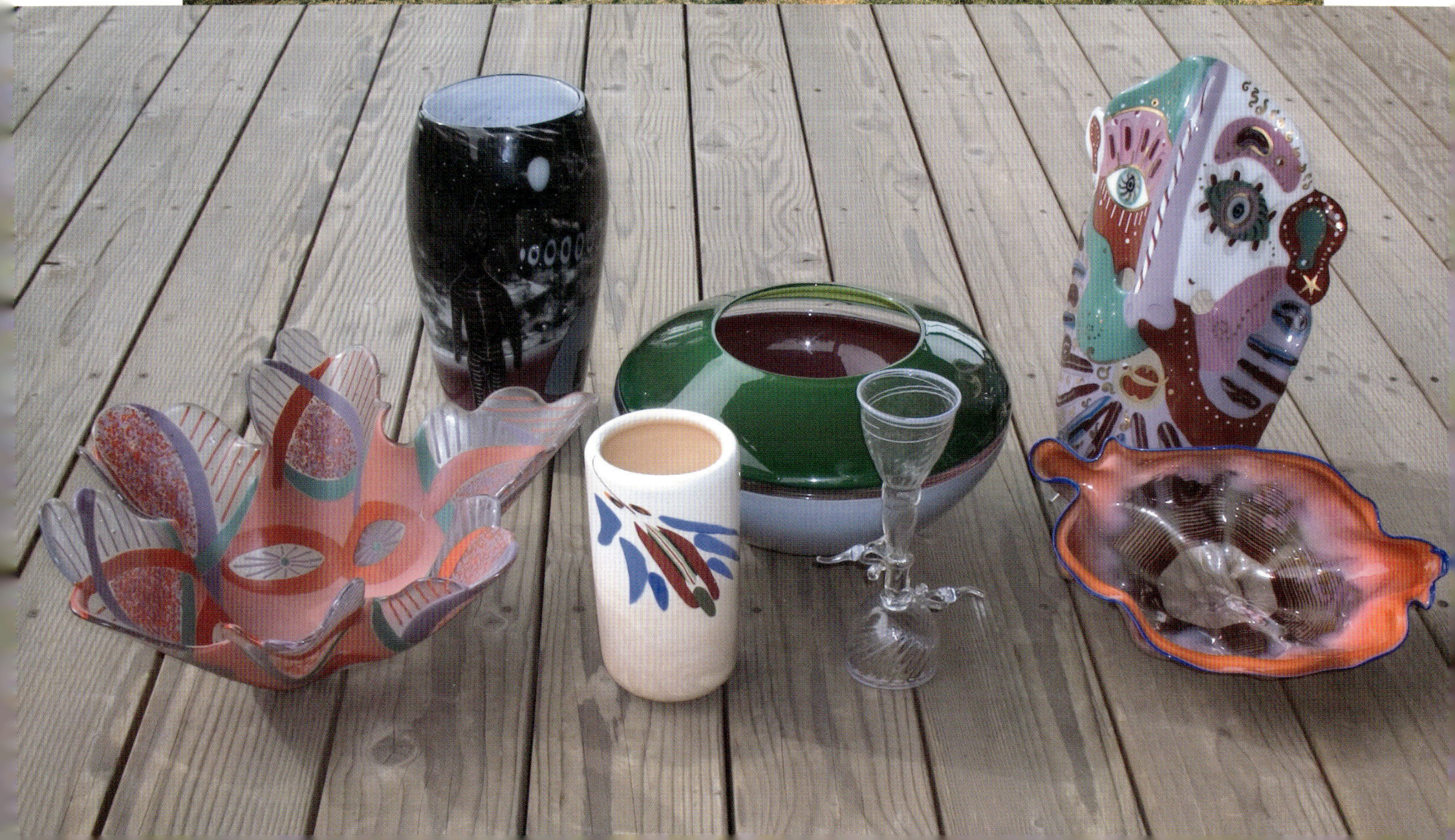

experimental glass: 1960's - 70's

The Studio Glass Movement

The story that is generally told is that the studio glass movement in the United States began as a result of two 1962 workshops by Harvey Littleton and Dominick Labino at the Toledo Museum of Art in Ohio. Before this time, glass designers were academy or university trained; glass blowers learned through apprenticeship. Designers gave blowers the designs that they would then create. Harvey and Dominick built a small glass-melting furnace – suddenly, the artists could be both designer and craftsman, blowing the pieces themselves and creating the freedom to experiment.

Early glass enamelists encouraged the Studio Glass movement. The 1962 workshops didn't appear from a void. In 1957, craftsmen Michael Higgins, Edris Eckhart, and Maurice Heaton gave talks about glass at the First Annual Conference of the American Craft's Council at Asilomar in Pacific Grove, California. At that time, Frances and Michael Higgins, who knew ceramicist Harvey Littleton, corresponded with Harvey to encourage experiments in glass blowing.

In 1959 Frances and Michael Higgins joined Earl McCutchen on a panel chaired by Harvey Littleton at the Third National Conference of the American Crafts Council in Lake George, New York. Harvey proposed that artists should begin to explore hot glass techniques.

The 1961 Fourth National Conference of the American Crafts Council was held at the University of Washington in Seattle. Harvey Littleton talked about his glass blowing experiments; also on the panel were Michael Higgins, Edris Eckhart, Russell Day, and lampworker John Burton. They urged Harvey Littleton to develop glassblowing for the individual craftsman. What followed were the revolutionary 1962 Toledo Workshops where glass engineer Dominick Labino and ceramist Harvey Littleton introduced artists to the small studio furnace for melting glass. Frances and Michael Higgins dropped by during the first workshop to observe the results.

Many early glass blowers had a ceramics background. Harvey Littleton was head of the University of Wisconsin, Madison ceramics department; his first students formed glass departments at colleges and universities and trained more glass artists. These students included Marvin Lipofsky (University of California, Berkley, fall 1964), Robert Fritz (San Jose State College, fall 1964), Fritz Dreisbach (Toledo Museum, Ohio, 1967), Dale Chihuly (Rhode Island School of Design), and Daniel Schwoerer and Ray Ahlgren, who, together with Boyce Lundstrom (who studied with Robert Fritz at San Jose State) founded Bullseye Glass Company.

upper left:
The hot shop built in 1974 on the campus of the Pilchuck Glass School, founded in 1971 by Dale Chihuly just north of Seattle, Washington. Photo 1981.

middle left:
The Pilchuck lodge built in 1978, photo 1981.

middle right:
View of the Pilchuck hot shop with Tee-Pee roof allowing natural ventilation; the flat shop which was built in 1976 is on the left, photo 1981.

lower:
Pilchuck Glass 1974 – 1986. These pieces are from a few of the many artists who have taught at Pilchuck Glass School and live in the area. Collection of Richard La Londe. (left to right)

Richard La Londe 1983
Paul Marioni 1984
Rob Adamson 1974
Sonja Blomdahl 1981
Fritz Dreisbach 1978
Ruth Brockmann 1983
Dale Chihuly 1986

Marioni's piece is 12 in. (31 cm) tall for scale.

Glass enamelists of the 1950's also inspired a few people to try fusing stained glass, but glass incompatibility kept this from going very far. We see a few wind chimes and flattened whiskey bottles but not much more. Small projects, for which pieces were barely fused together and contained a lattice-like open space, seemed to stick and stay together. Fusing glass that was cut from the same sheet usually was successful. Blue and green from the same glass company was probably compatible but usually not if fused with the red or yellow. Neither a complete color pallet of fusible glass nor a reasonable method for testing compatibility was available. That would have to wait for Bullseye Glass Company and the 1980's.

Kay Kinney wrote the book Glass Craft: Designing, Forming, Decorating, Chilton/Haynes, 1962. This book taught glass crafters how to melt bottles and stained glass into plates, wind chimes, ashtrays, and other craft projects.

I checked this book out in 1980 from my local library, and she inspired me to throw some glass into a kiln. As a glass separator on the shelf, I used whiting (calcium carbonate), which stuck to the glass, but did the job. That glass just happened to be Bullseye solid color opals, which I used for my stained glass pieces, and they stayed together, probably because they were fused to stick. This was before I had any idea about compatible glass.

Harriet Anderson took a class from Maurice Heaton, experimented with fused glass and wrote the book Kiln-Fired Glass, Chilton 1970. In 2006 I purchased a used copy of this book, and, reading it for the first time, I was astounded as to how much technical vocabulary was already in use. She refers to sagging, slumping, coefficients of expansion, testing fused sample strips of enamels for compatibility, overglazes to cover fingerprints, molds, and firing schedules.

Keith Cummings
In England, Keith's research of ancient glass techniques led to the book The Techniques of Glass Forming, Batsford Ltd, London, 1980, and more recently to Techniques of Kiln-formed Glass, A & C Black London, 1997. The dust jackets state that during the early 1960's he worked for Whitefriars Glass and in 1967 became a senior lecturer in glass design at Stourbridge College of Art; later he was head of the Glass Department at Wolverhampton University, where he retired from teaching in 1994. His kiln experiments include fusing, slumping, sagging, hot glass pouring, mosaic glass, cane making, and lost wax sculpture. His personal artwork is displayed in museums, and he has influenced artists through his writing and teaching. Keith's first book, written in 1980, mentions very little about glass compatibility and nothing about compatibility testing, which shows how far we still had to go.

The 1960's and 1970's were about experimentation. These were the "hippie years" and the "what can we do with this stuff" period. Early blowers worked with a clear tank furnace, using a small multi-color pot furnace and silver nitrate for color. Cold working, kiln forming, acid etching, and sandblasting began to be incorporated.

Pilchuck Glass School began the summer of 1971 when Dale Chihuly and eighteen college students set up a furnace on a tree farm near Stanwood, Washington where they lived in tents and handmade houses. During the mid-1970's, German Kugler color rods introduced new techniques for coloring glass, and the use of small color pot furnaces pretty much disappeared.

The 1980's were about technique. Glass artists looked to European roots and studied with Swedish, German, and Italian masters, many of whom were brought to Pilchuck Glass School and helped expand the techniques of glass.

During this time the Studio Glass Movement was still mainly about blowing, but kiln forming was also being accepted. This is when the term "craftsman" slowly disappeared for the more PC (politically correct) "craftsperson."

The early 1990's were about bad glass sculpture as art. This is the period where glass craftspeople decided they were artists and worked too hard to prove it. Just look at the awful sculptures from this era in the Corning Glass New Glass Review, www.cmog.org

The New Millennium 2000-plus is about art that is too serious and slick. It's all about $$$$. Don't get me wrong – I can use money, too, but I long for the "hippie days." What happened to the fun?

The Stained Glass Movement
From about 1200 A.D., European cathedrals included stained glass as part of their architecture. In the United States, beginning around 1900 and continuing through the Tiffany era, a profusion of stained glass windows were produced. Many small "Mom and Pop" stained glass shops sprung up to fill the need. In the cities, houses were built right next to each other, and wasn't it nice to put a bit of color in the window to block the view of the neighbor's house. This collapsed with the Great Depression of the 1930's. Stained glass pretty much disappeared except for churches, and that was rather limited. Stained glass became "old fashioned."

By 1972 in America, only a few "church window companies" and three colored glass manufacturers remained; supplies were limited. The stained glass available was "Tiffany-style" streaky opalescent glass and simple "cathedrals" from Kokomo and Wismach. Blenko Glass Company made a few transparent colors of blown cylinder glass that was small in size, maybe 14 in. (35 cm) x 18 in. (46 cm), that went from ½ in. (12 mm) on one end to ⅛ in. (3 mm)

on the other. A small amount of very expensive imported European stained glass was around.

In 1974, Bullseye Glass Company and Genesis in Portland, Oregon were the first new stained glass manufacturers since Tiffany's time to make hand rolled stained glass. Within ten years, over twenty companies were making sheet glass in the USA; most of these companies didn't survive.

The "hippie" craft revival.
The late 1960's and early 1970's spawned a group of experimental stained glass artists on the west coast of the United States. Artists such as Paul Marioni, Kathy Bunell, Dan Fenton, and Narcissis Quagliata in the San Francisco Bay area and James Hubbell near San Diego pushed traditional stained glass into new and exciting realms. Ed Carpenter in Portland, Michael Kennedy in Seattle, and Peter Molica in the Bay area changed the look of "Architectural" stained glass. You can see their work, along with that of others, in the classic book <u>New Glass</u> by Otto Rigan, 1976, Ballantine Books, New York.

The revival was on, and it was like a gold rush! By the late 1970's stained glass shops selling supplies and teaching classes were sprouting all over the USA. Many students who had made only two or three windows were getting commissions. Lots of stained glass experiments, bad art, and sun catchers flooded the market. I have to say that I was part of it, but hey, ya gotta start somewhere. Like any "bubble," it had to pop – and it did in the early 1990's.

In general, the retail shops today are better in quality and classes, but I don't see as many residential commissions now; however, as long as the sun shines, sun catchers will always be around.

Many of the early glass blowers came from university ceramics backgrounds and most of the early Bullseye Glass fusers came from a stained glass background.

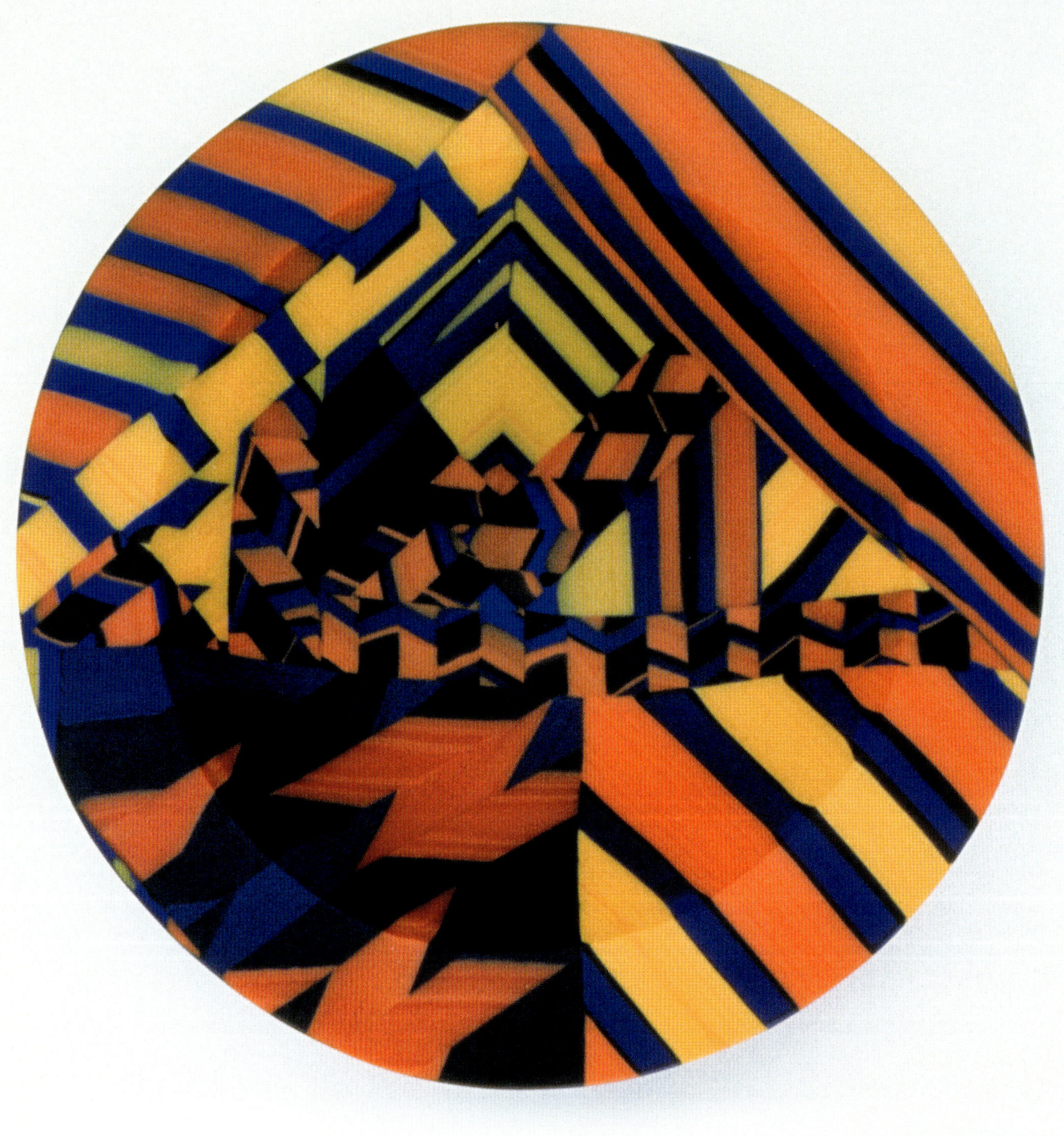

Past Influences Present: Klaus Moje

Klaus Moje (b. 1936)
Beginning at age 12, Klaus began cutting and grinding glass in his family's workshop in Hamburg, Germany for pocket money. Klaus continued his apprenticeship there (1952-1955) and further studied at the glass schools of Rheinbach and Hadamar (1957-1959) earning a master's certificate. In 1962 he started a studio with Isgard Moje-Wohlgemuth; they created cut lead crystal sculptures.

During the early 1970's, in the Hessen Glas Werke near Frankfurt, where his clear crystal blanks for cutting were made, he found some 4 foot (122 cm) long solid colored rods used to make glass buttons and jewelry. Klaus cut these rods into strips and rounds with a diamond saw, laid these on asbestos, and fused them together in a brick kiln. His fused glass was compatibility tested by doing – if it worked, it worked; if it didn't, then he didn't use it. Even though Klaus didn't know about annealing, the glass seemed to hold together – probably because his brick kiln cooled slowly. His pieces were covered with a "crust" (devitrification), which he ground off on a glass cutting lathe.

By 1975 Klaus was making vessels that were influenced by ancient Roman mosaic bowls. His technique was in three steps:
(1) Lay out glass pieces in a precise design, using a diamond-saw to cut glass rods and then fuse them together flat.
(2) Slump this fused piece into a thick silica/plaster mold.
(3) Finish the bowl by grinding with a diamond wheel, creating a textured surface.

Klaus, an innovator and working alone, developed techniques by trial and error. By sawing, assembling, and fusing followed by more sawing, reassembling, and refusing, he was able to create extraordinarily intricate patterned bowls that he finished with his trademark textured surface.

In 1979 Klaus and Isgard taught painting, fusing, and slumping at the Pilchuck Glass School. While at Pilchuck, he observed that glass in Europe was about technique with aesthetic rules that one didn't break; however, in America, glass art was about freedom of expression with no rules. Klaus taught his students that skill and technique must be combined with imagination and freedom.

Klaus returned to teach at Pilchuck in 1980 – 1982, 1984 and then many more times in the following years. As an instructor at Pilchuck, Klaus has influenced many glass artists, including me.

> "From niche to mainstream is a long way and as our field of glass work has reached the status of mainstream, within the contemporary glass movement, I am happy and proud to be part of it from the very beginning".
>
> Klaus Moje May 2006

Facing top:
Klaus Moje Bowl, 1981, 9.5 in. (24 cm) in diameter x 2 in. (5.5 cm).

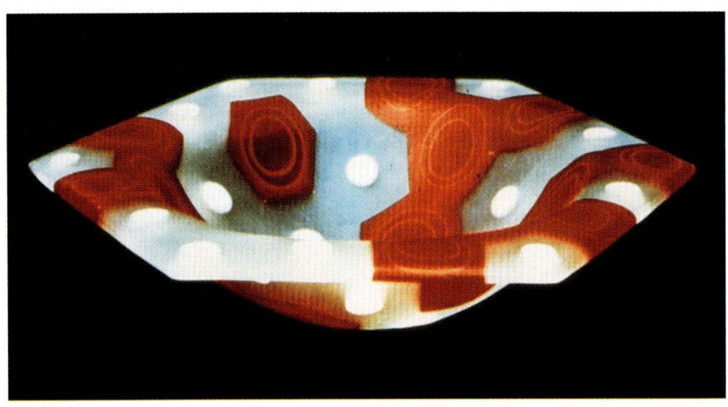

The 1981 Pilchuck catalogue describes Klaus' class. *"Special Class: Slumping, Fusing and Mold-Making.*
Klaus Moje, one of the most renowned glass artists in Europe, will be at Pilchuck creating mosaic bowls and vessels by using some of the old Roman techniques in combination with modern skills he has developed. Moje is considered the leading technical and esthetic authority on the distinctive approach to making glass art, which is not practiced in the United States. Klaus will teach students how to make the plaster molds, slump mosaic glass in the forms and how to finish the pieces on a glass lathe with stone and diamond wheels."

In 1980 Klaus met Boyce Lundstrom and Daniel Schwoerer, who talked about developing compatible glass. He visited the Bullseye Glass factory in Portland, Oregon.

In 1981, I was enrolled in a glass blowing session at Pilchuck; also at the same time, Boyce Lundstrom (co-owner of Bullseye Glass Company in Portland, Oregon) was attending Klaus' fusing class where he was fusing his color rods. In the blowing class I met Gil Reynolds, who became my glass blowing partner for that session; we both bought our stained glass from the Bullseye factory, and while at Pilchuck we talked a lot with Boyce about glass. We also kept our eyes on what was going on in Klaus' class, and after returning home, we independently began fusing our Bullseye scraps.

In 1982 Klaus left Germany for Australia where he became the Founding Head of the Glass

Workshop at the Canberra School of Art of the Australian National University.

During one of my visits to Bullseye to stock up on glass, in the fall of 1982, I saw a whole crate (60+ sheets) of various colors of tested compatible glass being packed to be sent to Klaus in Australia. I was so envious – a whole crate! I was there to buy what I could afford – maybe 12 sheets.

During his tenure at Canberra, Klaus trained and influenced many Australian kiln workers. Some of the first graduates were: Mezza Rijsdik, Kirstie Rea, Judi Elliott, and Richard Whiteley. He taught at Canberra from 1982 – 1992, after which he retired to pursue his artwork full time.

Klaus' trial and error experiments and innovation have been an enormous influence on the glass fusing that we do today. His art and his teaching motivate us to combine artistic freedom with technical skill.

Klaus Moje sets a high standard for all of us to follow.

Thank you, Klaus.

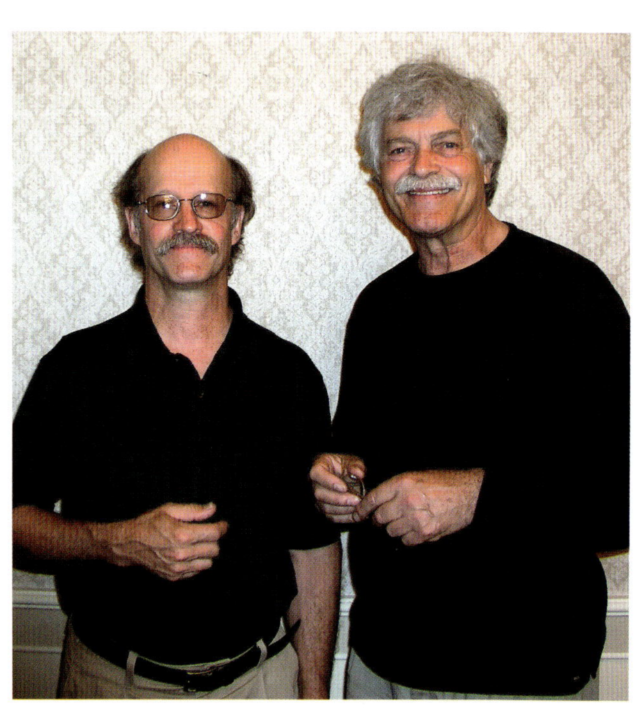

Facing top:
Red and White Bowl, 1977, 11 in. (28 cm) in diameter x 2 in. (5.5 cm). This piece is in the Kunstmuseum Duesseldorf, Germany.

facing bottom:
Richard La Londe with Klaus Moje at the BECon 2005, Bullseye Glass sponsored conference in Portland, Oregon.

top:
Moje Plate, 1985, 20 in. (51 cm) in Diameter x 3 in. (7.5 cm). Intricate $3/8$ in. (9 mm) thick strips of Bullseye Glass are laid side by side, fused, and then cut with a diamond saw; repositioned to give the zig zag pattern, re-fused, slumped, and then finished with a diamond wheel for texture. The clear zig zags are made by placing irridized clear strips on edge.

bottom left:
Combed Vessel, 1984, H. 13 in. (33 cm) x W. 13 in. (3 cm) x 2 in. (5.5 cm). Bullseye glass is combed, slumped, and diamond wheel textured.

bottom right:
Plate, 1996, H. 19 in. (48 cm) x W. 19 in. (48 cm) x D. (5.5 cm). Bullseye glass is heated to a higher temperature than full fuse, about 1650° F (900° C) and allowed to cook and mix. It is slumped during a second firing and then cold worked and textured with a diamond wheel.

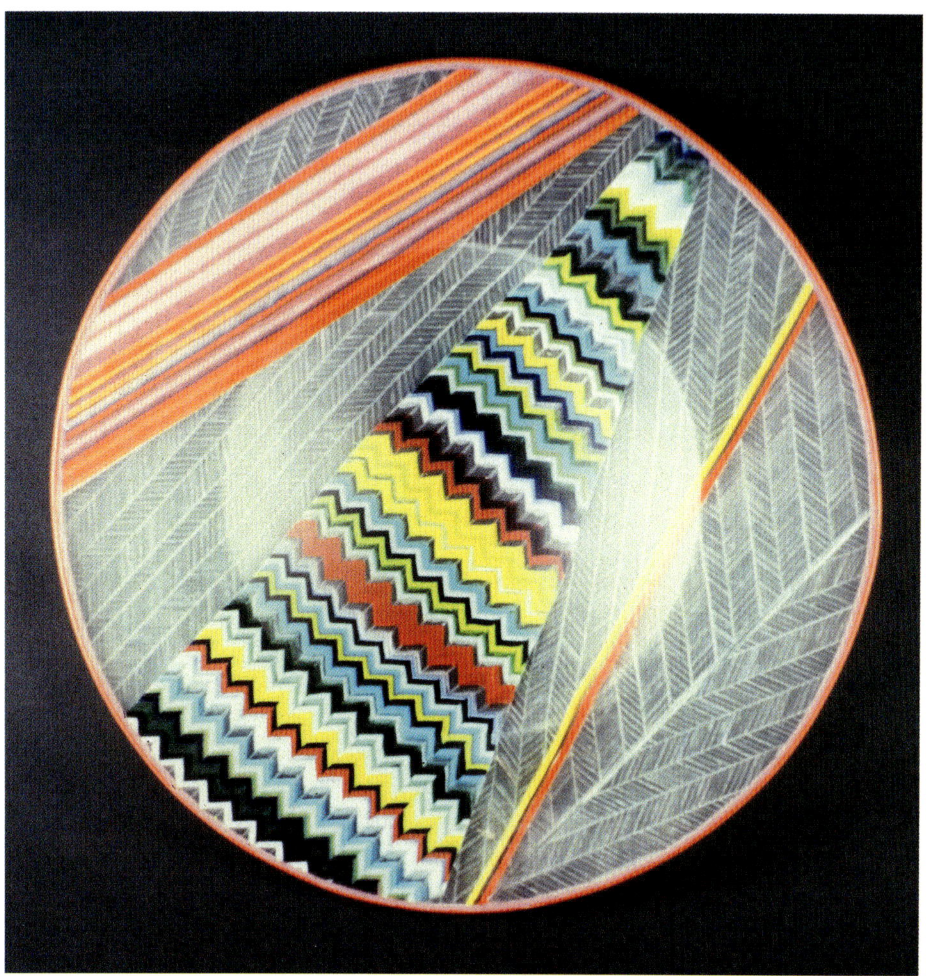

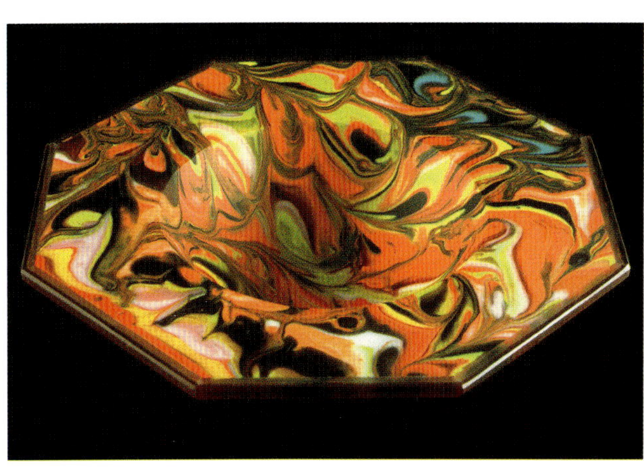

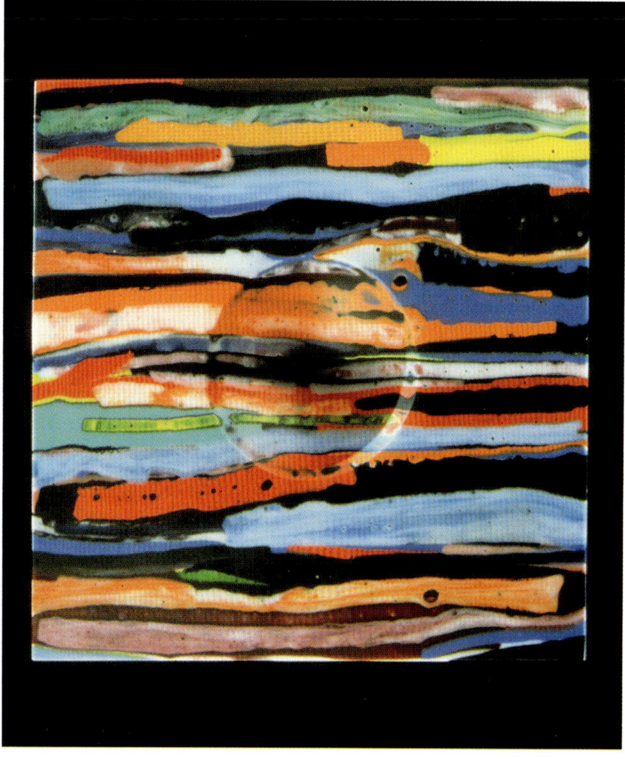

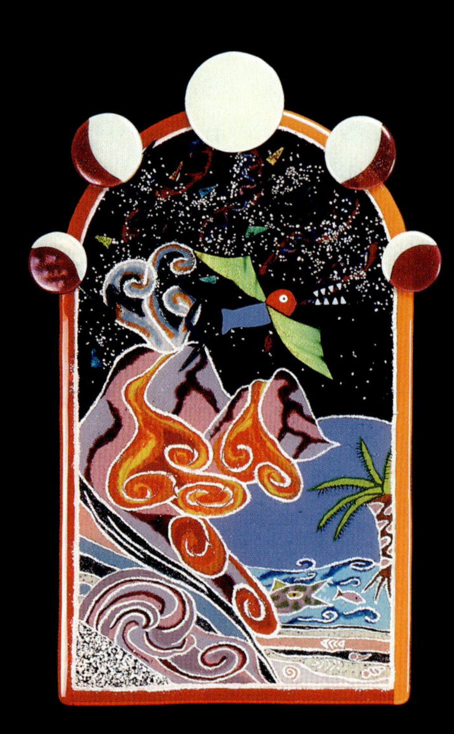
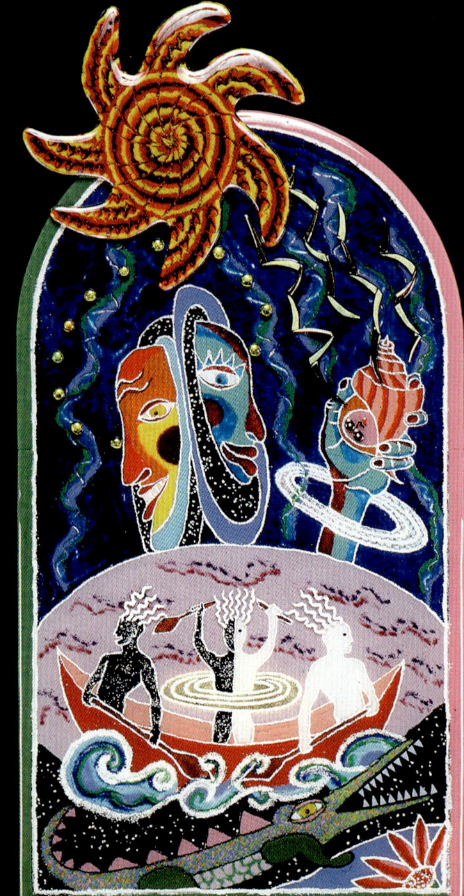
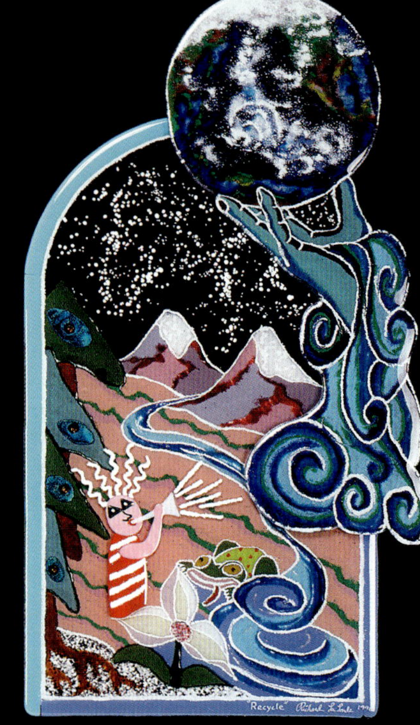
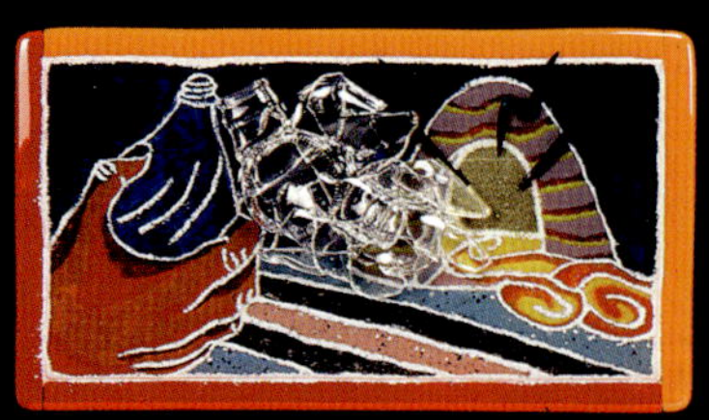
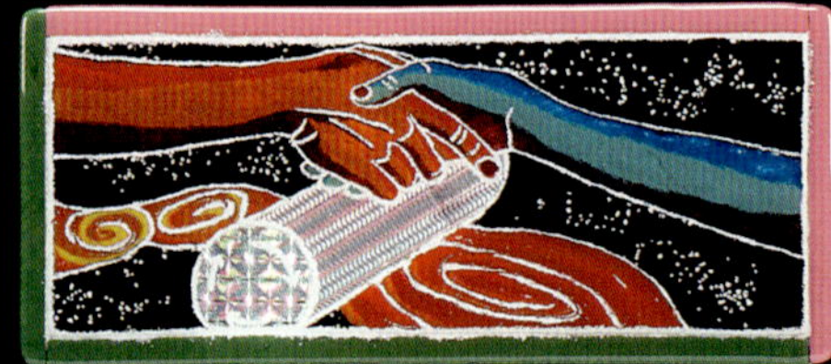
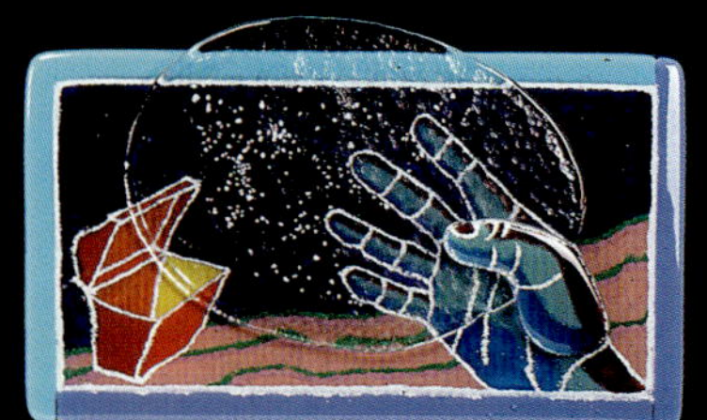
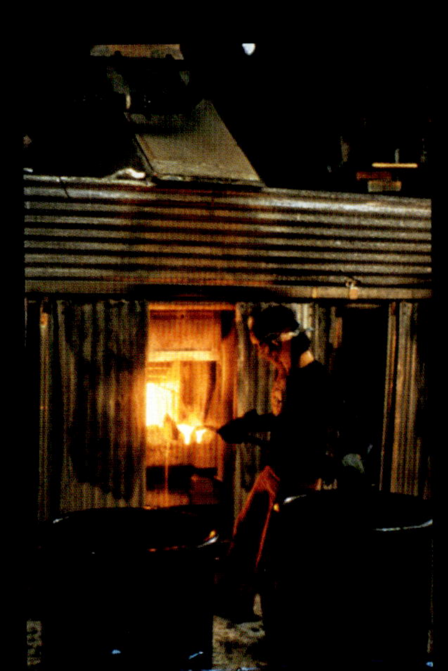
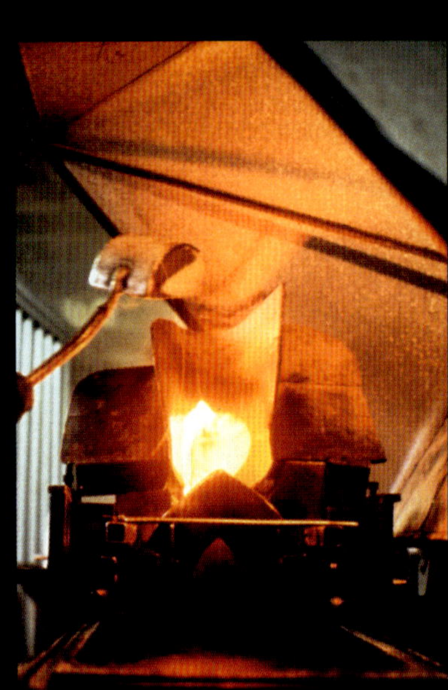
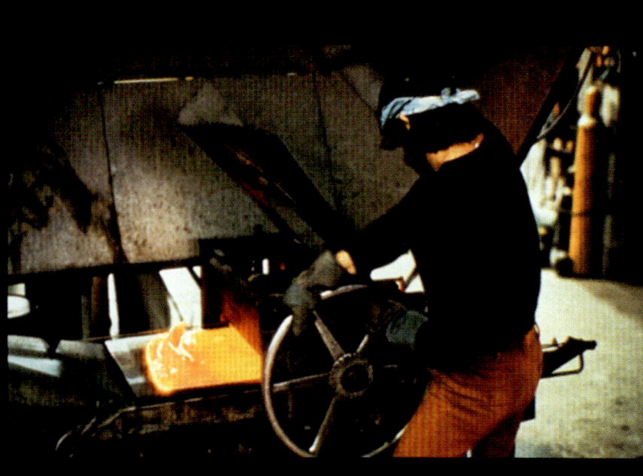
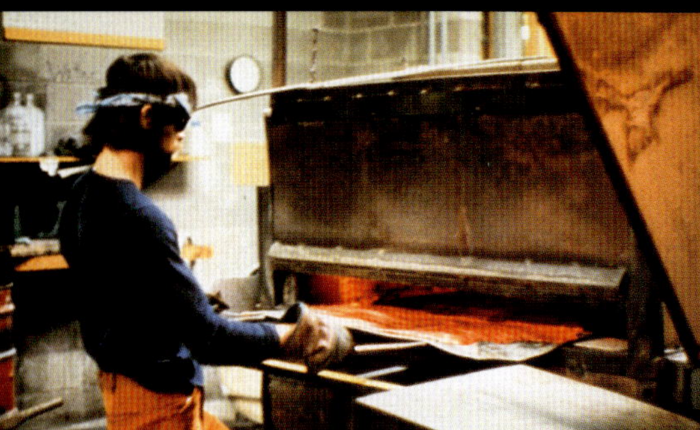

The Bullseye Fusing Movement

In June 1974, Ray Ahlgren, Boyce Lundstrom, and Daniel Schwoerer started Bullseye Glass Company in Portland, Oregon. They began making transparent and opalescent sheet glass for the reemerging stained glass movement that was mostly recreating Tiffany-style lamps and windows.

Prior to this, Boyce studied with Dr. Robert Fritz at San Jose State in California and set up a blowing studio in Corvallis, Oregon in 1968. Daniel and Ray studied under Harvey Littleton at the University of Wisconsin in Madison, and in 1969 Daniel started a blowing studio in Portland, Oregon; Ray joined him in 1971. They all first met while selling blown glass at the 1972 summer Bellevue Arts and Crafts fair. Together they set up Bullseye Glass to make and sell sheet glass, which would give them the money, time, and the studio to create blown glass art. Bullseye Glass Company was a big success, glass fusing interceded, and they never got back to blowing. Ray left the company in 1980 to pursue his own direction.

In 1974, I lived in the small town of Vancouver, Washington and went across the river to Portland, Oregon to a church restoration shop and purchased some red, yellow, blue, and green sheet glass and a few strips of lead came. At this time, no stained glass shops were selling supplies or teaching classes in Portland. The only sheet glass available, being made in the United States was Kokomo, Wismach, and some blown Blenko ovals that varied in thickness from ⅛ in. (3 mm) to ½ in. (12 mm).

From a picture in an article in Sunset magazine, I made my own came cutting knife from a sharpened putty knife and grozing pliers from a pair of Klines, a type of bull-nosed electrical pliers. I used a hardware store soldering iron, plumber solder, and a Red Devil glass cutter to create my first window. I couldn't figure out what whiting was, so I used cornstarch to dry up the putty in the window. My window was a little wobbly. Later I learned to stretch the came, which straightened and made it rigid, creating a stronger window.

When I returned to this restoration shop, they had some beautiful yellow opal glass that they said was made by a new company in town. In 1975, I stumbled into Bullseye Glass Company and couldn't believe what they were doing. Out front was a huge pile of broken clear bottles; inside were a bunch of "hippies" casting and rolling sheets of glass they had made from melted bottles (early recycling); racks of colored glass, oval in shape of varying lengths of about 24 in. (61 cm) - 30 in. (76 cm) by 18 in. (46 cm) or so wide,

"Recycle" H. 42 in. (107 cm) x W. 60 in. (152 cm), 1991.

This is the commissioned piece that I made for the Bullseye Glass Company. The left panel shows volcanos spewing molten lava and the smaller subplot under that, shows a hand throwing a bottle into the furnace to be melted. Bullseye glass used to be made from recycled clear bottles called cullet.

The middle subplot shows rolling the molten glass.

The right subplot shows taking the finished sheet from the treasure chest or annealer. In the very beginning Bullseye used to make oval sheets. I had them cast me a small sheet about 12" across.

1) ladling molten glass from the Bullseye furnace.
2) dropping the glass into the chute of the roller.
3) rolling over the glass on the casting table.
4) placing the still flexible sheet into the continuous annealing lehr. An ⅛ in. (3 mm) sheet takes about 20 minutes from being cast to removal from the annealer.

These photographs are from the "Bullseye $10 tour" slide show, 1985.

were sitting sideways in racks. Soon after this, Bullseye began producing more uniform sized sheets by cutting the ends off the top and bottom of the ovals so the sheets could be evenly packed into crates for shipping. I began buying all of my glass from the factory – with every visit, new colors, sheets of iridescent glass, and new textures – I felt like a kid in a candy factory!

1980 - 81: Bullseye Glass Company and the Compatible Glass Idea

One reason that before 1980 we had seen very little fusing of colored sheet glass was that when you melted colors together usually the blues and greens "sort of" stayed together and didn't crack and the yellow and reds "kind of" worked together, but fusing the blues and greens with the yellow and reds was usually a disaster. The people fusing enamels on window glass were able to get away with fusing multi-colors because they were usually either laminating (trapping) very thin layers of enamels (colored glass) between sheets of window glass or using thin layers of enamels called "micro-layers" by Frances and Michael Higgins. After fusing and annealing, the higher expansion enamels (laminated between pieces of lower expansion window glass) shrank more than the thicker window glass and pulled against it, creating tension similar to tempered glass. When incompatible glass pieces or thicker layers of enamel were fired to the surface of window glass they usually crazed or spalled off.

For years glass blowers had used the **pull test**, as a simple test for glass compatibility by pulling a thread of two colors of glass and seeing which way it bent. This test takes practice and skill, and it must be done exactly the same way each time. Place one piece of glass on top of another, heat them in a torch, and pull a flat thread, without rotating, keeping one color exactly on top of the other. The glass that contracts the most will bend the cane toward itself. This glass will have a higher expansion rate and will shrink more than the other when cooling. The more curved the thread, the more compatibility difference.

The **bar test** was the next evolution in testing. Strips ½ in. (12 mm) wide and about 18 in. (46 cm) long were cut and laid on top of strips from the same sheet of clear glass and then fully fused together on a kiln shelf. By measuring the curvature of these bars and factoring in the curve of the kiln shelf, it was a more accurate way to predict which glass pieces would successfully fuse to each other. The beauty of this test is that it replicated the fusing process.

In 1981, I visited Ray Ahlgren's studio, and he showed me his bar test device. I went home and welded a metal caliper (micrometer) to a straight 1 in. (2.5 cm) square steel tube with two supports to lay the bar on.

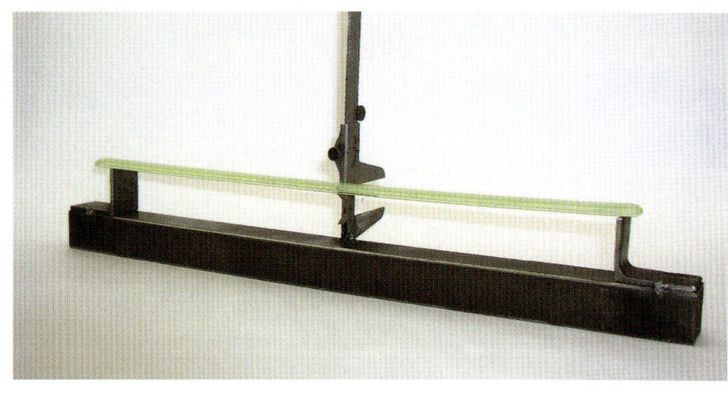

I tested all of my larger sheets of Bullseye against a sheet of Bullseye clear. I labeled all of these sheets with a number in millimeters of curvature, over the 16 in. (41 cm) measured in my device. Most bars curved up away from the clear which meant that they had a higher expansion rate than the clear; a few bent the bars toward the clear which meant that they had a lower expansion rate than the clear. The sheets from the bars that didn't bend more than ⅜ in. (9 mm) became my fusible glass. I labeled these sheets and put them in a separate rack.

At first Bullseye used the bar test, but it took too much time and glass to perform. By using a polariscope that had been used in glass laboratories since about 1920, Bullseye developed the **chip test** (see the section about compatibility) and by August 1982, Bullseye began selling its "Stressometer." Now people had an easy way to measure compatibility.

1982: The Bullseye Fusing Ranch

Within its factory, Bullseye created a separate area devoted to fusing and called it the Bullseye Fusing Ranch. Boyce Lundstrom headed up the Fusing Ranch and proselytized the virtues of glass fusing. Daniel Schwoerer was in the factory developing compatible glass.

Boyce was fanatic about glass fusing and pushed the ideas into the mainstream of glass art. He encouraged individual artists with slogans such as, "Never refuse to refuse."

Once Boyce told me that he visualized a time when fusing would be so common that every housewife would have a kiln in her kitchen to make bowls and plates. In my opinion, that initial emphasis on the hobby market caused fusing to lag in development. For years I could count on one hand the number of fusers doing anything more than earrings, plates and bowls.

In the beginning, the research and the effort to bring tools for glass fusing to the market fueled development. A Fusing Ranch ad in *Glass Studio Magazine*, August 1982, advertises kilns, the "Stressometer," and curious rods similar to Moje's button rods.

Problems still plagued innovators. When fused, some glass had a scummy surface called ***"devitrification."*** One way to "sort of" get around this was to fuse only the colors that didn't seem to devitrify and to quickly heat and cool through the devitrification range of 1350°F – 1450°F (730°C – 790°C). This meant that a quicker kiln had to be developed. The Bullseye Marathon 20 x 20 was the first to be marketed. It was insulated with ceramic fiber blanket which absorbs very little heat compared to soft fire brick pottery kilns. Also, in a pottery kiln, glass would be heated unevenly, so it could shatter from thermal expansion. The Marathon kiln had top-fired elements which would more evenly heat flat glass than the side heated pottery kilns that people were using at this time.

In early 1982, we were looking for an overglaze that would flux or seal the top surface of the glass and prevent devitrification. I remember testing a dozen or so overglazes from Seattle Pottery, and none were compatible with Bullseye. Boyce Lundstrom, however, found one, labeled it "Spray A," and rushed it to the market in late 1982. "Spray A" is a stable, 18% lead glass that has been powdered and placed in a liquid medium. It is brushed or sprayed onto the glass surface and melts at a slightly lower temperature than full fuse; since it's usually applied in a very thin layer, there is less of a compatibility problem. Around 1990, Daniel Schwoerer reformulated his glass at Bullseye so that it is not as sensitive to devitrification; today "Spray A" is rarely used.

Tested Compatible Glass

By August 1982 Bullseye began marking the glass that had been tested for compatibility. The labeling went through a series of changes over the years.

bottom: Bullseye "Tested Compatible" labels on the right corner of their sheet glass. 1982 just had the letter F.

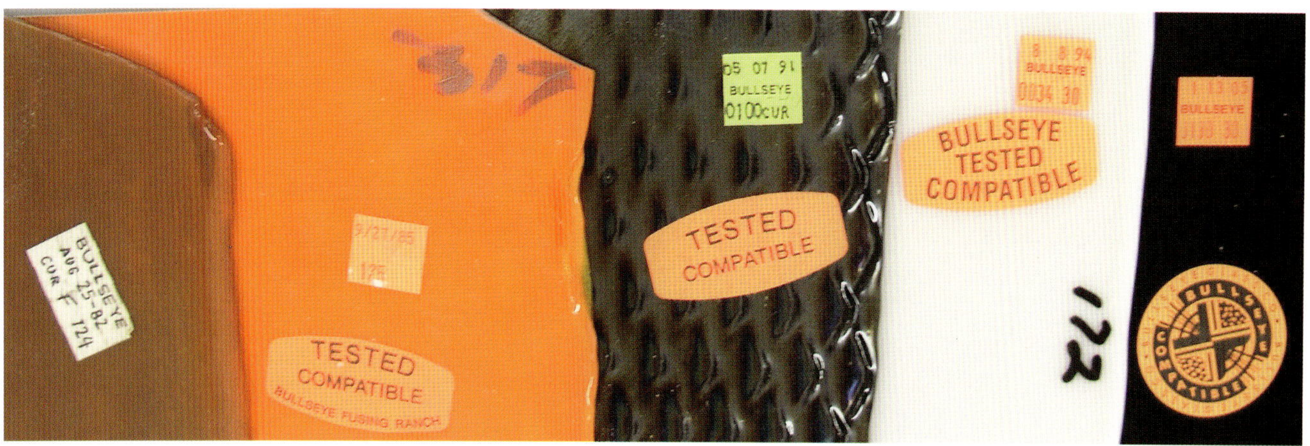

BULLSEYE FUSING RANCH

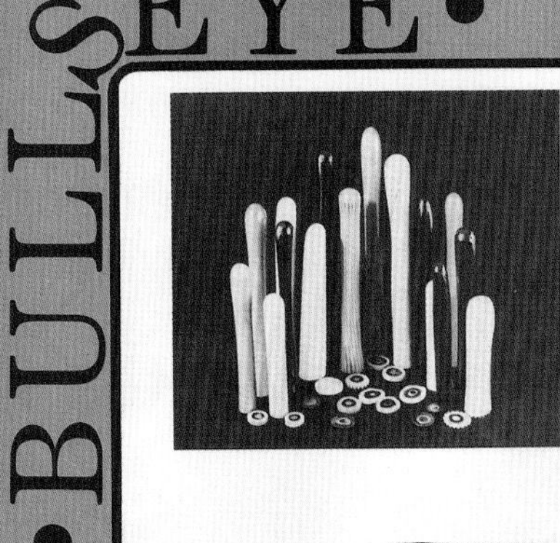

If you know how to use them —
Bullseye Fusing Ranch has them.

The Bullseye Stressometer is a device for measuring the stress in all glasses related to a base clear of the same glass. The Stressometer reveals patterns of polarized light in stressed glass, which makes possible the visual observation of poor combinations.

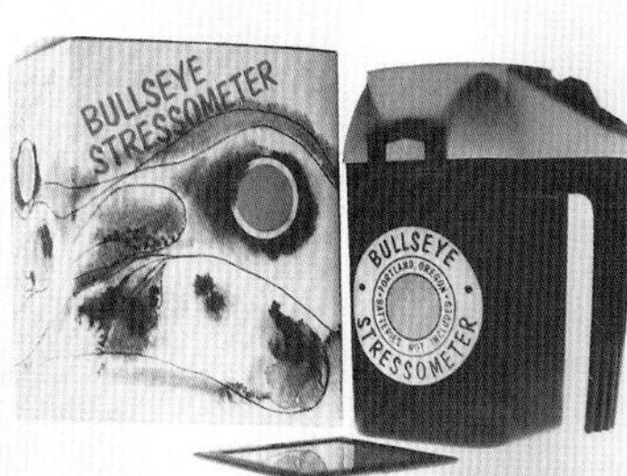

Stressometer includes instructions

$14.95

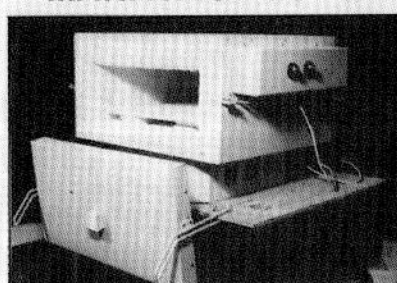

No Stress 0	Little Stress 1	Moderate Stress 2	Extreme Stress 3

This is a test strip showing stress in a clear base glass using the Bullseye Stressometer.

BULLSEYE FUSING PACKAGE

Designed specifically for fusing, laminating, and paint firing on glass

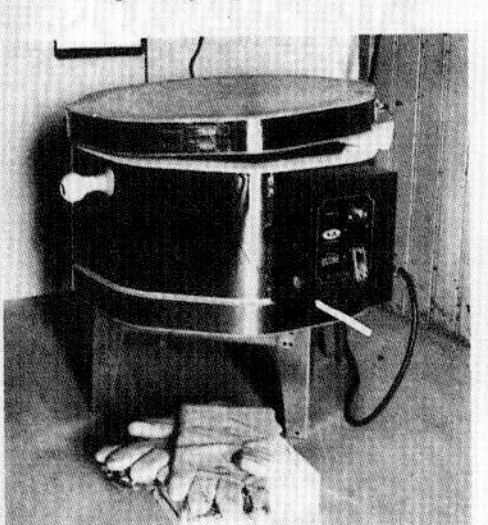

The Bullseye Fuser is a professional studio kiln designed specifically for fusing to 1650°F. The kiln will reach fusing temperature in 1½ hours. The kiln-setter acts as an automatic safety for oven firing and as a control shut off for production or class firing. The firing instructions for this fuser are located in the Bullseye Fusing Booklet.

The future potential of fusing is the largest new dimension in glass to come along since the individual glass blowing studio. The possibilities of using fused glass as a studio craft, in the making of plates, tiles, wind chimes, architectural wall, lights, etc., etc., are just starting and will continue to grow for many years. This kiln should give many years of constant and continuous use.

Package Price
$595.00

Kiln with Pyrometer only $485.00

Total Package Contains Kiln & Firing Instructions

- *220 Volt 15 Amp. Kiln & firing instructions*
- *Octagonal in shape with inside dimensions of 17½″ x 9″ deep*
- *Two 16″ kiln shelves*
- *Constructed of insulated fire brick with stainless steel jacket*
- *Elements are of highest quality. (Iron, aluminum & chromium — Kanthal type.)*
- *Infinite switch for controlling rate of temperature climb*
- *Kiln-setter which will control shut off time, with use of pyrometric cones.*
- *Pyrometer (temperature indicator) and thermocouple*
- *Glass separator*
- *Stressometer - for testing compatibility of glasses*
- *Soft brick shelf supports*
- *Pyrometric cones - 2 packs △ 012 △ 011*
- *Power cord adaptor*
- *Our best terry gloves*

HAND CAST GLASS
BULLSEYE GLASS COMPANY
SINCE 1974

3722 S.E. 21st
Portland, Oregon 97202
503-232-8887

Manufacturers of Cathedral, Opalescent and Specialty Glass
OPEN: Monday through Friday, 9:00 A.M. to 4:00 P.M.

FUSING KILN
BULLSEYE MARATHON 20 x 20

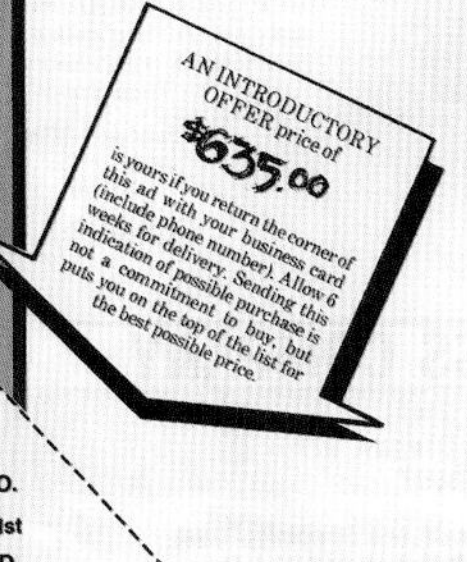

BULLSEYE now has a new kiln especially designed for fusing and painting glass. The elements are overhead so the glass is evenly heated. There is no other kiln on the market with all these features:

- 70° F to 1600° F in 30 minutes
- 20 x 20 fusing area
- Front loading
- Infinite switches
- 30 AMP, 220 Volts
- 100% ceramic fiber insulation
- Pyrometer and Thermocouple included
- Table-top stand

This fusing kiln is past the testing stages and is by far the top performer of all fusing kilns to date. Boyce says: "I don't know who would want more in a 20″ x 20″ than this kiln offers".

AN INTRODUCTORY OFFER price of **$635.00** *is yours if you return the corner of this ad with your business card (include phone number). Allow 6 weeks for delivery. Sending this indication of possible purchase is not a commitment to buy, but puts you on the top of the list for the best possible price.*

BULLSEYE GLASS CO.
3722 S.E. 21st
PORTLAND, OREGON 97202

BULLSEYE APPRENTICE PROGRAM

Become a Bullseye apprentice in residence. Live and work and learn at Bullseye. Living accommodations plus meal expenses will be provided.

Requirements

- *Glass Experience*
- *Layout Design*
- *Basic Photography*
- *Scientific Procedure*
- *No Heavy Thinkers*
- *No Daydreamers*
- *No Holidays*

This is an intensive learning and working program that takes a three month commitment. Apprentices will work on: 1) Glass Casting 2) Glass Photography 3) Kiln Construction 4) Technical Aspects of Fusing 5) Fused Glass Design and 6) Glass Blowing.

WE WILL ACCEPT 5-6 APPRENTICES TO START IN DECEMBER & JANUARY

Please send resume, and letter relating to present situation and commitments, plus three references in regards to the above listed talents to: Bullseye Glass Company, 3722 S.E. 21st Avenue, Portland, Oregon 97202. No phone calls.

BULLSEYE IS LOOKING FOR *HOST* STUDIOS AND RETAIL STORES TO CONDUCT FUSING WORKSHOPS

Bullseye Glass Company has a successful fusing program ready for your shop. We will send you a professional teacher, all the necessary equipment, fusible glass and advertising flyers.

Bullseye has a continuing teaching program for retail shops. The purpose of these well defined classes is to promote scientific fusing knowledge and teaching principals, so that fusing does not falter in the wake of mis-information.

Fusing is a simple procedure, in its basic concept, but testing must be learned. Annealing must be understood and design concepts are totally different than working with flat glass designs.

Please fill out the form below or a reasonable facsimile. Include all information and Bullseye will send you a packet that will explain the *total* teaching relationship.

These classes are set up to provide information so a shop owner can establish a profitable continuing fusing program.

BUSINESS NAME ________________
ADDRESS ________________
CITY ________________
STATE ________________ ZIP ________________
PHONE ________________ OWNED BY ________________

☐ *I would like to sponsor a fusing class.*
☐ *I would like more information.*

Clip and mail to: BULLSEYE GLASS CO., 3722 S.E. 21st, Portland, Oregon 97202

Bullseye Fusing Ranch: Teaching

Before 1980, only a few artists were experimenting with glass for fusing and included Klaus Moje, David Ruth and Boyce Lundstrom. In the beginning, all of the people fusing Bullseye glass either worked for Bullseye, bought glass for stained glass projects directly from the factory, or knew Boyce Lundstrom. The early fusers using Bullseye Glass by 1981 included Ray Ahlgren, Michael Barton, Ruth Brockmann, Richard La Londe, Boyce Lundstrom, Liz Mapelli, Marty McNelly, Gil Reynolds, and Rob Snyder. In 1982 Jim Bowman, Tony Parker, Klaus Moje, David Ruth, and Roger Thomas were also experimenting with Bullseye.

The August 1982 Bullseye ad in *Glass Studio* magazine was very exciting because it listed two Fusing Ranch projects, the Fusing Ranch apprentice program and the workshops. Participating in the "Bullseye Apprentice Program" were Peter Magdan, Linda Ethier, and Ma Anand Rupama.

The "Bullseye Fusing Workshop" as defined in the ad: "The purpose of these well defined classes is to promote scientific fusing knowledge and teaching principals, so that fusing does not falter in the wake of misinformation." Boyce Lundstrom was the first teacher. During the summer of 1982, Ruth Brockmann, Gil Reynolds, and David Ruth joined Boyce at the Fusing Ranch to play with fusing and to develop ideas; Ruth Brockmann began making her glass masks.

After commercial fishing for salmon in Alaska, I joined the group at the end of September. Boyce trained the four of us, and we became the first teachers for Bullseye Glass Company, going out to retail shops that purchased a package of two Octagon 16 in. (40 cm) pottery kilns with pyrometers, fusing supplies, and a case of glass for fusing. Early kilns didn't have kiln controllers (other than the person running the kiln). We taught what I called "The Big Three"; compatibility, volume

control, and annealing – and handed out a fourteen-page pamphlet called "Fusing, Fusing, Fusing," by Boyce Lundstrom. I taught my first class at the beginning of 1983 in Newport News, Virginia and continued teaching through this Bullseye Fusing Ranch program, around the United States and in Canada, for a couple of years. After that, people wanted advanced classes, which I put together, and I continued teaching on my own.

In August 1983, as a TA (teaching assistant) for Susan Stinsmuehlen, I taught fusing using Bullseye glass at the Pilchuck Glass School. In 1984, I returned to Pilchuck as TA for Toots Zynsky; Ruth Brockmann was TA for Klaus Moje the same session. Ruth and I were instructors at Pilchuck in 1985, and Gil Reynolds was our TA.

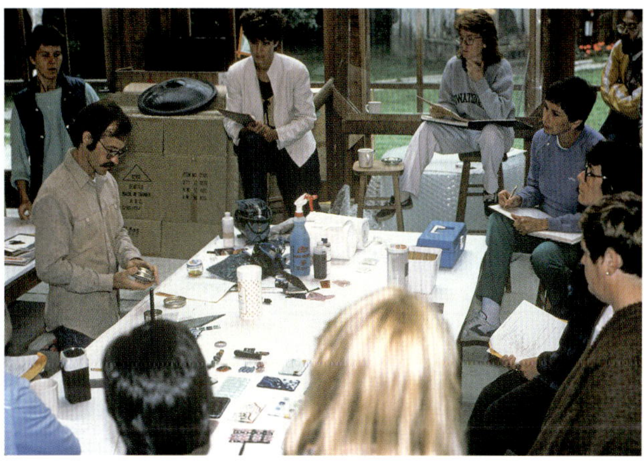

above: Richard La Londe in 1983, teaching the new technique of fusing Bullseye glass at Pilchuck.

The Bullseye Fusing Movement grew quickly. By 1986, many artists were fusing Bullseye, including Brock Craig, Melody Rowe, Leslie Rowe Israelson, Michael Dupille, Frank Vandenham, Roger Nachman, Hal Bond, Marlyn Nugent, Carol Hall, and Warren Langley. Klaus Moje's students at Canberra all worked with Bullseye. The first class graduated in 1986.

The next two pages contain artwork created in the early 1980's by the original fusing instructors for the Bullseye Fusing Ranch, Ruth Brockmann, Gil Reynolds, and David Ruth, (I was the fourth original instructor). Following that, Liz Mapelli with the first public commission to use fused Bullseye glass, 1981.

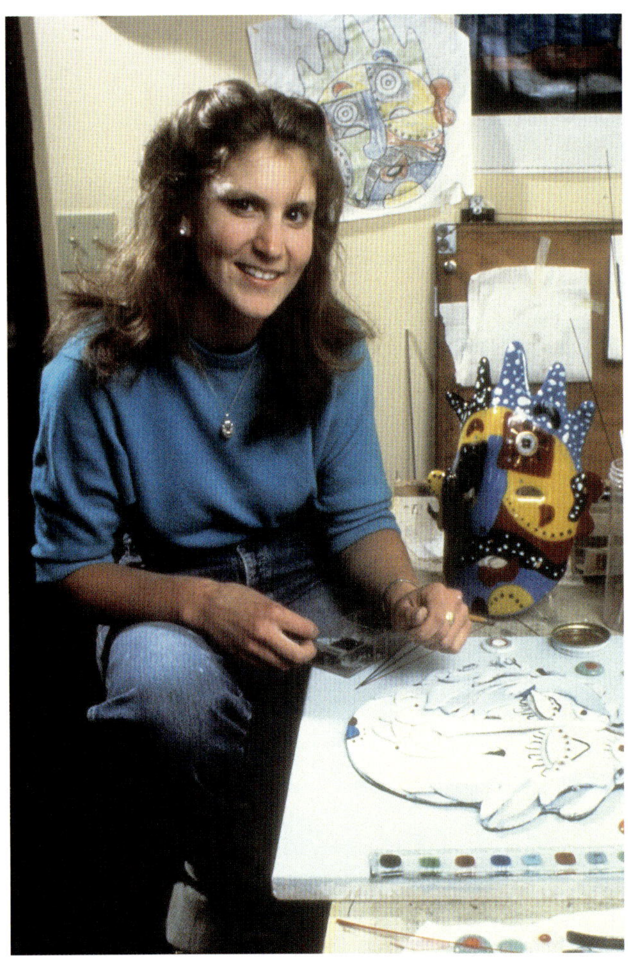

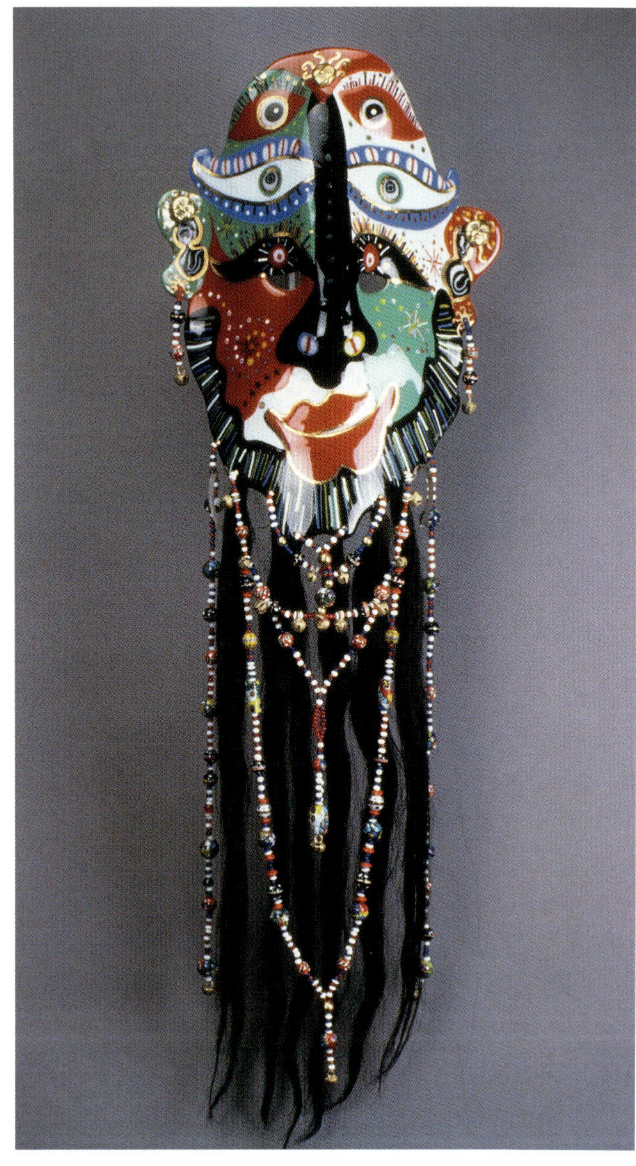

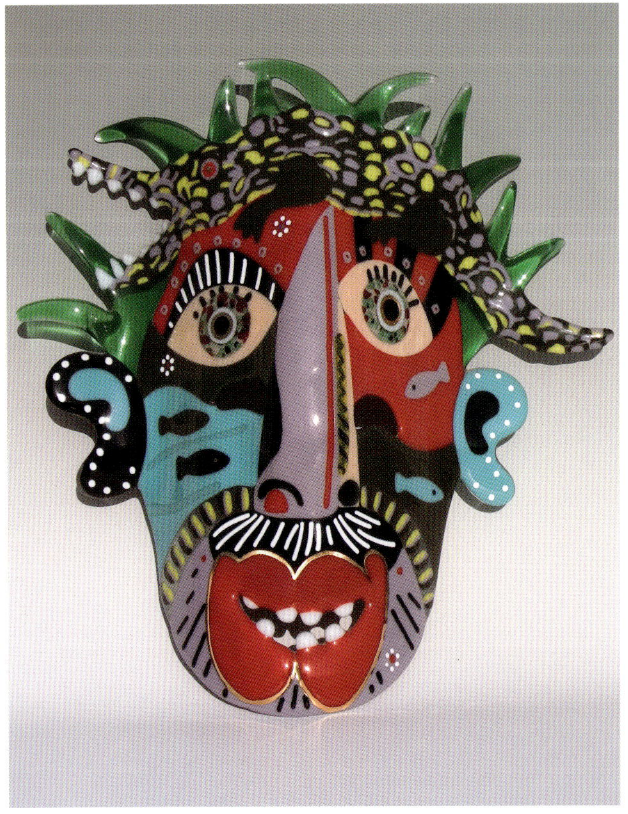

Ruth Brockmann (b. 1955)

After teaching a few workshops for Bullseye, Ruth became a successful gallery artist with her masks and kiln cast sculpture. In 1992 she created 2 large fused glass, kiln cast glass, and colored cement murals for the Portland State Office Building in Portland, OR.

above left: Ruth Brockmann, 1983, laying out a mask on a shelf, shows compatibility test strip and white "Spray A" covering glass pieces to prevent devitrification. This piece was fused flat and then slumped over a fiber mold.

above right: "Best Wishes Jinni," 1984, H. 33 in. (84 cm) x W. 11 in. (28 cm) x D. 6 in. (15 cm). Fused and slumped Bullseye glass with real human hair and beads.

bottom left: "Crocodile Shaman," 1985, H. 17 in. (43 cm) x W. 16 in. (41 cm) x D. 6 in. (15 cm). Fused and slumped Bullseye Glass.

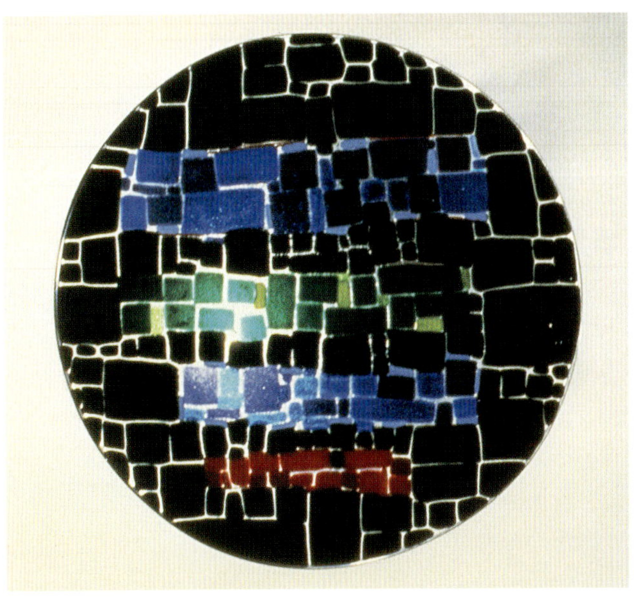

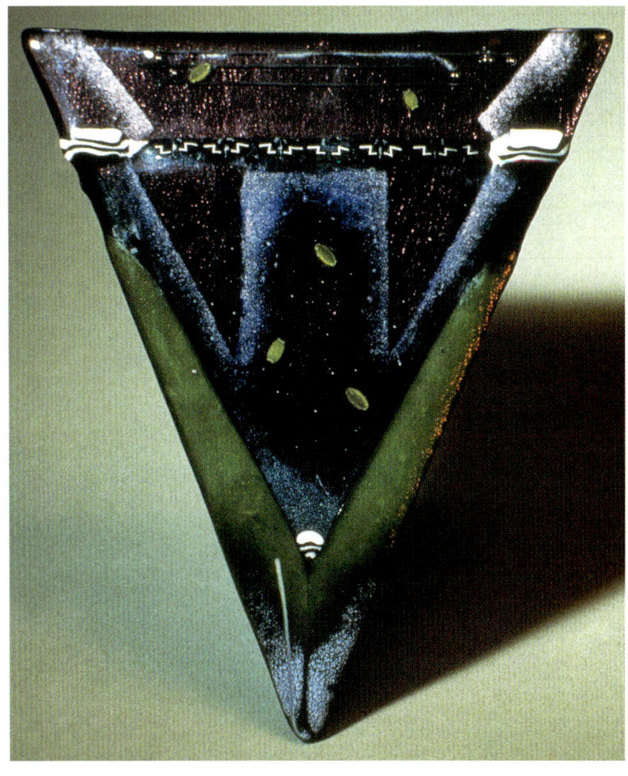

David Ruth (b. 1951)

David was the first glass caster for Genesis Glass Company in Portland, OR, and in 1980 he set up Ruth Glass, rolling beautiful sheet glass in Santa Cruz, CA. In 1982 he began teaching for the Bullseye Fusing Ranch. Today he creates large kiln poured and cast glass sculptures in Oakland, CA.

above left: David Ruth fused plate, 1983, 14 in. (36 cm) in diameter x 1 in. (2.5 cm), fused Bullseye glass.

below left: "Water Dancing," 1984. H. 72 in. (183 cm). Painted steel with glass.

Gil Reynolds (b. 1951)

Taught classes through the Fusing Ranch and went on to establish Fusion Headquarters, a retail supply company now located in Newberg, Or. In 1987 he wrote <u>The Fused Glass Handbook</u> and continues to teach classes. He organizes the Hot Glass Horizons conference. www.fusionheadquarters.com

above right: "Narsistic Firbosis" 1981 H. 10 in. (25 cm)
below right: "Ganymede," 1981 12 in. (30 cm) in diameter, fused plate.

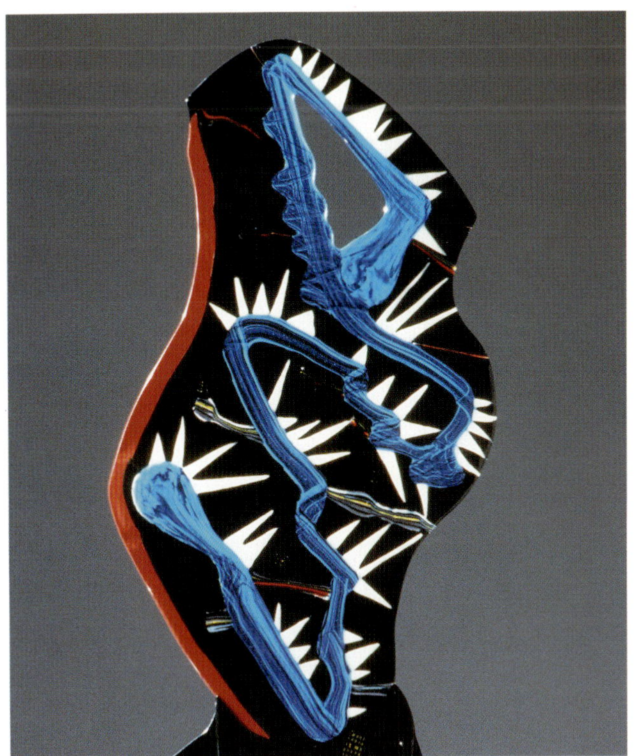

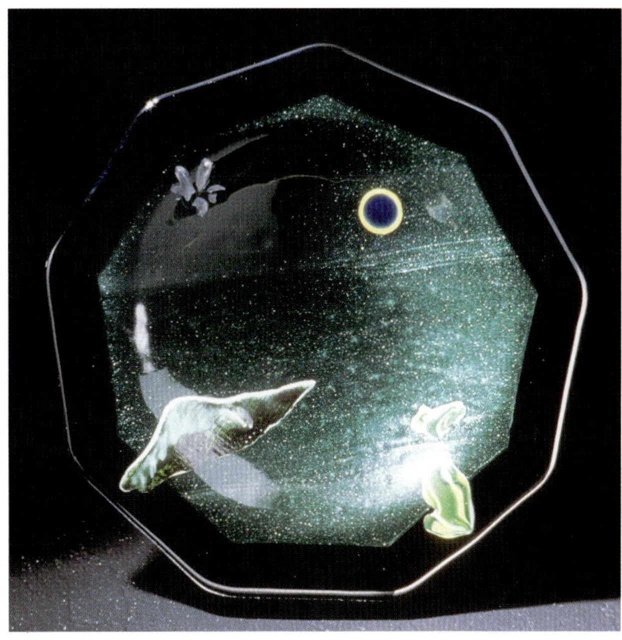

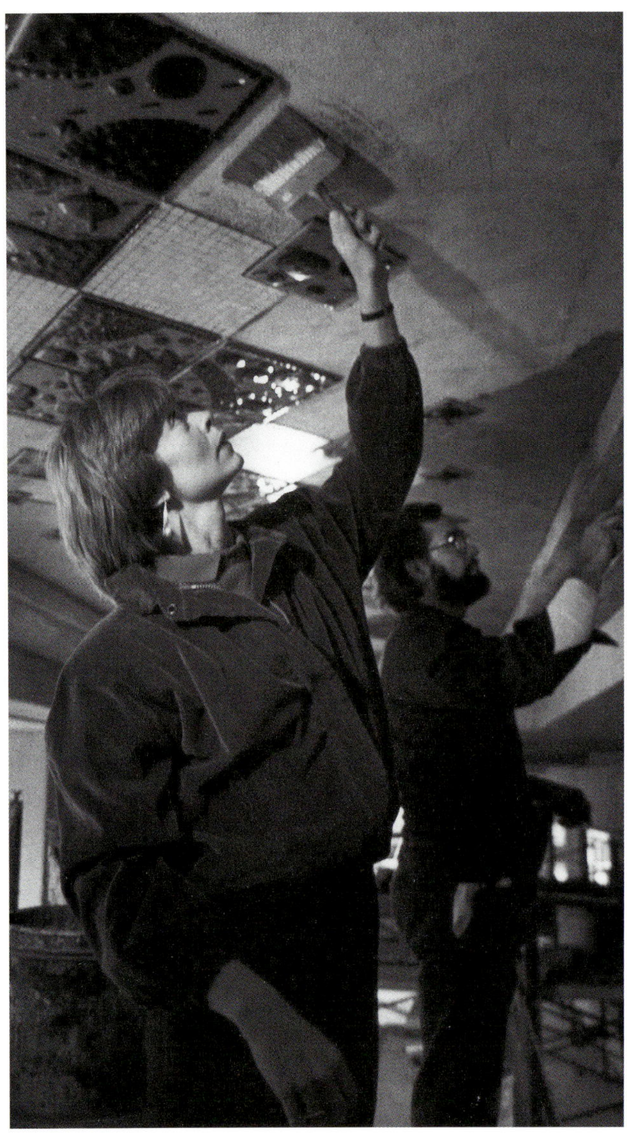

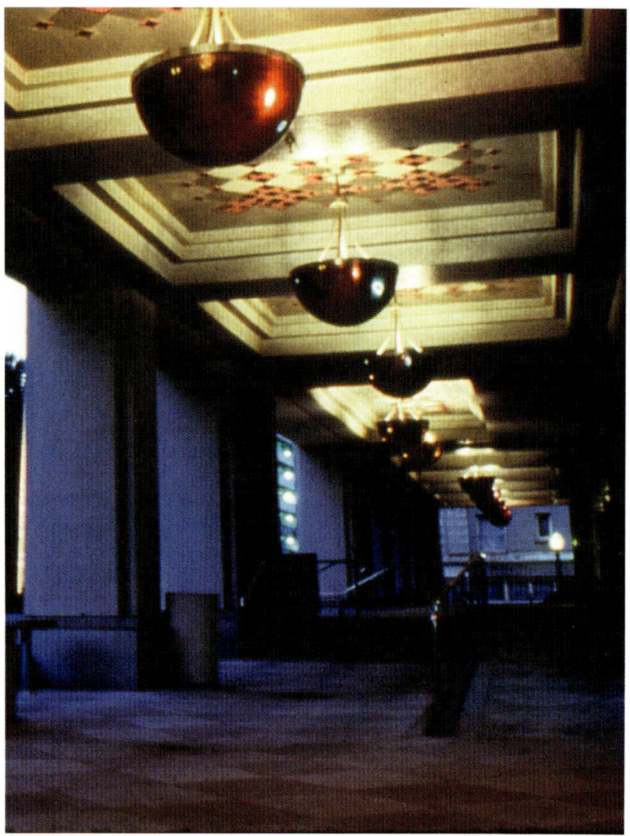

Liz Mapelli (b. 1948)

above right:
Fused Bullseye glass and Italian glass mosaic tile ceiling at the Justice Center Exterior Arcade in Portland, Oregon, 1983. 5000 square feet (465 square meters). This is the first public commission using fused Bullseye glass. Since this commission Liz has created many public and private fused and enameled glass wall pieces.

above left:
Liz Mapelli applying mastic to adhere her fused glass and Italian glass mosaic tiles to the Justice Center ceiling.

lower left:
Disk, 1981, 18 in. (46 cm) in diameter, fused mosaic technique. Many tiny square pieces of Bullseye glass were placed with the iridescent side down on fiber-paper and fused. Liz was one of the first artists fusing Bullseye to show at a major gallery, the Habatat Galleries in Michigan, 1981.

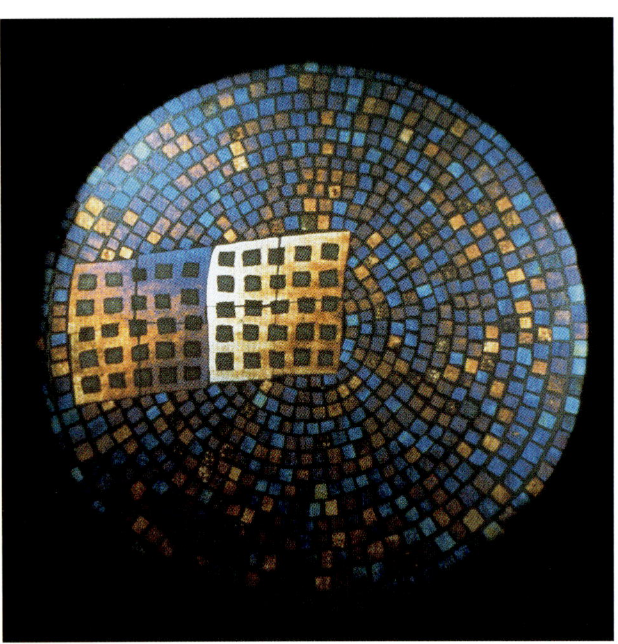

The Book
Glass Fusing Book One, published in 1983 by Boyce Lundstrom and Daniel Schwoerer, is still the quintessential book about glass fusing on the market today (in my opinion) covering the basics, including compatibility, volume control, annealing, kilns, firing, slumping, sagging, and molds. Today it is available under the title, Kiln Firing Glass • Glass Fusing Book One .

In 1985 Daniel Schwoerer and Boyce Lundstrom dissolved their partnership. Daniel took over glass making and the Bullseye factory; Boyce got the Fusing Ranch and fusing supplies. The supply line, including "Spray A," the "Stressometer," and shelf primer - is now sold by Ed Hoy's International; Ed has added many new products and markets under the name Hotline. Boyce moved the fusing ranch and reopened it as a summer school for fusing.

Camp Colton: 1986 – 1993
In 1985 Boyce and Katy Lundstrom purchased a rustic "Waldenesque" old summer camp called Camp Colton located thirty-five miles southeast of Portland, Oregon and set it up as their home and a camp for fusing. It was situated on fifty-six wooded acres with a trout pond, creeks, and large fir and cedar trees. The 1989 Camp Colton Program Guide states, *"students enjoy an intimate, yet elegant family-like camp stay."* There were cottages, studios, and a large dining hall-lodge. Kathy ran the camp and kitchen. Boyce and visiting instructors taught classes. The program advertised all aspects of kiln glass including fusing, slumping, moldmaking, casting, pâte de verre, enameling, torch and glory hole work.

In 1986, Ruth Brockmann and I taught at the very first session. We set up the large fusing kiln that I had built for Bullseye in 1982, and I donated my old glass furnace where we blew the first glass at the camp.

At Camp Colton, Boyce Lundstrom wrote Advanced Fusing Techniques: Glass Fusing

Book Two and Glass Casting and Moldmaking: Glass Fusing Book Three, both published in 1989 by Vitreous Publications. Michael Dupille, Ruth Brockmann, and Dan Ott did experiments and research for the books and are featured throughout.

From 1986 to 1993, many students from all over the world attended sessions at Camp Colton. One student, Tony Serviente, summed it up by saying, "I was at Colton in 1990 where Boyce infected me with his passion for glass. His personality struck me as a combination of 60 grit silicon carbide, a kiln element glowing to the point of burnout, an unabridged encyclopedia of glass, and street corner preacher. I still treasure the experience for what it taught me to do, as well as avoid."

After Colton, Boyce set up a couple of fused glass tile manufacturing companies, bought a marble factory, and today the larger-than-life Boyce Lundstrom lives in the world of myth, and his glass dreams are overflowing with ideas. Many artists fusing today experienced Camp Colton. There has never been anything like it since.

Thirty Something: www.bullseyeglass.com
Today, 2006, Bullseye Glass Company offers a wide range of compatible products and states on their website that "Bullseye's mission has been to develop and manufacture a fully integrated system of glasses which cross the borders of individual disciplines, fusing, blowing, torch work, casting, and the foundation flat glasswork." Bullseye sells compatible sheet glass, frit, rods, billets, tools & supplies all over the world. Through their Bullseye Resource Center, they sell glass and supplies and offer classes. Bullseye also sponsors conferences and competitions. The Bullseye Connection Gallery exhibits kiln formed glass art.

Pretty good for a bunch of "hippies" rolling sheets from melted pop bottles!

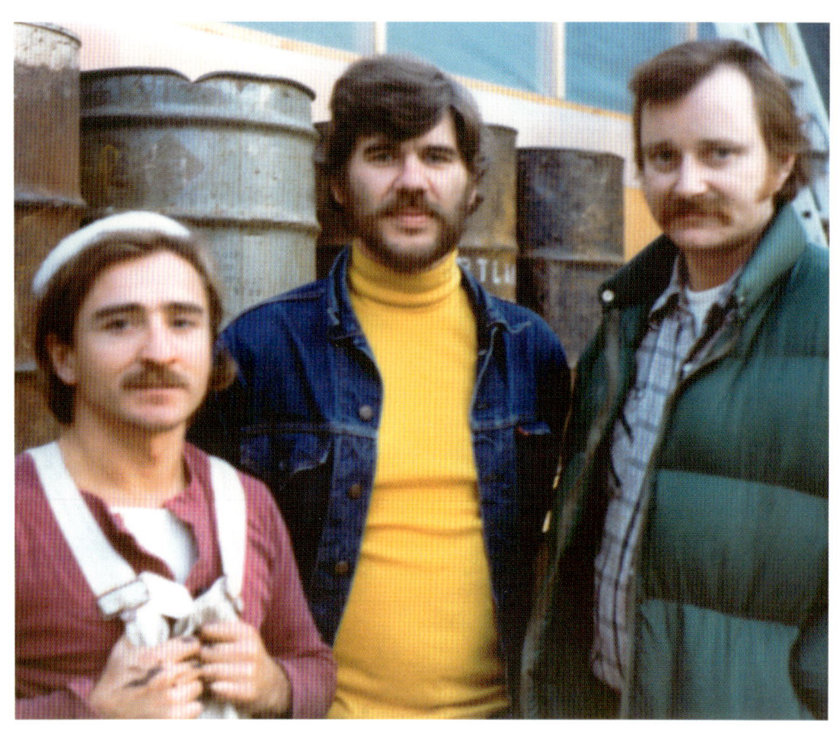

upper: **The founders of Bullseye Glass Company, Portland, Oregon.** (from left) Daniel Schwoerer, Boyce Lundstrom, Ray Ahlgren, 1977.

The Bullseye Fusing Ranch 1982
middle left: David Ruth.

middle: Richard La Londe.

middle right: (from left) Boyce Lundstrom & David Ruth, glass on punty rods.

lower left: Ruth Brockmann & Gil Reynolds, glory hole work with punty rods.

lower right: (from left) Gil Reynolds, David Ruth, & Ruth Brockmann glory hole.
Note: We were too busy having fun to take any decent photographs.

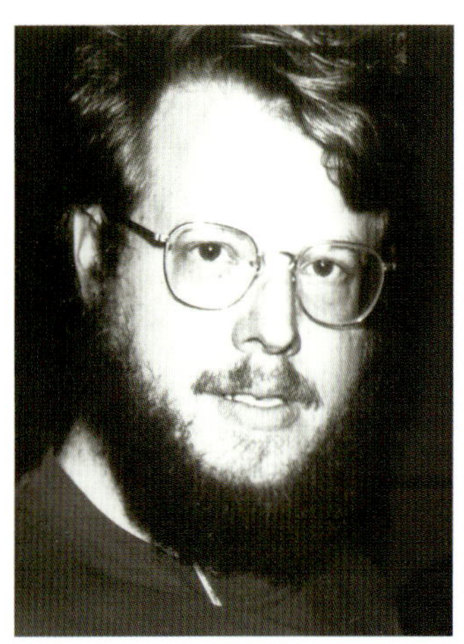

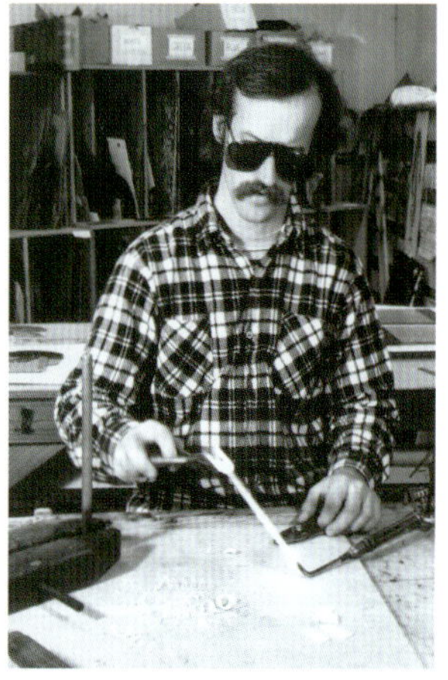

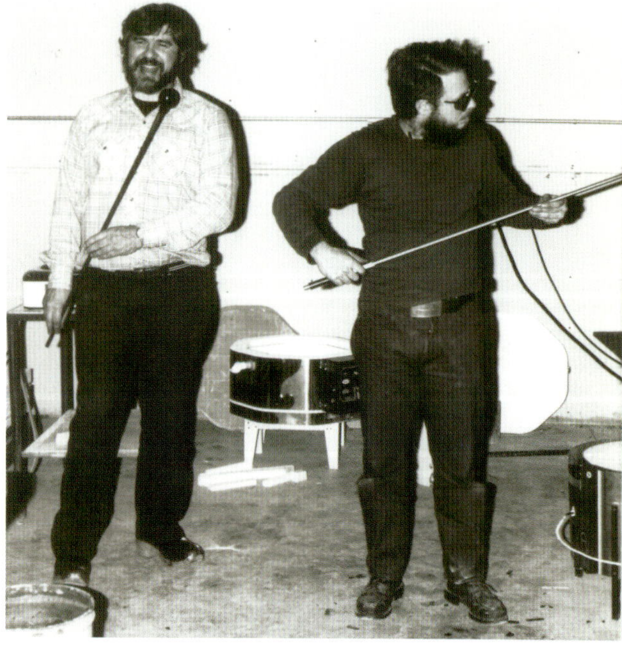

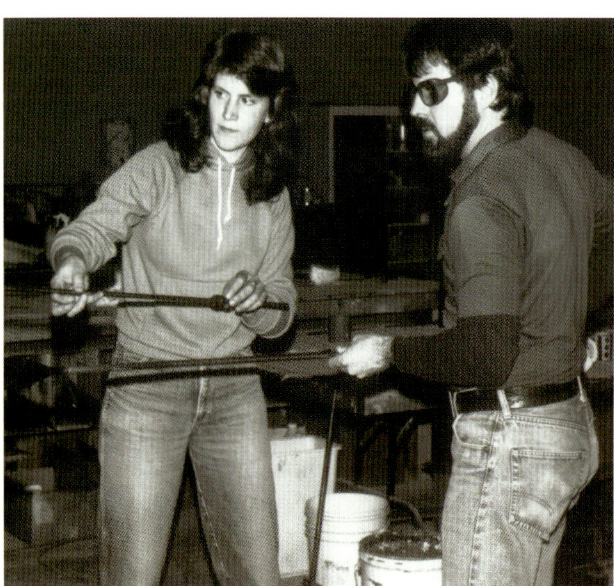

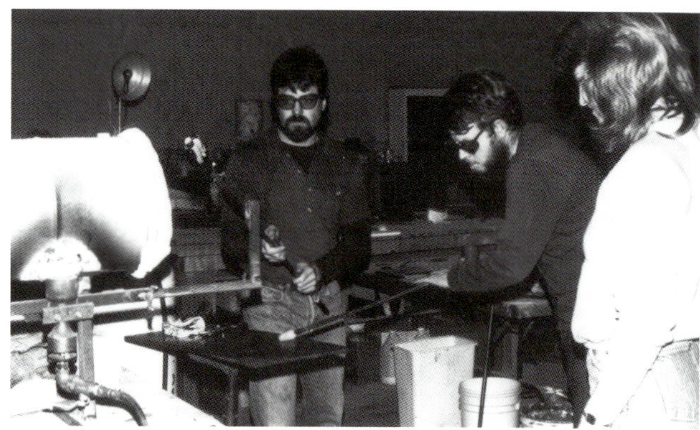

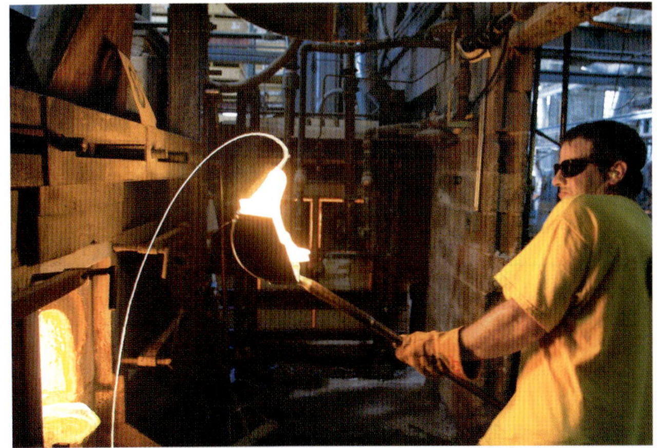

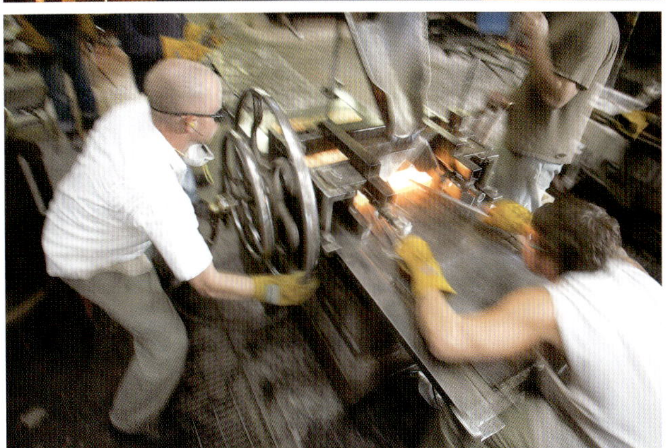

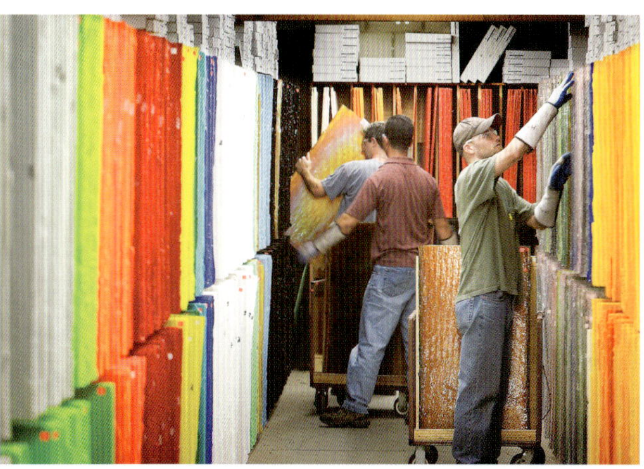

Bullseye Glass Company Today

upper left: Molten glass is ladled out of a furnace and carried to the glass casting table.

middle left: The fast-paced action of hand-rolling a sheet of glass on the casting table.

middle right: Racks and racks of the beautiful finished sheets of Bullseye glass in the warehouse.

lower: Located next to the factory is the Bullseye Resource Center which has kilnworking classes, hosts artist lectures, and sells glass, books, tools, and supplies. (Photos courtesy of Bullseye Glass Co.)

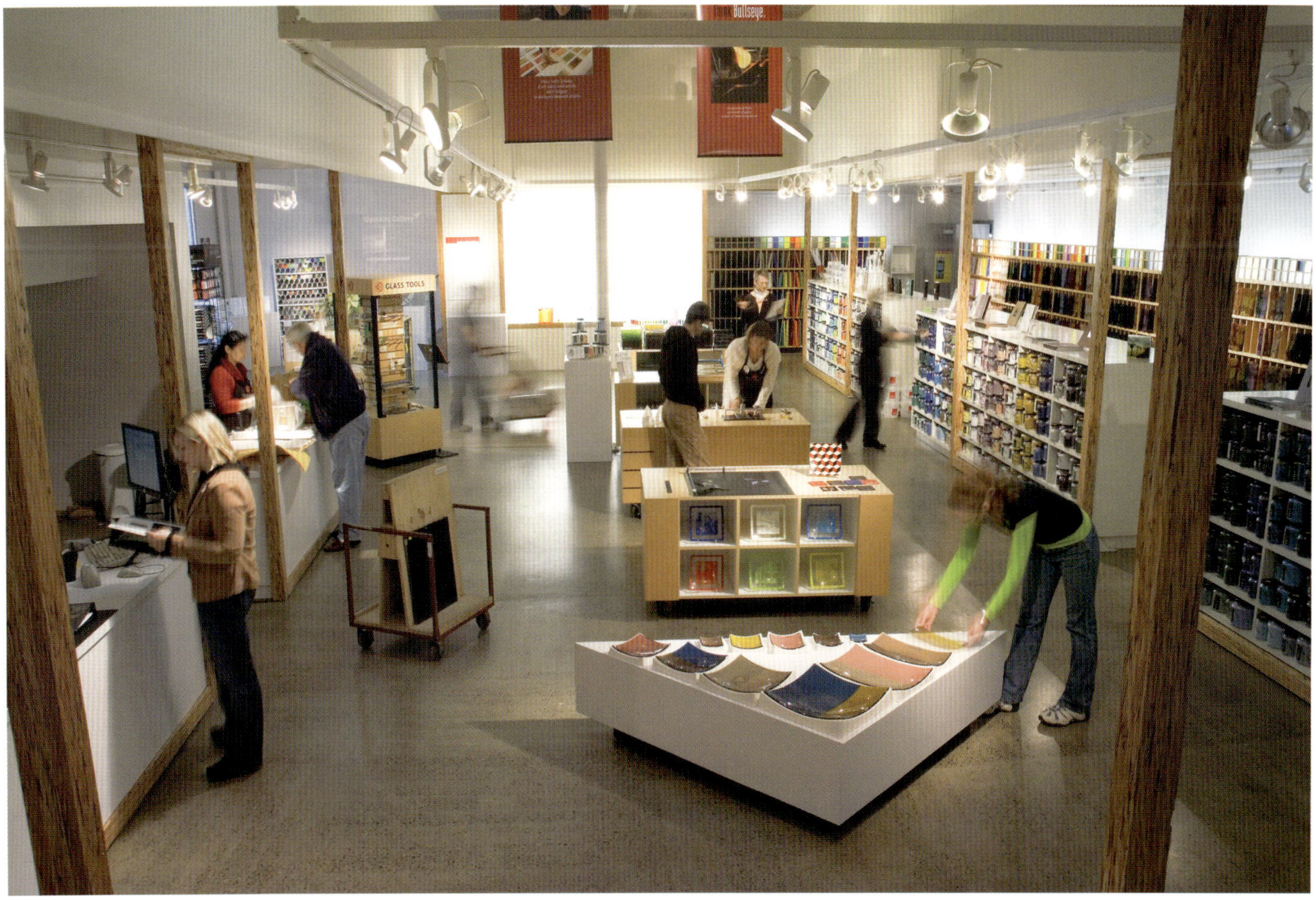

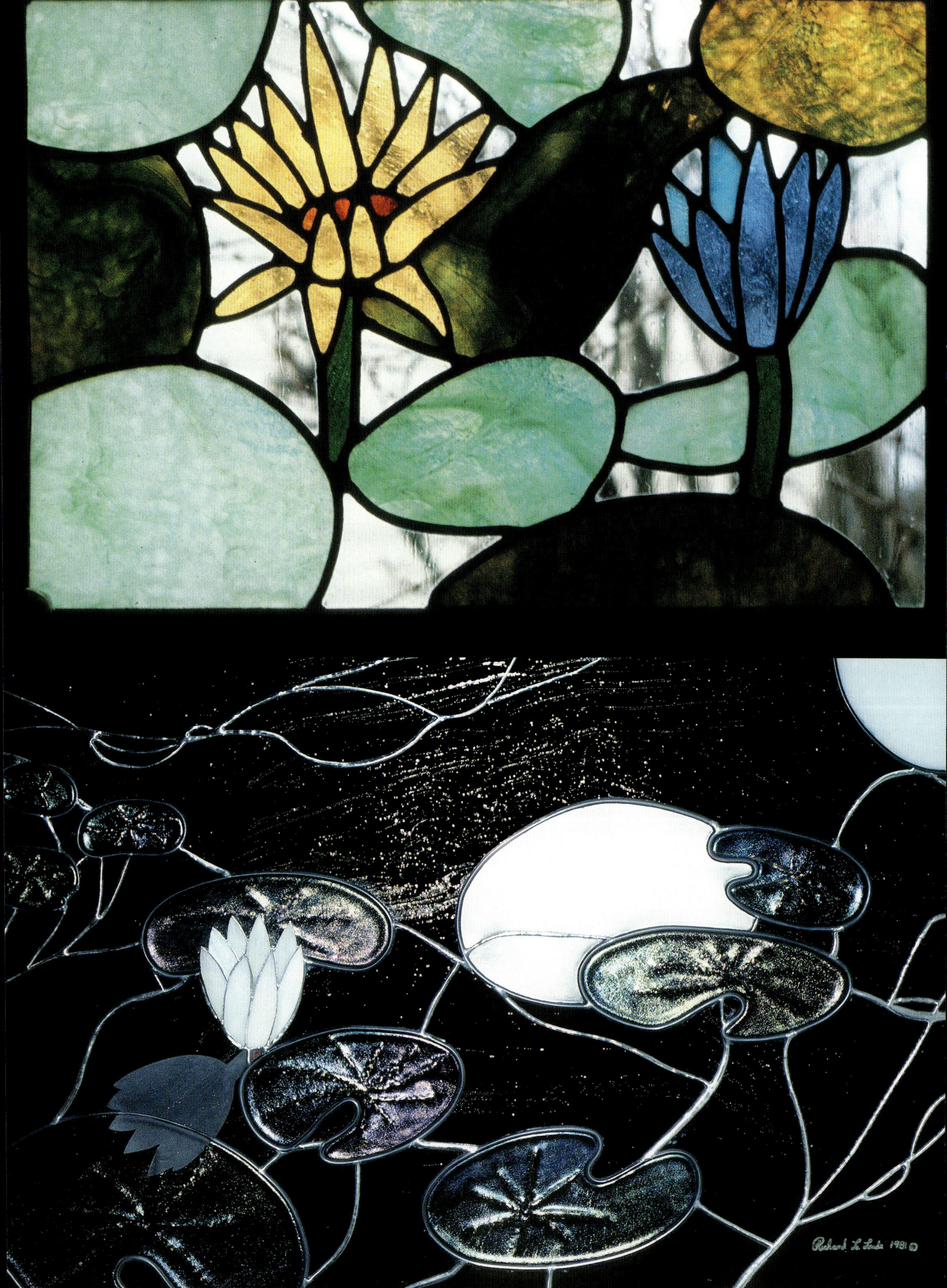

Richard L. Lala 1981

Part 2: Richard La Londe

The Beginning: My Path

"I am on a path and I know where it is only when I fall off!"

Circumstances and Location

Fusing glass involves the right sequence of actions, the right combination of planning and luck. Likewise, my involvement in the glass fusing movement wouldn't have happened if events in my life hadn't unfolded in just the right sequence, with little planning but lots of luck.

Born on June 30, 1950, my life in the "All American" mill town of Vancouver, Washington didn't foreshadow life as a glass artist. But as a kid, I stumbled into opportunities that paved the way. When my parents didn't buy the toys that I wanted, I had the resources to start making them, becoming very good with tools and with using my hands. In the eighth grade, I received the "Best Woodshop Student of the Year Award," which was dedicated to a previous shop teacher who got his arm wound up in the drill press. The award failed to impress others as a sign of my destiny as an artist.

After the Soviets launched the first satellite, Sputnik, people encouraged me to become a scientist. In 1972, I received a degree in Geology from the University of Washington in Seattle. My desire to create combined with the impetus of the hippie movement, and the next year I abandoned science for a six-month, self-guided tour of European art. That adventure included hanging out on the island of Crete and traveling two thousand miles through Turkey. Inspired, I returned home to purchase an oxyacetylene torch to make sheet metal sculptures. One day I turned my torch on an empty beer bottle to see if it would melt; the bottle exploded, giving me my first introduction to thermal shock and maybe my inclination to know more about glass.

I am on a path and I know where it is only when I fall off !

I wanted to add color to my metal art, but under the unwritten rules of the 1970's "hippie crafts revival," painting just wouldn't do. Rather, the emphasis was on traditional materials and techniques, so in 1974, exploding beer bottle aside, I turned to colored glass. This pre-dated stained glass popularity, so no shops sold supplies or taught classes. I began by teaching myself stained glass techniques from an article in a magazine. Then I found a church window repair shop jammed with streaky Tiffany-style glass. I talked the owner

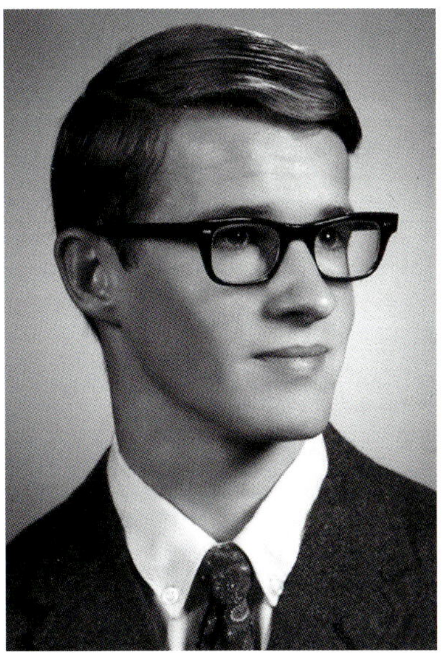

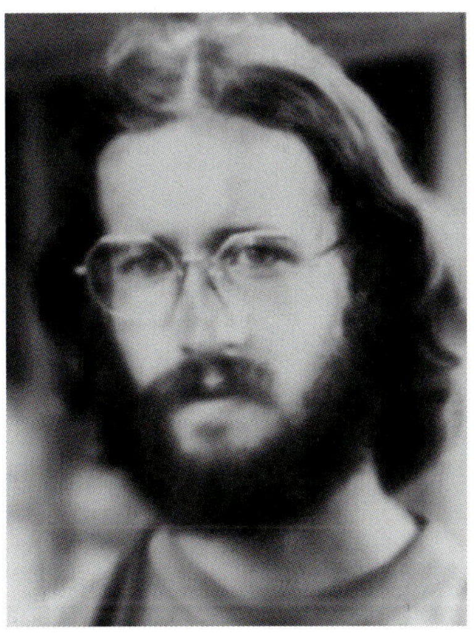

upper: Richard La Londe as a high school graduate, 1968.

lower: Richard in Istanbul, 1973. A street photographer shot this photo, developed it in trays of chemicals inside of the camera, and gave it to me wet.

facing upper: "Water Lily" window, 1975, H. 16 in. (41 cm) x W. 24 in. (61 cm).

facing lower: "Midnight Water Lily," 1981, H. 24 in. (61cm) x W. 36 in. (91 cm). For the glass lily pads, I fused iridescent Bullseye from the same sheet and had no compatibility problems. The glass is copper-foiled and soldered together, a technique that Tiffany developed.

into selling me some yellow, red, blue, and green glass. I sharpened a putty knife to cut lead and made glass grozers from a pair of electrical pliers; my cheap Red Devil cutter came from a hardware store. With these tools and that colored glass, combined with some clear window glass, I built my first stained glass window.

In 1975, I discovered hand-rolled glass from the Bullseye Glass factory. Here a bunch of hippies operated massive furnaces to make the glass. Like a kid in a candy factory, I prowled through racks of glass looking for big, bold, solid colors. Meanwhile, to cover more mundane expenses, I worked at Acme Metal Company in Portland, Oregon; I think I made the stuff for Wile E. Coyote, but over those few years, I became a journeyman welder. During the off time, I grabbed my volume of Jack London's Tales of Adventure and headed to southeast Alaska where I commercial fished salmon during the summers of 1974 and 1975.

In 1976, I met Ruth Brockmann and the next year we married and moved to Gig Harbor, Washington. We both commercial fished in Alaska the summers of 1977 and 1978 and during the winters we built our own house and studio where we created commissioned stained glass windows.

In 1980, the idea of blowing glass inspired me to build a furnace that instantly gobbled up both a thousand gallons of propane and my idea of making a living blowing glass. Glass art remained a dream while I earned money by combining my skills: forging ornamental railings; carpentry; electrical wiring and welding on fishing boats. Meanwhile, I checked out Kay Kinney's book Glass Craft from the library and, by luck, fused some Bullseye scraps left over from stained glass. It worked!

The Right Place at the Right Time
In 1981, I attended a glass blowing session at Pilchuck where I became better acquainted with Boyce Lundstrom, co-owner of Bullseye Glass Company, who was attending Klaus Moje's fus-

ing class. I also met Gil Reynolds who was my glass blowing partner for that session, and we immediately saw the potential of fusing. After that session I focused on fusing Bullseye Glass.

During the economic downturn of 1982, I headed off to the fishing grounds one more time. I finished the season, but my thirty-two-year old bones gave notice that this would be the end of my commercial fishing. Back at home, I enjoyed a reunion with Ruth Brockmann, Gil Reynolds, and David Ruth, all of whom had spent some of the summer working with Boyce Lundstrom at Bullseye, now becoming known as "The Fusing Ranch." So it was, in the fall of 1982, that the four of us became the first fusing instructors for Bullseye and traveled around the United States and into Canada to teach fusing and to promote both new fusing equipment and Bullseye Tested Compatible Glass.

The Early Mechanics of Fusing
From the beginning, fusing glass was magical. Each step involved a new process, a new technique, and more excitement. For me, the early days were really about the mechanics of fusing rather than the art.

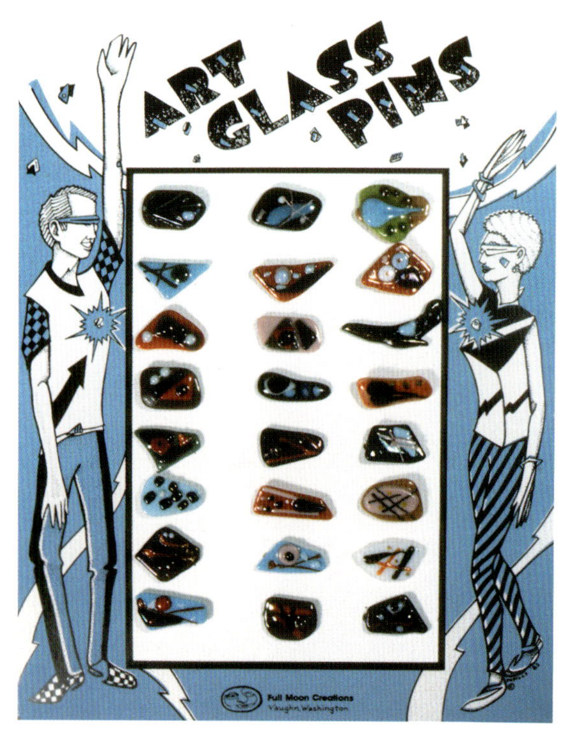

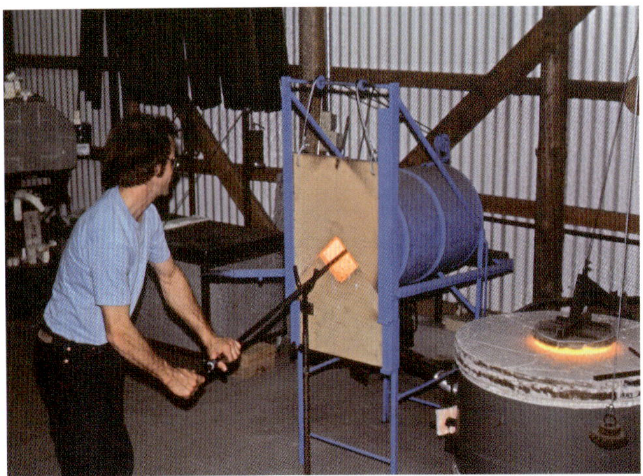

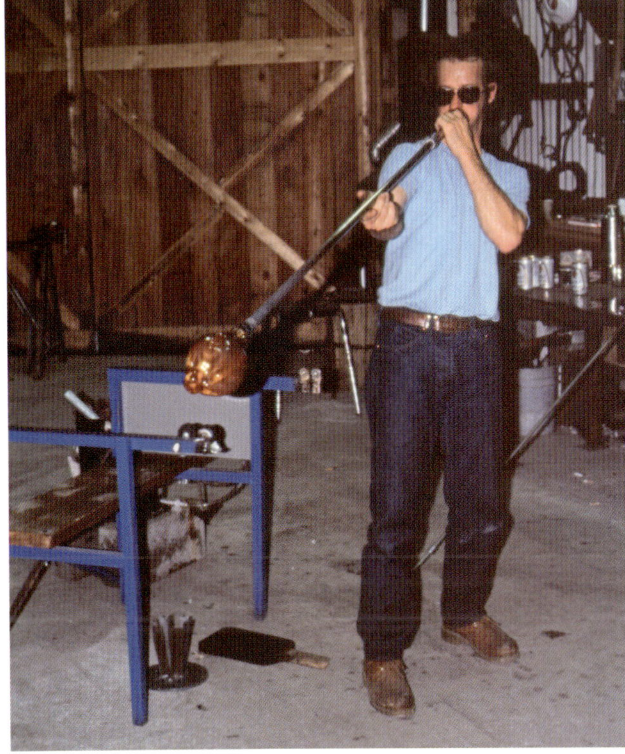

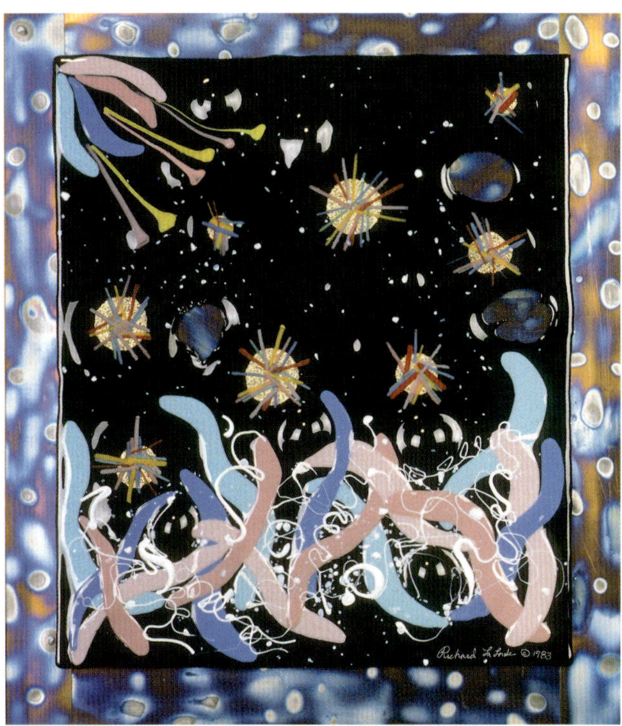

The folowing letter is about the above piece.
I guess if you put it out there, it's out there.

Wednesday, October 05, 2005 12:07 PM

Dear Mr. La Londe,
Thank you for your quick response to our e-mail. The receptionist at the Bullseye Connection's 300 NW 13th Ave site, did recognize your name and work, but as to value, she could not give Ken any help. She suggested we e-mail photos of the piece to the gallery then the gallery would contact you and you would be the one to suggest a value.

We had checked for your work on the internet, which is where we found the Bullseye Connection address but couldn't quite believe the $5 garage sale purchase could be for real. We wanted to do some more checking on our own. I decided the easiest way was to just e-mail photos directly to you to see if it was your work. We did not want to bother the gallery if the piece was really just worth the $5 Ken paid for it.

Thanks again for your help. I don't know if Ken will contact Mr. Schwoerer as you suggested, put it up for sale on Ebay or just keep it as his "great find."
Sincerely,
Lynn and Kenneth

facing: **Every One Starts With Pins!**
These are pins that Ruth Brockmann and I made in 1981. Our friend Michael Dupille designed the display for us. They didn't sell too well; I guess that we were just ahead of the time.

upper left: Richard La Londe heating glass in his glory hole in 1980 with his propane-fired, crucible furnace on his right.

lower left: Richard blowing glass.

upper right: "Untitled," 1983, experimental panel, H. 21 in. (53cm) x W. 19 in. (48cm), with popped bubbles, glass threads pulled in a little glory hole, foil-backed clear areas, and torch-colored titanium border.

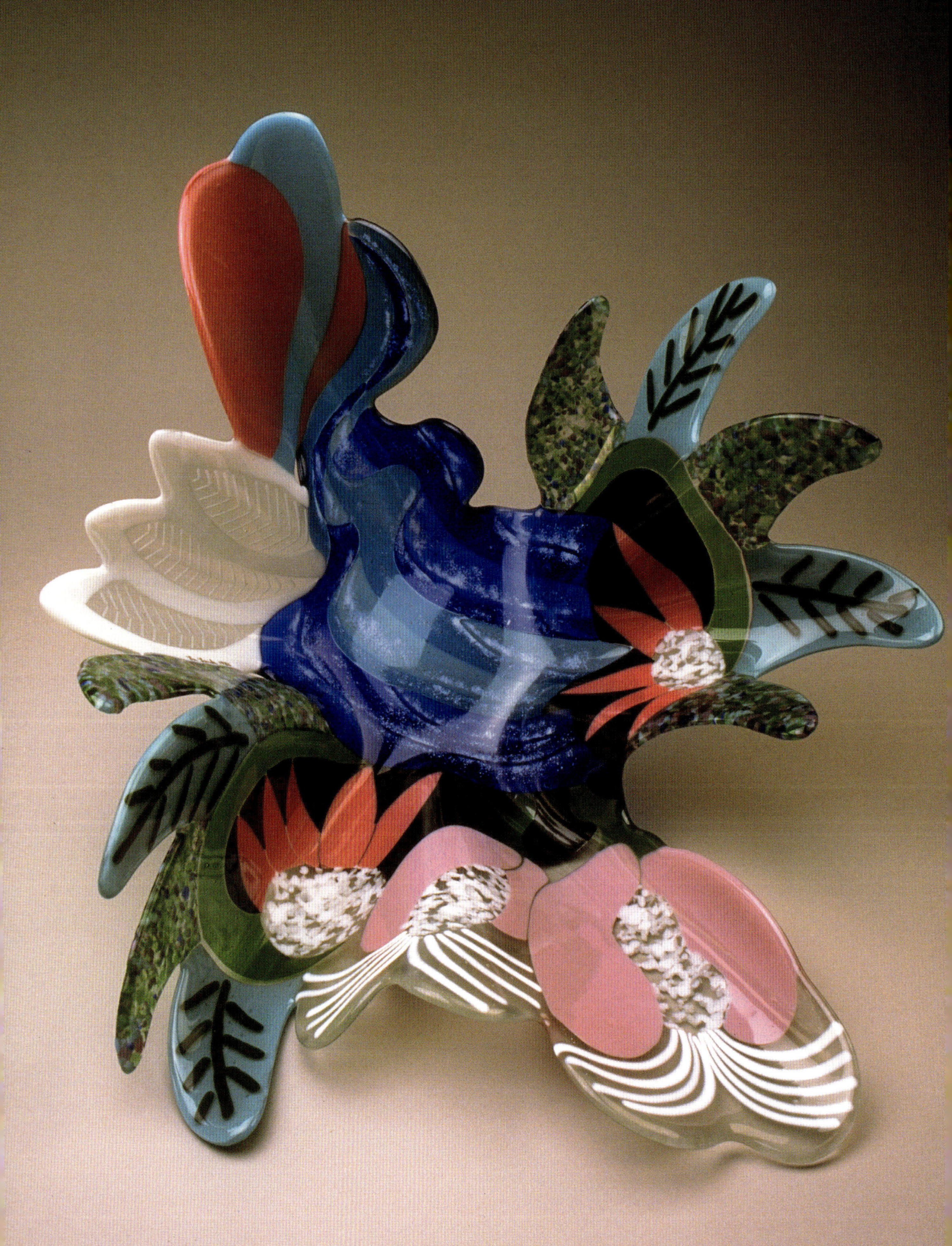

Cut Sheet Glass 1983-1988

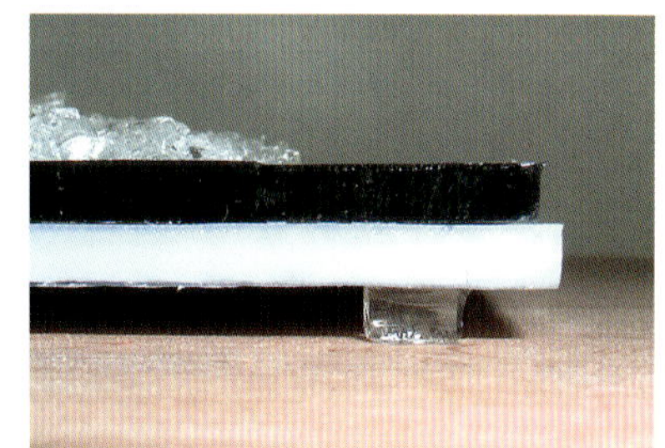

I created twelve wall panels and one hundred twenty-five vessels between 1983 to 1988 with the cut sheet glass technique.

In the beginning, I used the same techniques that I'd used for stained glass windows to cut and assemble my fused pieces. In 1983, I created my first large mural, "Neptune's Waltz." Following a design on paper, I cut the individual pieces from different sheets of colored glass and then fused them together in a brick pottery kiln. The work is composed of twelve fused glass tiles, for an overall size that is 48 in. (122 cm) high by 65 in. (165 cm) wide.

Each tile began with a 16 in. (41 cm) x 16 in. (41 cm) sheet of clear glass for the bottom layer. I created the second layer by placing colored pieces cut to fit exactly next to each other as if this were a stained glass window.

By using two layers, each ⅛ in. (3 mm) thick, the tile maintained its original size and had nice rounded edges after fusing, but until the two layers are fused there is a possibility of huge air bubbles between the shelf and glass destroying the glass project. I describe the reason for this in detail in Part 4: Techniques, in the section about volume control.

Two techniques eliminate this bubble problem. (1) Fire on ⅛" fiber paper, which allows the air to escape; (2) Put two or three small ⅛ in. chips of clear glass along the front edge under the bottom of the tile. This second method elevates the tile, and as it slumps it squeezes out the air between the glass and the shelf.

I decorated the glass surface of the mural with torch-bent glass stringer that I pulled from sheet glass heated in a very small "glory hole." This is a propane-fired glass reheating furnace that I made in a coffee can insulated with high-temperature ceramic fiber wool. I also sprinkled frit on top of the glass. I smashed glass into this "frit" ranging in size from powder to large sand grains, with a steel mortar and pestle that I welded. The smashed glass sorts to size when sifted through screens that are easy to make. Small amounts of stringer and frit don't push the tile edges out of shape.

In 1981, I began building top-fired fiber insulated kilns, specifically designed for fusing glass, and in 1984 I put together a kiln controller so I no longer needed to constantly monitor my kiln firings or set my alarm for 3:00 in the morning and run out to the kiln to make an adjustment.

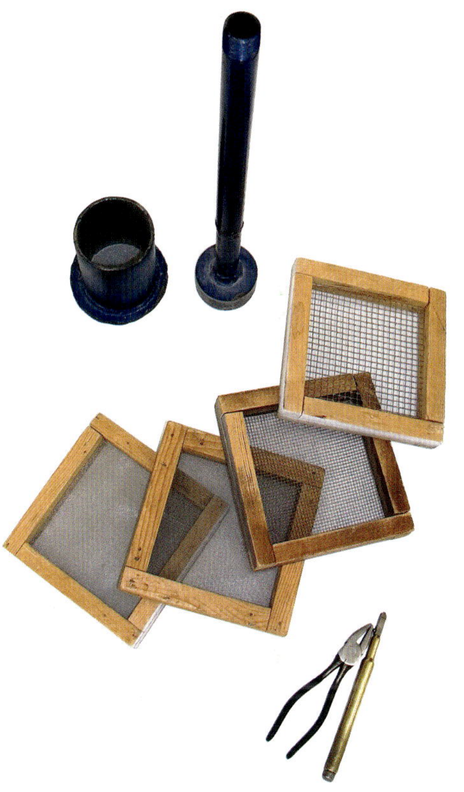

facing:
"Saturn's Serenade," 1986,
H. 14 in. (35 cm) x W. 19 in. (48 cm) x D. 21 in (53 cm).

upper: a chip under the glass helps let the air out and stop huge bubbles from forming.

lower: frit smasher and screens.

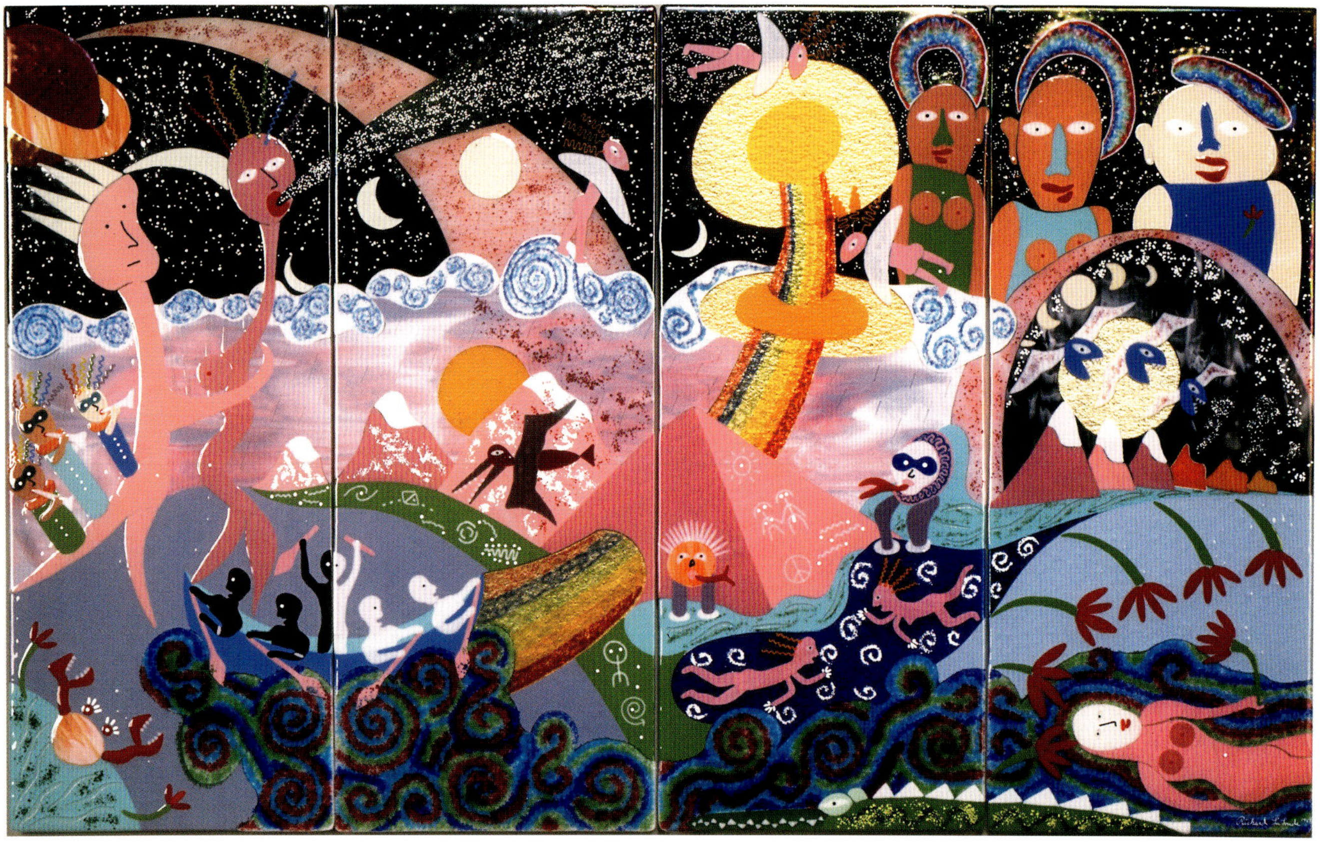

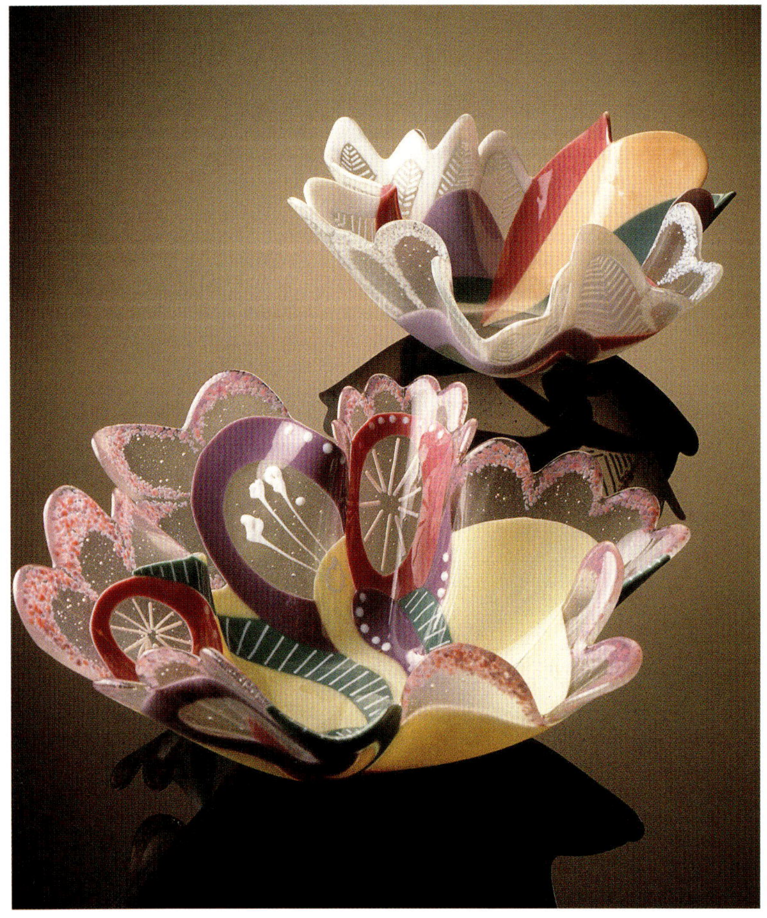

upper:
"Saturnian Song," 1987,
 H. 40 in. (102 cm) x W. 64 in. (163 cm).

lower:
"Buttercream Post Contemporaries," 1985,
H. 6 in. (43 cm) x W. 17 in. (43 cm) x D.
17 in. (15 cm).

facing upper:
"African series," 1984, largest piece H. 6 in.
(43 cm) x W. 14 in. (36 cm) x D. 14 in. (43
cm), combed glass.

facing lower:
Richard La Londe with "Neptune's Waltz,"
1983, H. 48 in. (122) x W. 65 in. (165 cm).
The gold areas are foil wrappers from
Almond Roca candy bars mounted behind
a clear area in the mural and covered
with duct tape on the back and siliconed
between the glass and aluminum backing
plate. I later learned gold leafing.

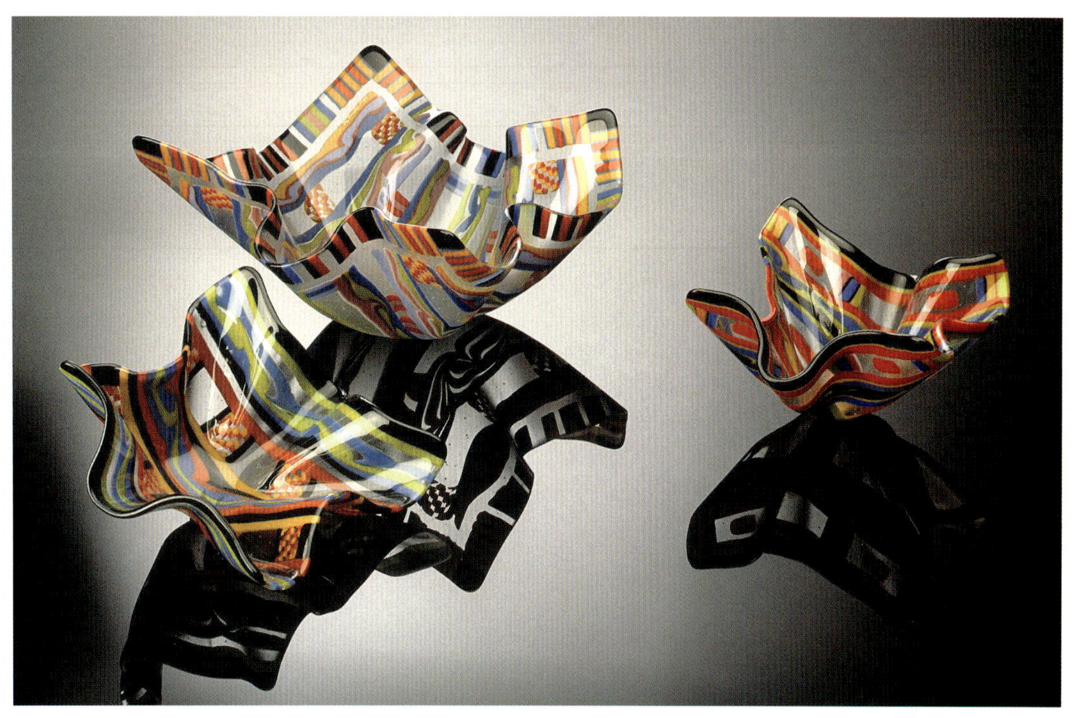

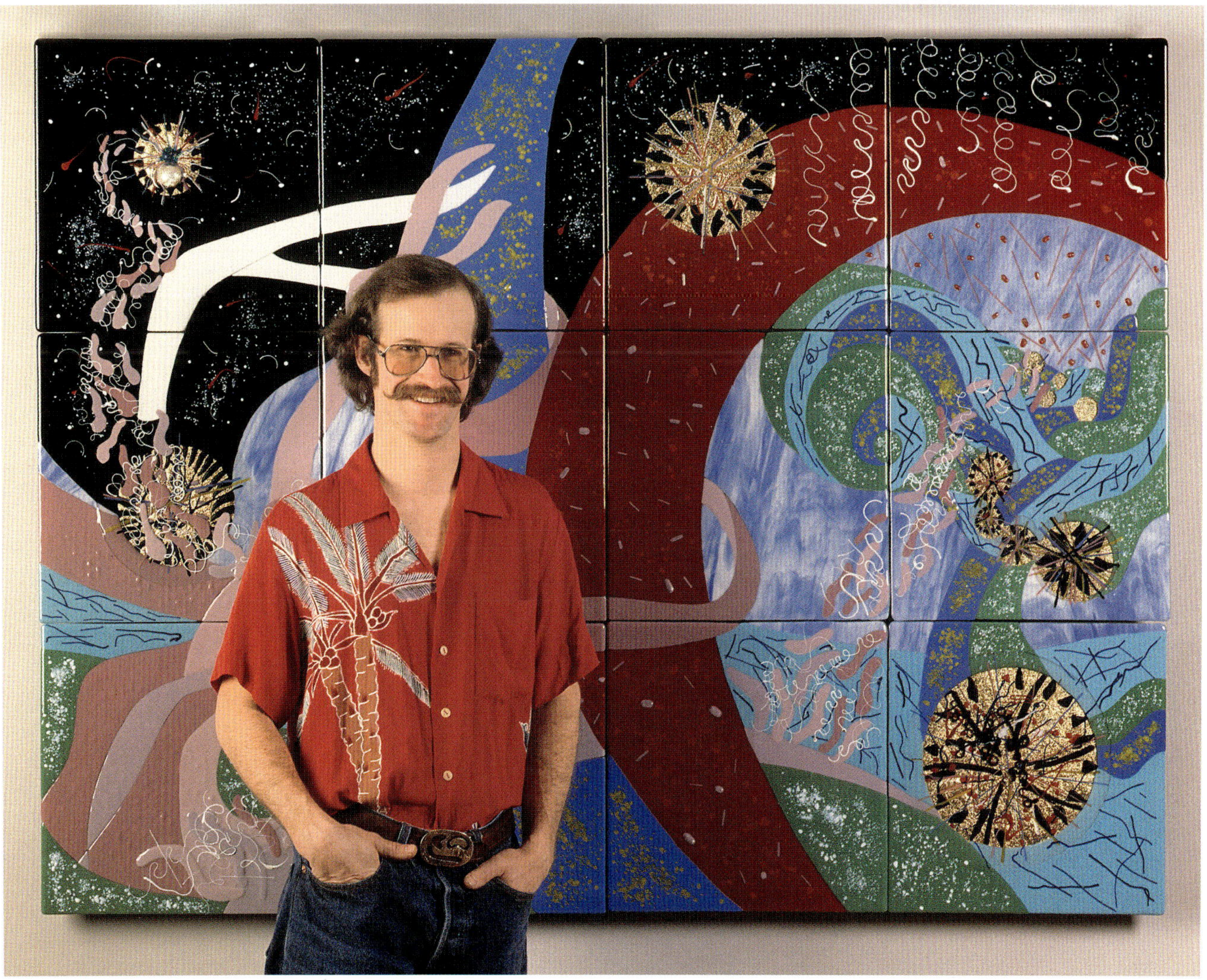

Cut Sheet Glass Vessels

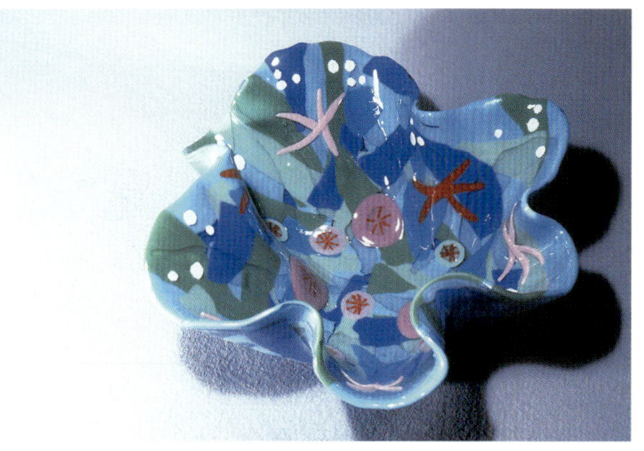

"Blue Tide pool," 1982, H. 6 in. (15 cm) x W. 15 in. (38 cm) x D. 14 in. (36 cm).

Tide Pool Series 1982

This was my first series of bowls. I cut and layered pieces of sheet glass, added glass nautical creatures that would be found in a tide pool, and fused this in my electric kiln. I created my first stainless steel mold to slump the glass into and have used it for over twenty years.

6 pieces total

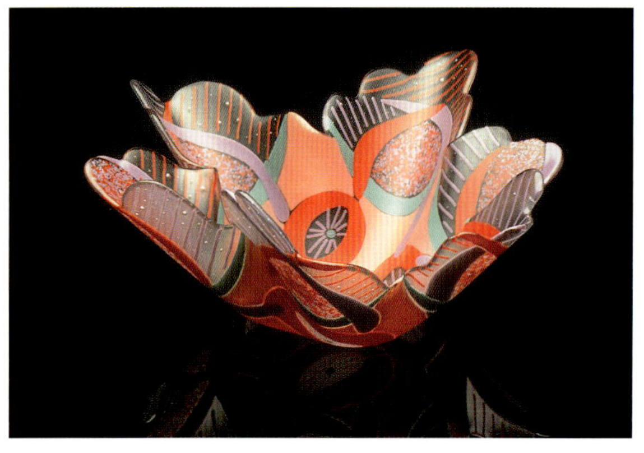

"Post Contemporary," 1983, H. 7 in. (18 cm) x W. 16 in. (41 cm) x D. 15 in. (38 cm).

Post Contemporary Series 1983 – 1985

I began this series at Pilchuck Glass School during the summer of 1983. I cut sheet glass pieces and fused them with crushed glass and glass threads. I slumped the flat fused shape into my metal mold. Some of these were sandblasted before the slump which produced a matte finish. Later pieces were shiny.

50 pieces total

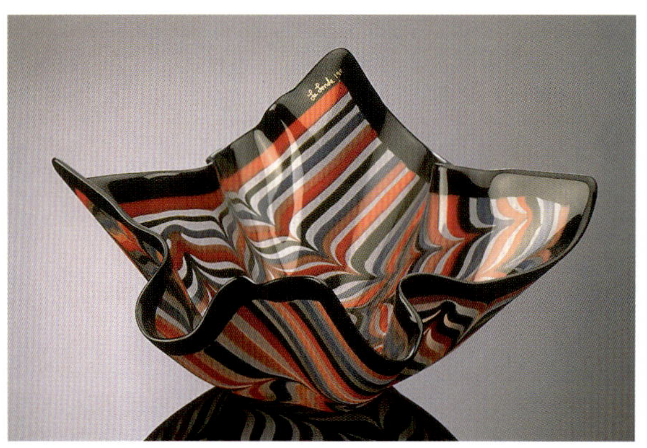

"Zig Zag" Series, 1984, H. 8 in. (20 cm) x W. 14 in. (36 cm) x D. 13 in. (33 cm).

Zig Zag Series 1984 – 1987

I laid strips of cut, colored sheet glass onto a sheet of clear glass. This was heated in an electric kiln to 1600° F, and then I combed the glass with a hooked steel rod. The sheet was cooled and then slumped.

35 pieces total

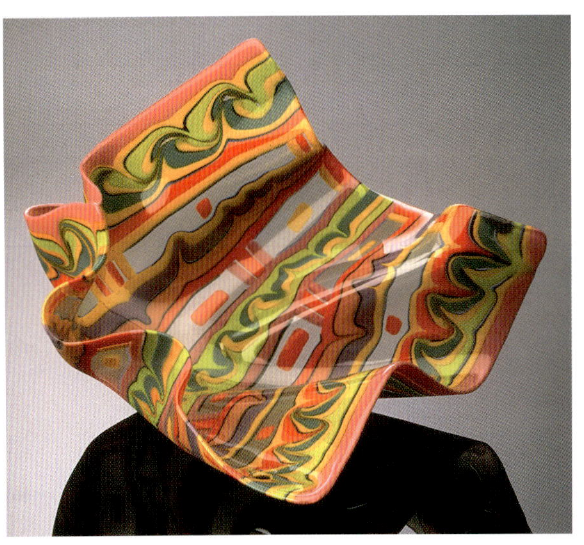

"African," 1984, H. 11 in. (28 cm) x W. 16 in. (41 cm) x D. 15 in. (38 cm).

"Tropical Moon," 1986, H. 10 in. (25 cm) x W. 20 in. (51 cm) x D. 20 in. (51 cm).

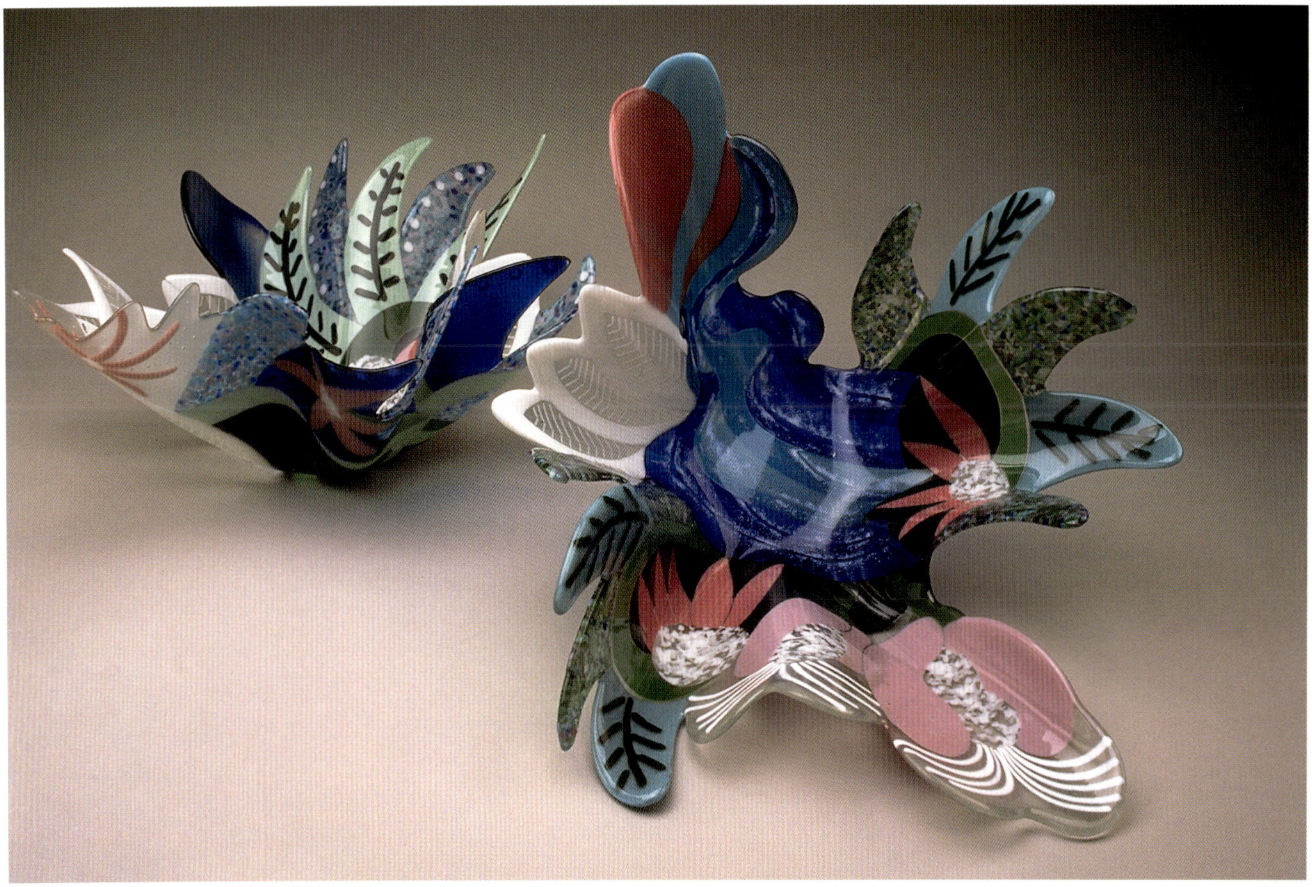

Botanical Series   1985 – 1986

These were created with cut sheet glass shapes, glass threads, and chunks of crushed glass. They were large and labor intensive. The pieces were fused and cooled and then slumped in a second firing into a large metal mold. I used my big fiber kiln with an inside dimension of 44 in. (112 cm) x 44 in. (112 cm) x 24 in. (61 cm) for these pieces. 24 pieces total

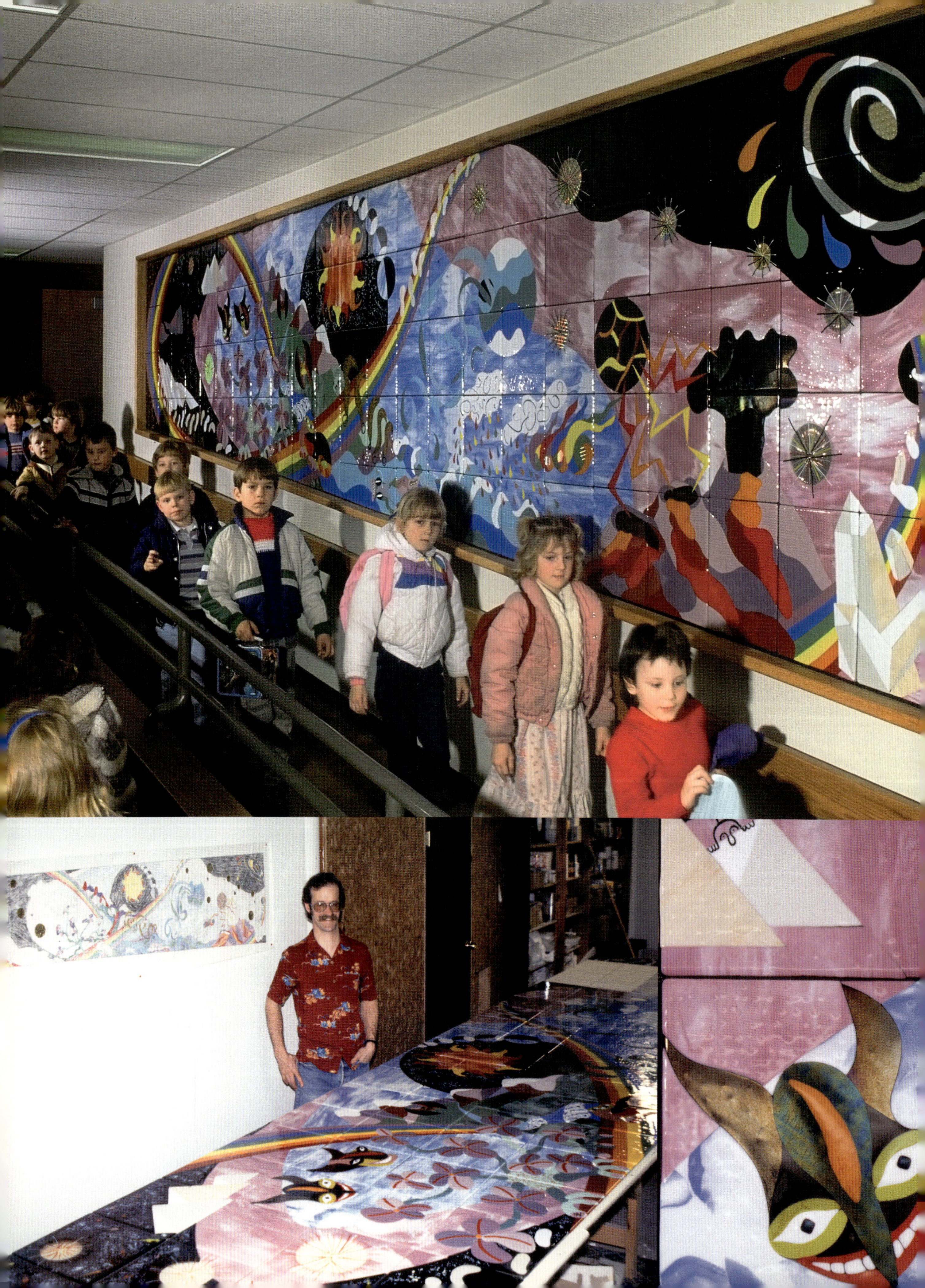

Black Lake Elementary School

My First Public Piece

Washington State was one of the first states in the country to pass legislation for art funding providing for ½ percent of State-funded public building and renovation money to go to art for the buildings. A committee selects an artist from an image slide bank of juried artists from around the country. Having completed two glass murals – "Neptune's Waltz," H. 48 in. (122 cm) x W. 65 in. (165 cm) and "Moon Dance," H. 72 in. (183 cm) x W. 42 in. (107 cm) – I wanted to try public art. Because I felt that I needed a larger portfolio, I created six miniatures and photographed them. My pictorial fused glass murals were a totally new idea at the time, so I hoped they would have a chance on that basis. I wrote on the slides, "architectural model" as small as I could and sent them into the Washington State Arts Commission. Days went by, and I forgot about the submission.

One day, a man phoned and said, "I'm from the Washington State Arts Commission, and you have been selected by committee to design a wall mural for the Black Lake Elementary in Tumwater, Washington."

Stunned, I nonetheless galvanized into action to meet the group, and they showed me a hallway wall with an inclining ramp going up to the Music Room. The wall looked enormous. The budget also looked huge to me at that time: $8,500 to create glass art! So what to do? I had dreamed of a chance to create a huge public piece, and now the opportunity gaped in front of me.

I set about designing a piece that would have fused glass tile sections 12 in. (30 cm) x 12 in. (30 cm). I had to trust that silicone sealant, which doesn't say "adhesive" on the tube anywhere, would hold the piece up for at least fifty years. Silicone had been available to the general public – me – for only a few years, but the manufacturer claimed that it was guaranteed for twenty-five years. I could never figure that one out. Nonetheless, I took them at their word and used silicone to adhere the glass sections to a sheet aluminum background that I screwed to the wall.

I believe that public art is for the public – in this case, elementary kids from five to twelve years old. In order to try to think like the kid that I had once been, I designed a scale drawing using color crayons. I presented that drawing, a model of the mounting system, and a fused example of my work to the committee. They went for it! Now I had to do it!

One criterion for the commission was that the kids had to be able to touch the glass and that made me nervous!

Touching is one thing; rambunctious kids shoving each other into the glass is another. I figured that if I surrounded the glass with an oak frame, then when kids banged against the mural they might bash their heads but not break the glass.

facing upper: "Metamorphosis," 1985, left side H. 46 in. (117 cm), right side H. 69 in. (175 cm) x W. 24 ft. (7.3 m), created for the Black Lake Elementary and funded through the Washington State Arts Commission.

facing lower left: Richard La Londe with his mural on the table. The design hanging on the wall was done with color crayons for the elementary school.

facing lower right: Detail of creatures nicknamed, "flying hood ornaments"; also notice the Kilroy-like figure overlooking the pyramid. I tried to put a variety of things in for the kids to notice and to make them laugh.

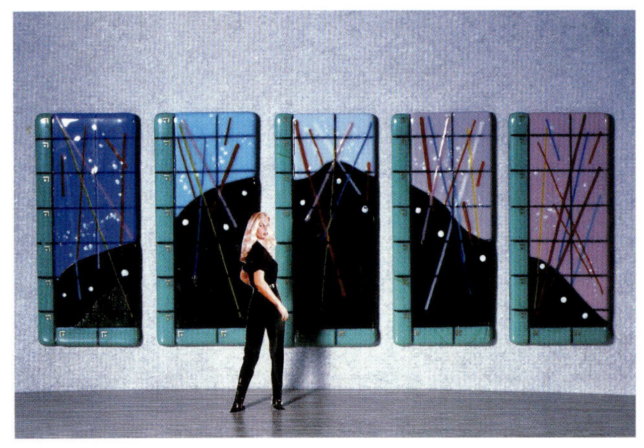
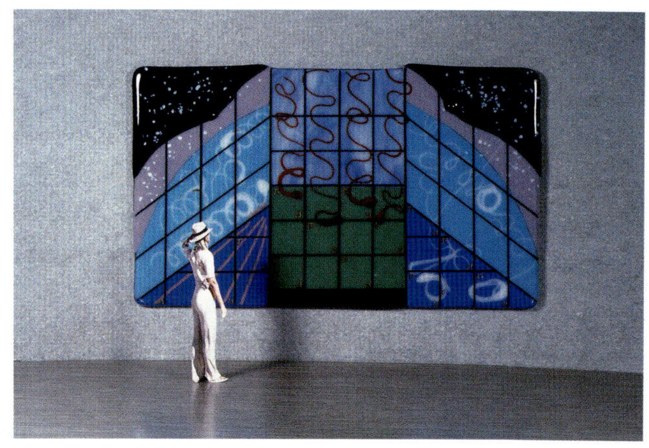

upper left and right: Two examples of architectural models where the 6 in. tall fused glass pieces are duct taped to a background; the ladies are cut out of magazines and positioned in front of the piece; the miniature scene is photographed, 1983.

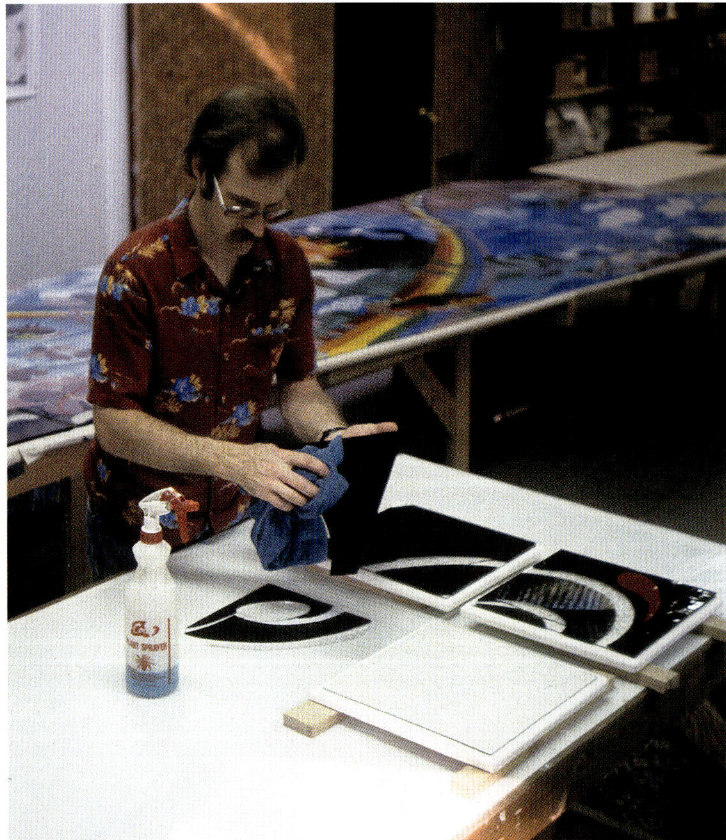

middle left: Richard La Londe assembling tiles on kiln shelves for firing. The tiles are made by fusing one layer of ⅛ in. (3 mm) Bullseye pieces on top of a ⅛ in. (3 mm) clear base. This gives the magic thickness of a little over ¼ in. (6 mm), so that when full fused the edges are rounded and the tiles are very close to the original 12 in. (30 cm) x 12 in. (30 cm) square. I did no edge grinding on this piece. This is an example of volume control.

lower left: (9) 12 in. (30 cm) x 12 in. (30 cm) tiles in my large fiber kiln before firing; some of the glass has been sprayed with white "Spray A" overglaze to control devitrification or surface crystal growth that can create a scummy look on the glass.

lower right: The tiles are full fused after firing.

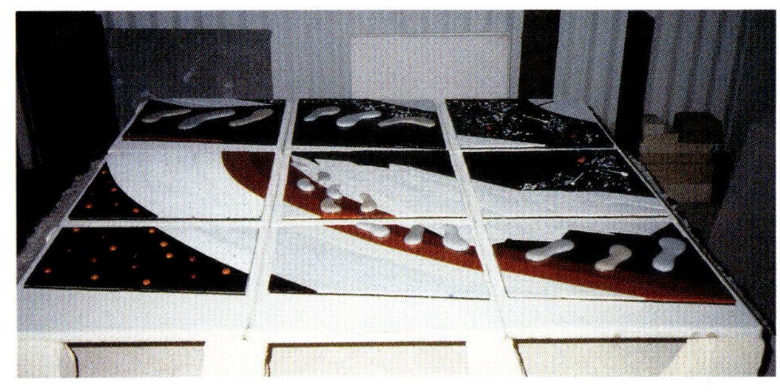

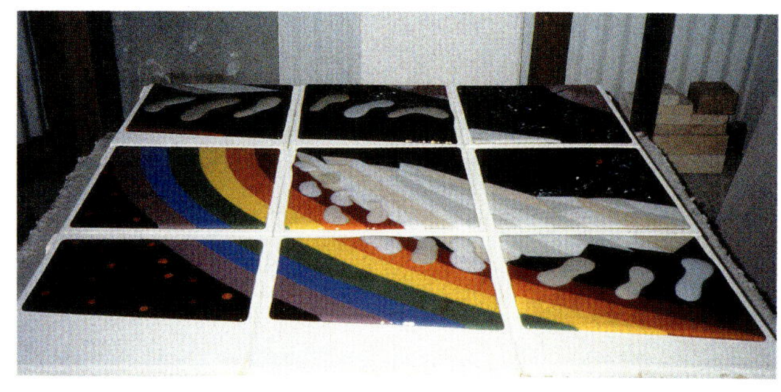

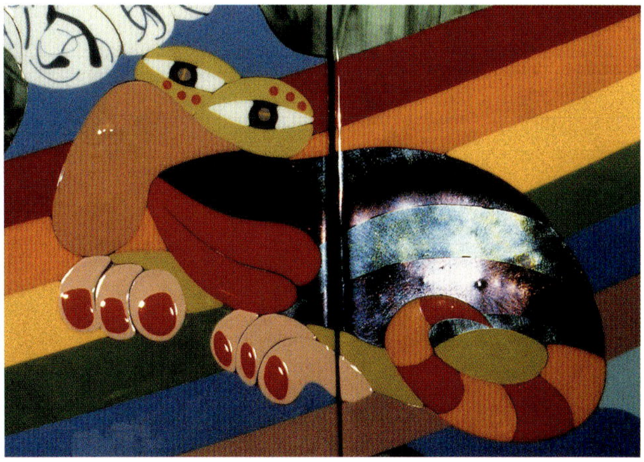

upper right: One of the fused glass creatures in
the Black Lake Elementary piece "Metamorphosis." I
included many fun things for the elementary school
kids to look at.

middle right: I cut an upper layer of Bullseye sheet
glass pieces to fit side by side like pieces in a stained
glass window. They are sitting on a bottom layer of
12 in. (30 cm) x 12 in. (30 cm) clear Bullseye pieces.
By fusing exactly two layers, the tiles end up very
close to their original size after firing.

lower: detail of upper left section of the mural
"Metamorphosis."

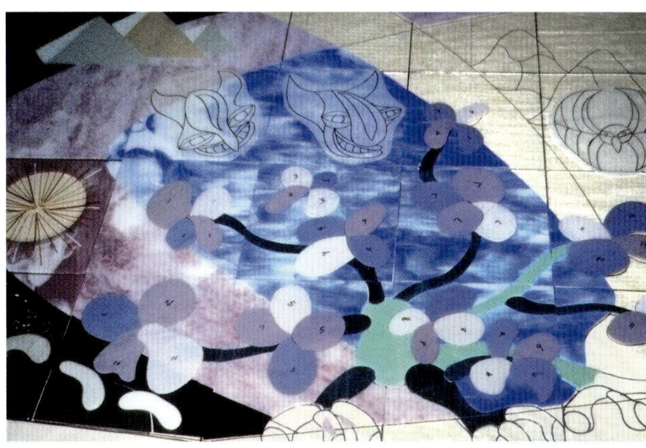

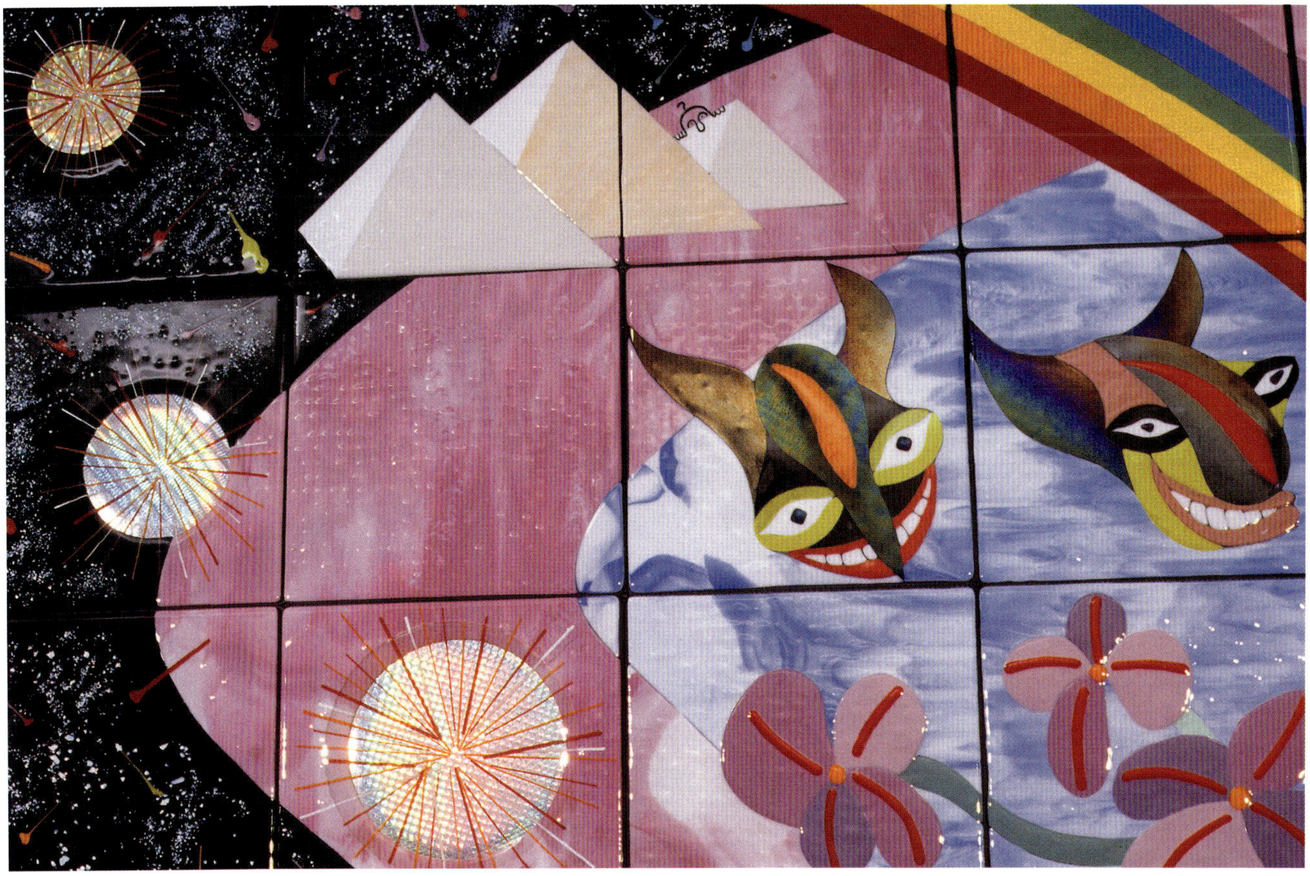

Making "Metamorphosis"
In March of 1984, I began by blowing up my color crayon drawing to full size on white butcher paper. I outlined the pieces with a Sharpie felt-tipped marker. I laid out this pattern on an improvised huge table, and then, first step, cut out all of the clear base tiles.

Using a second pattern and beginning on the left side, I cut individual pieces from sheets of compatible Bullseye glass on my light table. I had done a chip test on every sheet to see (1) if they were compatible, (2) what color they might change to when fired, (3) if they devitrified, and (4) how their relative hardness and softness (viscosity) compared.

I laid out this second layer, sprayed "Spray A" on the devitrifying colors, laid small threads of color and glass that I crushed by hand on top, and began to fire nine tiles at a time. I continued moving to the right—cutting, laying out, and firing as I went along. Working alone in this manner, I had all of the glass tiles done in three months.

The first of June, I started the mounting system by taking ½ in. (12 cm) plywood and attaching an oak 2 x 4, (5 x 10 cm) protective frame to it. The plywood covered a large enough area that anchorage to wall studs would be assured. The mounting board needed to be 69 in. (175 cm) high on the right side and then tapered along 24 feet (7 ½ meters) to 46 in. (117 cm) high on the left side; this was in three sections.

Next I went to purchase the aluminum to mount my glass on but couldn't bring myself to spend $600; instead, I bought galvanized 16-gauge steel, $\frac{1}{16}$ in. (1.5 mm) thick and very rigid. I took these sheets to a metal fabrication shop and had them cut pieces on their large mechanical shear. This allowed me to butt the steel backing plates perfectly tight. I laid this out in the wooden frame and began running beads of Dow Corning #732 clear sealant vertically to the back of the glass; then I positioned the glass on the metal.

If you try this, don't run the silicone all the way around the edge of the tile because the sealant in the center will not dry, and you won't have much adhesive holding the tiles to the wall. Leave about 2 in. (5 cm), between the vertical strips of silicone, and air will flow in and around the strips, curing the silicone. I glued four tiles to a section of metal. On the bottom row, I made the tiles longer to accommodate the taper.

I mounted the metal with the siliconed tiles to the plywood background with pan head sheet metal screws. To disguise these fasteners, I painted the edges of the metal and screws flat black. Caution! Every public art piece will at sometime be removed, relocated, or trashed, so give the future art movers an obvious place to start! Leave a screw or joint exposed to show how things went together. Being slick won't do the art much good when they take it down with a sledgehammer.

I installed "Metamorphosis" at Black Lake Elementary in Tumwater, Washington in July, 1984. Installation, with two helpers, took about six hours. It's important to do much of the work in your studio so that installation at the site is easy.

"Metamorphosis" is about evolution and change; however, I couldn't use the word "evolution" in my statement for the school, so I wrote: "Metamorphosis" depicts the changes in a fantasy planetary system portraying beginnings, fire & water phases, and plants & animals. Arriving at the pyramids we encounter two creatures resembling automobile hood ornaments pointing backward, and we ask ourselves, Which way are we going?

It is also inevitable that I'm asked to explain my imagery. I'm a visual artist and not so much into the literary, so it's difficult for me to write about what I do from my gut. Perhaps, however, "Metamorphosis" was part of my evolution as an artist.

Note: Don't ask artists to explain what they do – they just do it!

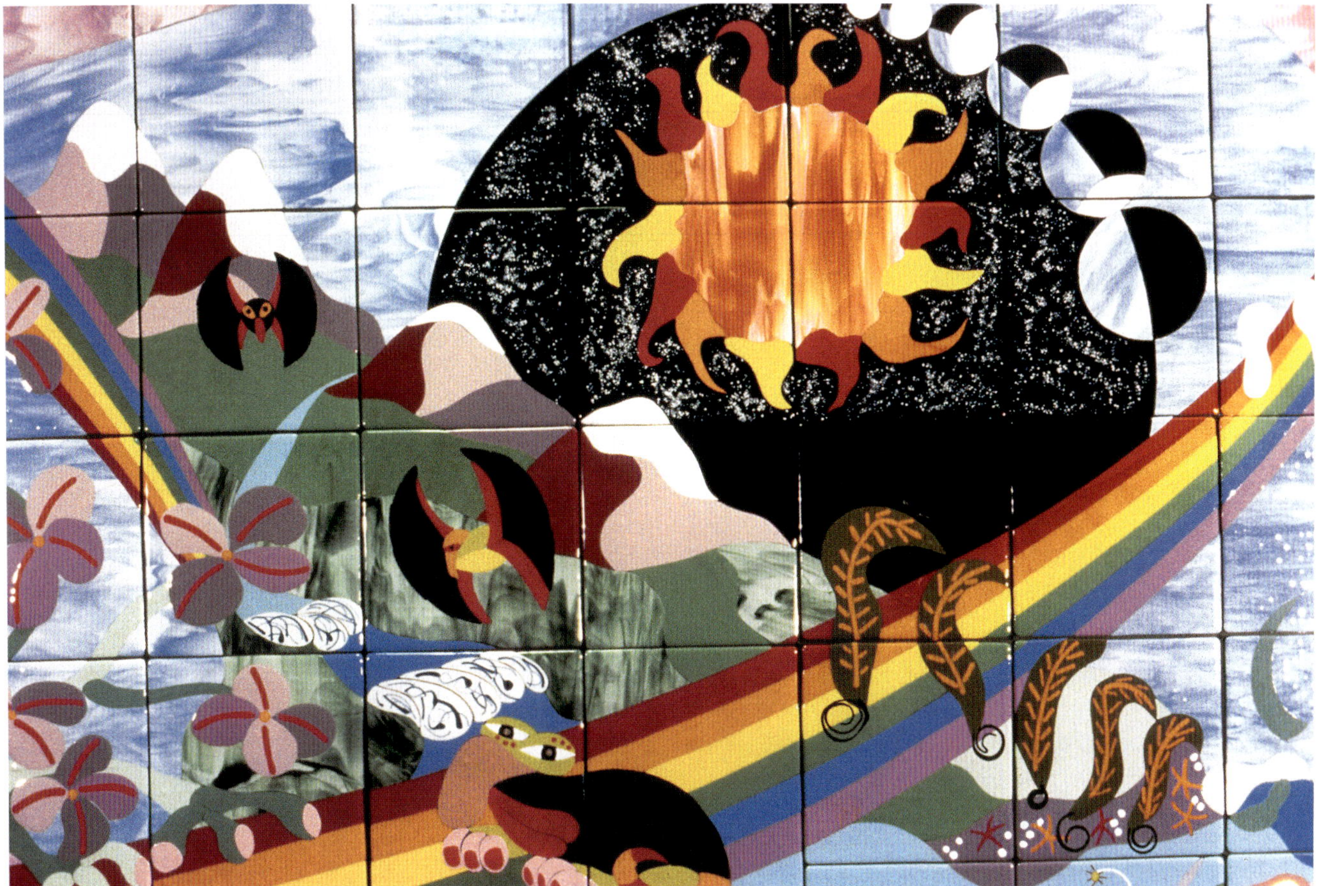

My art allows viewers to interpret the work themselves through their filters of philosophy, stuff, and junk that they have accumulated during their lives. I strive to put layers of imagery into my pieces, hoping that people will see something new every time they look at my artwork. Personally, I get tired of looking at art that has the "been there, done that" feel. The viewer looks quickly, is bored quickly, and the artwork recedes into the background like wallpaper. I like to challenge viewers to dig and ponder, "What does this mean?"

"Metamorphosis" includes creative qualities kids like: lots of color, movement, and quirky things to look at. Today I see too much "serious" art; no wonder some people don't have much fun today.

Twenty years after I installed "Metamorphosis," a man called and said, "We gotta take your mural down." The shock was worse than when I received the call accepting my idea for the mural. Had it been up that long? I felt old and disappointed: my art should be around for a while, not taken down. Had it fallen out of fashion?

My disappointment eased when they told me that the building was outdated, not my artwork. The structure needed to be brought up to code and strengthened against earthquakes. I made a deal to take it down and pack it for storage; I'd reinstall it when they were done, and they would pay me about one-fourth of the original cost to do this work.

In my studio, I designed and built custom cardboard boxes to fit the tiles. In the field, by myself, I took the mural down and packed it in one day. When the building was ready, my friend, Michael Dupille, and I reinstalled the mural in six hours. This is recorded on the next two pages up to and including our exhausted smiles when done. And so I repeat: Just remember, leave a trail so those who remove your work won't use a bulldozer on it.

Richard La Londe and Michael Dupille reinstalling "Metamorphosis" December 2005.

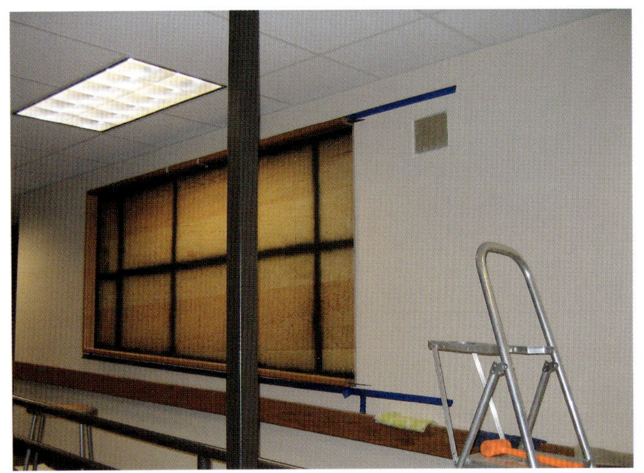
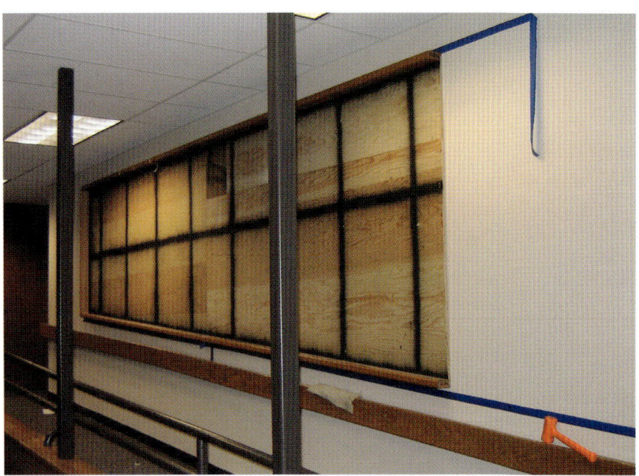
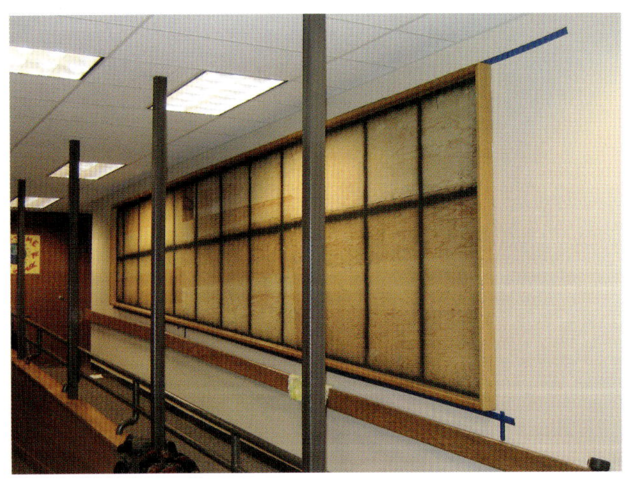
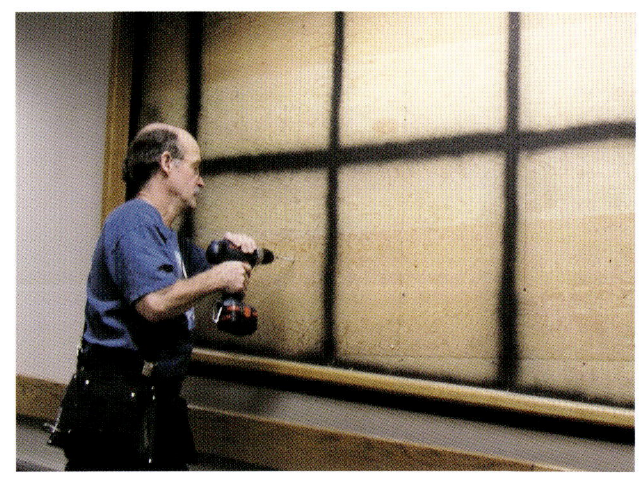
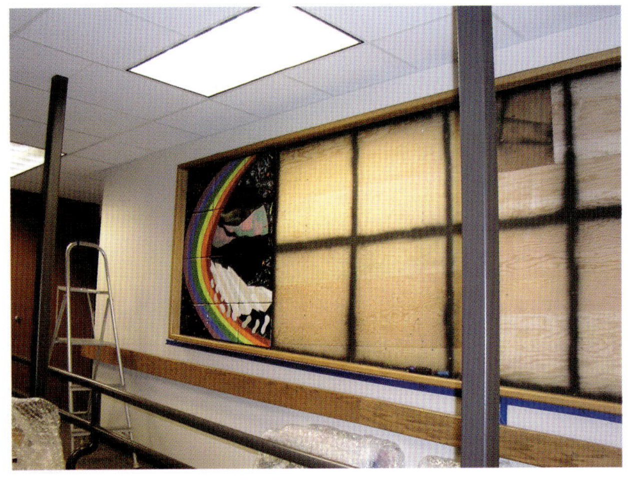
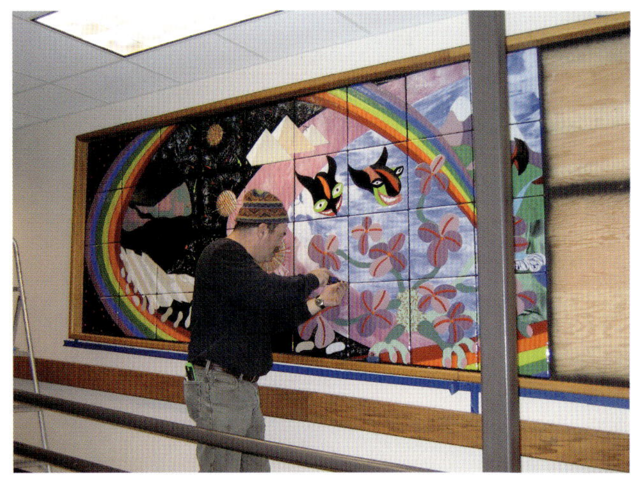

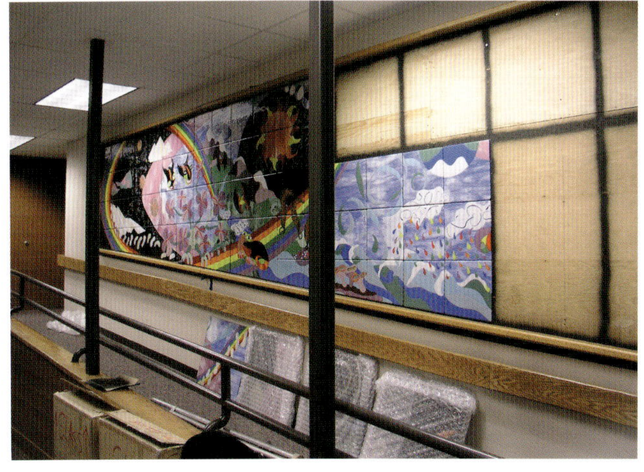
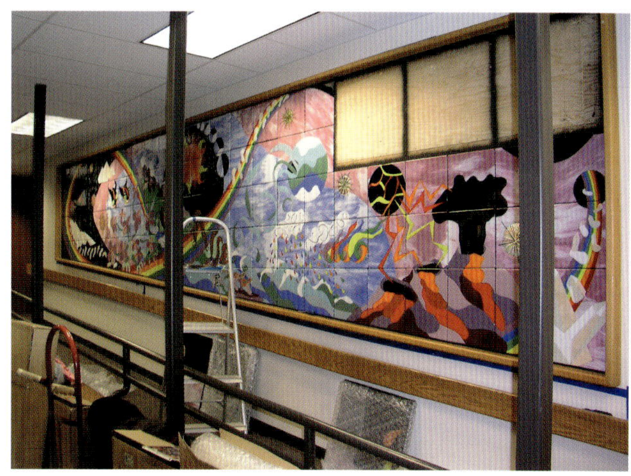
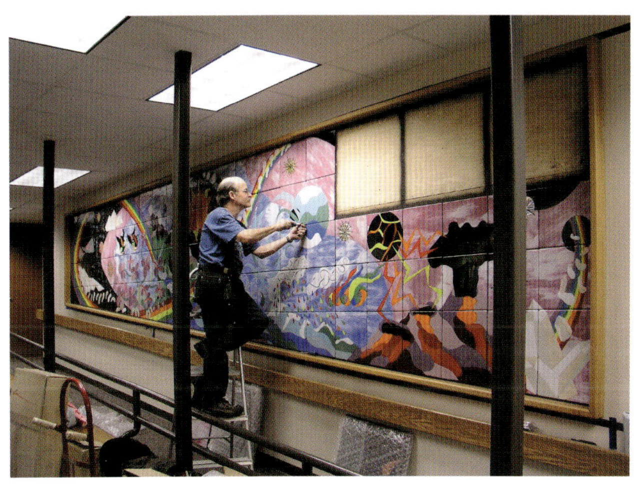
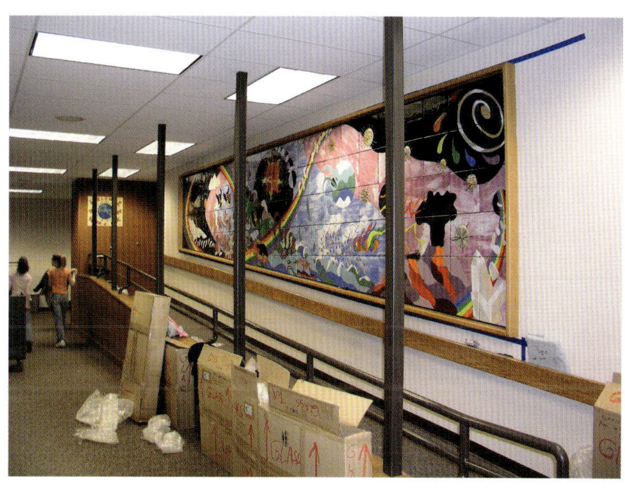
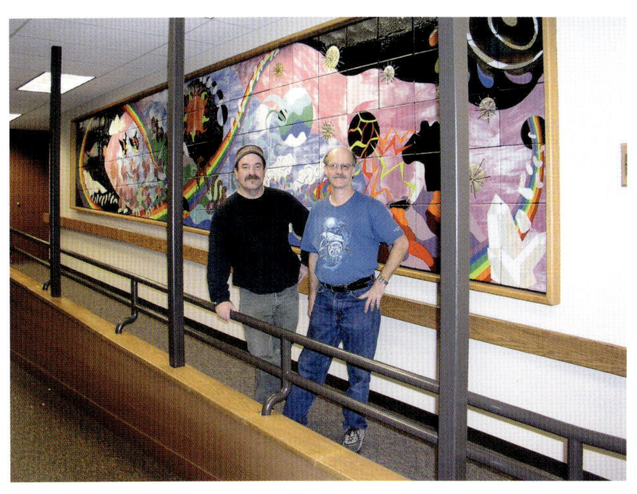
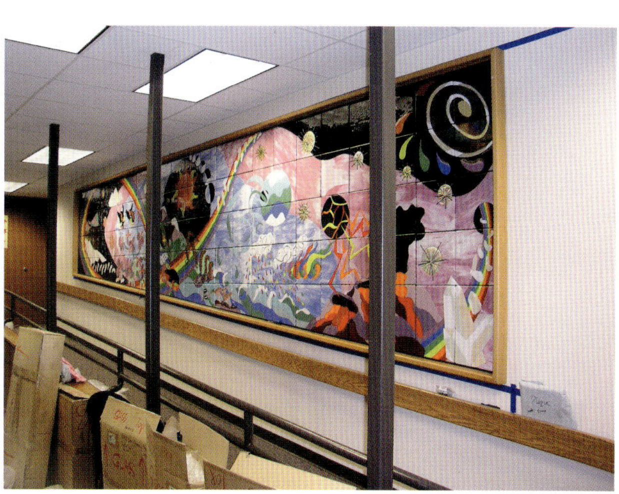

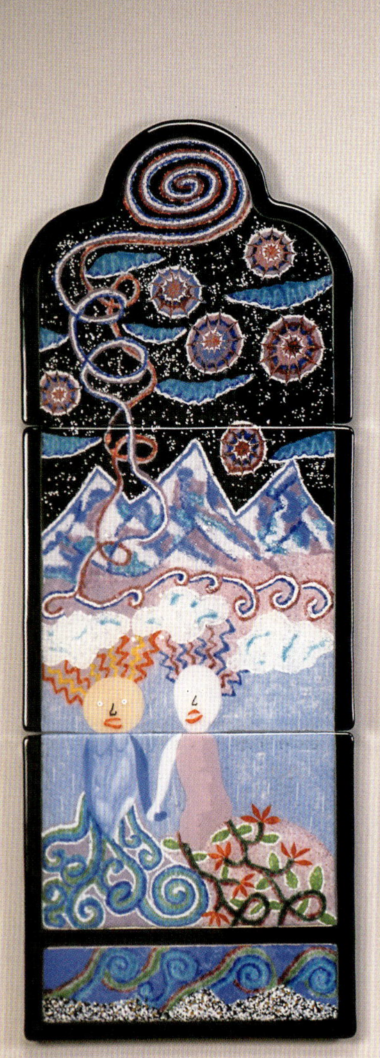
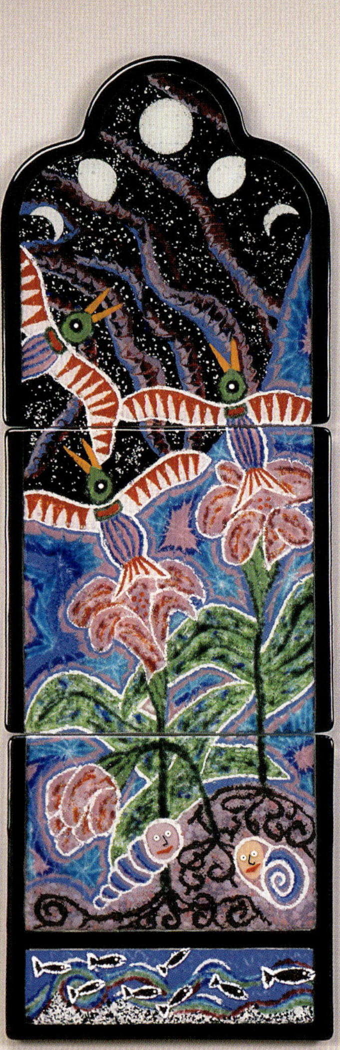
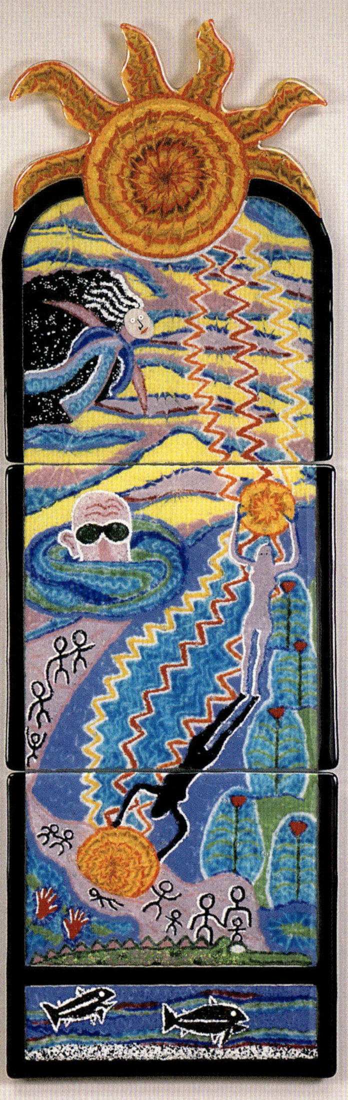
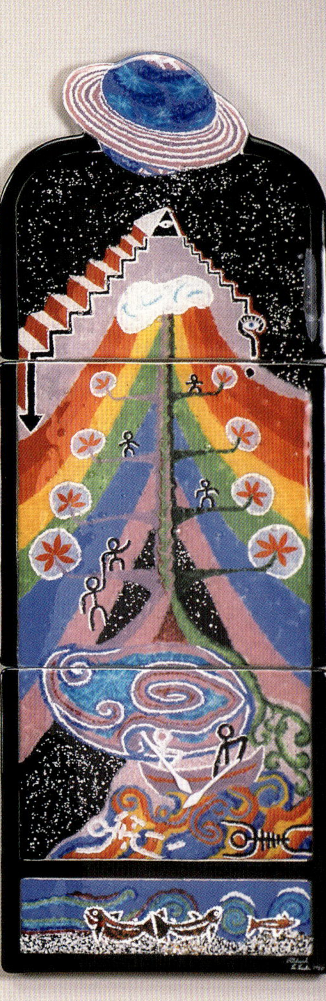

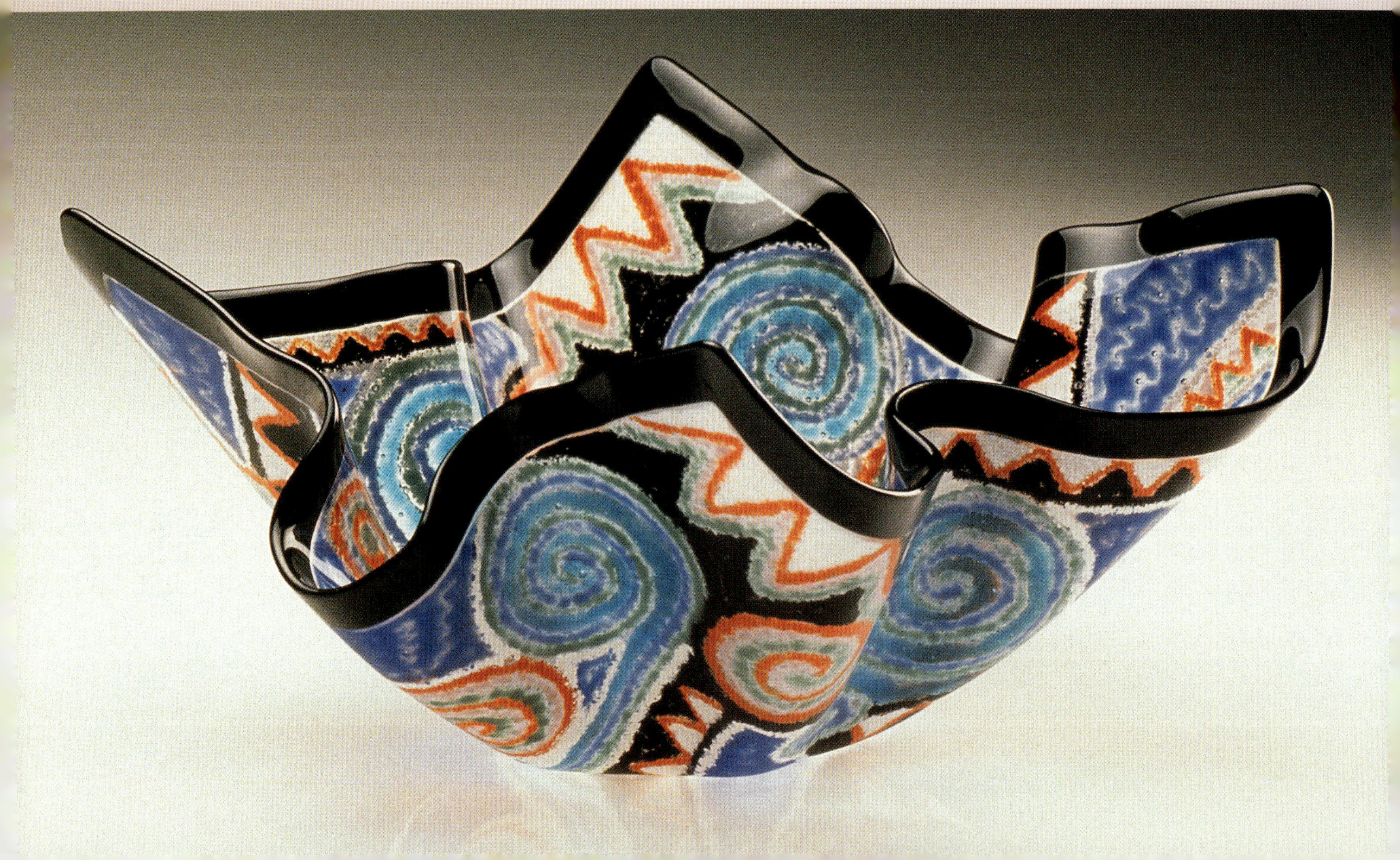

free design frit: 1988 - present

I created 5 wall panels in 1988 using my "free frit design" technique and today I still make some of my vessels this way.

As I continued developing my work, each glass piece that I hand cut and decorated was becoming more and more intricate, taking longer and longer. I cut pieces using my diamond saw, pulled many glory hole threads, hand-smashed, magnetically removed iron particles and screened more frit. One day I created a hat for one of my characters by laying different colors of frit onto the surface and combing it with the end of a sharpened paintbrush. I loved this look but was scheduled the next day to leave for a 34-day tour of the Mayan ruins of Yucatán in Mexico and Guatemala. I vowed that I would do something with this new idea when I returned.

During that trip, I had a vision of sketching with glass powders without a preconceived design, just like drawing on paper with a pencil or creating a sand painting. Back at home and ready to put my vision to work, I took two full sheets of clear ⅛ in. (3 mm) clear single-rolled Bullseye; they didn't have ¼ in. (6 mm) at that time and put a ½ in. (12 cm) iridescent black Bullseye strip of glass around the edge as a border. I hand smashed glass in a large mortar and pestle and then put the glass in a folded piece of postcard with one end taped closed; I experimented with this until the glass flowed readily from the postcard, and then I began to lay down sketch-like lines of crushed glass. After I completely covered the clear glass with powder, I full fused this on a piece of ⅛ in. (3 mm) fiber paper.

I sandblasted the fiber that stuck to the back of the glass. About sixty bubbles had been trapped between the two clear sheets. I drilled tiny holes into these with a ¹⁄₁₆ in. (1.5 mm) diamond bit in a rotary Dremel tool. I then coated the sandblasted side with "Spray A" that I applied with a 4 in. (10 cm) foam brush. Prior to this I had used an airbrush to spray this on, but the room filled with nasty glass dust. "Spray A" is a stable lead-bearing glass, and the micro particles of "Spray A" contain a huge amount of surface area, so if breathed or ingested the lead can possibly be leached out of the glass by your body. After the glass has been fused flat and there is less surface area to be chemically attacked, the lead is harder to break out of the glass. When using an airbrush, a respirator is essential. This is why I prefer to use a foam brush – to keep the "Spray A" out of the air.

To review: I laid the frit onto two sheets of clear glass, full fused it, flipped it over, drilled out the bubbles, sandblasted the surface, blew the sand out of the drilled bubble holes, brushed on "Spray A," and then I put it back into the kiln and fused it a second time. Whew!

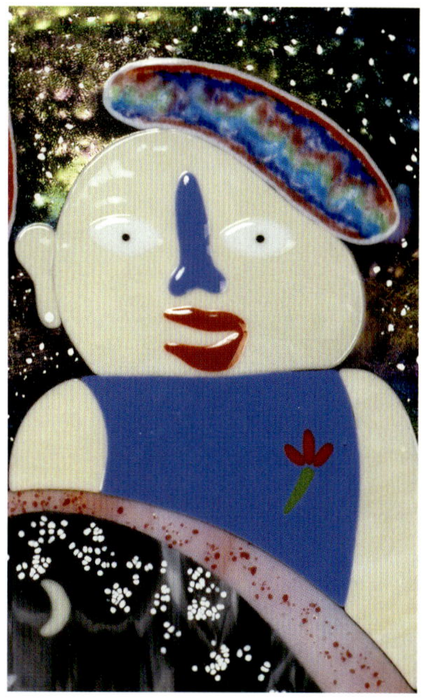

facing upper:
"The Four Seasons,"
H. 58 in. (147 cm) x W. 78 in. (198 cm), 1988. Fused crushed glass is laid down without a pattern, free design.
I know it's corny, but I played Vivaldi's Four Seasons while I created this piece. For example I listened to the "Winter" part over and over while I sketched with crushed glass the panel on the far left, then "Spring," and so on. At the bottom of the piece, there is a subplot that contains salmon eggs for Winter, salmon fry for Spring, adult salmon for Summer, and returning-to-spawn salmon for Fall; this is the cycle of life, the "Four Seasons."

facing lower:
"Black Rim Bolero," H. 8 in. (20 cm) x W. 15 in. (38 cm) x D. 15 in. (38 cm), 1988. Fused crushed glass is laid down without a pattern, free design, fused, and then during a second firing, slumped into a stainless steel mold.

After that, I mounted it to aluminum or slumped it into a bowl. My goal was to give more spontaneity to my work by not using a paper pattern, but the process was labor-intensive.

How much fun is hand-smashing lots of compatible glass scraps? Not much. So I looked for a machine and found one for crushing gold ore. I could then cut whole sheets of Bullseye into 2 in. (5 cm) x 3 in. (7.5 cm) pieces and feed them to "the machine," which ground the glass and screened it to 01 sized frit (table sugar size) and finer powder. This was a very dusty, outside, wear-a-respirator, change-your-clothes kind of operation that still wasn't much fun, but it did produce gallons of crushed glass that was perfect for my drawings.

Drilling all the bubbles wasn't much fun either, but on a buying trip to Bullseye, I saw some ¼ in. (6 mm) thick sheets of single-rolled black glass hot from the annealer. I asked Daniel Schwoerer what these were for, and he told me, "They are going to Mexico to be ground and polished into bevels, go figure, black bevels, huh?"

A light clicked on in my head, and I asked, "Can you roll ¼ in. (6 mm) glass in clear?"
Daniel said, "Sure, but you have to buy a case."

So I committed to my first full case of glass, which was a big deal for me, and Bullseye rolled their first ¼ in. (6 mm) clear, which later showed up in their catalog; with the overseas market they started calling it 6 mm. My piece "Recycle," which is in the Bullseye collection, was made with crushed glass that I ground in my gold ore machine and then fused on this ¼ in. (6 mm) glass: no bubbles. No drilling.

A careful look at the edge of those clear sheets reveals a range in color from turquoise to green to gray. This seemed to dull the bright colors of frit that I liked to use, so on another trip to the factory, I spied some ⅛ in. (3 mm) sheets of "crystal clear" and ordered another case of this in ¼ in. (6 mm). Today I'm really delighted that Bullseye offers large, flat, super-clear sheets of double-rolled, virtually bubble-free glass that they call Tekta.

Using the "free design crushed glass" technique, I created five wall panels in 1988, and I continue using the technique for some vessels; however, with each new piece the design became more complicated so I began designing on paper again.

lower:
"To Love You Must Let Go," H. 40 in. (102 cm) x W. 23 in. (58 cm) including frame, 1988. Fused crushed glass on two sheets of ⅛ in. (3 mm) clear Bullseye.

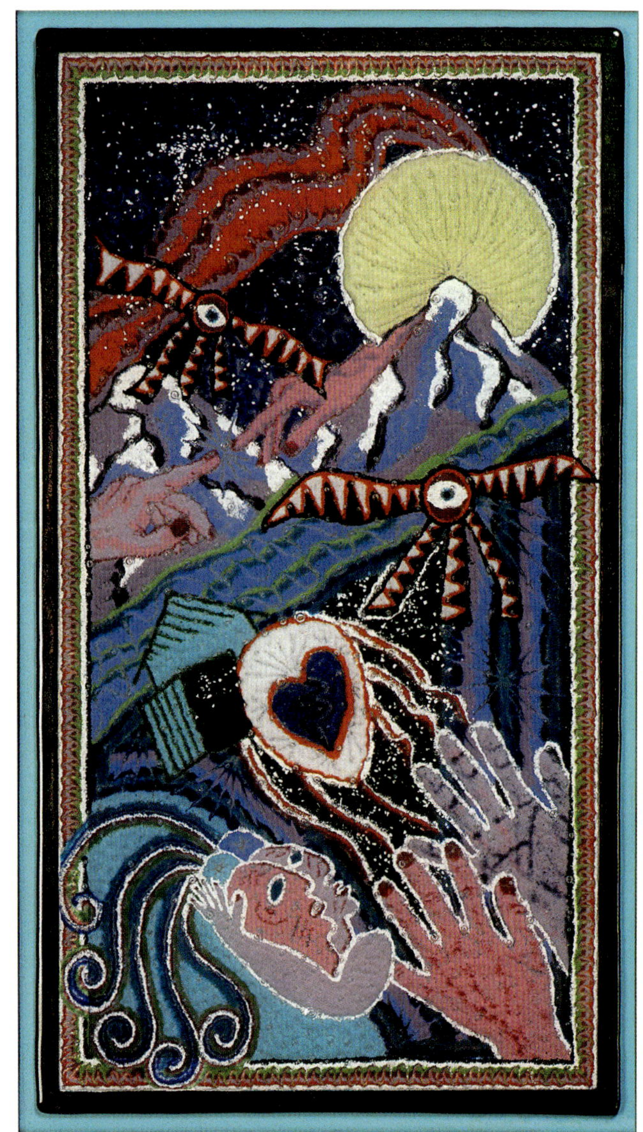

frit smashers

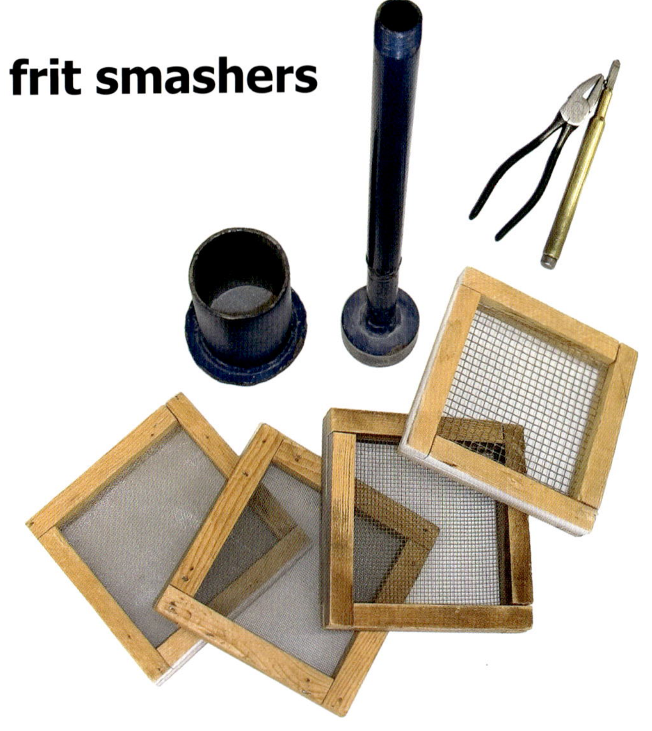

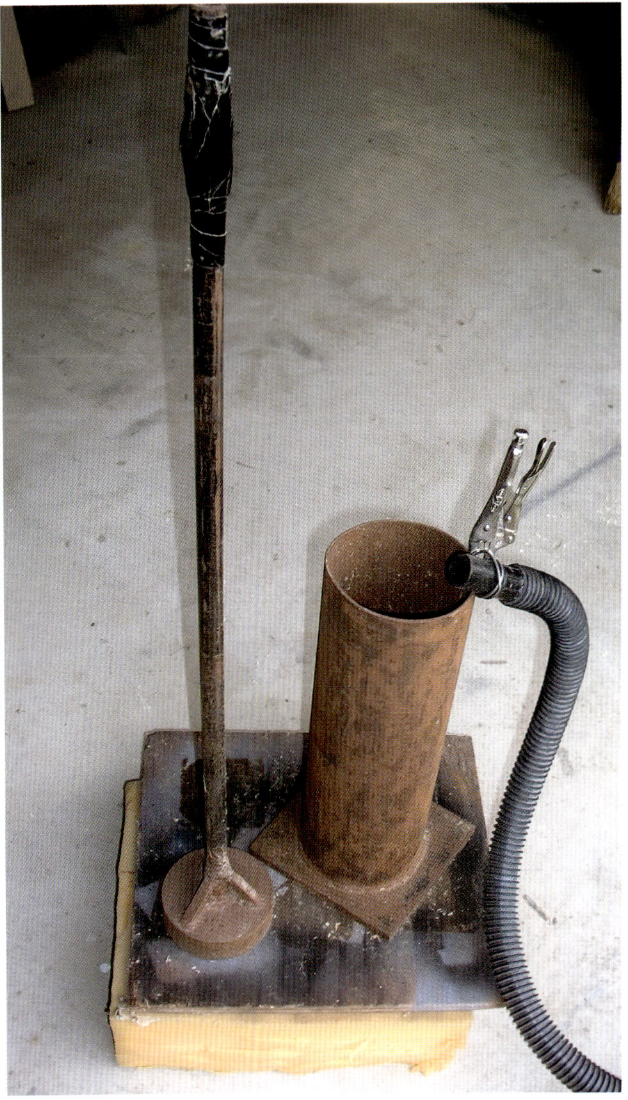

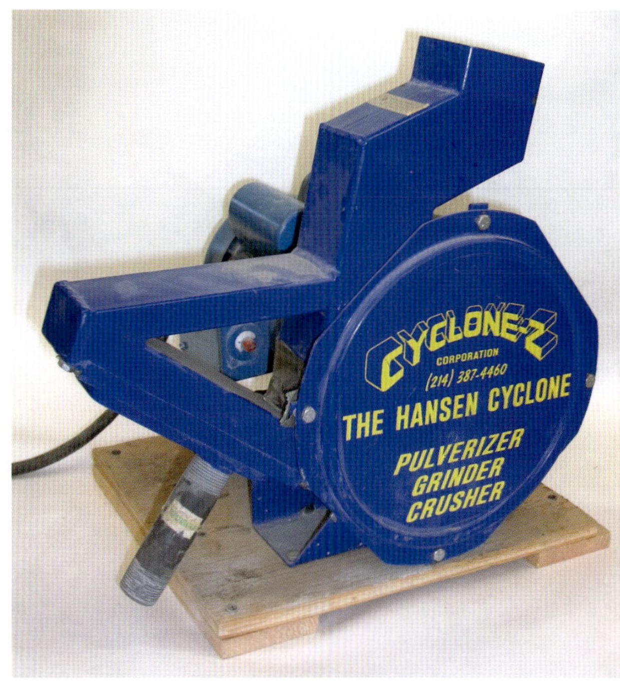

upper: Frit smasher, circa 1981, in a 3 in. (8 cm) pipe. I purchased the metal screen at a hardware store at different sizes of ¼ in. (6 mm), ⅛ in. (3 mm), 1/16 in. (1.5 mm) window screen, and a finer wire mesh; each is mounted in a wooden frame. I smash frit to accent my artwork and sort to different sizes by pouring it through the screens. I wear a respirator when crushing glass and working with glass powders

lower left: I turned scrap glass into frit with my frit smasher, circa 1983, in a 6 in. (15 cm) pipe, 18 in. (46 cm) long. I put it on top of a piece of plywood on a 3 in. (8 cm) piece of dense foam-rubber to absorb the blows and cut down on the noise. I placed a shop vac at the opening to suck the powder away and cut down on the dust. I wear a very good respirator and do the smashing outdoors. It's dusty.

lower right: Glass crusher, circa 1988. I purchased this machine designed for milling gold ore to crush my glass. It's made to run with water, but I run it dry outdoors and produce an enormous amount of dust. This crusher uses large links of chain to beat the glass into frit that passes through a fine screen as a mixture of about 01 sized frit and finer powder. I wear a super-duper respirator, use a shop vac to suck away the escaping dust, and change my clothes when I am done. I cut whole sheets of Bullseye and feed them to my machine. It's a nasty job!

Once upon a time, the Bullseye Fusing Ranch sold little packets of frit; they didn't sell well, and so they stopped. For years I ground my own glass, and I'm very thankful that Bullseye now sells frit again!

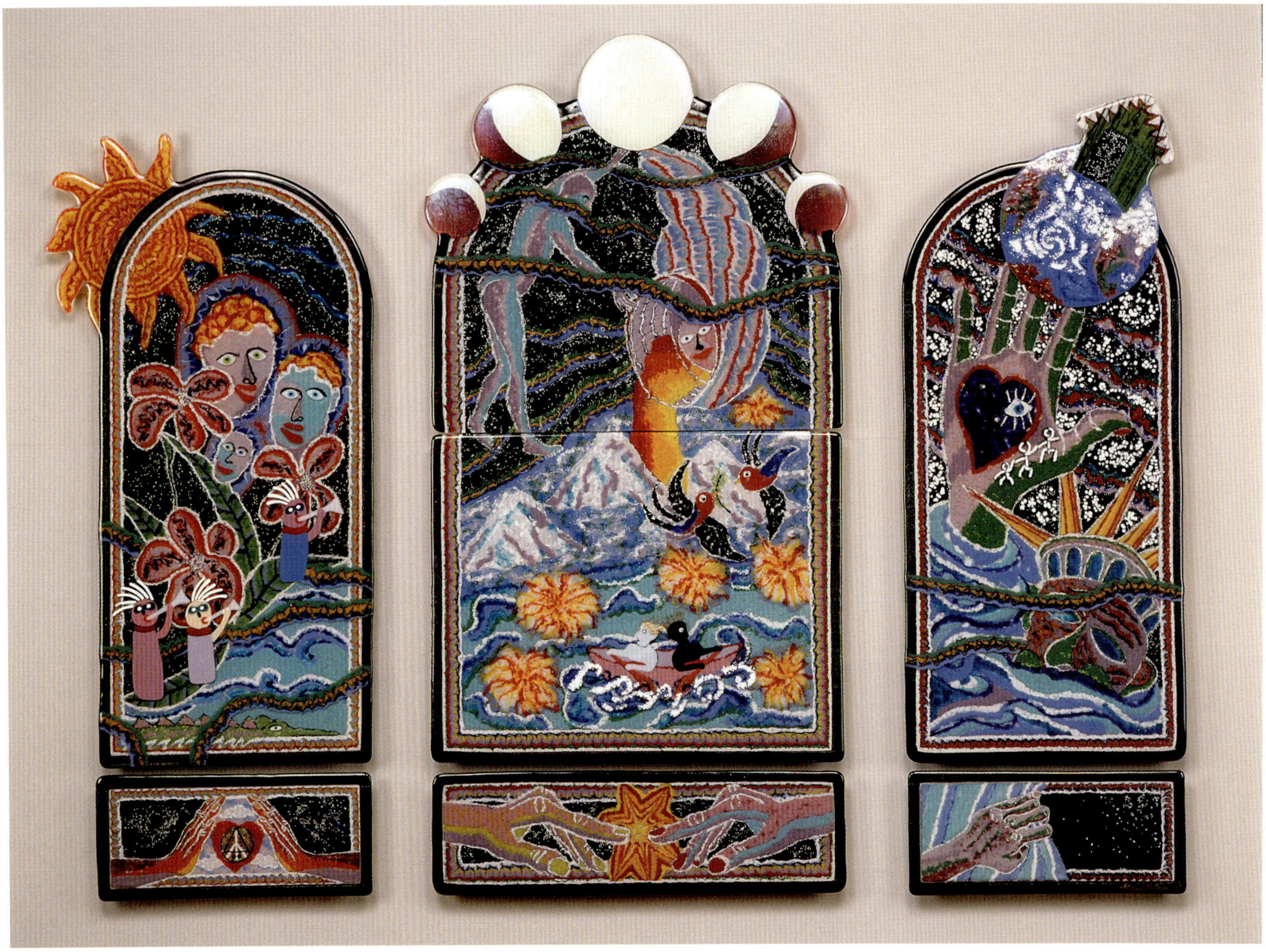

upper:
"Cornucopia," H. 50 in. (127 cm) x W. 68 in. (173 cm),
1988. Free designed with frit with no sketch drawn first or
paper pattern.

Free Design Frit Vessels

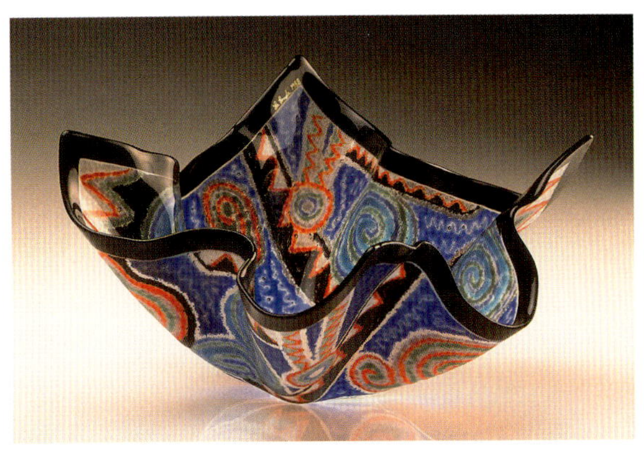

Bolero, 1988, H. 8 in. (20 cm) x W. 15 in. (38
cm) x D. 15 in. (38 cm).

Bolero Series   1988 – 1992
I laid crushed, colored glass, table sugar size, onto
a sheet of glass. Free-formed spirals and lines were
sprinkled on in a manner like sand painting. The
pieces were fused and flipped over, then fused a
second time and slumped into my metal mold on
a third firing.

70 pieces total

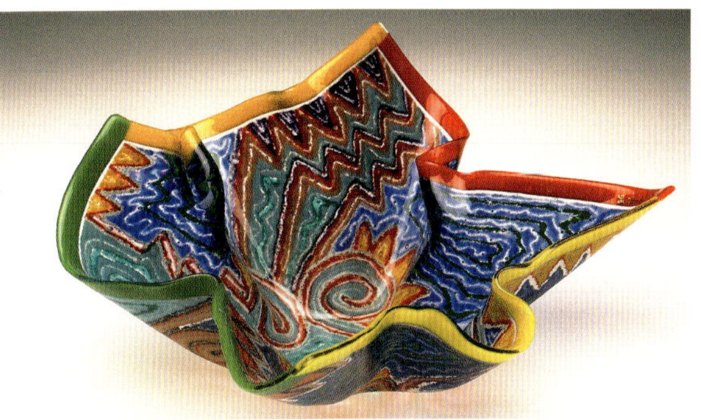

Calypso Series 1989 H. 8 in. (20 cm) x W. 16 in. (41) x D. 15 in. (38 cm).

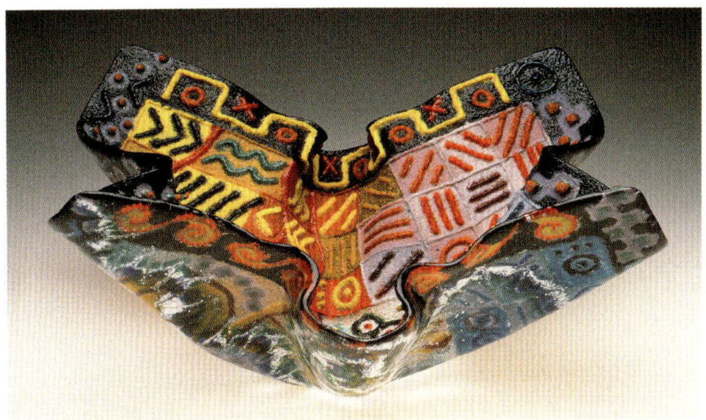

Vitroglyph 1989 H. 8 in. (20 cm) x W. 16 in. (41 cm) x D. 15 in. (38 cm).

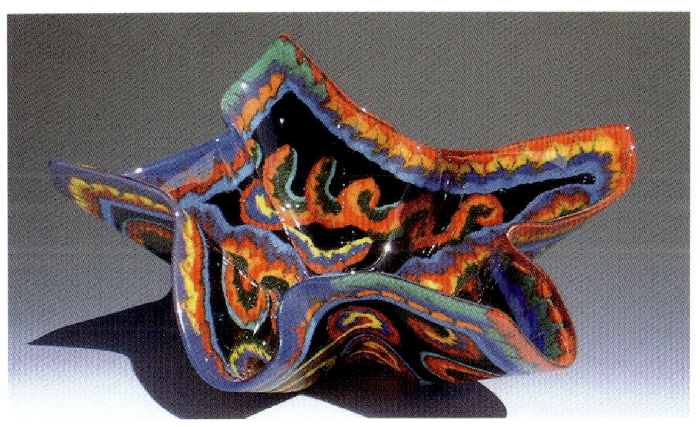

Fiesta   2002   H. 10 in. (25 cm) x W. 19 in. (48 cm) x D. 17 in. (43 cm).

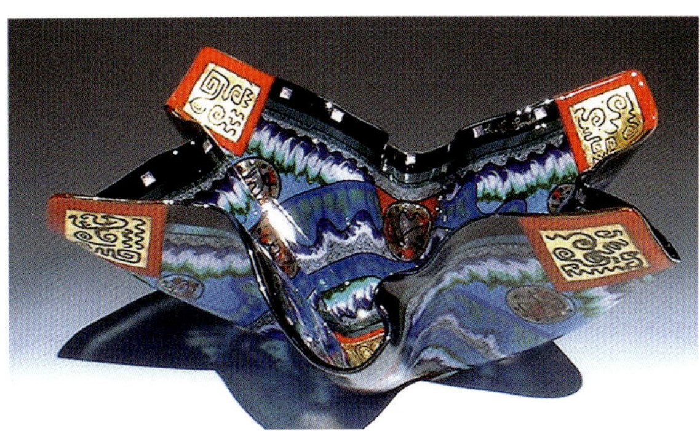

Mandala   2003   H. 10 in. (25 cm) x W. 19 in. (48 cm) x D. 17 in. (43 cm).

Calypso Series 1989

I began this series in the cold of winter when I wanted to warm up my colors. This is constructed similar to the Bolero I Series.

12 pieces total

Vitroglyph Series   1989

I pressed a design into a wet sand and clay mix on a kiln shelf. Then I laid crushed colored glass into this and fused a clear sheet of glass on top. I flipped the dimensional surface up and slumped it in a metal mold.

9 pieces total

Fiesta Series 2002

I began this series to create more spontaneity in my vessels. After laying crushed glass on a kiln shelf, I dragged a pointed stick through it to create a feathered look. I laid a piece of clear glass over the crushed glass and fuse this in my kiln. During a second firing I slump it into a metal mold.

10 pieces total

Mandala Series 2002 – present

This series uses all of the techniques that I have developed. I am creating a concentric "Mandala" pattern with cut sheet and crushed glass. Thin copper foil produces a bubble pattern when it is fired, and I use gold foil that I etch designs into by hand. I also blend the crushed glass (frit) to look like granite rock. These pieces use more subtle colors. I am striving to create a meditative, harmonious feel. This is my current series.

45 pieces (2002 – 2005)

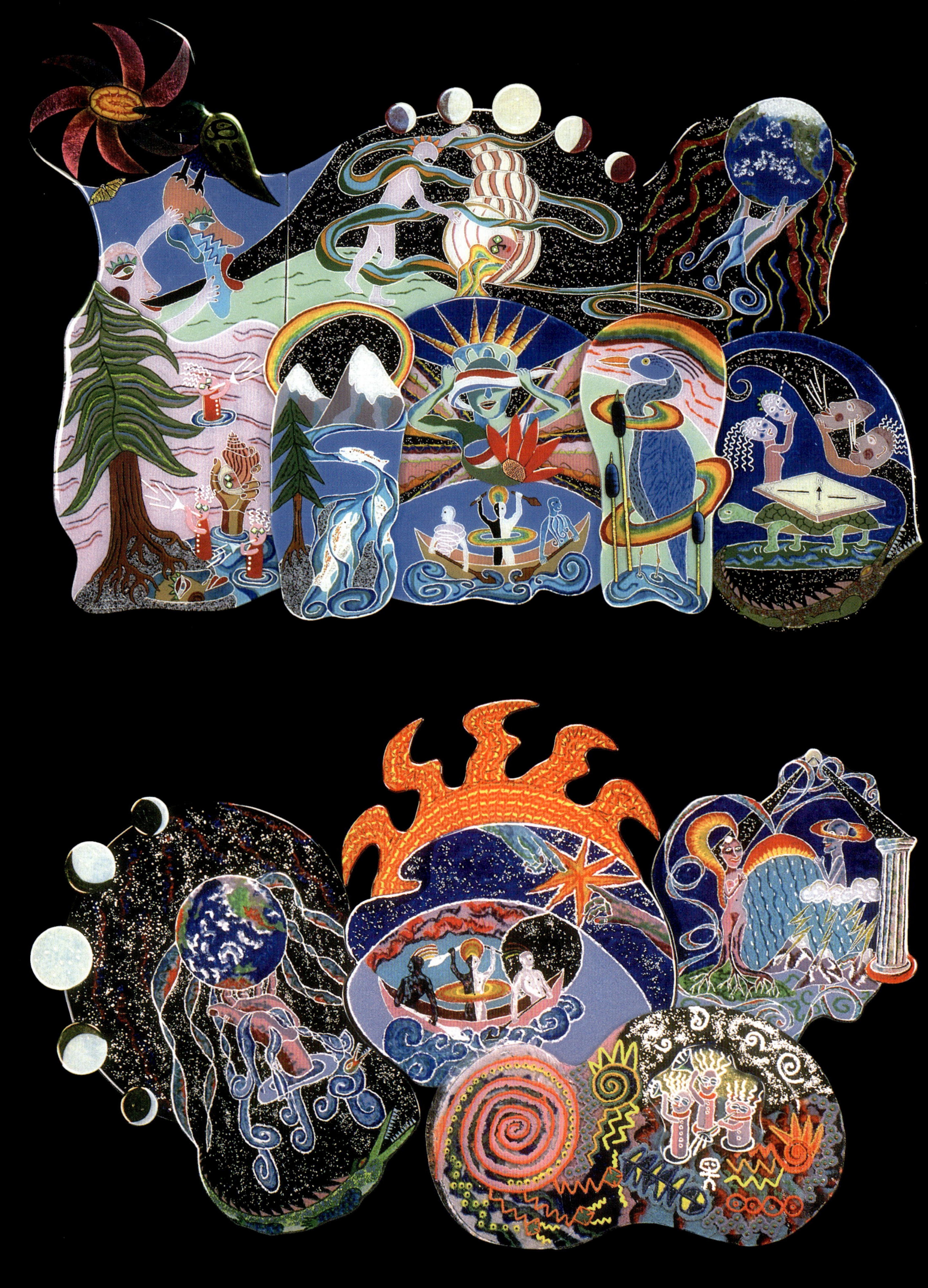

frit follows design: 1989 - 1993

52 wall pieces were created between 1989 and 1993 using "frit follows design" technique.

Paper patterns gave me more control of my design; however, once again my artwork was getting more and more complicated, and I needed to create an easier and fun way to work. I went back to designing full-sized patterns on butcher paper with Sharpie markers. I flipped my patterns upside down on a light table, laid clear glass on top of the upside down pattern, and outlined the design with black or white crushed glass. I swept errant frit pieces back into their places with a small paintbrush, and I would fill in between these outlines with colored frit. Very carefully, I would carry the sheets of clear glass with their loose crushed-glass designs to the kiln. Those who saw me do this would inevitably say, "I hope you don't sneeze!"

I also began fusing small additions of dichroic glass that is coated with a very thin layer of metal, and I applied gold and silver leaf after the piece was fused.

facing upper:
"Look Too See," 1992, H. 52 in. (132 cm) x W. 76 in. (193 cm). This piece is built in eight sections, which are tiered and overlap each other. The fish and the heron bottom panels stand 1 ½" away from the wall and overlap the panels on either side, which are 1" from the wall and overlap the upper row, which is ½" from the wall.

facing lower:
"Remember the Stars," 1989, H. 48 in. (122 cm) x W. 72 in. (183 cm). The bottom right panel is cast dimensionally in sand.

lower:
"Whirlwind," 1990, H. 42 in. (107 cm) x W. 60 in. (152 cm).

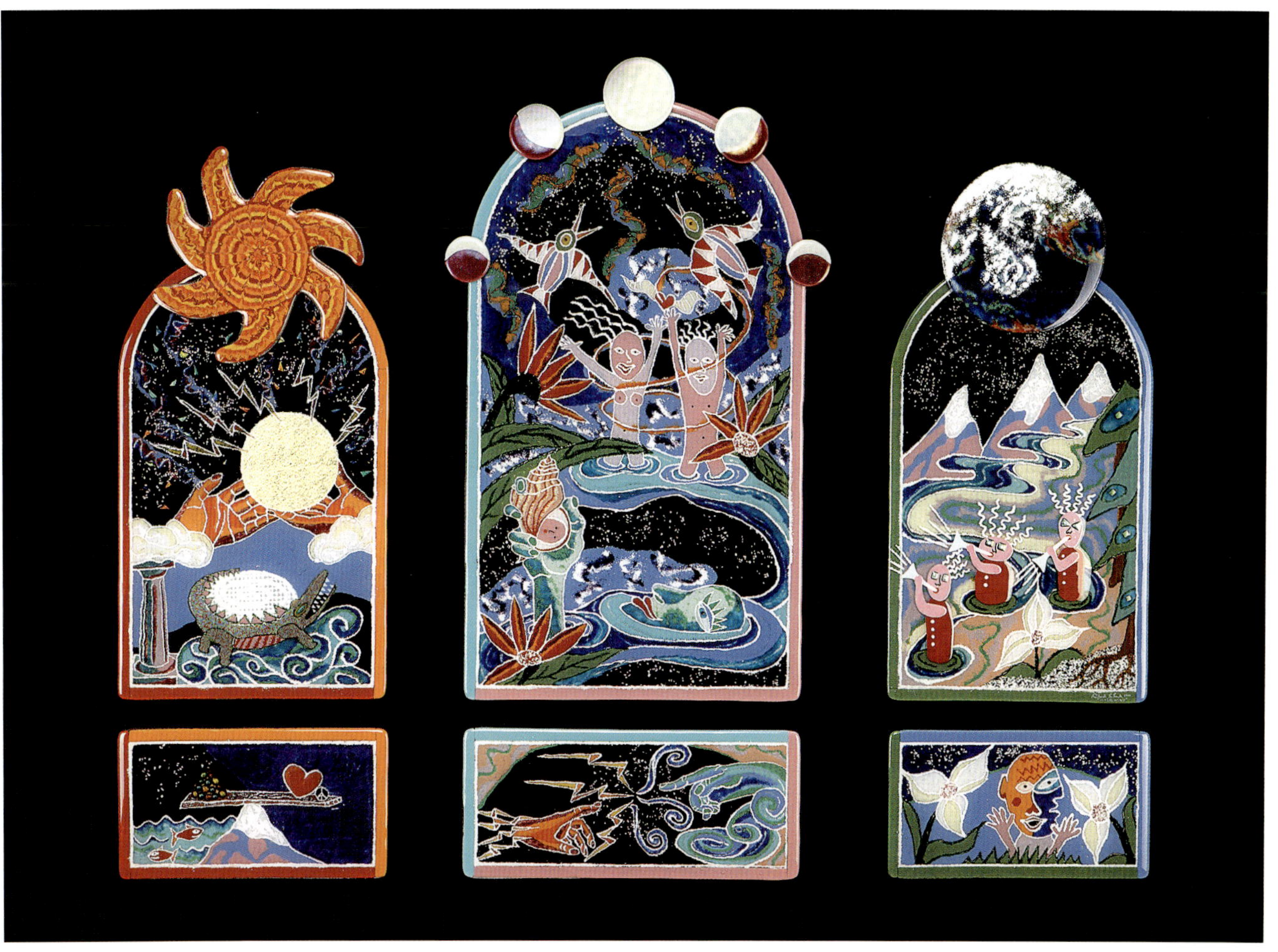

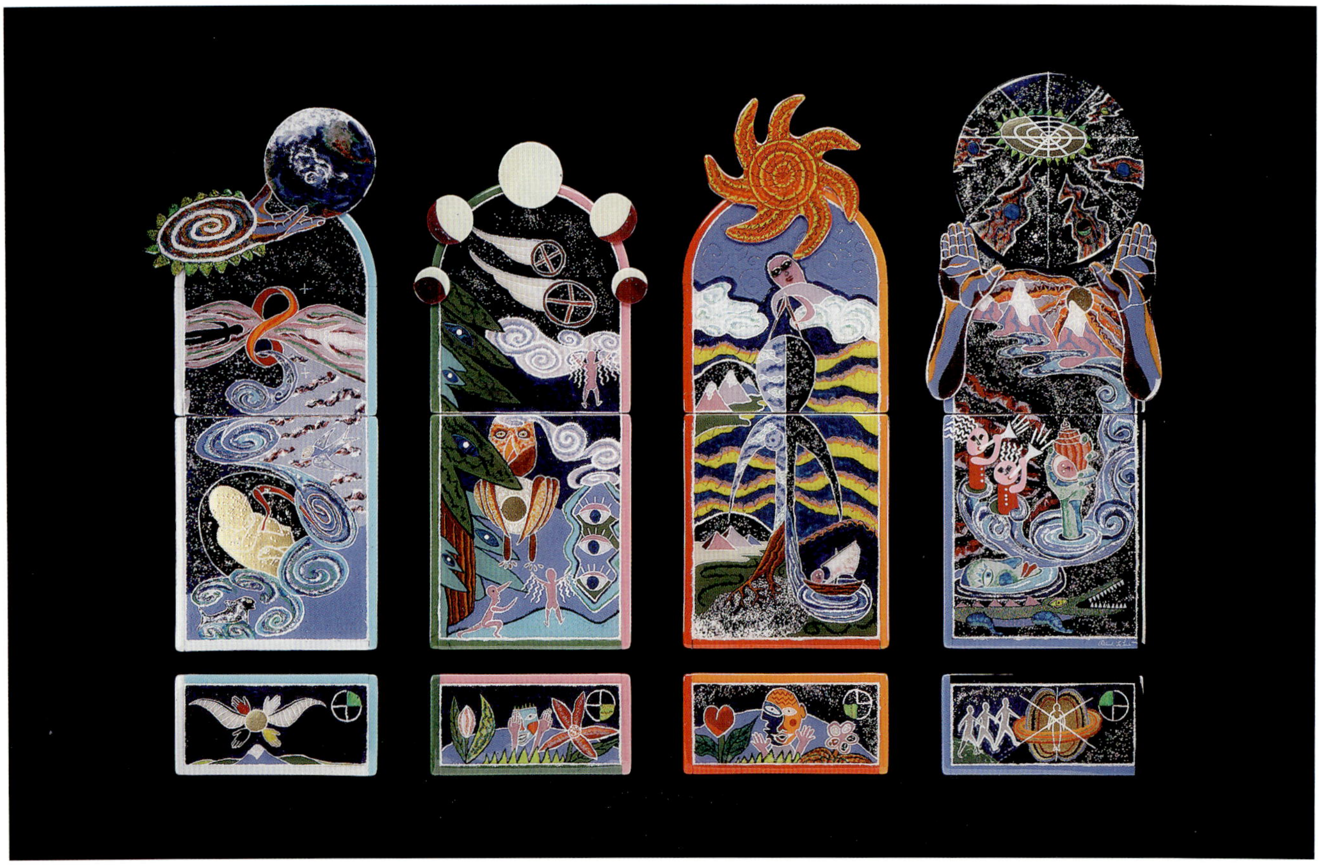

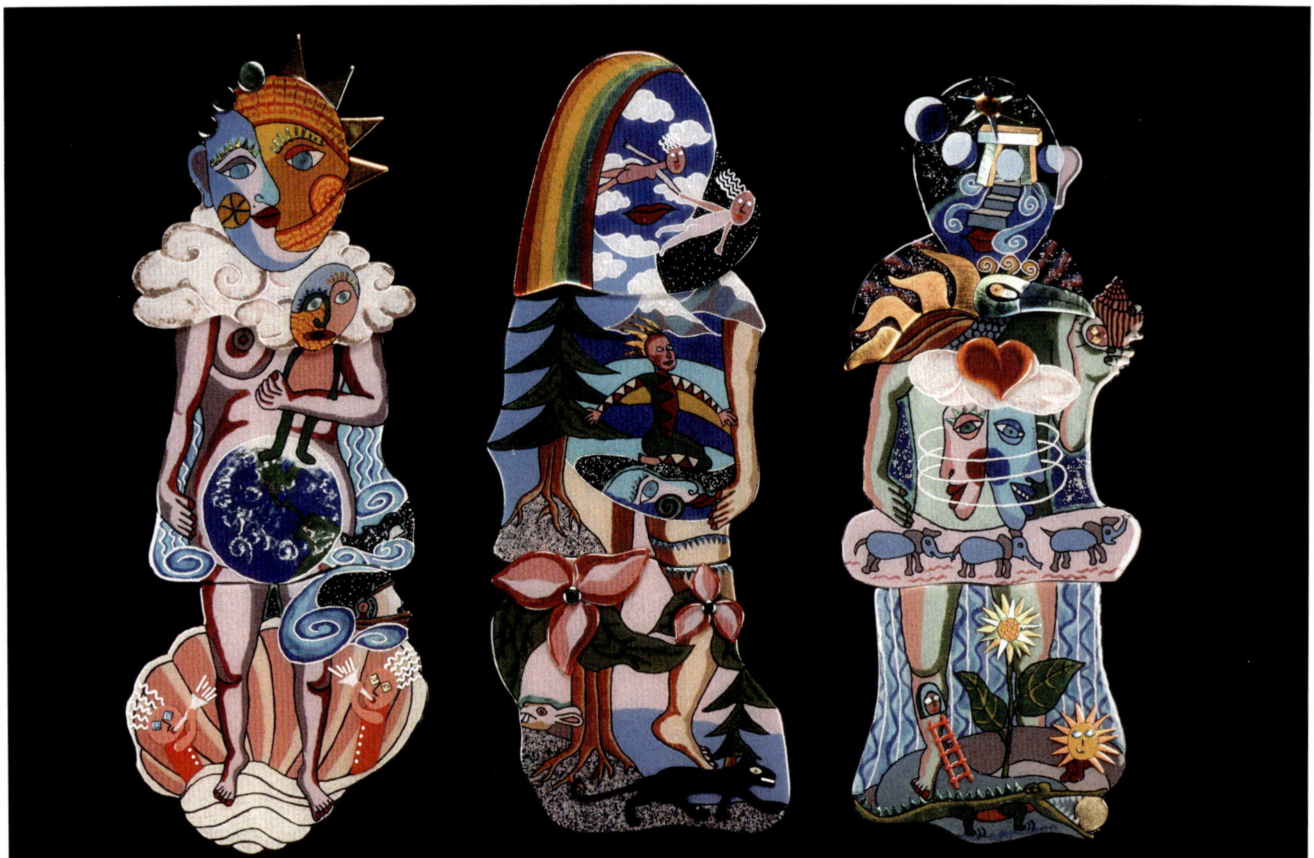

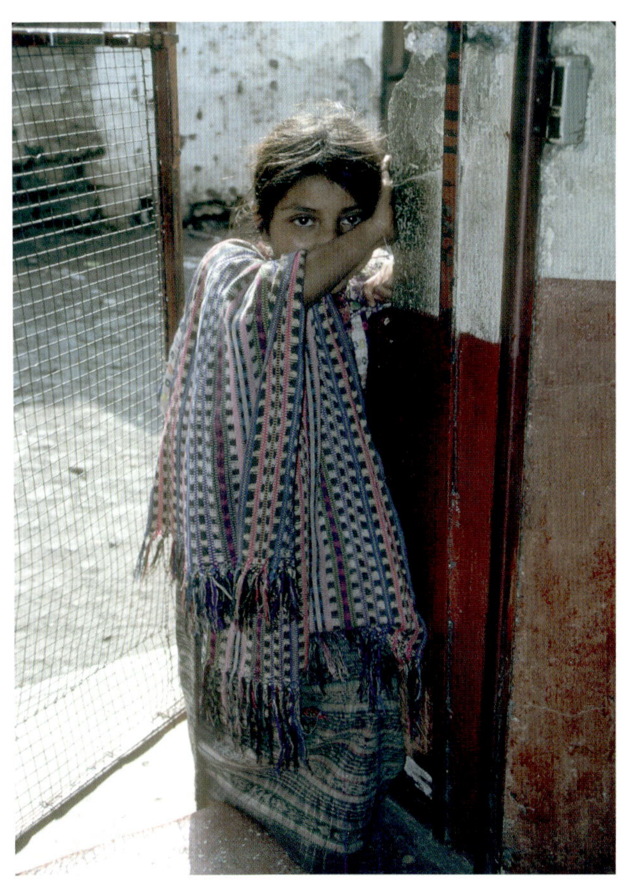

facing upper:
"The Four Directions," 1991, H. 51 in. (130 cm) x W. 84 in. (213 cm).

facing lower:
"Three Figures," 1993, H. 56 in. (142 cm) x W. 66 in. (168 cm).

upper:
Girl in Guatemala, 1988. I used the idea of the shawl over the girl's arm as the curtain in the piece below.

lower:
"Touch," 1989, H. 56 in. (142 cm) x W. 62 in. (157 cm).

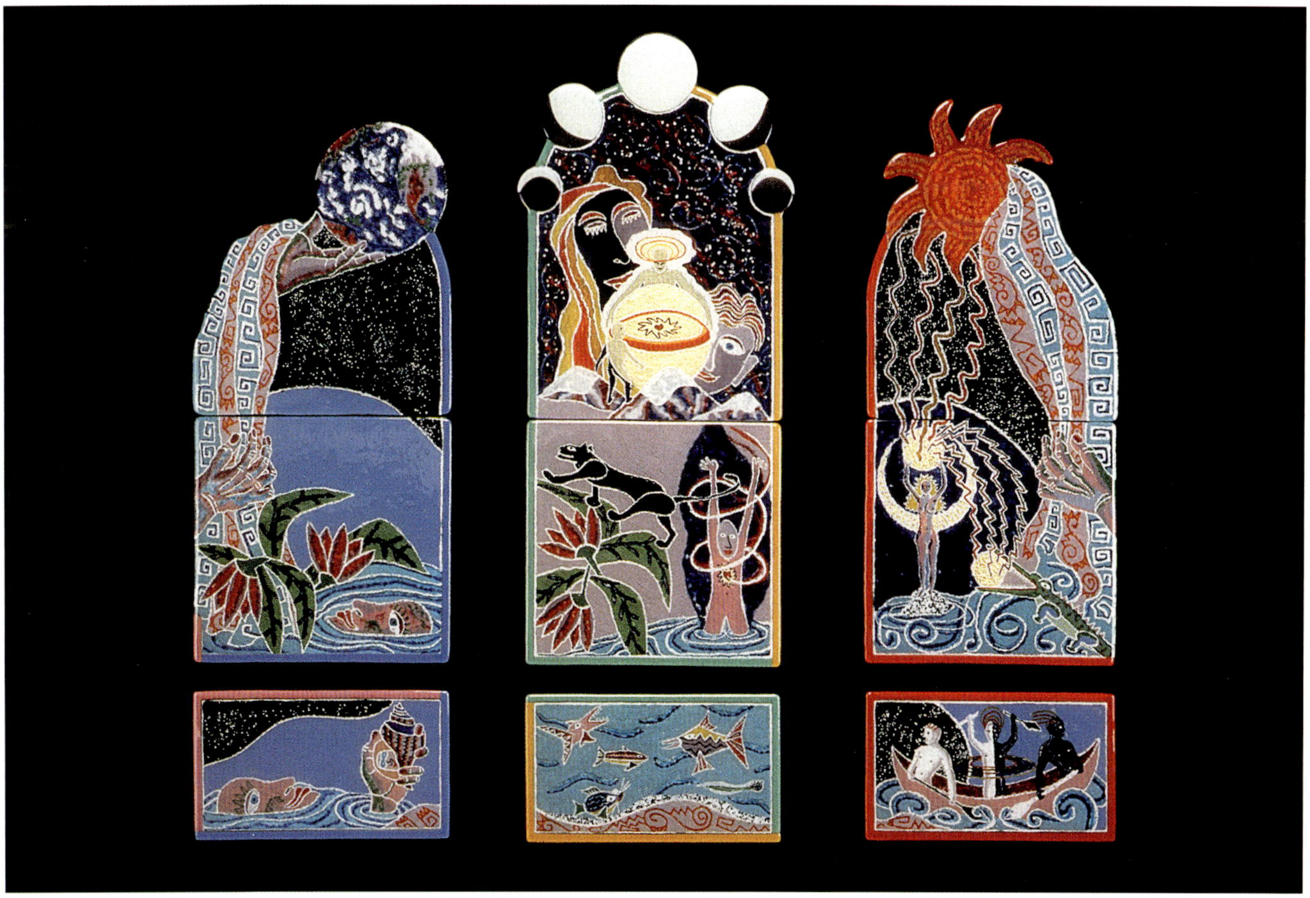

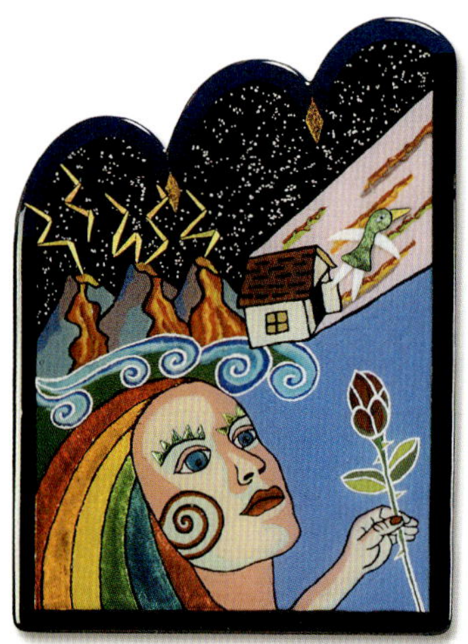
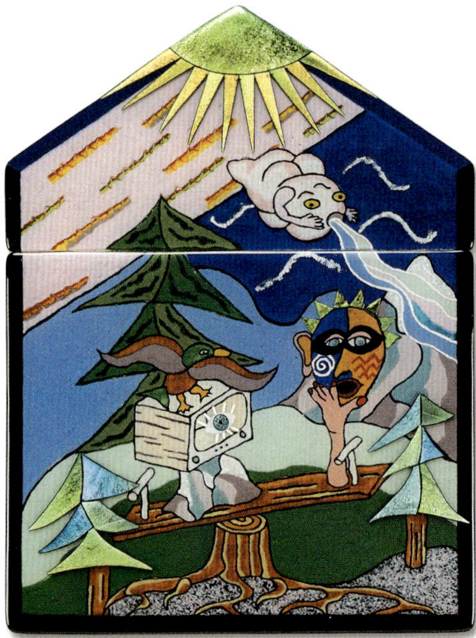
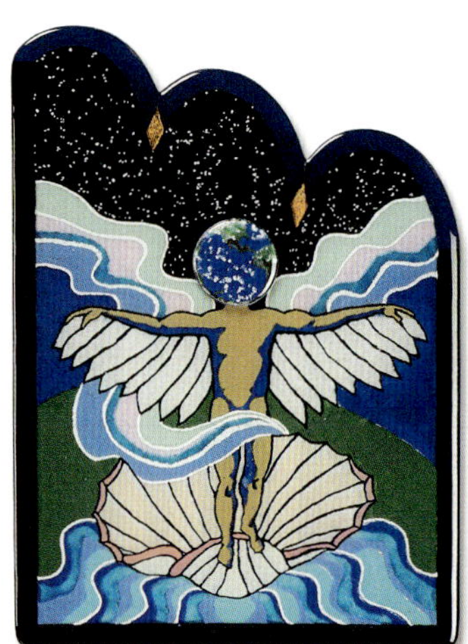
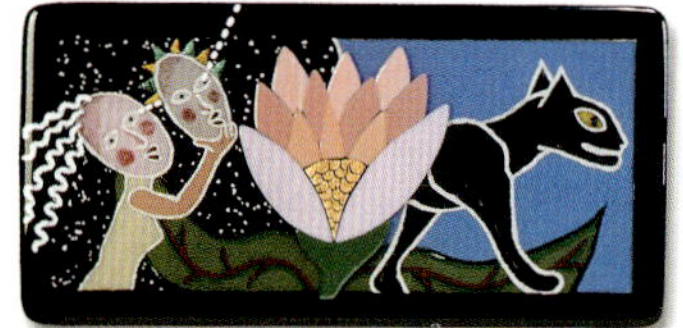
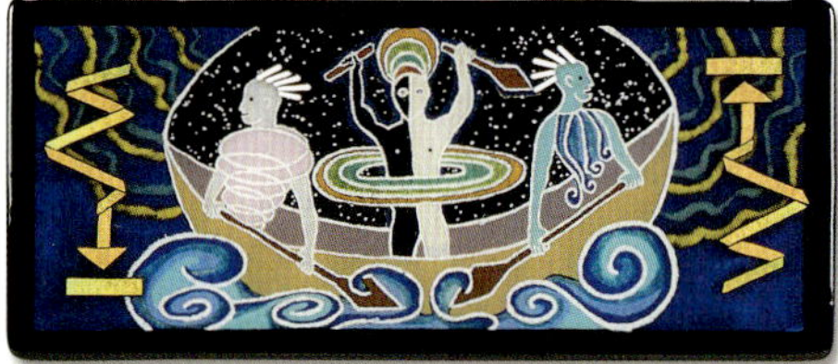
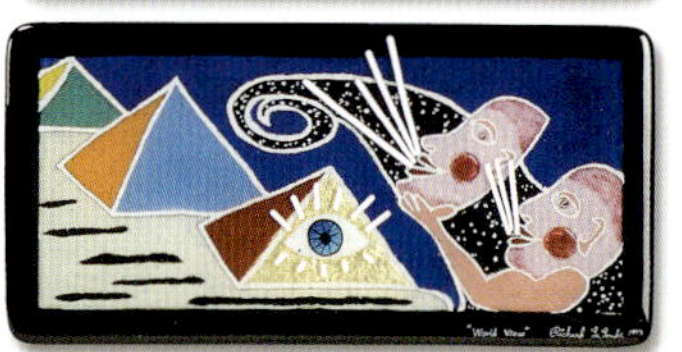

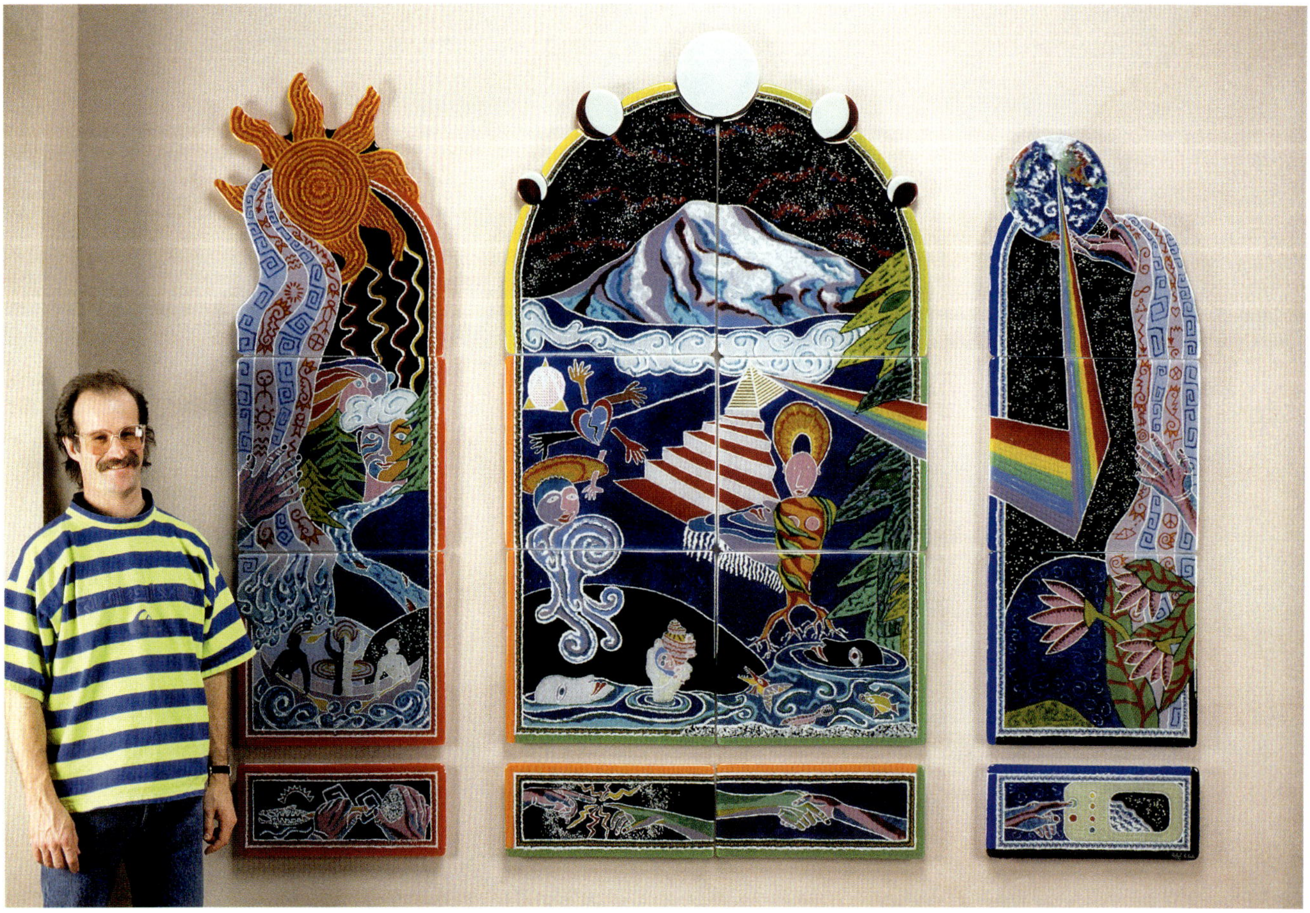

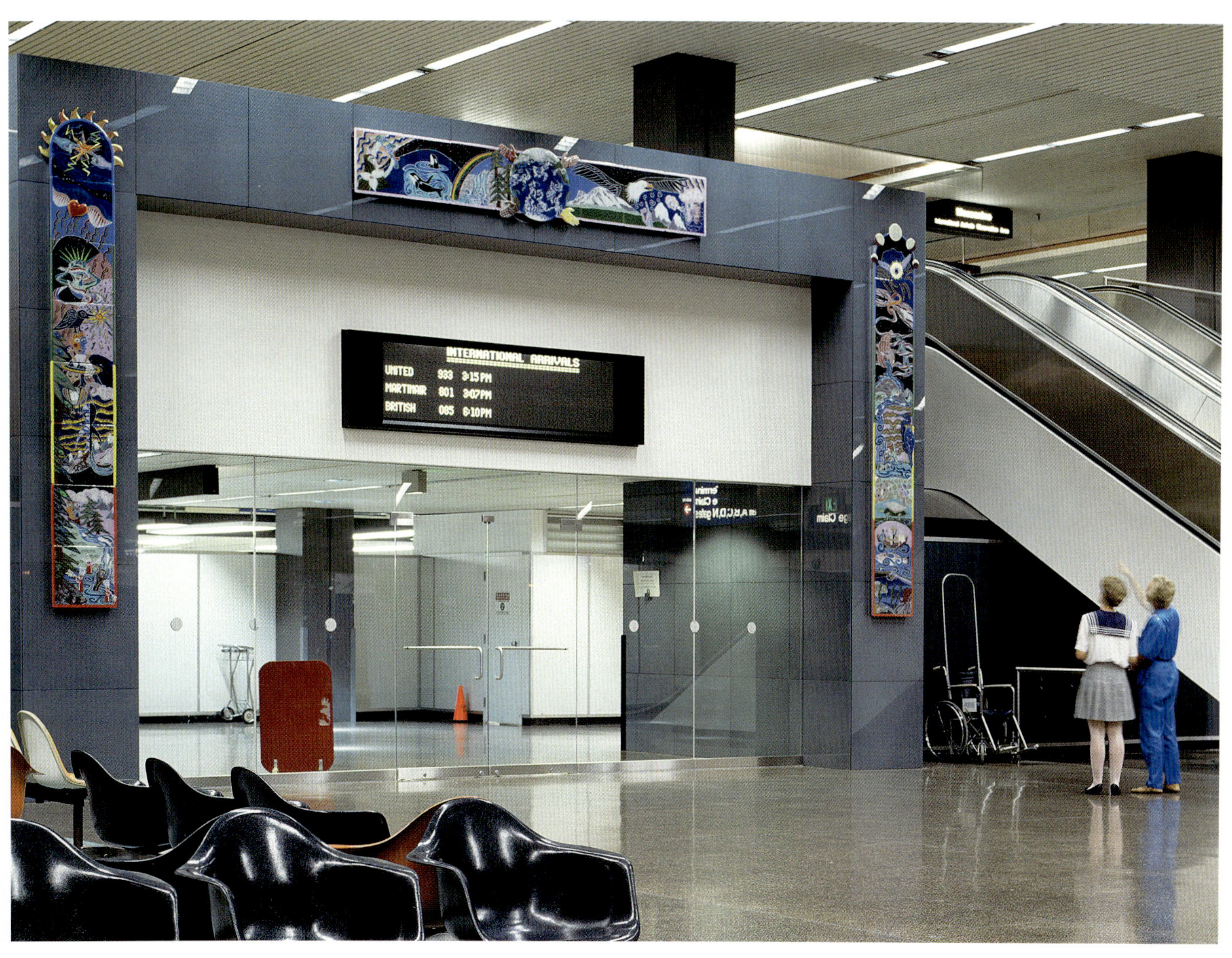

facing upper:
"World View," 1993, H. 43 in. (109 cm) x W. 66 in. (168 cm), Evanston Public Library, Evanston, IL. Private Commission for the library.

facing lower:
"The Hand of Humankind," 1990, H. 56 in. (142 cm) x W. 74 in. (188 cm). The Parkland-Spanaway Public Library, Parkland, WA. The Friends of the Library/Pierce County Library Commission.

upper:
"Into The Mythos," 1992, 3 sections 158 in. (400 cm) x 24 in. (61 cm). International Arrivals Gateway at the Seattle/Tacoma Airport, SeaTac, WA. Port of Seattle Commission.

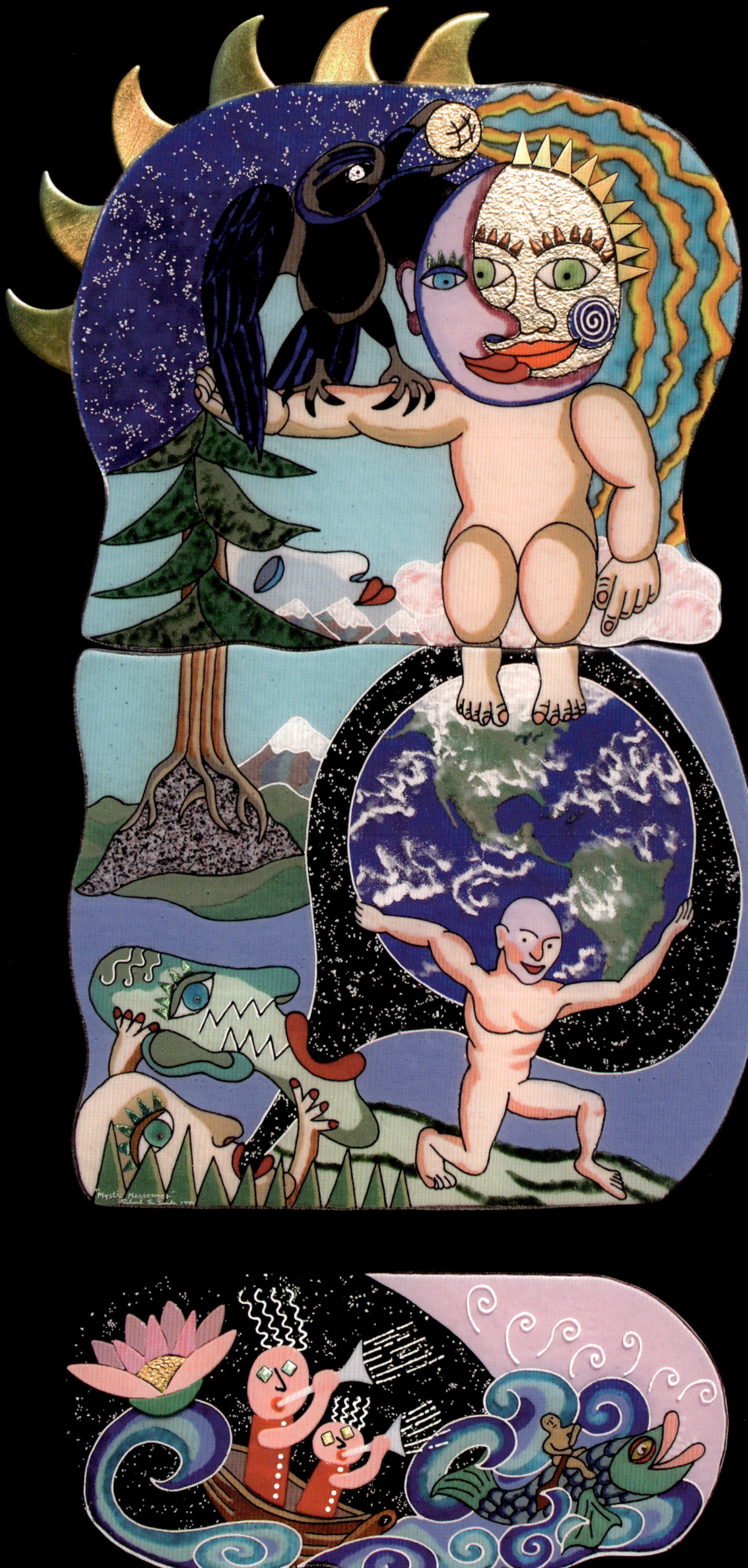

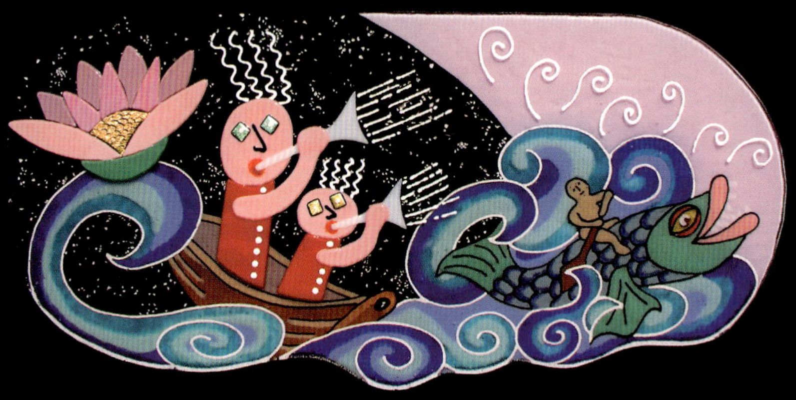

"Mystic Messemer"

liquid glass line: 1993 - present

I created 54 wall pieces and 203 vessels between 1993 and 2003 using my "liquid glass" technique.

From the beginning of creating crushed glass murals I outlined areas that I would fill with color. To start, I laid a line of crushed glass that I smoothed and straightened with a paintbrush. In order to create a thinner outline, I developed a technique of laying a line with fine powdered glass in a "liquid glass" medium, which was applied with a squeeze bottle. I would then fill this area with crushed glass.

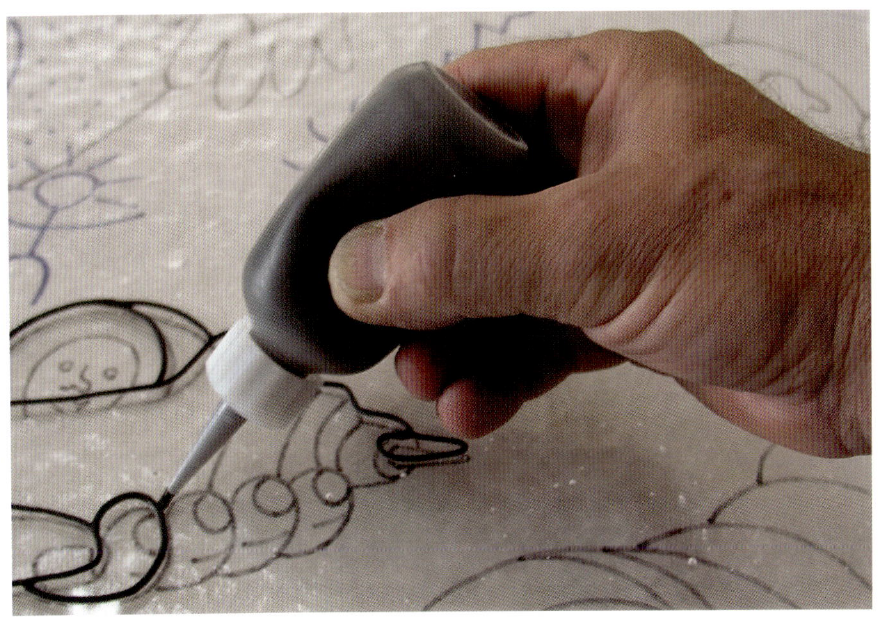

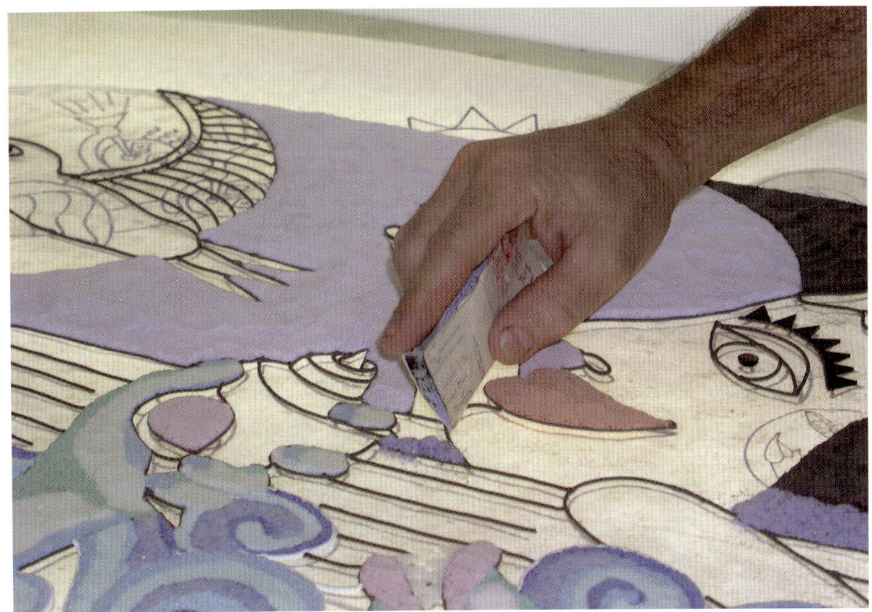

facing:
"Mystic messenger," 1994,
H. 56 in. (142 cm) x W. 28 in.
(71 cm).

upper:
Laying down the liquid glass line using a squeeze bottle.

lower:
Applying crushed glass with a folded postcard.

next two pages:
"The Four Directions" (left) and "The Four Elements" (right), 1994 — present, H. 24 in. (61 cm) x W. 20 in. (51 cm). Eight of fourteen panels used as illustrations for my self-published book Heart of The World. These panels are available in a limited edition of ten each and sold as sets of the four Directions or the four Elements as well as some individual panels.

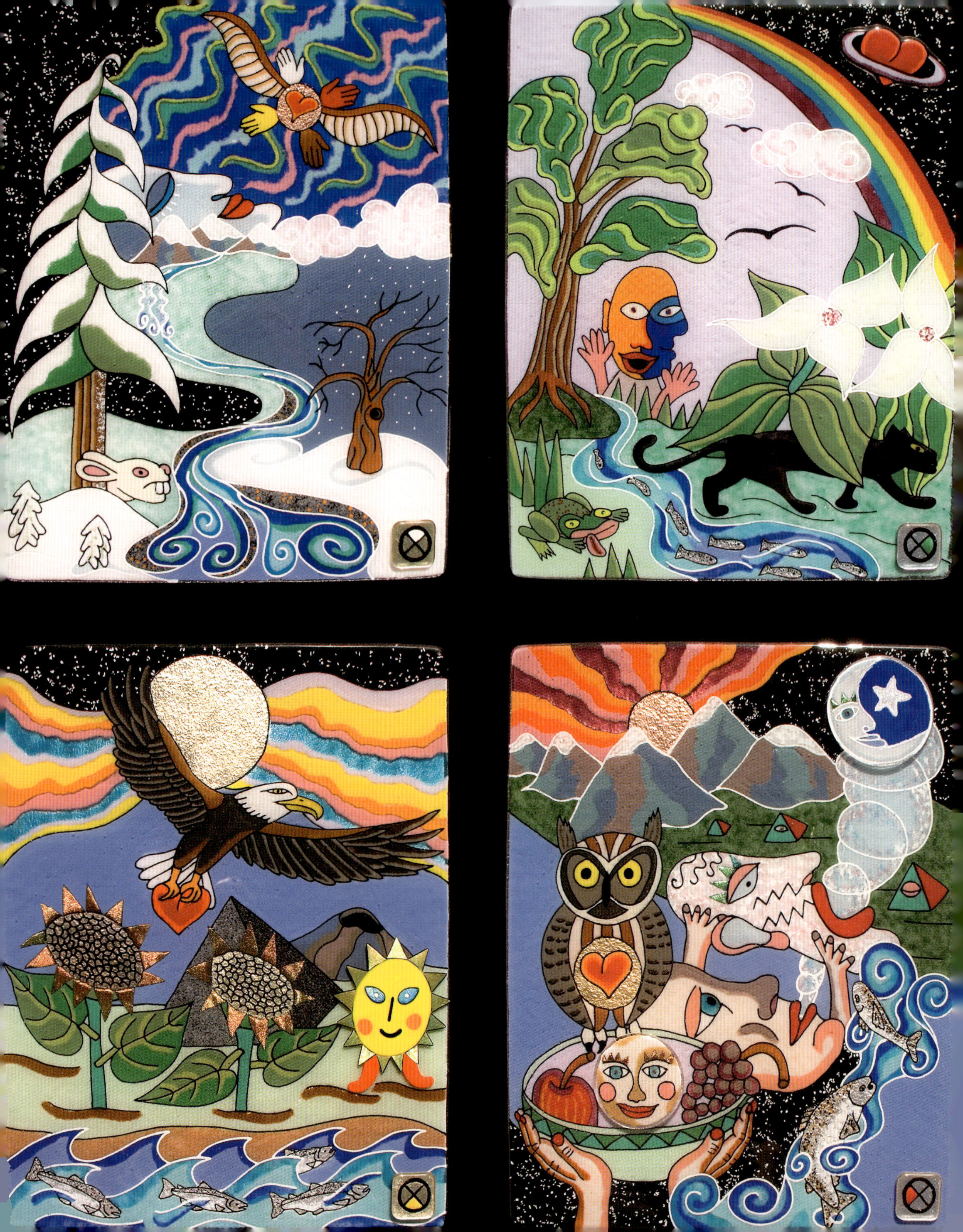

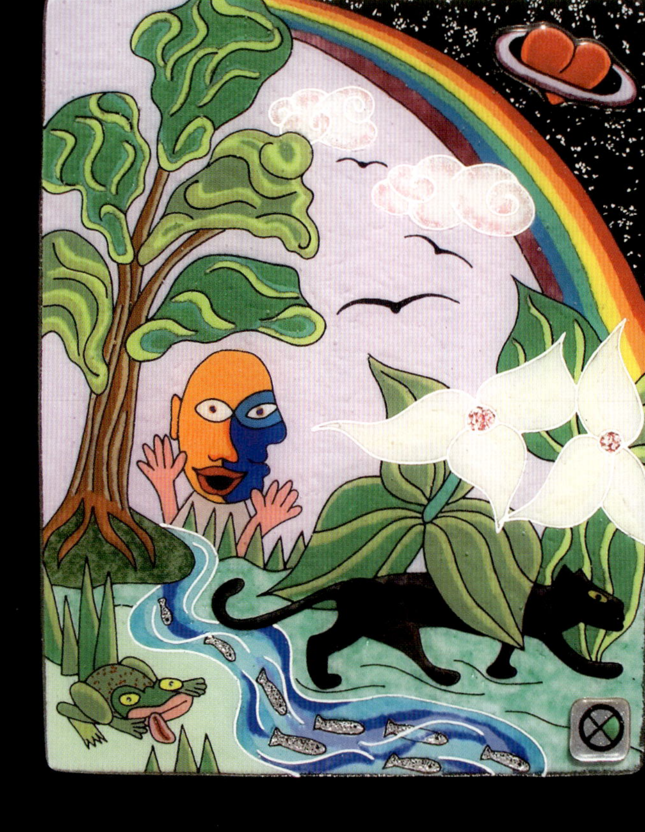
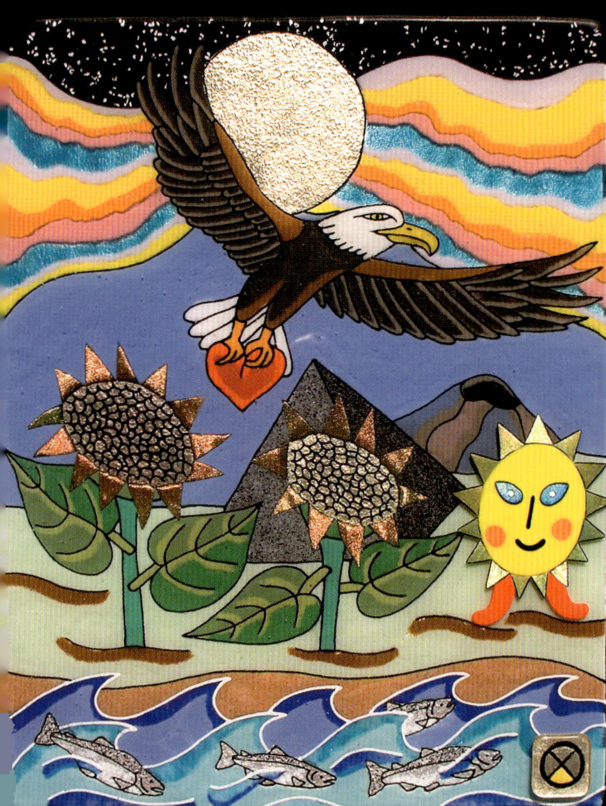
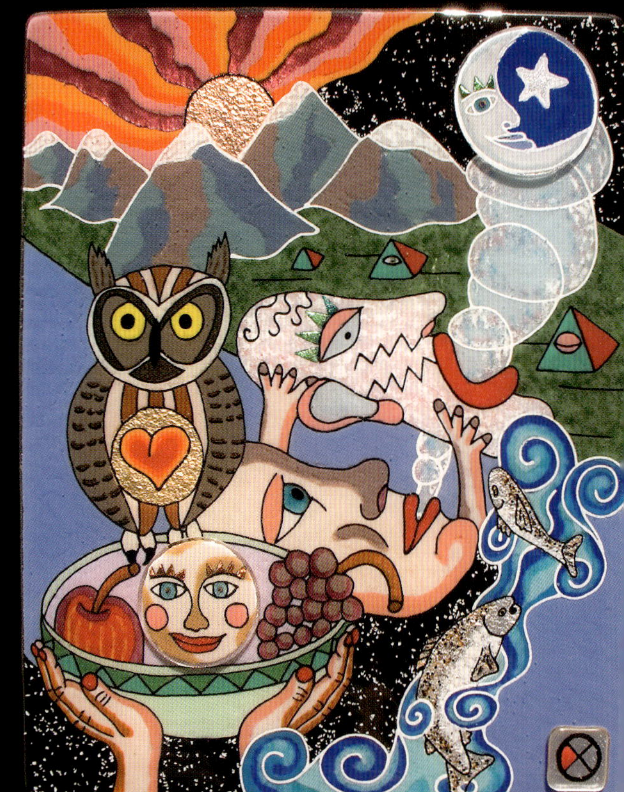

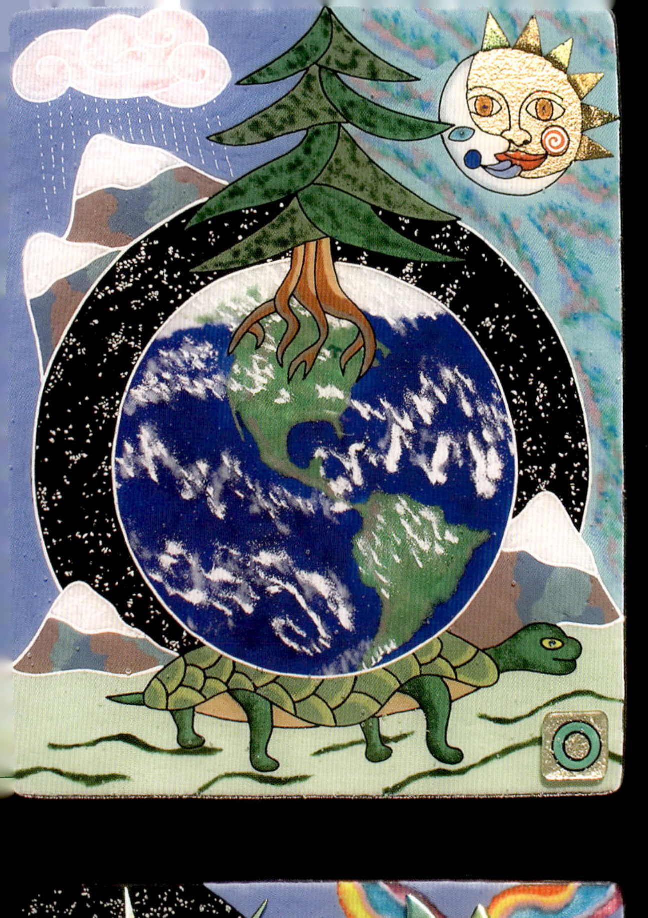
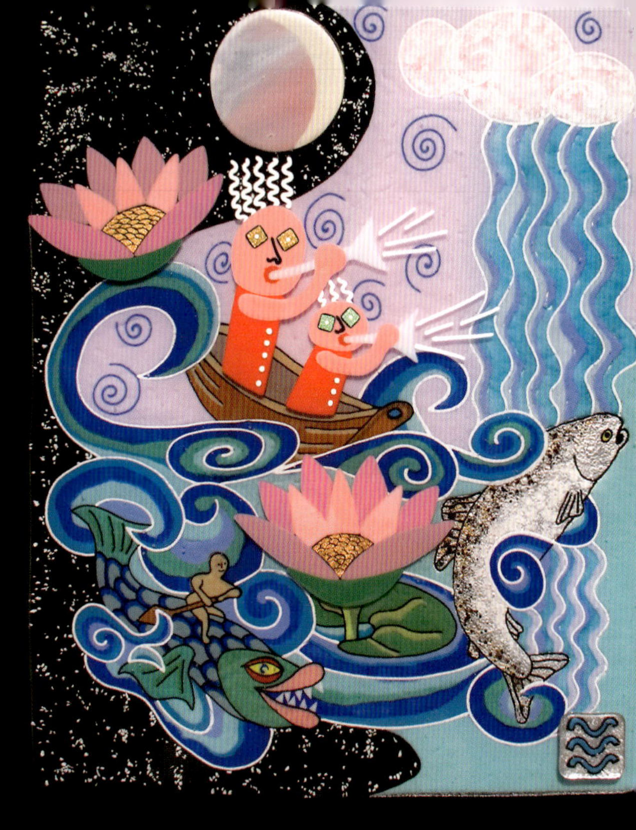
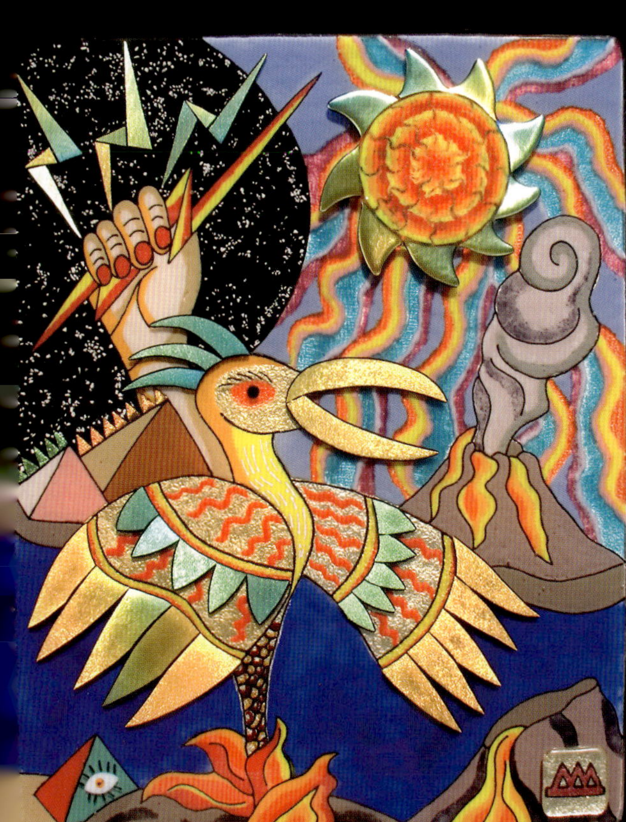
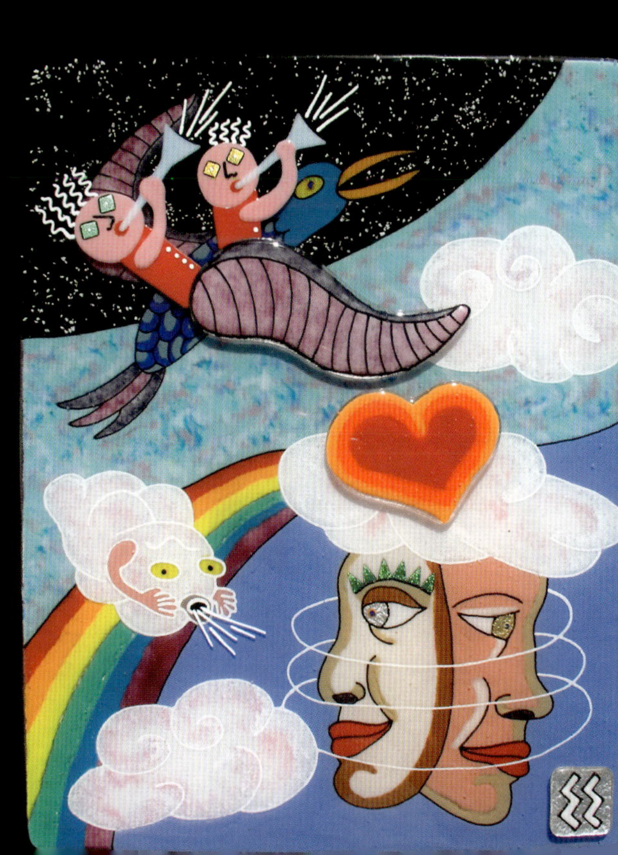

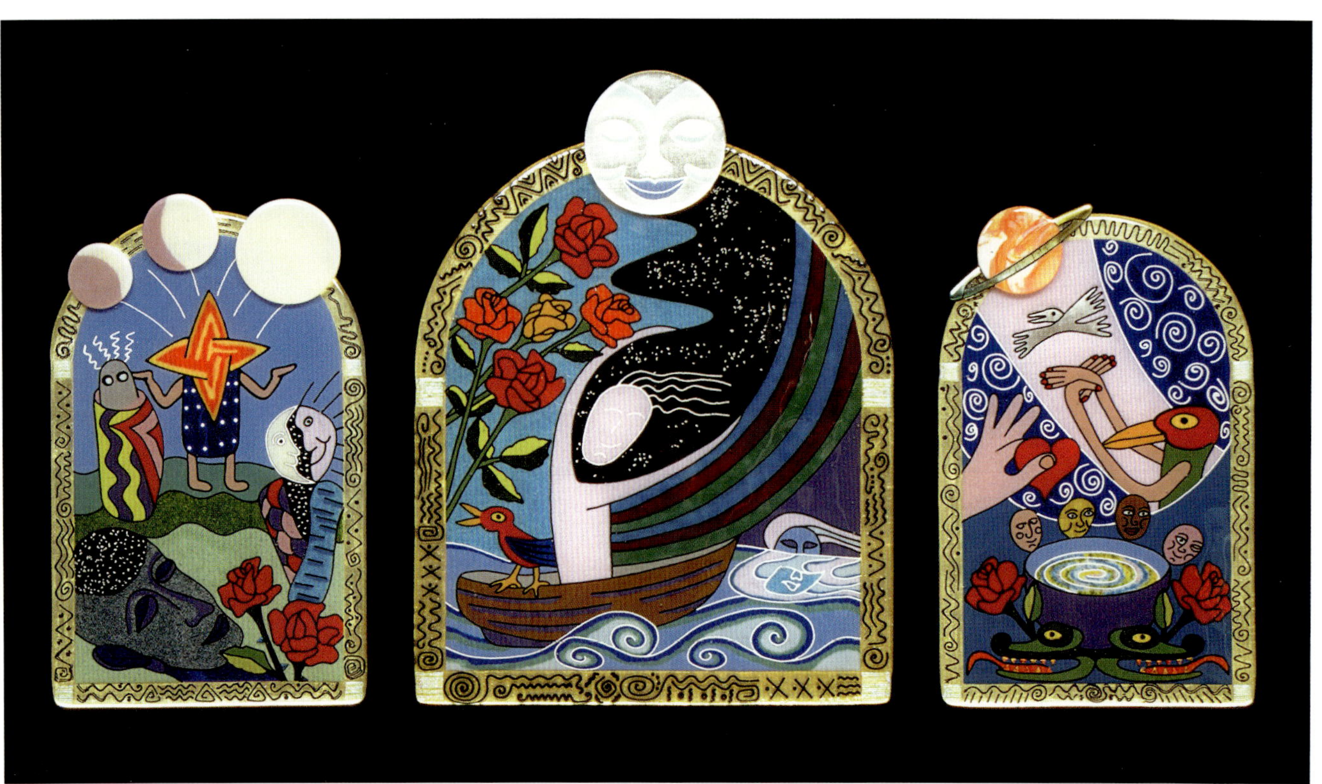

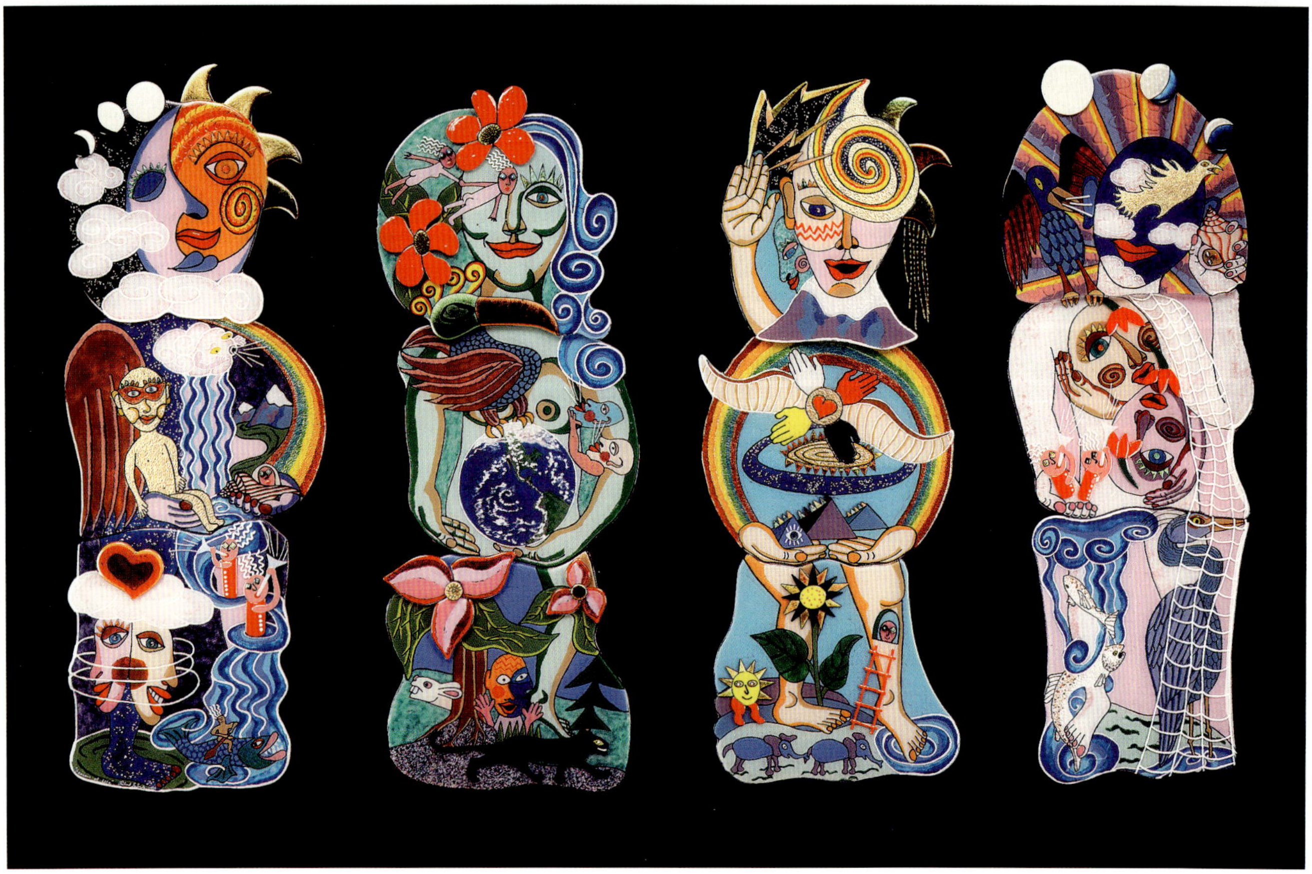

upper: "Roses & Moonbeams," 1999,
H. 26 in. (66 cm) x W. 50 in. (127 cm).
Gold leaf under the glass frame.

lower: "Seasons of Life," 1993,
H. 56 in. (142 cm) x W. 96 in. (244 cm).

94

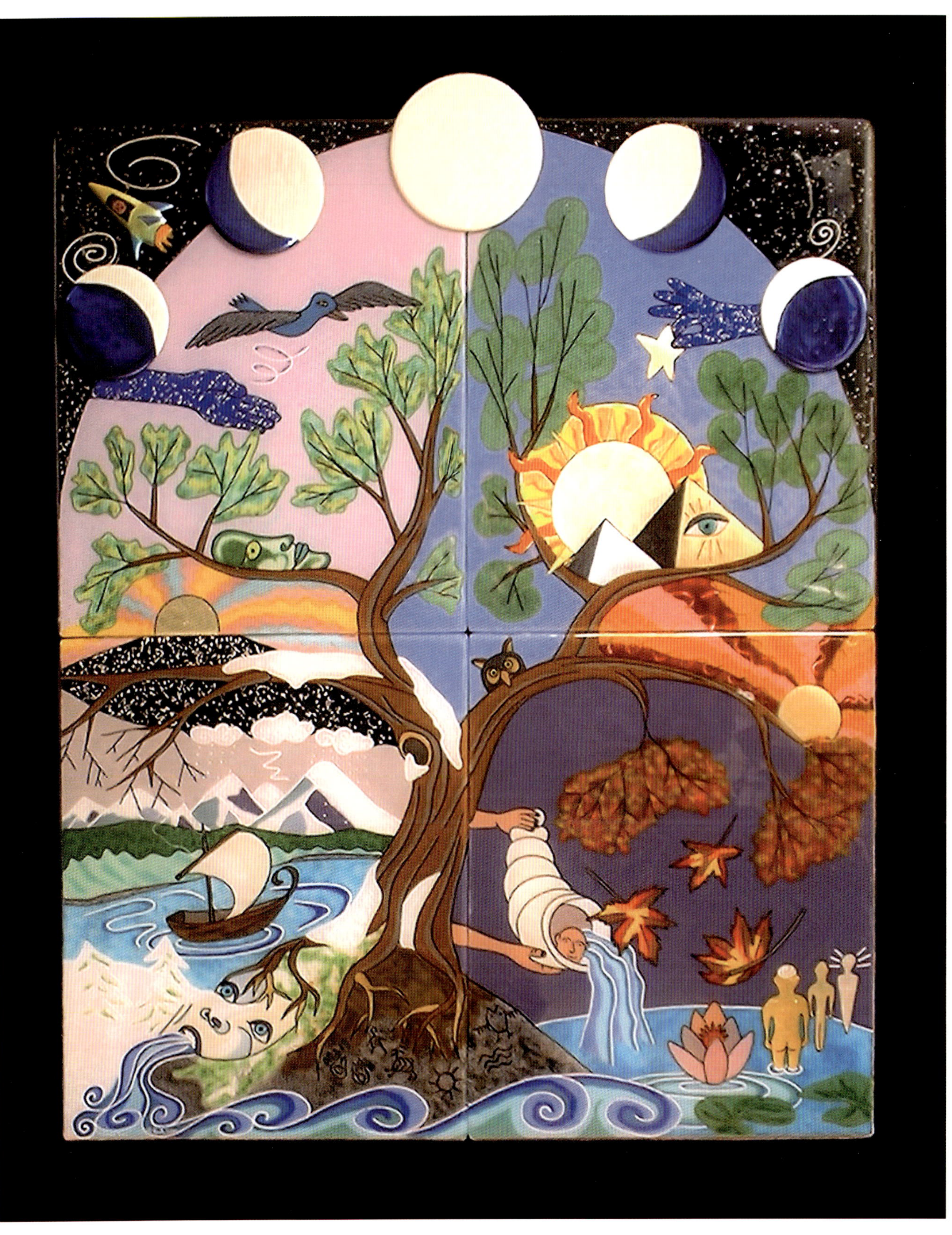

above: "Season Tree," 2000,
H. 48 in. (122 cm) x W. 39 in. (100 cm).

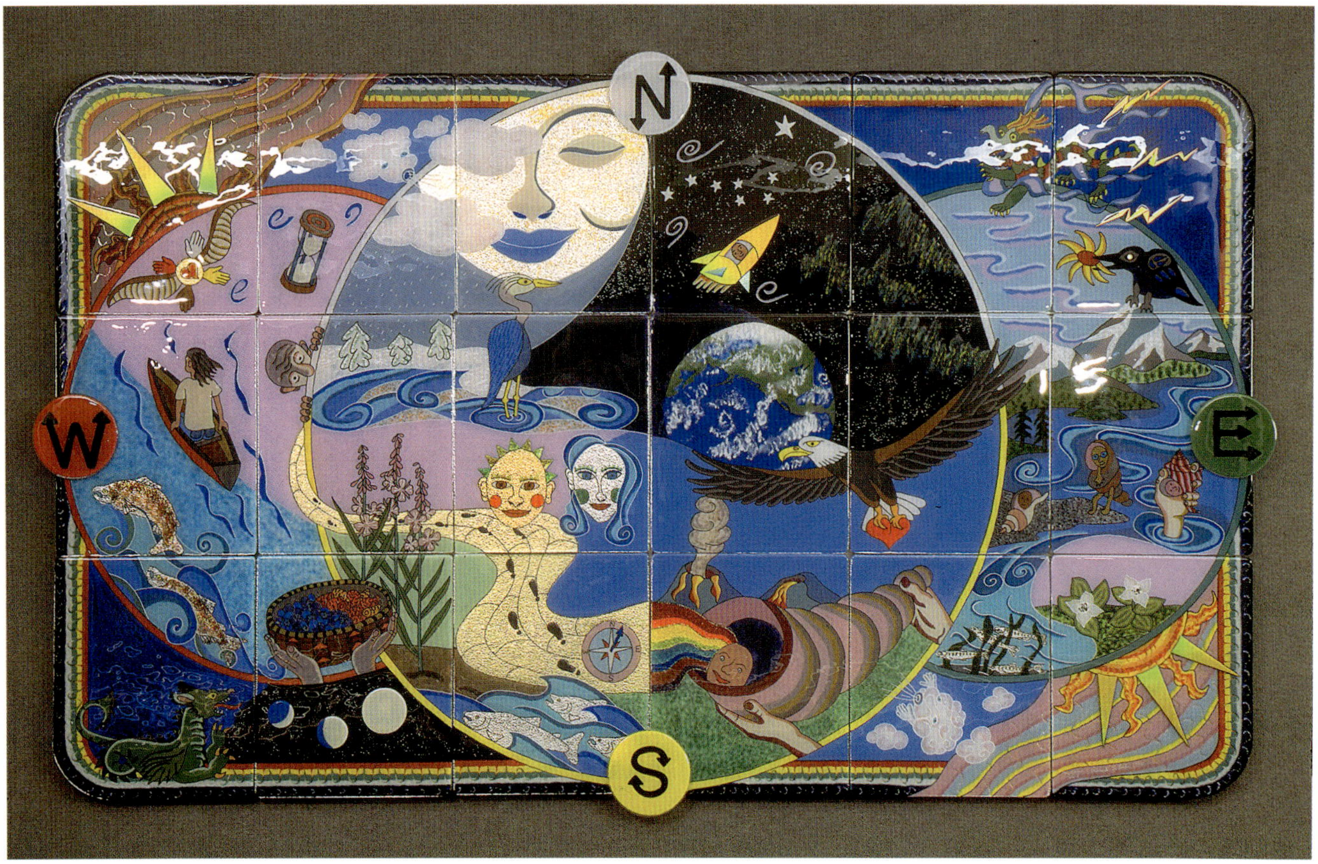

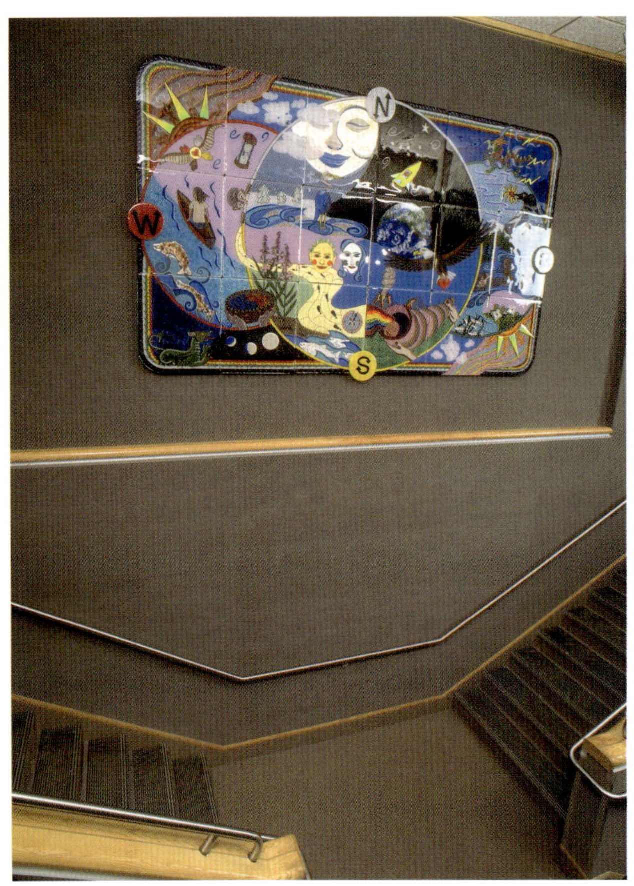

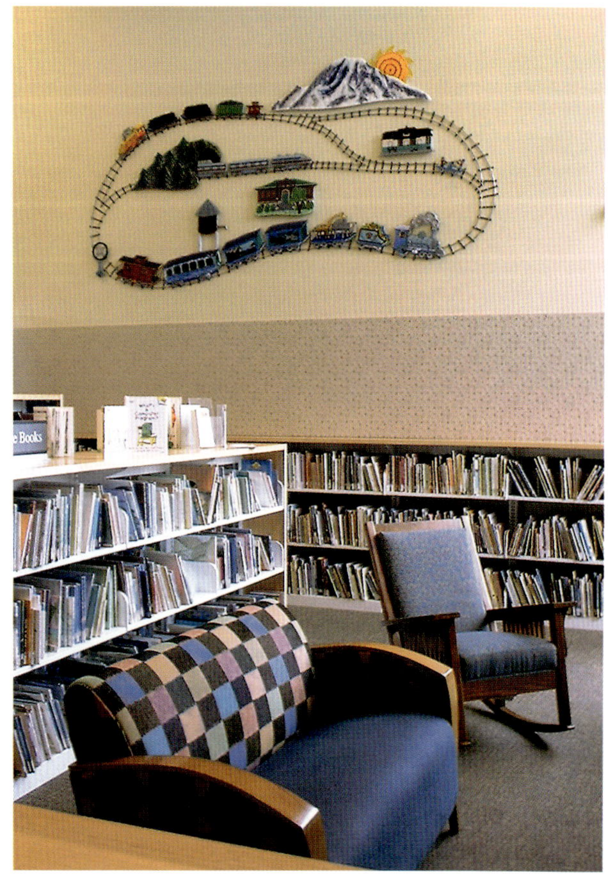

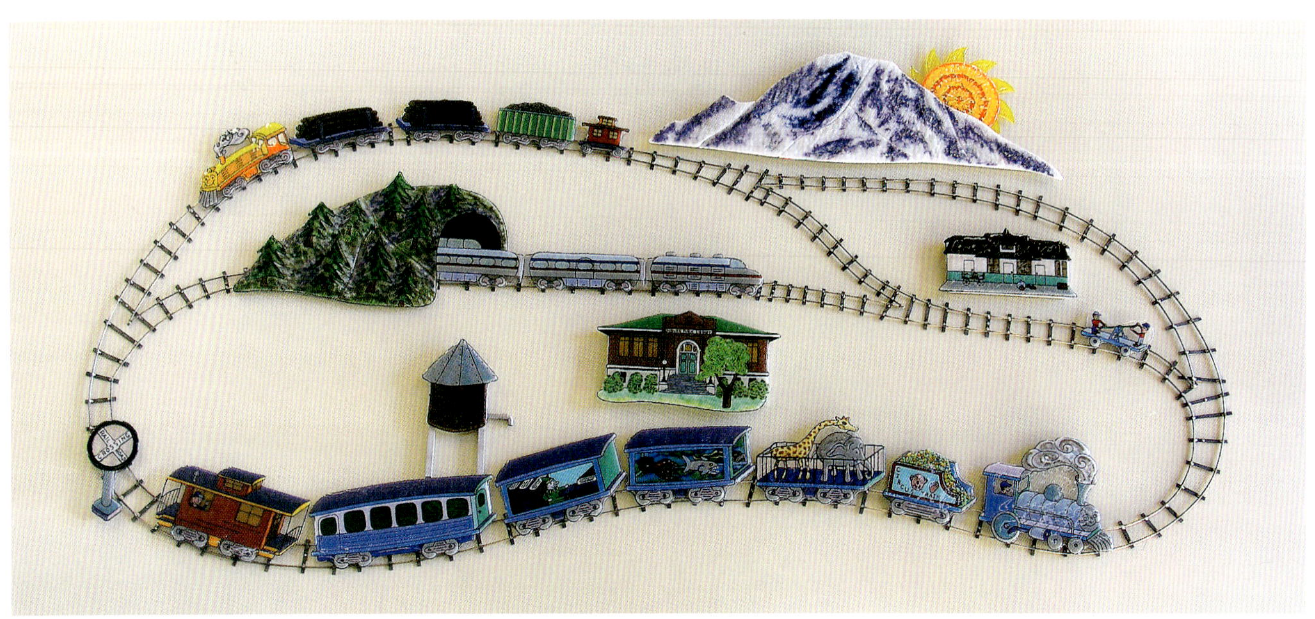

Public Art

facing upper: "Journey of Life," 1996, H. 72 in. (182 cm) x W. 120 in. (305 cm). Dzantiki Heeni Middle School, Juneau, AK. Alaska Percent for Arts Program.

facing lower left: "Journey of Life" installation.

facing lower right: "Circus Train" installation.

upper: "Circus Train," 2002, H. 70 in. (178 cm) x W. 140 in. (356 cm). Auburn Public Library - Children's Area, Auburn WA. Commissioned by the Friends of the Library, fused glass train on a stainless steel track.

lower: "Healing Hands and Caring Hearts," 2005, H. 39 in. (100 cm) x W. 70 in. (178 cm). Good Samaritan Hospital, Puyallup, WA. Private commission.

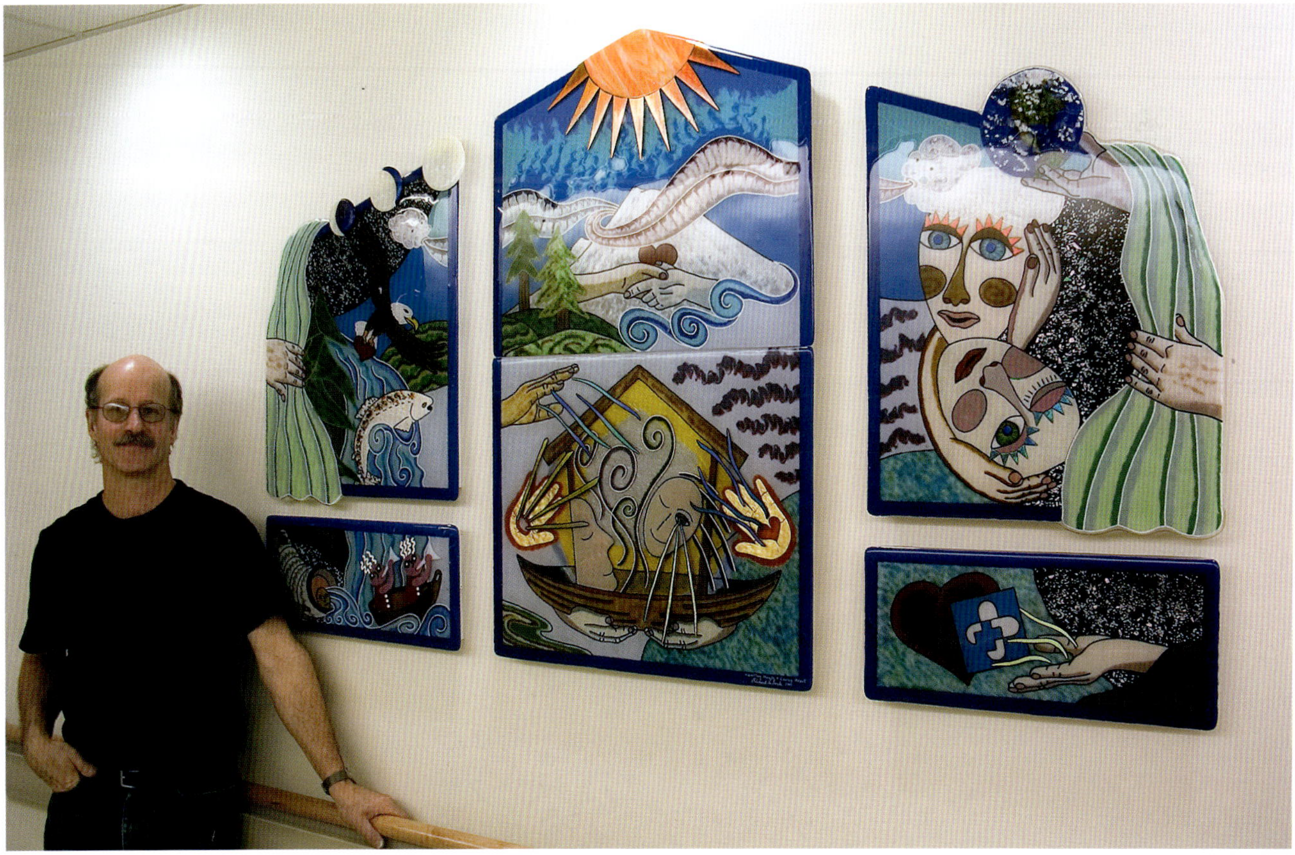

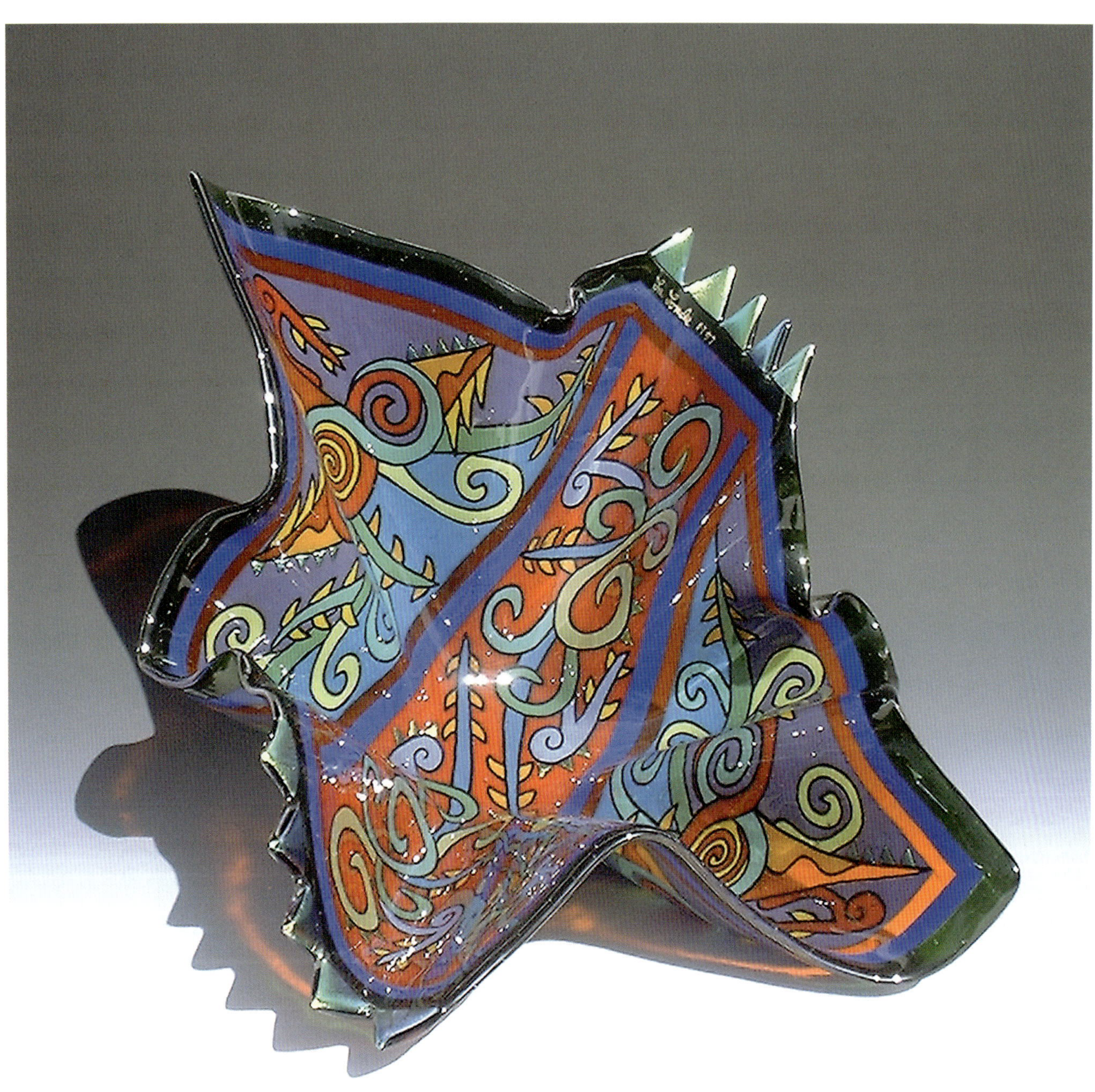

BOLERO II SERIES   1993 – 2001

Outlined designs were created with fine powdered glass in my " liquid glass" medium which
was applied with a squeeze bottle. These areas
were filled in with crushed glass and fired in my
electric kiln four times.

1993 73 pieces, 1994 25 pieces, 1995 16 pieces,
1996 14 pieces, 1997 26 pieces, 1998 18 pieces,
1999 10 pieces, 2001 1 piece   183 pieces total

above:
"Red Stripe," 1997, H. 16 in.
(41 cm) x W. 19 in. (48 cm) x D. 17 in. (43 cm).

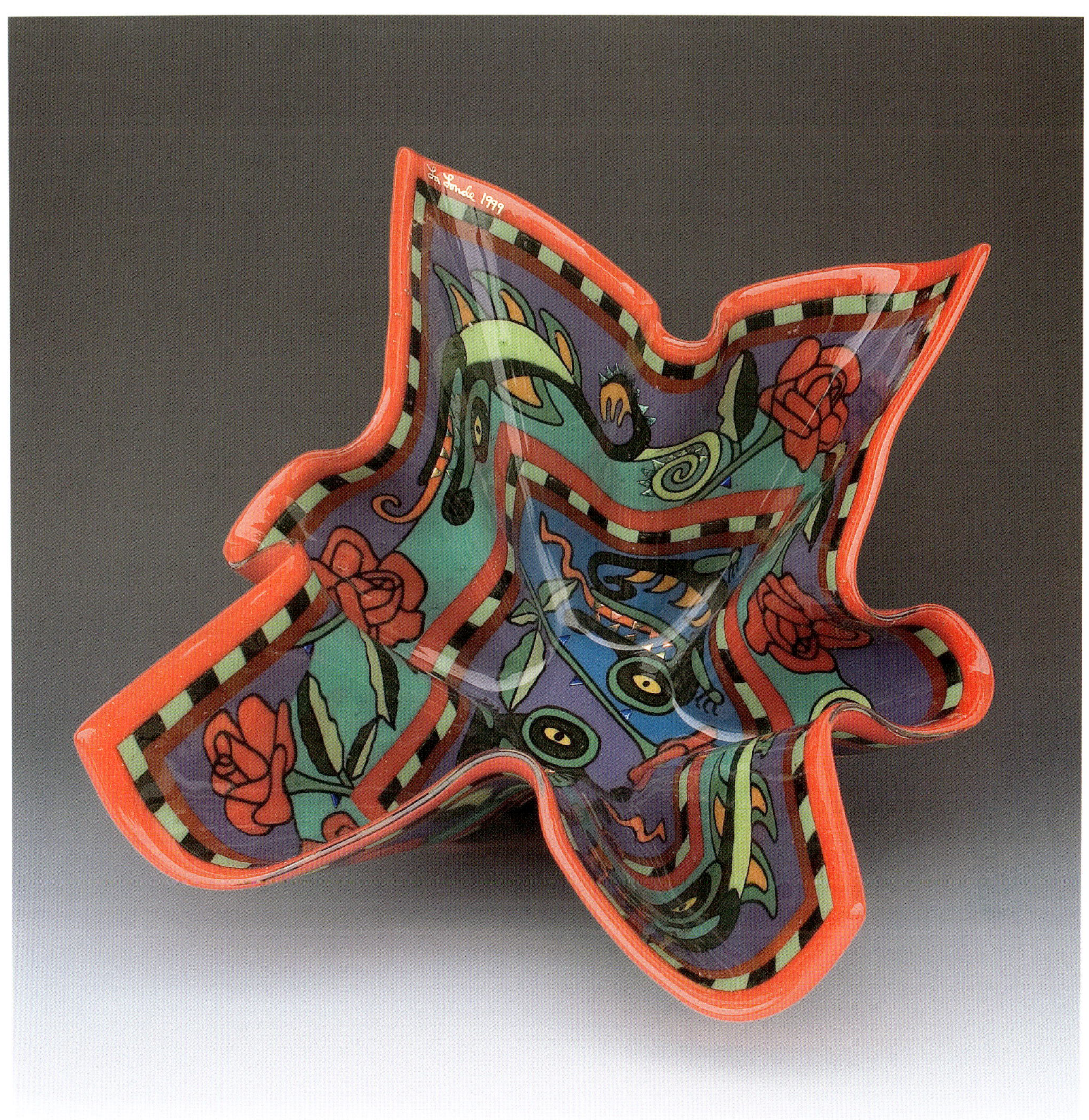

DRAGON SERIES   1998 – 1999

The most detailed Bolero-type vessels with
dragons, roses, and botanical motifs. They were
in the kiln four times.

20 pieces total

above: "Dragon & the Rose," 1999, H. 13 in.
(33 cm) x W. 19 in. (48 cm) x D. 17 in. (43 cm).

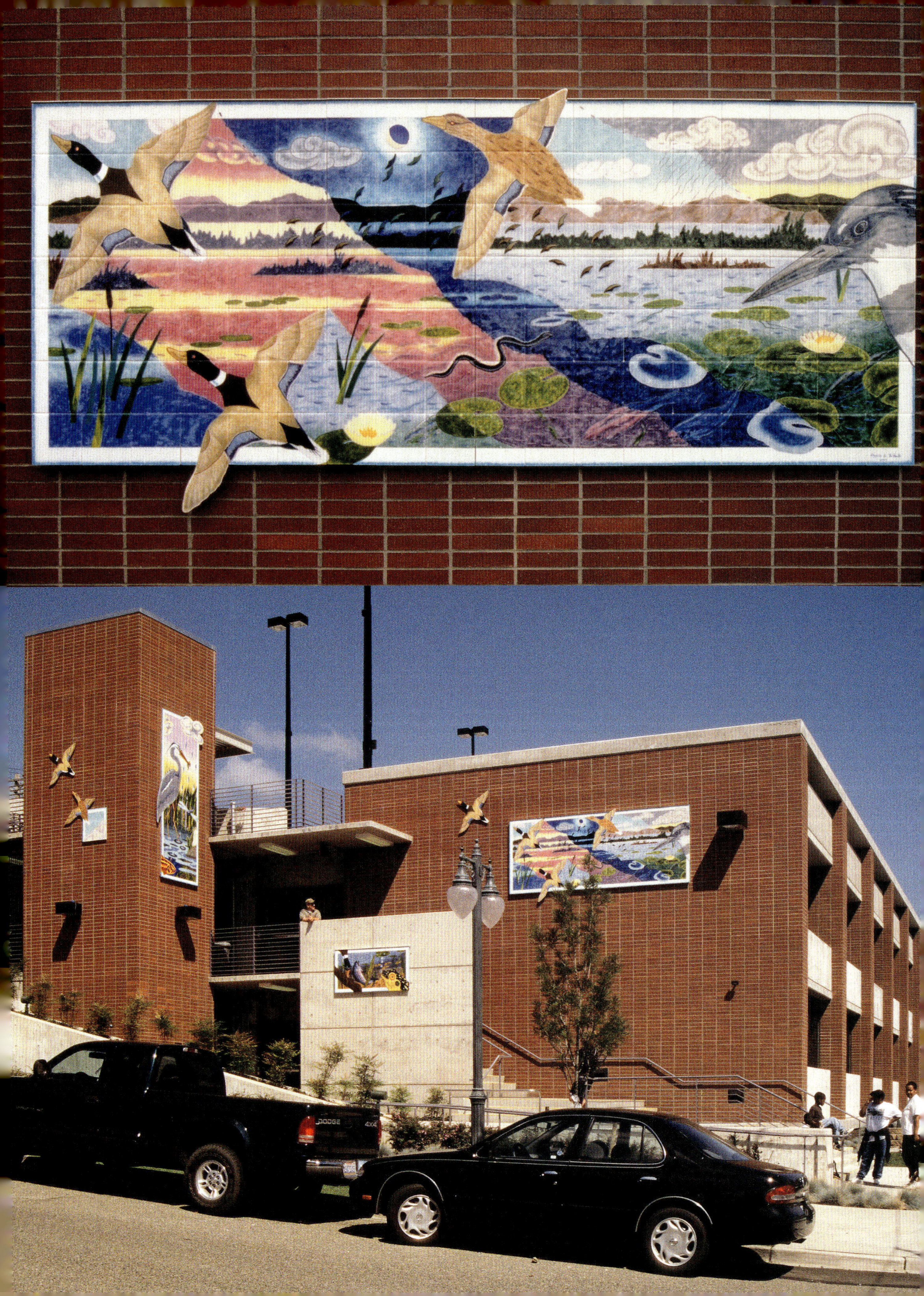

collaboration: 2000

My good friend Michael Dupille and I combined our techniques and created a series of exterior fused glass murals, "As Above, So Below," for the Pierce County Arts Commission at the County/City Court-house in Tacoma, Washington. We placed layers of crushed colored glass on ⅛ in. (3 mm) white sheet glass 8 in. (20 cm) square tiles and covered this with clear frit which was then fused in a kiln. These were adhered to marine aluminum with industrial silicone. The aluminum is screwed to a stainless steel frame that is bolted to the brick wall. The theme of local vanishing wetlands was chosen by the art committee.

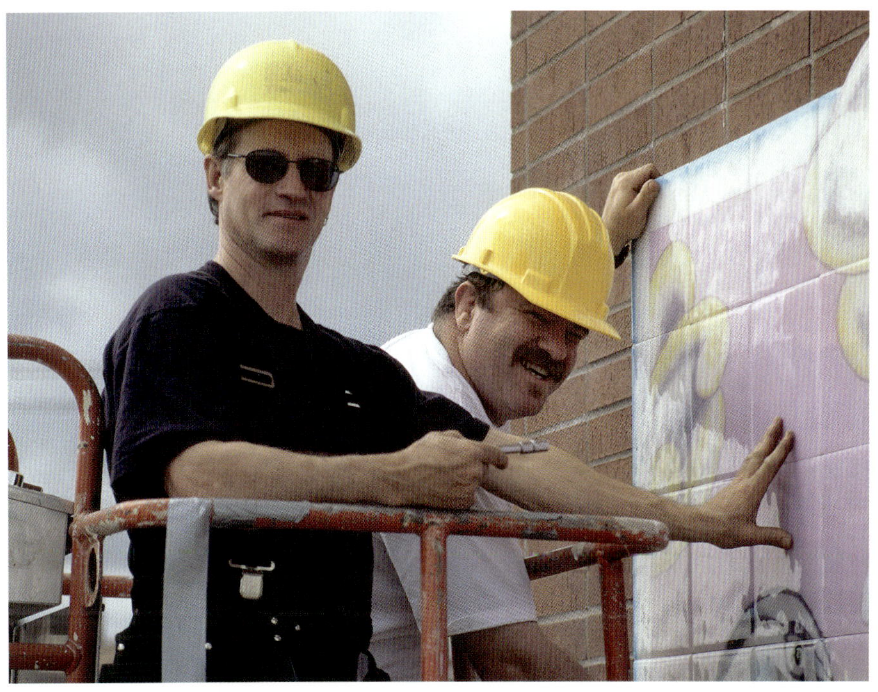

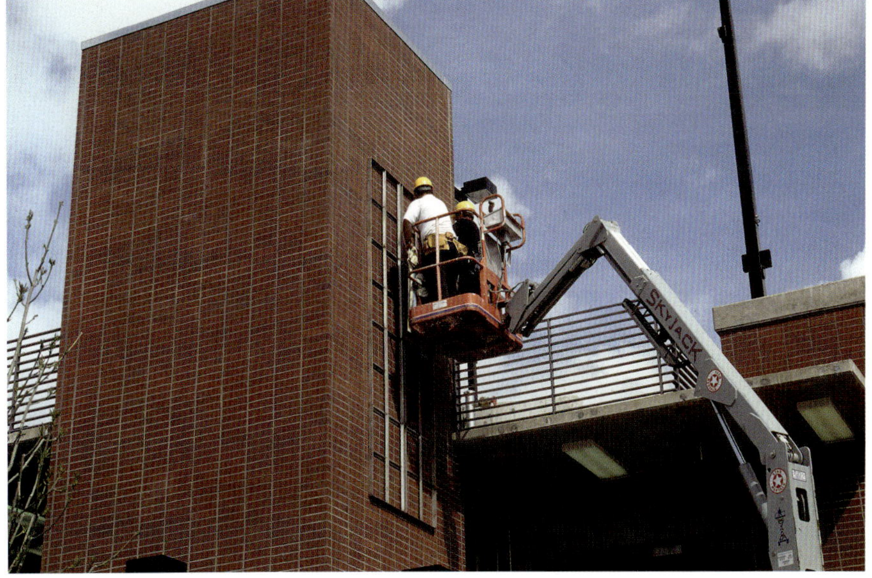

"As Above, So Below" artists collaboration of Michael Dupille and Richard La Londe during the year 2000. This piece is located on the south facing exterior wall of the County/City Courthouse Parking Annex, on 10th and Yakima in Tacoma, Washington, just a few blocks away from the Glass Museum. Our piece is an oasis of color amid grey and tan buildings, brick walls, and black pavement.

facing upper: "Ducks," H. 63 in. (160 cm) x W. 162 in. (412 cm).

facing lower: Shows the murals mounted on the building.

upper and lower: Richard La Londe (dark shirt) and Michael Dupille (white shirt), installing the Heron mural from a man-lift, 24 feet (7.3 meters) in the air.

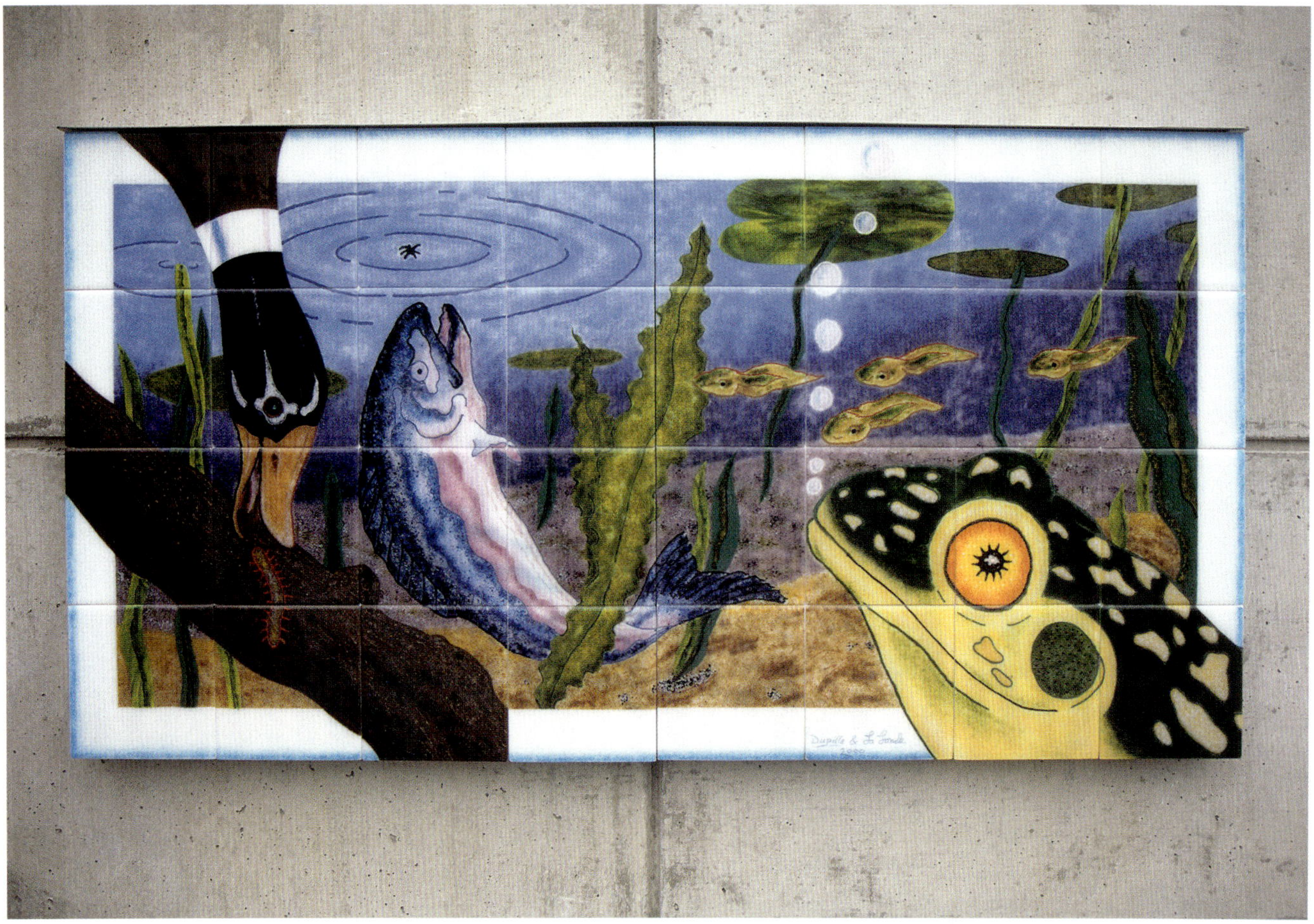

facing: "Heron," H. 144 in.
(366 cm) x W. 54 in. (137 cm).

upper: "Frogs," H. 36
(91 cm) x W. 72 in. (183 cm).

right: Duck mural on table
in studio.

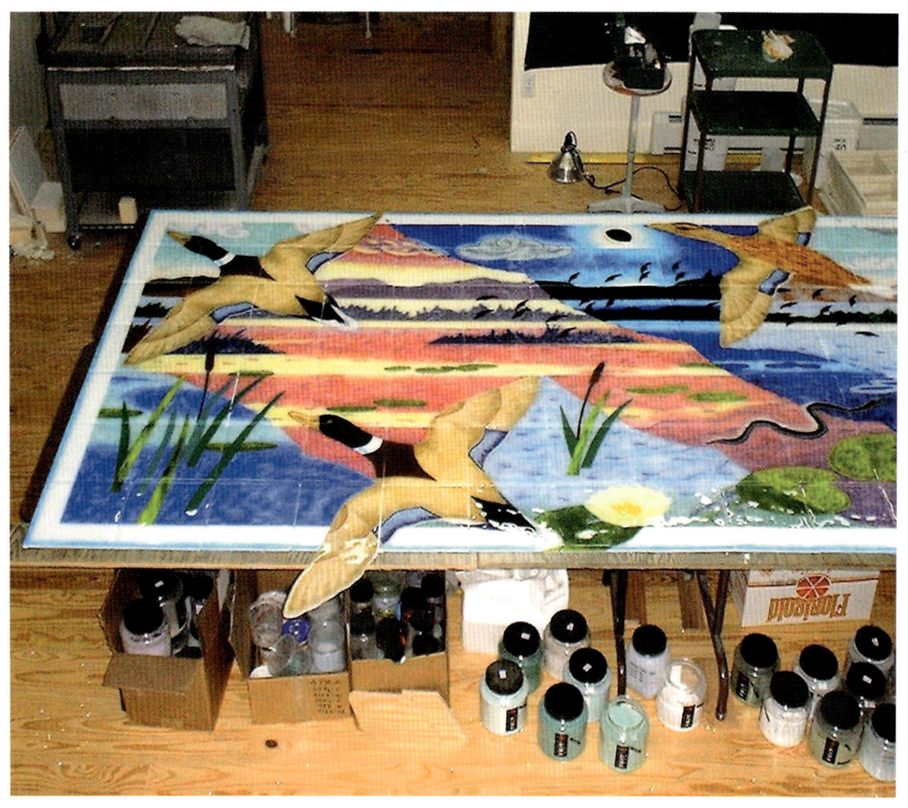

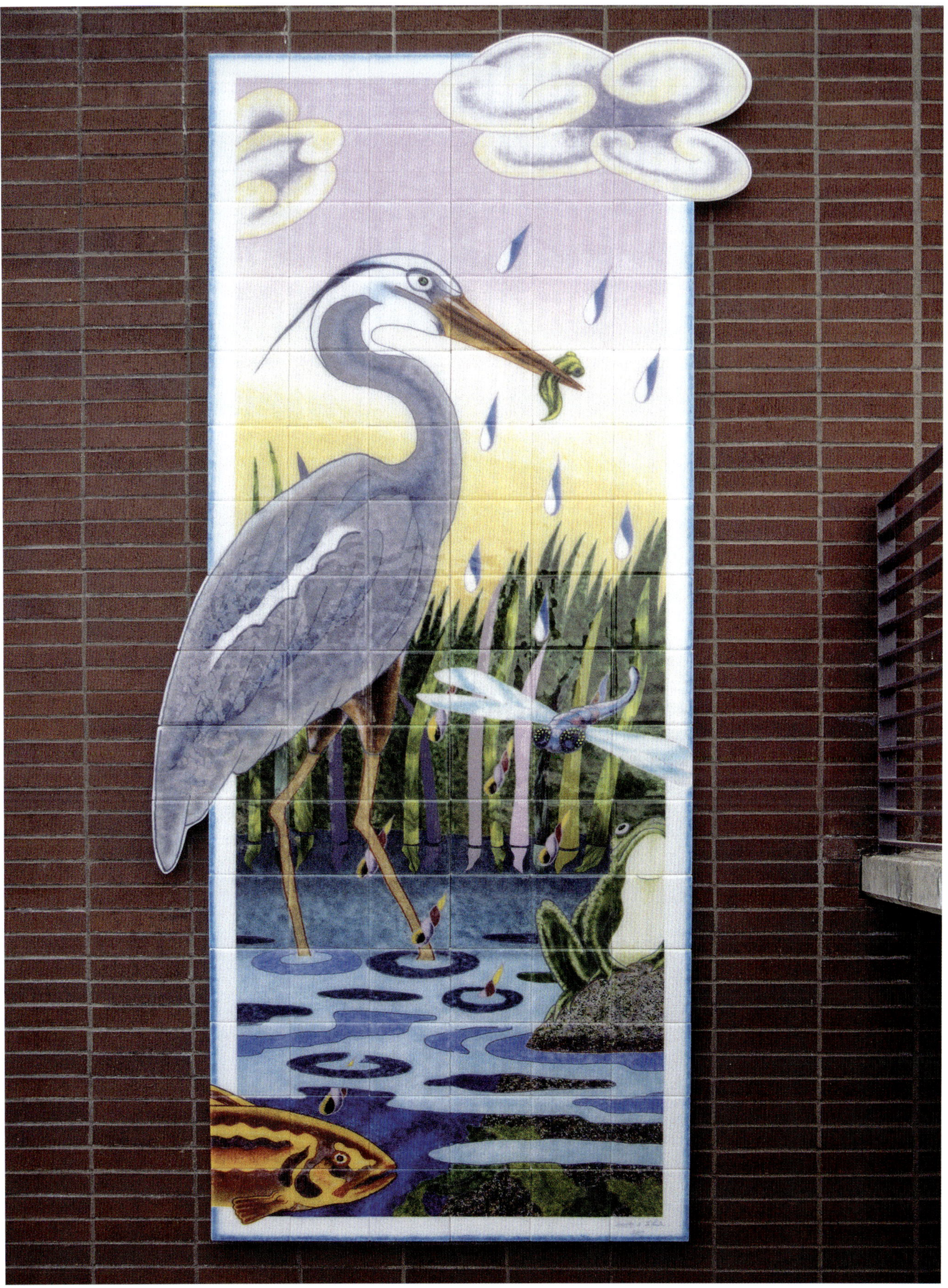

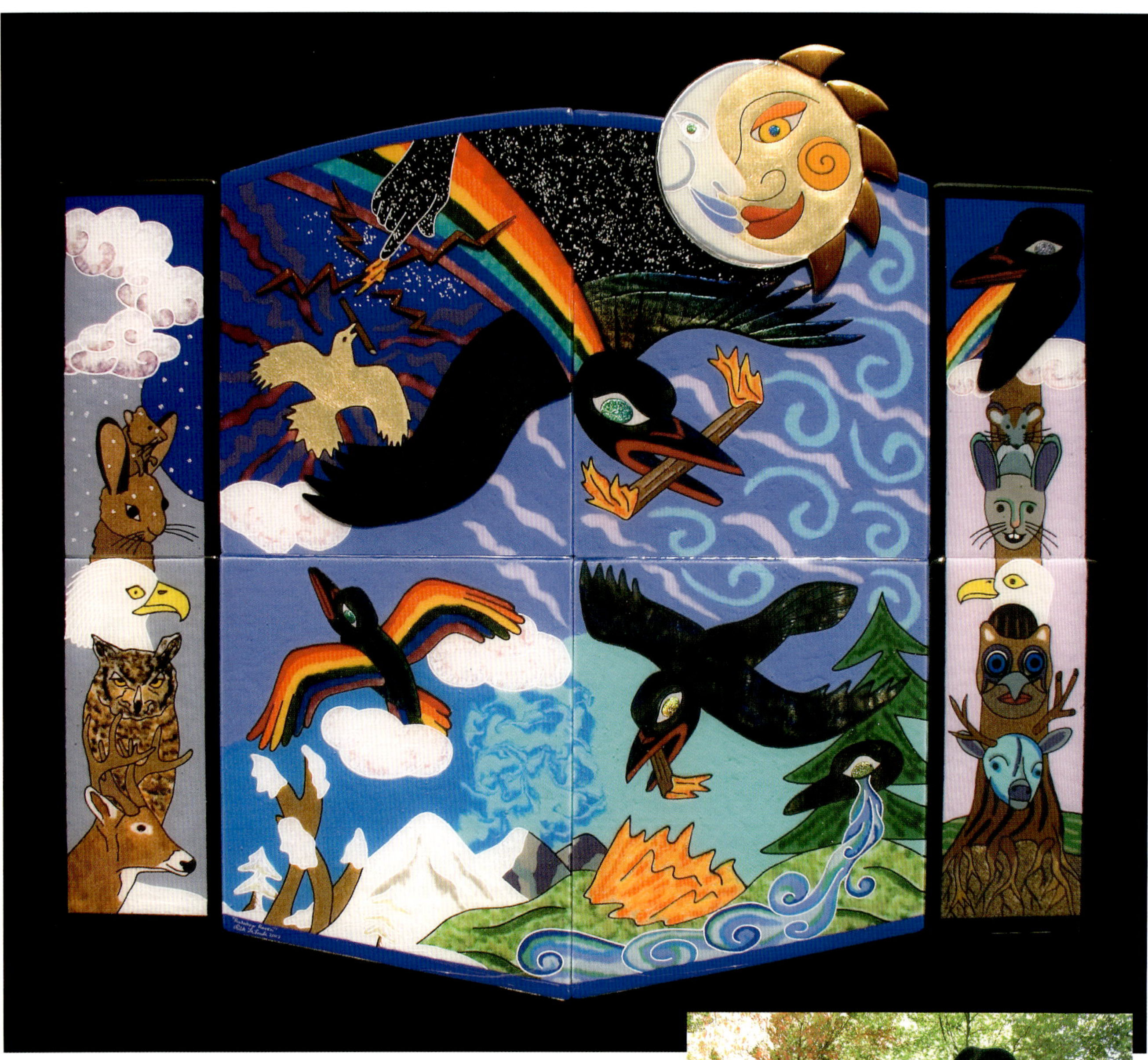

above:
"Rainbow Raven," 2003, H. 52 in.
(132 cm) x W. 57 in. (145 cm).
I interpreted into glass the story of Rainbow Raven
as retold by Grey Eagle.

below: Grey Eagle and Richard La Londe, Autumn 2004.
Grey Eagle (Ojibwa) has traveled worldwide telling stories
and taught Native American studies and journalism at the
University of Washington, 1973 — 1993.

Rainbow Raven (short version)   retold by Grey Eagle

Long, long ago, before the two-legged walked on Mother Earth, the animals had it very well. They were all part of the same family and lived in harmony in a world that was rich and luxuriant since the weather was always warm. But then the first snow came to that part of the world. No one knew for certain why Earth was covered with the blizzard. Some said that North Wind was showing how strong he was by blowing snow from the very top of the world. Others said it was to punish the animals who were no longer living in harmony with each other. The snow got so high that the smaller animals were sitting on the larger one's heads or clinging to their antlers.

Who should go for help? The animals were pleased that Rainbow Raven would be their messenger. His rainbow-colored feathers were brilliant even in the grey of the storm. He flew beyond where any bird had been before to the lodge of The Good Spirit. Rainbow Raven sang out a respectful greeting to her in his lovely voice. He told her about the animals being covered with snow. The Good Spirit placed fire on the end of a long stick and gave it to Rainbow Raven.

On the first day that Rainbow Raven flew down, sparks from the fire stick landed on his tail, turning it dark. On the second day, the fire burned fiercer and Rainbow Raven's feathers were covered with soot. On the third day, the fire burned brighter still and Rainbow Raven's feathers were singed jet black. On the fourth day, smoke and ash from the fire blew into Rainbow Raven's mouth turning his throat croaky and hoarse.

When Rainbow Raven got back to earth, everything was covered deep in snow, only the tips of the tallest trees could be seen. He flew about with the fire stick, melting the snow. The animals were grateful for being saved and wanted to honor Rainbow Raven, but he was nowhere to be seen. Where could beautiful Rainbow Raven be?

"Here I am," croaked Raven. But of course he was all black now, not with the striking colors of before. "Who are you?" the other animals asked. "We're looking for Rainbow Raven to return so he can tell us in his beautiful voice how he flew to the lodge of The Good Spirit and came back to melt the snow." "But that's me," the black bird said in his croaky voice. The other animals laughed, "We know what Rainbow Raven looks like and sounds like and that's certainly not you." Rainbow Raven tried to explain, "I carried back a fire stick to melt the snow and it blackened my feathers and cooked my voice," he said. "Take that story somewhere else," the animals said, "We're looking for the real hero,"

Poor Rainbow Raven had lost his beautiful feathers and his lovely singing voice. He flew off to a tall tree and sat on a limb and wept. The Good Spirit heard his weeping and came down to comfort him. She said the two-legged would never hunt Raven for his meat, which now tasted like smoke, or for his beautiful feathers, which were now black. They would never cage him to hear his lovely voice, which was now a raspy croak. For his bravery he would be honored and his image would be carved high on totem poles.

Raven felt much better. He flew back to where the other animals were. They could see the colors of the rainbow reflected on the shiny black feathers. They gathered in a circle and had a great celebration to honor Raven as the bravest and cleverest of all of the birds.

That's how it was, and that's how it is.

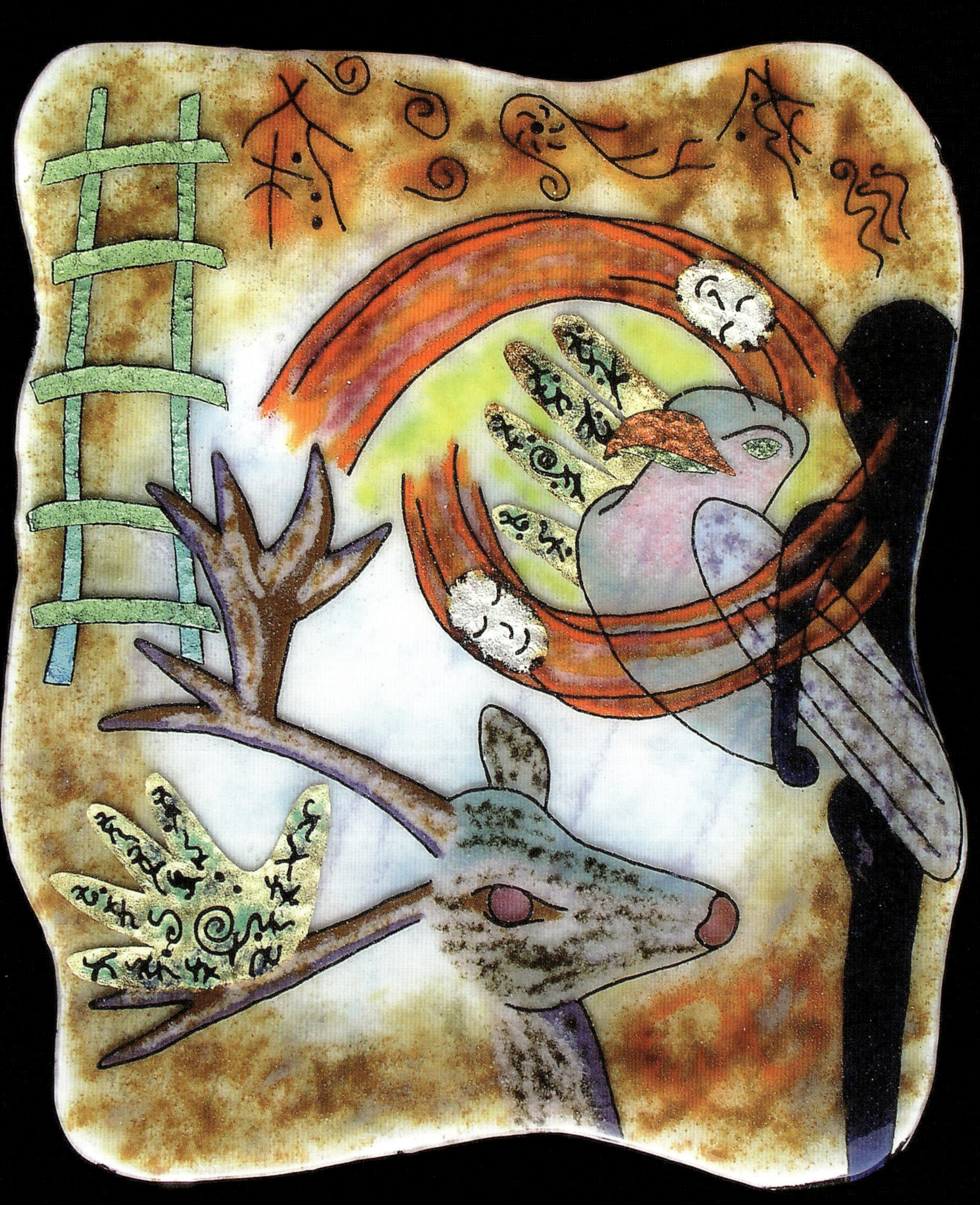

multilayers: 2004 - present

Building on the techniques from my collaboration with Michael Dupille, I developed a more spontaneous way of working.

This process is complicated and utilizes most of the techniques that I have devised over the past twenty-five years. You will find more information about these methods in the "Techniques" section.

First, I sprinkle a background design of crushed glass colors onto a kiln shelf that has been coated with shelf primer. Next, I put silver and gold foil under and on top of a clear sheet of glass, which I place on top of the crushed glass background. On this clear sheet, I outline some areas with "liquid glass" lines and then fill them with colored crushed glass. Finally, I sift on glass powders with stencils, add dichroic cut glass pieces, and cover the entire piece with coarse clear frit. I then place the shelf into my electric kiln and fuse the glass.

This is the most spontaneous yet controlled way of working with frit that I have devised so far.

facing:
"Spirit Animal Dream," H. 19 in. (48 cm) x W. 17 in. (43 cm), 2004.

lower:
"Spirit Dream," H. 23 in. (58 cm) x W. 39 in. (100 cm), 2004.

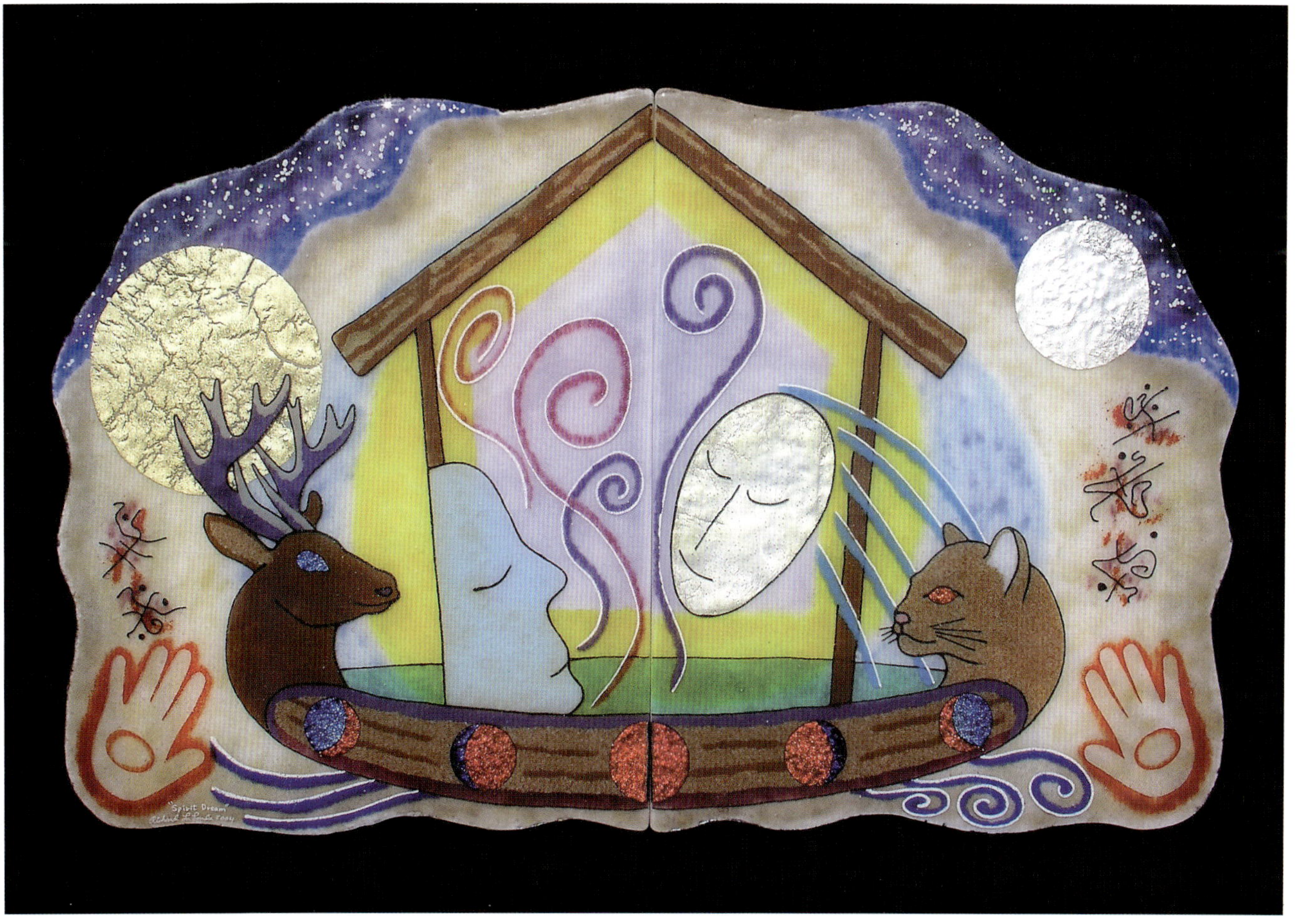

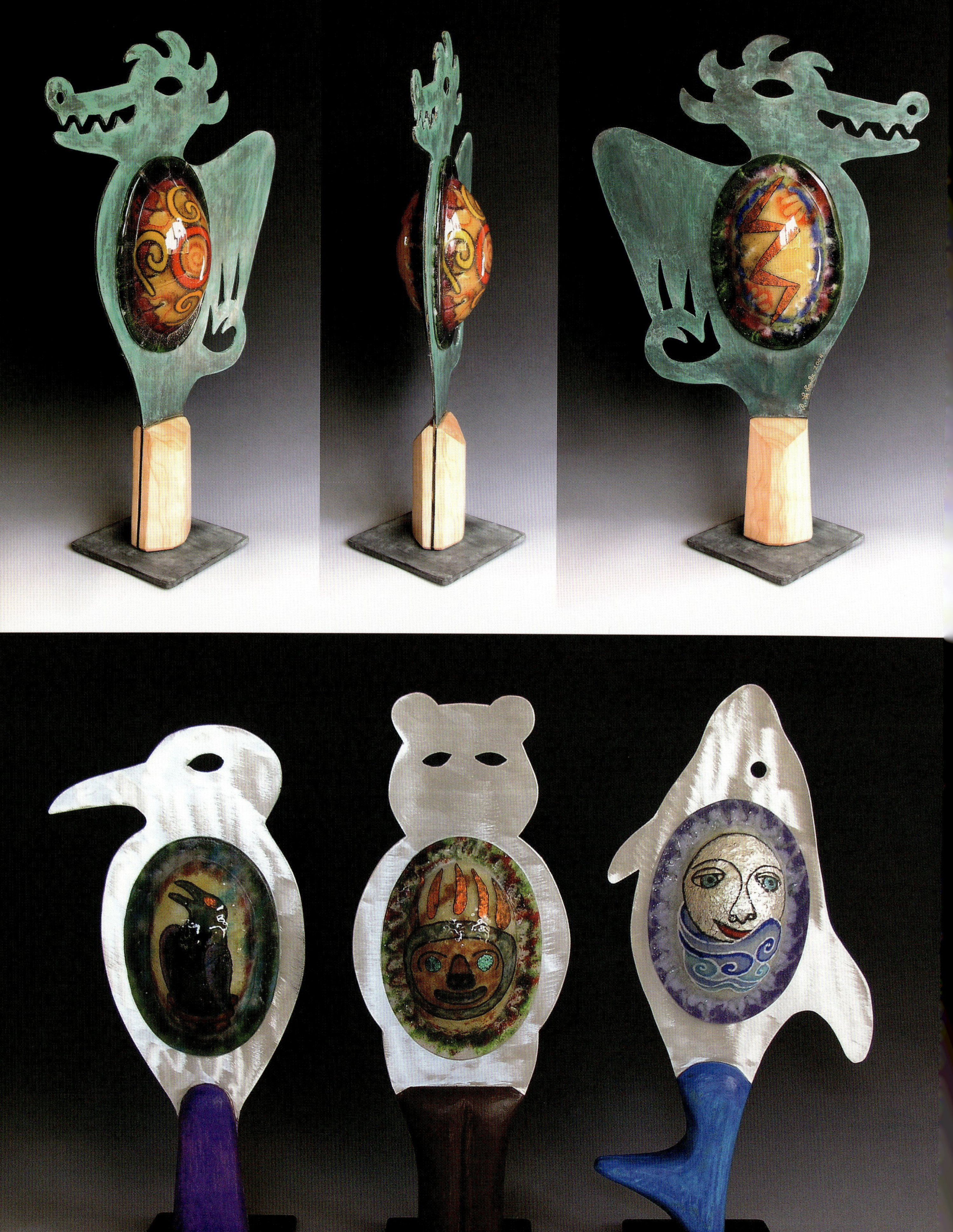

Both living in the Pacific Northwest temperate rainforest and commercial fishing in the fjords of Southeast Alaska exposed me to the rich cultural storytelling of native people. Those stories inspired me to create Rattle Shakers as a sculptural way to display fused glass and, at the same time, tie together my love of artifacts and mythology.

The idea for the rattles first came to me one day in 2003 with the notion of gluing two glass hemispheres onto a ⅛ in. (3 mm) piece of metal. I ran a test to see if my idea would work. First, I fused two glass ovals using my multilayer technique of frit on the shelf covered with a sheet of clear glass; I added more colored frit and then a final covering with clear frit. I sagged these through an oval dropout mold that I made.

Using an electric sabre saw, I cut a piece of ⅛ in. aluminum into the rattle form, including a cutout hole for the inside of the rattle. To make the handle, I took two ¾ in. (2 cm) thick pine boards from a Bullseye packing crate and glued them to the aluminum. I colored the handle with pastel chalk and sealed it with clear plastic spray sealer. After that, I siliconed the two-dimensional glass pieces – enclosing metal BB's to make a rattle sound – onto the aluminum handle, over the center hole.

The rattle shaker sits on a 4 in. (10 cm) long by ⅛ in. diameter (3 mm) steel rod that sticks straight out from the heavy metal base (see the section about mounting systems). You can rotate the rattle on its base or take it off for shaking.

In 2004 I made a series of rattles for an exhibition at the Glass Gallery in Bethesda, Maryland. This show included my "Golden Bear Rattle Shaker" that was 36 in. (91 cm) tall (pictured in the section about precious metal foil). I colored the bronze with various patinas.

I teach a Rattle Making Workshop in which participants make an aluminum rattle form, fuse and sag glass rattle pieces, add a handle, and make a base. They personalize their rattles by attaching lampworked and fused beads, feathers, and other special items.

facing upper:
"Dragon Rattle Shaker," 2004, H. 20 in. (51 cm) x W. 13 in. (33 cm) x D. 3 in. (8 cm). Bronze, fused and sagged glass with a curly maple handle.

facing lower:
"Rattle Shaker Group," 2003 – raven, bear, orca, (left to right). Orca H. 19 in. (48 cm) x W. 9 in. (23 cm) x D. 3 in. (8 cm). Aluminum, fused and sagged glass, colored pine wood handles.

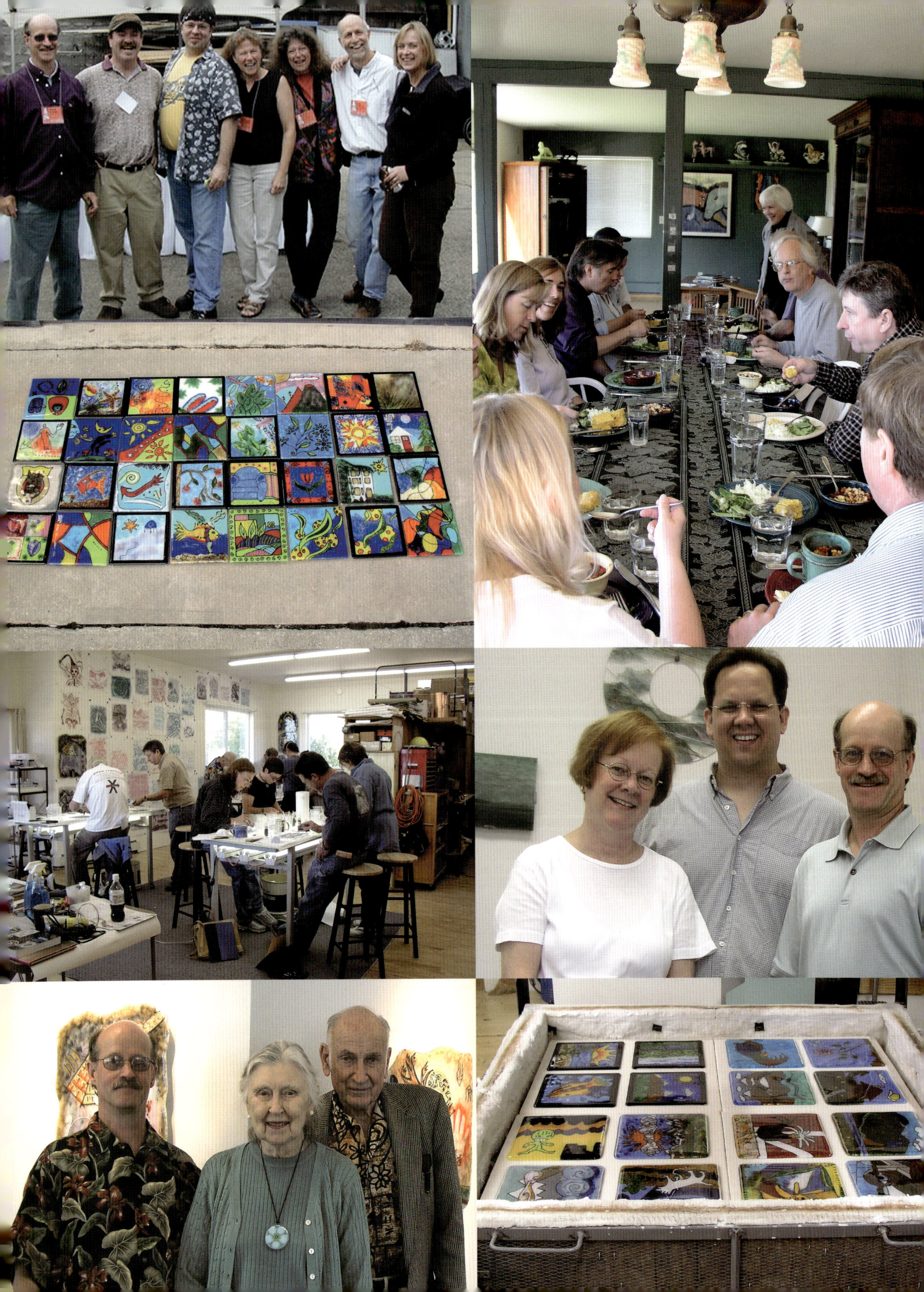

Part 3: Fusing Concepts
THE BIG THREE

Compatibility
Volume Control
Annealing

When I began teaching for Bullseye Glass Company in 1983, to become a successful fuser one had to know the basics, what I called The Big Three: Compatibility, Annealing, and Volume Control. As this book goes to print, I find that many glass fusers don't really know the basics.

- Today, by fusing "tested compatible" glass, one can bypass incompatibility and testing.
  Is ignorance bliss?

- Today, many people believe that huge bubbles in their work are caused by water in the kiln shelf and not volume control.
  What does turning down the radio have to do with fusing?

- Today, by programming a kiln controller from a chart in a book, one can fuse without understanding annealing.
  Can what you don't know hurt you?

In 1981, learning skills and trying to figure out this new stuff called glass fusing breathed life into my work. Those early days were really about the mechanics of fusing, rather than the art.

I learned that once I understood how fusing worked, I could develop new ideas. I turned mistakes into techniques. This hasn't changed.

First, to be a successful glass fuser, learn the basic skills! Understand THE BIG THREE: Compatibility, Volume Control, and Annealing!

Second, work backwards!
Once you know the concept behind what you want to express, then:
(1) figure out how you want to display or hang your piece, if you do.
(2) consider how or if you want to bend or shape the piece.
(3) plan how to build and fuse the flat blank that you will work with.

The challenge of combining quality technique with personal art is part of becoming a Master; the beauty is that you are always on that path without ever totally knowing where it will lead.

upper left:
"Old Time Fusers" at the GAS Conference, Seattle, WA. 2003
left to right,
Richard La Londe, Michael Dupille, Gil Reynolds, Leslie Rowe Israelson, Melanie Rowe, Roger Nachman, Patty Gray.

upper right:
lunch at Richard La Londe's 2004 Spring Fusing Workshop at his home and studio.

upper middle left:
workshop projects at Vitrum Studio, 2004.

lower middle left:
Spring Workshop participants at Richard La Londe's studio, 2004.

middle right:
Judith Conway, Kevin O'Toole, and Richard La Londe at his workshop at Vitrum Studio, 2005.

lower left:
Richard La Londe at his exhibition with Sally and Ned Hansen at the Glass Gallery in Bethesda, MD. 2004.

lower right:
projects in Richard La Londe's big kiln at his Spring Workshop, 2005.

Compatibility

The bigger your piece, the more affect compatibility has. You might successfully fuse a tiny earring, but compatibility is more critical in a huge wall panel. Multiple firings can also alter the compatibility. If I have a problem or I suspect a color shift or reaction color change, I fuse a quick test.

Most materials expand when heated and shrink when cooled. When different glasses are heated in a kiln and fused together, they need to cool – to shrink and contract – at the same rate, or incompatibility stress will build up during cooling, and the glass will crack.

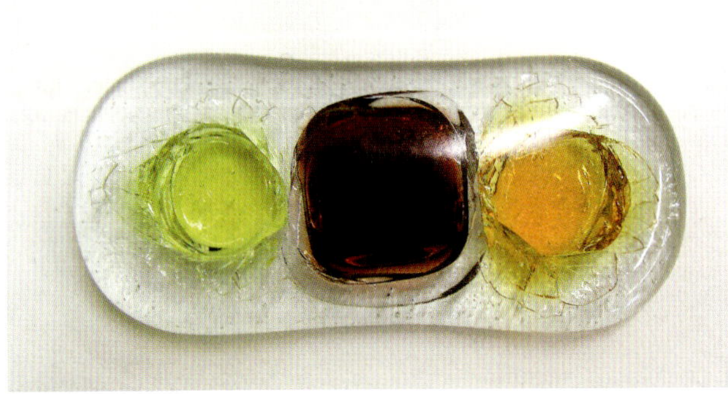

above: Breakage caused by incompatible glass.

The clear has a higher expansion rate than the yellow samples on either end; as it cooled, the clear shrunk more than the yellow, shattering the clear.

The clear has a lower expansion rate than the red sample in the center; as it cooled, the red shrunk more than the clear and pulled away, causing a break in the clear all the way around the red.

Today, most people, including me, just buy fusible glass and don't test for incompatibility; however, I know how to do it and occasionally when something doesn't work or I need to know about the properties of the glass, I use a "polariscope" to test my glass. This is also a good method for glass blowers to check compatibility or to set up a palette from a glass company like the German glass GNA that is not listed as compatible.

When in doubt, test it out!
Use a "polariscope" and the "Stressometer Test," originally described in <u>Glass Fusing Book One</u> by Lundstrom and Schwoerer, Vitreous Publications, 1983.

This test will show you:
(1) **Compatibility**
(2) **Color Change** -some glass changes color after firing.
(3) **Devitrification** - the surface of some glass looks scummy from surface crystal growth.
(4) **Relative viscosity** of the glass, hard vs. soft, or which melts sooner.

This is how I do the "Chip Test" to set up a compatible pallet of glass.

Cut a 2 in. (5 cm) x 18 in. (46 cm) strip of clear glass. This is the base glass to test against.

Cut a triangle off one corner and place it on the clear strip. This is to indicate whether the strip has been properly annealed.

Cut pieces about ½ in. (12 mm) x ½ in. (12 mm) from the glass to be tested and place them on the clear strip with 1 in. (2.5 cm) between the chips.

Label the chips with a felt tipped paint marker which will fire onto the glass.

Fire this strip in a kiln to a full fuse flat and then anneal.

Place this fused strip between two pieces of a polarizing film. You can buy a "Stressometer" or make a "polariscope" by purchasing a sheet of polarizing film from Edmund Scientific and cutting it in two pieces.

Take a light source, place one piece of polarizing film over it, and place the fused glass test strip on top of that.

View the fused glass test strip through a second piece of polarizing film. Rotate the upper film until it is at its darkest position.

Check to see that no annealing stress shows on the cut corner fused on itself. If there is stress, it will show up as a halo of light, and affect your compatibility test, giving you a false reading.

Next check for incompatibility which will show up as a halo of light on the corners of the chips. No halo, no stress. I fuse glass that shows no

halo or just a slight hint of light – see the chip test photo below; more than that can produce problems in large fused pieces. You can get away with more incompatibility, more halo, in a very small piece of jewelry.

The idea is that if chip A of the glass being tested is compatible to the clear base, and chip B is also compatible to the base clear, then chip A should be compatible to chip B. The beauty of this test is that "Stressometer Test" replicates glass fusing. Additional tests can indicate if the glass has a higher or lower expansion rate than the base clear, but I don't find such tests necessary for the fusing that I do. If you do another compatibility test, place a piece of the original base clear on it, to see if the new base that you are testing remains the same. Label your glass fusible and put it in a separate rack. away from all other glass in your studio. Besides compatibility this test shows color change, devitrification, and relative viscosity.

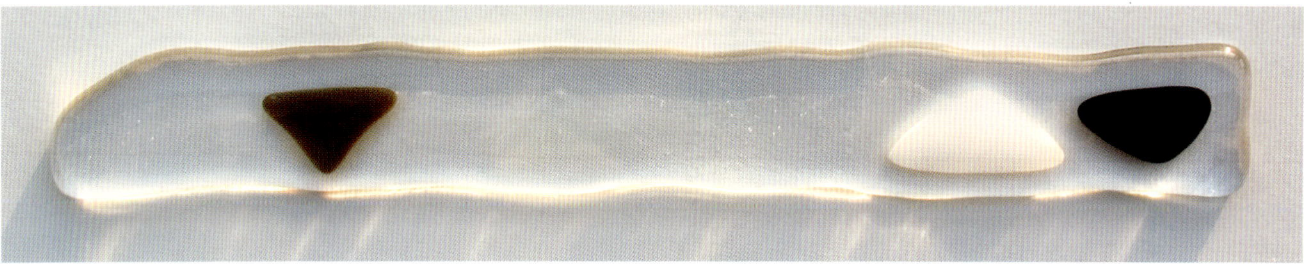

Chips above are viewed under natural light, full fused onto a strip of a base of Bullseye 1101 clear glass.

1   **2**   **3**   **4**   **5**   **6**

Chips above are viewed through crossed polarizing filters; stress shows as halos.

1 The corner or the base clear is cut off and fused onto itself to check for annealing stress.
2 Mystery glass shows way too much halo - not compatible to the base.
3 Window glass shows some devitrification and is not fully fused - not compatible to the base.
4 Spectrum Clear also shows too much halo - not compatible to the base glass.
5 Mystery White, no halo - compatible to the base.
6 Bullseye black 0100, no halo - compatible to base.
#5 & #6 are fusible to each other and also to the base clear, giving me three glasses to probably successfully fuse, indicated by this test.

Volume Control

The most important and least understood of "The Big Three" is how to make the glass do what you want it to do! This has to do with the different thicknesses that you work with – in other words, controlling the volume of glass. As you will see, most of my technical developments and breakthroughs involved Volume Control.

Various glasses have different viscosities, so they act differently as they are heated; for example, window glass needs a higher temperature than Bullseye to full fuse. You'll also find fusing temperature differences within the Bullseye palette. Another factor is that dark opaque glass absorbs heat faster than a transparent light-colored glass.

Time and Temperature
Glass has a chance to absorb more heat in a soft brick kiln, which tends to fire slower than a fiber kiln; firing schedules will reflect this difference. Consequently, full fuse in a brick kiln will occur at a lower temperature than in a faster fiber kiln.

My fiber kiln, with a 21 in. (53 cm) x 21 in. (53 cm) x ⅝ in. (16 cm) thick shelf and a piece of 20 in. (51 cm) x 20 in. (51 cm) x ¼ in. (6 mm) glass, goes from 1100 – 1550°F (595 – 845°C) full fuse in fifteen minutes. The same glass and shelf in a Paragon brick GL24 full fuses at 1500°F (815°C) and might take thirty-five minutes or more to get there. You need to know, for the kiln that you use, at what temperatures your glass does what it does. Variables are many.

What Glass Does

Temperatures will vary with:
(1) different types of glass
(2) different kilns
(3) soak times
(4) transparent vs. opaque glass
(5) where you place the thermocouple that measures the temperature in the kiln.

These temperatures are based on my experience with Bullseye Glass.

1200° – 1300°F   (650° – 705°C)
Begins to slump.
Glass starts to move slowly, bending under its own weight.

1300° – 1350°F   (705° – 730°C)
Slumps and begins to tack fuse.
Sharp edges may round slightly.

1350° – 1450°F   (730° – 790°C)
Fuses to stick and semi-fuse.
Devitrification Range
A ⅛ in. (3 mm) thick piece of glass begins to pull up. The glass is moving and the viscosity is decreasing. The surface tension is greater than the pull of gravity. Trapped air between the shelf and glass may create large bubbles.

1450° – 1500°F   (790° – 815°C)
Semi fuse to full fuse.
The glass is less viscous, movement increases and as the pull of gravity overtakes the surface tension, the glass begins to flatten. Bubbles between the shelf and glass pop and make holes.

1500° – 1550°F   (815° – 845°C)
Full fuse flat.
When full fused, the surface tension and gravity reaches an equilibrium at the magic thickness of just a little over ¼ in. (6 mm).

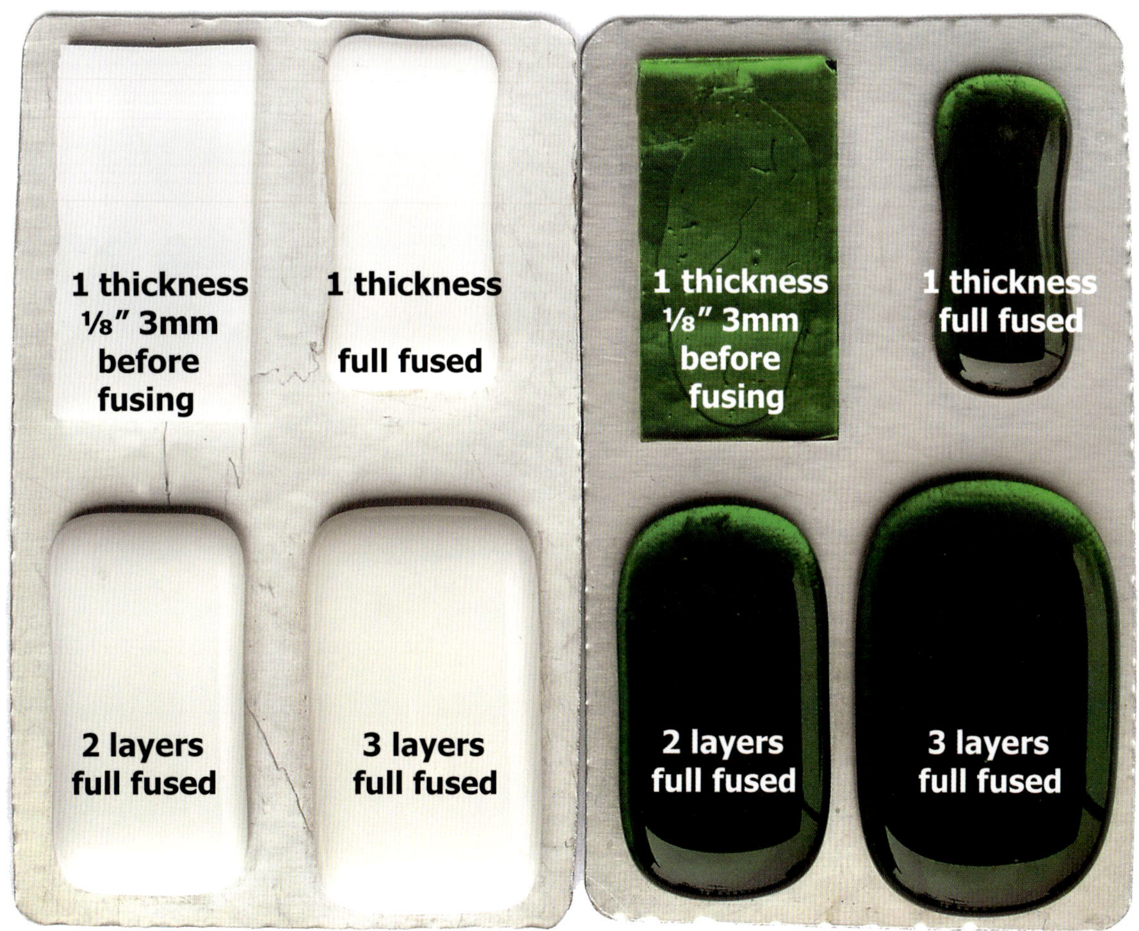

Bullseye white opal 0113   **Bullseye green transparent 1107**

The above glass samples are from my 1983 teaching kit and show the effect of volume control. The white and green samples were fired in the same kiln, right next to each other at the same time. You will see the original size in the upper left hand corner for both the white and green glass.

Observe the effect of surface tension and gravity.

One thickness tries to pull up to the magic ¼ in. (6 mm)-plus thickness and, in the process, rounds the corners and thins the middle. The surface tension is greater than the pull of gravity and consequently pulls on glass.

Two layers stacked one on top of the other full fuse to almost the same size as the original piece except the corners are rounded. Surface tension and gravity are equal.

Three layers stacked on top of each other full fuse to a larger size than the original piece, trying to achieve that ¼ in. (6 mm)-plus thickness. Gravity is greater than surface tension, and the glass flows until tension and gravity are equal.

Note that the green transparent is more rounded and that it moved more than the white; the green glass is less viscous than the white.

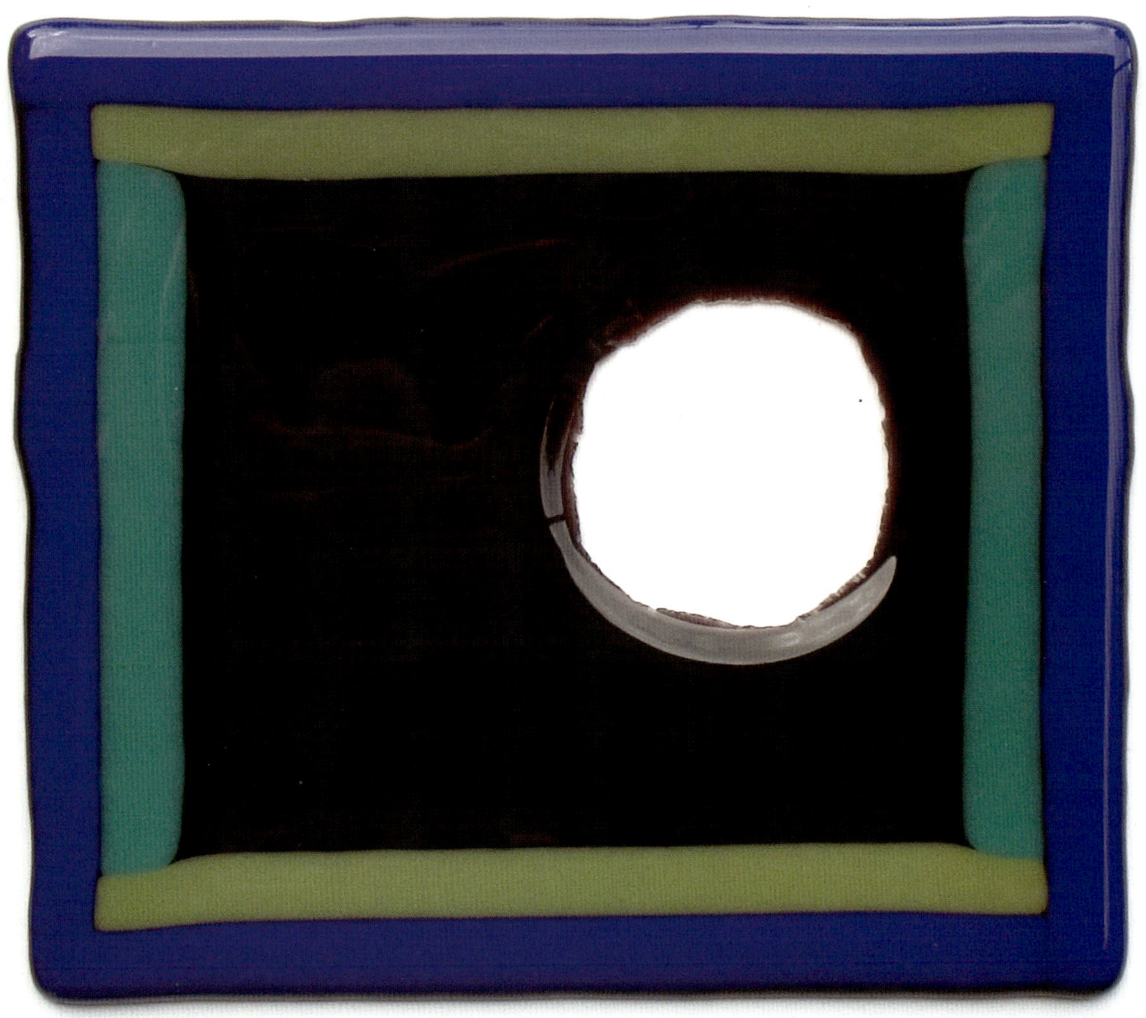

Big bubbles are not caused by wet kiln shelves!

When I was first trying to figure out what fused glass could do, huge bubbles, some as big as 3" (7.5 cm), appeared when the glass reached full fuse temperature. Getting angry didn't eliminate bubbles, so I turned the mistake into a technique: I opened the kiln and popped the bubbles with a pointed metal rod; the glass pulled back, and the edges of the hole became round.

I backed the holes with surplus titanium that I purchased at Boeing Surplus (the airplane manufacturer in Seattle). I colored the titanium by heating it with a torch. This became a series of glass art.

At the time, I thought that wet kiln shelves were the bubble-creating culprits. I prefered the kiln shelves, but bubbles continued to form. Finally,

I eliminated the bubbles by firing on ⅛ in. fiber paper.

Eventually, I reasoned that the bubbles formed because air, trapped between the shelf (covered with shelf primer) and the glass, expanded as the heat increased; the air couldn't escape because, as the temperature rises in the kiln, the glass becomes soft, sealing against the primered kiln shelf. As the temperature continues to rise, the thin layer of trapped air begins to expand and to move toward the area where surface tension has begun to pull and thin the glass. The expanding air forms a bubble. Fiber paper allowed the air to escape. Later, I firgured out how to use chips of glass under one edge instead of fiber paper, see page 65.

facing: big hole from a popped bubble.

right: "Shift Right," 1981, H. 21 in. (53 cm) x W. 19 in. (48 cm). Fused multiple layers of Bullseye glass with glass threads pulled in a small glory hole and backed with torch treated titanium surrounded by a gold anodized aluminum frame. I created a series of 10 of these panels.

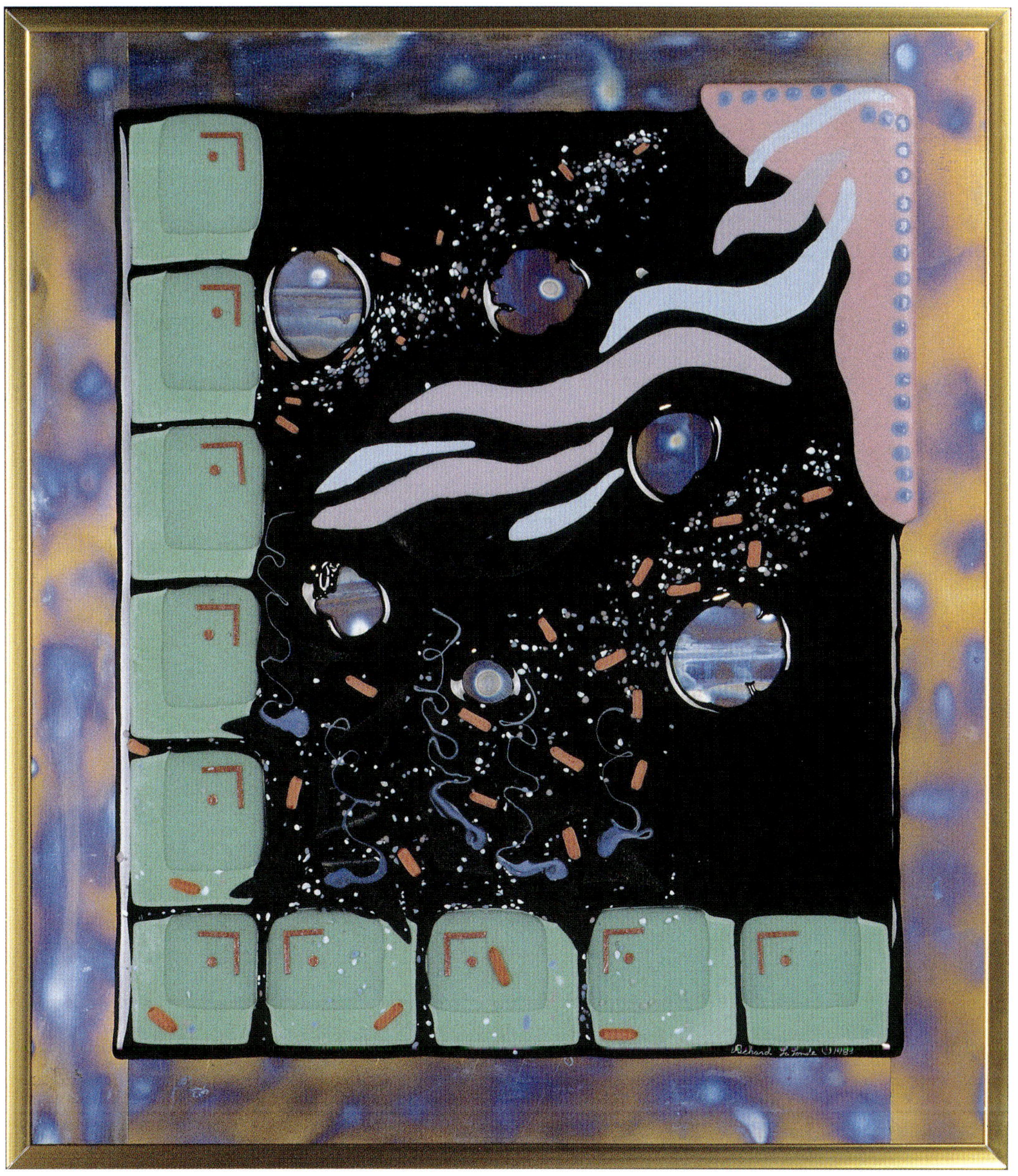

Air must be the bubble culprit – water, at sea level, turns to steam at 212°F (100°C) and couldn't exist inside of a kiln at 1400°F, around the temperature at which the glass seals to the shelf. This proves that bubbles aren't caused by a wet kiln shelf or water trapped between the glass and the shelf. It all had to do with volume control and not wet kiln shelves.

My suspicions about volume control issues are confirmed by studying my art piece, "Shift Right." The large holes happen only in the area with one layer of a very soft black glass. Where there are

second layer elements, bubbles are less likely to occur. Also, notice the pink glass where it meets the black on the top and right side; these started out with a flush edge, but the single layer black pulled away trying to get to that magic ¼ in. (6 mm)-plus thickness, which is the same as two ⅛ in. (3 mm) pieces of glass stacked on top of each other. The edges of the single layer black glass also have a sharp saw-toothed edge, rather than the rounded edge and corner of the pink glass.

It's all about volume control!

Annealing

Ideas and definitions about annealing glass are prolific. Get a group of scientists, engineers, and artists together and you'll likely get a variety of different explanations: the scientific definition, an economic definition, and then...The La Londe version.

Personally, as an artist, I like to think of annealing as more of a philosophy than a science. Simply put, glass is a viscous material and gets stiffer as it cools. For our discussion, annealing is a controlled cooling through the zone where the glass goes from being plastic to solid.

Trying to understand annealing has always been a brain puzzler for me, so I devised an oversimplified literary picture to describe it.

Annealing occurs when the glass is cooled slowly enough to allow the inside and the outside of the glass to pass from a plastic state to a rigid state at roughly the same time so that stress is minimized. My mental picture is that the outside surface, which cools first, will "lock" and for all practical purposes become a rigid solid. Next the inside continues to shrink, pulling on the locked surface as it cools, until it "locks" as a rigid solid. If the stress between the outside and the inside is too great, the glass will crack. The idea is to slow this cooling so that the inside and outside become rigid at roughly the same time.

You can get real technical – or philosophical – about annealing, but what you really need to know is how to do it to get your glass out of the kiln in one piece – and keep it that way.

Your annealing will take longer if:
(1) Your piece is thick.
(2) Your kiln doesn't cool evenly.
(3) You use a dam, a thick shelf, or a mold – the time increases if these are insulating (for example, a fiber shelf).
(4) The shape of your piece is intricate with lots of sharp angles and internal cutouts.
(5) Your piece varies dimensionally and is thick and thin or tack fused.
(6) You have a transparent glass fused right next to opaque color – sometimes they loose heat at different rates, so allow a longer annealing time.

Also, if glass is poorly annealed, it's more susceptible to breaking if extra stress is added by other outside forces, such as heat (for example, placing a thick piece of poorly annealed glass in a hot window or dishwasher). Incompatibility also adds to the stress.

For most of my work I use the anneal soak temperature recommended by Bullseye Glass Company for their glass: 960°F (516°C).

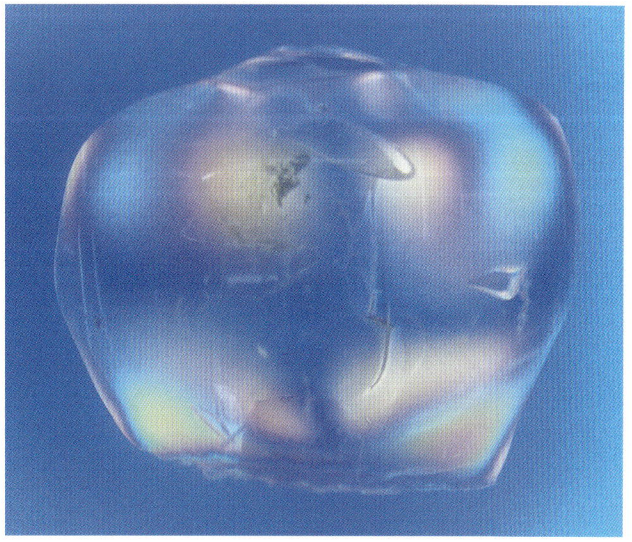

above:
this is what clear glass that has not been annealed looks like under polarized light. This piece is about the size of a golf ball and I picked it up from the floor of a blowing studio. You can check your clear glass for annealing with a polariscope, "stressometer."

I don't have too much trouble with annealing because: my kilns cool very evenly; my work is usually regular in shape with very few sharp angles; my glass is generally no more than ½ in. (13 cm) thick and is fused on ⅝ in. (16 mm) or 1 in. (25 mm) mullite shelves; and I slump in very thin stainless steel molds. The only problem that I have had is in transparent areas of glass that extend all the way to the shelf, next to a opaque color; under these circumstances, I have to slow my annealing down or end up with a broken piece.

So let's get a bit more technical. A solid has an arranged characteristic order. For example the molecules of water, frozen into ice, are lined up into a lattice structure and act like a solid. When ice is heated and its atoms absorb enough energy to overcome their lattice bonds; they collapse into a liquid. As water freezes back into ice, its molecules reorganize in the lattice structure again.

On the other hand, glass is so viscous and its kinetic energy is so low that as it cools, glass rarely has a chance to set up a lattice structure and become an ordered solid. Some people refer to glass as a liquid, but I prefer to talk about glass as a plastic; it exhibits some of the properties of a solid and some of the properties of a liquid.

As glass cools, at a certain temperature it begins to change from being plastic to solid. This beginning transition point is called the *"annealing point"* and is located at the upper temperature end of the *"annealing range."* The lower temperature end is referred to as the *"strain point,"* where glass begins to become rigid and behaves like a solid.

The *"annealing range"* is a transition zone where glass goes from being plastic to solid and occurs over approximately a 100°F (38°C) interval; it is where annealing takes place. The molecules of the glass are moving faster at the upper temperatures of this zone; consequently, glass anneals much faster than at the lower end of the annealing range. A temperature of 960°F (516°C) for Bullseye Glass seems to be the most economical place to soak the glass. But you still have to get through the lower end of the zone and that requires slow cooling.

To make it more complicated, different glasses have different annealing ranges. By doing an anneal soak at 960°F (516°C), we are trying to average the relief of stress for the different glasses that have fused together. Some glasses such as the gold-containing Bullseye 0334, 1334 or 1311 have an even lower annealing range, and when I use a substantial amount of these I do a second anneal soak at 890°F (477°C).

Even after an anneal soak where you have allowed the inside and the outside of the glass to reach the same temperature of 960°F (516°C), you still have a long way to go to get out of the annealing zone. A continued slow cooling is still needed to get out of the annealing range without putting intolerable stress back into the glass.

Once below the strain point, you still need to cool very slowly for the next 100°F (38°C). And then you get into the *"thermal shock zone"* where the glass can break either during the heat up or cool down – whenever the temperature difference between the inside and outside puts too much stress on the glass. It's like putting a glass plate (non-Pyrex) into a hot oven or taking a hot piece of glass from your kiln and running cold water on it to cool: "KaBoom."

You really can't anneal something too long, so the idea is to:

• Soak at 960°F (516°C) for a sufficient time. see Bullseye Annealing Thick Slabs chart (appendix).

• Really slow cool to 800°F (427°C).

• Cool slowly to room temperature – that point where you can hold your hand on the piece before you take it out of the kiln.

Don't Rush It!

Devitrification

Sometimes the surface of the glass puckers and looks scummy. This is devitrification, caused by crystal growth in the glass, and usually appears on the surface and edges. See the example below.

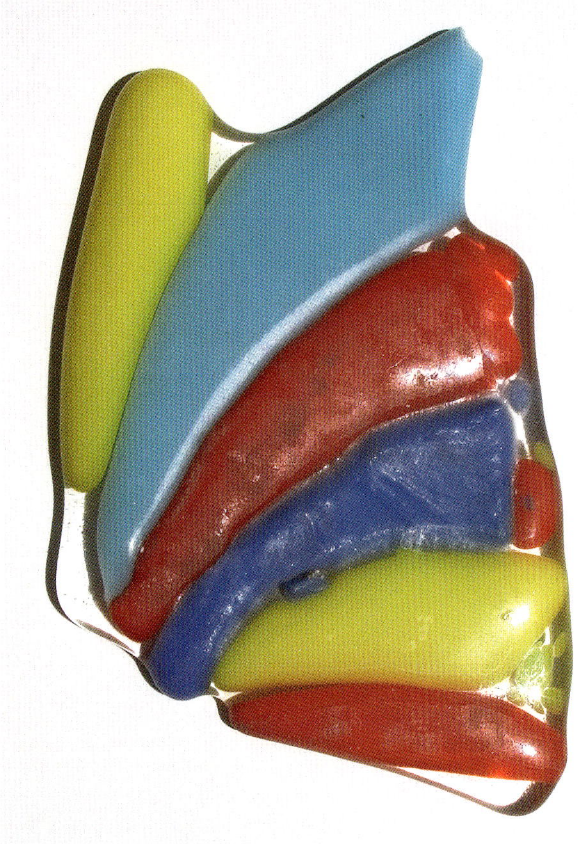

Devitrification first occurs when something – such as oil and dirt – gives the crystals a nucleus to grow around. Cleaning the glass before fusing helps avoid this. Some glasses are more prone to "devit," but can be covered with a low temperature fluxing glass called an "over-glaze," such as the lead-bearing "Spray A."

Devitrification can occur during firing and during cooling, whenever the temperature increases the kinetic energy available to the molecules and they have enough time to arrange themselves into a lattice structure. The process stops when the crystal structure breaks down because the molecules are moving too much. For common fusible glass, the "devit" range is usually between 1350°F – 1450°F (730°C – 790°C).

Fighting devitrification was the reason we initially designed fast fiber kilns, to go through the "devit" range as quickly as possible and decrease the crystal growth. Bullseye altered their glass formulas to lessen devitrification, and this major problem has now become a slight nuisance.

Window glass is prone to "devit." It is sometimes called "float glass," because it is pulled across a molten tin surface as it solidifies, so that the bottom side remains flat and shiny. Depending on the manufacturer, devitrification can occur on either side of the glass, but it's usually worse on the side of the glass that was against the tin.

To remove devitrification, sandblast the "devit" off, cover with an "overglaze," and refire.

To avoid devitrification:

(1) Choose a glass that doesn't devitrify easily.

(2) Fire and vent quickly through the "devit zone," 1350°F – 1450°F (730°C – 790°C).

(3) Clean the glass and handle by the edges.

(4) Apply an overglaze to the glass.

left: The multi-colored fused glass example shows surface scum and puckering called "devitrification."

right below: The overglaze "Spray A," used to prevent devitrification. I prefer to use a foam brush for application rather than to spray it with an airbrush which puts lead-bearing glass dust into the air and environment.

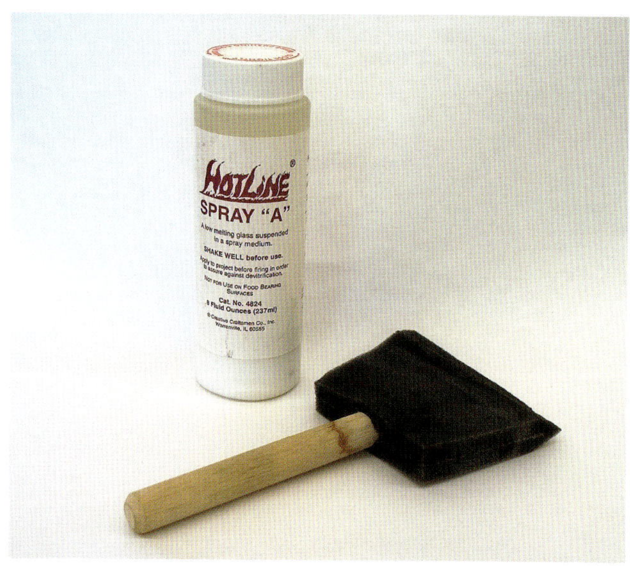

Color Reactions

Some colors don't mix as you might expect! Screams of horror often resound when a student first notices that a combination of two elegant colors produces black. This reaction occurs when glass containing copper or silver is placed next to glass containing sulfur, producing a sulfide (copper sulfide or silver sulfide) that causes the characteristic black color. Both transparent and opaque color glass is vulnerable. As with other glass surprises, this can be avoided – or converted into a technique. The black intersections of Egyptian Blue with French Vanilla have become a common artistic touch. Take care when combining copper and sulfur glasses – and when in doubt, test it out.

Copper reacts with sulfur!

Copper: Turquoise, some Blues, some Greens.

Sulfur: Yellows, Oranges, Reds, Ambers, & French Vanilla.

The fused tile below shows a black reaction where the two lines of frit intersect and have been stirred together with the end of a paint brush.

Some Bullseye Glass Containing Copper
(Lines of frit mixed together, showing the black copper/sulfur reaction where they intersect)

| Egypt Blue 0164 | Steel Blue 0146 | Turquoise 1116 | Teal Green 0144 | Jade Green 0145 |

Some Bullseye Glass Containing Sulfur

French Vanilla 0137

Medium Amber 1137

Sunflower Yellow 0220

Orange 1125

Red 0124

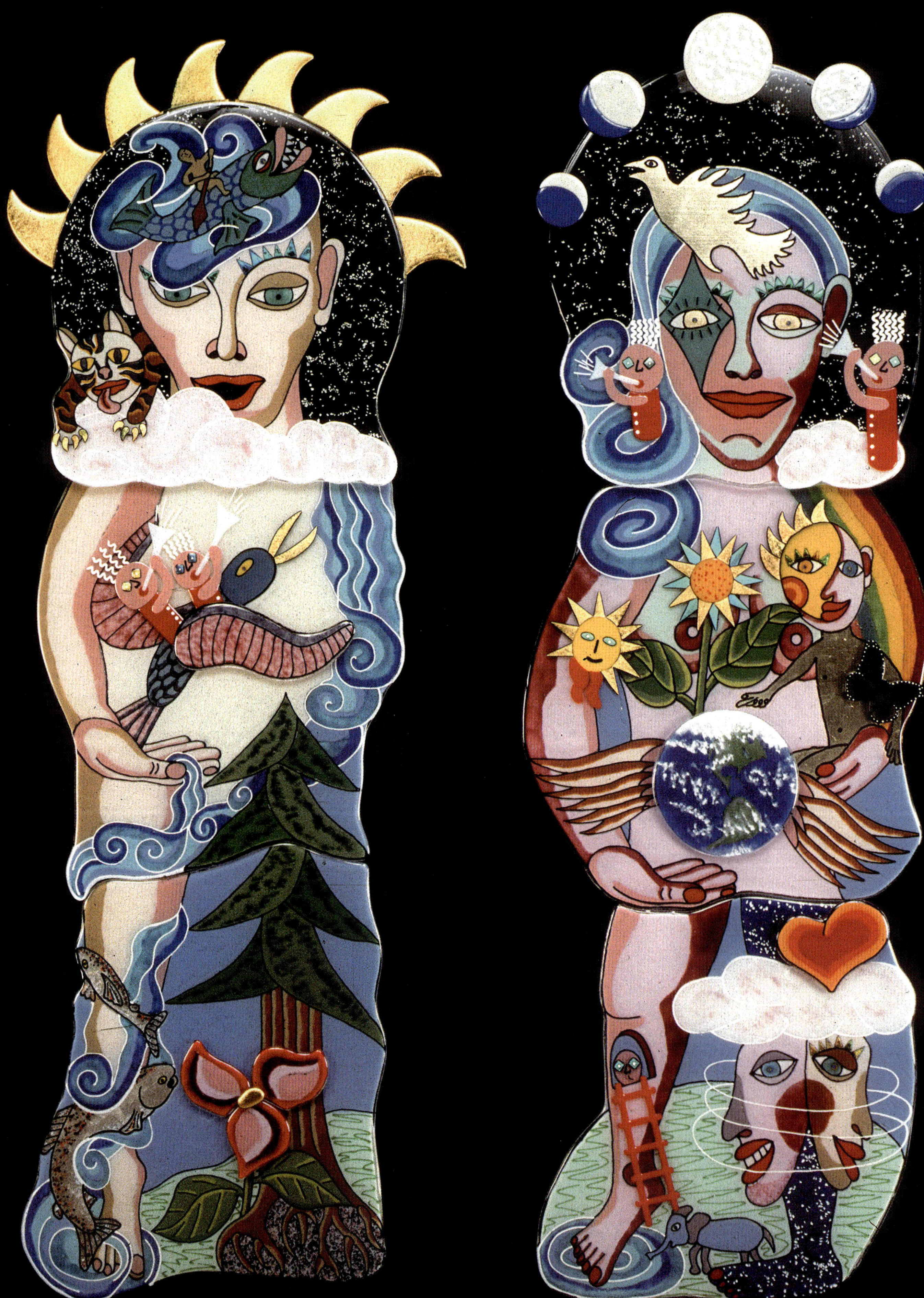

Part 4: Technique
liquid glass line

In 1993 I developed this technique in order to create an outline that could be filled in with colored frit. Many years later, I realized that this is similar to the wire and enamel technique used for cloisonné.

Make the Liquid Glass Goop
To get started, go to a ceramic supply place, such as Seattle Pottery Supply, and purchase a one-pound bag of CMC (carboxy methyl cellulose). This product is used for ceramics and also as a food additive (check the ingredients list for tortillas).

Boil water and then pour one pint of the hot water into a heat proof container. Add five heaping tablespoons of powdered CMC and stir for about thirty seconds. You will have to experiment with the amount of CMC because it differs between manufacturers and comes as either granules or flakes. Mash the lumps, but don't worry about those chunks that don't seem to want to break down. After the mixture cools and sits, say overnight, it will be a clear gel; the chunks should have dissolved. As with a good cup of coffee, I prefer to make it thicker rather than thinner. You can always thin it with water, but you can't make it thicker; if it's too thin, start over.

To create the "liquid glass," I mix a ratio of about $\frac{1}{3}$ CMC goop to $\frac{2}{3}$ glass powder (I use 08 Bullseye powder) in a squeeze bottle. Experiment with this ratio to get the right proportions until you can lay a nice even round line onto a piece of glass. A mixture that is too thin will flow and spread out. A mixture too thick will be too hard to squeeze through the nozzle. You can achieve some nice effects by spreading this mixture with a pallet knife or smearing it with a paintbrush. Fusing the line to stick will produce a dimensional line, and, of course, full fuse will make it flat. Either way, the CMC burns off clean.

Liquid Glass Line Tool Kit

(1) **squeeze bottle** - a bottle over 3" is too hard to squeeze.
(2) **stir rod with handle** - use a round shaft Phillips screwdriver.
(3) **small paint brush** - sharpen the end and use it to push the line around.
(4) **flat bottomed spoon** - used for tamping the frit down.
(5) **straightened paper clip** - use to clean out the nozzle.
(6) **folded card** - tape one end closed and use for applying frit.
(7) **razor blade** - use to cut and remove the liquid glass line.
(8) **ultra fine Sharpie marker** - use for drawing on the glass, it burns off in the firing.
(9) **paper towels** - use for cleaning the liquid glass off of the stir rod.
(10) **CMC goop -** for mixing with fine glass powder.
(11) **glass powder** - I use size 08 or finer.

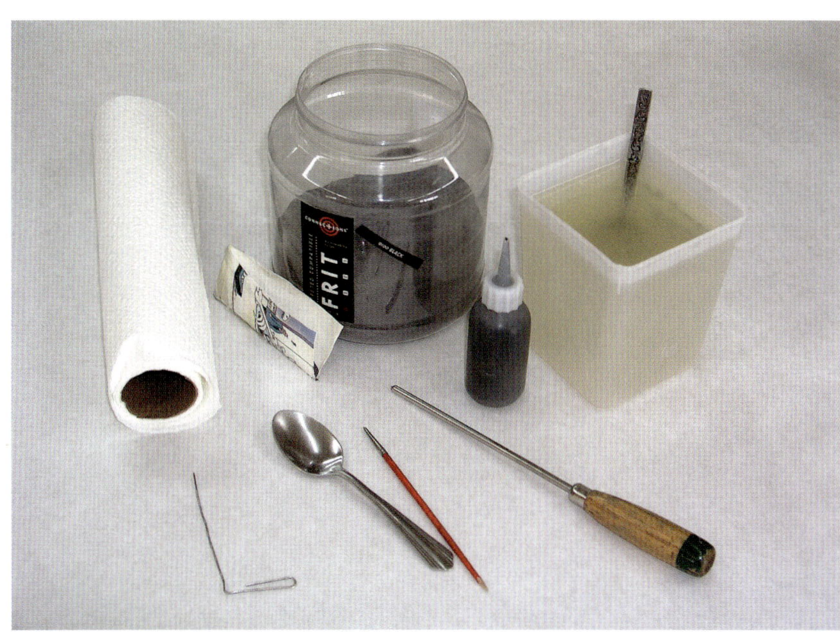

facing:
"Guardians," 1994, H. 58 in. (147 cm) x W. 42 in. (107 cm).

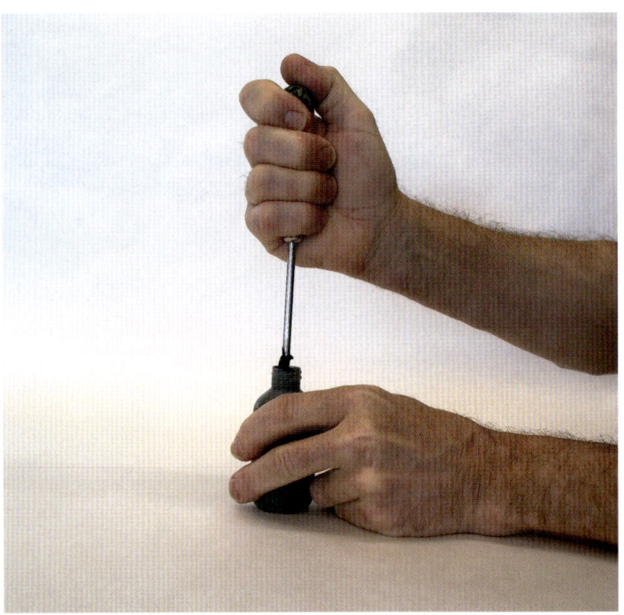

(1) Drizzle about $^1/_3$ CMC goop to $^2/_3$ glass powder (size 08) into the squirt bottle and mix with a stir rod. Wrap a piece of paper towel around the bottle neck and withdraw the rod. This keeps the liquid glass in the squirt bottle. Some people premix in a jar and then put it into the bottle or a small pastry bag. You will have to restir occasionally as the powder will separate with time.

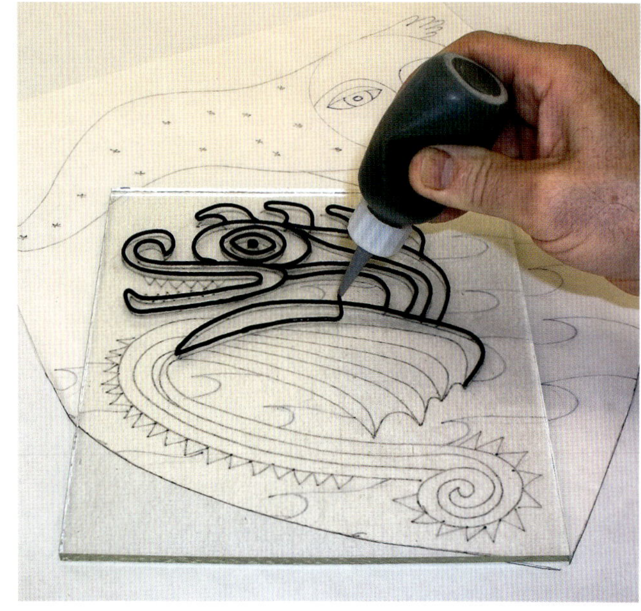

(2) Working in reverse, place ¼ in. (6mm) glass on your drawing that has been flipped over. Squeeze and touch the liquid glass to the clear sheet, lift up ½ in. and let the glass line drop into place. It should flow easily but not expand sideways. If this occurs, add more glass powder and restir. The clear glass is ¼ in. (6mm) thick to prevent the huge bubbles discussed in the volume control section.

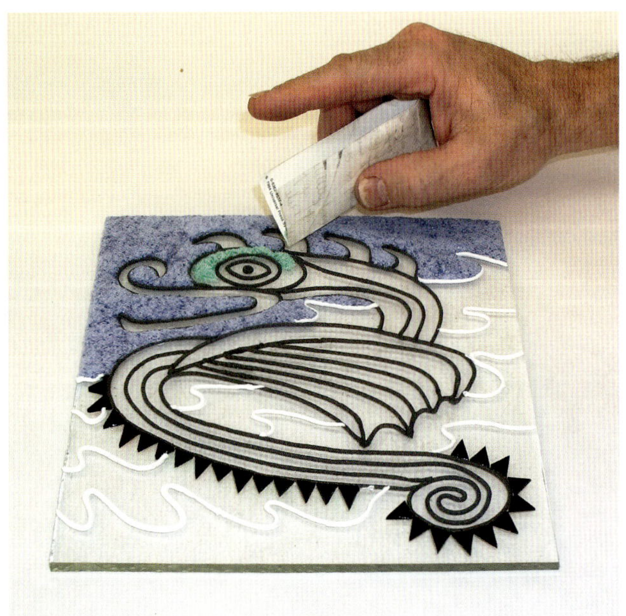

(3) I mix 50/50 size 01 fine frit with 08 powder which makes a mixture that flows easily from the tapper. I take a folded piece of postcard about 1 ½ in. (4 cm) high x 4 in. (10 cm) long and tape one end closed. I place the frit mix into it with a spoon and tap with my finger allowing a controlled and steady flow of glass powder.

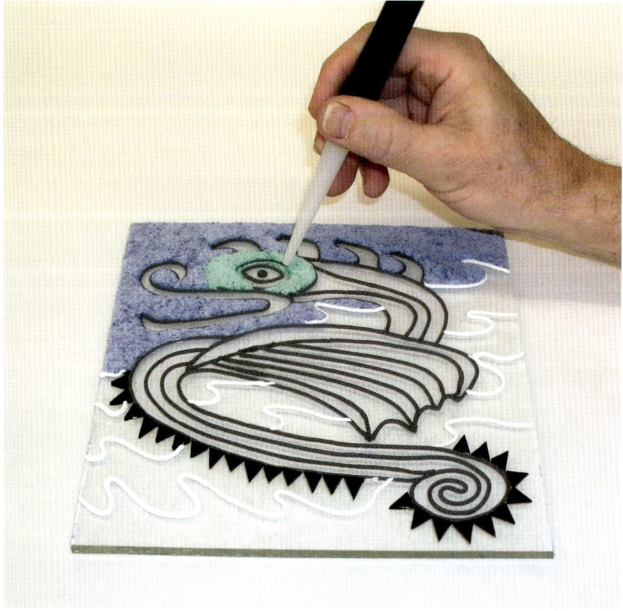

(4) I clean up the spillover with a vacuum pen. I describe how to make this in the equipment section.

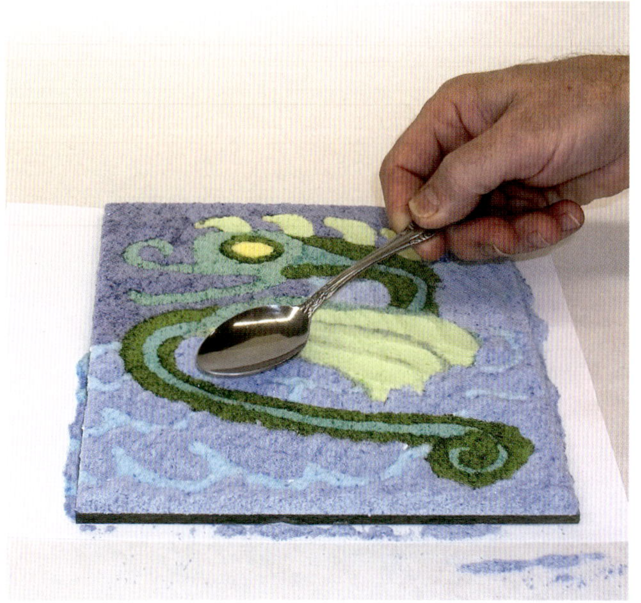

(5) I tap the frit down with the back of a spoon. You must apply at least ⅛ in. (3 mm) of frit (as it is about 50% air and fluffed up), so that after it full fuses it is about 1⁄16 in. (1.5 mm) thick. Crushed glass frit is much less dense in color than glass enamels and it takes more volume to cover an area. Place the light and transparent colors last.

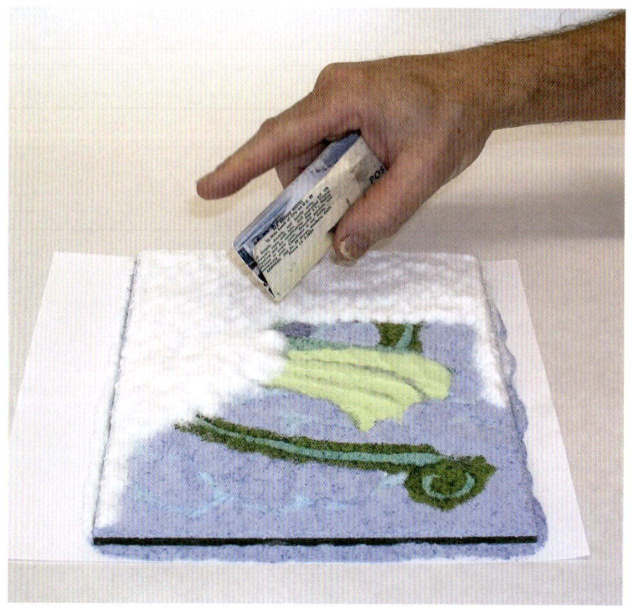

(6) I cover all of the previously applied frit with a 50/50 mix (size 01 & 08) of white frit for a wall piece or clear for a bowl. This layer keeps all the different colors from pulling up and leaving exposed areas as I discussed in the section about volume control. Tap it all down flat with the back of a spoon. I fuse the frit so it sticks to the glass but does not full fuse, about 1310° F to 1380° F, depending on your kiln.

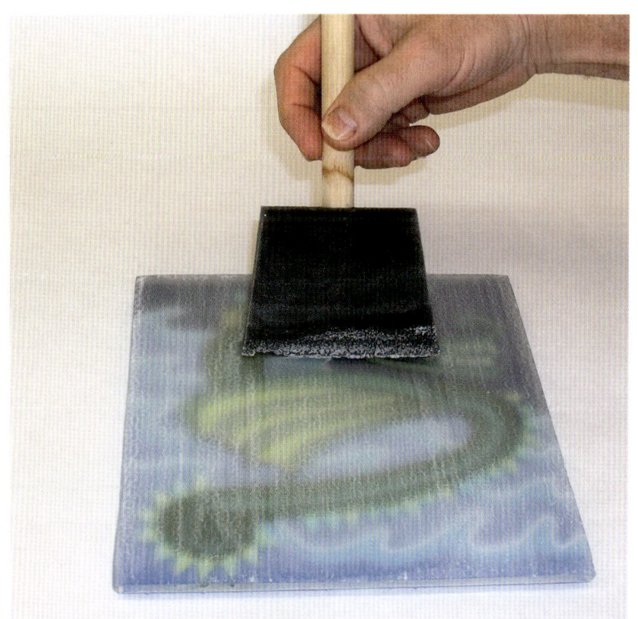

(7) After the first firing I take the piece out of the kiln, flip it over, and clean the surface with glass cleaner and a rag. In the past I sandblasted this surface, but now I just apply a very thin layer of "Spray A" with a foam brush, which takes care of any extraneous junk picked from the first firing. The "Spray A" should be applied thin enough to see through. Put the piece back into the kiln and full fuse the glass to 1500° F - 1550° F.

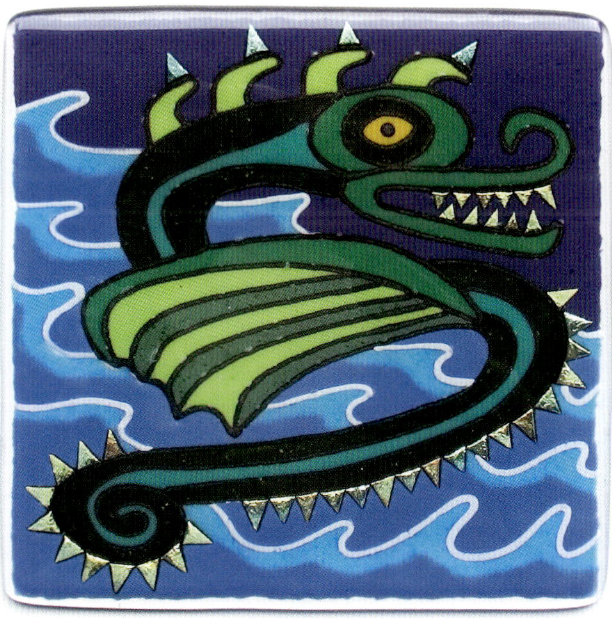

(8) The finished tile after firing to a full fuse. Firing schedules are located in the back of the book. There will probably be a clear line around the tile because the volume is a bit thicker than the magic ¼ in. (6 mm). This can be prevented by placing a dam made from a sawed mullite kiln shelf around the tile and then grinding and polishing the edge.

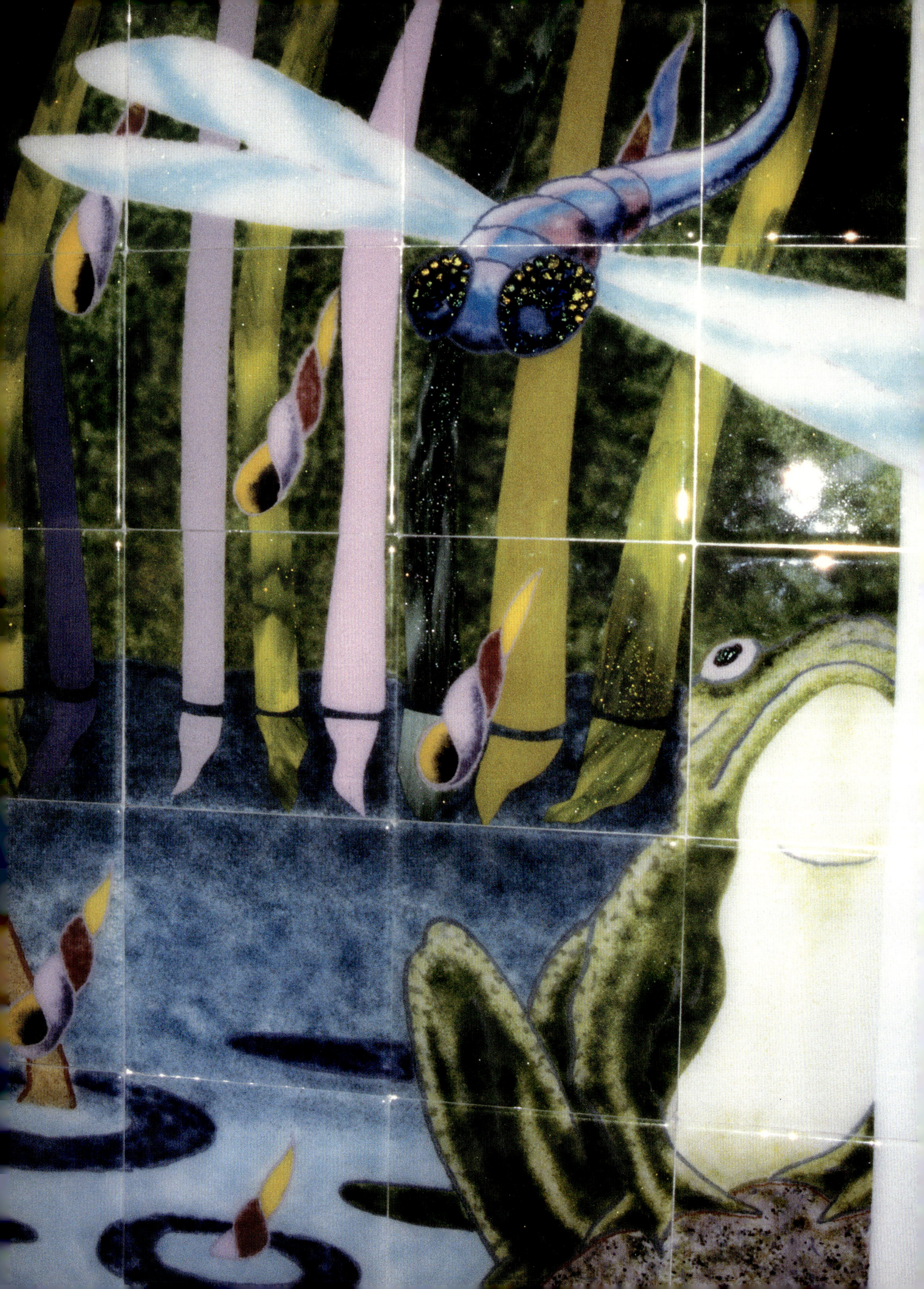

clear frit overlay

(1) The following describes making the "Home Sweet Home" tile utilizing the clear frit overlay technique. Using an ultra fine Sharpie marker, I draw my design onto an 8 in. (20 cm) x 8 in. (20 cm) x ⅛ in. (3 mm) piece of white glass. I cut a border of ⅛ in. (3 mm) black glass and glue it down with blue gel Elmer's Washable School Glue. I place cut sheet glass for the eaves of the house and a piece of dichroic for a moon. The "Sharpie" marker and blue glue burn off cleanly.

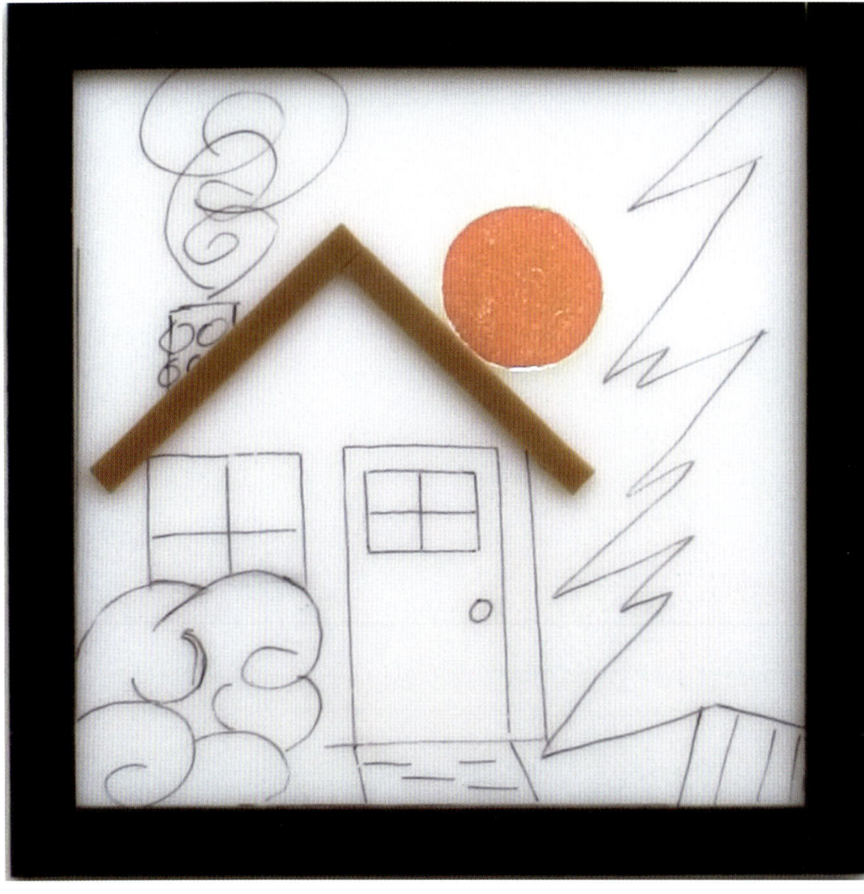

(2) I outline some of the details with a squirt bottle using (08) powdered black glass in a CMC medium as I described in the last chapter about liquid glass line technique.

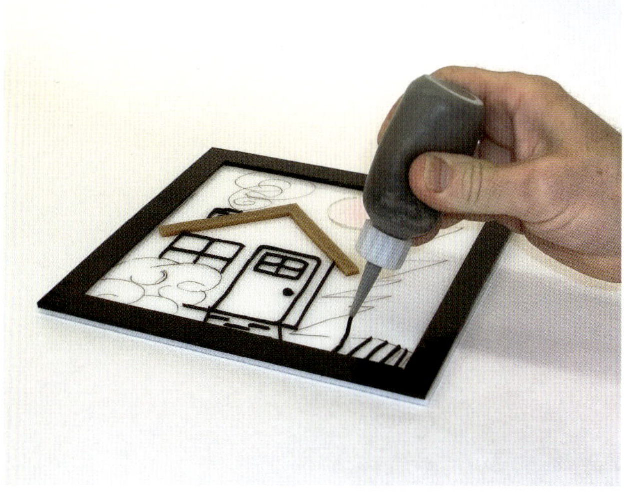

facing:
Detail from the "Heron" panel, 2000, H. 144 in. (366 cm) x W. 72 in. (183 cm). From the suite of murals titled "As Above, So Below," an artists' collaboration of Michael Dupille and Richard La Londe during the year 2000. This piece is located on the south facing exterior wall of the County/City Courthouse Parking Annex on 10th and Yakima in Tacoma, Washington, just a few blocks away from the Glass Museum.

These murals were constructed using the "clear frit overlay technique."

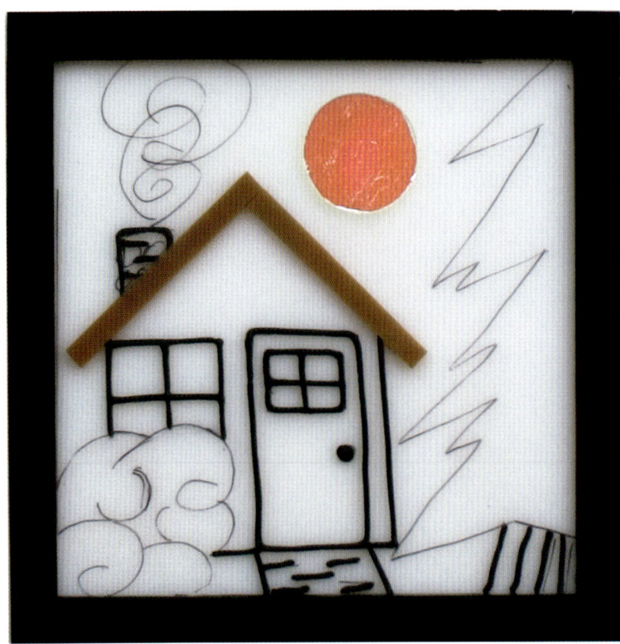

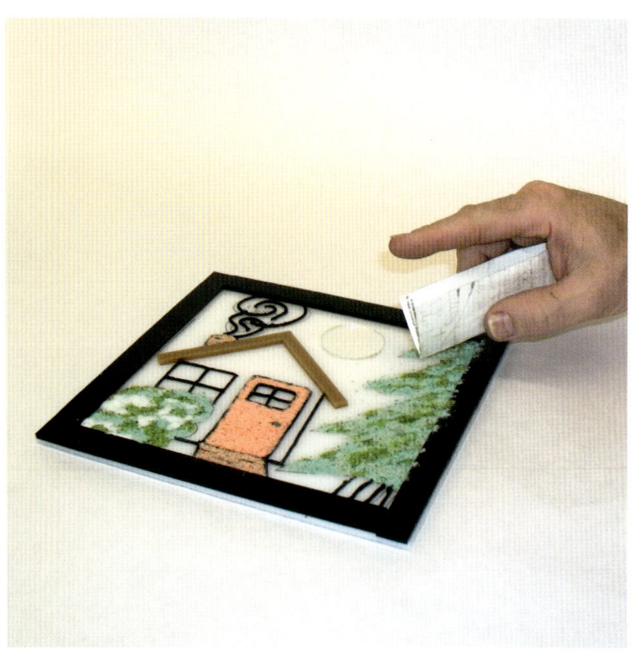

(3) I dry the "liquid glass" lines with a hair dryer. Because lines are an accent in my drawing, I don't put them everywhere. The clear frit overlay technique allows me to achieve a painterly blending of line and color. I've moved the moon, which looks better higher in the sky.

(4) I place powders onto the glass with a folded piece of postcard with one end taped closed. I use a mixture of 50% size 01 frit and 50% size 08 powder. The frit doesn't have to be as heavy as that used in the liquid glass line technique.

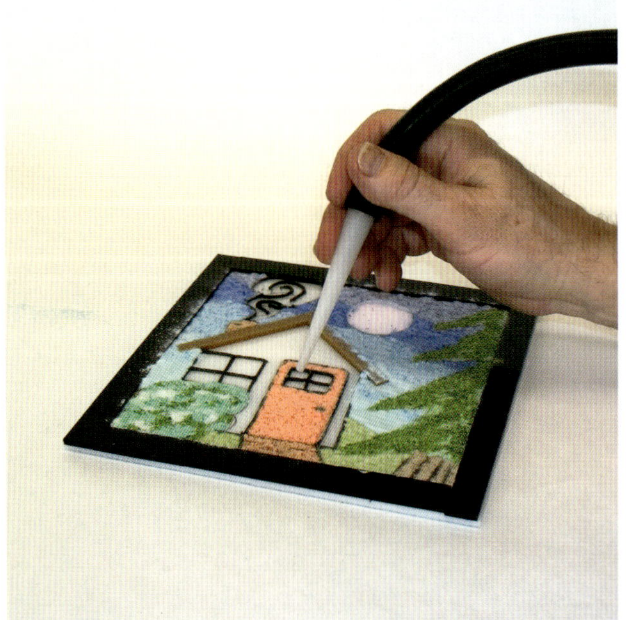

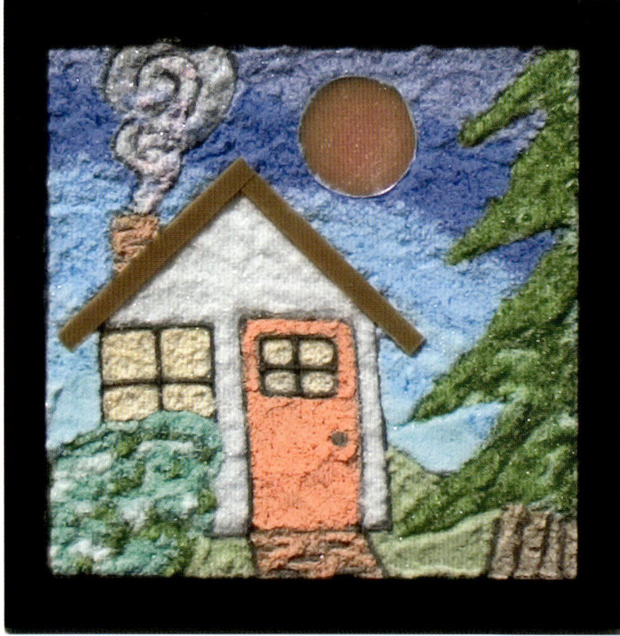

(5) The vacuum pen removes frit from areas where it is not wanted; building this tool is described under the special shop equipment section. The shop vac sits outside of the studio to keep the vented glass dust out and to reduce the noise.

(6) I have finished placing the colored frit onto the tile. By placing this tile on a light table I can see where the thin areas of color are, and I can fill in where necessary. I vacuum the extra frit from the sheet glass areas and border. I also sweep the excess frit off of the black lines with a small paint brush.

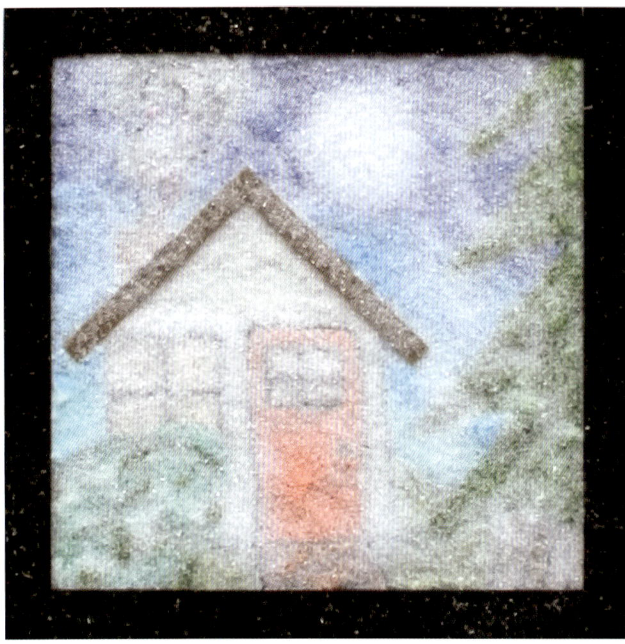

(7) I apply a thin layer of 01 clear frit on top of the colored frit. This acts as a cushion for the larger frit that I place on top. Without this layer the larger frit sometimes looks like raindrops have punched into the glass. Make sure that you just barely cover the black lines and solid pieces of glass.

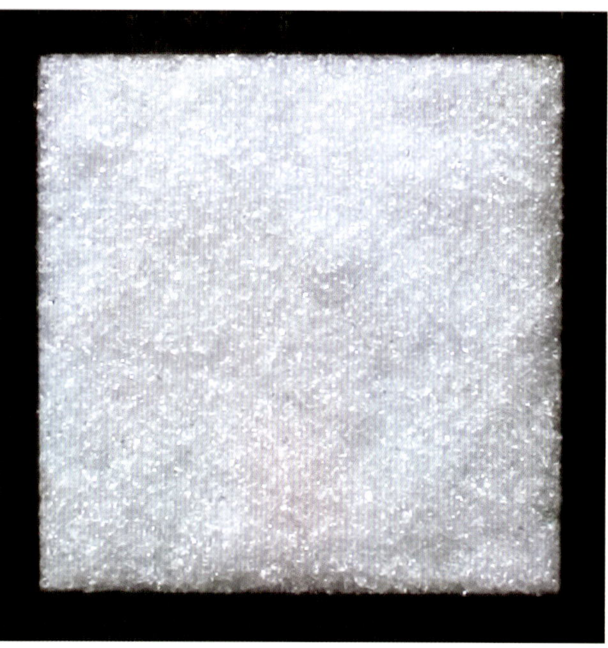

(8) I cover the bottom layers with a thick layer of 02 clear frit. This should stick up above the black border as frit is usually about 50% air and compresses as it melts.

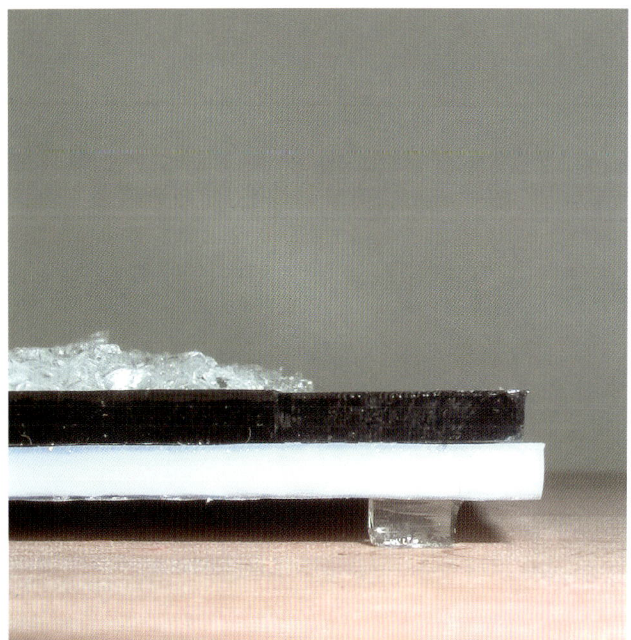

(9) I put this tile on two clear corner chips to let the air out between the kiln shelf and the glass as it full fuses. This keeps huge bubbles from occurring (see the Basic Fusing chapter about volume control). You can also fire on ⅛ in. (3 mm) fiber paper. Thin fire shelf paper sometimes causes bubbles by not allowing the air to escape between the shelf and the glass.

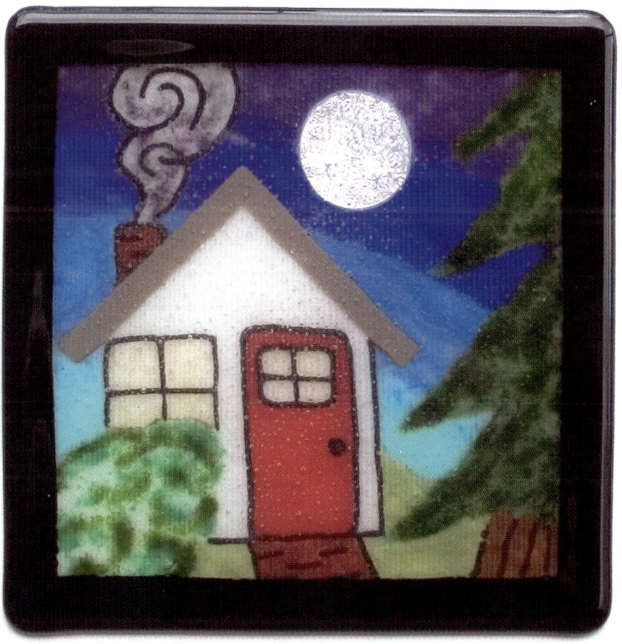

(10) "Home Sweet Home," the finished tile after firing to a full fuse. Allow at least one hour and thirty minutes between 1100° F - 1550° F so the bubbles can escape from the frit. Firing schedules are located in the back of the book. For a more detailed piece add more frit, lines, and stringers as another layer and fire again.

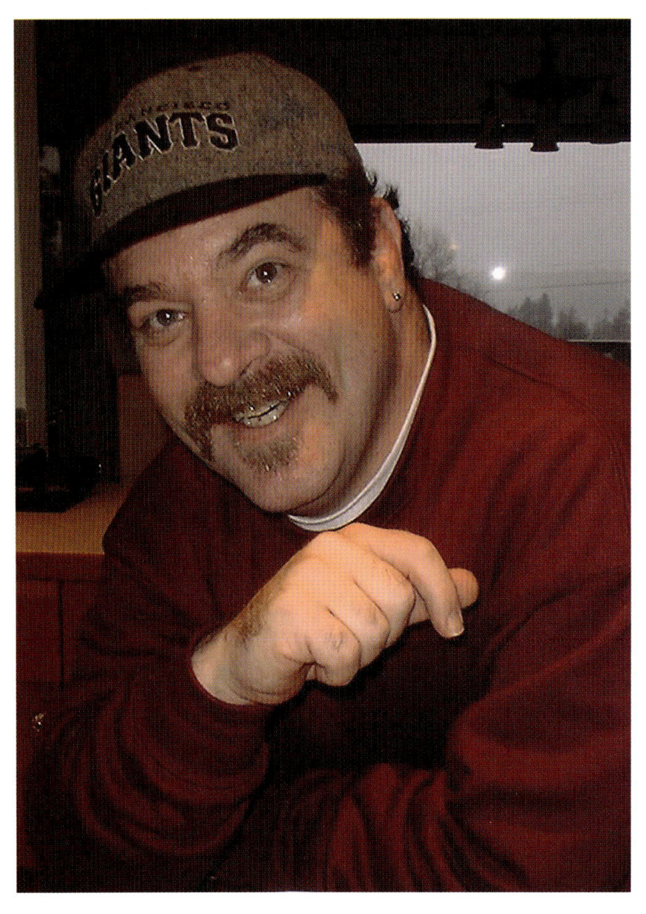

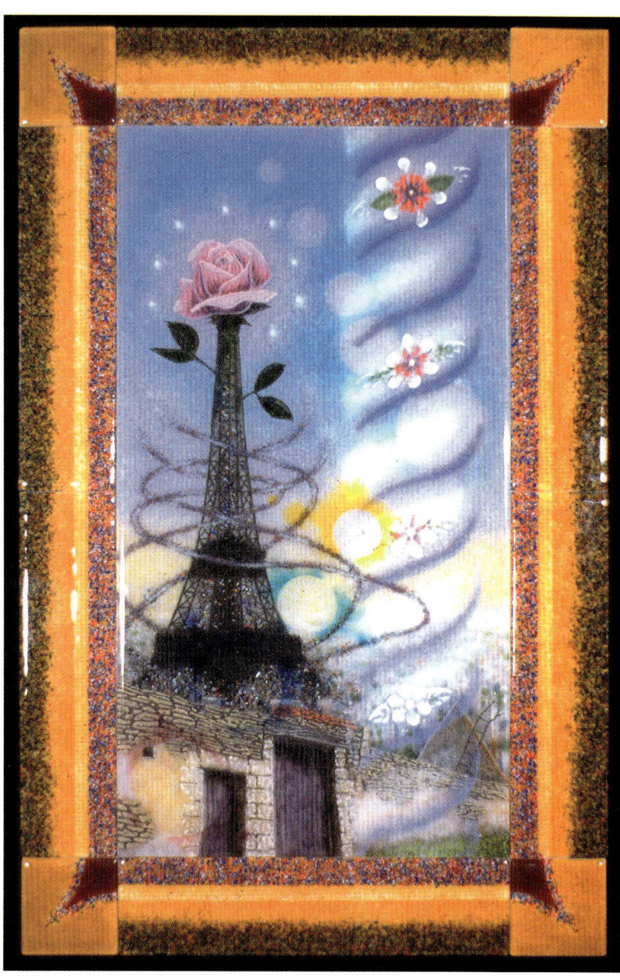

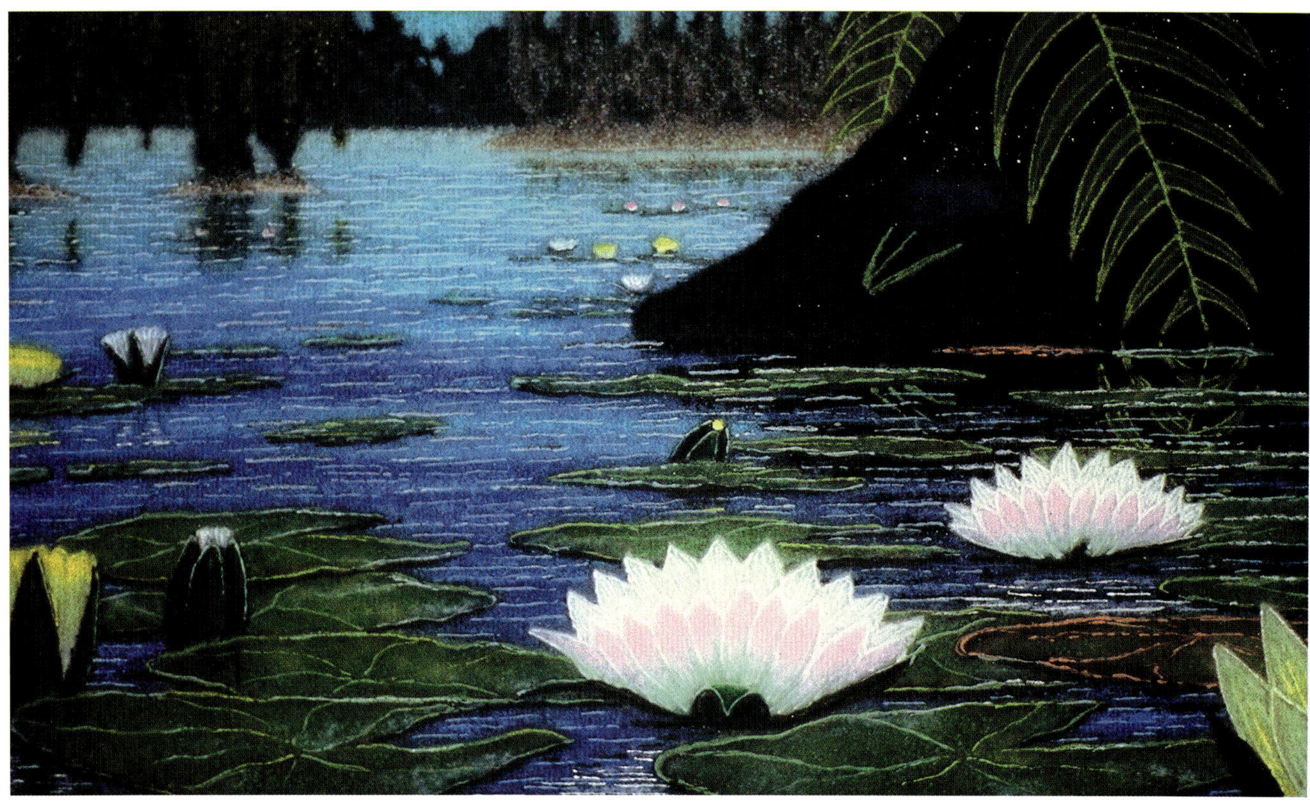

Michael Dupille (b. 1955)

facing upper left: Michael, 1999.

facing upper right: "From Ruins to a Rose," 2000, H. 42 in. (120 cm) x W. 27 in. (69 cm).

facing lower: "The Pond," 2005, (detail) H. 18 in. (46 cm) x W. 32 in. (81 cm).

upper right: "The 18th Tee," 1999, H. 19 in. (48 cm) x W. 19 in. (48 cm).

lower: "Onlookers," 1999, H. 11 in. (28 cm) x W. 21 in. (53 cm).

Michael Dupille uses layers of detailed frit and line work, and he fires his pieces multiple times to achieve realism with his painterly style that he calls "fritography."

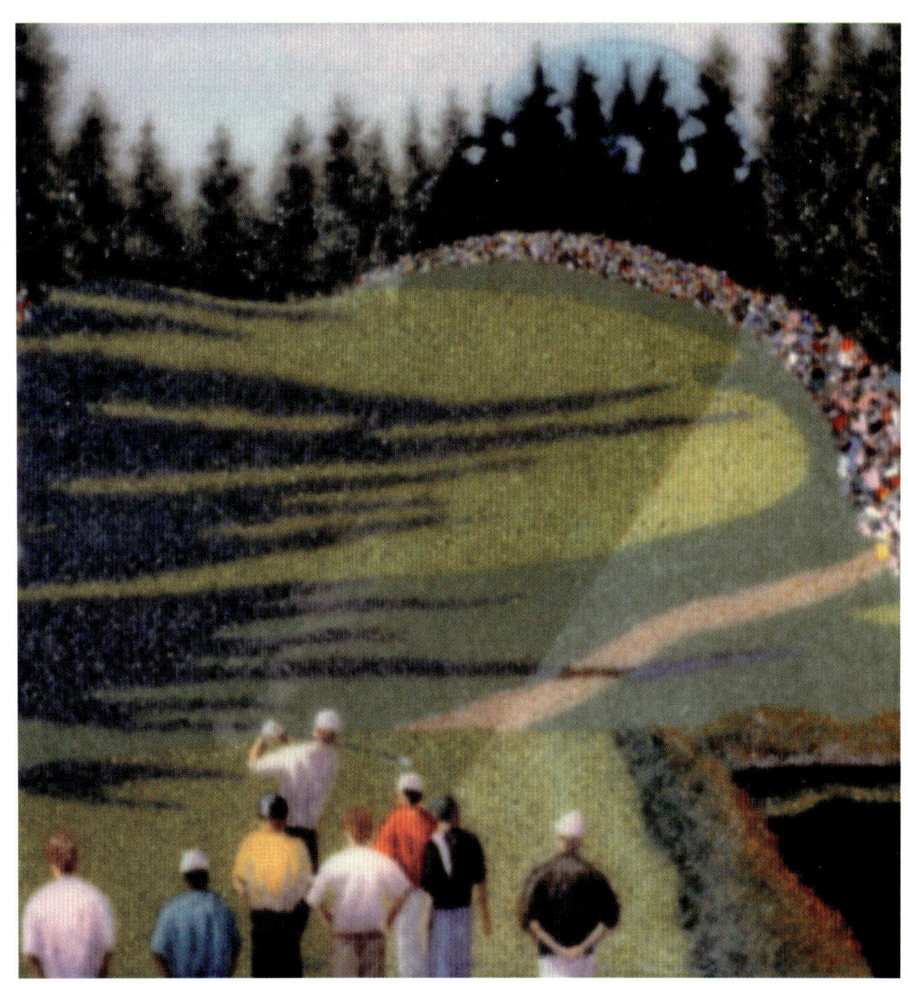

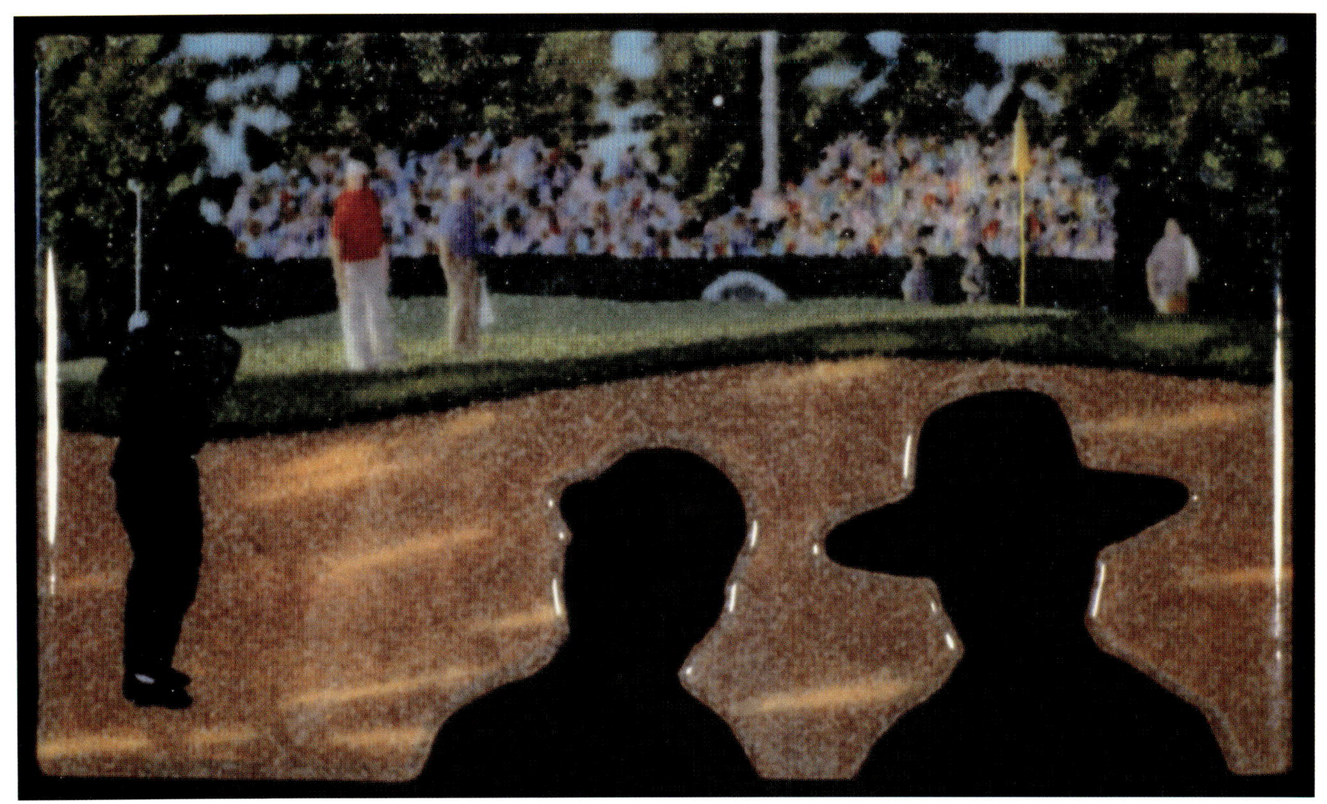

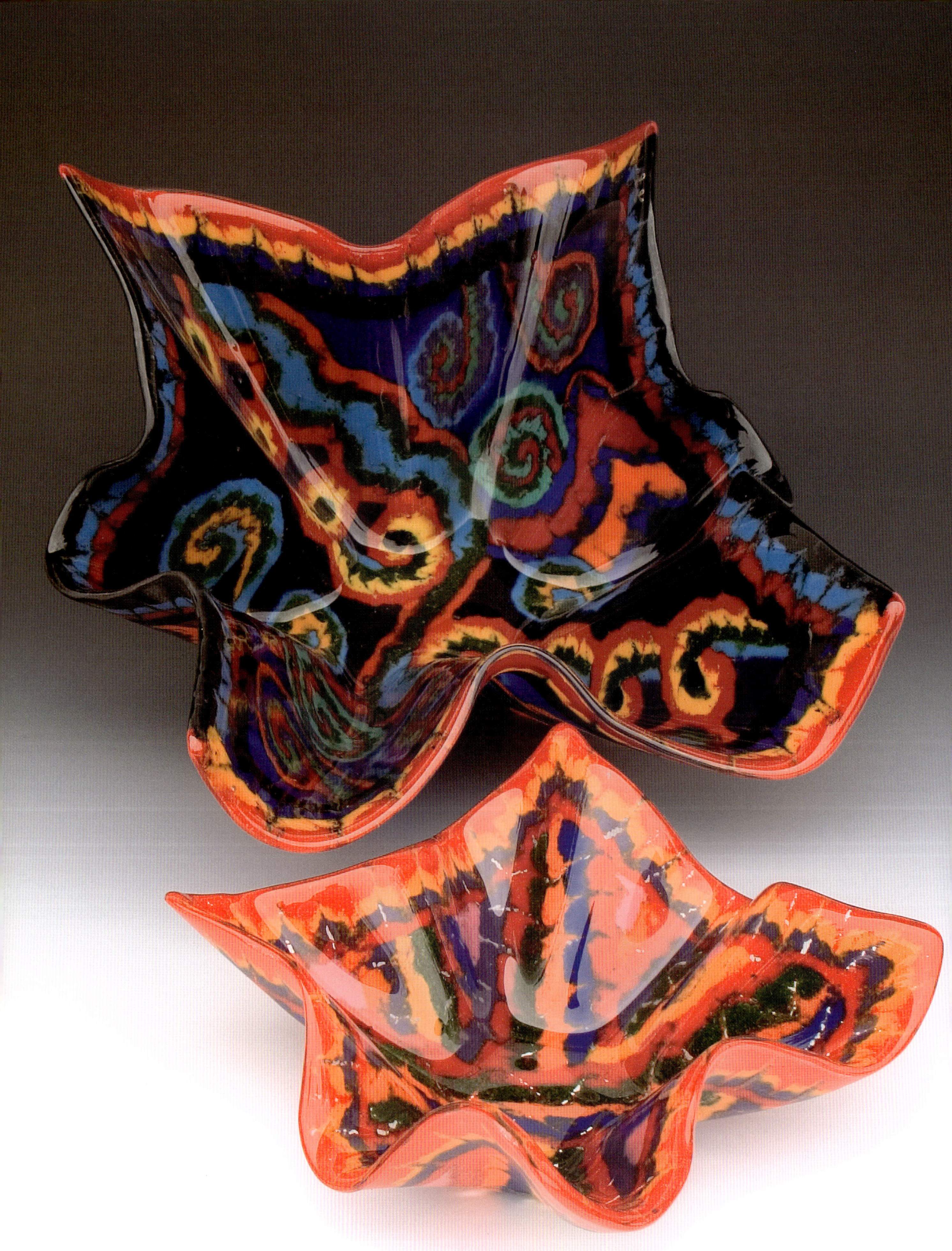

(1) To create a "frit on the shelf" piece, I place crushed glass directly onto a mullite shelf that has been coated with shelf primer. I use a folded piece of paper (postcard) that has the back end closed with tape. I use a 50/50 mix of powder and fine Bullseye 08 & 01 which flows easier from the "tapper" than either the powder or the fine frit alone. I tap the edge with my finger and the glass sprinkles out. Mound the glass about ¼ in. - ⅜ in. (6 - 9 mm).

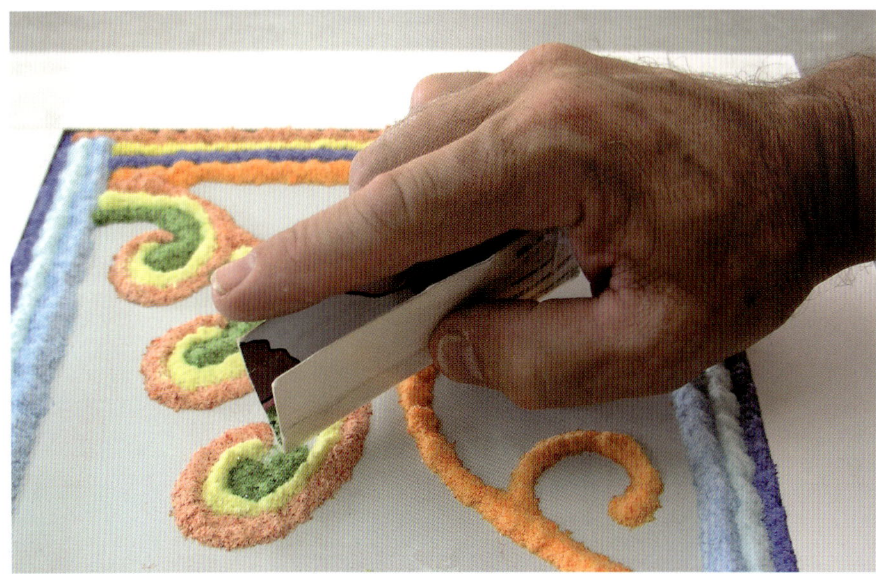

(2) I completely fill in all areas with crushed glass. You can leave some blank areas if you want. If you are using transparent glass be careful about overlapping colors. In this photo you can see how the crushed glass overlaps the adjacent colors. Light opaque colors should be applied on top of the darker colors, for example white overlapping black. I use a frame of ⅛ in. (3 mm) matte board to keep the edge straight. Make it ⅜ in. (9 mm) larger on all sides than your desired finished size. The glass shrinks as it fires; this is discussed in the section about volume control.

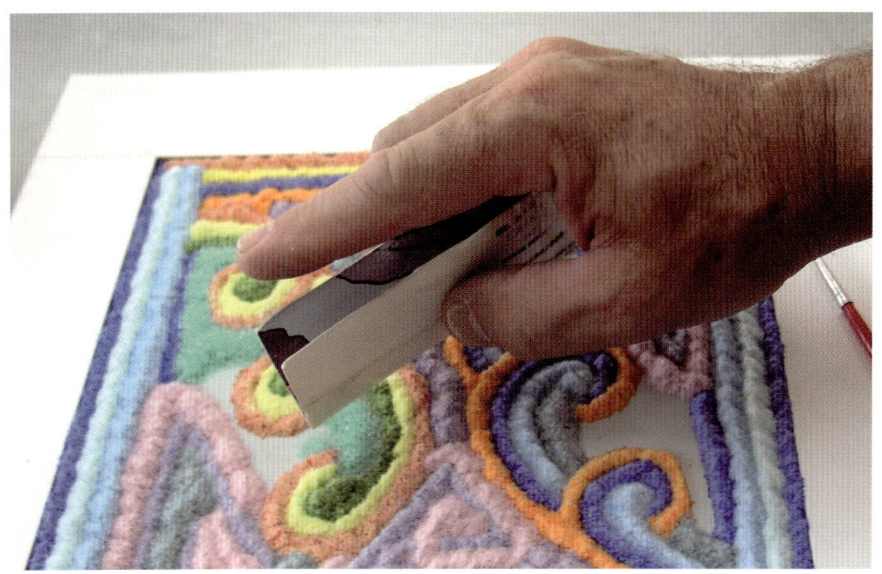

facing page:
fiesta vessels, 2002

"Black and red rim fiesta," H. 10 in. (25 cm) x W. 19 in. (48 cm) x D. 17 in. (43 cm).

"Red rim fiesta," H. 3 in. (7cm) x W. 8 in. (20 cm) x D. 8 in. (20 cm).

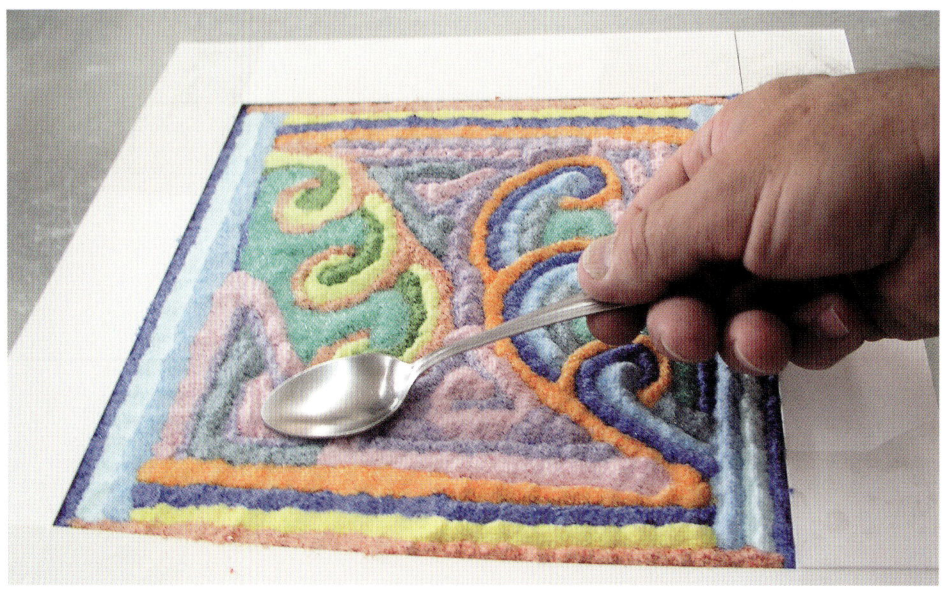

(3) I tap the glass down with the back of a shallow spoon. This compresses the glass. The mixture of powder and fine crushed glass helps fill in the voids between the particles of glass.

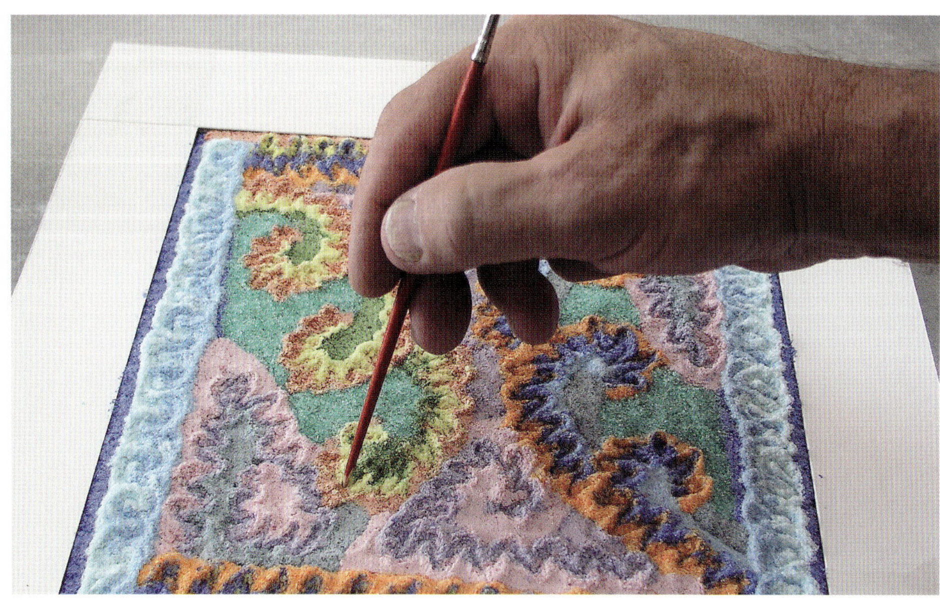

(4) I sharpen the end of a paintbrush and use it to "comb" and mix the colors around. I then flatten this with a spoon. Sometimes for a different effect, I don't compress it with a spoon, and then the lines become more pronounced after firing. You can experiment to see which effect that you prefer – or use both. Remove the border of matte board and straighten the frit edge.

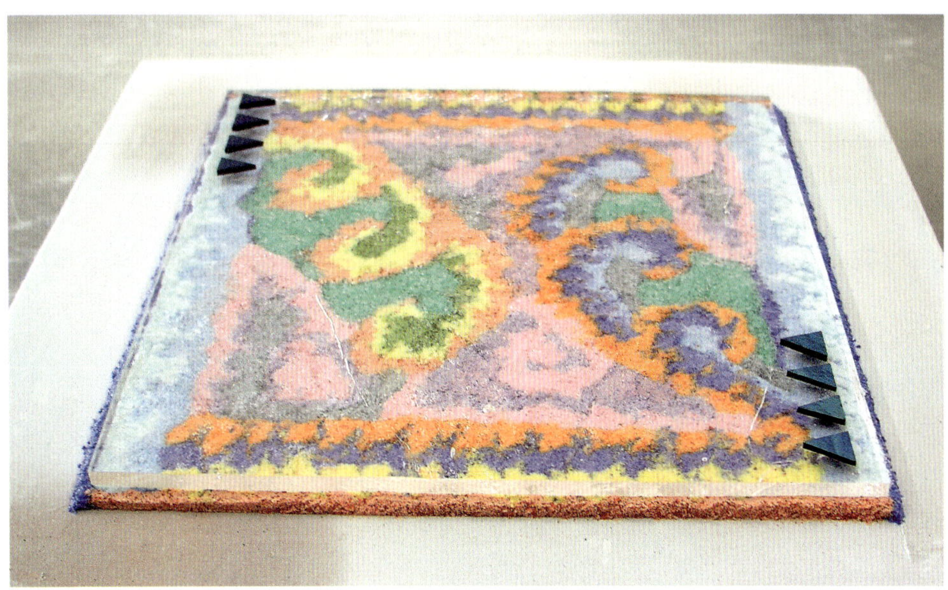

(5) Next I lay a piece of clear ¼ in. (6 mm) compatible glass on top of the crushed glass. Sometimes I add a few bits of thin dichroic sheet glass or more powder on top of this layer. I make sure that I don't cover up the bottom design. The crushed glass sticks out about ³/₈ in. (9 mm) from the clear glass on all sides; this is to allow for the shrinkage as the powder layer pulls inward.

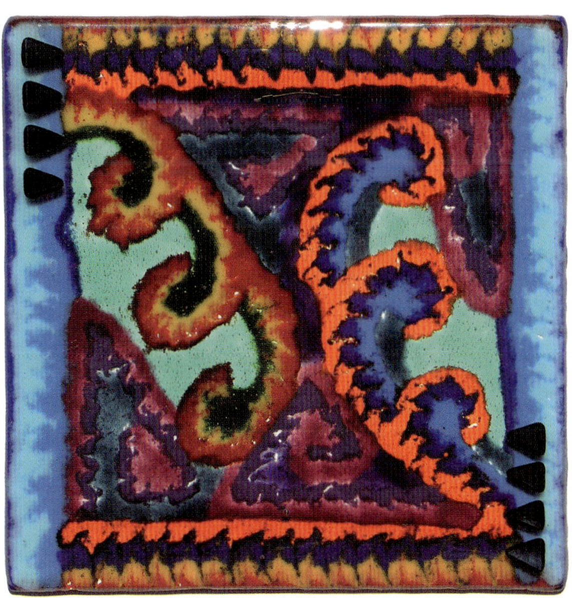

(6) This is the tile after full fusing flat. I have fused up to 23 in. (58 cm) x 23 in. (58 cm) directly on to a kiln shelf that has been coated with shelf primer without incurring any bubbles. This works because the glass cover layer is already the magic ¼ in. (6 mm) thickness that the glass wants to fuse to, as explained in the section on volume control. You can also fuse the frit on top of fiber paper. This piece can be flat or slumped in a mold.

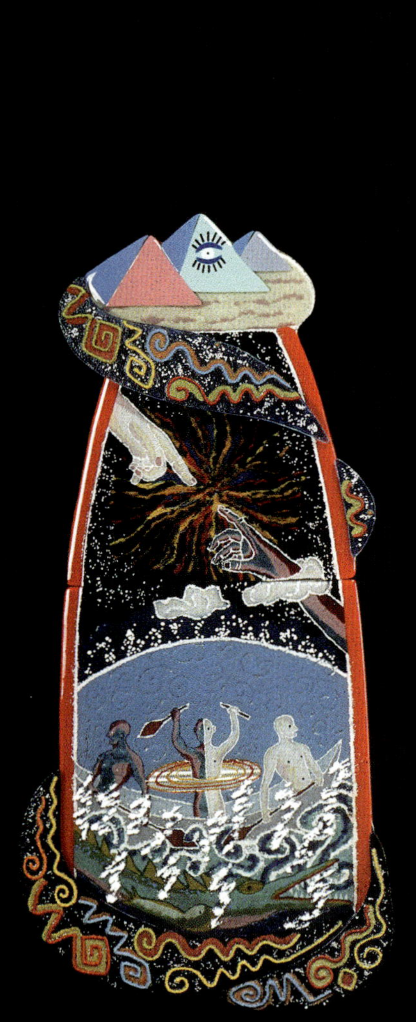 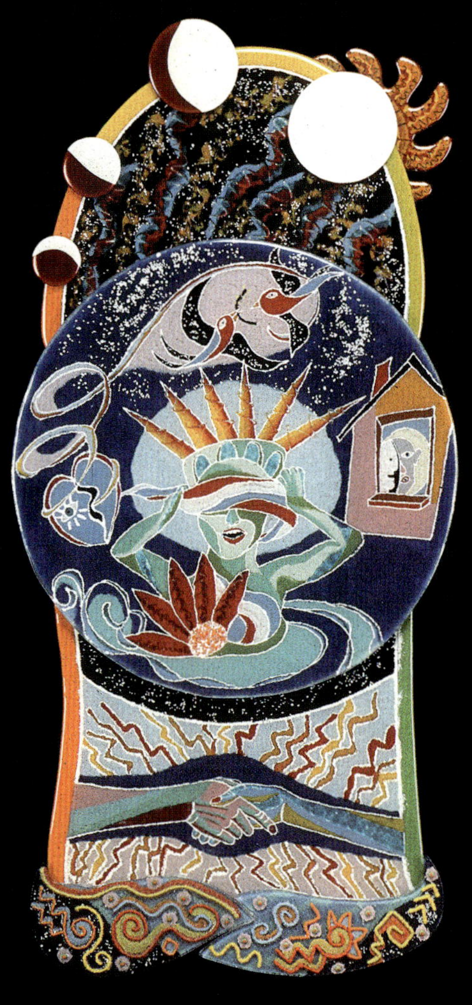 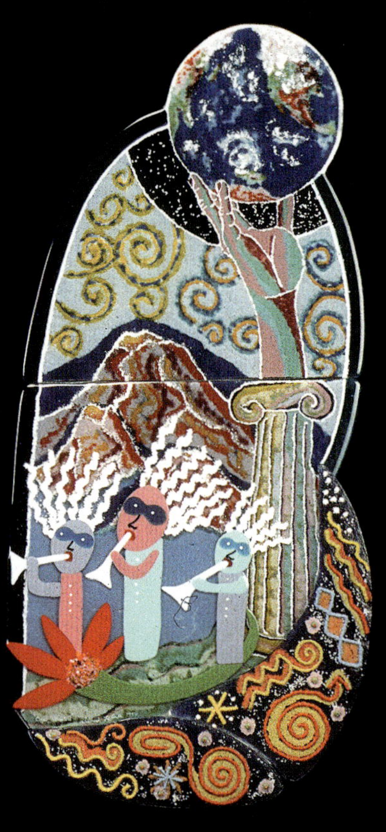

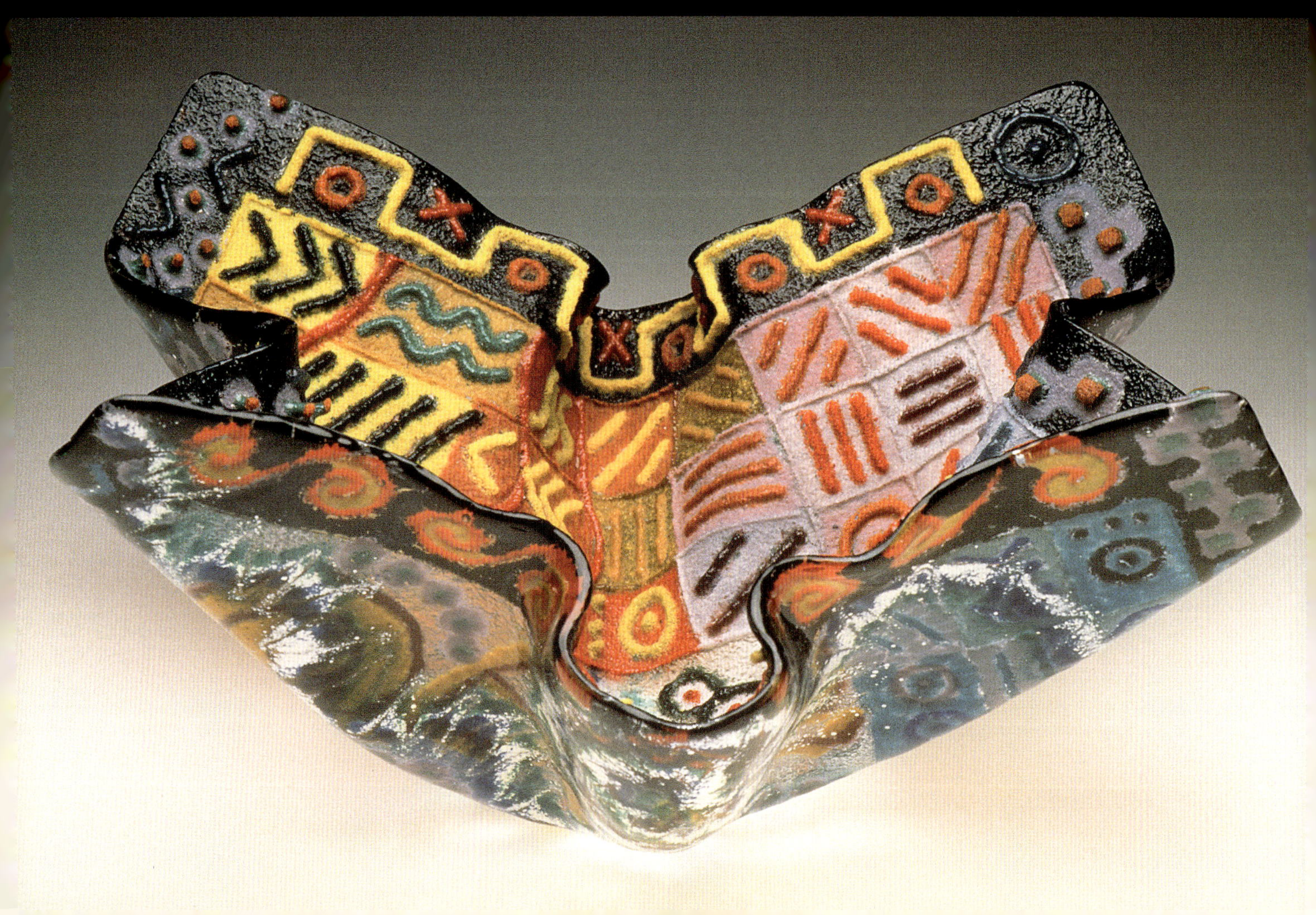

frit in sand

During the summer of 1989, I attended Pilchuck Glass School as a teaching assistant in an experimental Masters Glass Casting session. This gave me the idea to put a sand casting mixture on a kiln shelf, indent a design into the sand, fill that in with colored frit and fuse a sheet of glass on top of it all. I tried it, and it worked. I slumped this into my bowl mold and the Vitroglyph series was born.

With this technique, I also created sections for two murals, "Remember the Stars" and "One World." The next pages describe how to do this technique.

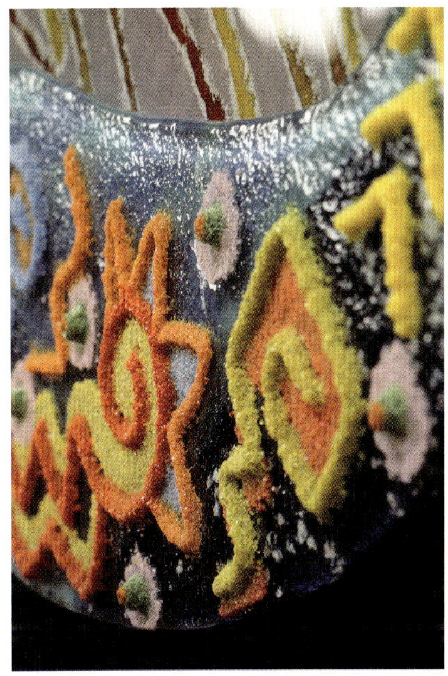

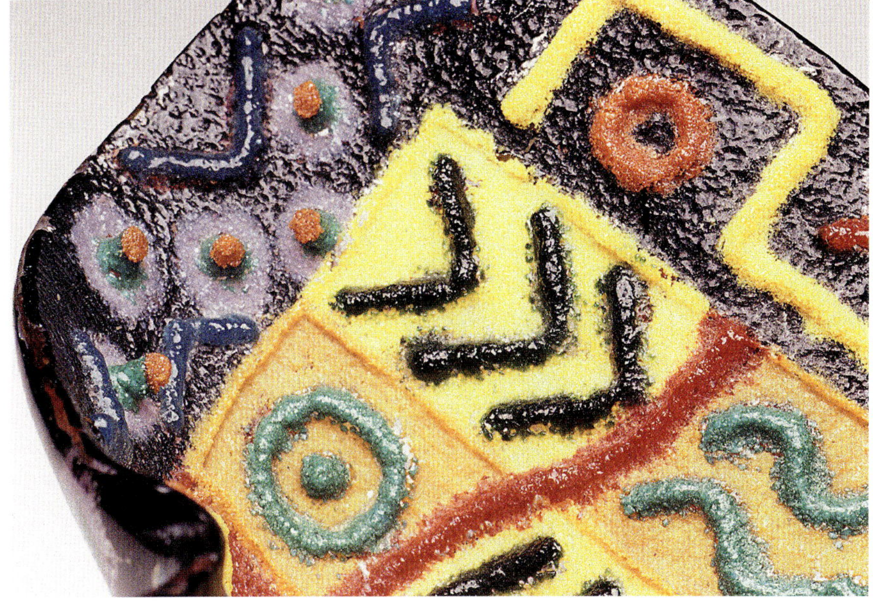

VITROGLYPH SERIES 1989
I pressed a design into a wet sand/clay mix on a kiln shelf. Into this impression I laid crushed colored glass and fused a clear sheet of glass on top. I flipped the dimensional surface up and slumped it in a metal mold.   9 pieces total

facing upper:
"One World," 1990, H. 56 in. (142 cm) x W. 74 in. (188 cm). Fused crushed glass with some areas fused into sand, creating a 3-D look.

upper:
Detail of "One World" showing frit fused into sand.

facing lower:
"Vitroglyph," 1989, H. 9 in. (23 cm) x W. 16 in. (40 cm) x D. 14 in. (35 cm).

lower:
Detail of "Vitroglyph."

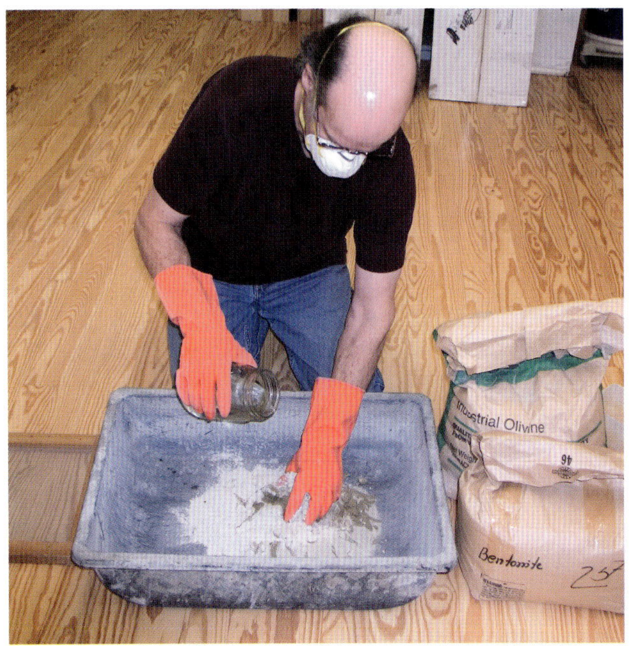

(1) Wear a respirator! Mix 95% olivine sand with 5% bentonite powdered clay. Wet the mixture with water and mix with gloved hands until you can squeeze a handful into a ball. For this technique it should be like wet beach sand by the ocean. I don't recommend silica sand as it is very dangerous to breathe. This mixture for hot glass casting is much fluffier.

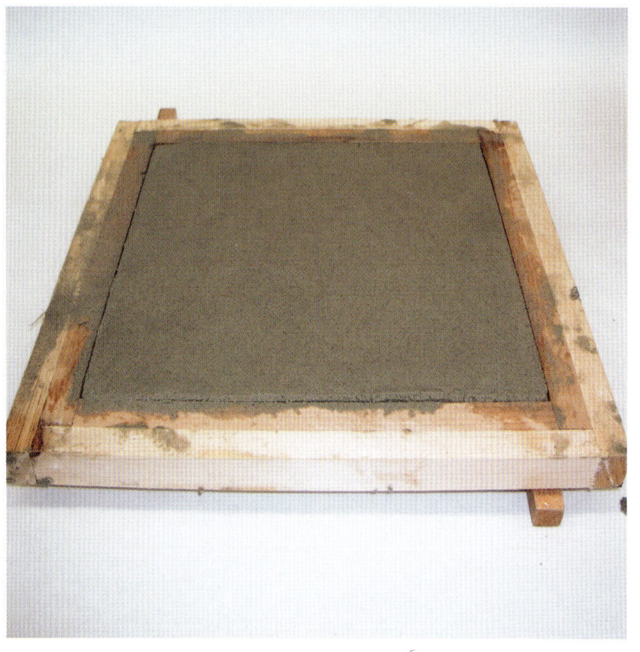

(2) I built a wooden outer frame around a kiln shelf and then nailed a second frame about ¾ in. (2 cm) thick to the inside of that, so it sits on the shelf. This allows me to make a ¾ in. (2 cm) thick clay tile. Press the sand/clay mixture into this form and smooth it with a steel cement float or trowel. Spray water to create a smooth surface when troweling.

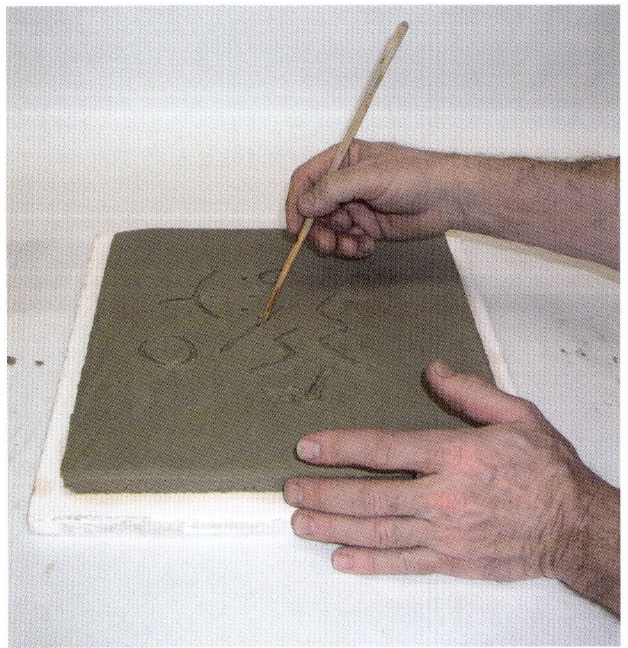

(3) Run a knife around the edges of the sand/clay tile and remove the wooden frame. Depress and carve a dimensional design into the damp mixture.

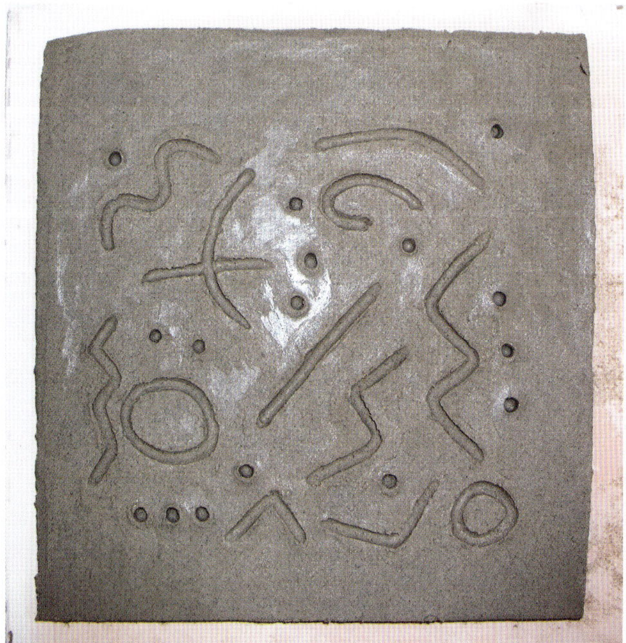

(4) These lines in this design are about 3/16 in. (5 mm) deep. You can use all sorts of tools for carving: screwdrivers, wood carving tools, sticks, nails, and so on. Remove the excess sand and smooth with a wet finger or trowel.

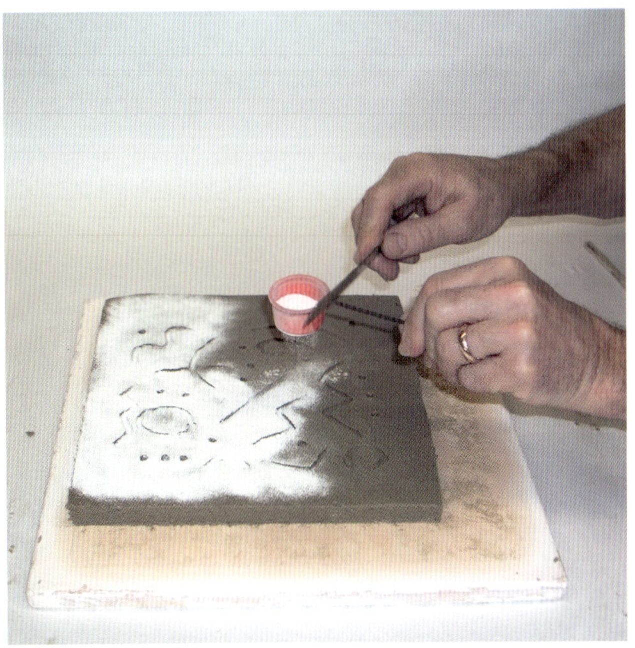

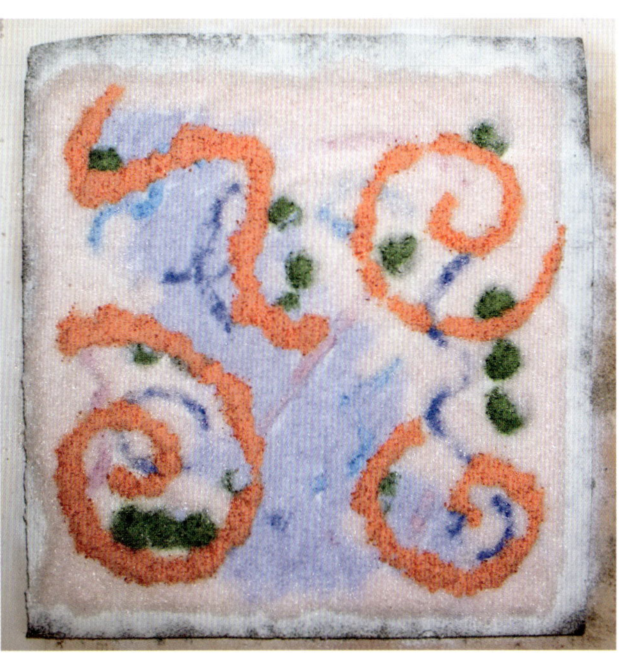

(5) Sift dry "Plaster of Paris" or "hydrocal" onto the wet sand/clay tile. Use an enamel sifter and drag a piece of metal across the ridges in the handle to vibrate the sifter and deliver the plaster. Put on a layer thick enough to cover the sand but not fill the indentations.

(6) Using a folded cardboard tapper (see the liquid glass line section), fill the groves with a 50/50 mixture of 01 and 08 frit. Mound it above the tile and then put a layer of color or clear frit, about ¹⁄₁₆ in. (1.5 mm) thick all over the sand/clay tile.

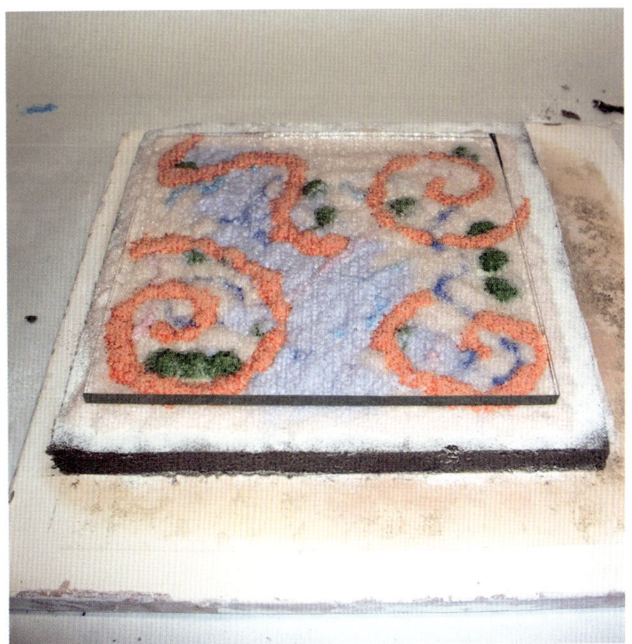

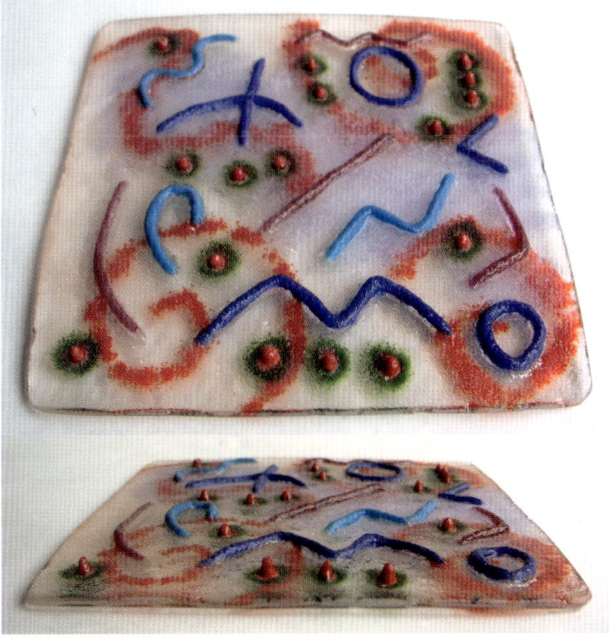

(7) Place a piece of ¼ in. (6 mm) glass on top of the frit on the sand/clay tile. Place this wet tile, which is on a kiln shelf, into the kiln and fire, using a regular firing schedule, to full fuse for the size and thickness of the glass. Higher temperatures and a longer soaking time will produce a more vitrified look. For a more granular effect, cut back on the time and temperature.

(8) After annealing and cooling, the tile should pop out. The sand/clay mix should be hard but fragile; if you are careful removing the tile, you might be able to reapply the plaster and get one more firing from this mold. Clean the plaster and bits of sand from the glass with soap and a soft bristle brush. Remove stuborn particles with a wire brush.

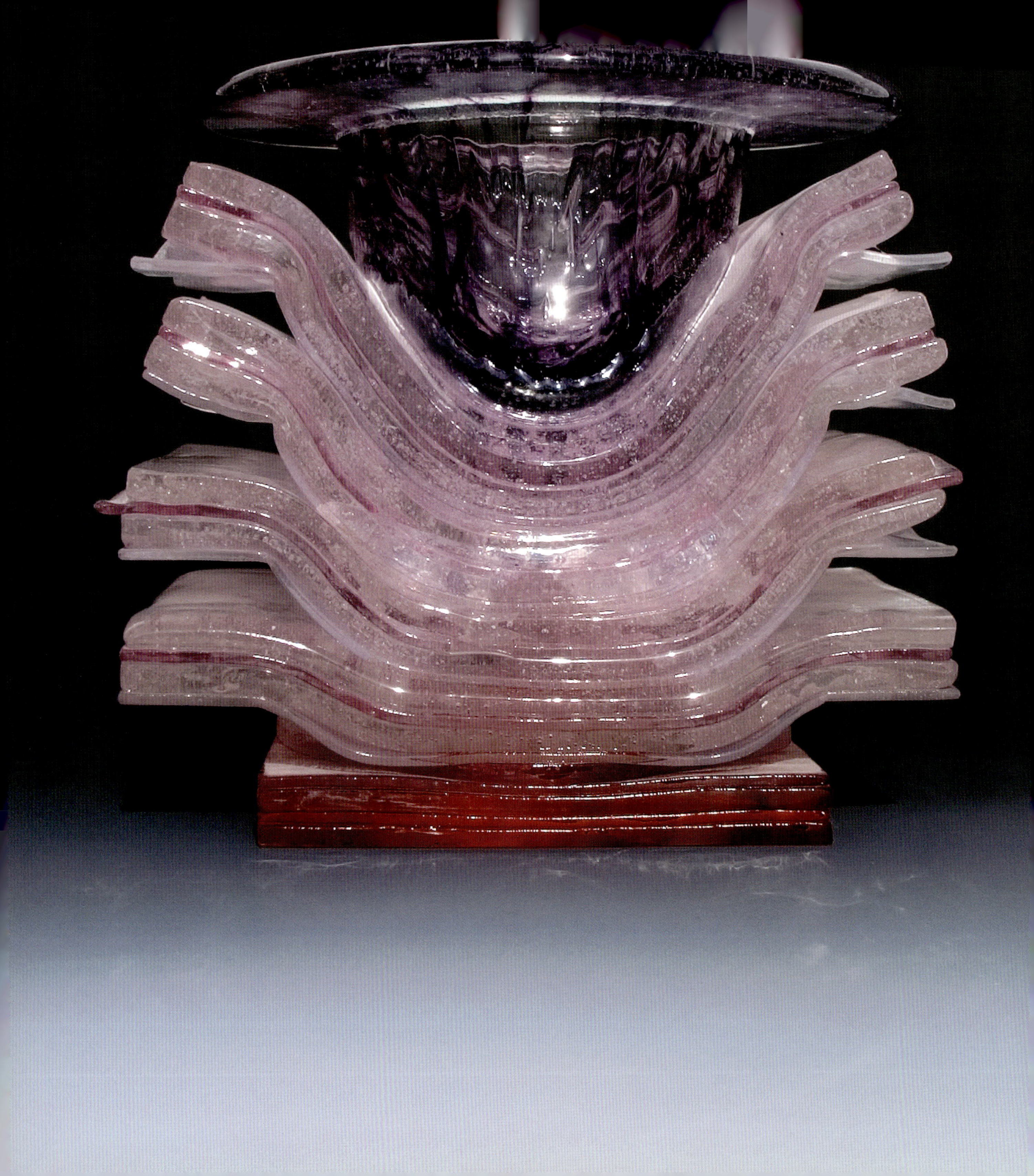

slumping, sagging, and molds

Molds for shaping glass can be made from any material that won't burn, melt, or give off poisonous fumes. You can use a clay flower pot, a stainless mixing bowl, shaped refractory fiber blanket, or you can make molds from clay, plaster/silica mix, soft and hard bricks, kiln shelves, metal, and other materials. You can bend glass over or into molds.

I prefer stainless steel for my molds! Stainless steel can be very thin, 20 gauge, $\frac{1}{32}$ in. (.75mm) or less, and unlike mild steel, it doesn't flake at slumping temperatures of 1250° – 1450° F. Thinner molds allow glass to heat and cool faster than do thicker, denser molds. Stainless can be bent into a curve such as a half-cylinder but resists bending into a compound curve such as a hemisphere; spinning stainless on a lathe will stretch it into shape without wrinkles.

I slump my vessels into molds that I make myself by bending and fluting a sheet of stainless steel. To give vessels a flat bottom, leave the bottom of the mold open to the kiln shelf. Molds can be fastened together with pop rivets. I make molds that I slump glass over by using expanded mild steel mesh. Expanded stainless would be better but is difficult to find. Heat the metal molds to 250° F in a kiln and brush or spray shelf primer onto them as a release. If you use a mixing bowl, drill a small hole in the bottom to let the air out.

You can usually slump into clay and over metal. A metal mold shrinks more than the glass and can crush it unless the glass can move and slip upward as it does in a tapered mold.

Slumping bends glass into a mold without a noticeable change in thickness; during **sagging**, the glass thickness changes. Francis and Michael Higgins invented the "dropout" mold technique: multiple layers of glass are placed on a ring mold, and with heat and gravity the glass drops through the hole and stretches. Glass for sagging must be thicker in order to accommodate stretching and thinning. For example, glass $\frac{3}{8}$ in. (9 mm) thick, if sagged six inches, would have a finished wall thickness of about $\frac{1}{8}$ in. (3 mm).

facing:
"Pink Compression," 1999,
H. 8 in. (20 cm) x W. 9 in. (23 cm) x D. 8 in. (20 cm) slumped and sagged glass.

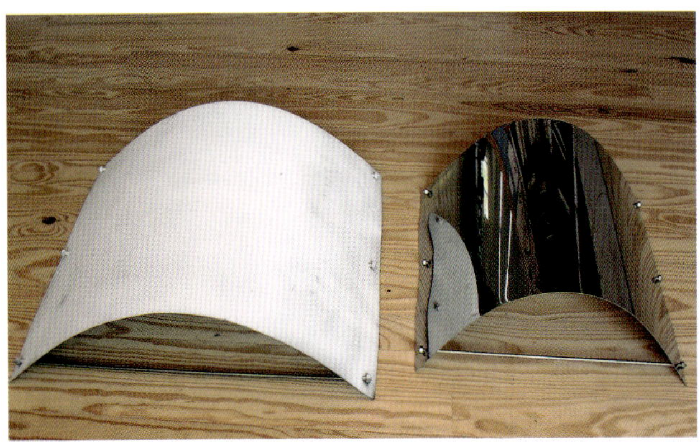

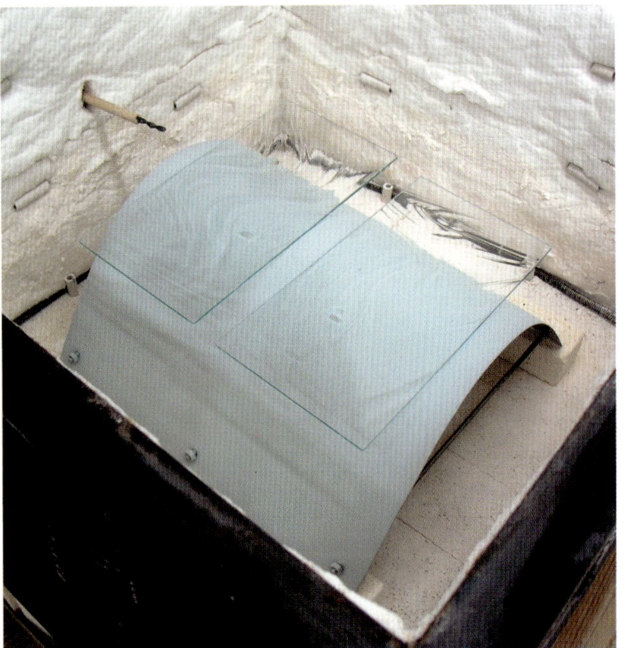

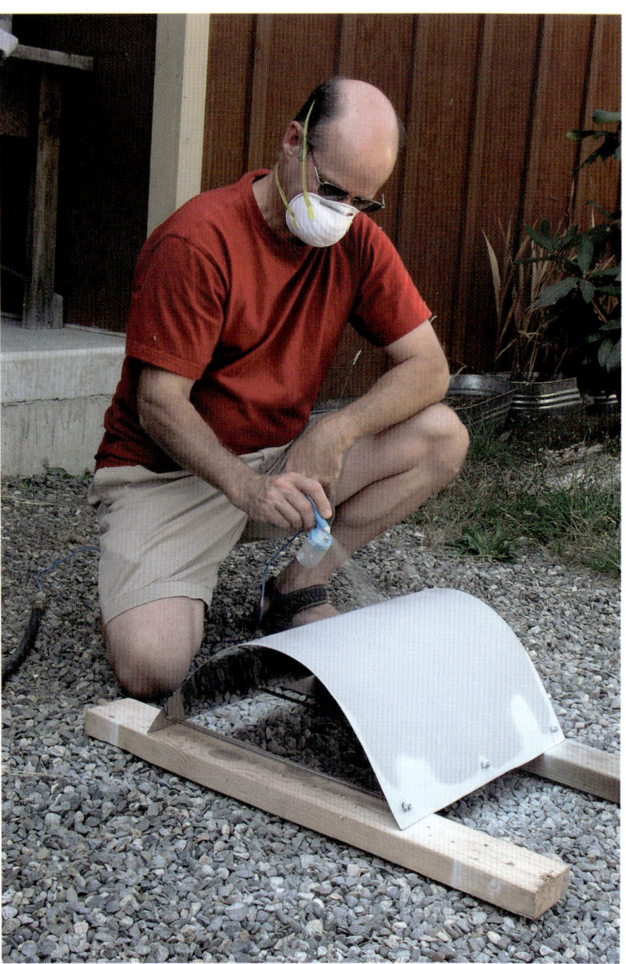

Glass Bending

upper left: the 18 gauge stainless steel is drilled in six places near the bottom edge. Then the sheet is bent and held by nuts on three threaded rods extending through the holes to hold the curve.

upper right: spraying shelf primer onto a hot metal form that has been heated to 250° F in a kiln.

lower left: glass balanced on the form. Sometimes ceramic props hold the glass level and are knocked out of the way just as the glass begins to bend, around 1100° F. Bending at a lower temperature by soaking the glass picks up less texture on the back than bending at a higher temperature.

lower right: bent glass on the form after cooling.

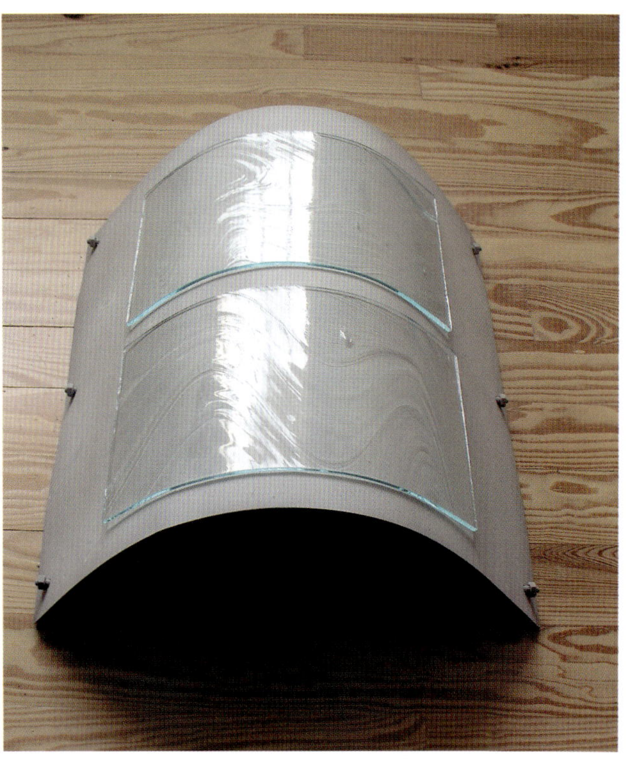

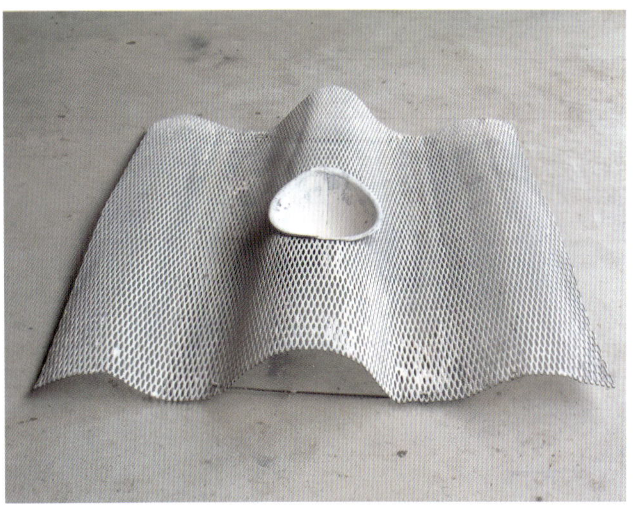

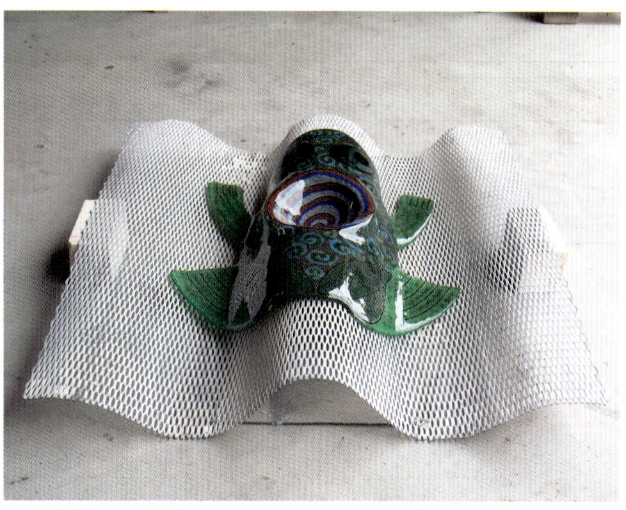

upper left: a bent, expanded steel mold coated with shelf primer. The center hole contains a stainless steel mixing bowl. Soak and slump the glass at a lower temperature to minimize transfer of the screen texture to the glass.

bottom: "Clear Gravity," 1986, H. 5 in. (13 cm) x W. 8 in. (20 cm) x D. 5 in. (13 cm). Glass slumped between electric motor winding cores consisting of many layers of thin metal that were able to move and slide, so the glass didn't crack.

upper right: glass "Frog Effigy Bowl," 2001, H. 19 in. (48 cm) x W. 15 in. (38 cm) x D. 3 in. (8 cm), after slumping on the mold.

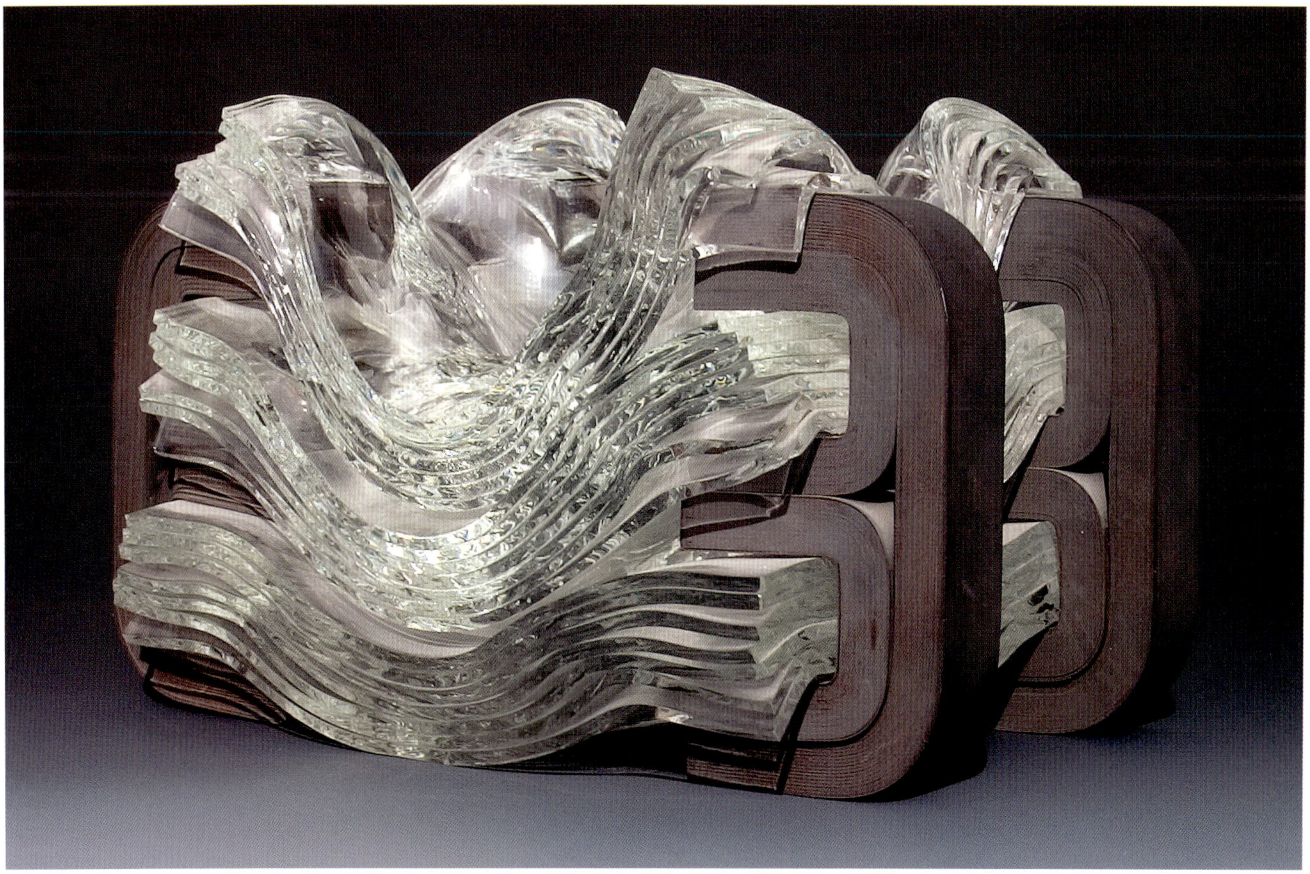

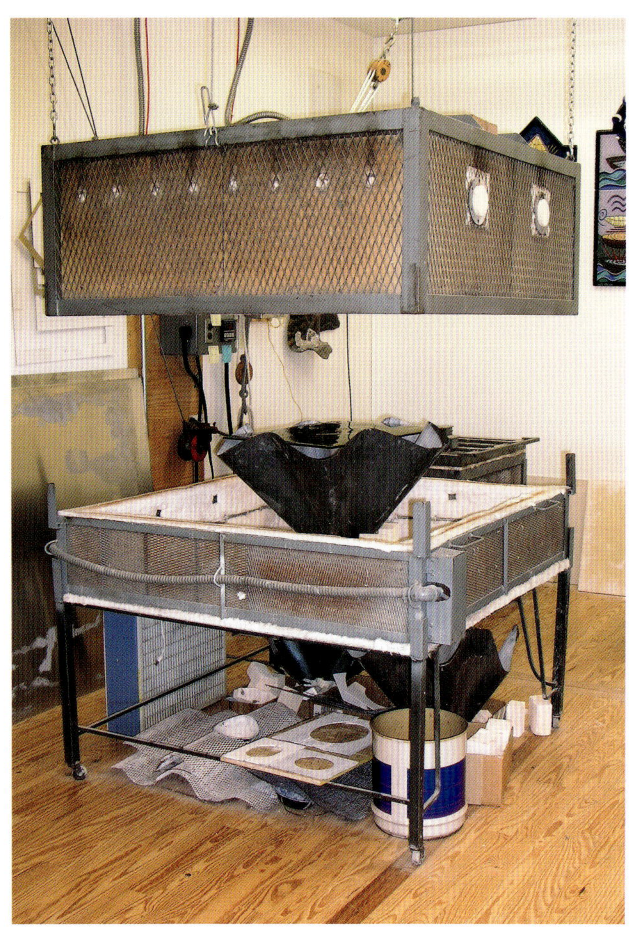

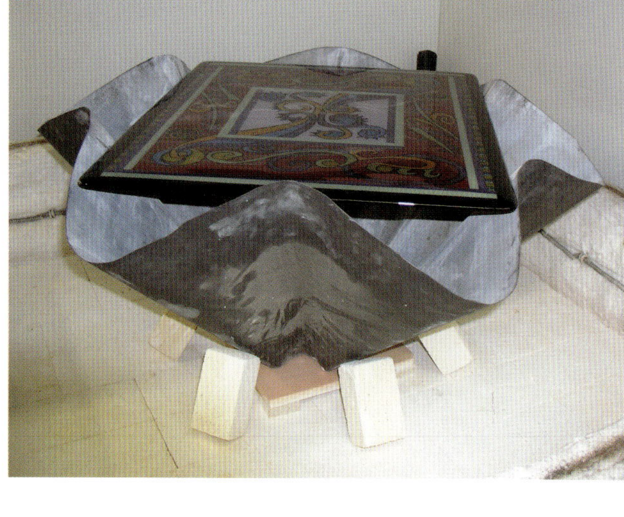

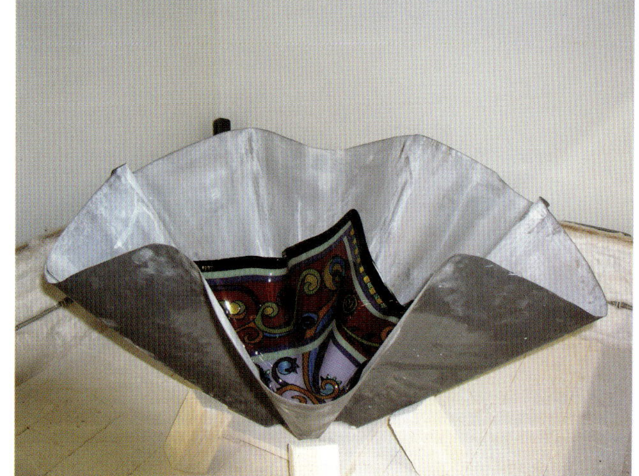

Glass Slumping

upper left: stainless steel mold with glass ready to slump in my big fiber kiln with an inside dimension of 24 in. (61 cm) high x 45 in. (114 cm) wide x 45 in. (114 cm) deep. Notice the ring molds, fluted metal molds, and expanded mesh mold under the kiln.

upper right: fused glass for "Bolero" vessel placed in the fluted stainless steel mold, which sits on a small kiln shelf and is braced by kiln bricks. The mold has been sprayed with shelf primer so the glass won't stick to the metal.

middle: glass in mold after slumping.

bottom right: finished "Bolero" displayed sitting on its side, H. 12 in. (30 cm) x W. 17 in. (43 cm) x D. 19 in. (48 cm).

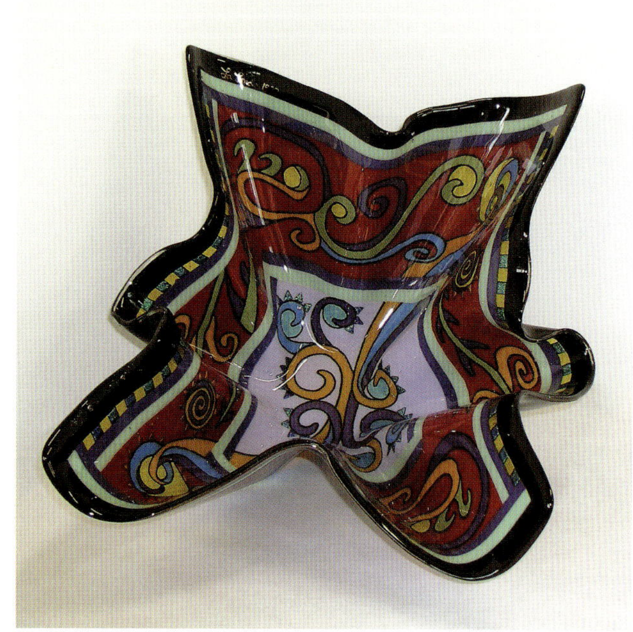

144

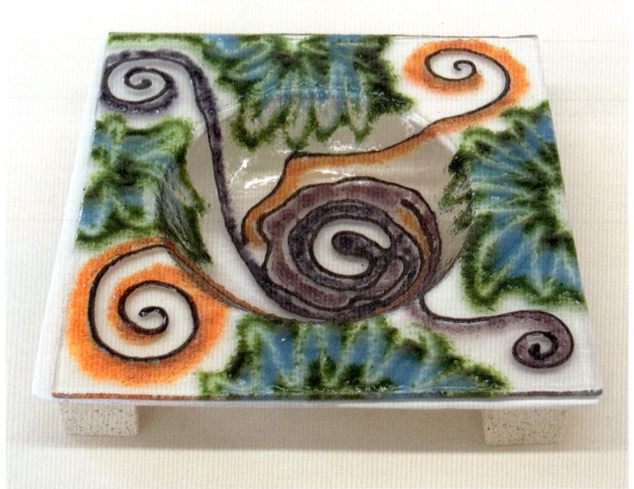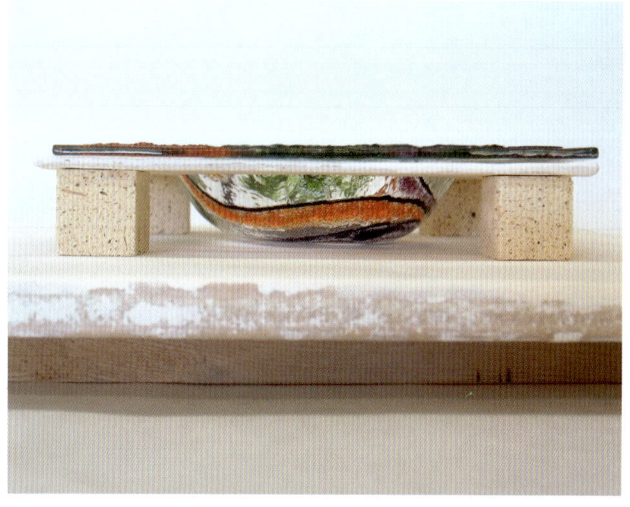

Sagging Glass

upper left: frit is placed onto a ⅛ in. (3 mm) thick x 6 in. (15 cm) x 6 in. (15 cm) piece of clear glass, which is sagged through a ring mold to create a flat bottom against the kiln shelf. The ring mold is made from rigidized fiberboard and is held 1 in. (2.5 cm) above the shelf with kiln brick pieces. The frit and liquid glass line will "fuse to stick" onto the glass during the sag.

upper right: side view of the fiberboard ring mold, brick posts, and sagged glass on a kiln shelf.

bottom: "Green Pagoda," 2002, H. 8 in. (20 cm) x W. 10 in. (25 cm) x D. 10 in. (25 cm). Pieces of glass are set on a four tiered square ring mold that has removable sections and then sagged onto a base. The glass is hotter in a sag than a slump, so frit and pieces of glass stick together.

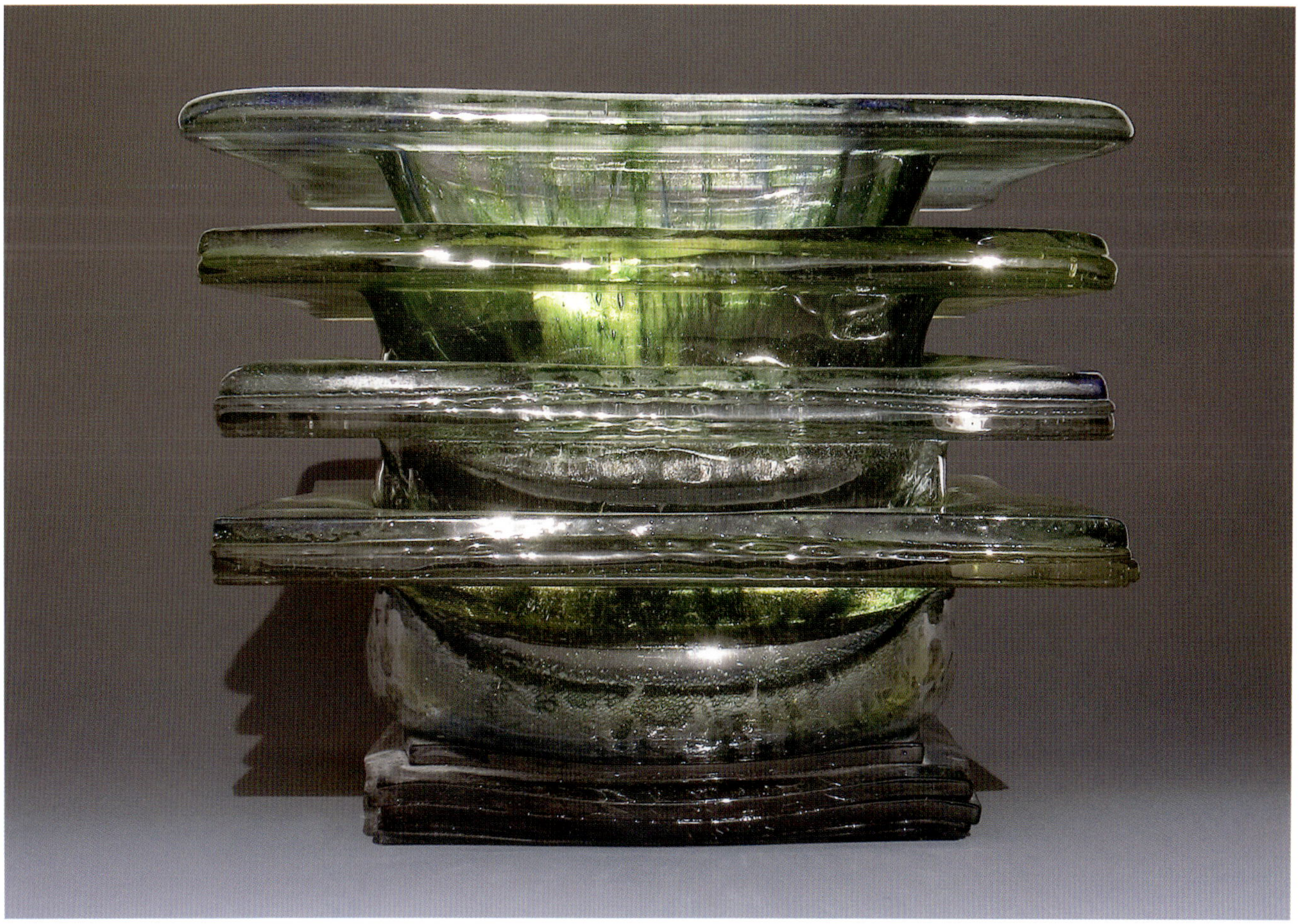

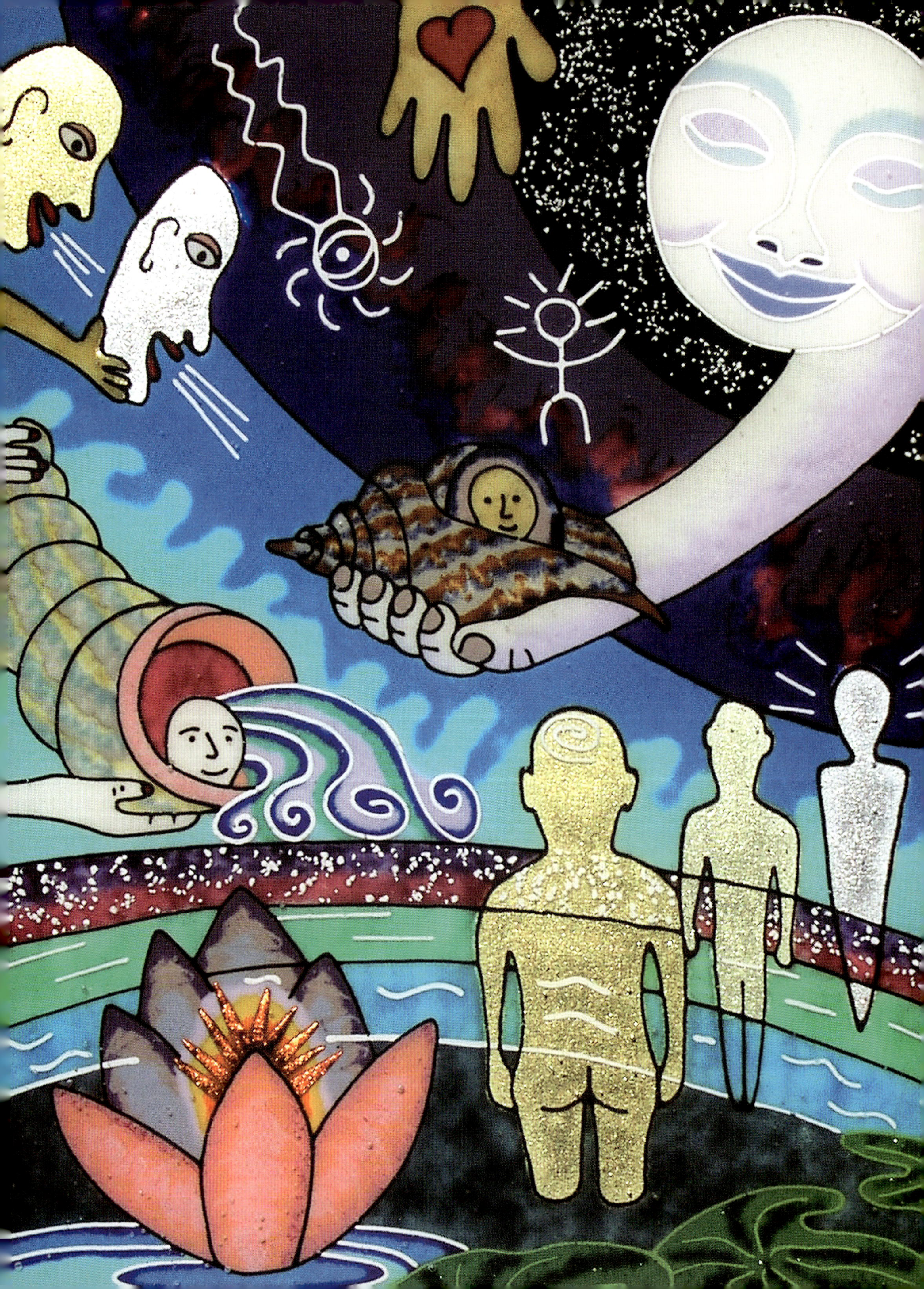

precious metal: leaf and foil

I use three different techniques with gold and silver in my artwork: (1) leaf under glass, (2) leaf on top of glass, and (3) foil fused in glass.

Precious Metal Leaf

Most hobby stores sell a 6 in. (15 cm) x 6 in. (15 cm) "imitation gold leaf," which is a mixture of mostly copper with a little tin; this tarnishes easily. Don't mistake this for real gold leaf! "Imitation silver leaf," which is aluminum, is also available, as is real copper leaf. When imitation gold or real copper leaf are fused between glass, the leaf disintegrates into beautiful turquoise bubbles. Aluminum turns gray. This can be a disaster or a great artistic success. The latter is worth exploring.

Leaves of gold and silver adorn some artifacts from Egypt, Mesopotamia, China, Peru, and many other ancient cultures. We still use leaf today as a decorative material in artwork, furniture, and picture frames; gold leaf is even eaten in fancy desserts. These precious metals are malleable and can be beaten into sheets. Gold leaf today, only a few millionths of an inch thick, easily disintegrates if touched by hand; if blown on, it can also be destroyed. It's a very interesting and challenging material to use.

Most gold leaf is available in 3 ⅜ in. (85 cm) x 3 ⅜ in. (85 cm) squares in a "book" with twenty-five leaves. Sheets of thin paper that won't stick to the leaf separate the individual leaves. To make leaf, metals are melted and poured into a rectangular mold. When the strip of metal has cooled, it's flattened in a rolling mill; the long ribbon this creates is cut into pieces that are placed between vellum, special rice paper, or plastic. This is pounded for final thinning to leaf thickness, which is then trimmed and put into the books. Hand-beaten leaf is still made, but today most is mechanically created. Thickness varies between manufactures, most of which are located in Germany, Italy, France, and Japan.

Most leaf is a mixture, "alloy," of gold, silver, and copper with a variety of color options to enhance your art. I especially like Lemon Gold, 18kt. (karats). Other leaf colors that I use are Glass Gold 23kt., Red Gold 23 kt., and Moon Gold 22kt. Gold, platinum, and palladium are fairly non-reactive metals, so they don't "tarnish." The higher the gold content, expressed in karats (24kt. is pure gold), the more durable the alloy is. Silver leaf is thicker than gold leaf; with silver, I have to take care that it doesn't oxidize (tarnish). Copper leaf is especially prone to oxidation – just compare a new penny to an old one. This "problem" can become another technique – coloring silver and copper with patinas can be one effect that you might want to try with leaf on top of the glass.

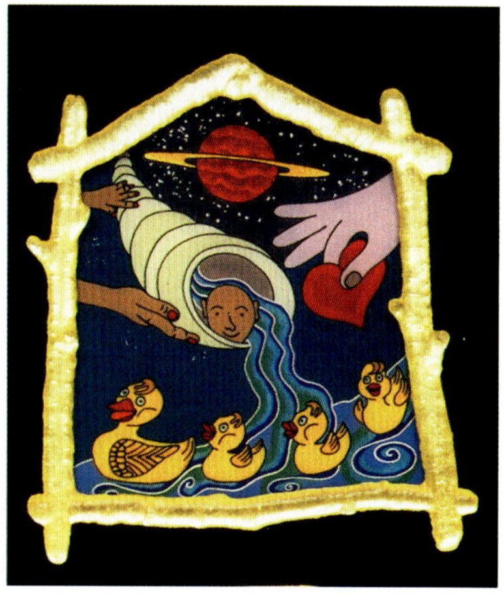

above: "All Lined Up," 1999, H. 24 in. (61 cm) x W. 21 in. (53 cm). Clear glass was kiln fused in a sand mold and gold leafed on the back.

facing: "Intuition," 2003, H. 23 in. (58 cm) x W. 19 in. (48 cm). One of eight panels commissioned for the Washington State Public Health Laboratory in Shoreline, WA. through the Washington State Arts Commission.

This panel illustrates the "Leaf Under Glass" technique. Glass is fused leaving clear areas "windows," which are then leafed on the back. The largest figure is done with Glass Gold leaf. The middle sized is Lemon Gold leaf; and the smallest is real silver leaf.

The face in the upper left is Glass Gold leaf holding a real silver leaf mask. Texture on the back of the glass and bubbles in the glass create an interesting effect. Sometimes I fuse on the back side of fiber paper, which gives a rough texture and enhances the leaf.

Leaf Under Glass

Twenty years ago my friend Roger Nachman gave me a thirty-minute demonstration of gelatin water size leafing. I've refined these techniques to leaf my fused glass. In 2005, I purchased a copy of <u>Gold Leaf Techniques</u> by Kent H. Smith and realized that I probably don't do things like a professional leafer. Get a copy of the book; it's a great resource. In this section, I'll tell you how I do it.

Leaf is adhered to the backside of clear glass with a gelatin water size. To make this mixture, purchase empty gelatin capsules, used for containing medicine, from a drug or health food store. I use medium-sized capsules, #0, which are ⅞ in. long and just over ¼ in. diameter, but all sizes will work. Don't use gelatin that is for cooking.

In a glass container, boil ¼ cup of distilled water in a microwave oven. Boiling tap water in a stainless steel kettle will work, but any dissolved minerals in the water might affect the leaf. Open and separate six #0 capsules. Remove the water from the heat source and add the capsules, which will begin to dissolve, a process you can encourage by mashing and stirring. When you can no longer see the capsules, the water size is ready to use. After one or two days, gelatin water size clouds up and should be tossed out.

To apply the mixture, I use an inexpensive 2 in. wide synthetic-hair paintbrush, used for latex paint. Keep this in your leafing kit and use it only for water sizing. The glass should have no oil on it, or the leaf won't stick; a freshly fused glass surface that you've cleaned with dish soap and thoroughly rinsed works well. Glass cleaner and alcohol also help. Remember, no oil.

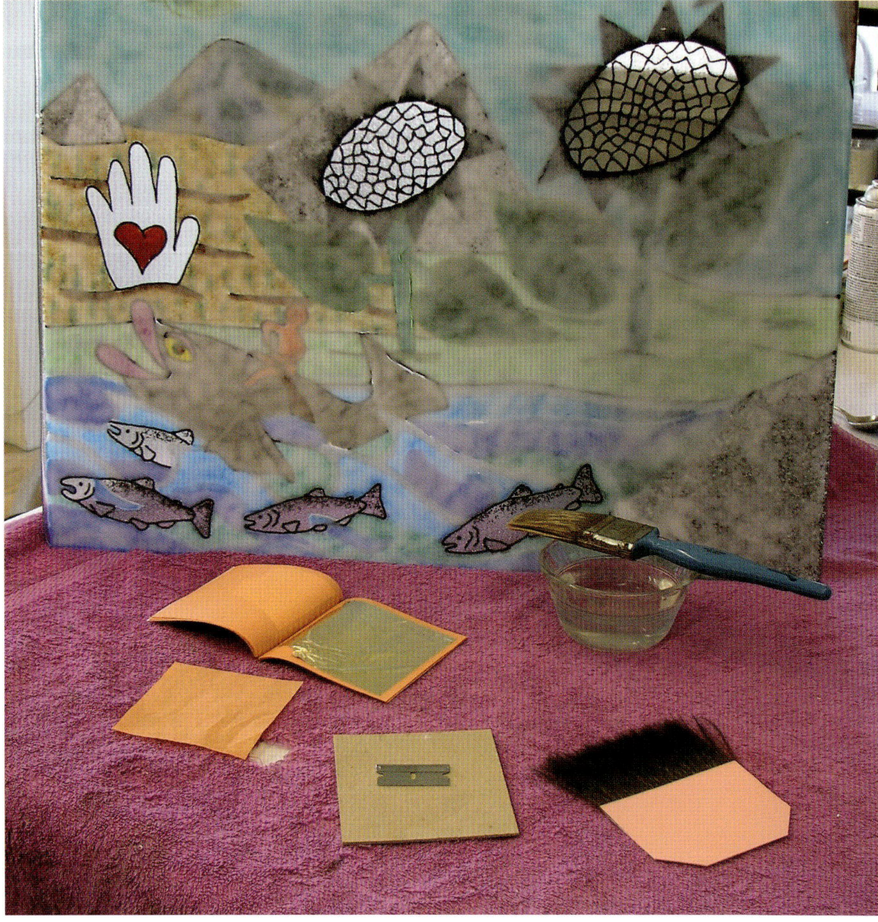

Right: The glass ready to leaf is propped almost vertical on a towel. All of the materials and tools are laid out. The leaf book is open. I cut a piece of leaf with a sharp razor blade, backing it with cardboard. The extra sheet of paper is to lay over the leaf when I cut it. The gilders tip brush is in the bottom right and the water sizing is in the glass container with the sizing brush laid across it.

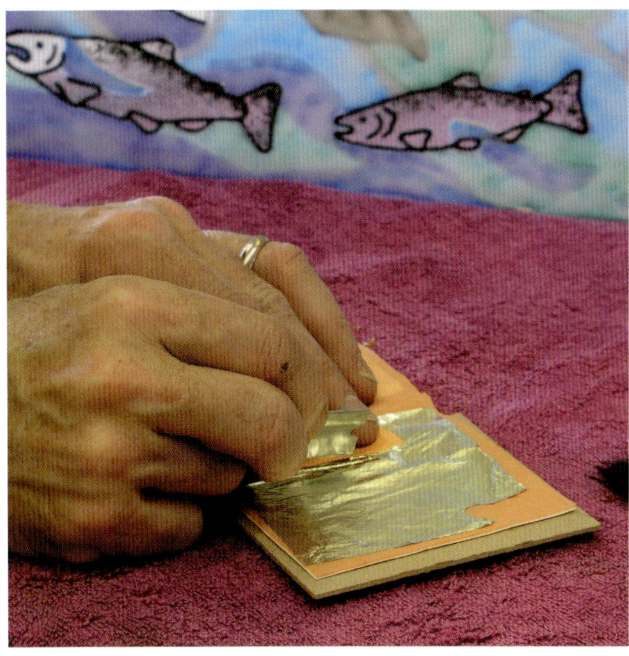

(1) Open the gold leaf book starting at the back and place a piece of cardboard under the last tissue with leaf on it. Place a sheet of tissue on the leaf to hold it down and make a line of little cuts about ⅛ in. long. Pick, pick, pick - little tears make the cut. You can also use a special guilders knife.

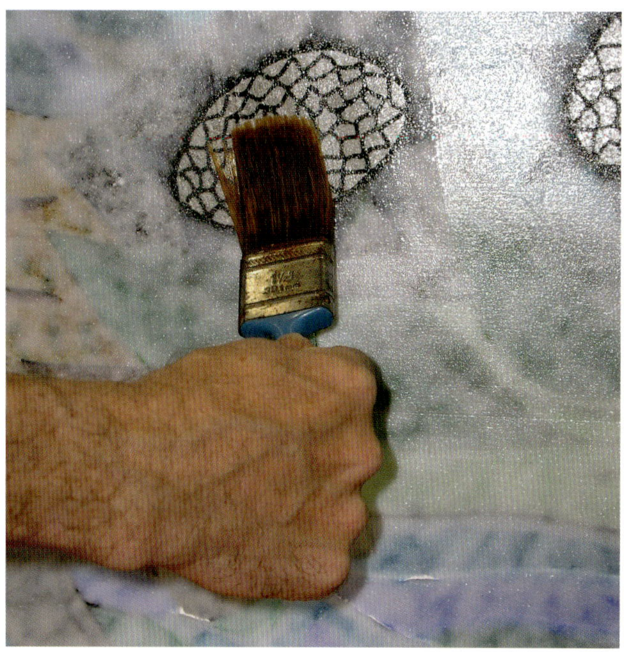

(2) Brush gelatin water size on the area to be leafed. One advantage of this method is that the leaf can be moved and positioned. If the leaf begins to dry, flowing extra water size from the brush tip and between the glass and leaf allows for repositioning.

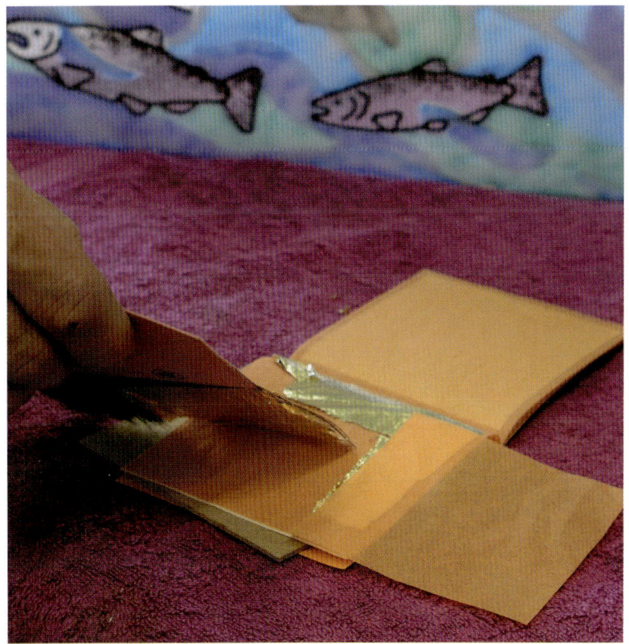

(3) The gilder's tip is a thin brush made from squirrel hair held between pieces of cardboard. Brush the bristles through your hair or, better yet, against your cheek or bald head to pick up oil from your skin. Then lay the bristles against the leaf and lift it up.

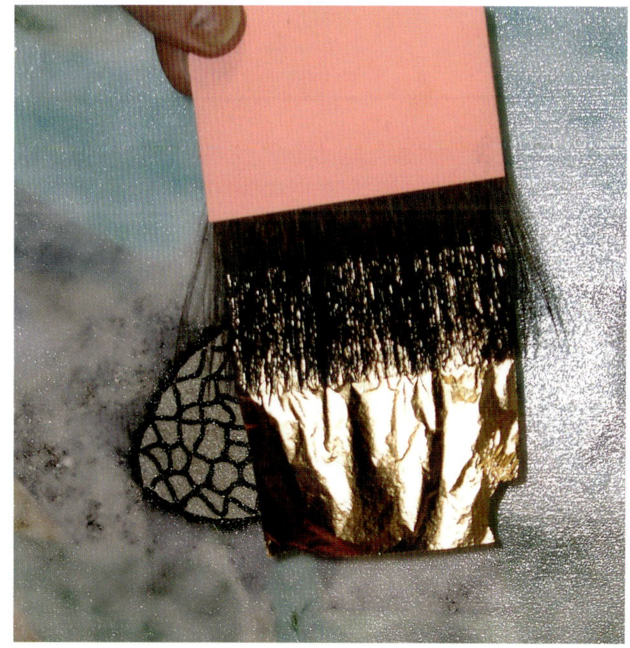

(4) Slowly bring the gilder's tip and leaf toward the glass but do not allow the leaf to touch. Notice that the hanging leaf moves toward the glass. Pull it back and the leaf swings away from the glass. When you are ready, move the gilders tip quickly and touch the glass. It will stick, and the hanging part will also swing and stick. This may take some practice.

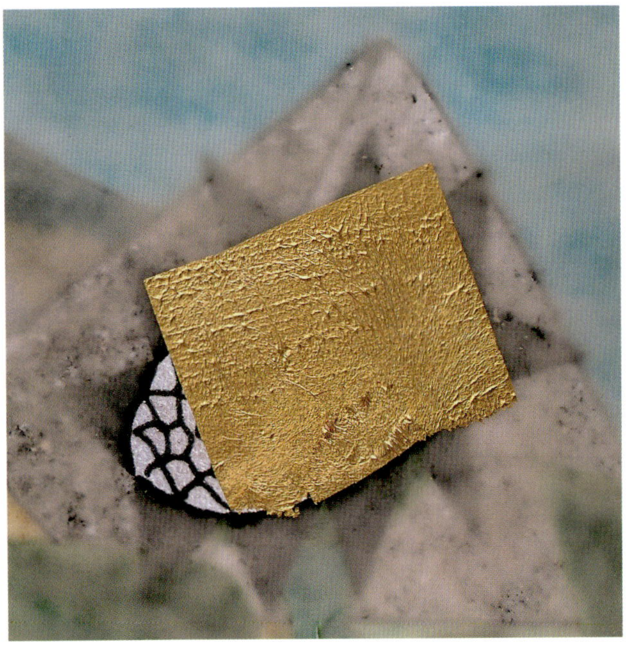

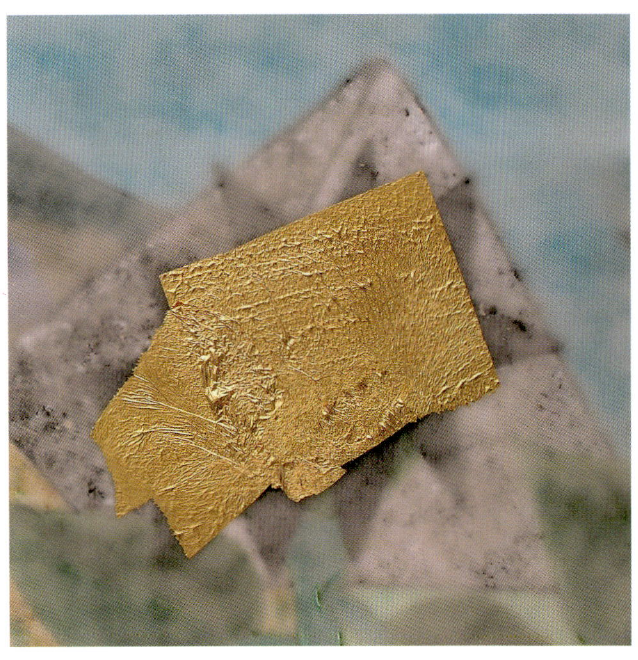

(5) Placement of the first leaf. The Leaf shows the texture of the back of the fused glass. On window glass there is no texture and the leaf can be smoothed to a mirror polish.

(6) Placement of two other pieces of leaf. They should overlap slightly.

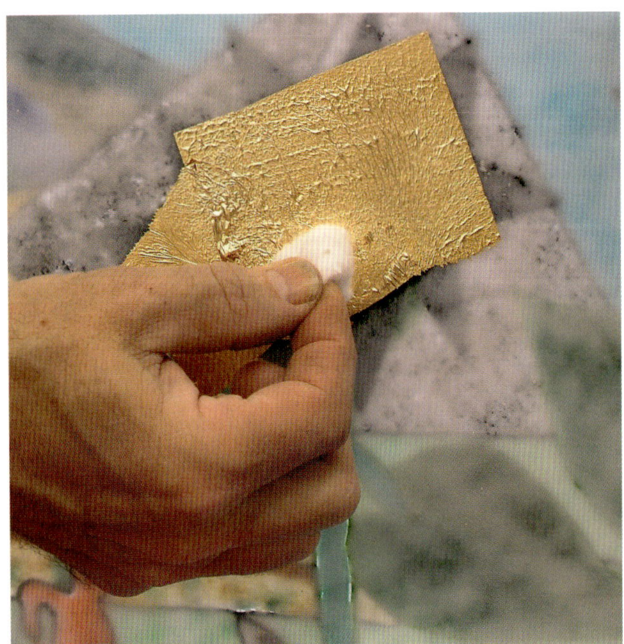

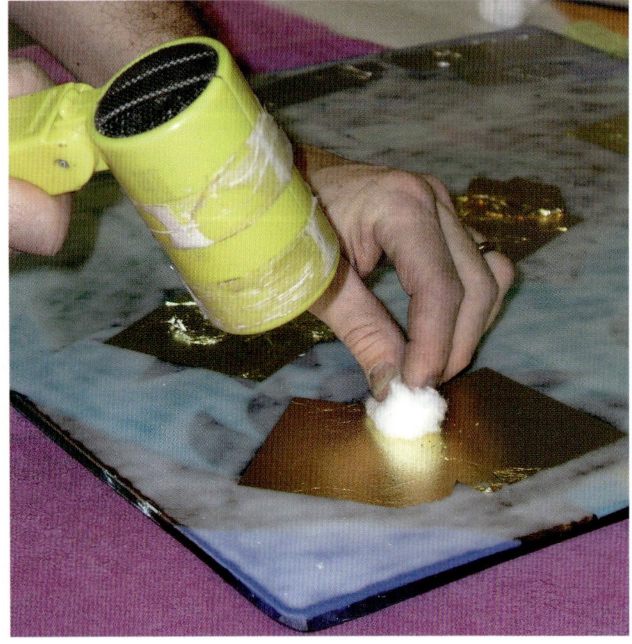

(7) Lightly press excess water from under the leaf with a pure cotton ball; replace the cotton ball as soon as it gets damp. Lean the glass in a sunny window or dry overnight for the best results. If you are in a hurry, you can use a hair dryer.

(8) With a hair dryer, press the cotton ball lightly into the leaf. As the leaf drys, rub ("burnish") the leaf to smooth the wrinkles. The leaf should get shiny. Be careful - the back surface of fused glass can be rough, or if it is wet, pieces of the leaf will tear away. After it's dry, go back and brush the leaf again with gelatin size and patch these holes with more leaf.

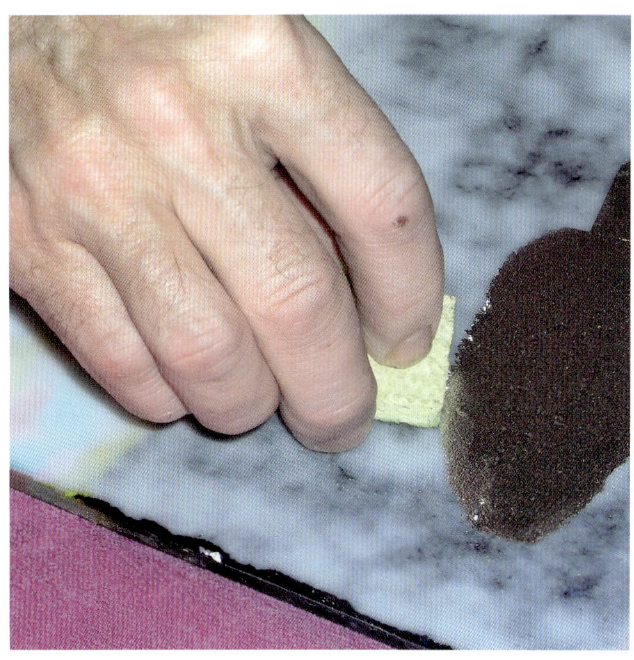

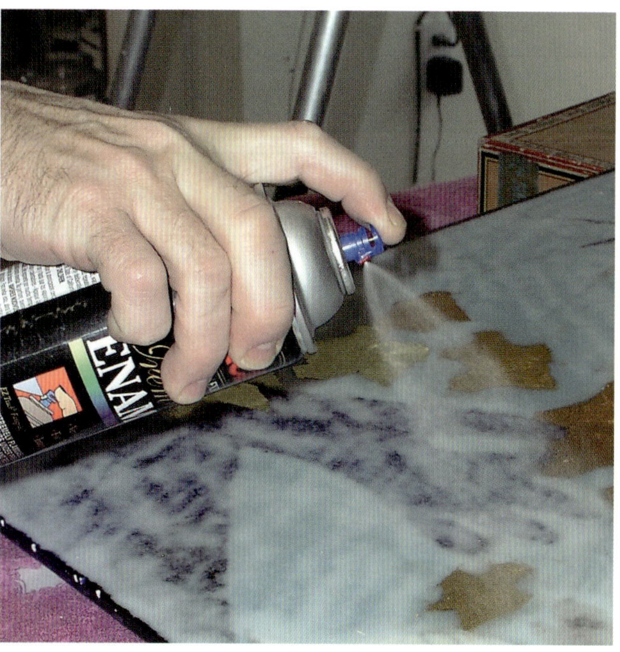

(9) Leaf that overhangs the clear area can sometimes show through the glass. Rub away the excess with a piece of green scrubby sponge.

(10) The leaf has to be covered because the sizing is water soluble. When the leaf is thoroughly dry, spray on clear plastic enamel to seal.

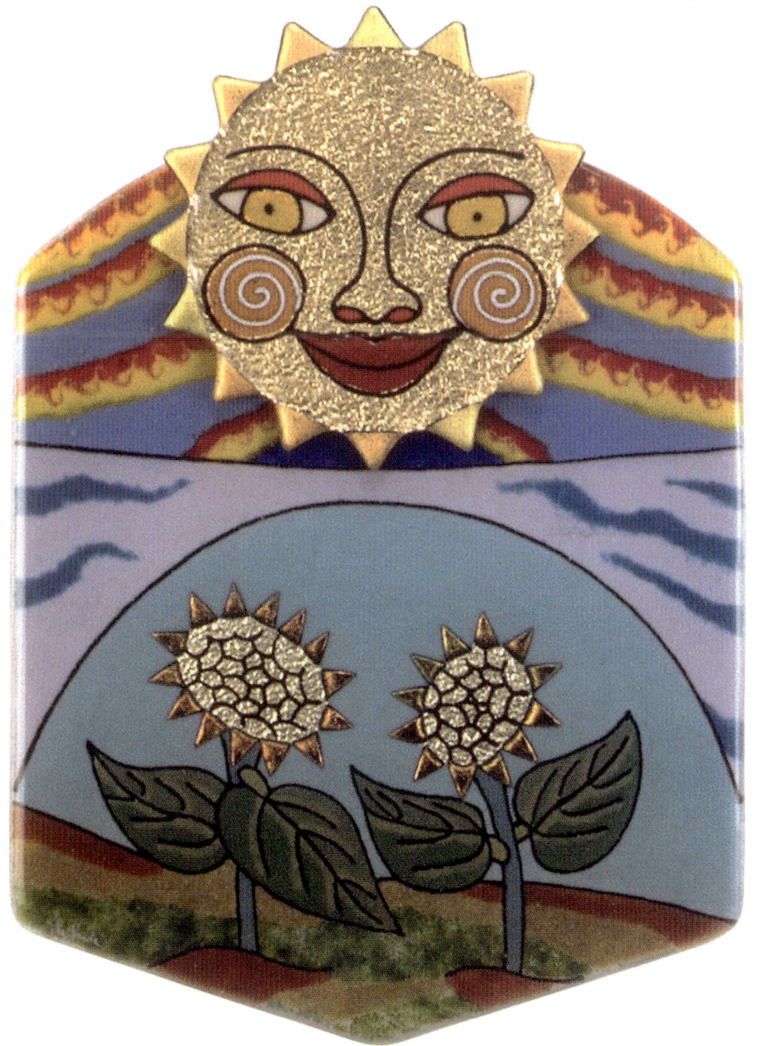

"Summer," 1995, H. 16 in. (41 cm) x W. 12 in. (30 cm). The tile and the sun were fused on the rough side of ⅛ in. fiber paper. When this textured surface is leafed, it scatters light and creates depth in this piece. Further sense of dimension is created by attaching the sun to the background tile with silicone adhesive.

Leaf On Top Of Glass

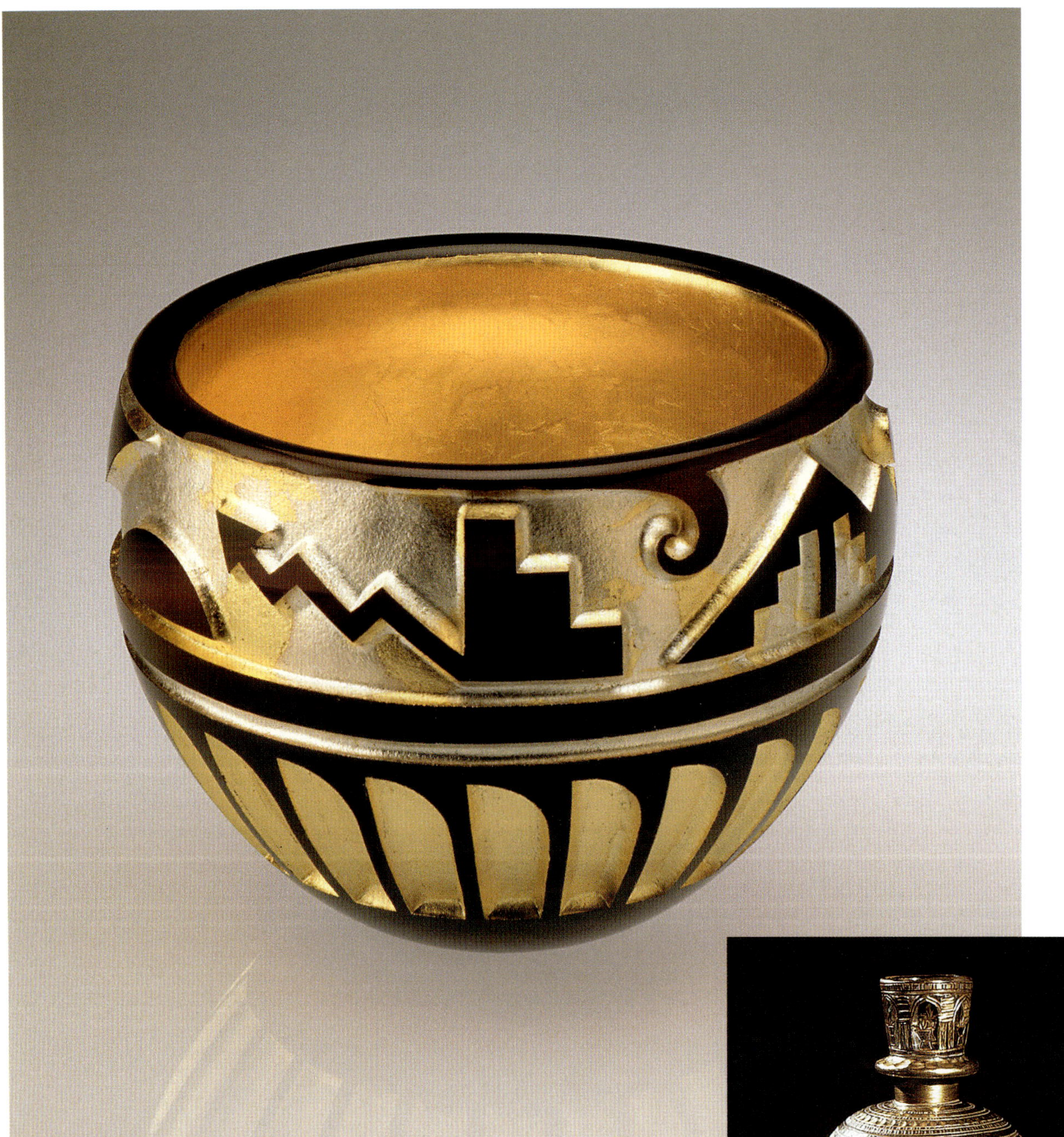

upper: "Golden Dreams," 1999, H. 8 in. (20 cm) x 10 in (25 cm) in diameter. Rob Adamson blew this vessel and deep carved the design with a sand blaster using silicon carbide as an abrasive. The gold leaf was applied to the inside of the vase and also to the exterior carved areas.

inset right: hookah base, blown, cut, and gilded with gold from 18th century India, H. 7 in. (17 cm). Adamson had not seen this earlier work, but developed his technique independently. Photo courtesy of the Corning Museum of Glass.

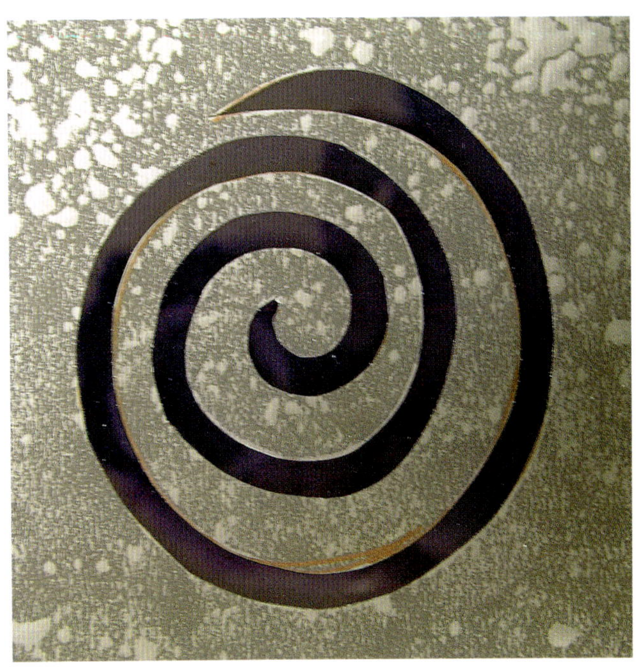

(1) The glass is covered with a self-sticking plastic resist. A design is cut into the resist with a razor knife to reveal the glass to be sandblast etched.

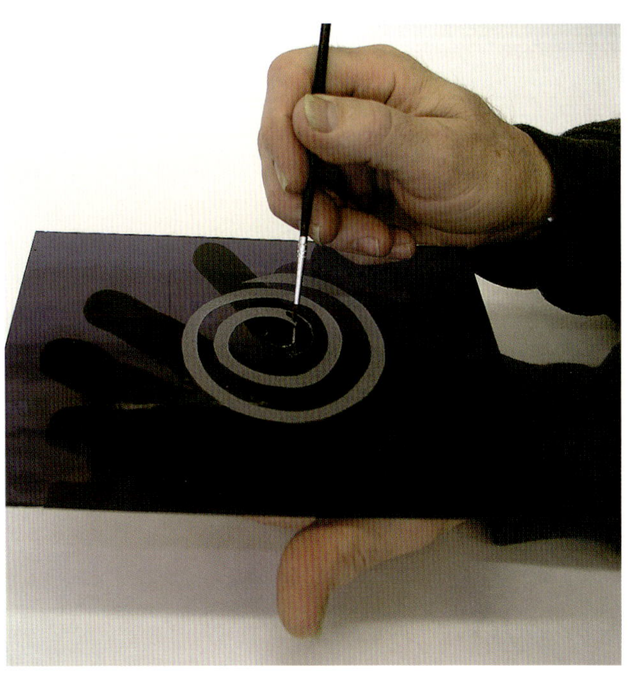

(2) After sandblasting, the resist is removed, and a quick drying varnish size is carefully applied with a brush. Quick size is ready to accept leaf in 1 - 3 hours.

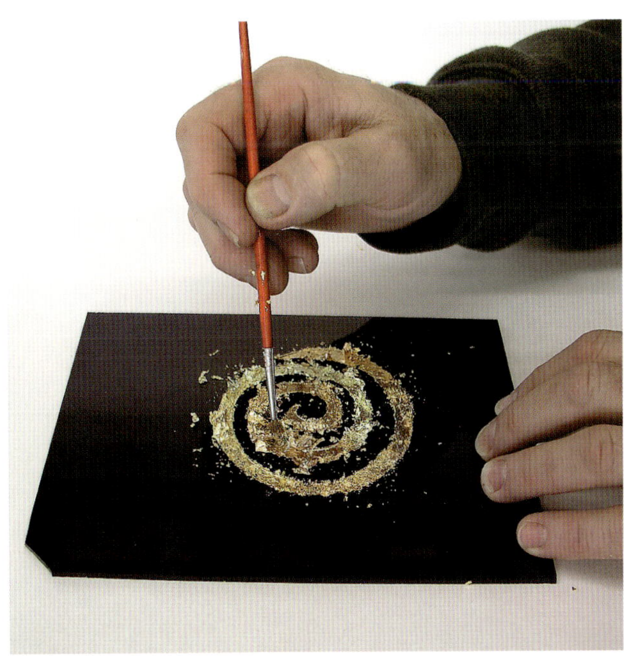

(3) Various colors of real precious metal leaf are applied and tamped down with a dry stipple brush. I don't use silver as it will tarnish.

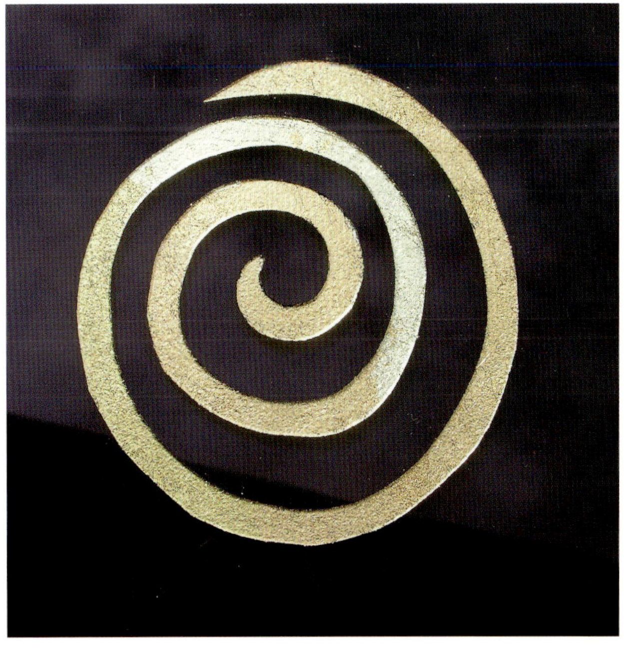

(4) The leaf that doesn't stick is brushed away. You can apply more size and leaf, only after the first application is totally dry. Real gold doesn't need a sealer for protection. I used three colors of gold for this tile.

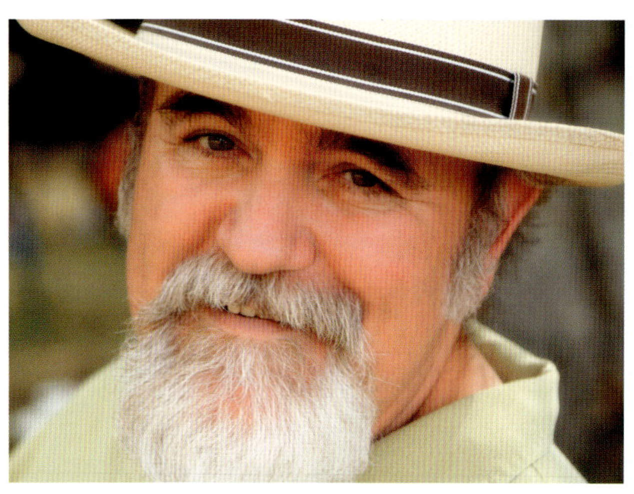

Rob Adamson (b. 1945)

upper left: Rob Adamson, 2005.

upper right: "Geo," 1999, H. 14 in. (35 cm) x 8 in. (20 cm) in diameter. Sand carved vessel with gold leaf.

lower left: "Maple Leaf Vessel," 1999, H. 12 (30 cm) x 10 in. (25 cm) in diameter. Sand carved with gold and white gold leaf.

lower right: "Golden Vessel," 1999, H. 7 in. (18 cm) x 9 in. (23 cm) in diameter. Sand carved vessel with gold leaf.

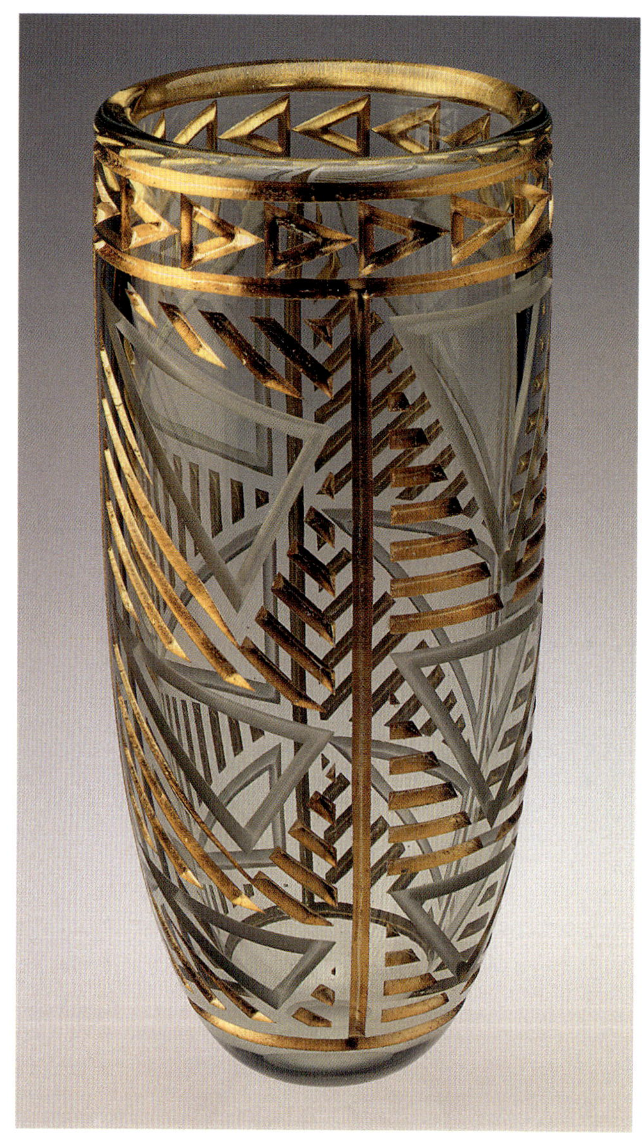

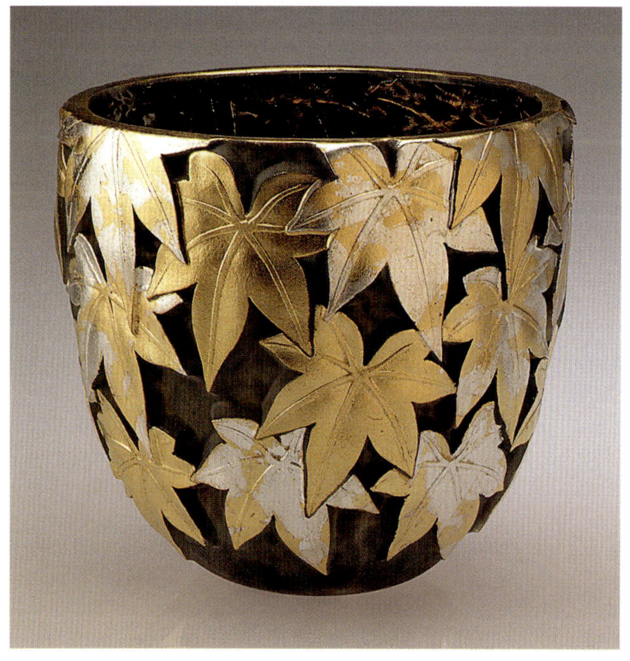

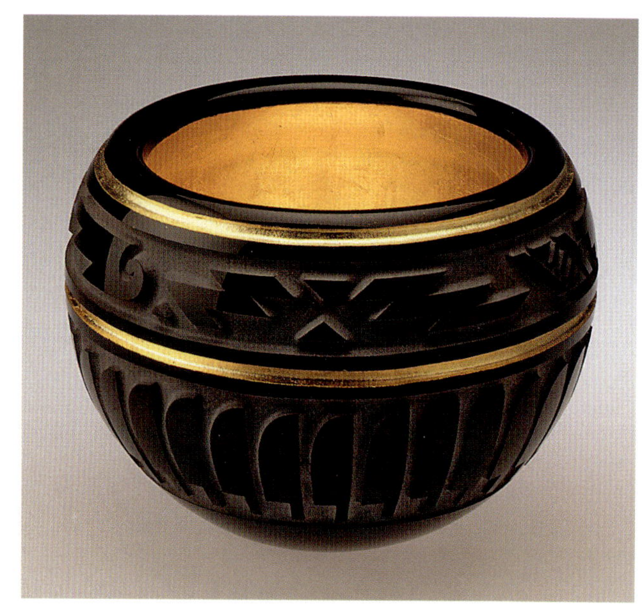

Foil Fused In Glass

Gold and silver leaf is so thin that it pretty much disappears when fused into or on top of glass, so I use the thicker gold and silver foil for fusing. Gold is non-reactive, and silver is very reactive to chemical influences during firing, which presents some challenges.

Japanese silver foil is 9 ½ in. (24 cm) x 9 ½ in. (24 cm) at 2 microns thick; Japanese gold foil comes in 8 in. (20 cm) x 8 in. (20 cm) sheets at .68 microns thick and is about seven times the price of silver. You can buy these as single sheets or in packets.

lower:
"Talking Raven," 2004, H. 20 in. (51 cm) x W. 20 in. (51 cm). The moon face is silver foil which has reacted with the glass and turned slightly golden in color. The sun is gold foil, and the center is silver foil. The lightning is dichroic glass.

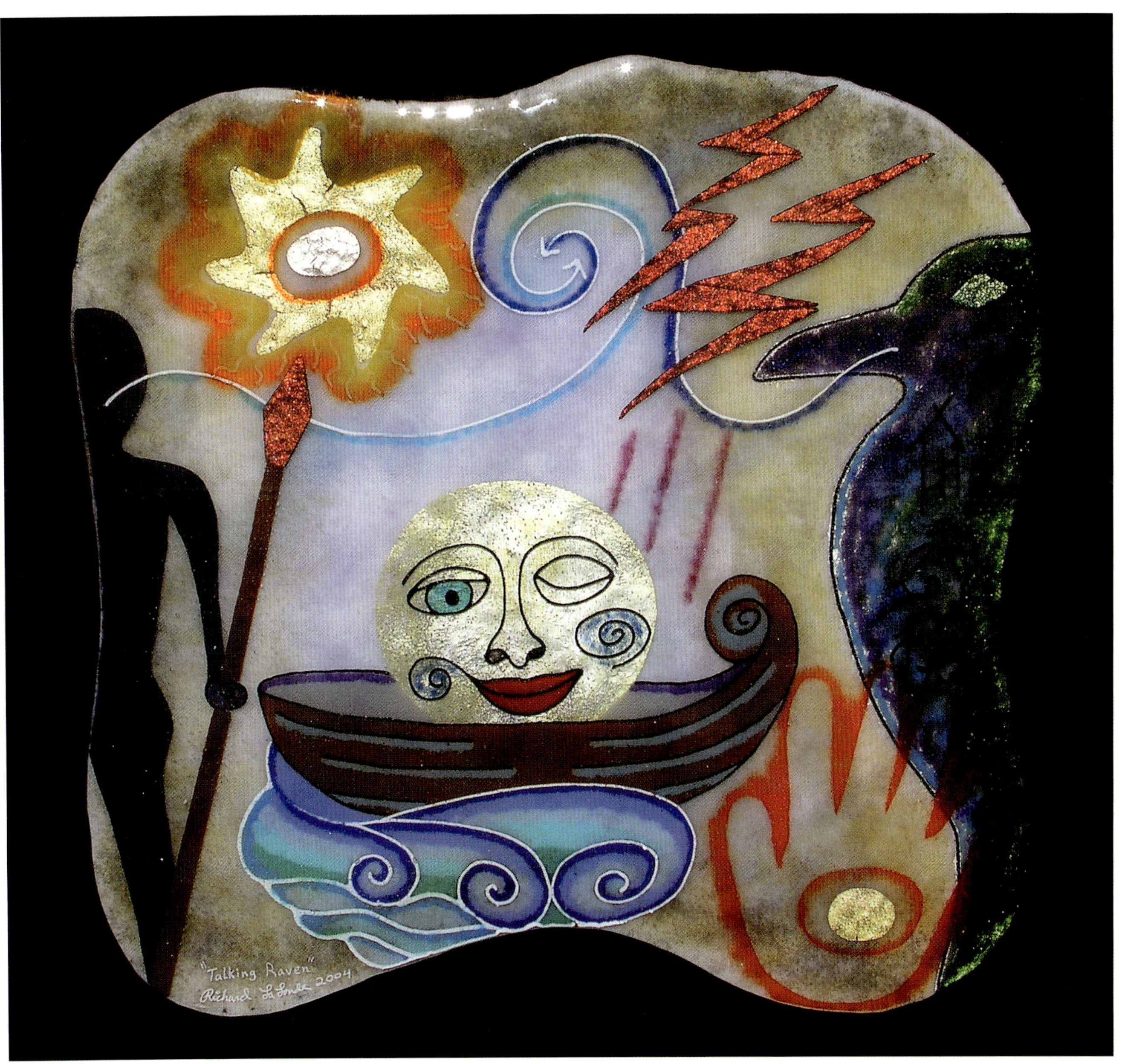

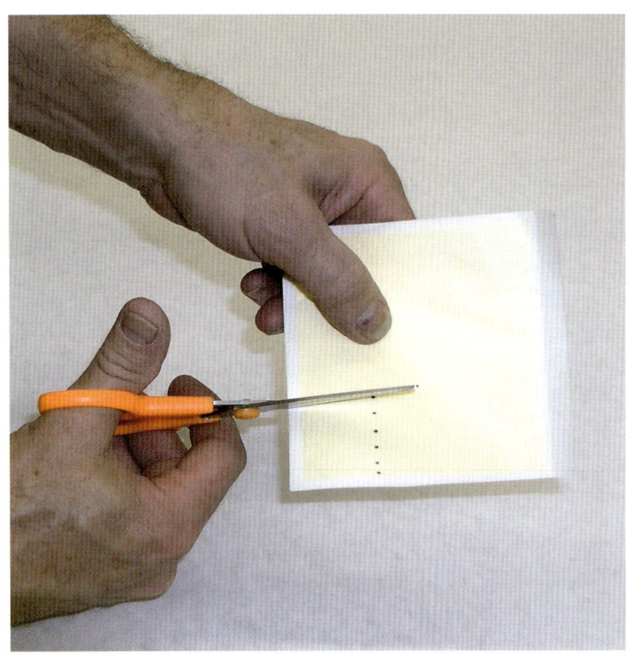

(1) Slide a sheet of foil onto a piece of copy paper. Unlike leaf, foil can be carefully handled with dry fingers. Make a line of felt pen dots outlining the area to cut and place a sheet of translucent tissue over it. Cut on the dotted line with sharp scissors.

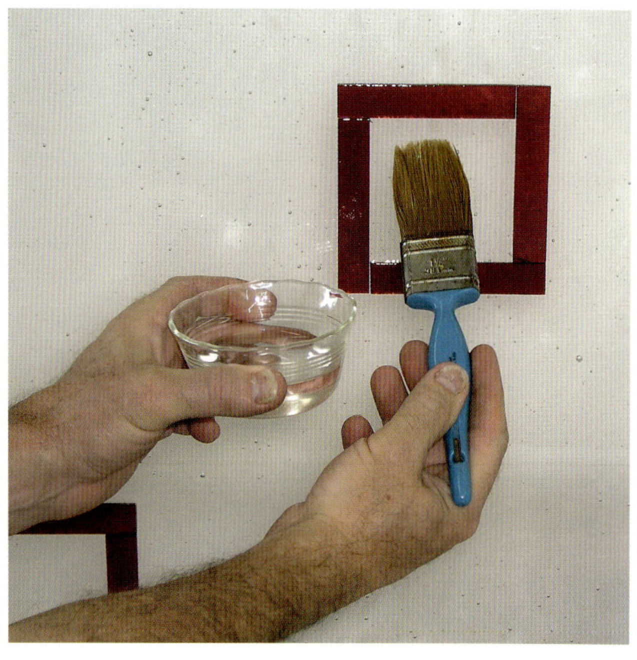

(2) Apply the gelatin water size.

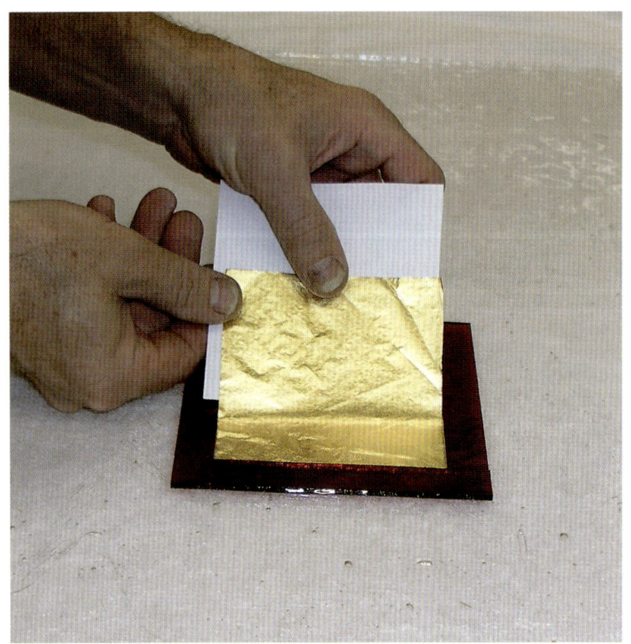

(3) Slip the foil off of the paper onto the glass

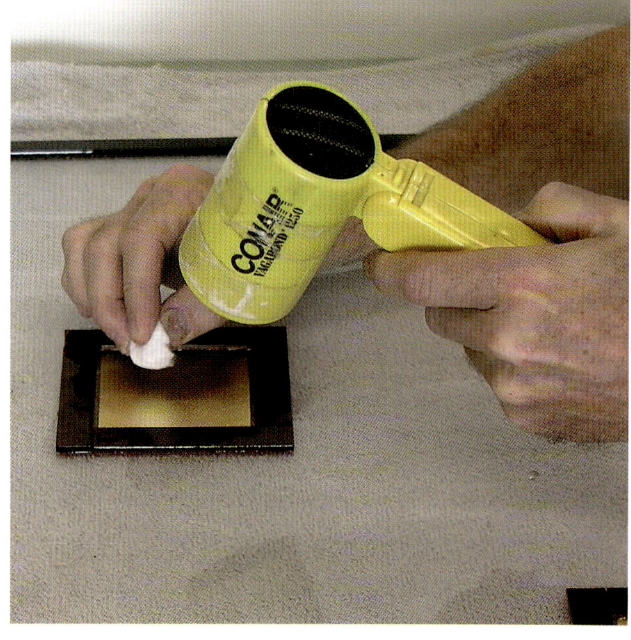

(4) Dry and carefully blot and push the water from under the foil with a cotton ball. For best results, let it dry in the sun or overnight.

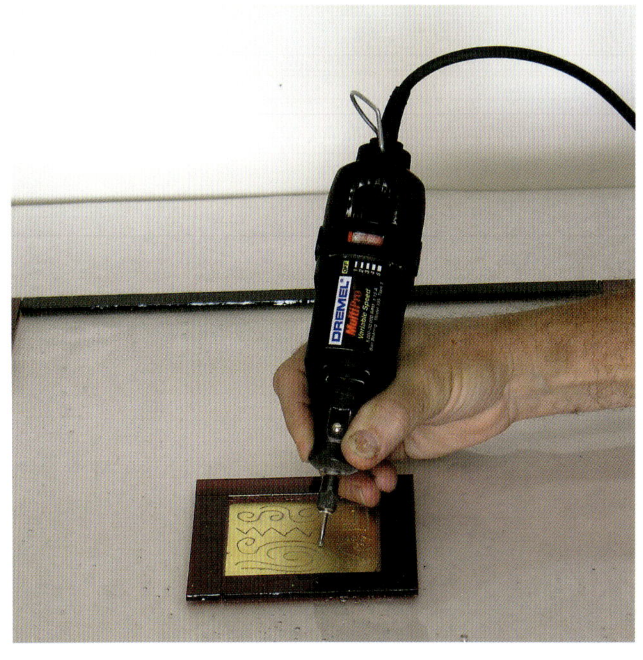

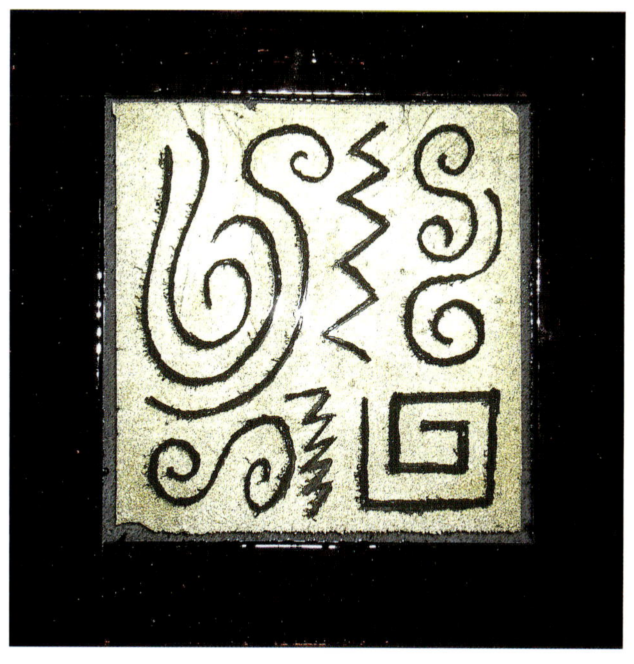

(5) Etch a design in the gold foil with a diamond burr and rotary tool.

(6) Etched design in gold foil.

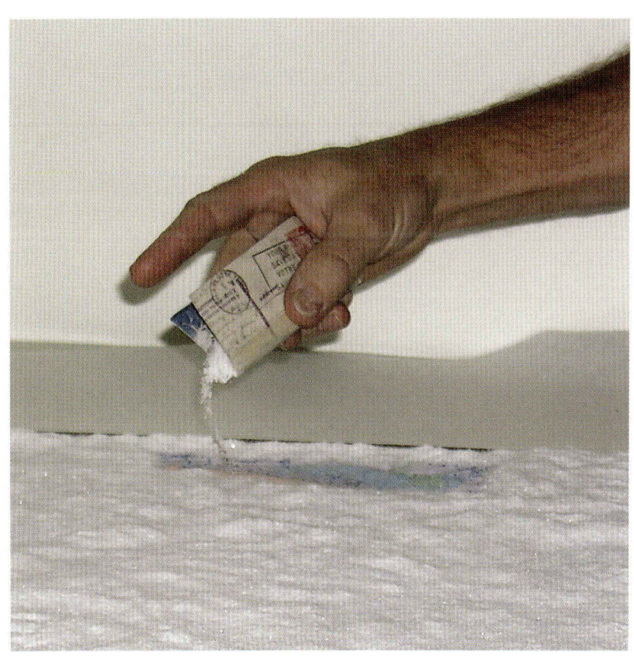

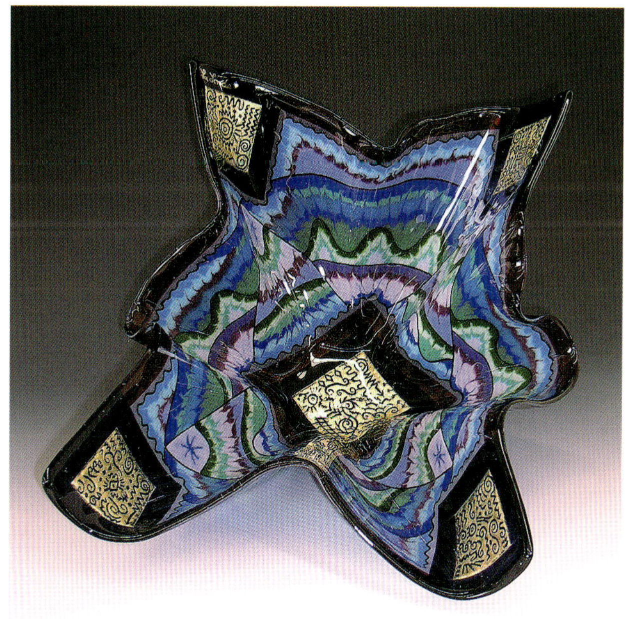

(7) The foil and other glass powders are covered with crushed clear glass.

(8) Mandala Vessel with etched gold foil, 2005, H. 12 in. (30 cm) x W. 17 in. (43 cm) x D. 19 in. (48 cm).

Technical Note: Silver is a very reactive metal

(1) Firing silver foil in a kiln where volatile organic materials are present can change the foil in both color and volume.

When the binder "burns" out from the shelf paper it produces a reduction atmosphere, carbon, which reacts with the silver. The test below illustrates this reaction which causes the silver to thin out and disappear in some places. For best results with silver, fire on predried shelf wash or prefired fiber paper. Do not fire on "Thin Fire" paper, a high temperature shelf paper which contains a binder.

Japanese Silver Foil Test

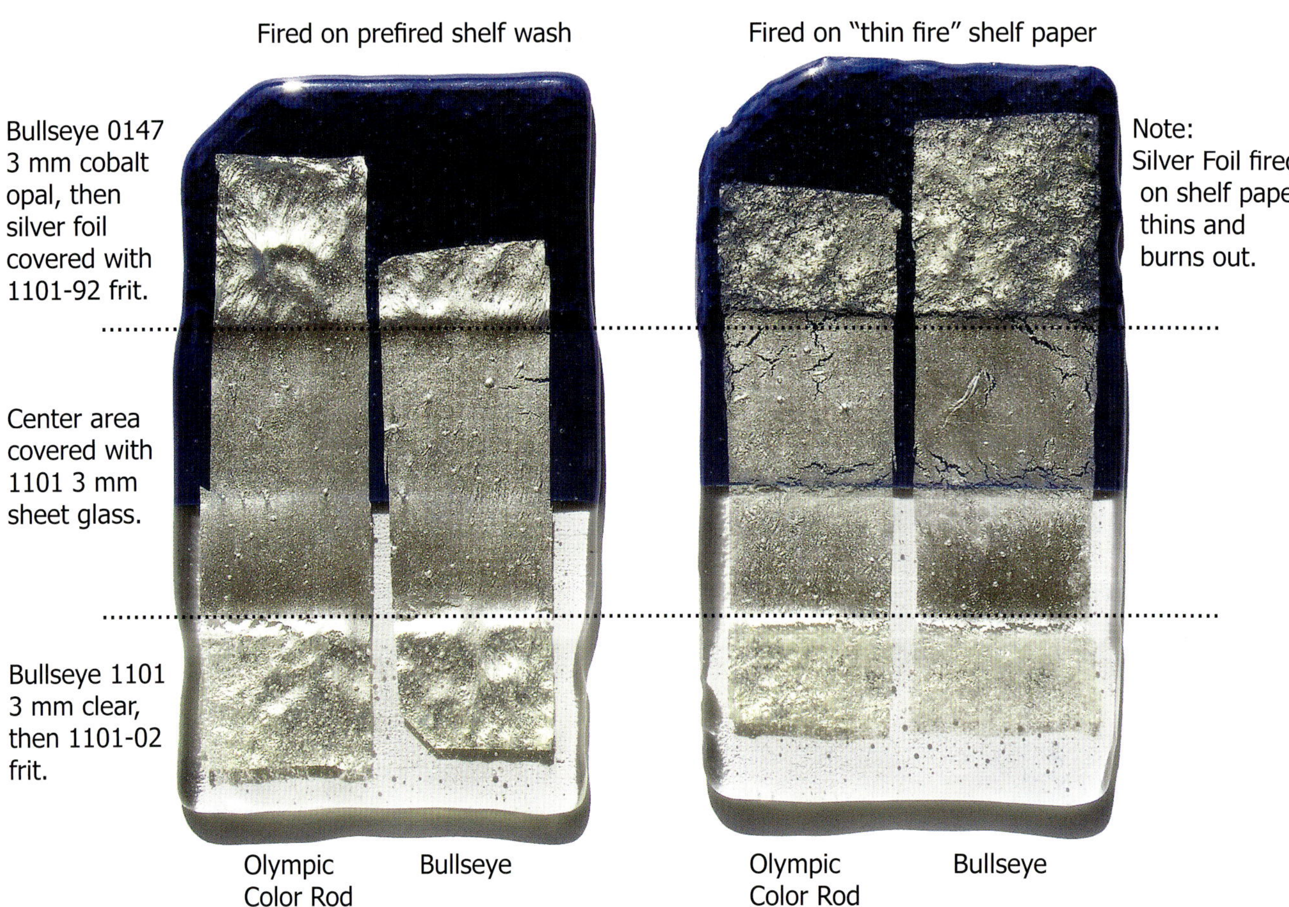

Note: This test uses both silver foil purchased from the Bullseye Connection in Portland, Oregon and Olympic Color Rod in Seattle, Washington. There was no noticeable difference between the silver from these suppliers. Thinning of the foil occurred in a slightly reducing kiln atmosphere created when the binder burned out from the "Thin Fire" paper. This can be noticed in the tile on the right where the foil that is cracked seems to disappear.

(2) Silver also reacts with elements in the glass.

Silver foil fired on glass containing sulfur - as in Bullseye reds, yellows, and french vanilla - can cause a reaction where the silver meets the glass. This can become a technique or a disaster, depending on how you view it. Notice a black line around and on some foil samples. The french vanilla sample (1) shows amber 1137 frit on top of the silver foil turning black; (2) gold foil with turquoise frit 1116 shows no reaction; (3) silver foil with a black edge line and (4) shows that transparent yellow 1120 flipped over is black between glass and silver foil.

Silver & Gold Foil Fused on Bullseye Glass

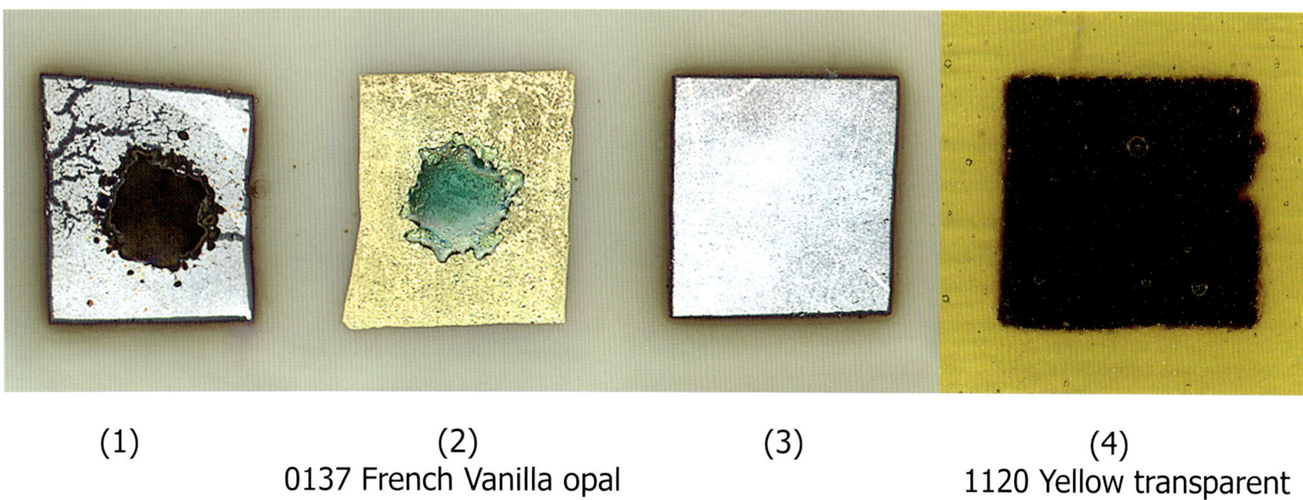

(1)	(2)	(3)	(4)
	0137 French Vanilla opal		1120 Yellow transparent

(1) Silver reaction with the glass black edge line and 1137 Amber frit on top turns black
(2) Gold Foil No Reaction 1116 Turquoise frit on top
(3) Silver reaction with the glass black edge line
(4) Silver reaction (black color), is viewed through the yellow transparent

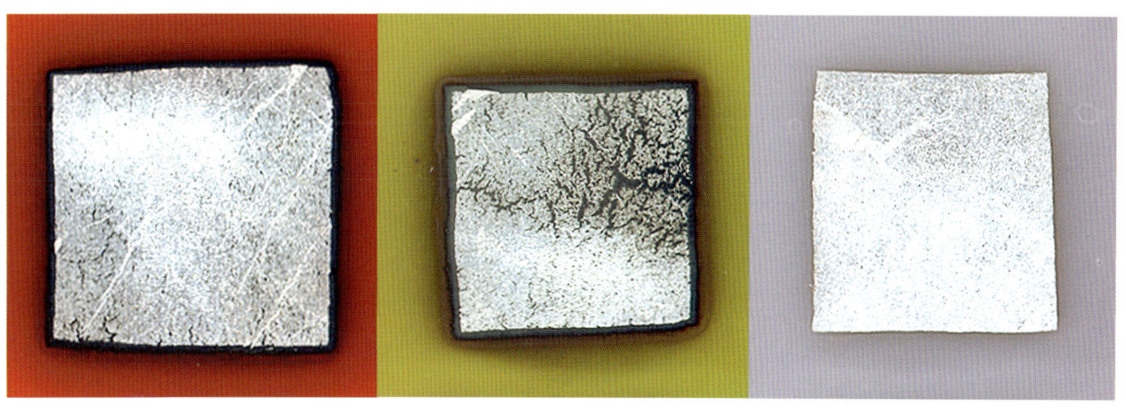

0124 Red opal	0220 Yellow opal	0142 Neo-Lavender opal
Reacts black edge line	Reacts black edge line	No Reaction

(3) Silver foil can change from bright silver to yellow when fired against clear glass.

This silver staining seems unpredictable; my tests of silver foil against Bullseye 1101, 1401, and Tekta clear don't give me a clear answer as to when and how this happens. It might have to do with the brand of silver foil, the glass composition, sizing, and/or the amount of time in the kiln. Sometimes foil turns yellow and sometimes it doesn't. This remains one of those artistic mysteries that I haven't figured out how to control, but I do like the effect.

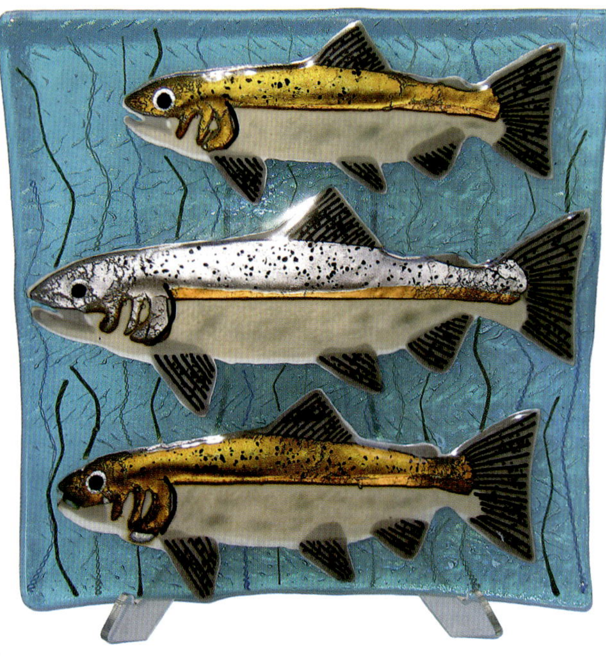

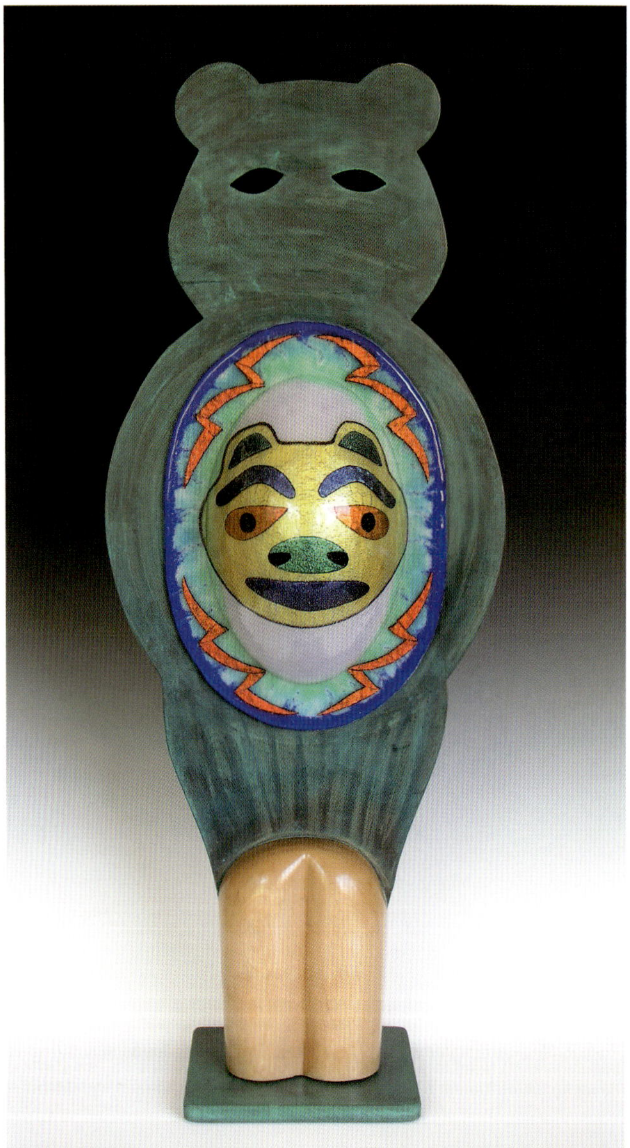

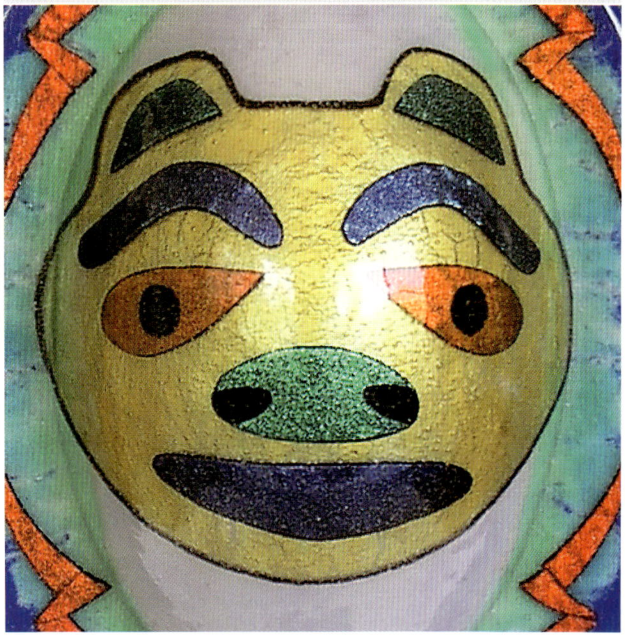

left: "Three Trout," artist D'Arcie Beytebiere, 2006, H. 15 in. (38 cm) x W. 15 in. (35 cm). The wonderful golden color is a silver foil reaction.

above right: "Golden Bear," 2005, H. 36 in. (91 cm) x W. 14 in. (36 cm) x D. 7 in. (18 cm). Fused and sagged glass with patined bronze with a maple handle. This sculpture uses the rattle form and makes noise if shaken. The gold color is really a silver foil reaction.

lower right: detail of "Golden Bear."

upper right: "Medallion with portrait,"
3rd century A.D., 2 in. (4.9 cm) in
diameter. Roman Empire, Italy, perhaps
Rome, colorless and translucent blue
with gold foil; gold sandwich. Courtesy
of the Corning Museum of Glass.

lower: "Fish," 1995, H. 10 in. (24 cm)
x 16 in. (41 cm), Higgins Glass Studio.
Prefired gold luster on window glass,
cut into pieces and fused with clear
and enameled window glass.

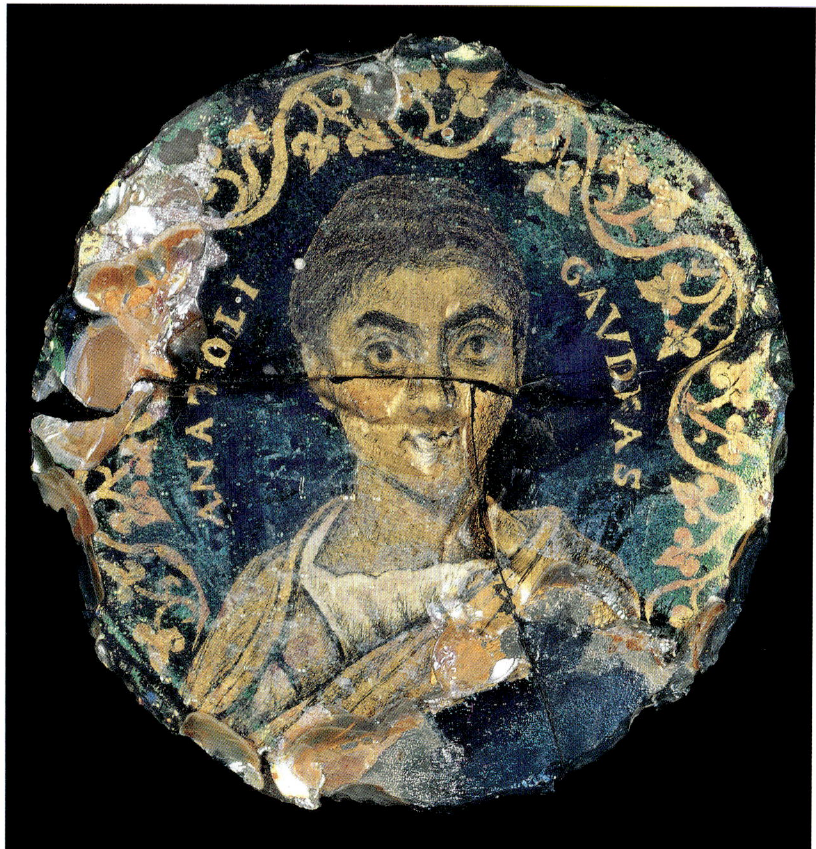

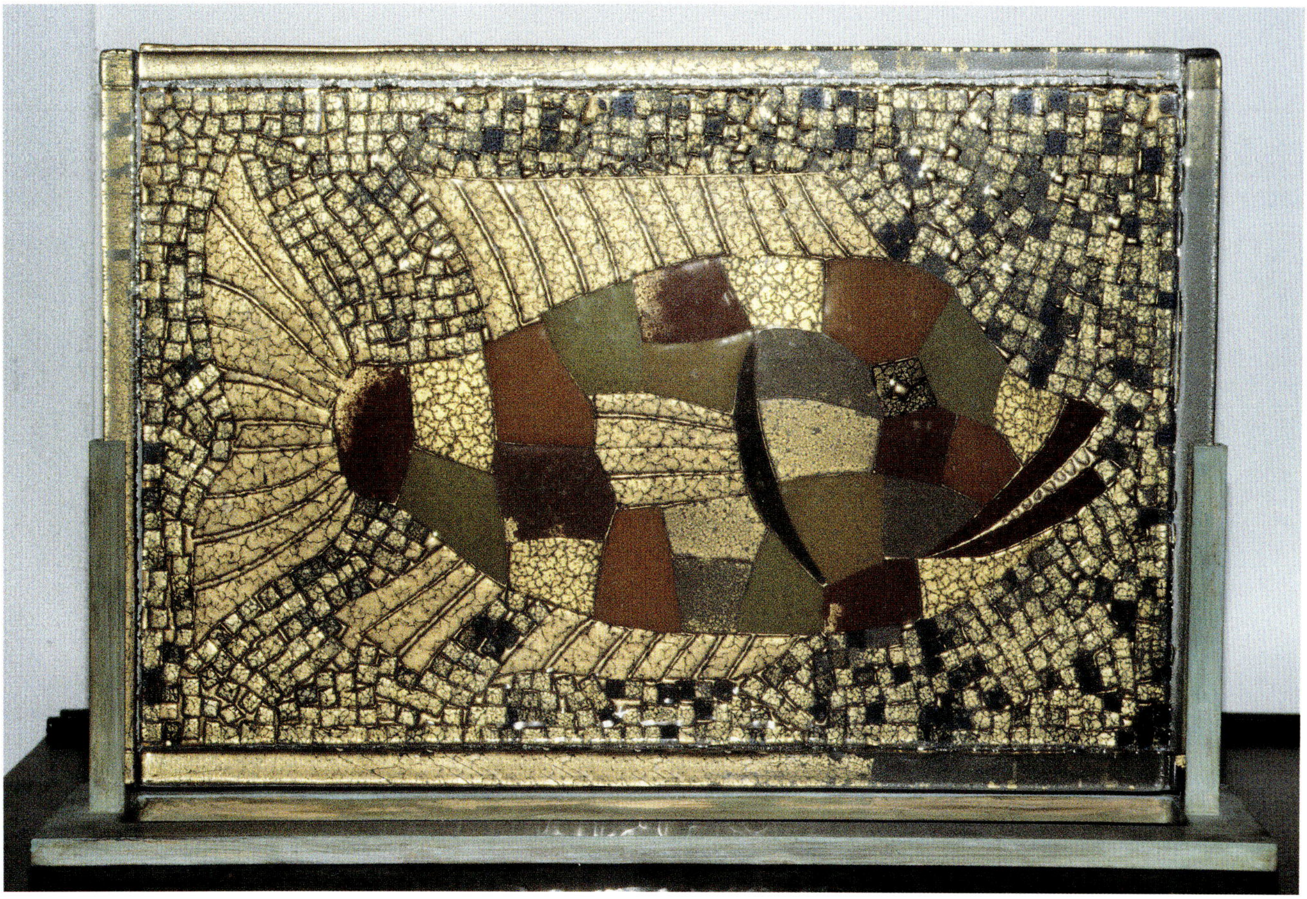

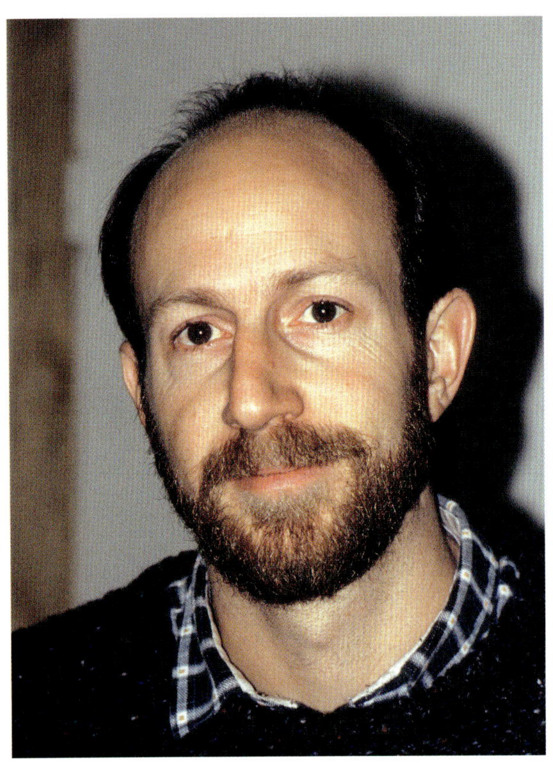

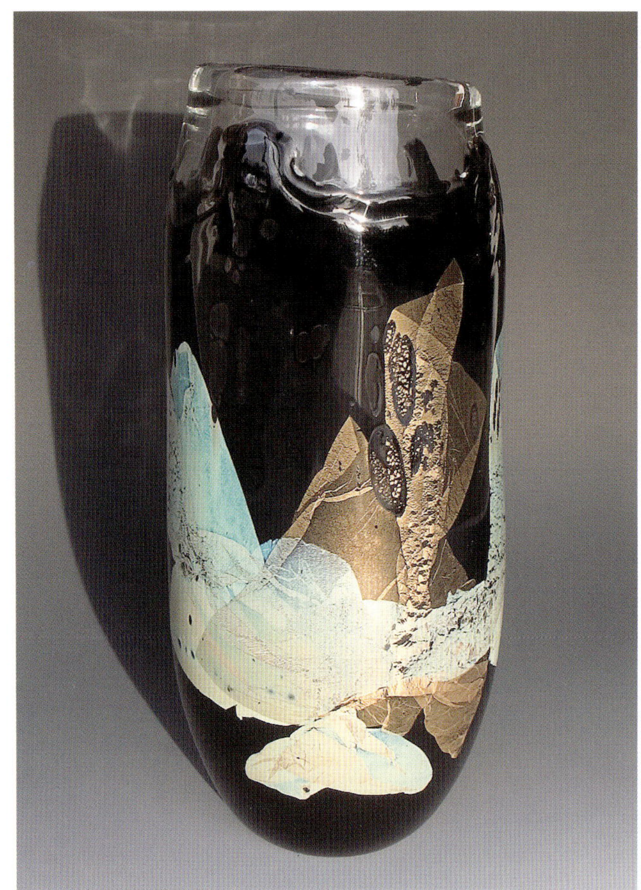

Roger Nachman (b. 1953)

left above: Roger 1986

right above: "blown gold and silver leaf vase," 1987,
H. 5 in. (13 cm) x 13 in. (33 cm) in diameter. Leaf
picked up on the outside of the vessel.

right middle: detail of "Zoe."

bottom: "Zoe," 1988, H. 3 in. (8 cm) x 18 in. (46 cm)
in diameter, fused glass with gold and copper leaf.
The copper turns into turquoise-colored bubbles
when fused. Slumped in a second firing.

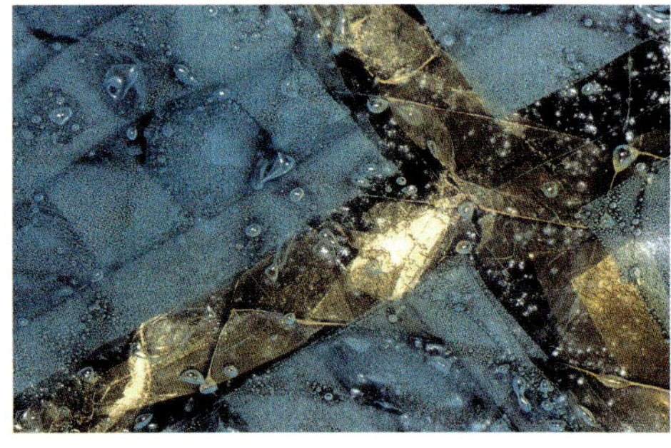

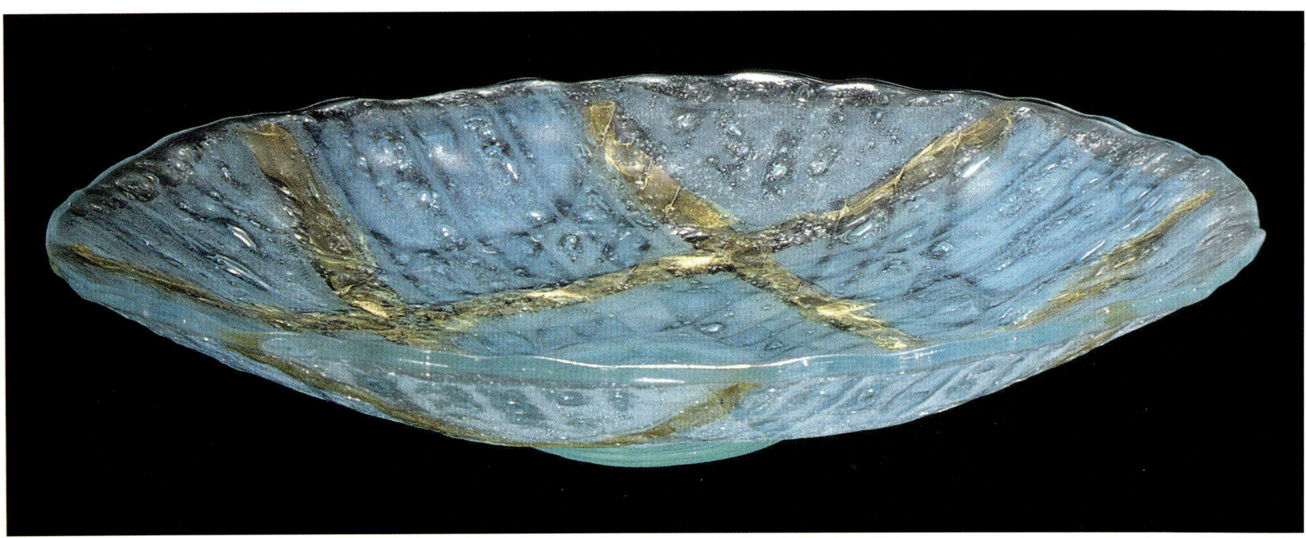

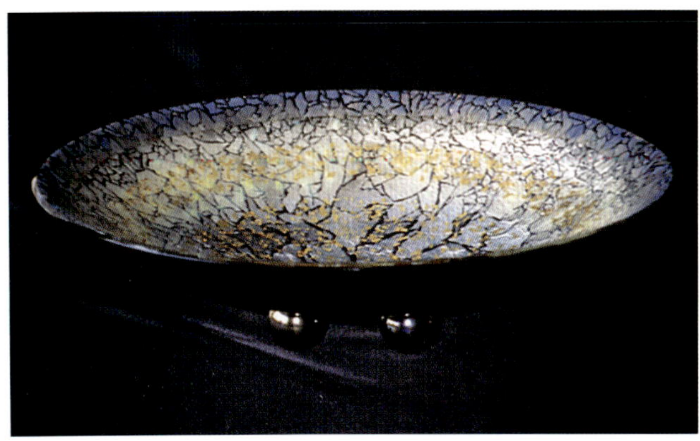

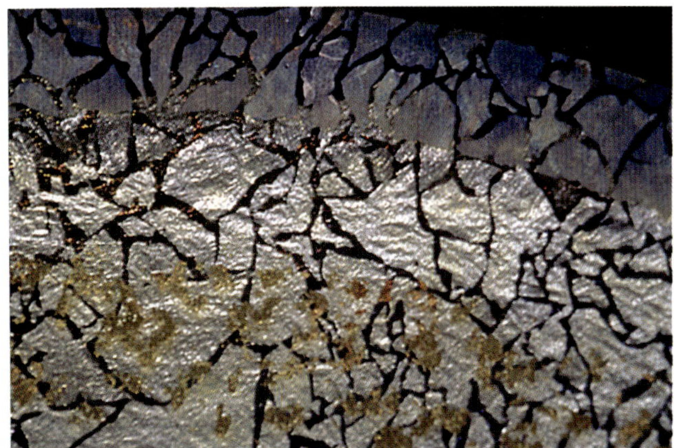

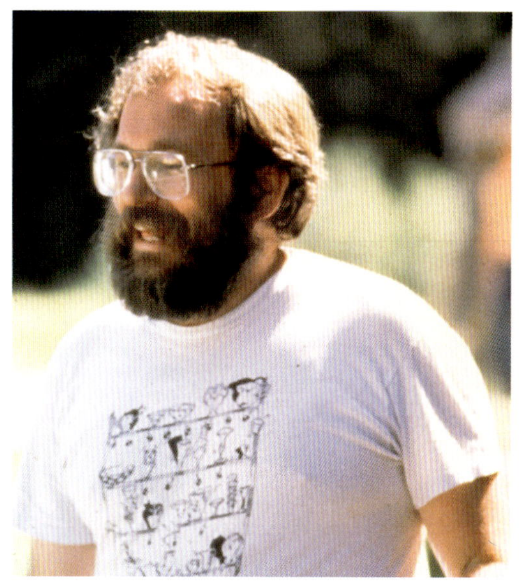

Brock Craig (b. 1947)

left above: "Footed Bowl," 2004. Silver and gold foil fused onto the surface.

left middle: detail - also shows the silver foil treated with liver of sulphur changing the color around the outside edge.

above right: photo of Brock Craig at Pilchuck, 1985.

bottom: "bowl," 2004, H. 3 in. (8 cm) x 16 in. (41 cm) in diameter. Silver foil with patinas and gold foil.

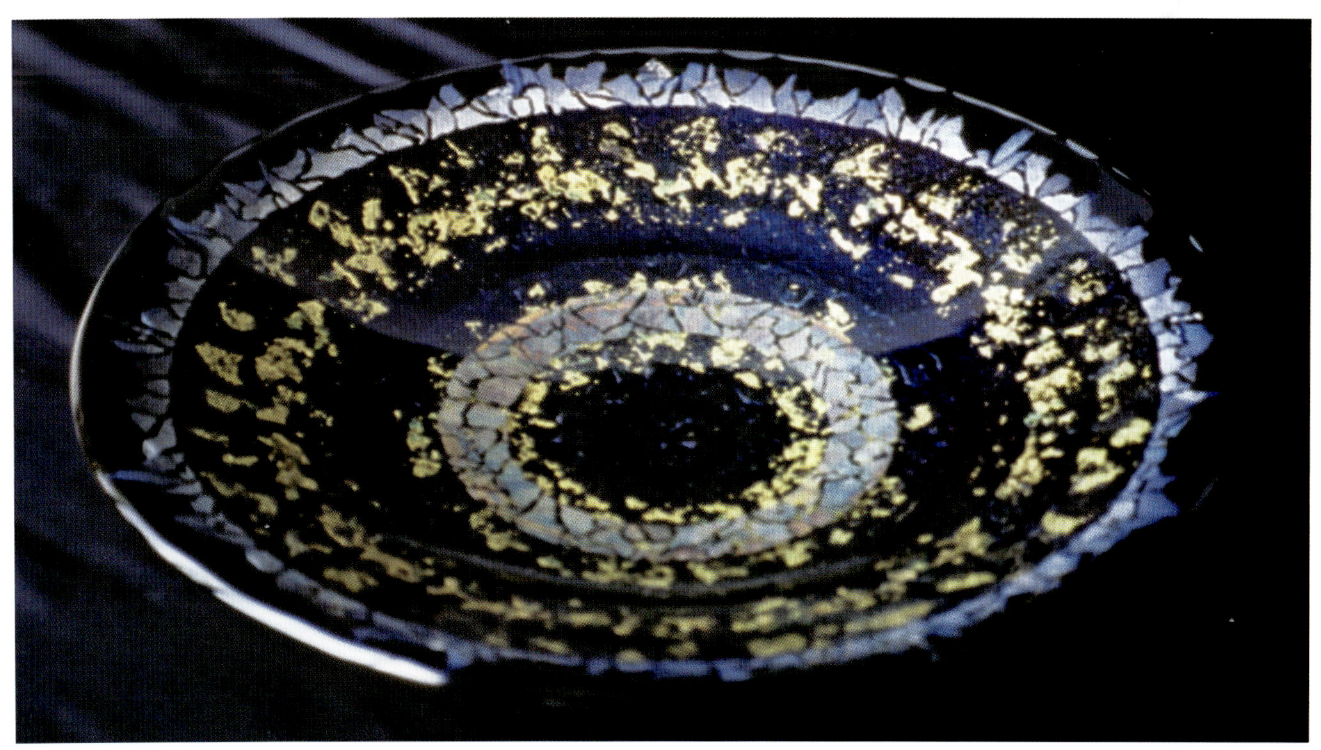

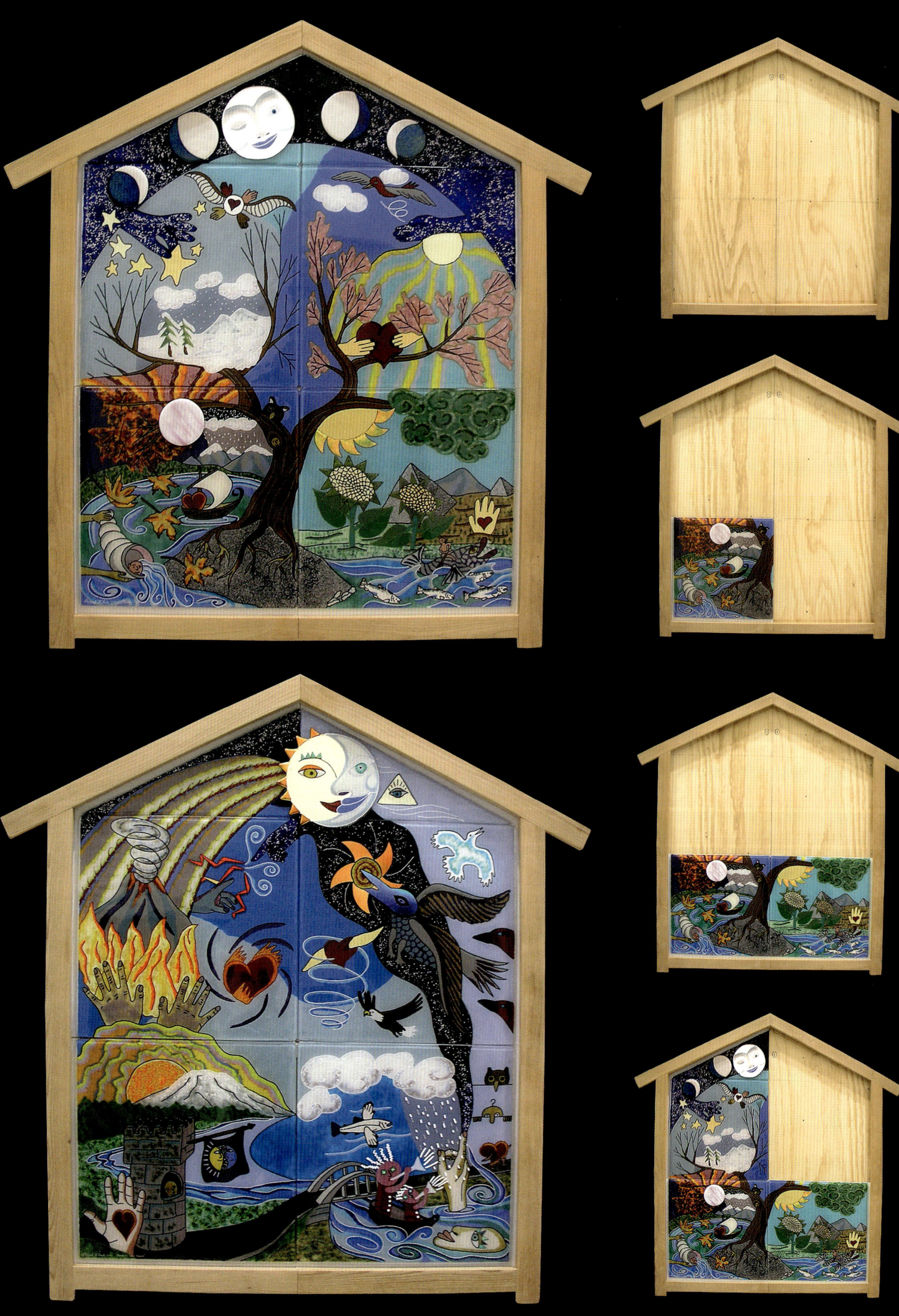

Part 5: Equipment
mounting systems

Work backwards.

Once you have a basic concept of what you want to express, first figure out:

(1) How you want to display or hang your piece.

(2) How and if you want to slump the piece.

(3) Then you are ready to fuse the glass that you will work with.

By doing it this way you won't get stuck in the end wondering how to display your piece.

- **Be creative with your mounting systems!**

- **Keep it simple!**

- **Leave a way for people in the future to easily figure out how you installed your piece, or they might just remove it with a wrecking ball!**

> **"Give me duct tape, silicone, and pop rivets and I can fix the world."**
> **Archimedes, Jr. 2006**

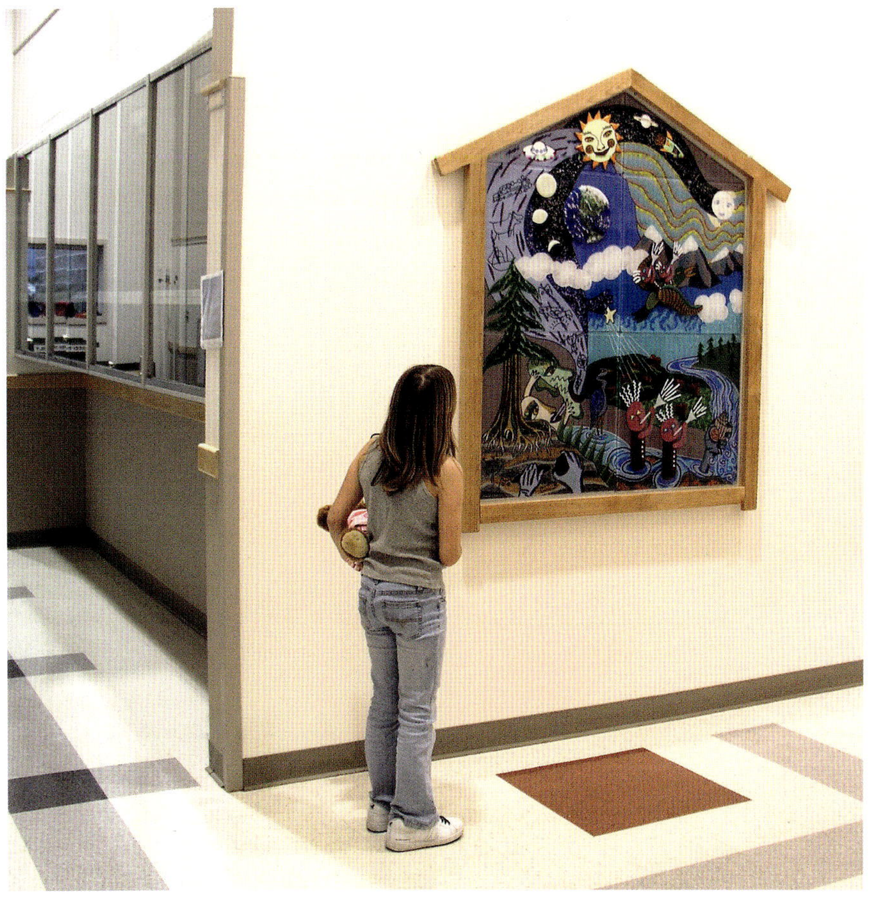

facing far left:
series of four photographs showing installation of glass sections at Evergreen Elementary School in Shelton, Washington, commissioned by the Washington State Arts Commission.

facing upper right:
"Season Tree," 2005, H. 64 in. (163 cm) x W. 60 in. (152 cm).

facing bottom right:
"Elements and Beyond," 2005, H. 64 in. (163 cm) x W. 60 in. (152 cm).

upper:
"Beginnings", 2005, H. 64 in. (163 cm) x W. 60 in. (152 cm).

bottom:
architectural setting of "Beginnings."

Public Art Mounting System

The following photographs show the mounting system for three glass wall pieces. They were commissioned by the Washington State Arts Commission and installed at Evergreen Elementary School in Shelton, Washington, 2005. Each panel is H. 64 in. (163 cm) x W. 60 in. (152 cm) and framed with maple.

Public installations have to be attached to the wall and are designed to deter theft. Do as much of the work in your studio as you can so that when you get to the site, installation will be easy.

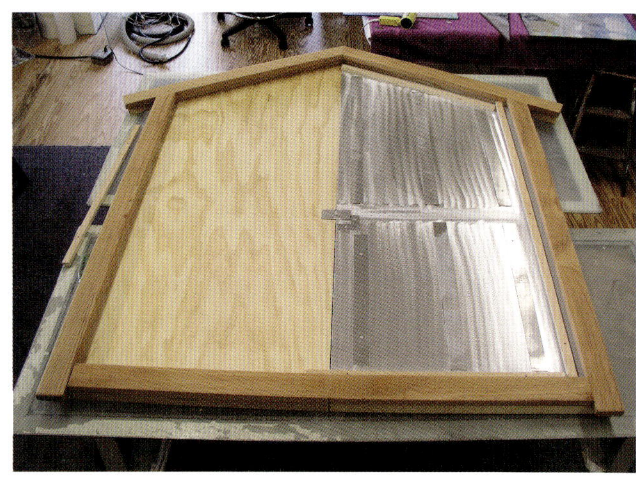

There are four aluminum backing plates that are held into the frame with surrounding wood moldings and the center section is held by a sliding clip, see below.

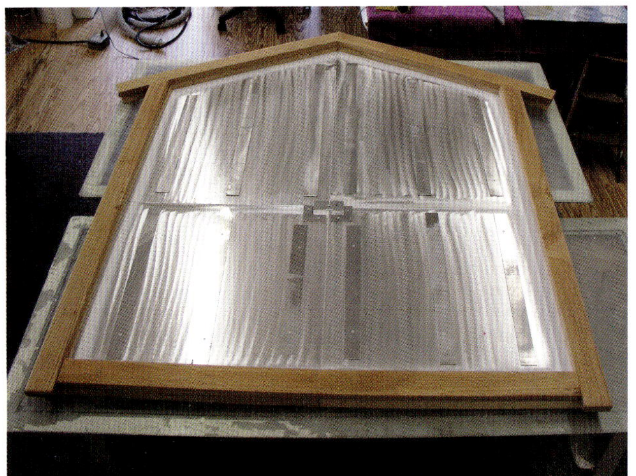

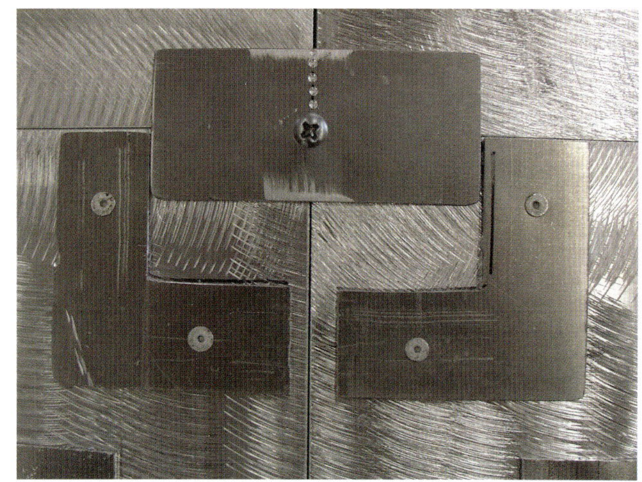

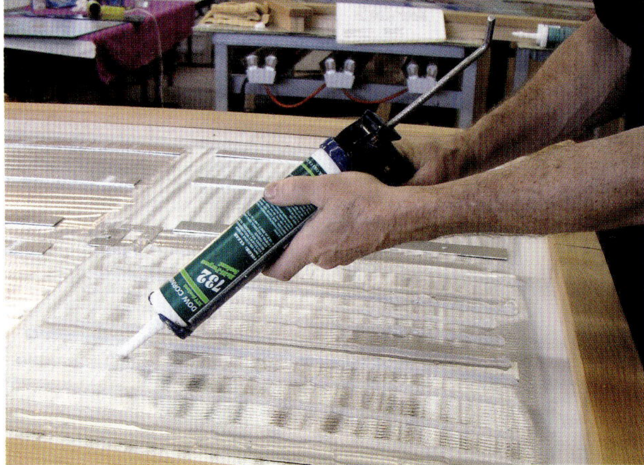

Silicone sealer is applied in vertical stripes allowing air circulation to cure the silicone.

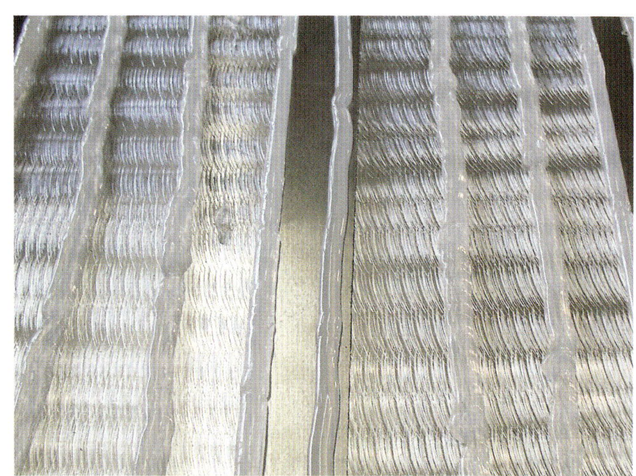

Rough up the aluminum and clean the glass with dish soap before applying the silicone.

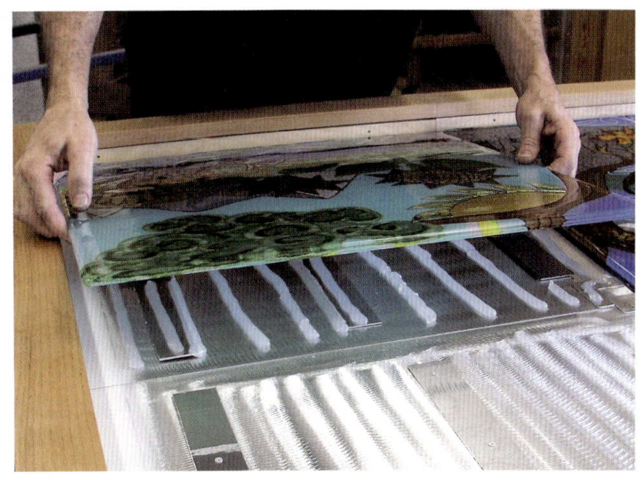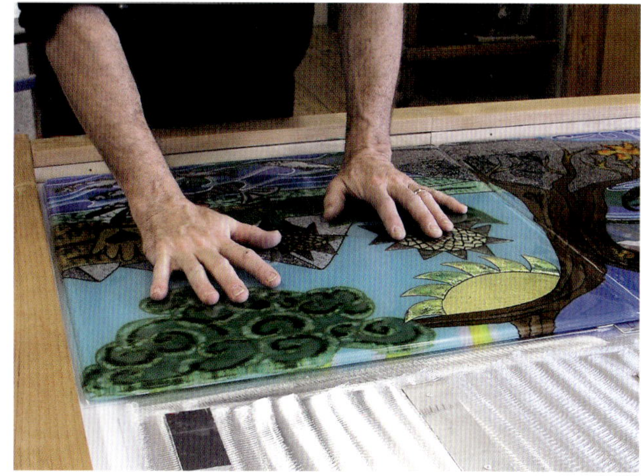

above: the glass panels are laid down and carefully pressed into place.

below: the finished wall panel, "Season Tree," in my studio.

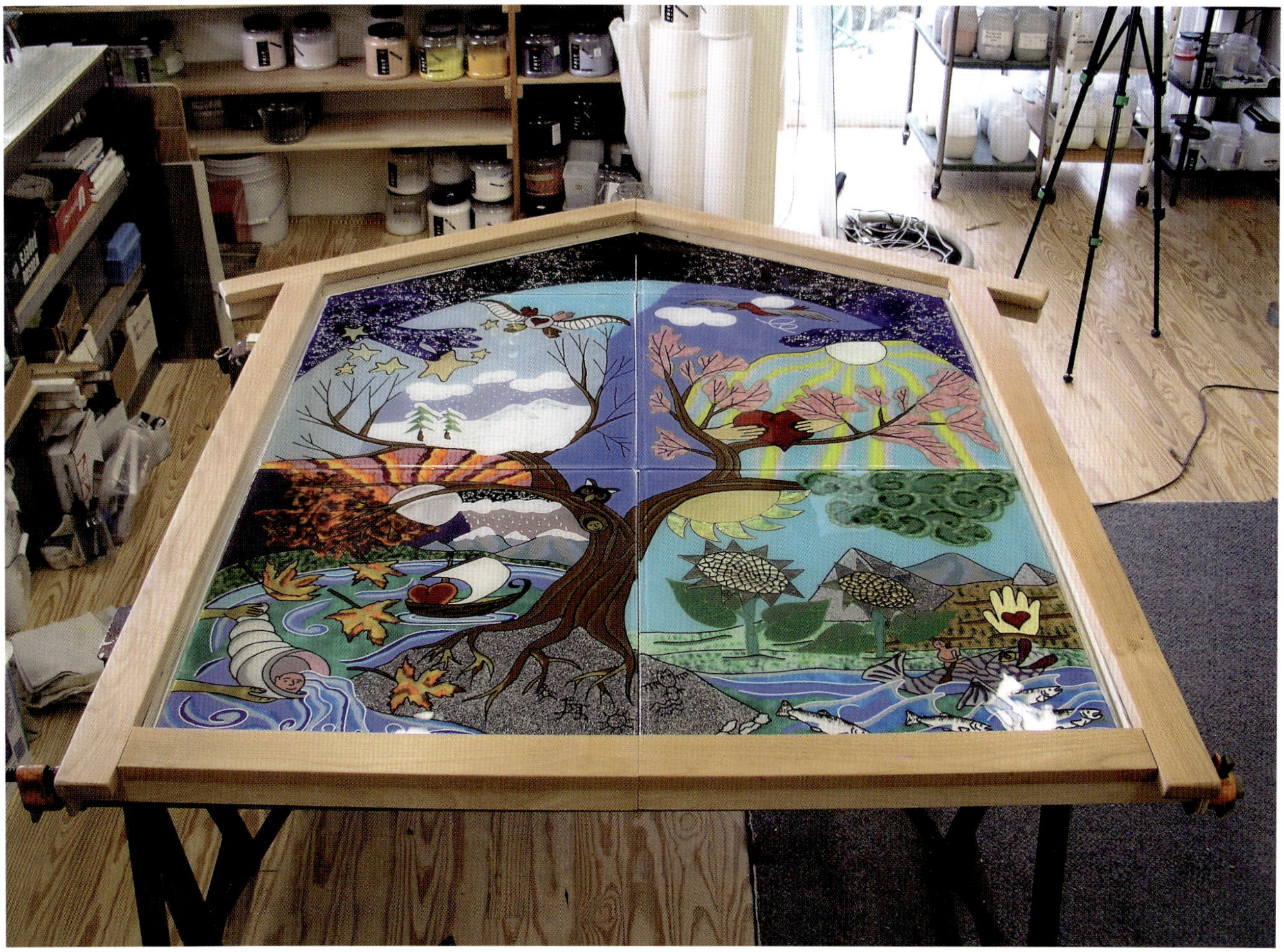

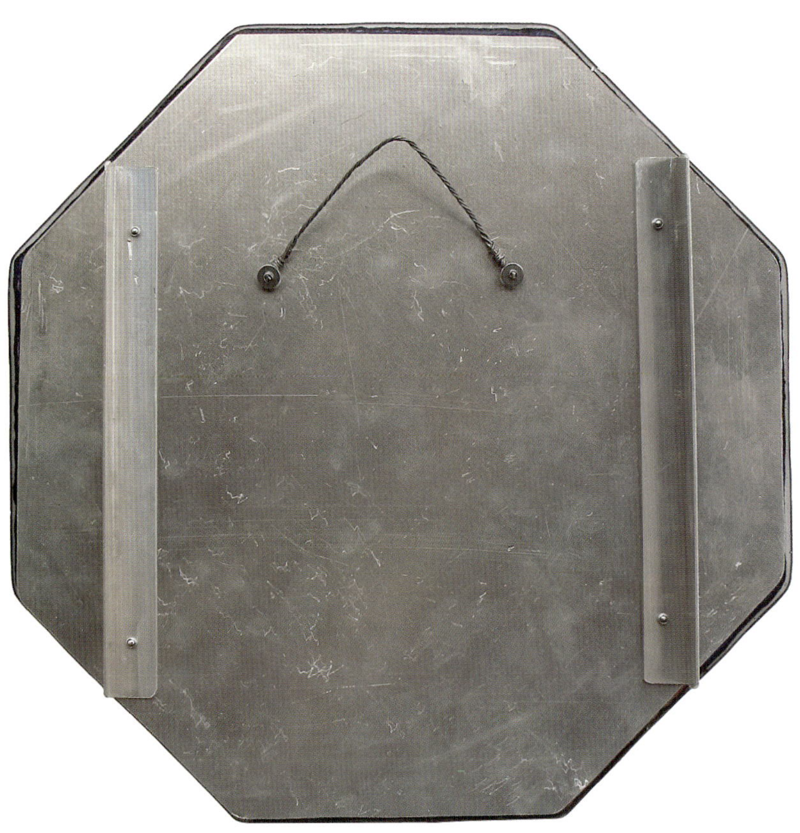

above: view of the back of my mounting system. I mount my fused glass wall pieces on a backing plate of surplus aluminum, which is cheaper than new, with a thickness of 16 gauge $\frac{1}{16}$ in. (1.5 mm). The aluminum can be stiffened with 1 in. (2.5 cm) x 1 in. (2.5 cm) x $\frac{1}{16}$ in. (1.5 mm) thick aluminum angles that are pop riveted to the sheet. These angles also hold the mount away from the wall to provide space for the mounting hooks. I roughen the mounting surface of the aluminum and use clear silicone sealer to adhere the glass. The rivet heads are on the side toward the glass and keep the silicone from being squished too thin and losing holding strength.

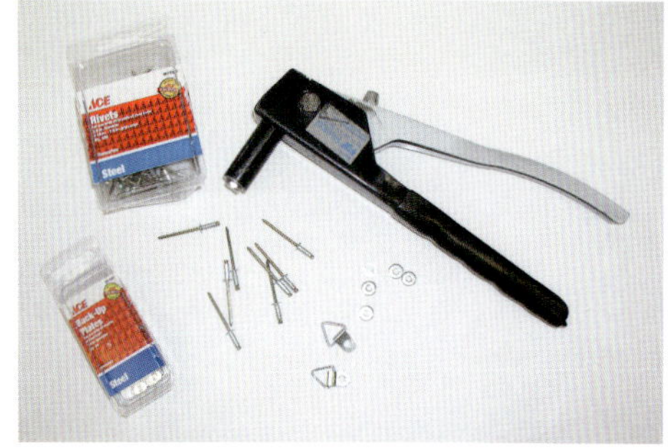

above: Pop Rivet tool, pop rivets, backing washers in case the hole is too big, and picture framing hooks for hanging.

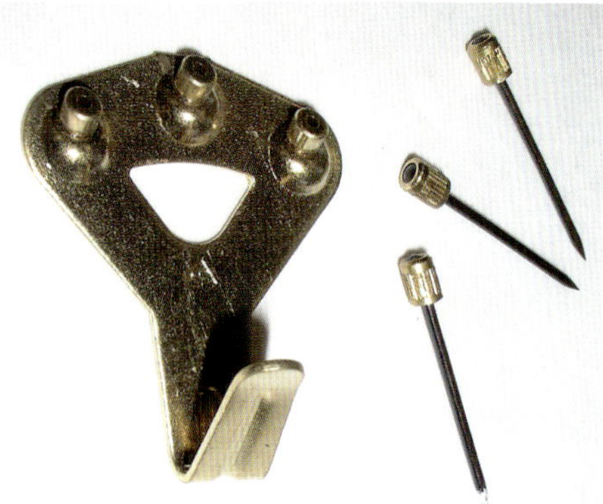

above: Floreat hook for hanging the wall pieces on wallboard. I use hooks rated for 75 pounds. They have three tempered nails that are guided into the wall through a cylinder to prevent wobble and tearing out of the wall. On my 20 in. (51 cm) wide panels, I use two hooks.

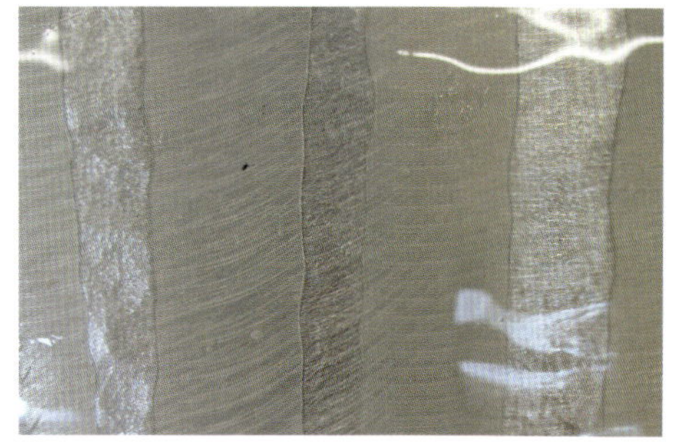

above: view through clear glass of the silicone. I use Dow Corning #732 clear silicone sealant that I buy from an adhesive supply company. I make vertical stripes and leave space for air to get in so them silicone will cure.

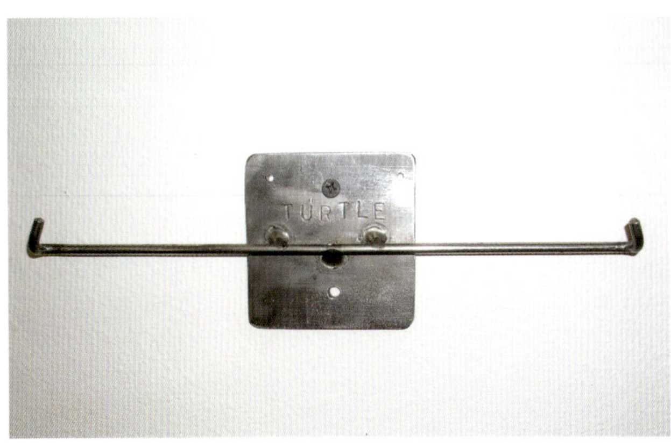

above: the mounting system for the turtle vessel. An ⅛ in. (3 mm) rod creates a holder into which the upper arms of the turtle slide. This is screwed directly into the wall.

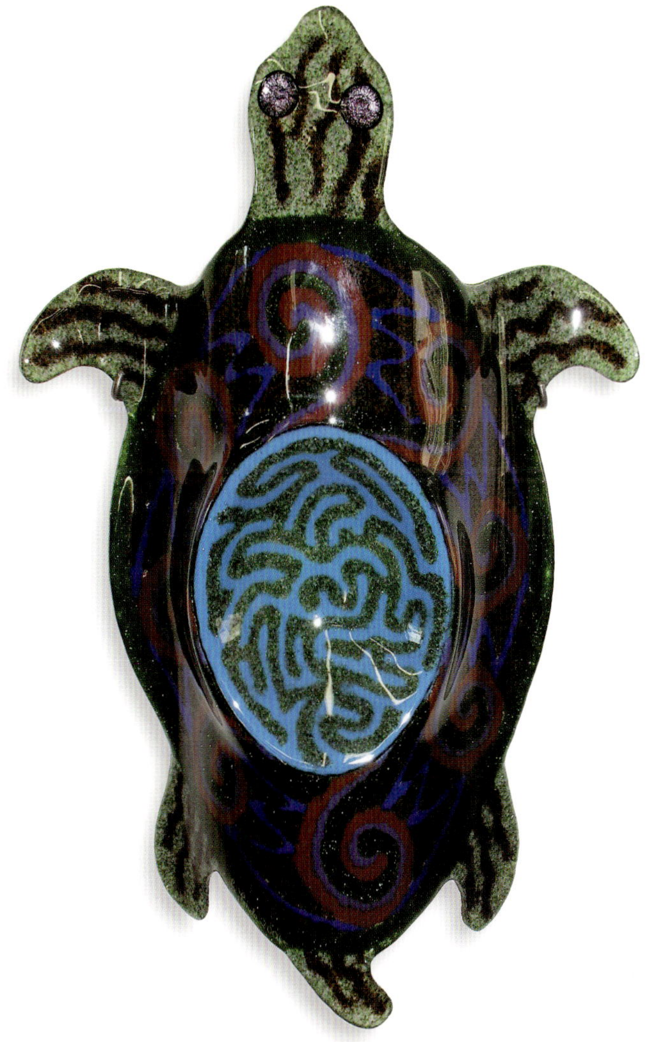

above: "Turtle Effigy Vessel," 2001, H. 21 in. (53 cm) x W. 15 in. (38 cm) x D. 3.5 in. (9 cm).

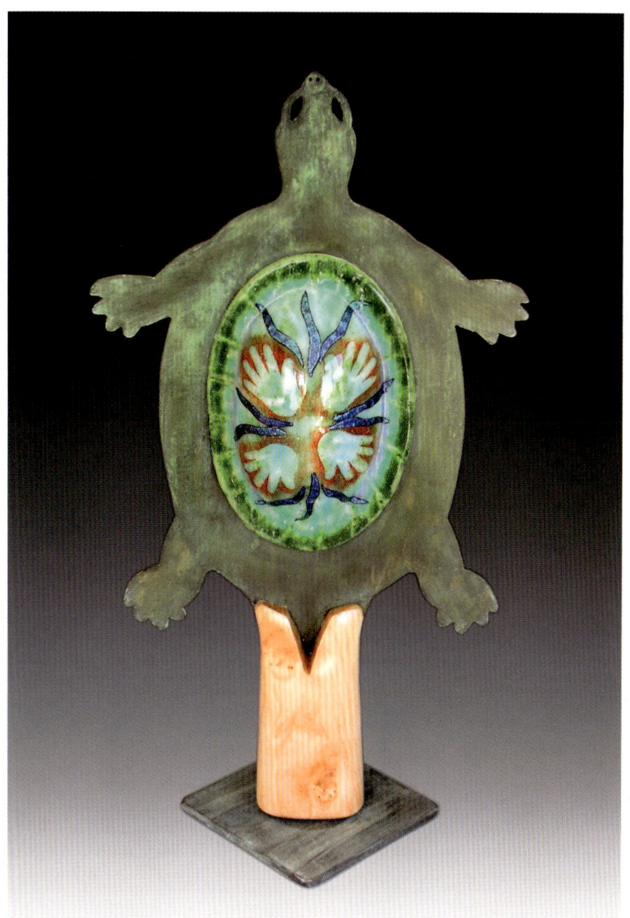

above: "Turtle Rattle," 2004, H. 19 in. (48 cm) x W. 11 in. x D. 3 in. (7.5 cm), 2004. Two fused and sagged hemispherical shapes are siliconed to a turtle shaped ⅛ in. (3 mm) sheet bronze from that has been patined. A curly maple handle is attached with epoxy.

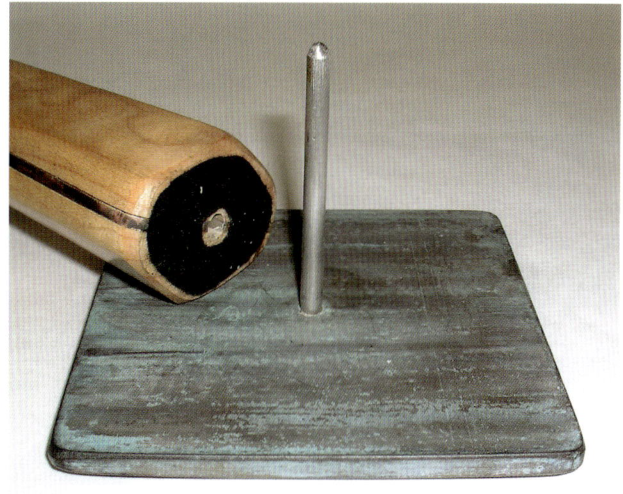

above: The rattle sits and can be rotated on the pin attached to the base.

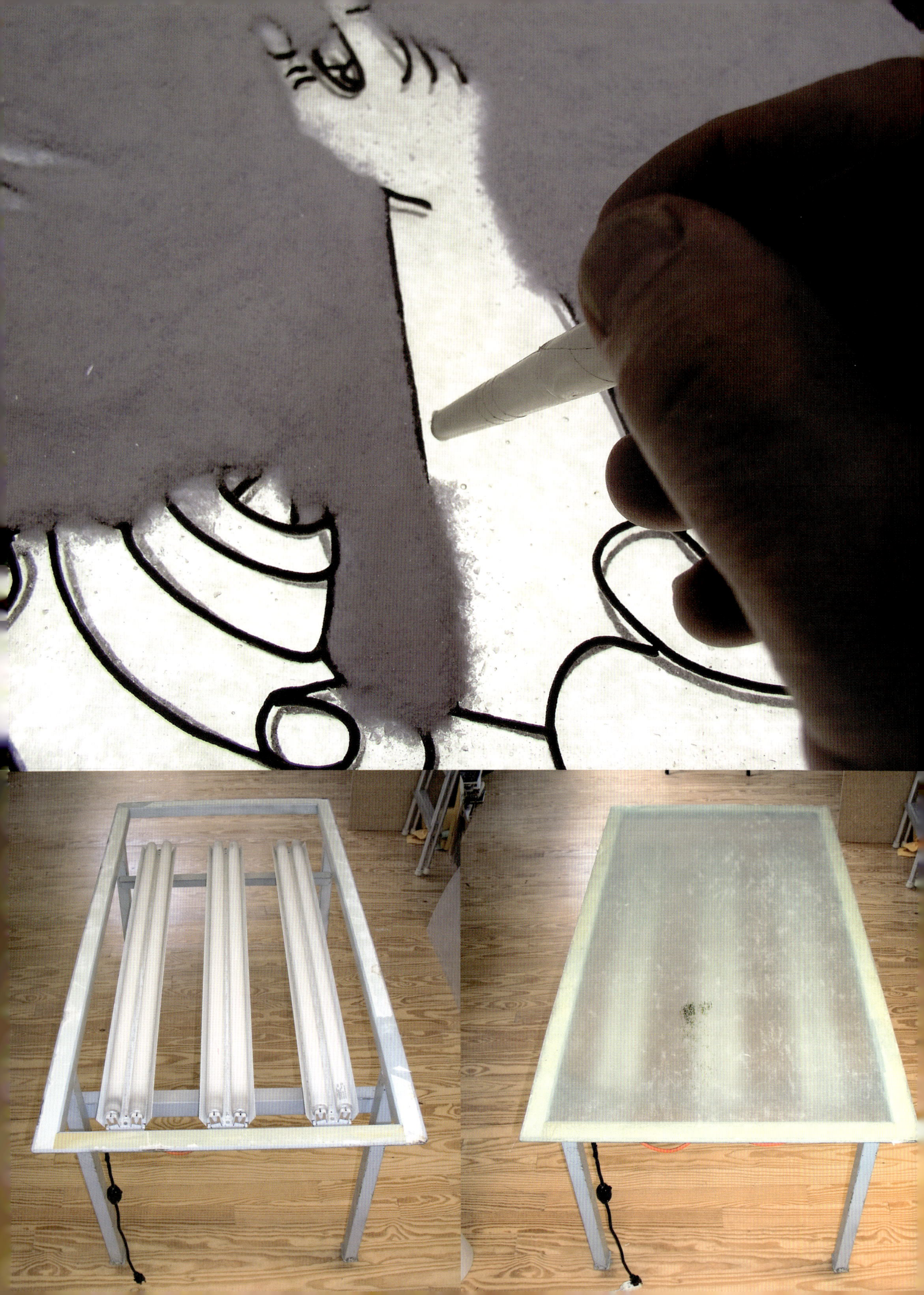

special studio equipment

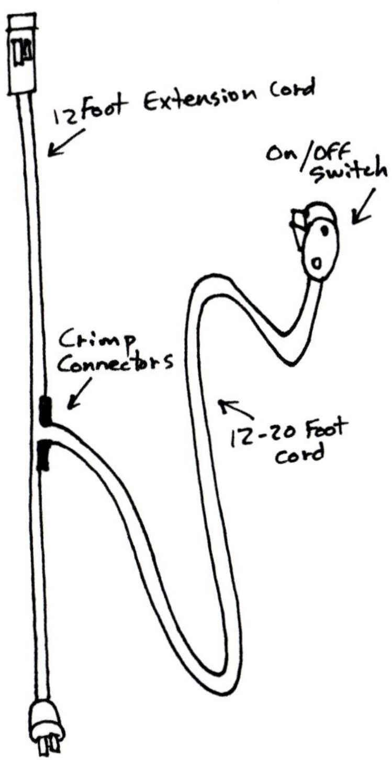

Make a switch extension
(left) Cut only one wire, the hot wire coming from the smaller prong of the male end of a 12-foot extension cord. Cut off the ends of a second 12 - 20 foot extension cord, or use a piece of equivalent wire, and splice it into the first wire with crimp butt connectors, as in the diagram. Tape over these connections with duct tape. Place a switch on the end.

Build a vacuum pen
(bottom) Neck down the hose from a shop vac with a plastic PVC pipe reducer and attaching a smaller diameter hose. Adding a plastic nozzle further reduces the hose – this time I used a plastic ballpoint pen case. I place the shop vac outside of my studio to eliminate the noise and glass dust; I turn the vacuum off and on with a switch on a longer cord.

facing upper:
using the vacuum pen to clean up the spillover of frit. The glass project is on the light table to help illuminate the frit.

Build a light table
(facing lower left) Use metal or wood and place inexpensive shop fluorescent lights 6 in. (15 cm) below the table top and no more than 6 in. (15 cm) apart. I put all of my tables on wheels, so I can reconfigure my studio easily.

(facing lower right) Place a surplus tempered glass shower door on top of the frame and run the glass all the way to the edge. I place a thin piece of Lasco "Crystalite" flat fiberglass reinforced acrylic on top of the tempered glass to protect it from nicks because they will weaken the glass. I cut my glass right on top of this sheet of plastic.

Build a polariscope
(bottom right) This small light box has a bulb inside. I've placed a 10 in. (25 cm) x 10 in. (25 cm) piece of polarizing plastic under a piece of window glass. View your test glass through another piece of polarizing plastic.

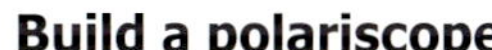

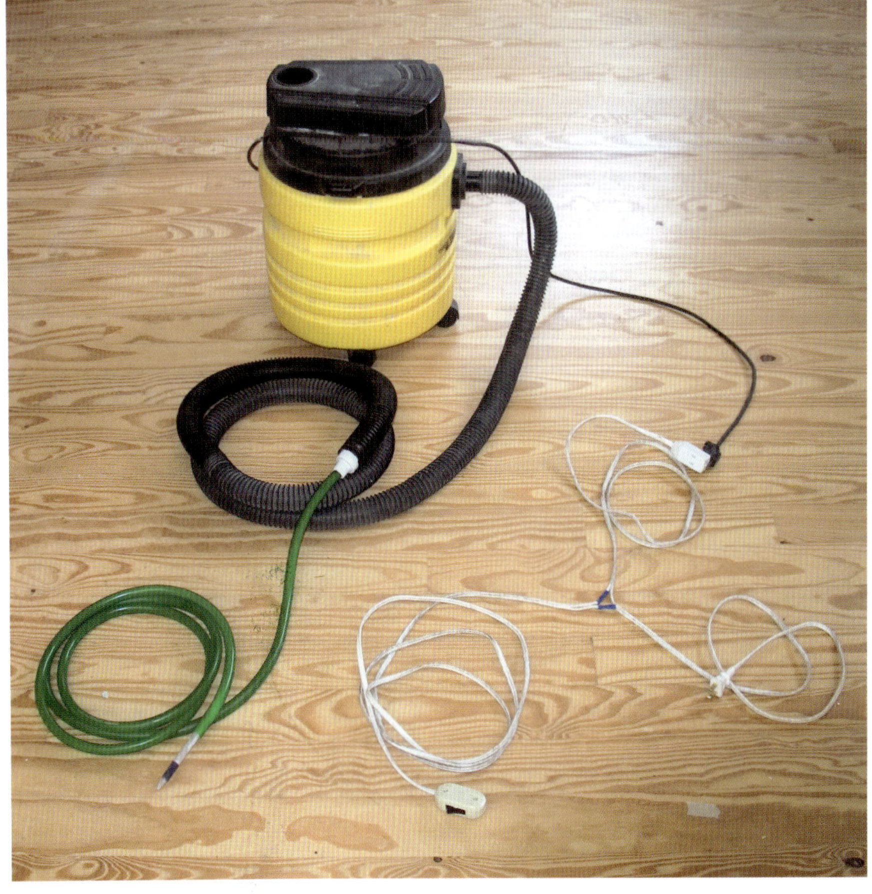

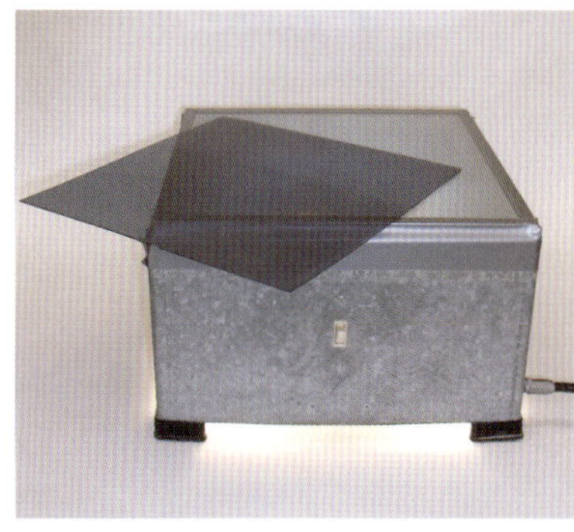

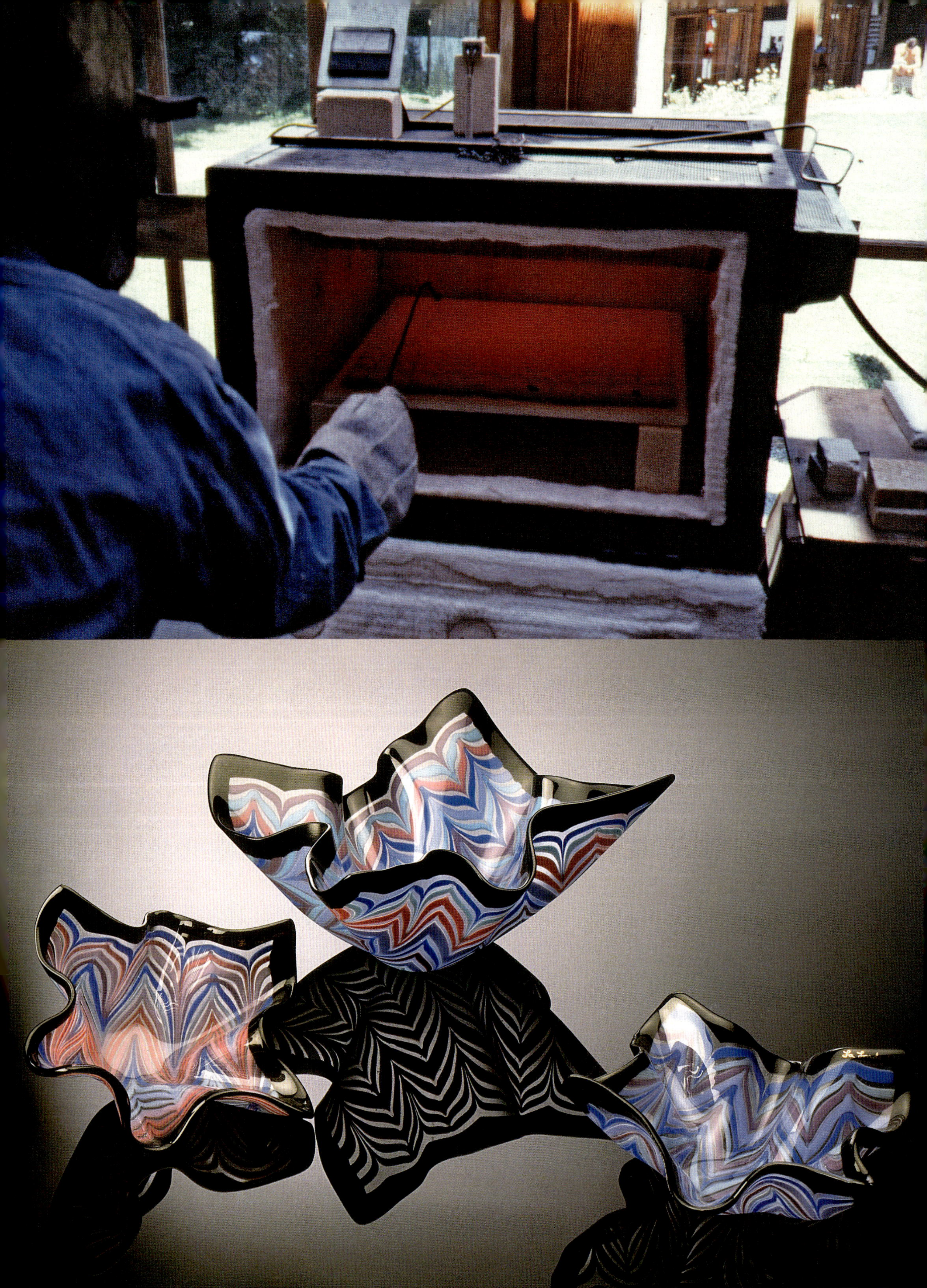

I'm a real fan of ceramic fiber kilns. They work great both for fusing and slumping glass up to 1 in. thick and for firing glass paints and enamels on sheet glass or blown vessels. Fiber kilns heat up quickly and cool down with limited or no venting. Fiber breathes, letting fumes and moisture pass through it. The ceramic fiber doesn't absorb much heat, so the outside of the kiln stays much cooler than a brick kiln.

High temperature mineral fibers have replaced asbestos, but they need to be used carefully. I use ceramic fiber blanket, rather than ceramic fiber board, because the particles become less airborne, but it's still best to avoid slamming the door on a fiber kiln and to wear a respirator when lining a kiln.

For thicker glass castings in molds I prefer an insulating fire brick (K23) kiln as it holds the heat better than fiber. Brick kilns take longer to heat up and cool down which is good for thicker castings.

In 1980, when I began fusing, no top element kilns (which give an even heat downward), were available. I fused on hexagonal kiln shelves in a side-fired hexagonal soft brick pottery kiln. In these side heating kilns, I had to fire slowly because if the difference in temperature between the outside edge and the center of the glass was too great, the outside edge expanded more, and the glass would crack.

The challenge was to have a top-fired kiln that would give even heat on the flat piece of glass. The Bullseye Marathon top-fired kiln was the first on the market. I designed my kiln with more interior height to both fuse and to slump deep bowls. I used ceramic fiber blanket, a material that I had used in my glass annealer, which is a box kiln for slow-cooling blown glass. This material comes in various sizes, but the most convenient and economical for my kilns is 1 in. (2.5 cm) thick and 24 in. (61 cm) wide in 25 foot (7.5 meter) rolls (called Fiber Frax, Kaowool, or Ceriblanket by different manufacturers). I support the electrical elements on ceramic rods at the top of the kiln. By welding a metal frame and holding the ceramic blanket against a wire screen welded in the framework, I was able to create a top-fired, square-sided kiln and fire on a square shelf.

Between 1982 – 1990, I built kilns for other artists including: Ruth Brockmann, Brock Craig, Roger Nachman, Sonja Blomdahl, Band-hu Dunhum, Bill Ayers, Rob Adamson, Bullseye Glass Company, and Pilchuck Glass School. Many artists still use my kilns today.

upper facing:
combing at Pilchuck, 1984.
I was a teaching assistant and brought my top element, front load, fusing kiln to the school and demonstrated the technique of combing glass in a kiln. This was before I had a kiln controller; the temperature was adjusted with infinite switches and measured with an analog dial pyrometer. The front door drops straight down to allow easy access.

lower facing:
Zig Zag series, 1984.
I laid strips of colored glass onto a sheet of clear glass. This was heated in an electric kiln to 1600° F, and then I combed the glass with a hooked steel rod. The sheet was cooled and then slumped during a second firing in a stainless steel mold that I made.

Building Kilns

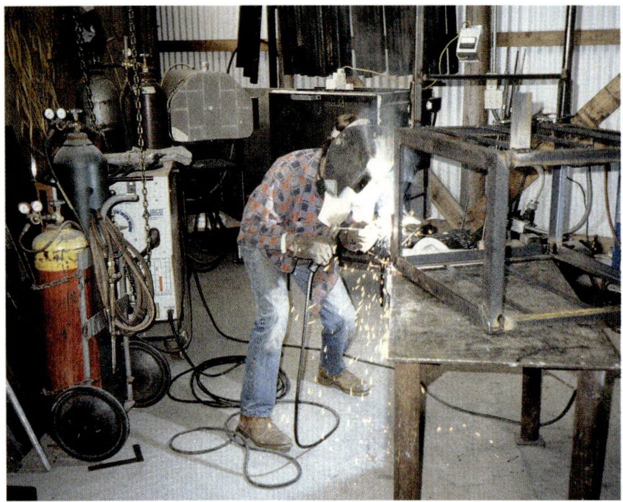

Originally, we fused in octagonal brick pottery kilns with side elements. This presented two problems: (1) uneven heating from the sides caused glass breakage by thermal shock, (2) and the kilns took too long to heat up - lingering in the devitrification zone too long caused the glass surface to appear scummy.

My fiber 20 x 20 kiln solved these problems: (1) top heating elements produced an even heat, (2) and the high-temperature ceramic fiber blanket allowed for a fast heat up and down through the devitrification zone. The front door dropped down, so it was easy to load the kiln, and I could get into it quickly for combing the glass. This kiln was also deep enough for slumping.

I built about twenty of these kilns for other artists. Brock Craig and Bill Ayers both manufactured more kilns of this design and still fuse glass in my original kilns after twenty years. In 1985, I built two kilns for Pilchuck Glass School; after much use and abuse, one is still in operation today.

The 20 x 20, named after the kiln shelf size, was controlled by electric oven infinite switches, had an analog needle pyrometer, and included a kiln sitter using ceramic cones to prevent over firing. I sold them for $750 in 1985. Today the Paragon GL24 is about the same size.

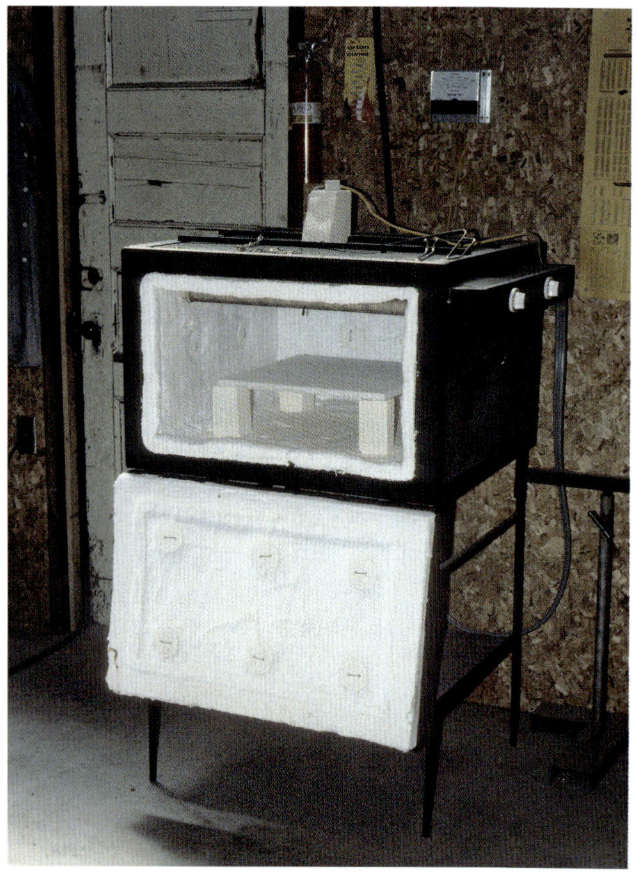

above left: Richard La Londe welding the kiln frame. The angle iron frame held an expanded steel screen that supported the high temperature insulating fiber, 1984.

above right: an original picture of my first 20 x 20 kiln built in 1982.

bottom right: six 20 x 20 kilns ready to go out the door. Two of these went to Pilchuck, 1985.

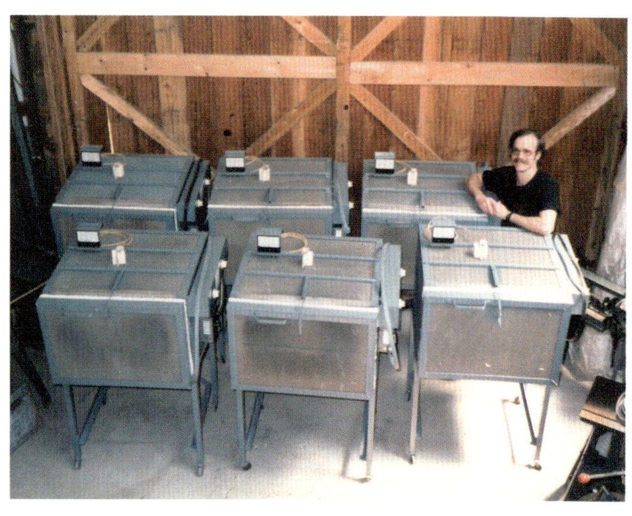

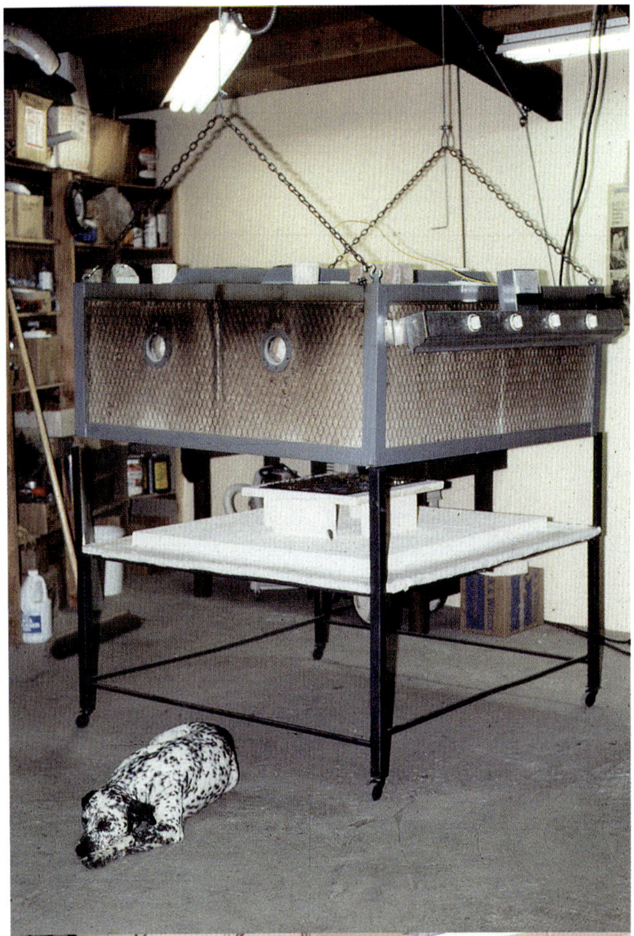

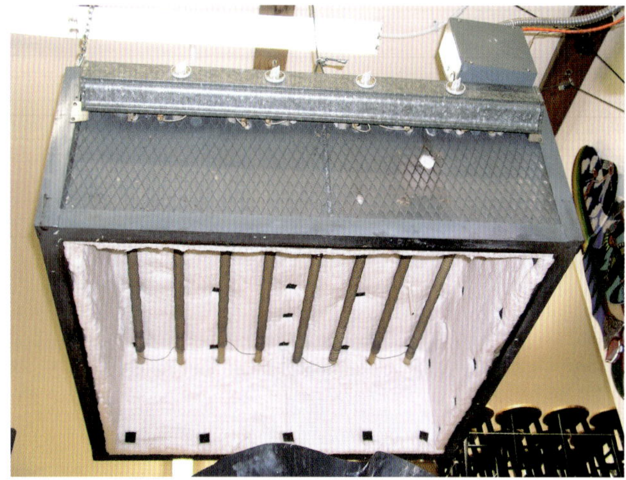

above left: my large Bell Kiln 45 in. (114 cm) x 45 in. (114 cm) x 24 in. (61 cm) inside dimensions & 240 volt, 60 amp - with Jack the dog. In October 1982, Bullseye gave me the materials to build two kilns, one for me and one for them.

above right: 60 amps of elements on 1 in. mullite ceramic tubes and the high-temperature fiber blanket lining.

bottom left: in 1984 I added a 30 amp ring with side elements for a total of 90 amps, 240 volts. It runs on (3) 30 amp breakers.

bottom right: shows the kiln lid lifted and my stainless steel mold for slumping my bowls.

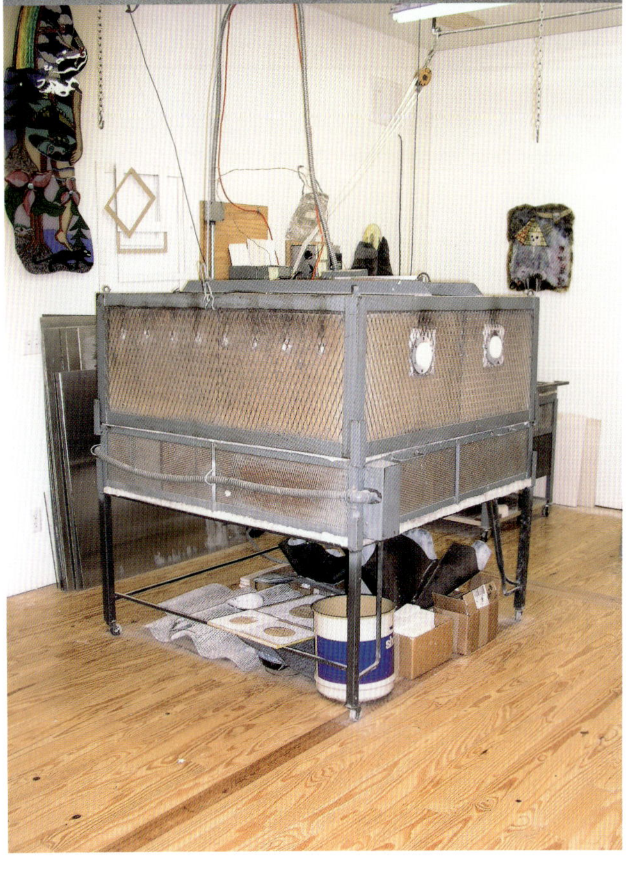

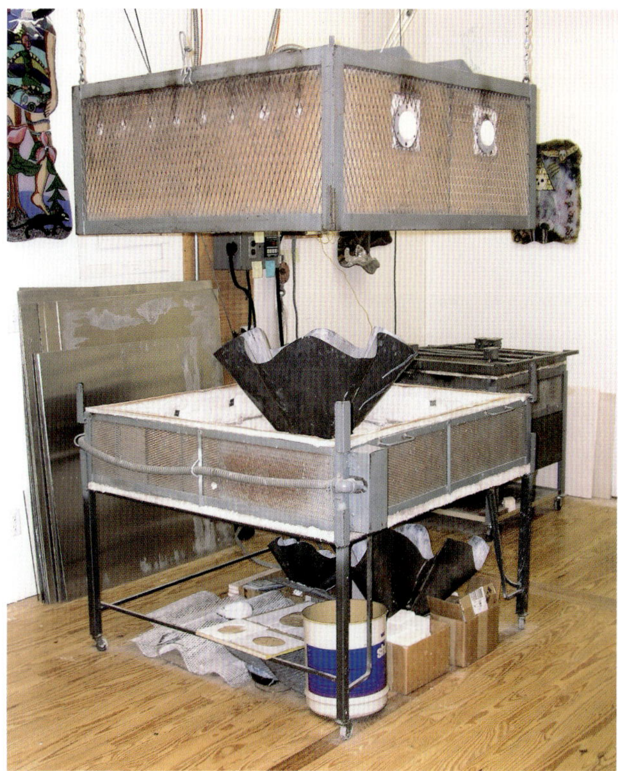

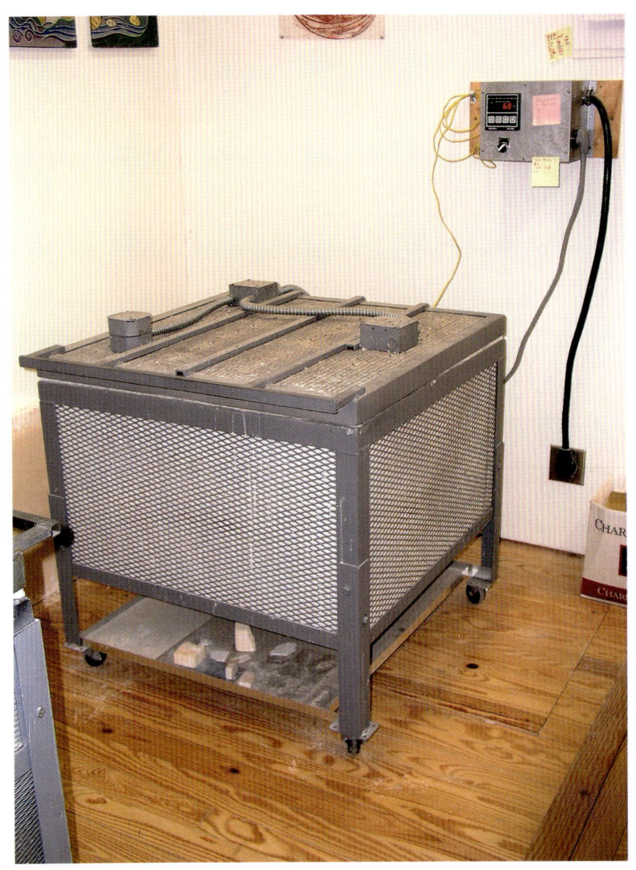

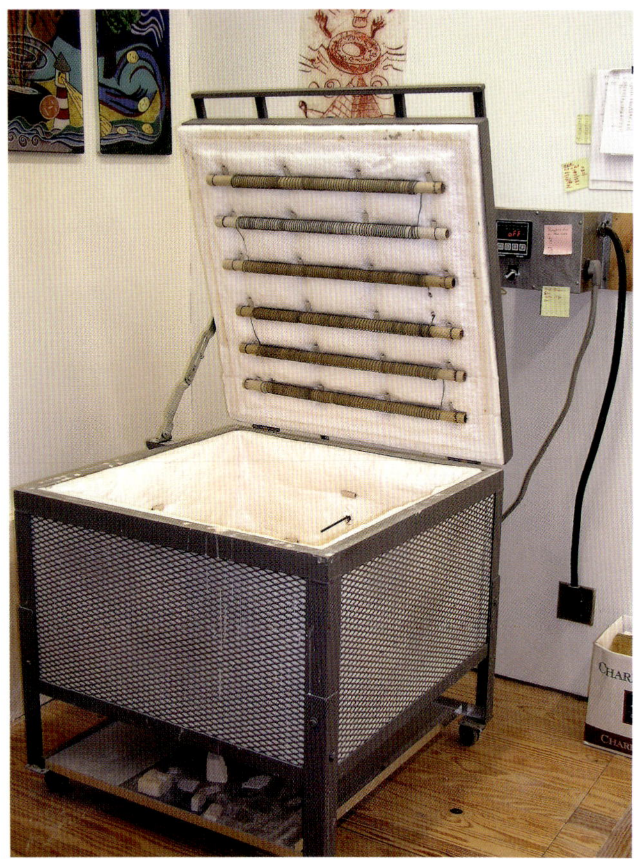

The top load kiln, my favorite kiln design today, has an inside dimension of 28 in. (71 cm) x 28 in. (71 cm) x 17 in. (43 cm) deep. It takes a 240 volt, 50 amp receptacle. This kiln has both top and bottom elements which help give it a more even heat. This is an easier kiln to load than the front loading kiln. I call this kiln the "geriatric kiln" because I use an overhead block and tackle hoist to load my kiln and save my back for my golf game.

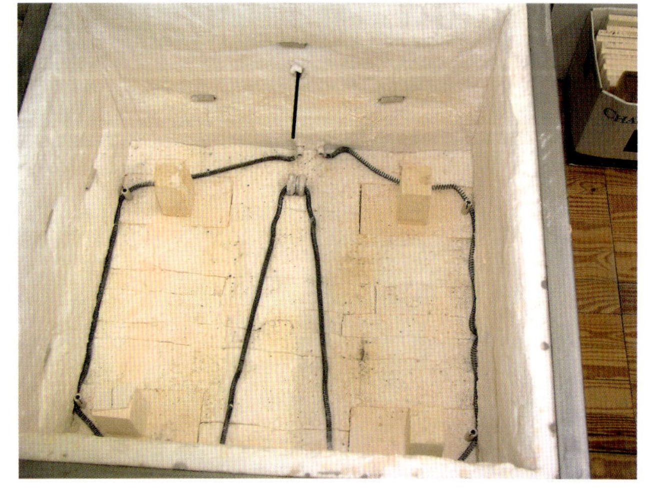

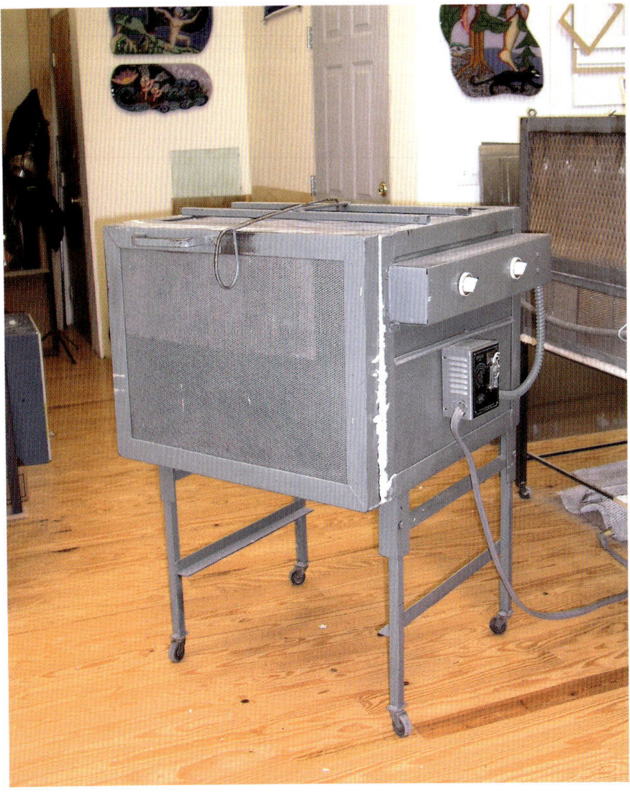

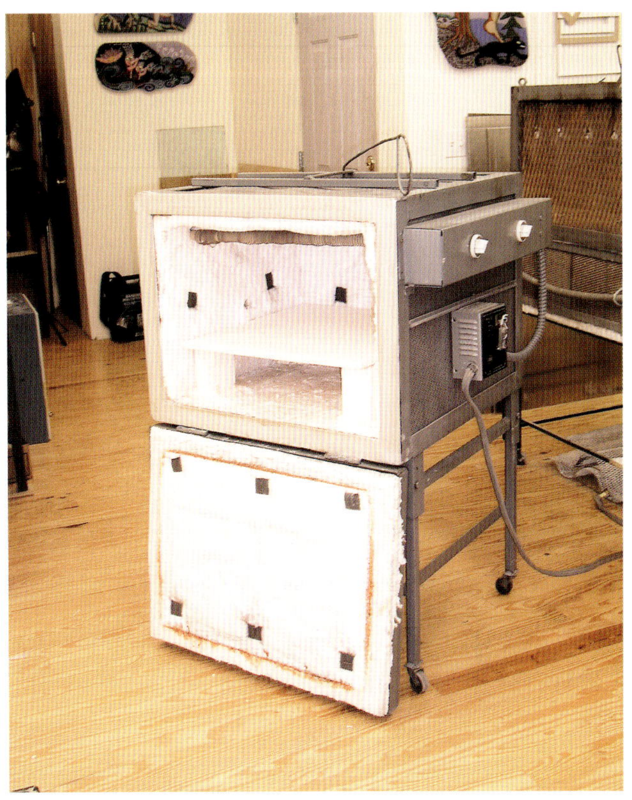

The 20 x 20 Front Load Kiln

Don't be afraid to build this kiln. It's only an insulated box with electrical elements!

<u>inside dimensions</u>
24 in. (61 cm) x 24 in. (61 cm) x 16 in. (41 cm).
<u>outside dimensions</u>
29 in. (74 cm) x 29 in. (74 cm) x 21 in. (53 cm).
33 in. (84 cm) wide, including control box.

<u>power</u>
Electric.
240 volt, 24 amps (30 amp breaker).
This kiln has top elements only.

The door can either drop down or swing to the side. This is a great kiln for combing as all of the heat does not go up into your face as with a top loading kiln.

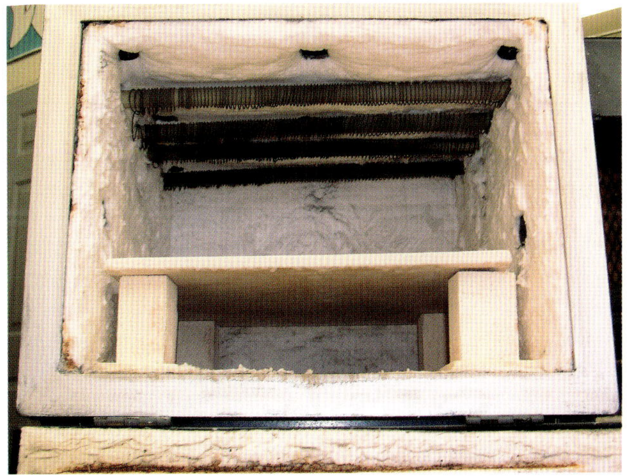

Note:
(1) It's a good idea to make the front door opening flange from stainless steel angle so that moisture doesn't rust it.
(2) The door can swing open on the right or left side and can include a peek hole. The drop front door allows for even venting when held open about 1 in. (2.5 cm), but the stand needs to be placed back 3 in. (8 cm) from the front to avoid being hit by the door when it opens.

20 x 20 Kiln Material List (measurements in feet ' & inches ")

Steel Supply Company

36' 2" x 2" x ⅛" steel angle
 (substitute 10' of stainless angle for the front
 door flange if you like)
10' 1 ½" x 1 ½" steel angle
10' 1 ½" x 1 ½" x 14 gauge square tube
 (adjust kiln leg length for your height)
12' ⅝" x ⅝" steel bar
 2' 1" x ⅛" flat bar
 4' 5⁄16" round bar
4' x 8' sheet ½" x 16 gauge expanded steel mesh
13" x 34" x 18 gauge steel for control box

Refractory Supply Company

Ceramic Fiber Blanket 2400° F
(1) box 1 ½" x 24" x 25'
(1) box 1" x 24" x 25'
 Sold under various names such as (Cerablan
 ket, Inswool, Kaowool). When installing this
 high alumina fiber blanket were a respirator.
 One box doesn't hold enough material to do
 a kiln, so you will have extra to build a glory
 hole or part of a second kiln).

Pottery Supply Company

(2) K 23 soft kiln bricks 2 ½" x 4 ½" x 9"
 210' of Kanthol 14 gauge element wire (180'
 to wind 2 elements, 20' to hold the fiber blanket tubes in place, 8' of extra.
 pyrometer and 12" long thermal couple if you
 are not hooking up to a kiln controller.

Appliance Repair Company

12) high heat spade connectors (to fit infinite
 switches)
20' 12 gauge high heat to hook up elements to
 switches.
(2) infinite switches 240 vole 15 amp (the type
 used in electric ranges.
(2) infinite switch knobs.
(1) electrical connector block to bolt the connections together.
(1) 30 amp dryer cord, 6' or longer
(1) roll high temp tape

Ceramic Rod Supply Company

(4) 30" x 1" diameter mullite tubes, open ended

(1) 50" x ½" mullite tube or length to cut
 into (18) lengths about 2" long to hold the
 blanket in place and (4) 3 ½" pieces for the
 element wire to pass through the insulation.
 I use the old knob and tube insulators for old
 houses that are 3 ½" long or longer.

Hardware Store

(1) small container of "Alumex" corrosion
 inhibitor for aluminum wire.
(4) bronze split bolt connectors for elements
(4) 360° swivcl rubber caster wheels 2" wheels.
(1) pair of 3 ½" door hinges (butt hinges)
(1) pair of 1" hinges for control box
(2) ½" nuts
(4) 5⁄16" x 2 ½" long bolts and nuts
 Primer and spray paint for kiln
 High temperature paint for door flange

Note:
Look up local suppliers in the yellow pages. The
internet is also a big help to run down odd supplies. Check the list of suppliers in the back of
this book. Don't forget it's sometimes cheaper
to have stuff shipped UPS than to drive all over
town looking for it.

Sometimes you can find some of the high temperature electrical supplies at a good hardware
store such as Home Depot. You can also find
mullite tubes at Seattle Pottery Supply although
they will probably be ¾", which is OK, but I like
the 1" diameter for the extra strength.

Kiln Frame Material & Cut List

Steel Cut List

(Cut with a metal cutting band saw or an abrasive wheel cutoff saw).

2" x 2" x ⅛" steel angle
Side Pieces   (4) 22 ½"

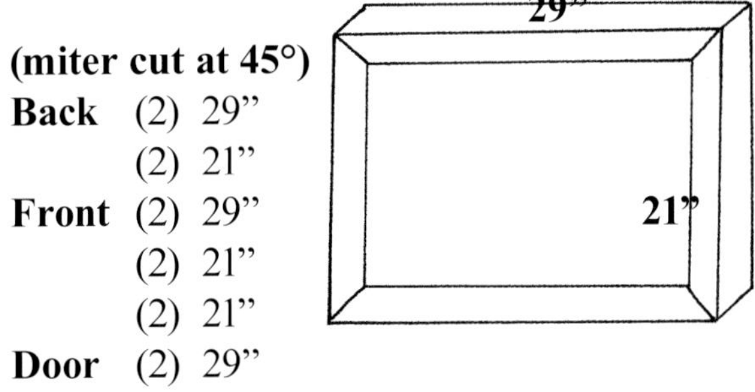

(miter cut at 45°)
Back   (2) 29"
          (2) 21"
Front (2) 29"
          (2) 21"
          (2) 21"
Door   (2) 29"
          (2) 21"

⁵⁄₈" x ⁵⁄₈" square steel bar
Roof Support Bars
          (2) 28"
Floor Support Bars
          (3) 25"

Stand

legs for stand
1 ½" x 1 ½" square tube
(adjust leg length to your height)
          (4) 24"
cross braces
1 ½" x 1 ½" x ⅛" angle
          (4) 23"
short kiln legs
1 ½" x 1 ½" x ⅛" angle
          (4) 6"

kiln sides
½" x 16 gauge flattened expanded steel
Top & Bottom (2) 28" x 25 ½"
Door & Back (2) 28" x 20
Sides   (2) 25 ½" x 20
(The screen may be cut with a saber saw using a metal cutting blade).

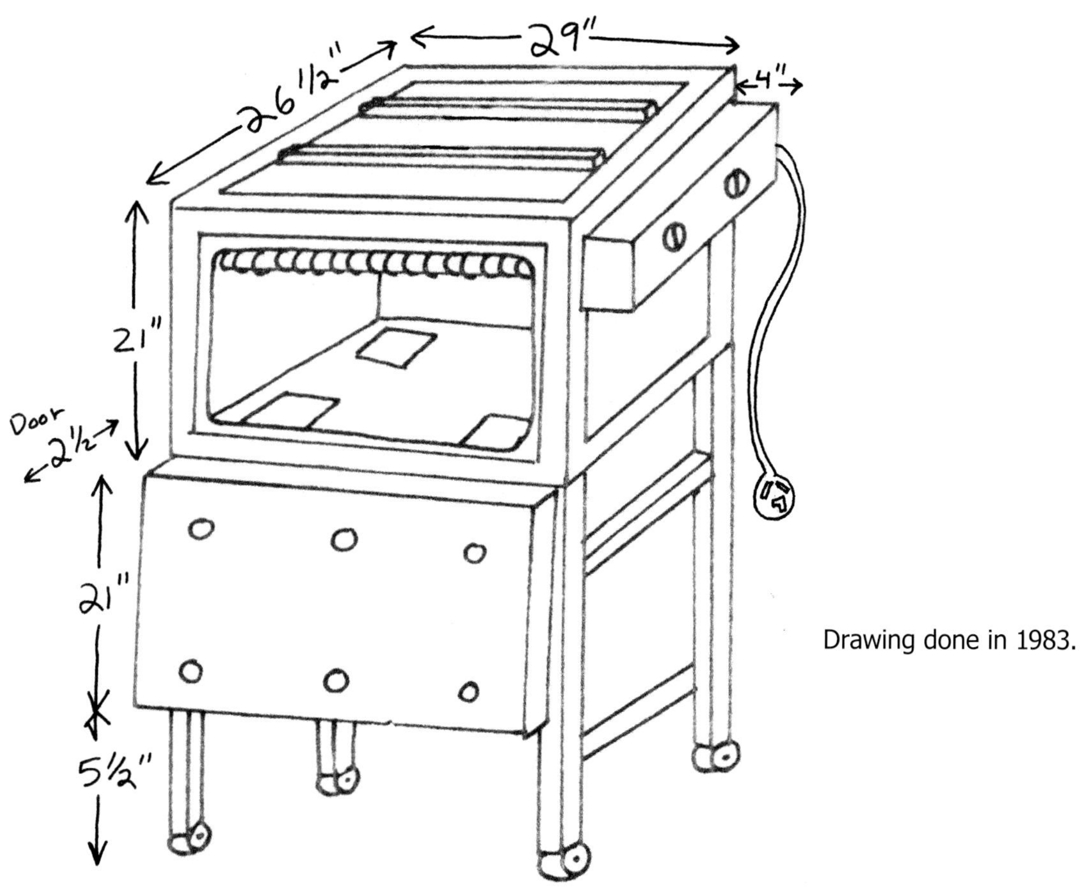

Drawing done in 1983.

Fabricate the Metal Frame

(1) Cut the kiln frame pieces from the cut list; use a metal cutting band saw or abrasive wheel cutoff saw.

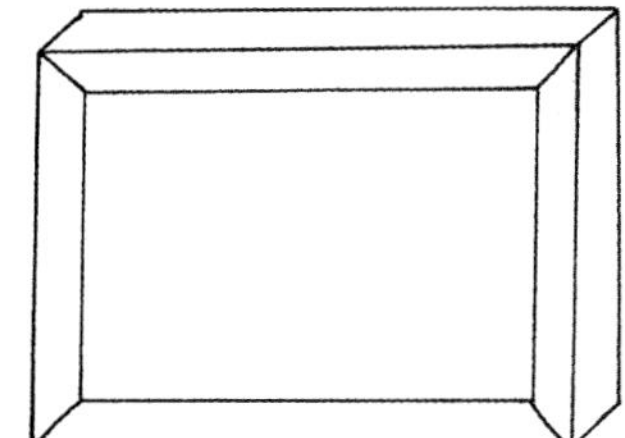

(2) Weld the front, back, and door frame sections.
Weld all corners and square up the frames.
Use stainless for front door flange if you want.

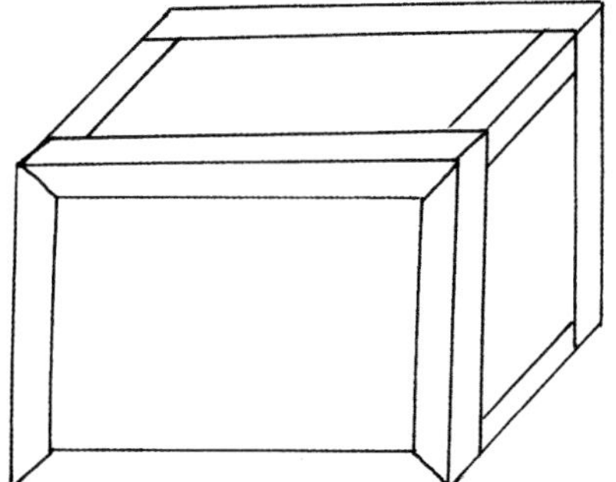

(3) Weld the side angle iron pieces between
the front and back frame sections.
Make sure the kiln box is square.
Grind the welds flat on the front face of
the kiln opening.

(4) Weld the top and bottom support bars.

 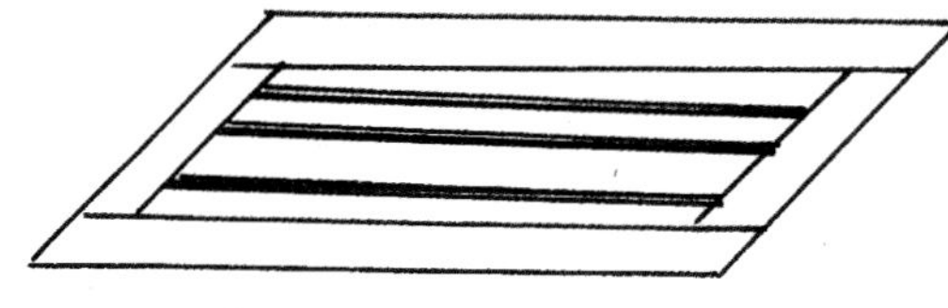

Top

Set the two top supports 8" from the
front and back.

Bottom

Place the front bottom support 4" from the front edge.
Put the back bottom support 6 ½" from the back.
Center the middle bottom support between them.

(5) Build the stand.

(6) Drill a ⅜" hole into the 6" kiln legs and through
the frame tubes and bolt with ⁵⁄₁₆" x 2 ½" bolts
to the frame. Place the frame with the legs onto
the bottom of the kiln box and all the way to the
back and weld into place. Flip the kiln frame back
over onto its wheels.

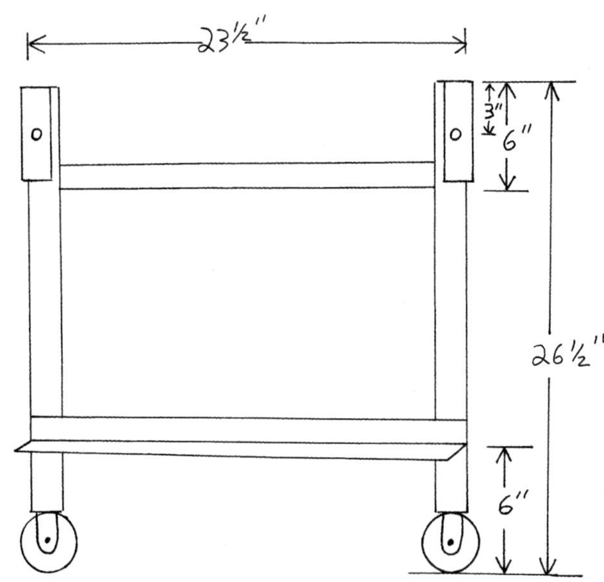

(7) Degrease the expanded metal sheet using lacquer thinner and a rag. Place the rag outside when you are done; the fumes are very strong. Cut the expanded metal with a sabre saw using a metal cutting saw blade. See the cut list for the kiln sides.

(8) Spot weld the expanded metal into the inside of the kiln frame and door.

(9) Spray paint the kiln using a metal primer and color.
Use high temperature paint on the front door flange (not necessary if it's stainless steel).

(10) The door will be installed later.

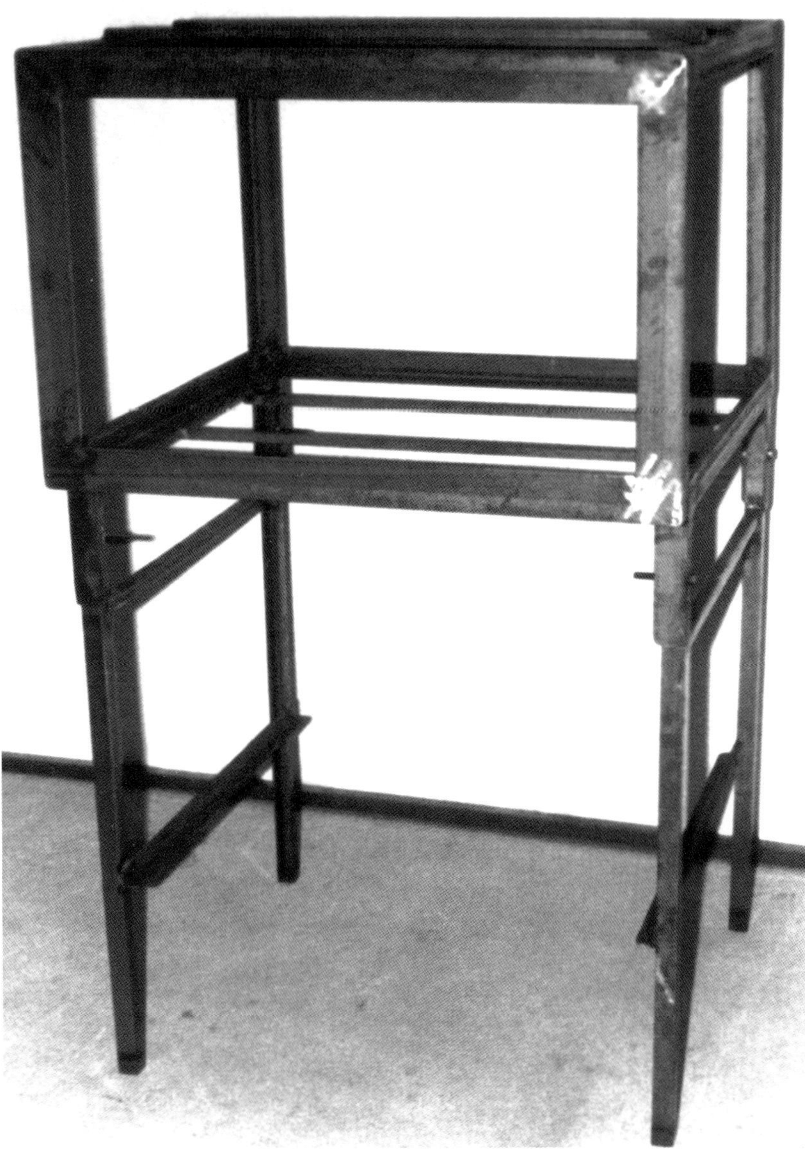

Welded kiln frame

- Weld all joints.

- Set the two top supports 8″ from the front and back.

- Check and square up frame.

- Grind the welds flat on the front face of the kiln opening.

- Place the front bottom support 4″ from the front edge.
Put the back bottom support 6 ½″ from the back.
Center the middle bottom support between them.

Welded kiln stand

- Put the bottom angle irons inside of the stand and bolt a ¾″ plywood shelf between them to stiffen the stand.

- Short welds hold wheel units to bottom of the tube (not shown in photo).

Install the Fiber Blanket

(1) Wear long pants and a long sleeved shirt. Wear rubber or cotton gloves and a good respirator. The fibers are dangerous to breathe.

(2) Lay the kiln frame on its back with the door opening facing up. Cut a 108" piece of the 1 ½" x 24" wide ceramic fiber insulation, roll up the insulation and place the roll into the kiln frame vertically and then unroll it. Place the seam at the bottom of the kiln and a bit to one side of the center line, press the blanket into the corners of the kiln (using a 26" long piece of 1" x 3" wood). Work your way around the kiln until you come to where the ends meet, and then trim the excess with scissors. Leave a little extra so that when you press the seam together, there is pressure to keep it closed. There will be a 1 ½" gap between the door opening and the edge of the wool. Take end cuts from the roll and fill this gap in tightly.

(3) Measure and cut a piece of 1 ½" blanket for the back of the kiln and press it into place. Also cut a 1" piece of insulation and place it into the back, for a total of 2 ½".

(4) Measure the remaining distance around the inside of the kiln; cut a piece of 1" fiber that long plus extra so you can trim the seam later and get it tight. Roll and unroll the fiber as in part #2 and press it tightly into the corners, (use a shorter board). The insulation should be tight between the back of the kiln and the door opening flange. The inside should be 16" x 24" x 24".

(5) Cut 1 ½" thick and 1" thick insulation pieces and put into the door.

(6) Make large U-shapes out of the Kanthol wire. Cut the wires 13" long and bend at 5"; place a piece of the 2" x ½" mullite tube onto the wire and bend again. Press these through the inside of the kiln insulation until the wires stick out from the expanded metal. Snug tight and bend over the expanded metal. To hold the insulation, space two per kiln wall, six in the roof and six in the door. In the previous photos of the completed 20 x 20 kilns you can see black oxidized metal clips where I've placed the mullite tube holders. I prefer the tubes to metal.

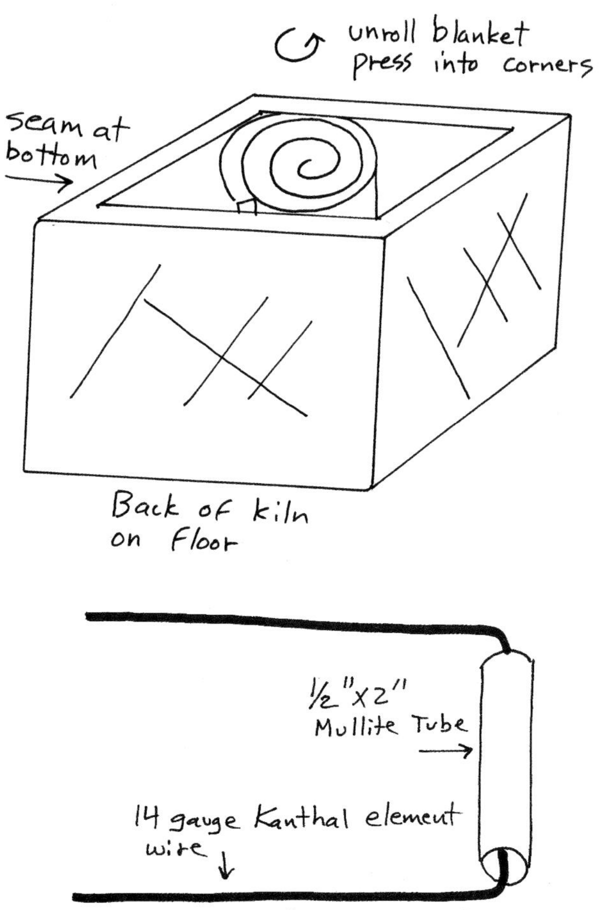

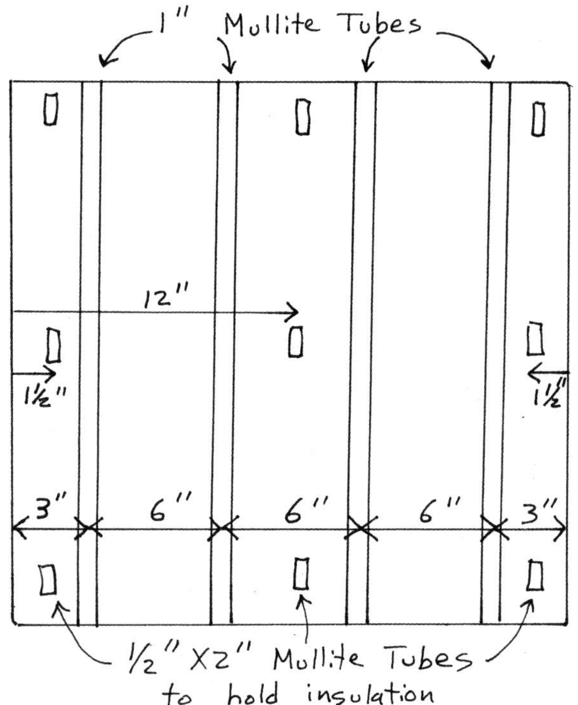

(7) Now with the kiln still on its back, position the door and drill; tap and bolt the hinges where they should go. This allows for the extra insulation to act as a door gasket.

(8) Stand the kiln up and put on the door handle. To keep the drop front door closed, I use a bent piece of ⅛" rod with a handle that hooks into the expanded metal. This can be used to vent the kiln by holding the door open at various spacings.

(9) Cut the soft insulating brick in half with a hack saw. Place the four 4 ½" x 4 ½" x 2 ½" thick bricks on the bottom of your kiln and outline around them with a felt pen. Cut tight holes in the insulation and work the bricks all the way to the bottom screen. These give you a solid base for your kiln shelf posts.

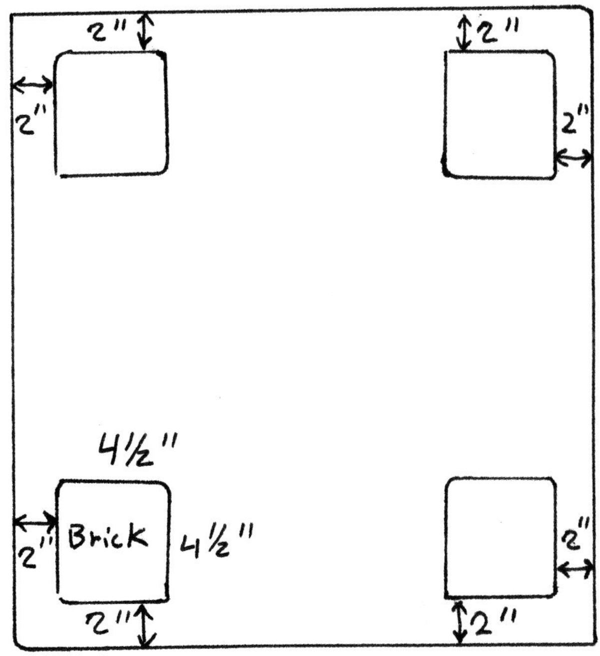

Wind the Elements

(1) Measure and cut 87 feet of 14 gauge Kanthal A-1 wire. The element is 86' plus 1' for the pigtail ends. If you use a different size of wire, have the supplier calculate the length that you need for a 12 amp, 220 - 240 volt element. The voltage will vary with your location, but 87' should be about right.

(2) To make the twisted pigtail end, bend 6" of the wire back on itself and grab the very end (bend) with a vice grip plier. Place the two wires between blocks of wood in a vice and twist until wound tight. Do the other end the same way.

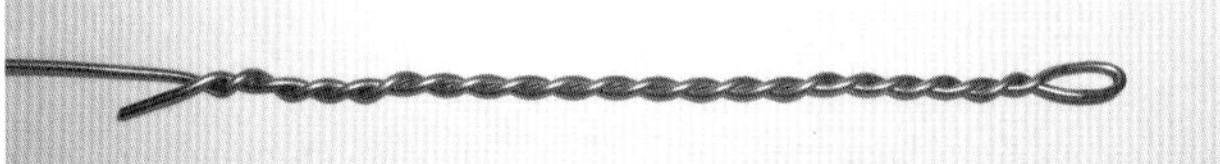

(3) Make an element winder (see photo below) out of a ¾" pipe. You can design a contraption using wooden blocks and a pipe with elbows and nipples to make a handle. I welded mine. It's 44" long. One end comes off so that you can slide the element off after it's coiled.

(4) Duct tape one of the pigtail ends parallel to the pipe and begin cranking the handle. With your other hand, feed the wire so it winds tight like a spring. When you come to the end, be careful when you let go as the end will whip around until it has unwound a bit.

(5) Remove the end support of the winder and slide the element off.

(6) Wind a second element. You need two for this project.

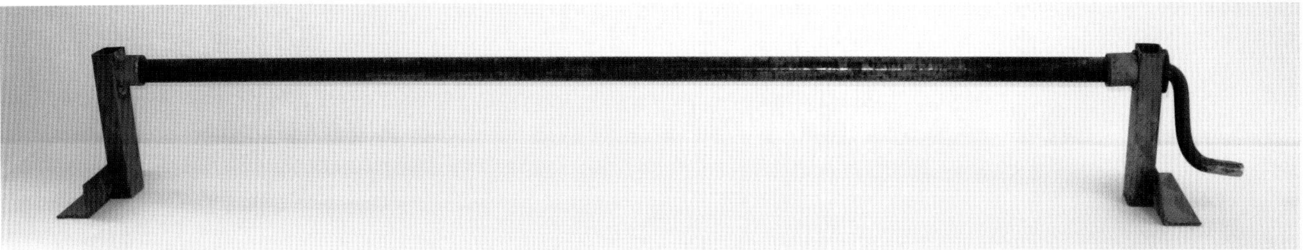

above: element winder - ¾" pipe with a 1" outside diameter, 44" long.

Place the Elements

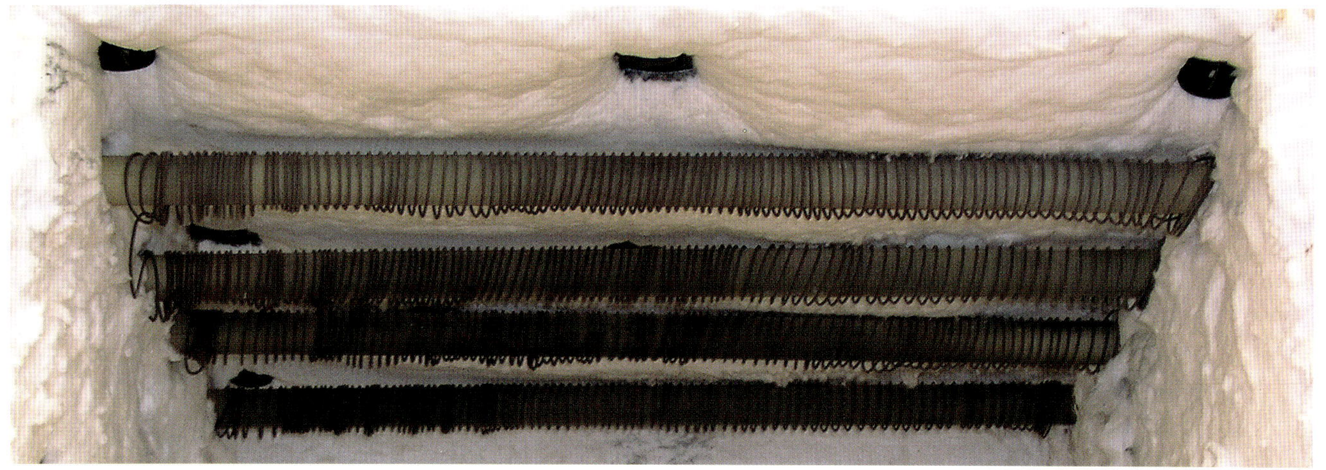

upper: elements in the kiln. If they bunch up in one section, unplug the kiln and spread them out with your hands. The insulation blanket is held with metal clips (Inconel) instead of mullite tubes.

lower: the 1" mullite element rods are plugged with fiber blanket insulation, and the element and wire split bolt-connectors are underneath the white high temperature tape.

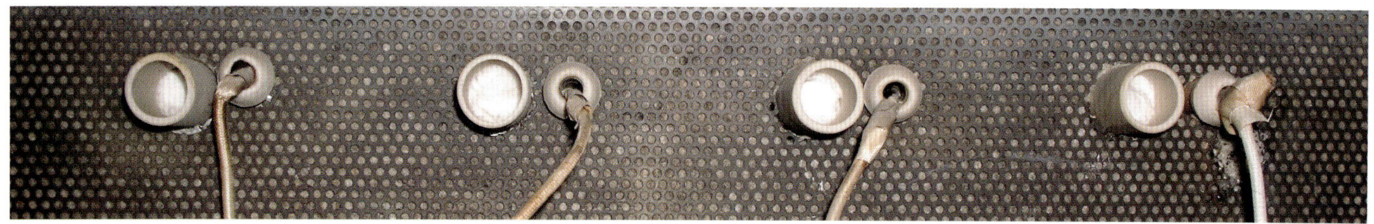

(1) Mark where the elements are to go with a felt pen on the ceramic fiber blanket. The elements enter on the right side where the control box is, go down one tube, cross over to the next, and then back making a U.

(2) With diagonal pliers, snip holes where the mullite tubes will go through the expanded metal and insulation at the control box. (See photo above, for this kiln I found some surplus perforated metal instead of expanded metal.)

(3) Bore and enlarge a tight hole through the insulation and also into the opposite wall. The top of the holes should be about ¼" below the inside roof of the kiln. This will give a small air space between the element and the insulating roof. It's OK if the elements touch the roof, but they should not be smothered by the insulation.

(4) Nip the screen about 1" away from the tube and bore a small hole in the control box area for the ½" mullite tube for the pigtail.

(5) Put about 2" of fiber into both ends of the tube to act as insulation.

(6) Find the center of the element coil and unwind about 6". Evenly stretch one-half of the element coil so that it lays at 26" after you let go, and then evenly stretch the other one-half of the coil at 26".

(7) Now make the element into a long U. You should have 26" of stretched coil, a bend of 90°, then an almost straight 6", a bend of another 90° and then the other 26" of stretched coil.

(8) Feed the mullite tube through the control box hole into the kiln, through one leg of the element, and into the hole on the opposite wall. Put the pigtail through the short length of ½" tube. Do this again for the remaining element leg. Repeat

this procedure for the other element. You should
have four pigtails sticking through the control
box wall. Wire a short piece of element wire
across the ends of the mullite tubes to keep them
from backing out (not shown).

Build the Control Box

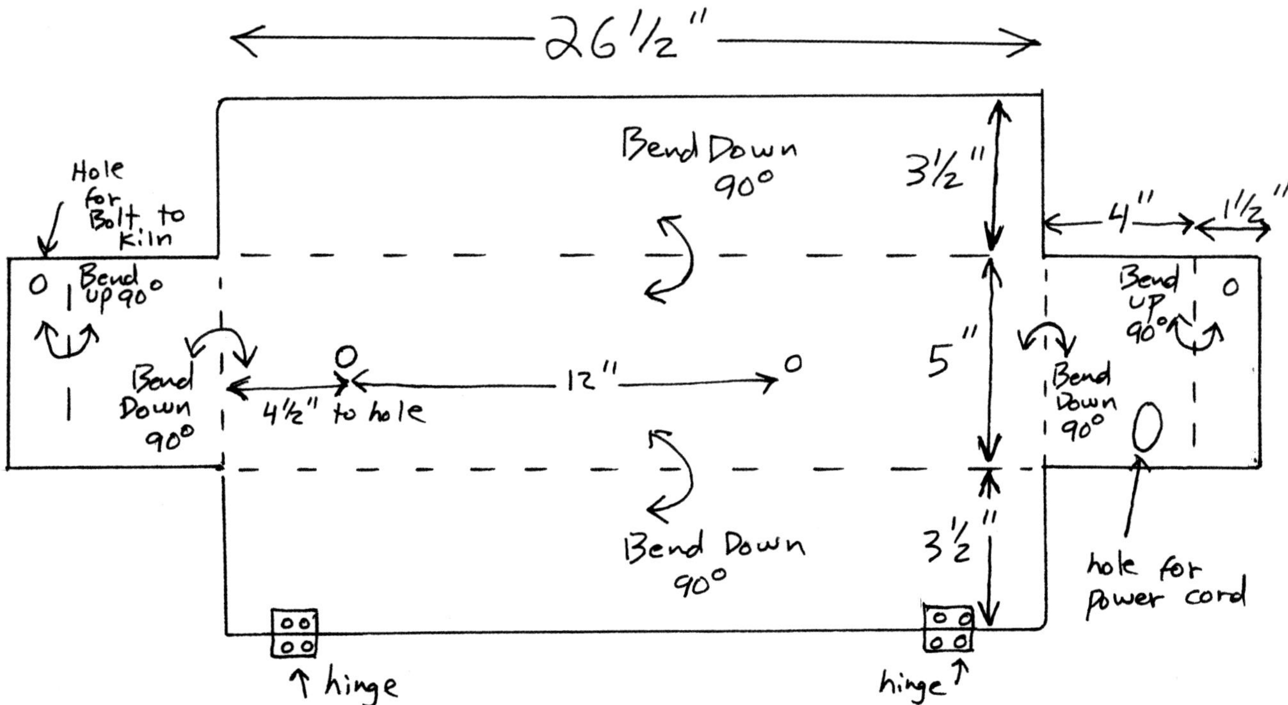

(1) Follow the diagram and cut out a piece of 18
gauge steel.

(2) Bend the metal into a box with a metal
bender or over a table edge with a mallet.
The ends will stick out ½" past the box; this will
hold it away from the kiln and allow air flow.

(3) Bend and tack weld the ends.

(4) Drill the holes for the switches and an
elongated hole for the dryer cord.

(5) Attach the 1" hinges.

(6) Paint the control box.

(7) Drill, tap, and bolt the control box over the
element pigtail area. Leave as much room as
possible in all directions so that the element
connectors won't contact any metal.

Wire the Kiln

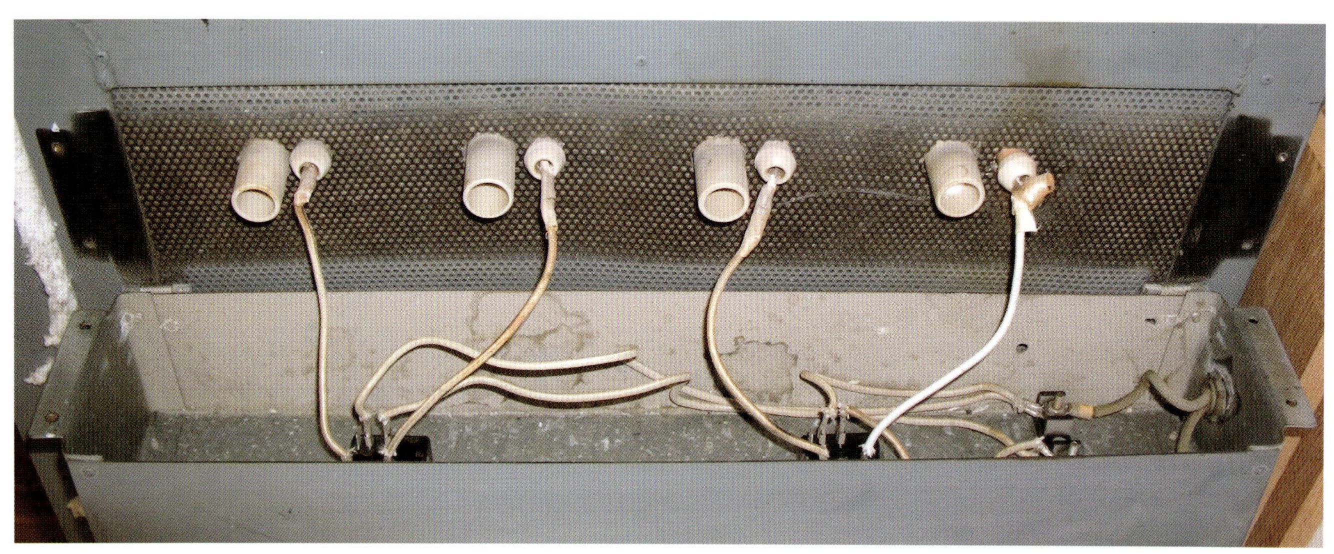

above: shows the control box hinged open.
far right: corrosion inhibitor and high temp tape.
below: wiring a kiln is simple - see diagram.

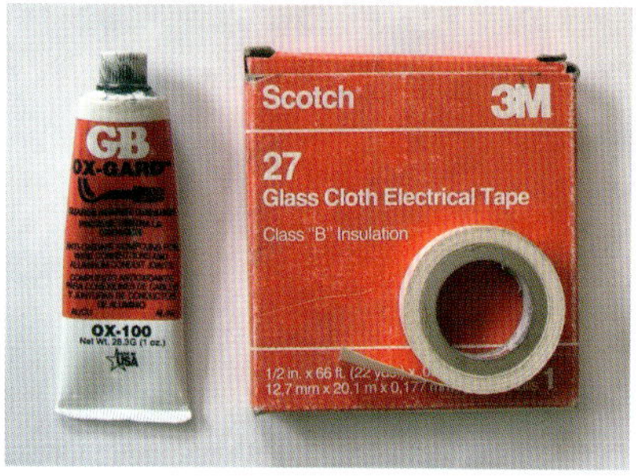

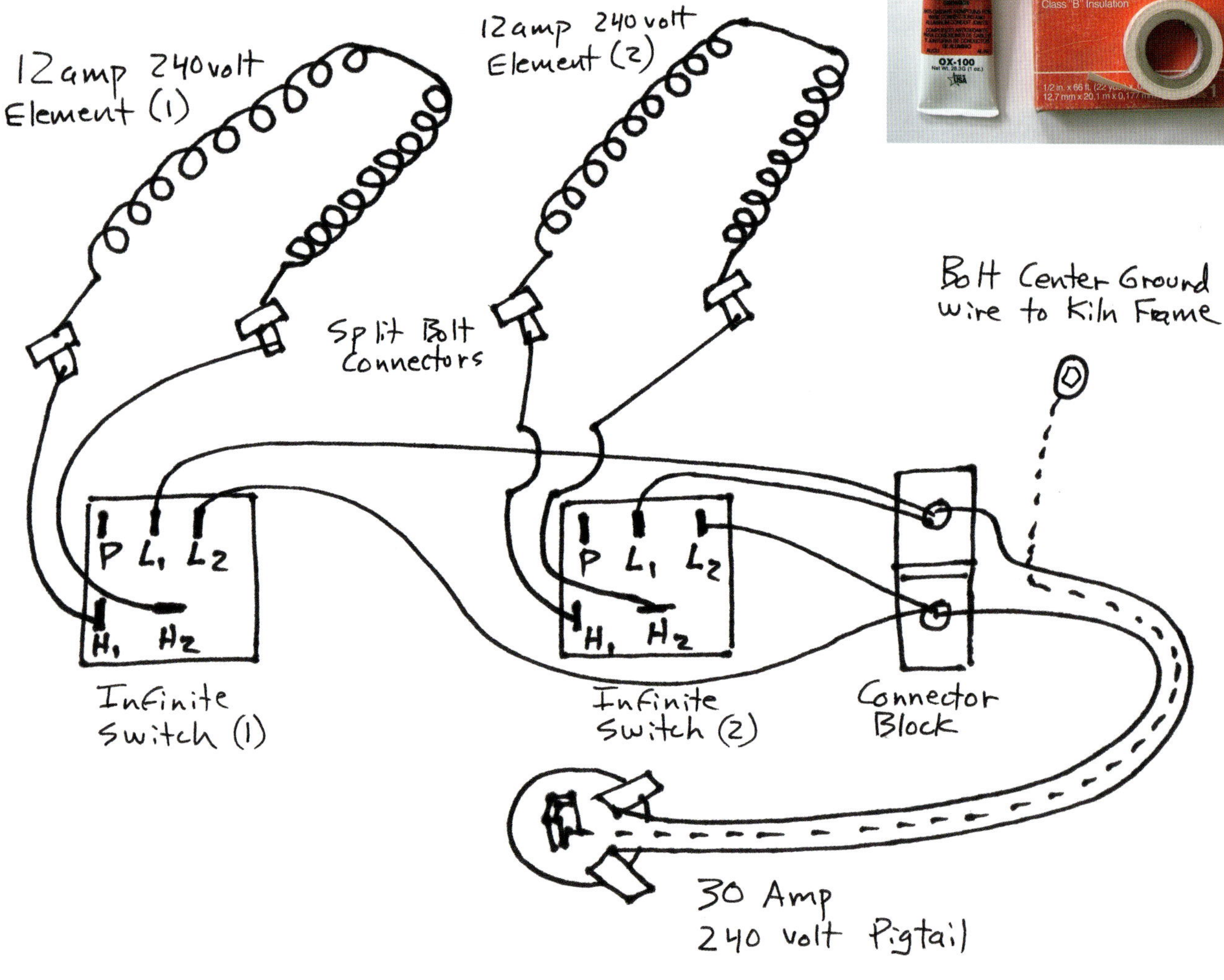

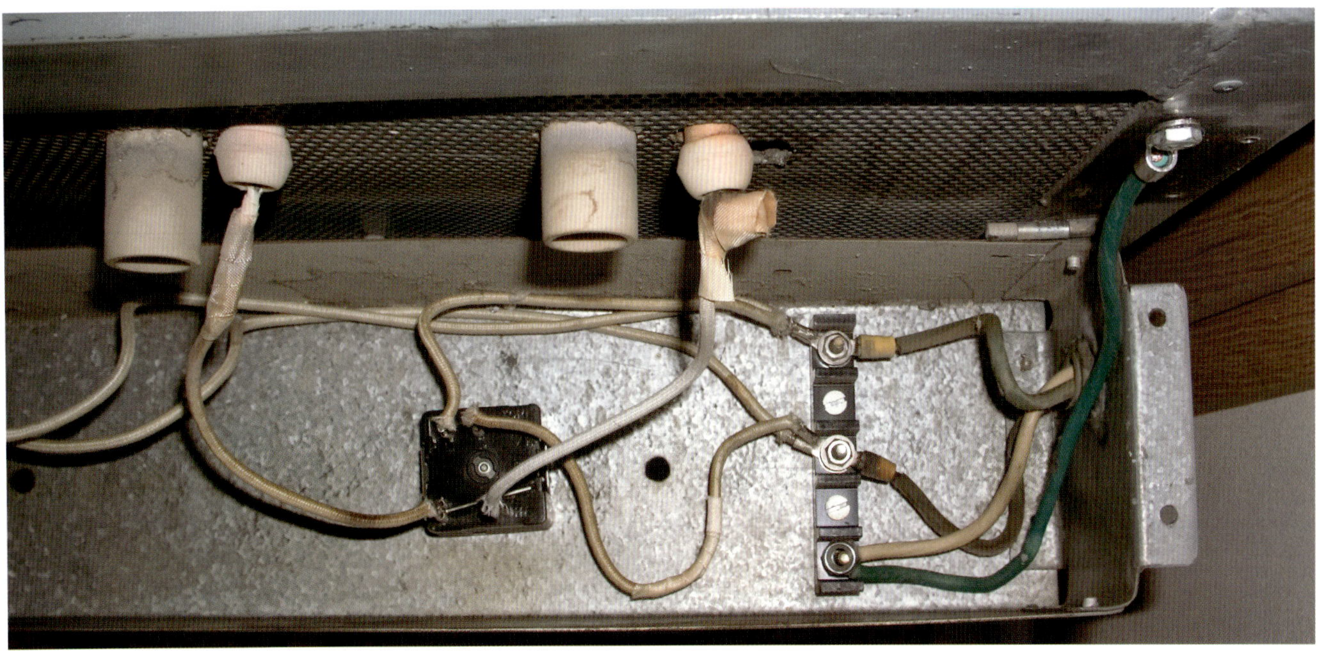

above: shows control box wiring and connector block.

(1) Mount the 3-bolt connector block to the wall of the control box.

(2) Place the 30 amp pigtail through the control box wall and secure with a wire clamp. Hook the hot leads to the connector block and nut them down. Nut down the center ground wire to the connector block. Take a #10 green wire with a ring connector on each end, and, with a second nut secure it directly to the side of the kiln, to the angle iron with a bolt into a hole that has been drilled and tapped. Allow slack for closing the control box.

(3) With a crimping tool, crimp extremely tightly the high temperature ring connectors to the 12 gauge high temperature insulated wire; run these from the connector block to the L1 and L2 spades of the infinite switches. Crimp the female connectors onto the ends and hook to the infinite switches.

(4) Crimp female connectors onto more 12 gauge high temp wire and run this wire from the H1 and H2 spades of the infinite switches to where the element pigtails stick about 1" through the small mullite tubes.

lower right: split bolt connector acts as a heat sink and creates a stable element/wire connection.

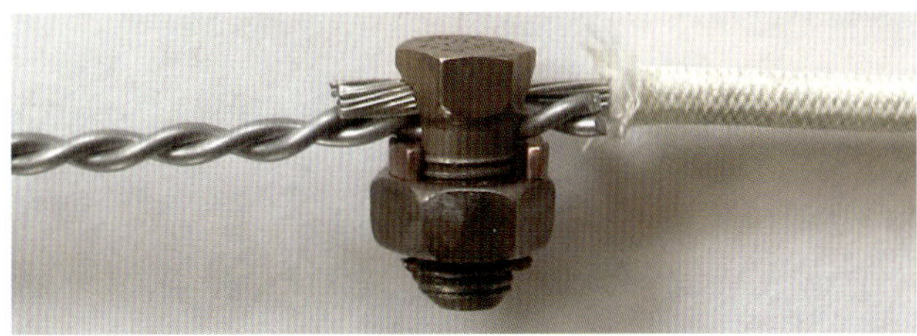

(5) Strip the high temperature wire and coat both it and the element pigtail with corrosion inhibitor. Place into the split bolt connector; with vice grips and a box wrench, tighten as tight as you can. This is where a loose connection will arc and burn out. Wrap with high temperature tape.

Programmable controller and thermocouple

Drill a hole through the side of your kiln and insert a 12' thermocouple probe horizontally so that it sits about 2" above your kiln shelf, which sits on four 4 ½" high K23 kiln bricks that have been cut with a hacksaw to use as kiln posts. Plug the kiln into a programmable kiln controller which is plugged into a 30 amp 240 volt receptacle - or plug the kiln in directly and use a separate pyrometer. You can adjust the infinite switches manually for your firing, just like we used to do in the old days. **Enjoy your new kiln!**

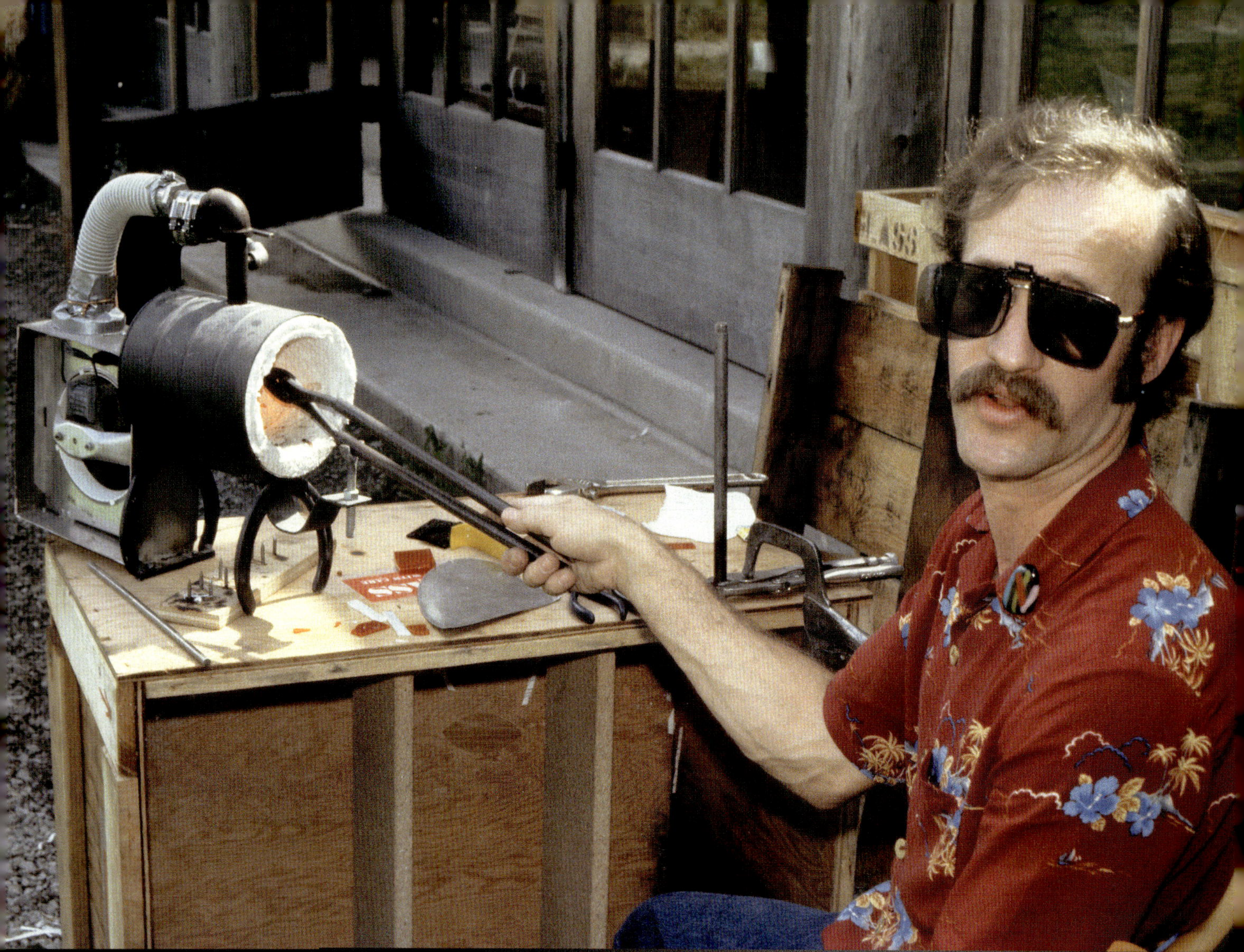

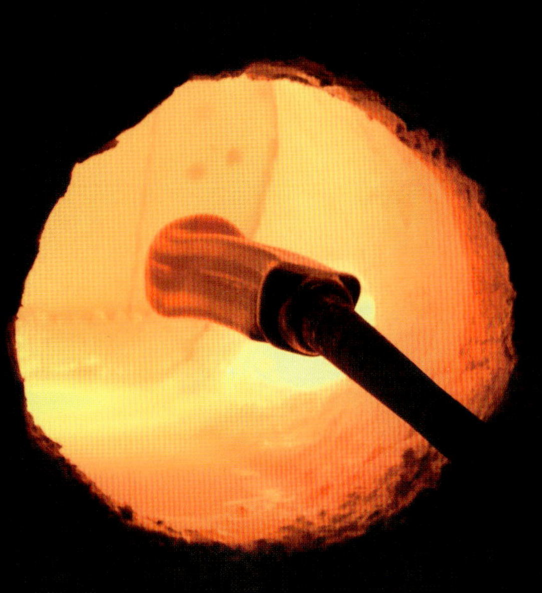

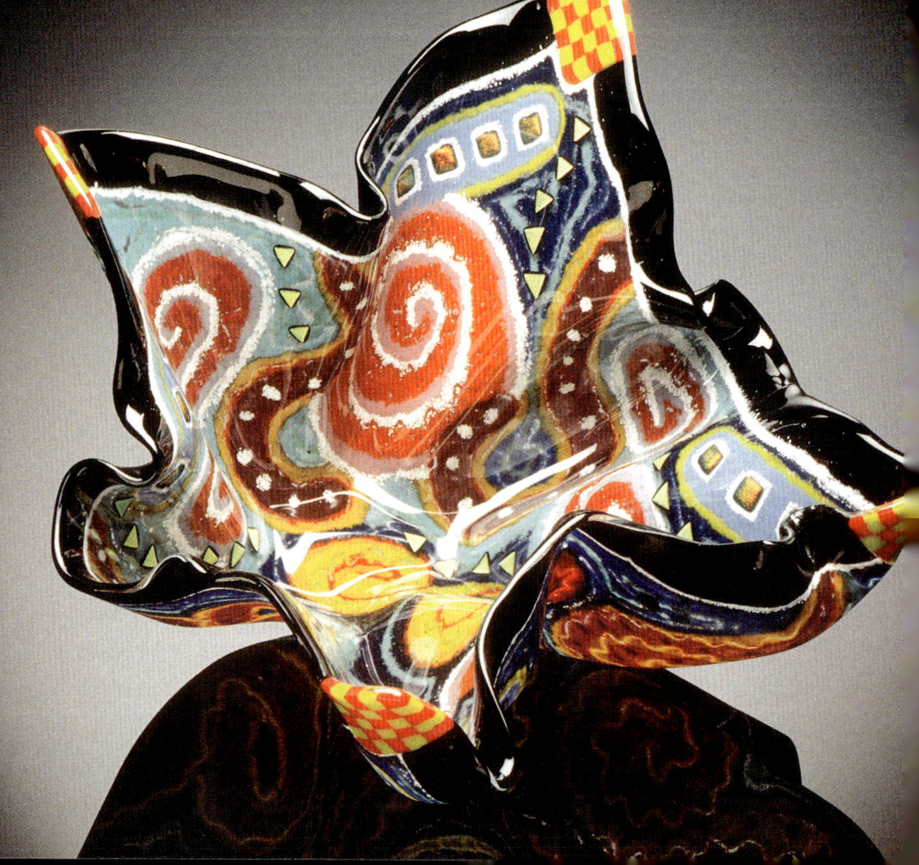

WARNING!
Glory holes burn natural gas or propane.
They can be dangerous. The gas can explode.

- **Have good ventilation in your work space.**
- **A nonflammable table and floor are best.**
- **Never leave a glory hole burning unattended!**
- **Don't wear open-toed shoes or plastic clothes!**
- **Wear dark glasses!**

I designed my small glory holes to use for a few hours at a time and I never leave them unattended! I am always in the room to turn off the gas if there is a problem, and I have a fire extinguisher nearby.

When lighting the glory hole, it is important to first turn on the blower for the air. If the blower is not turned on first, explosive gas might travel to the blower. Then, slowly turn on the gas and light the glory hole. If the gas does not ignite within a few seconds, turn it off, see what the problem is, and then try again. Never allow raw gas to flow from the glory hole. Natural gas and propane are heavier than air and they can form a layer of explosive gas on the floor and even go down sewer drains. If ignited with an electrical spark or flame, propane or natural gas can blow the building up, just like in the movies.

Now that I have said this, if you use precaution and understand what you are doing; you can have fun and make stuff with a glory hole. It is a good idea to take a hot glass class and find a glass blower to consult with when you build and fire up your first glory hole. If you have doubts about your ability to build your own glory hole, then buy a manufactured one. If you plan to run your glory hole for extended periods of time, or leave it running unattended, have a professional engineer design your burner and safety system, using a manufactured burner and a burner tip.

In 1981 I tried melting a small piece of glass over a butane torch and turned the glass gray. The year before, I built a hot shop for blowing glass which included a big glory hole, and I figured that I could heat small pieces in a miniature glory hole, so I designed "The 3 Pounder." By setting the ratio of gas to air, I can control the reduction atmosphere that discolored my glass. If I was working on a project and needed a certain color glass stringer, I can quickly heat up a small piece of glass, pull a thin glass stringer, and get back to work within a few minutes.

facing upper:
Richard La Londe in 1983 at the Pilchuck Glass School demonstrating his first version of the "3 Pounder" glory hole, made from of a three pound coffee can, a horseshoe, a surplus bathroom fan, duct tape, miscellaneous refractory materials, and a piece of shop vac hose. Upon seeing Richard, Dale Chihuly, with good humor asked, "What ya, doing, La Londe, roasting hotdogs?"

lower left: heating a bundle of strips of Bullseye for making a pattern bar.

Lower right: "Bolero", 1988, H. 8 in. (20 cm) x W. 15 in. (38 cm) x D. 15 in. (38 cm). The lime green and red checkerboard corners are made from a bundle of cut glass strips that are heated in a glory hole and swung into a pattern bar. After annealing, the glass is cut crosswise with a diamond saw.

On the following pages you will find a copy of the 1983 manuscript for "The Three Pounder" that I typed on my manual Olympic typewriter and that includes my drawings, misspellings, mark overs, and typos.

"The 3 Pounder"

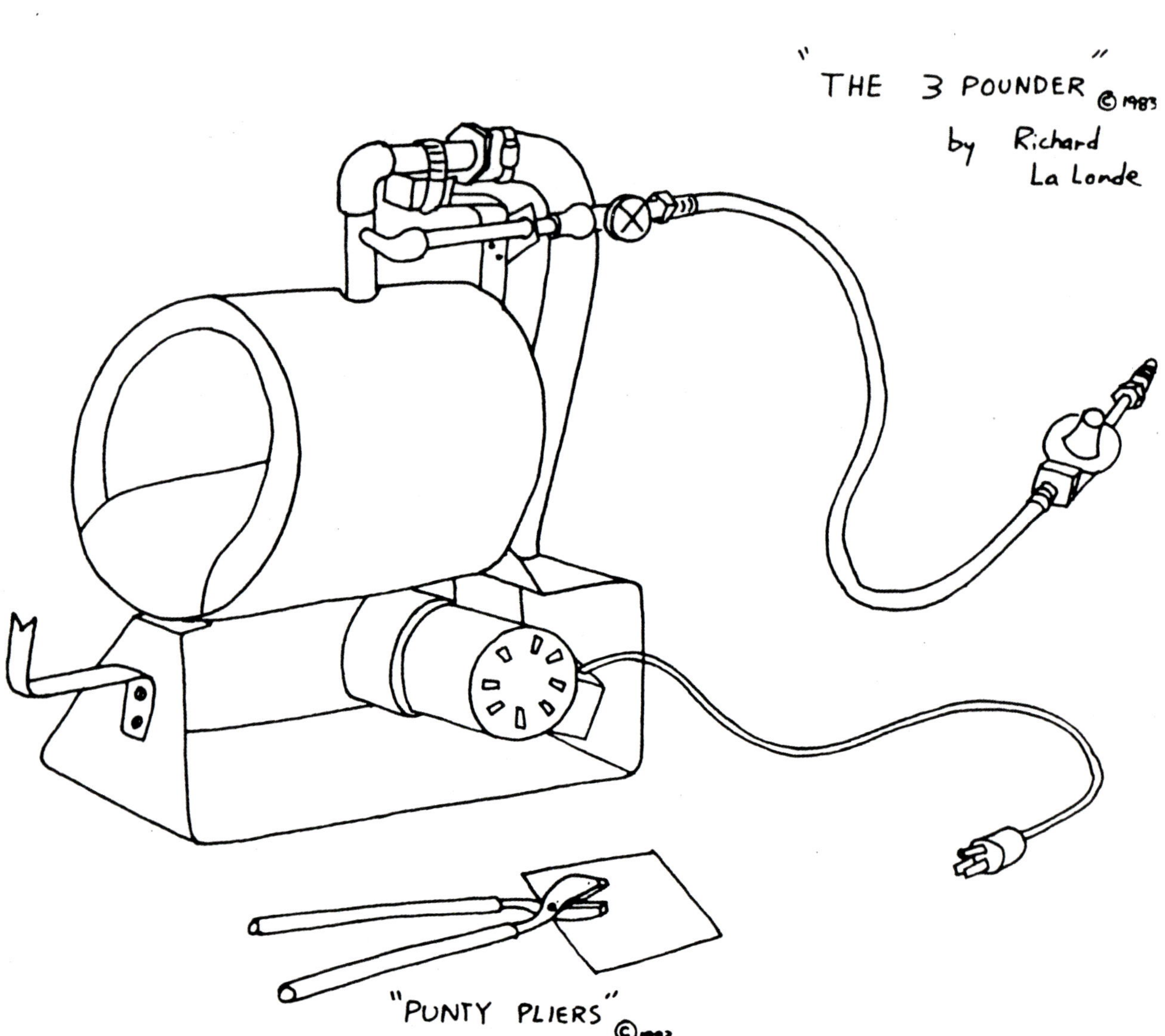

GLORY HOLE MATERIAL LIST

3 Pound Coffee Can

PIPE SUPPLY SHOP

Black Iron Pipe

    1/2" Nipple X 4" long
    1/2" Nipple X 2½" long
    1/2" Elbow
    1" X 1/2" Pipe Reducer
    1/8" Nipple X 4" long
    1/8" X 1/4" Bell Reducer
    1/8" Street Elbow

Pipe diameters are written as inside pipe measurements.

Use black iron pipe. You may substitute galvanized pipe except where the gas contacts the pipe & especially the burner pipe, (one going into the glory hole), must be black iron.

WELDING SUPPLY SHOP

1/4" pipe gas valve
6' of 1/4" LP-Gas hose with Female Propane (reverse thread) fittings, both ends.
Preset Propane Gas Regulator

Have the welding shop put the hose ends on for you.

AUTO PARTS STORE

14" of Flexible Hose 1⅜"-1½" I.D.
(3) 1¼"-1¾" Hose Clamps

Hose may be plastic or rubber.
I.D. means inside diameter.
O.D. means outside diameter.

JOHNSTONE SUPPLY CO.
or
ANY APPLIANCE REPAIR CO.

45 CFM (cubic feet per minute) FASCO Squirrel Cage Fan & Motor

You may use up to a 60CFM Fan but you must damper the air.
(See section on Fan installation.

HARDWARE STORE

6' 16/3 Wire (appliance cord)

(1) 3/4" Wire Connector   The threaded bushing is to lock wire

(1) 3 Prong Plug (grounded)   into the fan motor junction box.

(2) Wire Splicers (16 gauge)   The twist type wire nuts covered

(1) Spade Connector for Ground Nut   with electrical tape will work.

(6) 1/2" X 3/16" dia. Bolts, Nuts,   Twist wire around ground nut

     & Lock Washers.   will also suffice.

(12) 1/8" Steel Pop Rivets X

     3/8" long.

FIREBRICK & REFRACTORY SUPPLY CO.

1" thick Refractory Wool   Called Fiberfrax, Ceri-wool, Kaowool;

     Insulation 7" X 24"   depends who manufactures it. 2400° plus.

2# 2500°Refractory Cement

or Castable.

STEEL SUPPLY CO.
or
LOCAL WELDING SHOP

MISC. METAL

     1/8" X 1" X 24" long Steel Flatbar

     1" X 1" Square Tube X 1¼" Long

     16gauge Steel 6" X 24" (black or galvanized)

     Thin Wall Pipe (diameter of the flexible fan hose)

        1½" long (see Assembly part 6)

MISC. SUPPLIES

(1) Pair of inexpensive pliers   Hardware Store

(2) pcs. 3/8 pipe 12" long   Metal Shop

     Used for handles of "Punty Pliers"

(1) pc. Stainless Steel 18ga. or thicker

     Used for a "Marver"

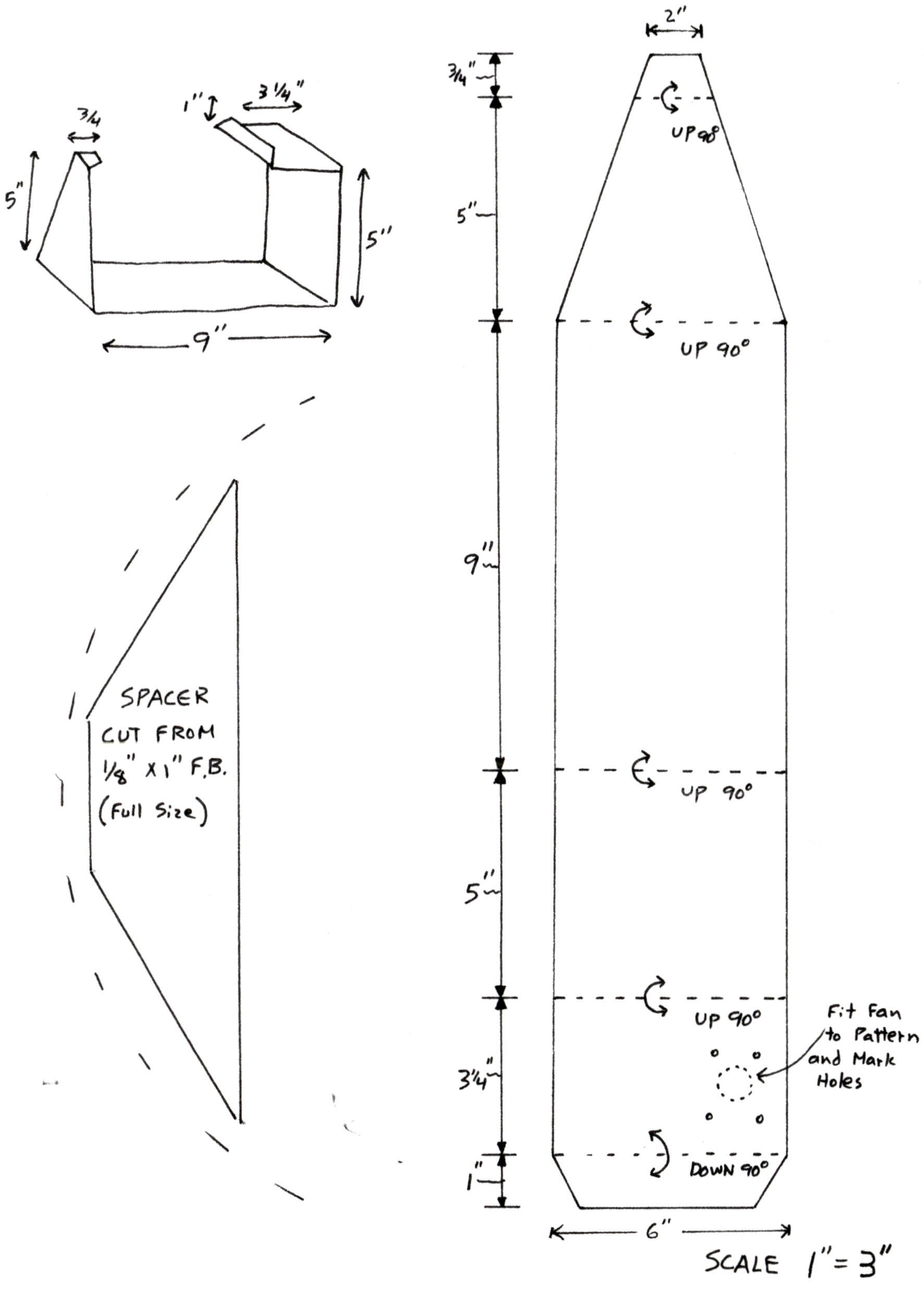

BASE PATTERN
3/4
1"
3 1/4"
5"
5"
9"
5"
SPACER
CUT FROM
1/8" X 1" F.B.
(Full Size)
2"
3/4"
5"
UP 90°
UP 90°
9"
UP 90°
5"
UP 90°
3 1/4"
Fit Fan
to Pattern
and Mark
Holes
1"
DOWN 90°
6"
SCALE 1" = 3"

ASSEMBLY

(1) Round up all of the material & tools.

(2) Cut out the base, using pattern found behind material lists. Use a fine tooth hacksaw or heavy metal shears or have it cut when purchased. Drill the fan mounting holes if using the Fasco 45 CFM fan; or wait & see how fan will line up after assembly. To cut the large hole, drill lots of little holes around the circle and then cut it out with a cold chisel.

(3) Follow directions on the pattern and bend over the edge of a work bench, using a hammer only when necessary. It should look like the following:

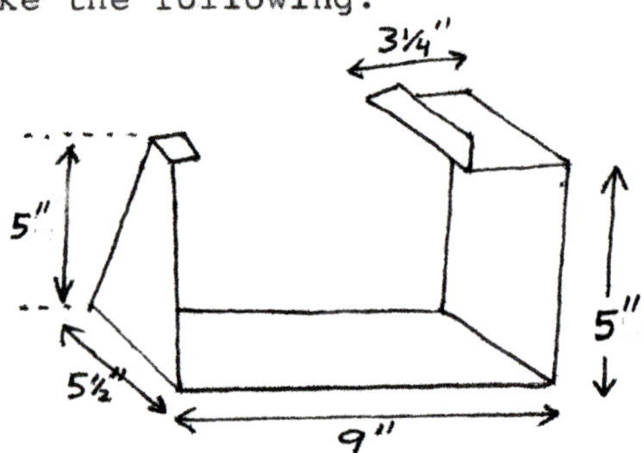

(4) Cut the 1/8" X 4" Spacer (See Pattern for Base).

(5) Hold can to the stand, line up and drill the 1/8" holes through stand. Mark spacer and drill those holes. Next drill one hole through can and using a pop rivet gun, rivit the can to the stand. Drill the second hole through the can and rivet and so on. The reason for drilling the holes one at a time is because the holes have to line up perfectly for the rivet and if one was to try to predrill all of the holes, chances are they wouldn't quite line up.

    Check to see if the can is level to the base, use a tape measure to check or a level.

Cut a 1" diameter burner hole using a drill to start and then taking small nibbles with tin snips to cut out the hole. Hole centered on top of the can.

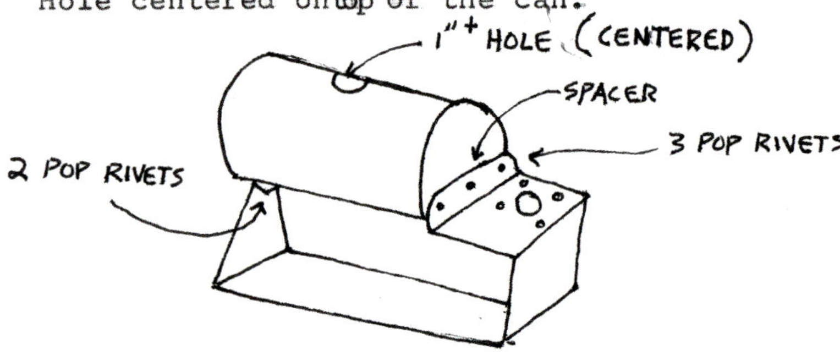

(6) Check to see if the fan fits the stand. Ream out fan motor
    mounting holes if necessary. Tack weld pipe for air hose over
    the fan hole. Or split the pipe with a hacksaw, bending the
    sections to form a flange, drill & pop rivet. You may also
    be able to find a pipe with a flange already attached, such
    as a drain pipe for kitchen sinks, cut to length, drill & pop
    rivet. Caulk any voids with silicon sealer, if it isn't tight
    air leakage may occur.

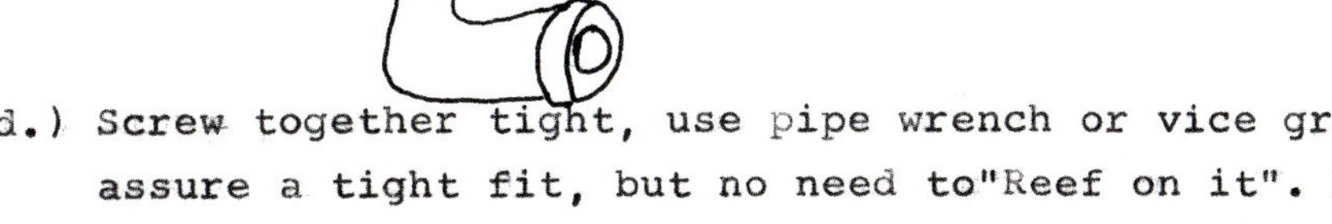

(7) Assemble Burner

    a.) Using a hacksaw (course tooth blade), cut the threads off
    one end of the 1/2" X 4" nipple (about 1"), file smooth
    inside & out.

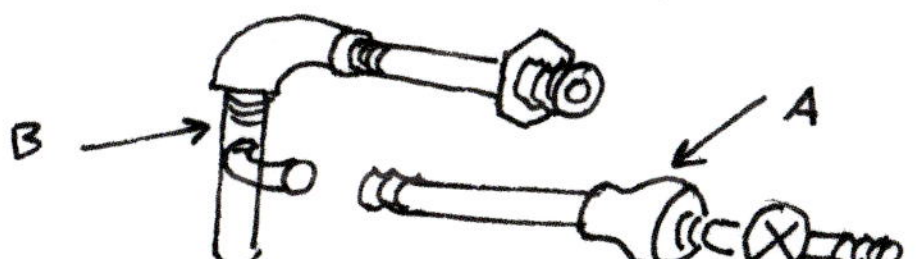

    b.) Drill an 11/32" hole in pipe from step a.), 1" below
    threaded end. Thread hole with a 1/8" pipe tap.

    c.) Close end of 1/8" Street Elbow by driving in a tight
    fitting round rod 1/2" long or welding closed. Drill
    a 3/32" hole (gas orifice). Do not bugger up the threads.

    d.) Screw together tight, use pipe wrench or vice grips to
    assure a tight fit, but no need to "Reef on it". No pipe
    caulking or teflon tape necessary. Do not tighten
    Section A to B until step (9).

(8) Figure height of support bar. The burner should go about
    1/4" into can. Pop rivet 1" X 1" X1¼" square tube to support,
    use two pop rivets. Pop rivet support to can. Insert burner
    and secure with a pipe clamp.

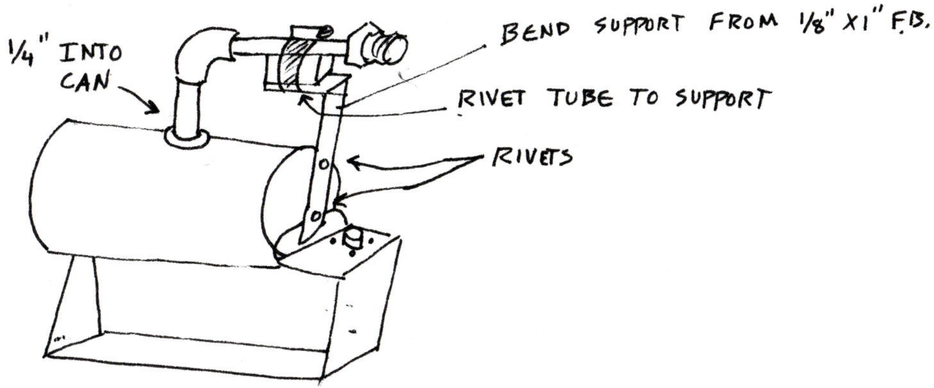

(9) Cut holder 1/8" X 1" F.B. (Flat Bar) X 2" long. Drill 1/2"
    hole & two rivet holes. Put Section A through holder piece.
    Screw Section A into Section B, tighten, locate holder, drill
    & rivet.

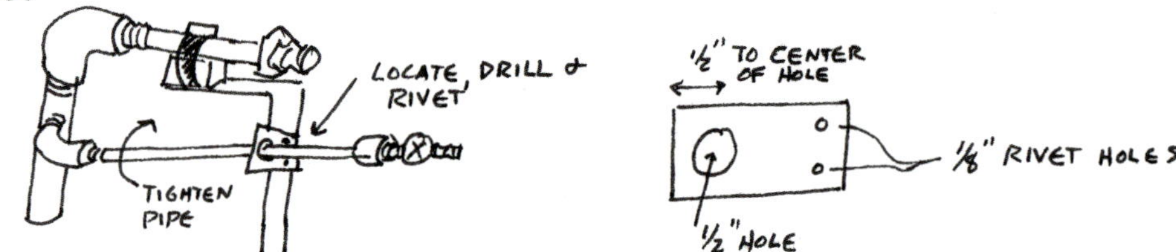

(10) Wear Respirator. Using a long thin knife, slice off 1/4"
     thickness of the 7" X 24" inswool.

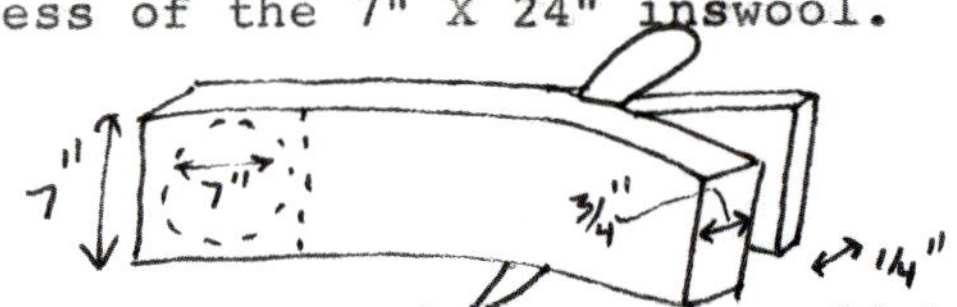

(11) Take can as a template, press slightly into wool to mark size.
     Cut out with scissors. Use one end of the 1/4" thickness of
     inswool.

(12) Place the 1/4" X 7" diameter inswool in the back of the can.

(13) Place the 3/4" X 7" X 17" in can and trim to fit. Place seam
     at the bottom of the can.

(14) Trim the remaining 3/4" X 7" X 7" inswool piece to fit into
     the inswool lined can, allow alittle extra for a tight fit.
     Tamp into the back of the gloryhole. It helps hold the sides
     up and seal the back.

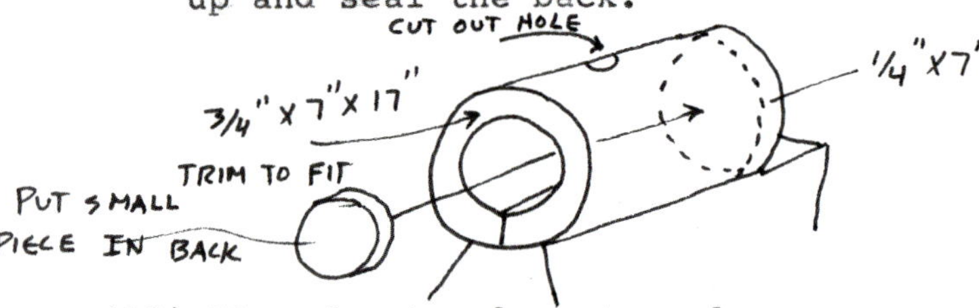

(15) Wire fan to element cord.

     a.) Punch out "knock out" of fan motor junction box. Screw
         in wire connector and put enough wire through the connector
         to make the connections. Tighten connector onto wire.

     b.) Clamp on wire connectors (splicers) or use wire nuts and
         tape. Make sure connections are tight.

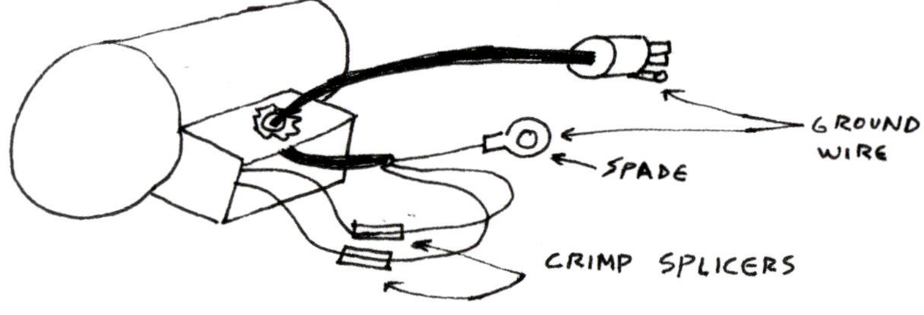

c.) Clamp on spade to ground wire.

d.) Drill hole in junction box (if needed), scrape away
paint and bolt spade ground to metal box, thus grounding
the glory hole. Use a 3/16" dia. X 1/2" bolt.

e.) Put on plug end, follow directions in package.

Wire in an optional, in-line off/on switch if wanted.

(16) Line up fan to base. Bolt with (4) 3/16" X 1/2" long bolts,
nuts, & lock washers. Seal air gap with silicon sealer or
a thin rubber gasket.

(17) Put on flexible hose from fan to burner unit with hose clamps.

(18) Mix 2500° Castible in a container. Add luke warm water a
little at a time until the consistency or brick mortar or real
thick pancake batter. Spread on the bottom of the glory hole ontop
of the inswool about 1/2" thick & taper up the sides part
way. Use a spoon back to trowel the surface smooth. Let
set overnight in a warm room. Do not fire for atleast 3 days
drying time in a warm room. (Firing may chip the castible,
then it needs to dry more.)

(19) Drill & rivet or bolt the stand for the "punty-pliers".
Bend out of 1" X 1/8" X 10" F.B.

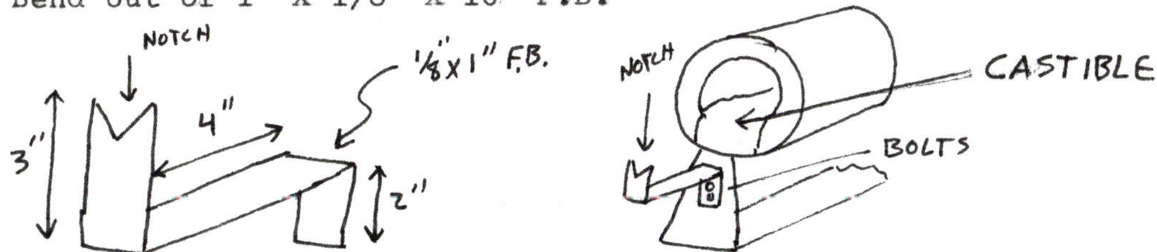

(20) Apply Sairset kiln brick mortar, (get 1 quart from Seattle Pottery Supply), with a 1" paint
brush, to the fiber blanket lining the glory hole to cover fibers and keep them from
becoming airborne.

(21) Check out the glory hole to see if you forgot anything. Hook up hose & regulator to small
propane tank, like the ones use for travel trailers or gas barbecues.

<u>OPERATION</u>

Set the glory hole up on a non-flammable surface (brick or
metal). A fire extinguisher near by and GOOD VENTILATION is a
must. A concrete floor is a good idea. Lighting the glory hole
is the most dangerous part and you should pay particular attention
to the lighting instructions and the order in which they proceed.
(1) Wear wool or cotton clothing, do not wear flammable plastic
    clothing. Plastic clothing is "tacky" anyhow!
(2) Wear dark glasses to protect you eyes from hot glass and infrared
    radiation (light rays).
(3) Ignite a piece of paper attached to the end of a 24" wire or
    better yet ignite a hand held propane torch.
(4) Turn on the fan
(5) Turn on the gas about 1 turn and immediately move the flame
    towards the opening of the glory hole. If the flame goes out or
    the glory hole does not ignite within a few seconds. Turn off
    the gas and try again. If the gas builds up,before it lights,
    it may ignite with a small explosion. Stay back from the opening
    when lighting as it usually belches out a large flame.
Once the glory hole is lit you must adjust the flame by cutting
back on the gas,(this will probably need to be adjusted again after
a few minutes and the glory hole has heated up). There are 3 flames:
            <u>Reduction</u>: More gas than oxygen, orange flame, may produce
                  Soot.
        <u>Neutral</u>: Sharp, defined blue flame.
        <u>Oxidation</u>: Very bright blue, sputtering flame, too much
            oxygen.
You want a neutral glame for most work. If you've installed a
45cfm fan, just cut back on the gas until you hear the glory hole
roar and the flame is a steady blue color, with a well defined shape.
If your fan is larger you might need to damper the air. Mount a
plate over the air intake and adjust.

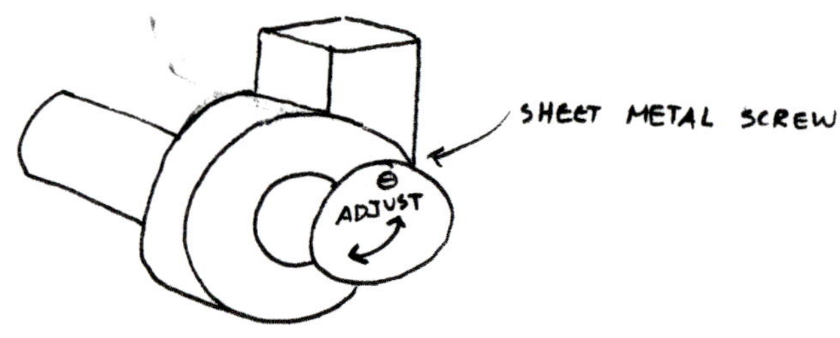

After you've successfully got "The 3 Pounder" under control
you can stick the "Punty Pliers" into the glory hole, under the flame
and warm them up. They don't need to turn bright yellow and melt,
but should show a slight color.

PULLING CANE

Pick up a piece of cold glass 1¼" wide and 2½" long, put this
into the pliers about 3/8" and plunge it into the glory hole, under
the flame and by resting one of the handles on the stand, rotate
from side to side to heat evenly.

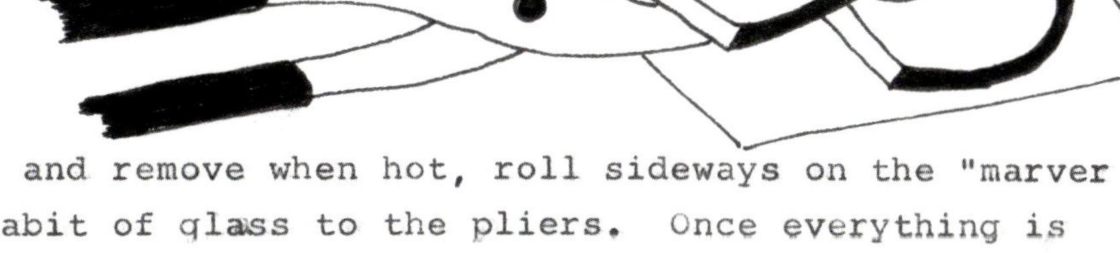

Once the glass begins to bend then bring it out and fold it
over using the "Marver Plate" or needle nose pliers.

Reheat again and remove when hot, roll sideways on the "marver
plate", sticking abit of glass to the pliers. Once everything is
hot, the pliers will collapse and the only thing holding the glass
will be that it has melted onto the pliers.

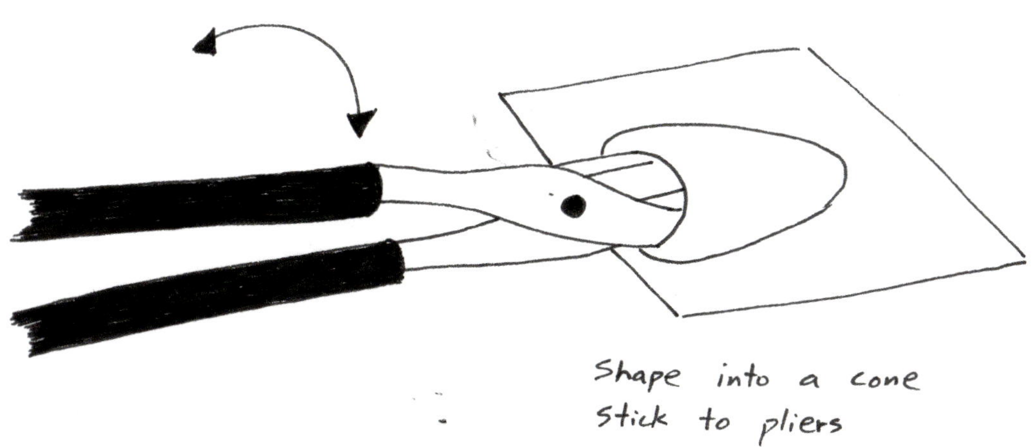

Reheat again and when the glass has coalesced into a solid
piece and begins to flop around as you rotate, then remove, grasp
the very end with a pair of needle nose pliers and wrap the end around
a nail stuck into your work table.

Stick the glass to itself. Then begin walking backwards, pulling
a string of glass cane. The slower you move the thicker the cane.
Experimenting will allow you to control the thickness. When the cane
becomes hard to pull, then stop and set the "Punty Pliers" on the floor.
Go back and cut the cane into usable lengths 12"-18" long.

If the glass pulls off the pliers then they are toohot. You
can chill them in water, but repeated chills will cause the pliers
to deteriorate, so keep this to a minimum. If you find that a fair
ammount of glass remains on the "Punty Pliers" then immediately
reheat on the "Punty Pliers" and pull again. Take care not to touch
the sides or bottom of the glory hole because you will pick up
impurities (stones).

ABSTRACT HOT LINES

Heat glass and marver the shape, when hot, then remove from
glory hole and pick at the glass lump with the needle nose pliers
to create an abstract mess.

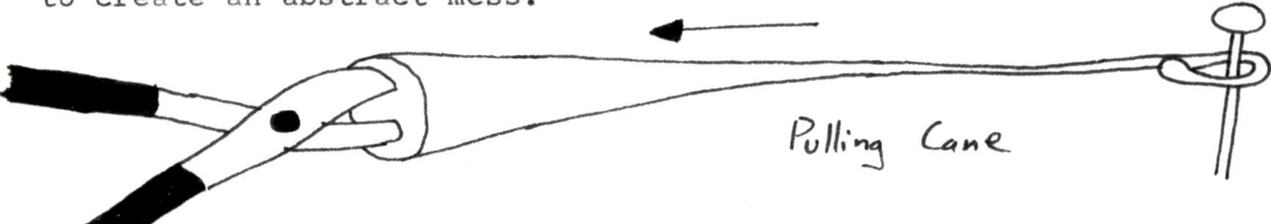

Pick and pull. Or you might get it real hot and then just let the
glass drip, moving it around to create a design. This mess may be
fused "as is" or sections cut out and design created with them.

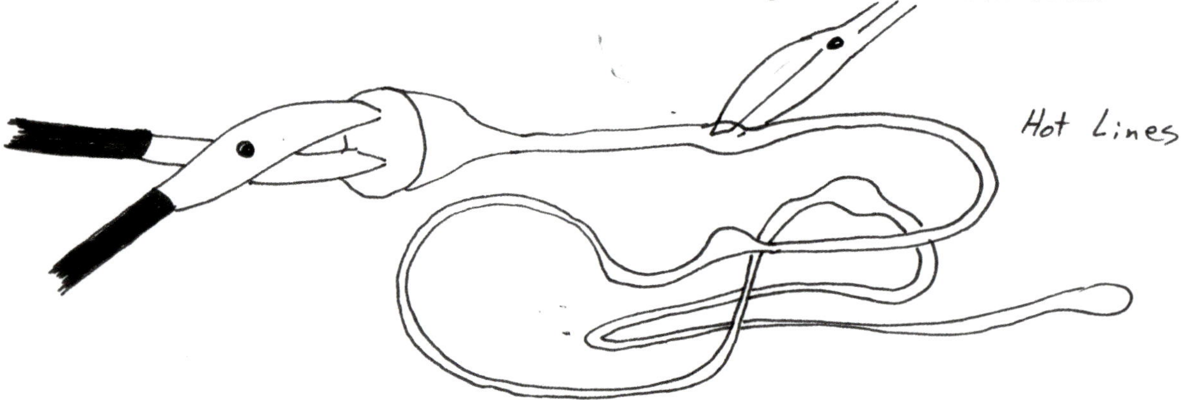

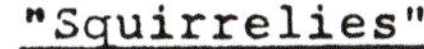

Again heat up the glass and then wrap around a metal pipe, square tube or between nails.

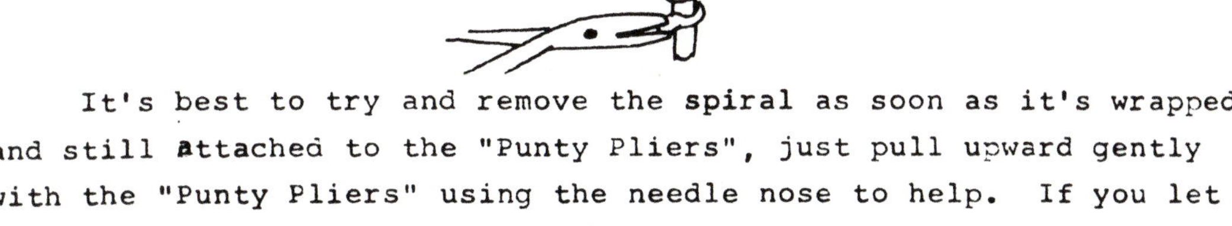

It's best to try and remove the **spiral** as soon as it's wrapped and still attached to the "Punty Pliers", just pull upward gently with the "Punty Pliers" using the needle nose to help. If you let it cool, it shrinks and becomes harder to remove.

These are just a few of the tings you can do with "The 3 Pounder". Again "You are only limited by your imagination" I wish you the best of luck and if you discover some new techniques or equipment, please write. If you build a successful "3Pounder", send photos.

left: "Carnival," 1983, H. 35 in. (89 cm) x W. 28 in. (71 cm) What I did with all of those "squirrelies," purchased by Genetic Systems for their main office, looks like it would fit the space.

right: Richard demonstrating making a "squirrelies" at Pilchuck, 1984.

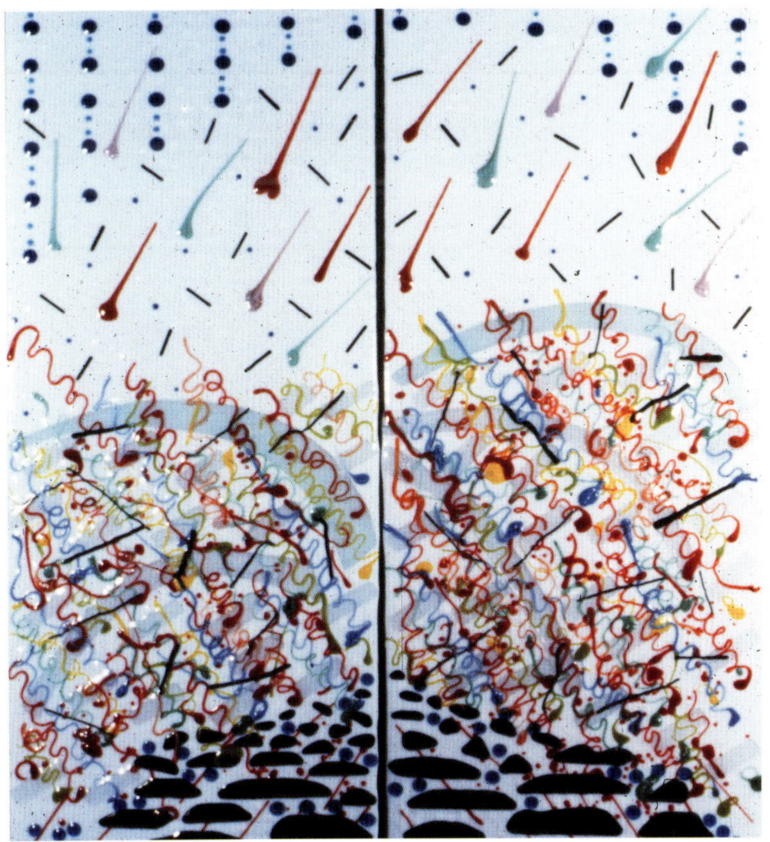

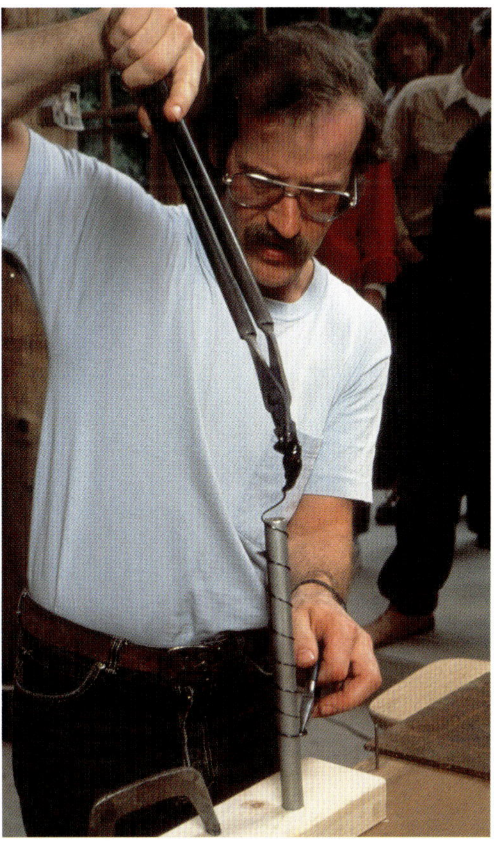

"The Bulldog"

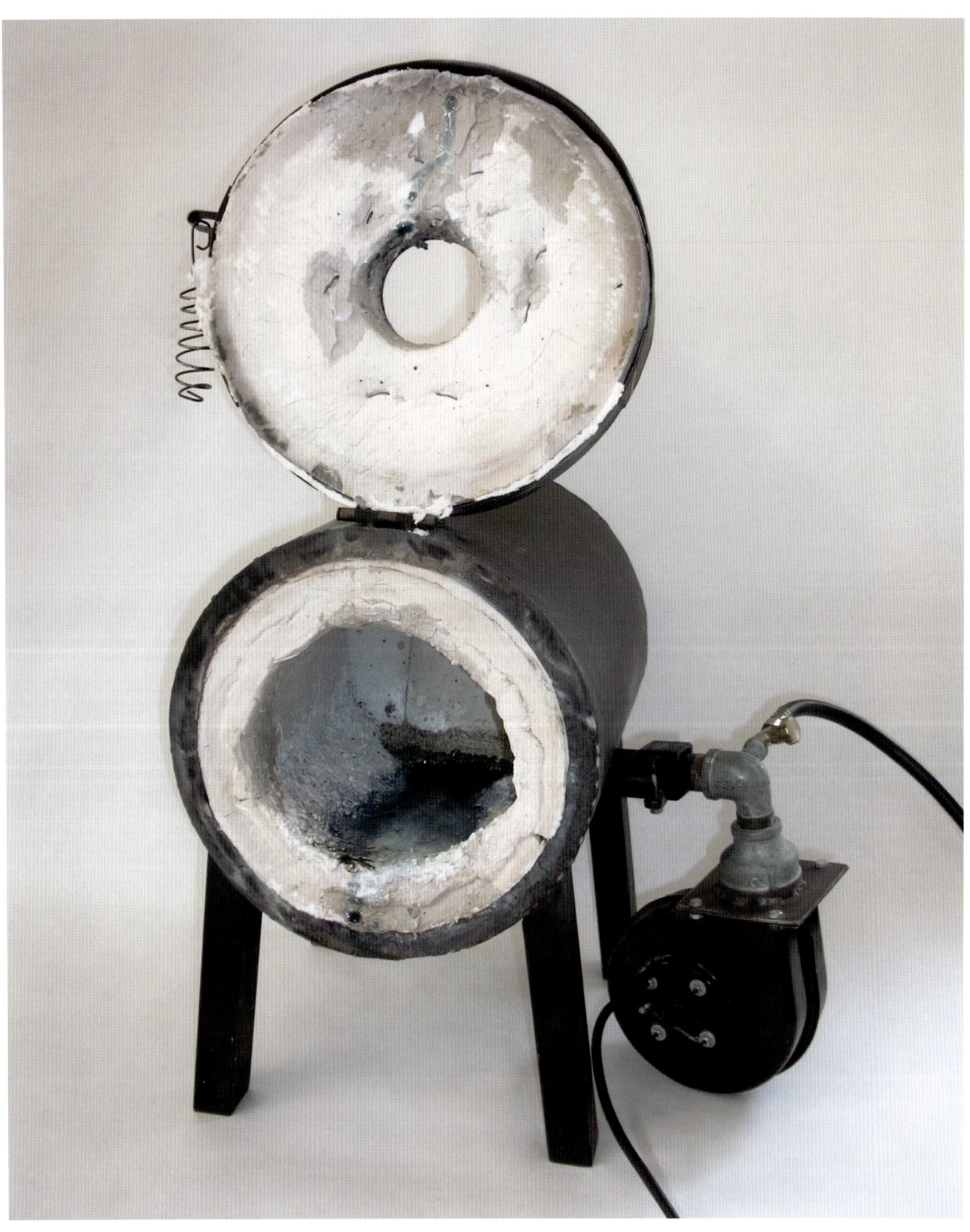

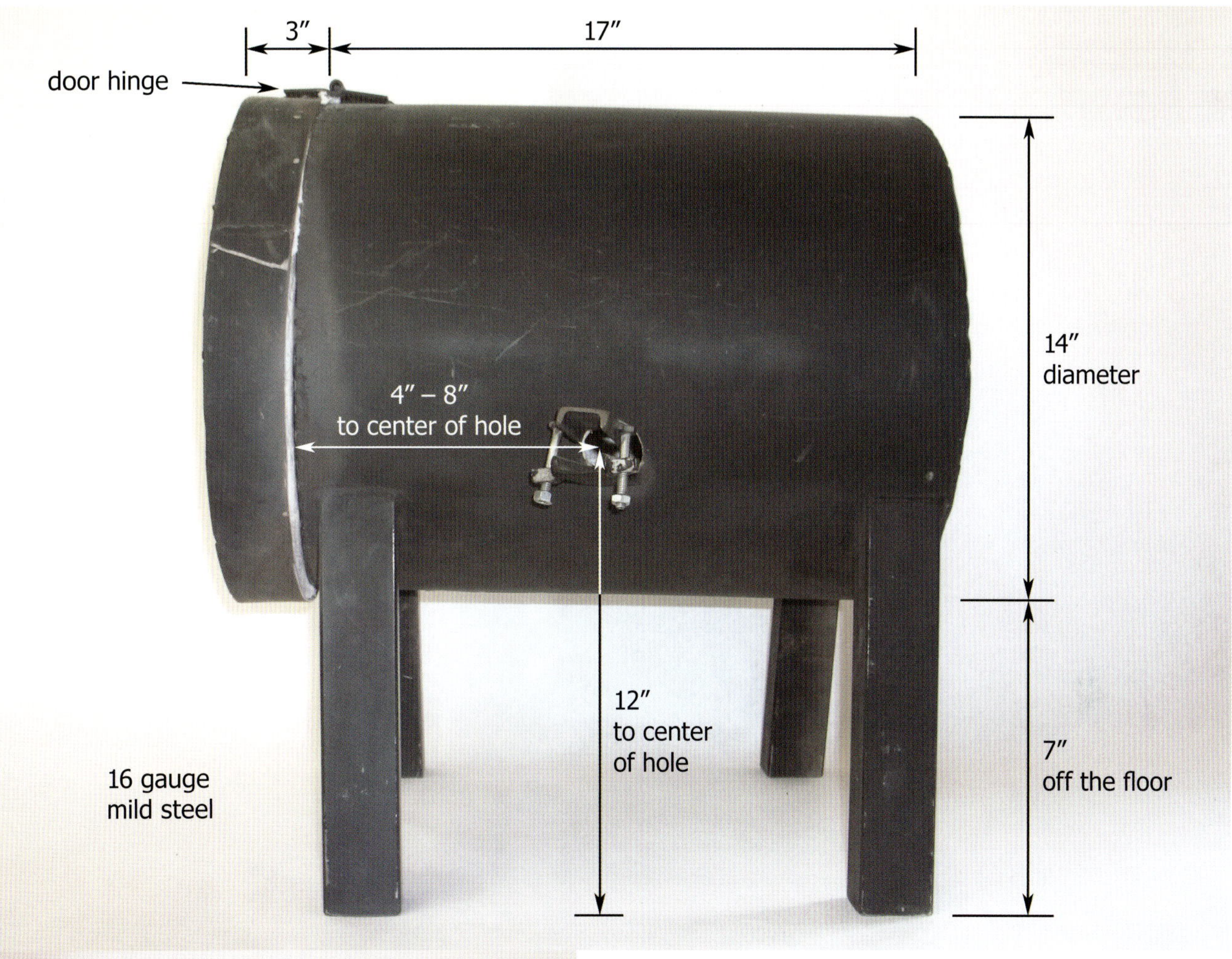

"The Bulldog"

You really need to have access to a welder to do a good job building this larger glory hole. I like the size and portability for pulling bundles of glass into cane.

(1) Familiarize yourself with the construction of the "Three Pounder."

(2) Find a metal bucket about 17" deep and 14" in diameter. If it is painted or galvanized, you'll need very good ventilation because the first few times that the glory hole heats up, the paint or any residue in the bucket will burn off. I couldn't find a bucket the right size so I rolled some 16 gauge mild steel into a cylinder and stitch welded, (weld•space•weld) a back onto it; a 1" ring welded onto the front makes it sturdier.

(3) Weld or bolt legs onto the bucket - make it sturdy so it won't fall over!

(4) The door is also 16 gauge mild steel; I stitch welded a 2" ring onto a round front with a hole. I welded a door hinge to the top edge. Gravity keeps the door closed. When I flip the lid up, it sits on a backward angle, so it won't fall forward while I'm working. I've used this glory hole since 1984, teaching many workshops with it, and it keeps on going and going.

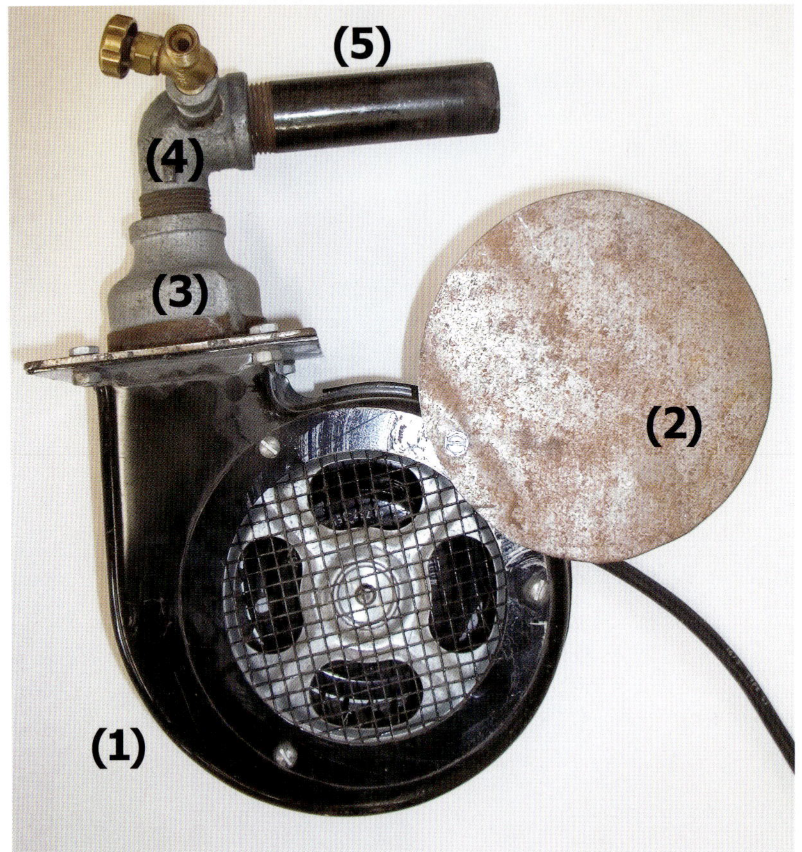

The Burner

(1) 105 cfm (cubic feet a minute) blower from Johnstone Supply # X89-32. The housing is about 8" in diameter and 4" wide. A fan up to 140 cfm works and can be controlled with the damper.

(2) circular rotating damper, a piece of sheet metal on a screw.

(3) 2" - 1" pipe bell reducer.

(4) 1" street pipe elbow.

(5) 1" black iron pipe 5" long, threaded on one end.

(6) $5/16$" nut brazed to the side of the 1" street elbow that is drilled into the pipe and tapped for $1/8$" pipe thread. This gives added support.

(7) $1/8$" all threaded pipe (find it in the lighting supply area), long enough to stick halfway into the elbow. The end is plugged and welded closed, and then a $3/32$" orifice hole is drilled into the plugged end.

(8) $3/8$" to $1/8$" pipe bell reducer.

(9) gas shut off valve. Hook this to a hose with a pressure reducer that can attach to a 5-gallon propane tank like those used for barbecues.

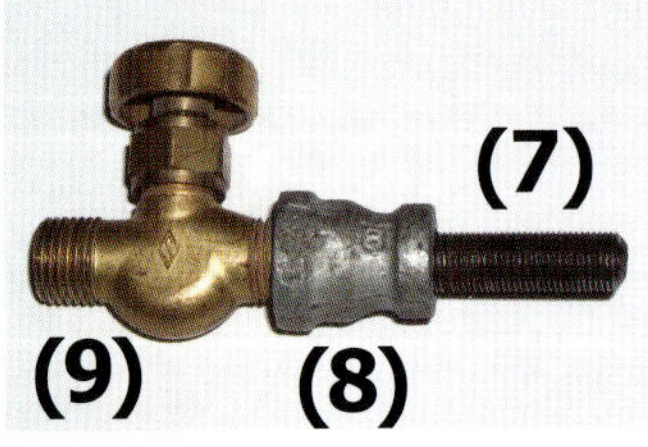

You should be able to find all of these parts at a good hardware store. Use black iron pipe fittings if you can find them; the burner pipe should definitely be black iron.

Plug and weld the end of the $1/8$" all threaded pipe and drill a $3/32$" orifice hole in the end.
The pipe sections screw together and should fit tightly, but they don't need to be sealed with gas-tight calking.

Assemble the burner; wire the fan to an electrical cord.

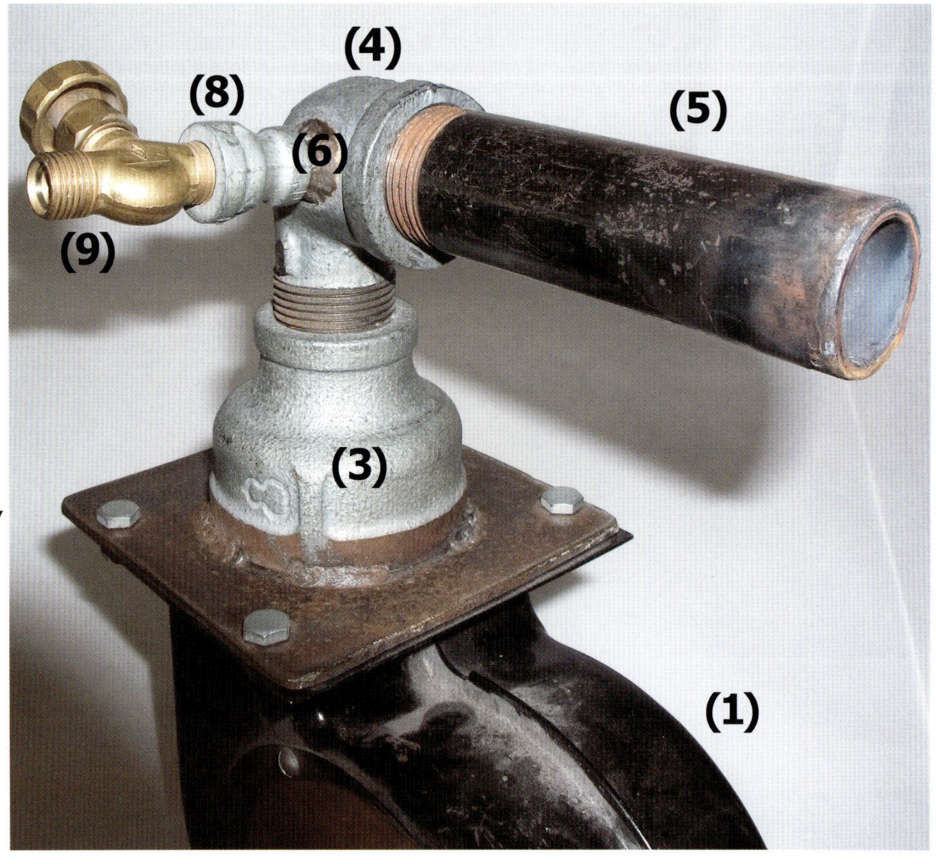

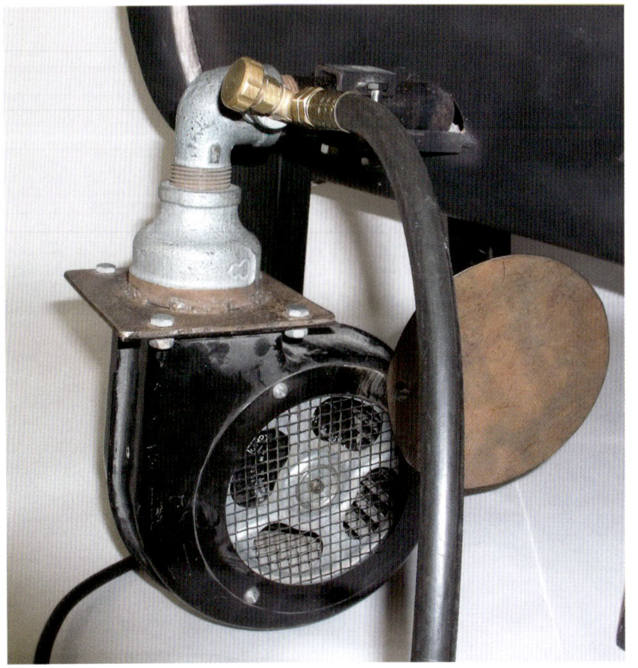 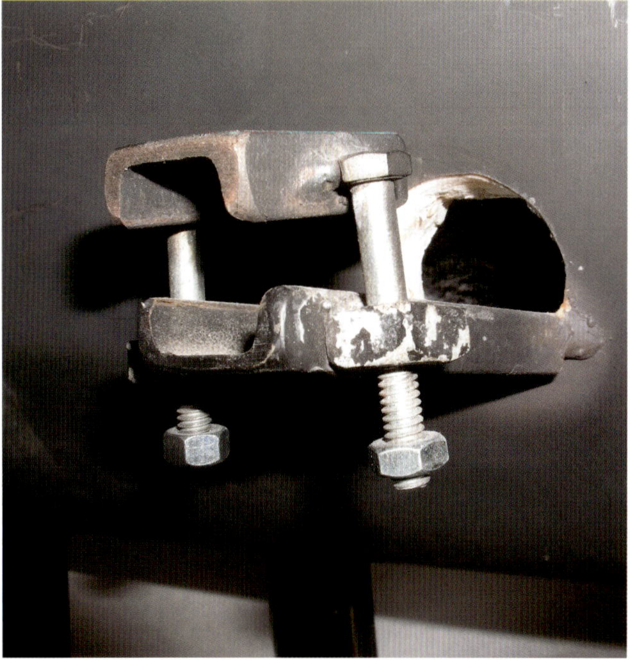

Create a welded channel or angle iron with a clamp system to hold the burner pipe into the glory hole.
The hole is just a little bigger than the outside diameter of the 1" pipe. The hole location is shown on the side view of the glory hole measurement diagram.

The burner pipe protrudes into the glory hole only about ½" and is angled towards the back of the glory hole (25 degrees from perpendicular and pointed slightly downward). The flame spirals down and toward the back of the glory hole, bouncing off of the back wall and then moving outward to the front opening - this way the glory hole is heated evenly. If you want the opening of the glory hole to be hotter, move the burner hole sideways and locate it about 4" from the front opening.

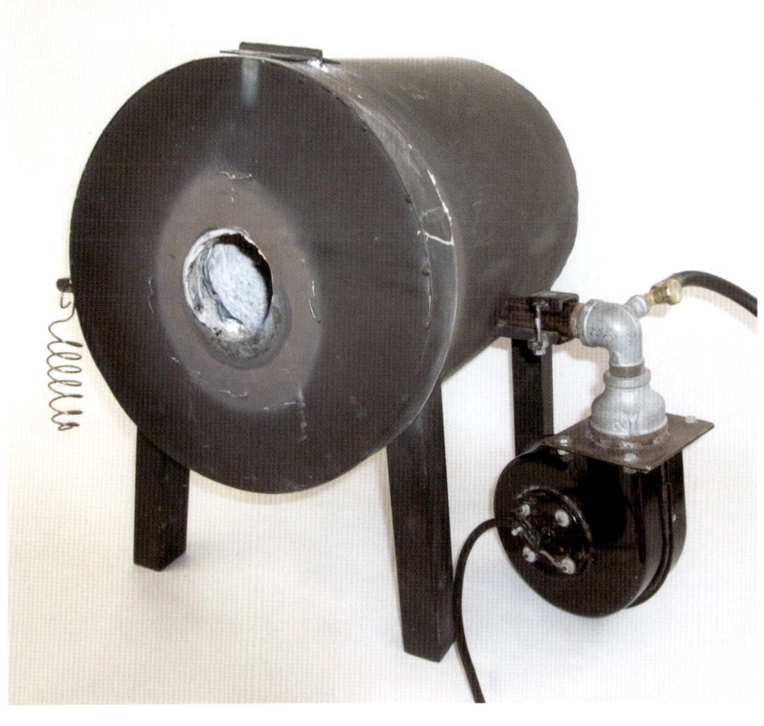

This view of the glory hole shows the burner pipe pointing back and slightly downward. Also notice the spiral wire handle for opening the door on the left side.

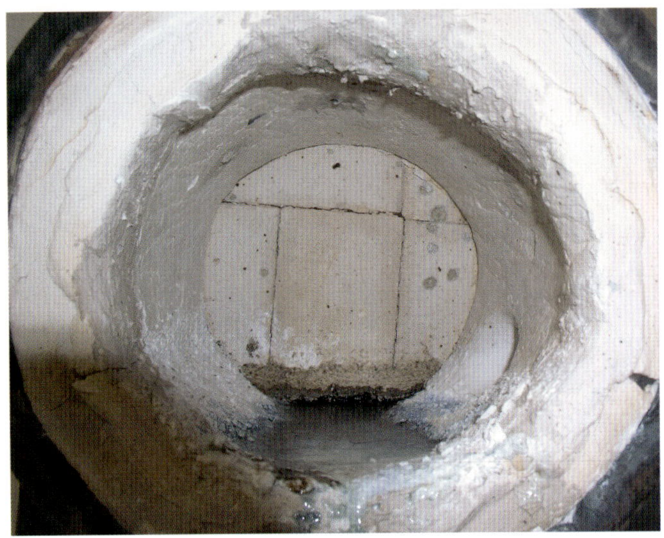

I lined "The Bulldog" with two layers of 1" thick 2600° F ceramic fiber blanket. It comes from different manufacturers with names such as "Inswool," "Ceriblanket," and "Kaowool." Wear a long sleeved shirt, rubber gloves, and a good respirator and change your clothes after you are done.

Place one layer of refractory blanket inside the metal glory hole frame and put the seam a few inches from the very bottom. Put a tight fitting circle of blanket inside and at the back end, which holds the cylinder of insulation in place.

Take a 4" strip of insulation that is the length of the circumference of the interior and thin it to ½" thick with a knife. Place this just inside the glory hole to create a lip.

Repeat the process and place a second 1" layer inside, but this time put the seam on the bottom. Put a tight-fitting circle of insulation at the back and form the insulation, using your gloved hands, around the tapered lip opening, which helps hold the heat in. You should have a 2" wall thickness all the way around and at the back and a flaring 2 ½" at the opening. I used a brick back in this glory hole because sometimes I stand it on end, put a crucible into it, and cast or blow glass. Fiber insulates better for the back wall of the glory hole.

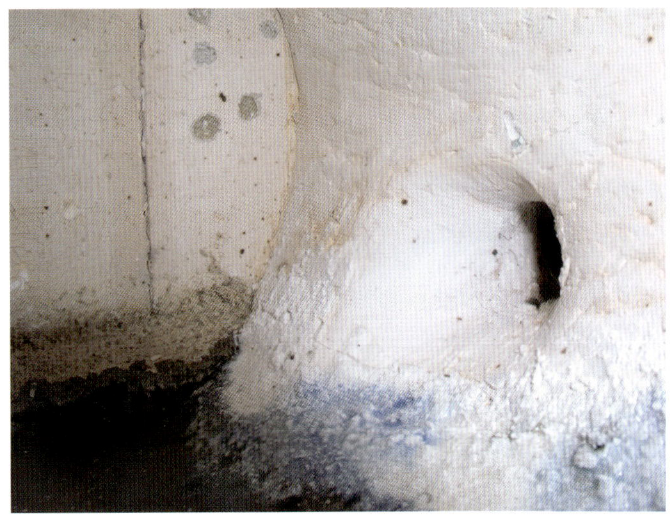

Cut with a knife and form the wool by tapering it away the burner hole, which creates a funnel type nozzle where the burner pipe enters. Notice that the burner pipe just barely protrudes into the insulation. If the pipe extends into the glory hole, it will melt.

Place 2" of refractory wool in the door and tie it to the front with 1" wide bent pieces of Kanthol element wire (which can take the heat).

Coat the entire refractory blanket with colloidal silica rigidizer, which is not sodium silicate (waterglass). You'll need at least one quart for this glory hole (purchase from pottery or refractory suppliers). Rigidizer prevents the fibers (which are not good to breathe) from blowing into your studio. Paint the rigidizer onto the blanket with a soft paintbrush – it takes some doing – and soak it at the lip and especially at the burner funnel. You can pat and form these areas with your rubber-gloved hands.

Put a ½" layer of refractory cement on the bottom and trowel it a few inches up the wall of the inside of the glory hole. This keeps errant chunks of glass from eating right through the ceramic blanket.

If you ever smell raw gas, except during the initial first few seconds of lighting, turn the gas off immediately. If the burner doesn't light within five seconds, turn it off, let the fumes dissipate, and try it again. If the gas builds up and then ignites, it can blow flames six feet up and out into the air. Do not stand in front of it when lighting.

Propane is explosive! Use in a well ventilated area! Light and use this equipment with extreme caution!

Lighting the Glory Hole

I stand to one side of the glory hole so that I am out of the way if flames shoot out - and they can explode and fly out and up six feet or more! Don't be in the way! (1) I turn on the fan and close the fan cover to cut down on the air for lighting. (2) I have my hand on the valve adjusting the propane. (3) I place a lit torch near the burner opening inside of the glory hole. (4) I slowly open the propane valve, and I count to four. If the glory hole has not lit by the count of four, then I turn off the gas, wait until the unlit gas has dissipated, and try again. (5) After the flame stabilizes and I have opened the propane valve all of the way, then I close the door to the glory hole to allow it to heat up.

- **Have good ventilation in your work space.**
- **A nonflammable table and floor are best.**
- **Never leave a glory hole burning unattended !**
- **Don't wear open-toed shoes or plastic clothes!**
- **Wear dark glasses!**

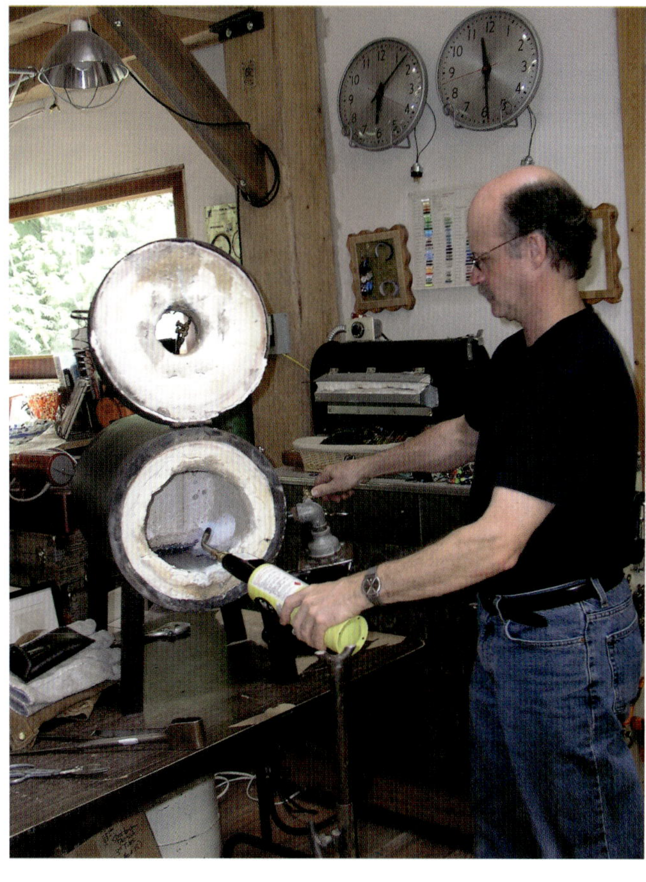

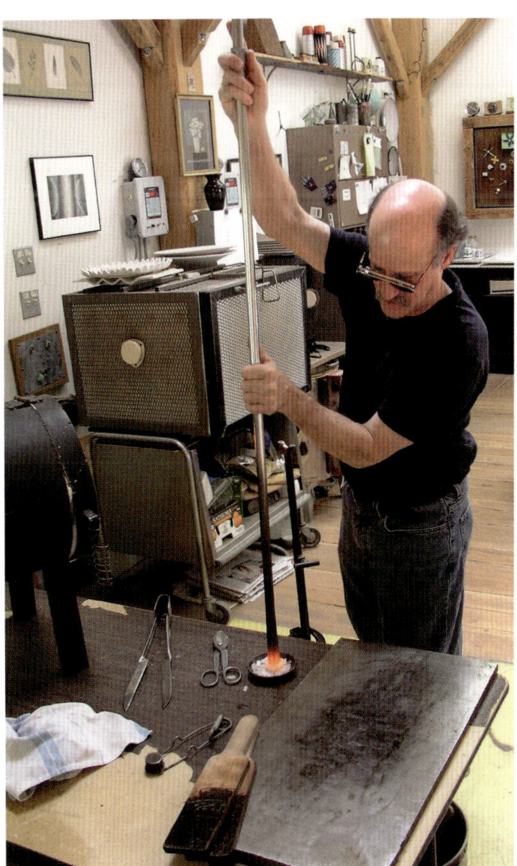

Making Pattern Bars

(1) I heat the punty rod until it glows orange and then press it into a pile of glass chips. I pick up a few and reheat in the glory hole. After I get some glass to stick to the metal, I continue picking up more glass and build up a button of glass about ¾ in. (2 cm) and ¼ in. (6mm) thick. I reheat and shape this button and then pick up a bundle of glass from the annealer, which, in this case, is a front loading kiln.

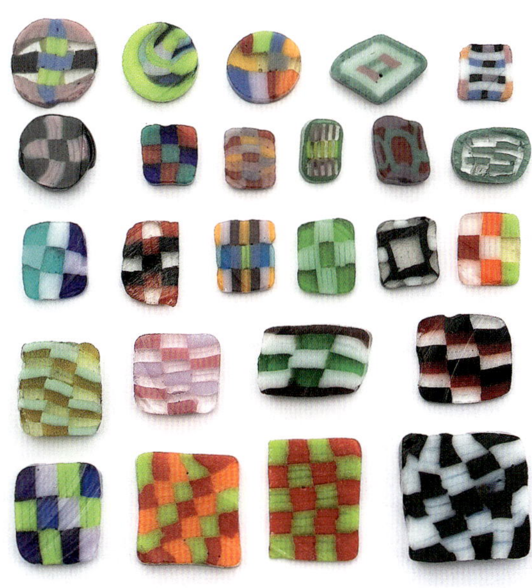

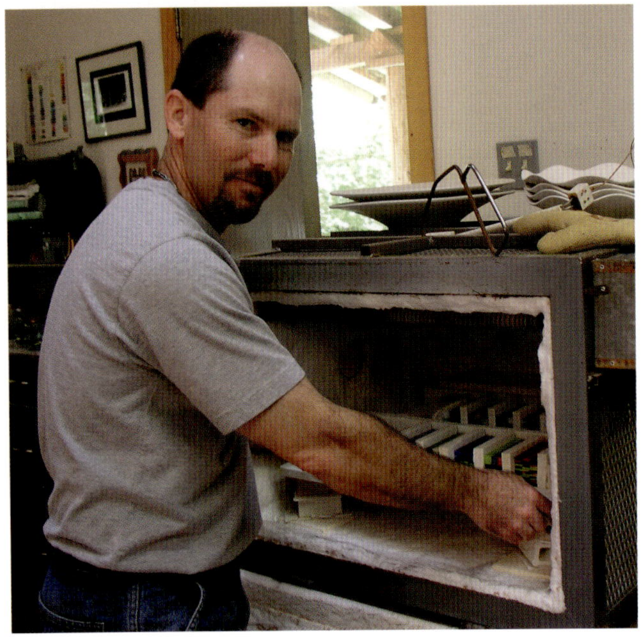

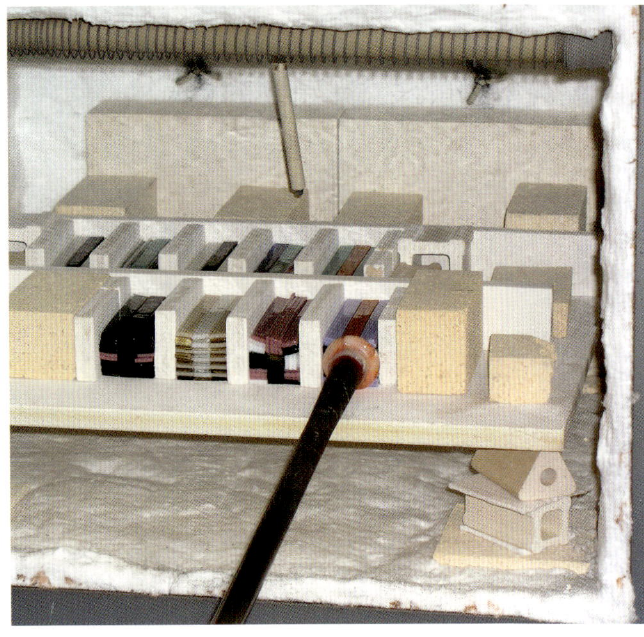

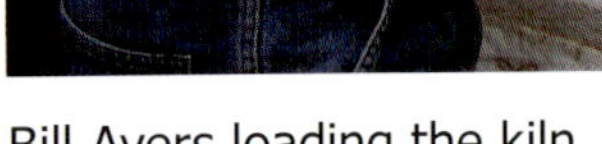
Bill Ayers loading the kiln.

Picking up hot bundles.

(2) I have placed stacks of glass into a front loading kiln on a kiln shelf. In this case the strips are ½ in. (12 mm) wide x 4 ¾ in. (12 cm) long. Each stack is twelve strips high and three rows wide. I've placed shelf primered pieces of cut up mullite kiln shelves around and behind the bundles. Because the glass is in small pieces I heat the glass up fast: 1 hour to 1100° F, full heat to 1390° F, soak 20 minutes (check to see if the strips are stuck together), then hold the kiln at 1015° F for picking up the bundles. In the above picture, the kiln is at 1015° F; the bundles have been fused together and the punty rod with a button of glass is centered and pushed into a bundle for pick up. The supporting shelf dividers continue all the way to the back of the kiln and give support for pushing into and picking up the bundle.

(3) I put the bundle on the end of the punty rod into the glory hole and heat until it begins to flop around. I "flash" the place where the rod meets the glass bundle by pushing it into the glory hole for a few seconds and then pulling it out just to the opening where I concentrate on heating the bundle. By regulating the glass, in and out, I can heat the bundle evenly.

With practice, you can make some very even pattern cane. Most of the canes in the facing bottom left picture were made by workshop participants who had never done hot glass before, and they did a great job. The photos were taken during glory hole workshop at Bill Ayers, www.rattarart.com, in Redmond, WA.

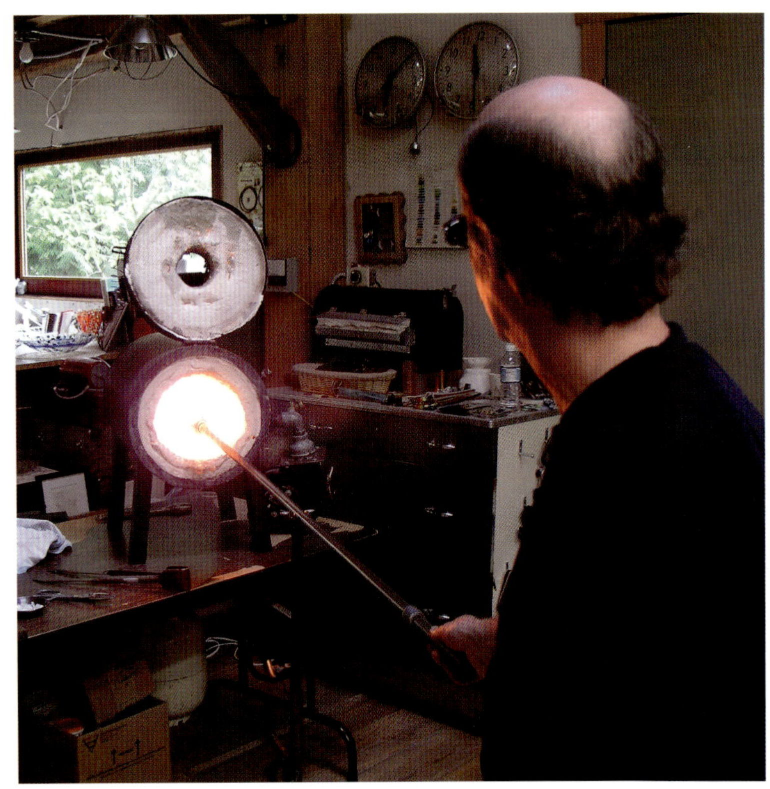

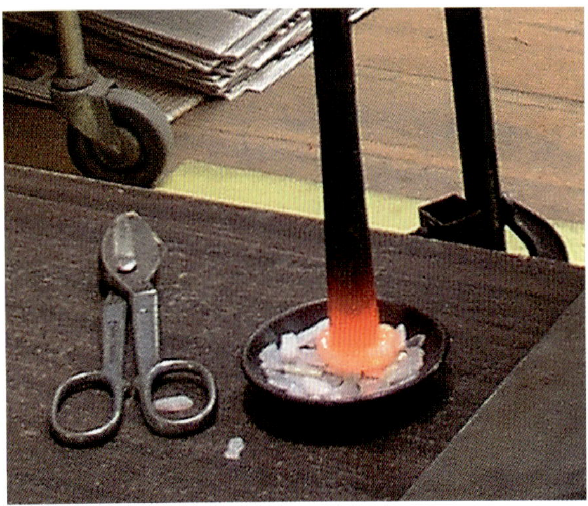

(1) Picking up chips of glass, for the first button.

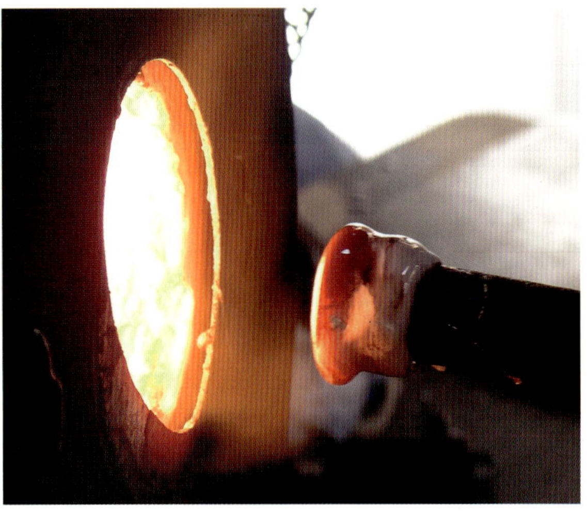

(2) Reheating the button of glass on the punty rod in the glory hole.

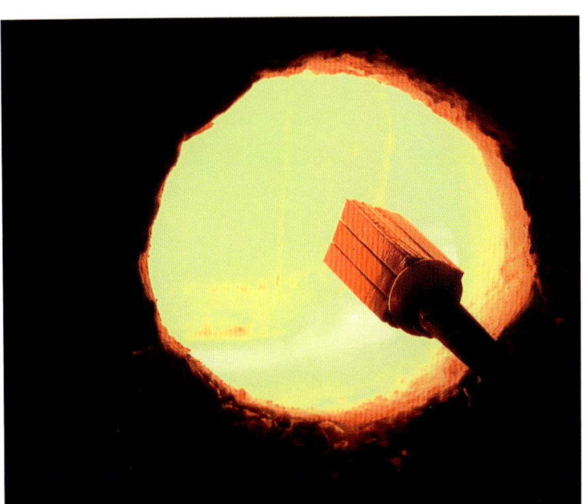

(3) The bundle of glass is picked up and placed in the glory hole to heat for the first time.

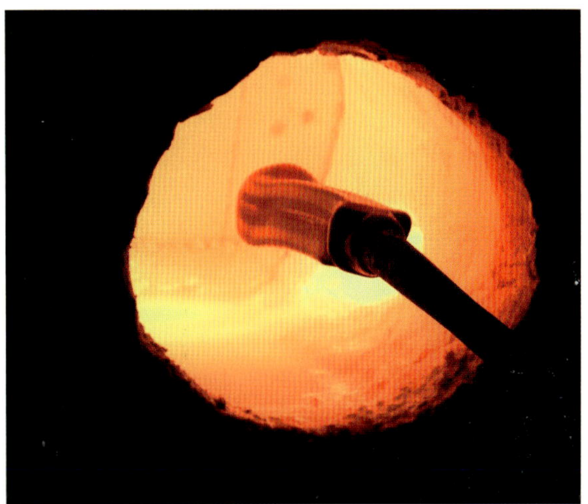

(4) After a few reheats and shaping on the marver, the bundle is softening and melting together.

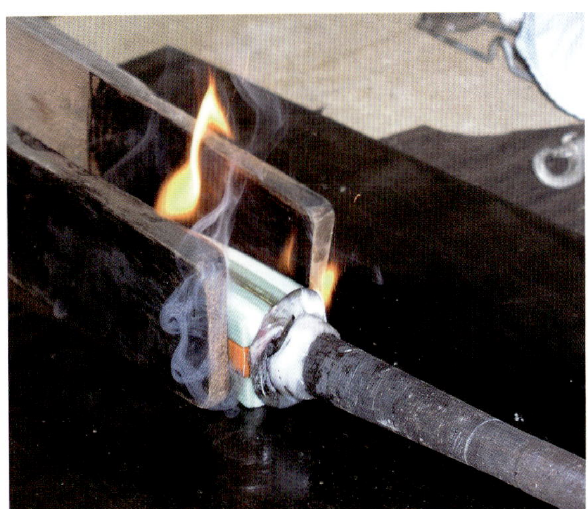

(5) Shaping the glass bundle with wet cherry wood paddles.

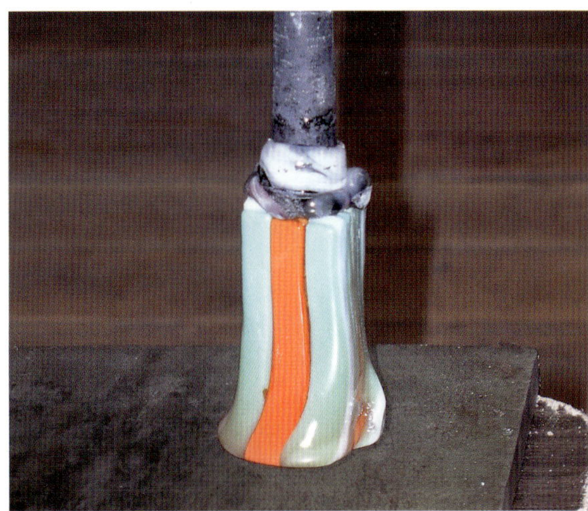

(6) Chilling and shaping the glass against the plate steel marver.

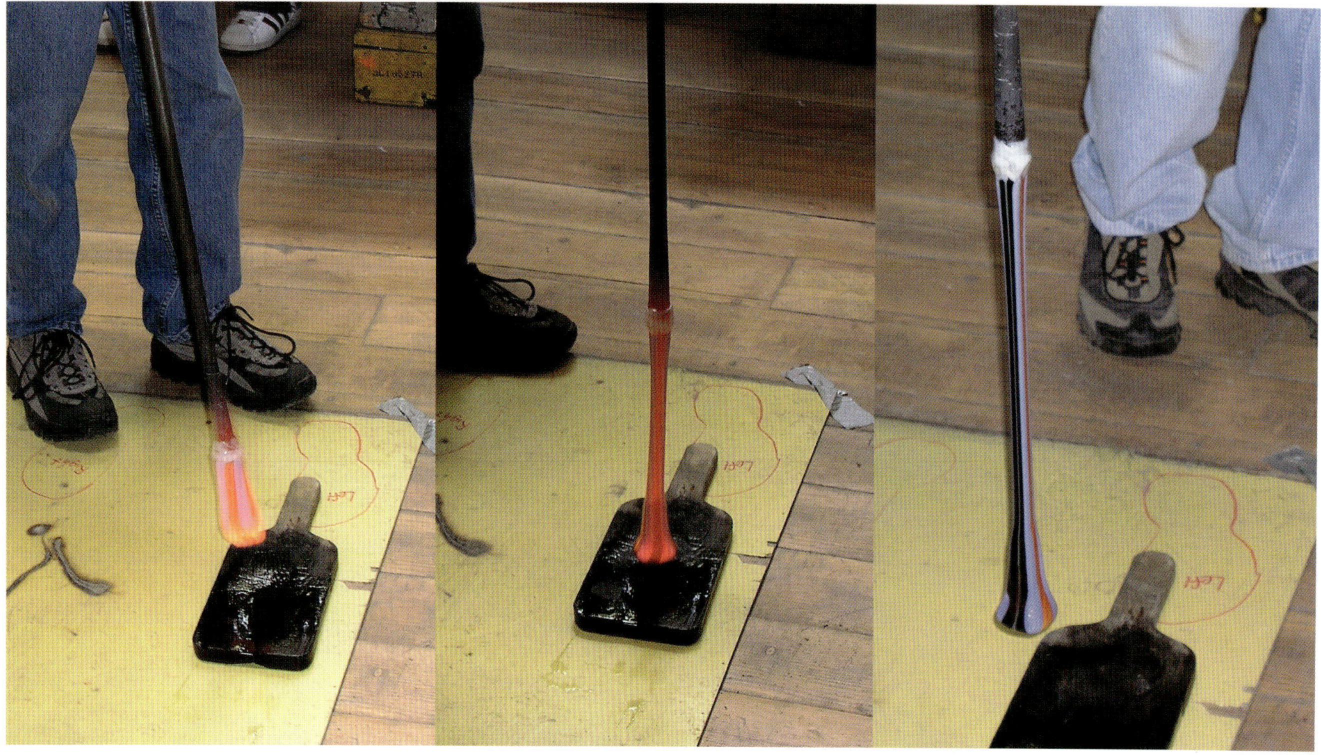

(7) Swinging out the bundle into a cane. Pulling the bundle is another method.

(8) A few careful swings elongates the cane. Swing harder when it gets stiffer.

(9) The cane is done. Better heating would prevent the end lump, but it can also be used.

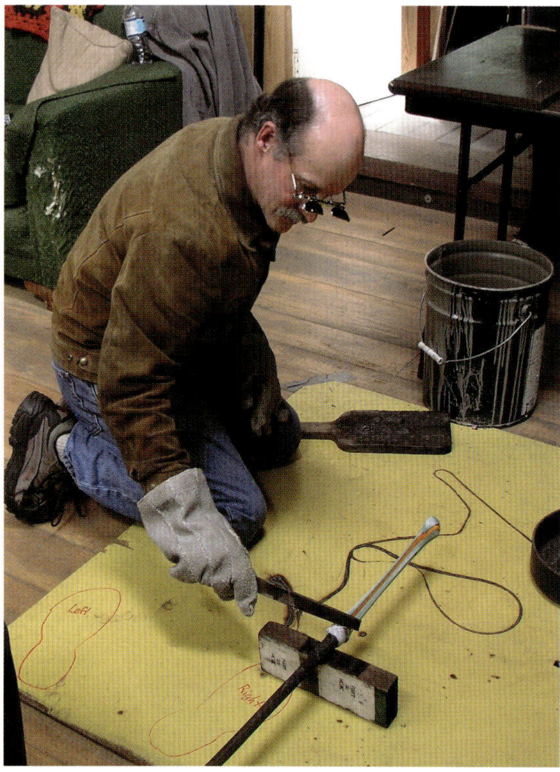

(10) With a few file scratches and some cold water dribbles into the file line, and a quick tap on the punty end will break the cane off.

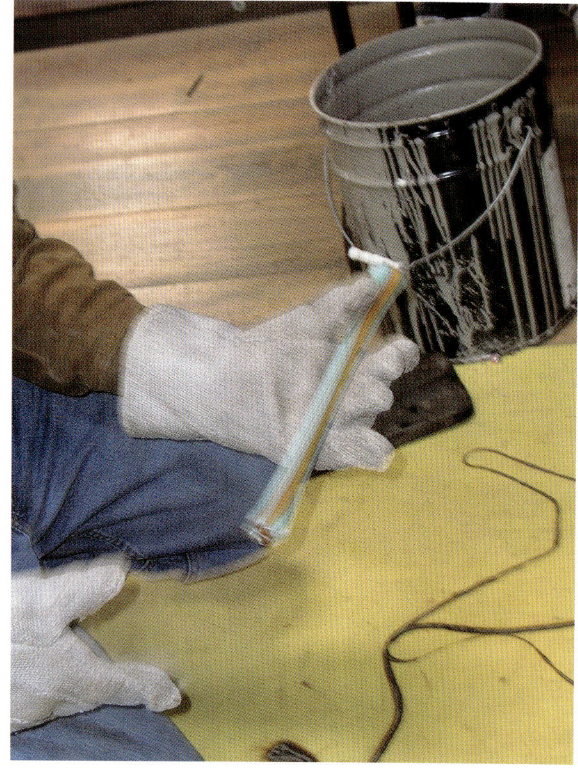

(11) Quickly glove the cane into the annealer where it hangs out at 1015° F until all of the canes have been pulled and they are all annealed.

Cynthia England (b. 1948)

After this workshop, she established the first hot glass studio in Alaska in Anchorage, 1985.

left above: Cynthia's first hot glass experience, gathering glass from an electric melt crucible furnace at a workshop put on by Ruth Brockmann (foreground) & Richard La Londe at their studio in 1984; Mark Olson is looking into the furnace. Cynthia told me in 2006, "if I had never gathered glass from that little pot, I would never have become a glassblower."

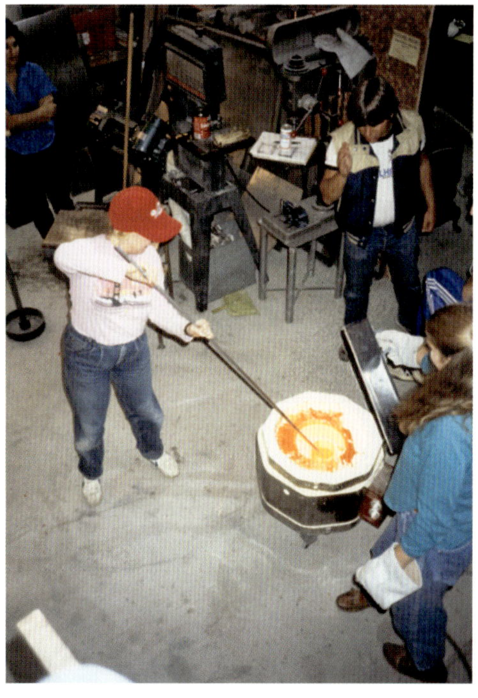

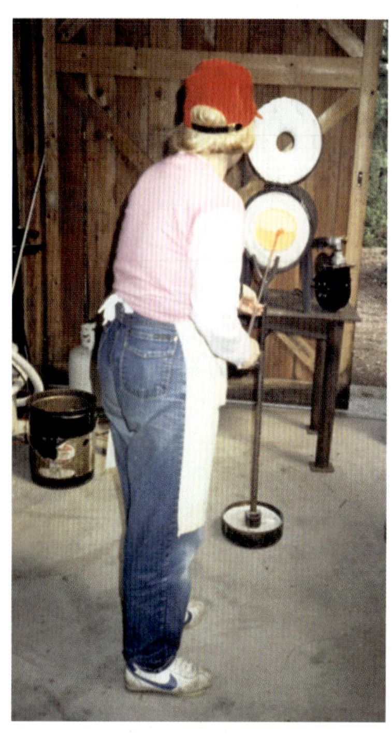

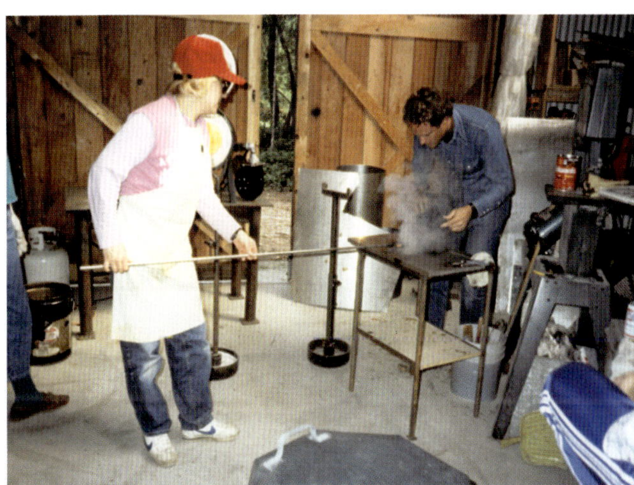

above right: Cynthia heating in "The Bulldog" glory hole.

middle left: Randy Gray paddling glass.

bottom left: stacked sheet glass canes.

bottom right: roll up 1995.

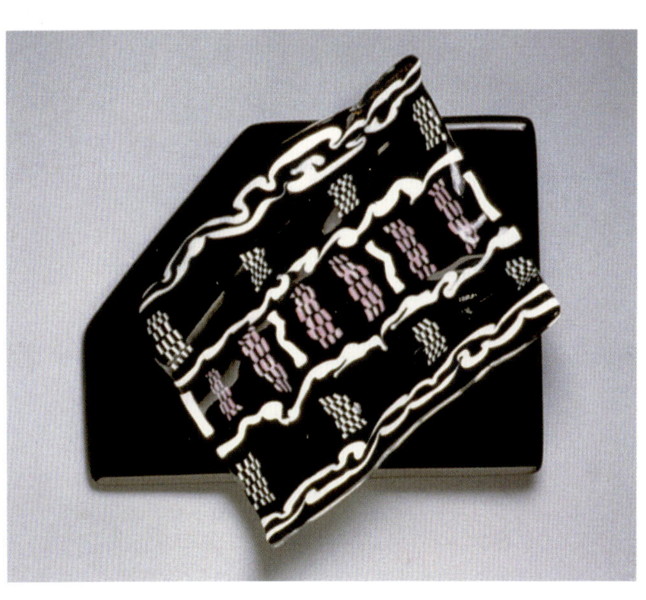

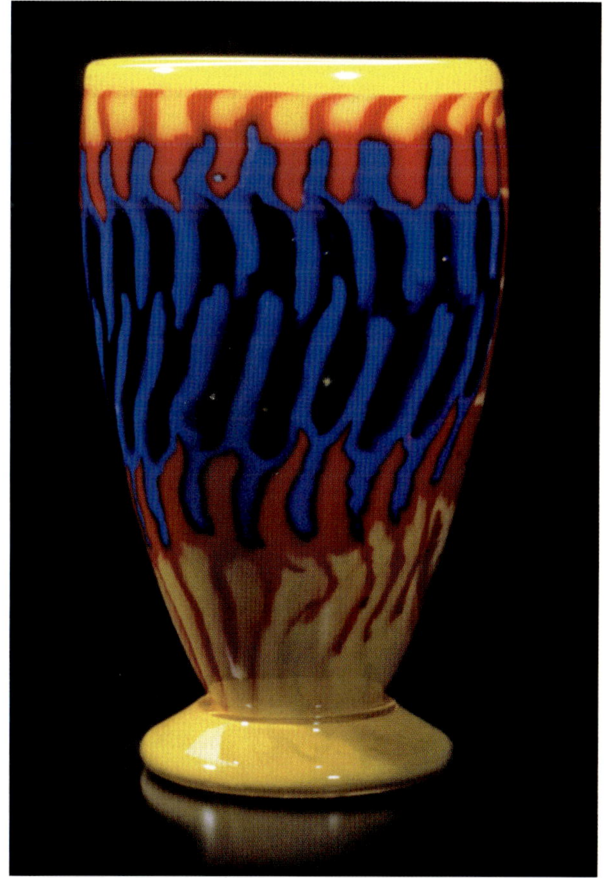

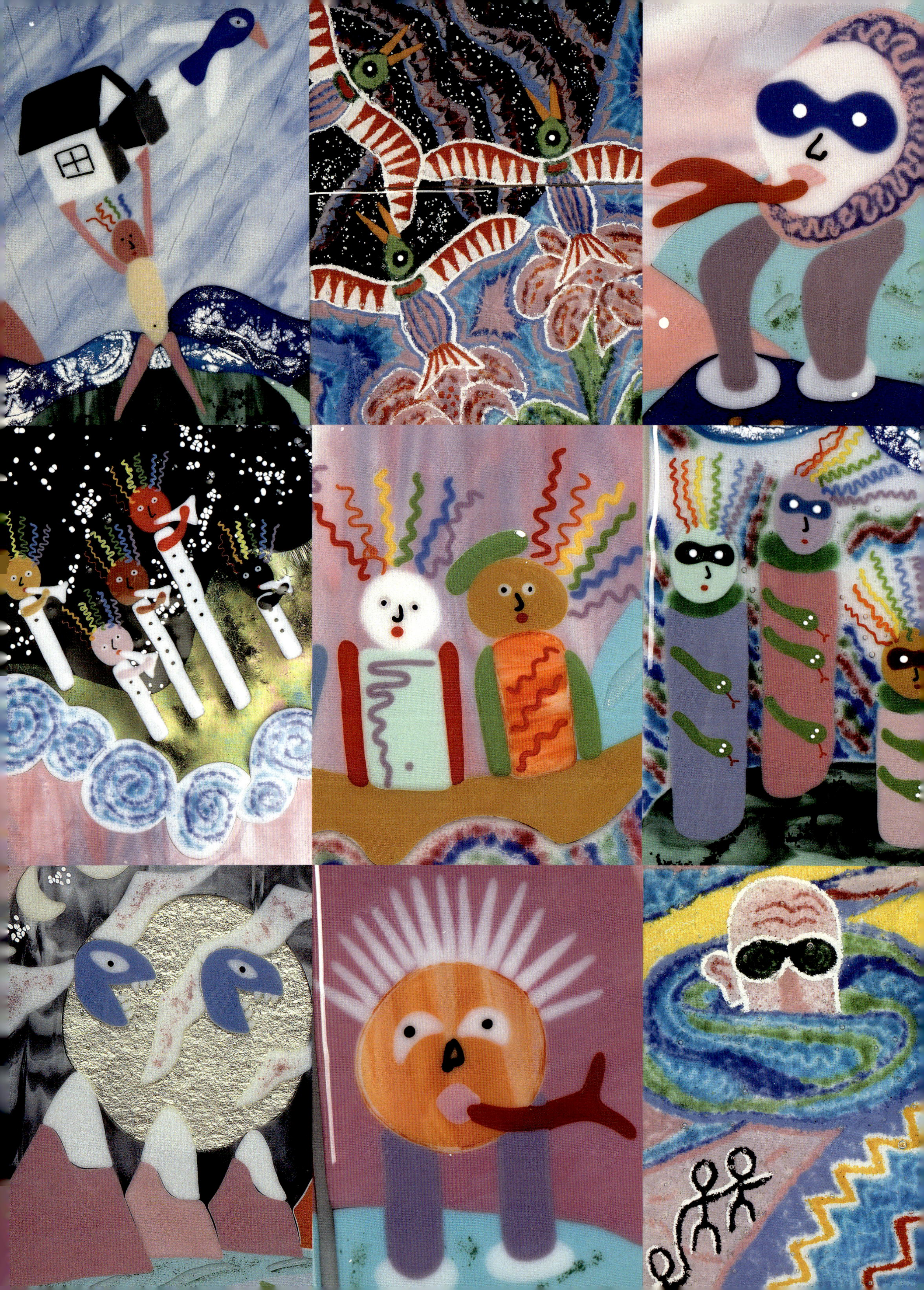

public commissions

murals

2005 Evergreen Elementary, Washington State Arts Commission
Shelton, WA three fused glass murals, H. 66 in. (168 cm) x W. 60 in. (152 cm) each.

2004 Good Samaritan Hospital
Puyallup, WA H. 30 in. (76 cm) x W. 90 in. (228 cm) triptych.

2003 Washington State Public Health Laboratory, Washington State Art Commission
Shoreline, WA eight fused glass panels, H. 26 in. (66 cm) x W. 22 in. (56 cm) and
one triptych H. 40 in. (102 cm) x W. 70 in. (178 cm).

2002 Auburn Public Library, Friends of the Library
Auburn, WA fused glass and stainless steel wall piece H. 72 in. (183 cm) x W. 144
in. (366 cm).

2001 Edgemont Junior High School
Edgewood, WA fused glass mural H. 24 in. (61 cm) x W. 96 in. (244 cm).

2000 Ptarmigan Ridge Elementary, Washington State Arts Commission
Orting, WA fused glass mural, H. 108 in. (274 cm) x W. 96 in. (244 cm).

1999 Tacoma / Pierce County Court House, Pierce County Arts Commission
9th & Yakima Parking Annex, (collaboration with artist Michael Dupille)
Tacoma, WA cxtcrior fuscd glass murals, H. 60 in. (152 cm) x W. 168 in. (427   cm),
H. 144 in. (366 cm) x W. 60 in. (152 cm), & H. 36 in. (91 cm) x W. 72 in. (183 cm).

1997 Frontier Junior High, Washington State Arts Commission
Graham, WA four fused glass murals, H. 52 in. (132 cm) x W. 46 in. (117 cm) each.

1996 Dzantiki Heeni Middle School, Alaska Percent for Arts
Juneau, AK fused glass mural, H. 72 in. (183 cm) x W. 120 in. (305 cm).

1993 Evanston Public Library
Evanston, IL fused glass mural, H. 43 in. (109 cm) x W. 66 in. (168 cm).

1992 Sea-Tac International Airport, Port of Seattle Arts Commission
SeaTac, WA fused glass gateway, 3 panels, each 156 in. (396 cm) x 24 in. (61 cm).

1992 Evergreen Hospital Lobby
Kirkland, WA fused glass mural, H. 60 in. (152 cm) x W. 84 in. (213 cm).

1989 Pierce County Library, Friends of the Library
Parkland, WA fused glass mural, H. 84 in. (213 cm) x W. 72 in. (183 cm).

1984 Black Lake Elementary, Washington State Arts Commission
Tumwater, WA fused glass mural, H. 60 in. (152 cm) x W. 288 in. (731 cm).

collections

vessels

The Corning Museum of Glass, Corning, NY
Notojima Glass Art Museum, Notojima, Japan
The Leigh Yawkey Woodson Art Museum, Wausau, WI
Museum Boymans-van Beuningen, Rotterdam, Netherlands
Glasmuseum, Ebeltoft, Denmark
Charles A. Wustum Museum, Racine, WI
Davis Wright Tremaine, Seattle, WA
McDonalds Corporation, Oak Brook, IL
Paccar - Kenworth Truck Division, Kirkland, WA
Prescott Collection, City Centre, Seattle, WA

murals

Colbey-Sawyer College, New London, NH
City of Lynnwood Planning Commission Office, Lynnwood, WA
Seafirst Corporation, Seattle, WA
Genetic Systems Inc., Seattle, WA
Bullseye Glass Company, Portland, OR

solo exhibitions

galleries

2004	The Glass Gallery	Bethesda, MD
2000	Museo Gallery	Langley, WA
1999	Glass Gallery	Bethesda, MD
1995	Marx Gallery	Chicago, IL
1994	Gallery Mack	Seattle, WA
1993	Vespermann Glass Gallery	Atlanta, GA
1992	Marx Gallery	Chicago, IL
1991	The Glass Gallery	Bethesda, MD
1990	Gallery Mack	Seattle, WA
1990	Vespermann Glass Gallery	Atlanta, GA
1989	Art Options	Santa Monica, CA
1988	The Glass Gallery	Bethesda, MD
1987	The Glass Art Gallery	Toronto, Canada
1986	The Glass Gallery	Bethesda, MD
1985	Edith Gottschalk, SM Gallerie	Frankfurt, Germany
1984	Gallery Mack	Seattle, WA

group exhibitions
selected
2006 "Ignite: Warm Glass International Invitational," Arrowmont, Gatlinburg, TN.
2005 "20 Artists/20 Years" New Glass Review, Bullseye Connection Gallery, Portland, OR
1999 "Hot & Cool Glass," (U.S. Museums Tour 1999 - 2001)
1997 Tucson Museum of Art, "Calido" Contemporary Warm Glass, Tucson, AZ
1992 "The International Exhibition of Glass Kanazawa 92," Kanazawa, Japan
     Contemporary Crafts Gallery "Kilnformed Glass," Portland, OR
1990 "The International Exhibition of Glass Kanazawa 90," Kanazawa, Japan
1987 Japan Glass Artcrafts Association "Glass 87 in Japan," Tokyo, Japan
1986 Huntington Museum of Art "New American Glass Focus." Huntington, WV
1984 The Leigh Yawkey Woodson Art Museum "Americans in Glass,"
     (European Museums Tour 1984 - 1986), Wausau, WI

publications
selected books, catalogs, & periodicals
2004 ***Stained Glass Source book***, Rockport Publishers, Gloucester, MA
2003 "Glass Craftsman" April / May 2003 Pioneers of Frit article by Judith Conway
1998 ***The Art of Stained Glass***, Chris Peterson, Quarry Books, Gloucester, MA
1997 ***Glass Art***, Peter Layton, U. of W. Press, Seattle & AC Black, London, England
     Calido, Tucson Museum of Art, Tucson, AZ
1992 ***Contemporary Kilnformed Glass***, Bullseye Glass Company, Portland, OR
     The International Exhibition of Glass Kanazawa 90, Kanazawa, Japan
1991 ***Out of the Fire***, Bonnie Miller, Chronicle Press, San Francisco, CA
1990 "Professional Stained Glass," March 1990, Chris Peterson, Brewster, NY
     The International Exhibition of Glass Kanazawa 92, Kanazawa, Japan
1989 ***Contemporary Glass***, Susanne Franz, Abrams Publications, New York, NY
     Glass: A Contemporary Art, Dan Klein, Rizzoli Publications, New York, NY
     "Glass Work Magazine," Portfolio, October 1989, Kyoto, Japan
     "American Craft Magazine," Portfolio, Feb/Mar 1989, New York, NY
1988 "New Glass Review 9," Corning Museum of Glass, Dusseldorf, Germany
1987 ***Glass 87 in Japan***, Tokyo, Japan
1984 "New Glass Review 5," Corning Museum of Glass, Corning, NY
     Americans in Glass, Leigh Yawkey Woodson Art Museum, Wasau, WI

bibliography (books in my library)

basic fusing

Boyce Lundstrom & Daniel Schwoerer, *Glass Fusing Book One*, Vitreous Publications, Colton, OR. 1983. The best book written about fusing basics, really covers annealing, compatibility and volume control. The "classic."

Brad Walker, *Contemporary Warm Glass,* Four Corners International, Clemmons, NC. 2000. A very good contemporary book about basic fusing.

basic fusing (pre-Bullseye)

Harriette Anderson, *Kiln-Fired Glass*, Chilton Books, Radnor, PA. 1970. A good classic book for your library, talks about sifted enamels, interesting for pre-Bullseye compatibility testing, and annealing.

Kay Kinney, *Glass Craft*, Chilton Book Company, Philadelphia, PA. 1962. If you want to fuse wind chimes out of wine bottles, this is the book for you.

kiln forming techniques

Boyce Lundstrom, *Advanced Fusing Techniques: Glass Fusing Book Two*, Vitreous Group - Camp Colton, 1989. Contains information about glory holes, slumping, enamels and lusters.

Boyce Lundstrom, *Glass Casting and Moldmaking: Glass Fusing Book Three*, Vitreous Group - Camp Colton, 1989. Contains good information about mold making and kiln casting. I was always disappointed that the last 36 pages in book 3 are copied from book 2. Combining these two books would have been a better book.

James Kervin, Dan Fenton, *Pâte de Verre and Kiln Casting of Glass*, GlassWear Studios, Livermore, CA 1997. One of the most comprehensive and detailed books about modeling, mold making, kiln casting and *pâte* verre.

Keith Cummings, *Techniques of Kiln-formed Glass*, A & C Black, London, England 1997. Has a good section about ancient glass history, covers kiln casting, including shots of David Ruth's studio.

other techniques

Kent H. Smith, *Gold Leaf Techniques*, ST Publications, Cincinnati, OH. 1998. A great book about precious metal leafing, under and on top of glass.

Frank E. Wolley, *Glass Technology for the Studio*, The Studio of the Corning Museum of Glass, Corning, NY 1999. A spiral bound collection of lecture notes about glass science, annealing, glass composition, expansion, and so on.

studio glass art

Ray & Lee Grover, *Contemporary Art Glass*, Crown Publishers, New York, NY. 1975. A wonderful book about the early studio glass pioneers, includes Edris Eckhardt, Maurice Heaton, and Frances and Michael Higgins.

Donald-Brian Johnson & Leslie Piña, ***Higgins Adventures in Glass***, Schiffer Publishing Ltd., Atglen, PA, 1997. Lots of photos of the artwork by the Higgins, their studio, promotional material, and interviews with Frances and Michael Higgins.

Bonnie J. Miller, ***Out of the Fire***, Chronicle Books, San Francisco, CA. 1991. A great book about 30 Northwest Glass artists in the early 1990's and a nice history of Pilchuck and NW glass.

Suzanne K. Frantz*, **Contemporary Glass***, Harry N. Abrams Inc. New York, NY. 1989. Documents the contemporary glass in the Corning Museum of Glass.

Dan Klein, ***Glass A Contemporary Art***, Rizzoli International Publications, Inc. New York, NY. 1989. A worldwide survey of 1989 artists working with glass.

Tina Oldknow, ***Pilchuck: A Glass School***, Pilchuck Glass School, Seattle, WA. 1996. A History of Pilchuck.

Otto B. Rigan, ***New Glass***, Ballantine Books, New York, 1976. The classic book about hippie stained glass that changed the way we make colored glass windows.

glass pamphlets

Contemporary Kiln Formed Glass, curators Lani McGregor and Daniel Schwoerer, Bullseye Glass Company, Portland, OR. Sept. 13 - Oct. 24, 1992. Great exhibition in a very nice book, hard to call it a pamphlet.

Edris Eckhardt: Visionary and Innovator in American Studio Ceramics and Glass, Henry Adams and Joeseph Kisvardai, Cleveland Artists Foundation, Lakewood, OH, Feb. 18 - Apr. 15, 2006 exhibition pamplet.

Earl McCutchen: Craftsmanship in Ceramics and Glass, Ashley Callahan, Georgia Museum of Art, Athens, Georgia, Oct., 19, 2002 - Jan. 12, 2003 exhibition pamphlet.

inspiration

James Yood & Tina Oldknow, ***William Morris: Animal/Artifact***, Abbeville Press, New York, NY. 2000.

Michael Kew, Macnair, Giles and McLennan, ***Susan Point: Coast Salish Artist***, University of Washington Press, Seattle, WA. 2000.

Rebecca J. Dobkins, ***Rick Bartow: My Eye***, Halle Ford Museum of Art, Willamette University, Salem, OR. 2002.

Fay Jones: a 20 year Retrospective, essays by Regina Hacektt and Sondra Shulman, Boise Art Museum Aug. 31 - Oct. 27, 1996, exhibition pamphlet.

Doris Shadbolt, ***Bill Reid***, University of Washington Press, Seattle/London, 1986.

material and suppliers

glass manufacturers

Bullseye Glass Company
3722 SE 21st
Portland, OR. 97202
(503) 232-8887
www.bullseyeglass.com

Spectrum Glass Company
PO Box 646
24105 Sno-Woodenville Rd.
Woodenville, WA. 98072-0646
(206) 483-6699
www.spectrumglass.com

Uroboros Glass
2139 N. Kerby Ave
Portland, OR. 97227
(503) 284-4900
www.uroboros.com

glass fusing supplies

Bullseye Resource Center
3610 SE 21st Ave.
Portland, OR. 97202
1-888-220-3002
www.bullseyeglass.com

Northwest Art Glass
9003 151st Ave NE
Redmond, WA. 98052
1-800-888-9444
www.nwartglass.com

Ed Hoy's International
27625 Diehl Road
Warrenville, IL. 60555-3838
(630) 836-1353
1-800- 323-5668
www.edhoy.com

suppliers

Dow Corning silicone #732

Atlas Supply
611 S. Charleston St.
Seattle, WA. 98108-5239
1-800-347-5767
(206) 623-4697

Refractories

EJ Bartells Co.
700 Powell Ave. SW
Renton, WA. 98057
1-800-468-9528
(424) 228-4111
www.ejbartells.com

Belts & Diamond Equipment

Covington Engineering
PO Box 35
Redlands, CA. 92373
1-877-793-6636
www.covington-engineering.com

Diamond Pads & Supplies

His Glassworks, Inc.
91 Webb Cove Road
Asheville, NC. 28804
1-800-914-7463
www.hisglassworks.com

Diamond Bits & Equipment

Lortone Inc.
12130 Cyrus Way
Mukilteo, WA. 98275
(425) 493-1600
www.lortone.com

Art Supplies

Daniel Smith
4150 First Ave. S.
Seattle, WA. 98124-5568
(206) 223-9599
www.danielsmith.com

Kilns, Chemicals, Etc.

Seattle Pottery Supply
35 South Handford St.
Seattle, WA. 98134
1-800-522-1975
(206) 587-0570
www.seattlepotterysupply.com

Sandblast Equipment

Tip Equipment
PO Box 649
Canfield, OH. 44406
1-800-321-9260

Gold & Silver Foil

Olympic Color Rod
818 John Street
Seattle, WA. 98109
(206) 343-7336
1-800-445-7742
www.glasscolor.com

Gold Leaf, Mica, Supplies,

Sepp Leaf Products
381 Park Ave South
New York, NY. 10016
1-800-971-7377
www.seppleaf.com

Polarizing Film

Edmund Scientific
60 Pearce Ave.
Tonawanda, NY. 14150
1-800-728-6999
www.scientificsonline.com

Gloryhole Fans

Johnstone Supply
www.johnstonesupply.com

Grainger Industrial Supply
www.grainger.com

Evidence of Glassmaking In Ancient Egypt Found

By Guy Gugliotta
Washington Post Staff Writer
Friday, June 17, 2005; Page A.03

Scientists said yesterday that they have unearthed the first conclusive evidence of a glass factory in ancient Egypt, offering new insights into production techniques for a commodity so highly prized that nobles used it interchangeably with gemstones.

Analyzing glass and clay fragments at Qantir-Piramesses in the eastern Nile Delta, researchers described a two-step process in which factories melted crushed quartz to form "semifinished" glass, then re-melted and colored it to make glass "ingots" for shipment to artisans elsewhere. They melted the glass again and shaped it into inlays, ornaments and other objects.

"For years, there was no direct evidence of the production of glass," said archaeologist Thilo Rehren of University College London. "Somebody was making it, but the only thing we had were museums full of glass objects."

Rehren, reporting in this week's edition of the journal Science, said he first visited Qantir 12 years ago to examine artifacts at the ruins of an ancient industrial complex dated 1250 B.C.

"There were lots of bronze castings, but among all the debris we found a number of things that didn't fit," Rehren said in a telephone interview. "It took me a year or two to figure out that the unusual finds were related to glass."

But it was not until additional excavations at Qantir in 2003 that researchers were able to say that Egypt had a thriving glassmaking industry of its own instead of simply importing glass from Mesopotamia. The Qantir artifacts have allowed archaeologists for the first time to show in detail how glass was made in the ancient world.

"We have thought that people were actually making glass in earlier excavations, but it has been very hard to interpret some of the evidence," said Egyptologist Christine Lilyquist of New York's Metropolitan Museum of Art. "Qantir is a very important excavation."

Common glass is made mostly of silicon dioxide – the same compound as quartz or sand – that has been melted and cooled rapidly so the molecules remain amorphous instead of forming a crystal lattice. Other compounds give glass its color or other properties.

Lilyquist said the first true glass appeared in Mesopotamia between 1600 B.C. and 1550 B.C. Ancient Egyptian texts describe how a pharaoh brought home skilled glassworkers, along with buckets of glass ingots, after a Mesopotamian expedition in 1500 B.C.

"The mainstream opinion was that the Egyptians were importing it from Mesopotamia," Rehren said. "In Egypt, we had only evidence that they were making it into artistic objects."

Glass was highly prized, not because it was inherently expensive but because "not that many people knew how to do it," Lilyquist said. Artisans used it as a gemstone equivalent in gold jewelry and in making small bottles, beads and sculptures.

It is unclear when glass production began in Egypt. At Amarna, archaeologists have found finished glass and intact furnaces from the time of the pharaoh Akhenaten, about 1350 B.C., but there is debate about whether the furnaces were for glass production or glassworking.

"We have wires of glass that are used for making objects, and it's true that glassworking doesn't necessarily mean glassmaking," said Cardiff University archaeologist Paul T. Nicholson, a glass expert who works at Amarna. "But I think we actually do have the factory."

Qantir, the ancient capital of the pharaoh Ramses II about 60 miles northeast of Cairo, has no intact furnaces or kilns but is littered with about 1,100 fragments of ceramic vessels marked by heat and frequently encrusted with bits of glass.

Rehren outlined a two-phase process that began by loading crushed quartz powder into half-gallon ceramic beer jars and heating it to about 1,650 degrees Fahrenheit. The quartz was mixed with an equal amount of ash from desert plants rich in sodium carbonate, which lowers the melting temperature of quartz.

Rehren said the artisans then crushed the semifinished glass into a powder and leached it with water to remove salt and other impurities. Then they put it into a flowerpot-shaped crucible and heated it to 2,000 degrees Fahrenheit, probably with the aid of a bellows.

"On the second melting, the gas bubbles disappear and you can get the colors," Rehren said. Qantir appears to have specialized in red glass, made by adding copper oxide during the second melting in carefully controlled amounts and conditions. Once cooled, the ceramic was broken and chipped off, and the ingots were sent away.

Richard La Londe   Workshop Firing Schedules

Paragon GL 24 brick kiln
hr. = hours   min. = minutes

Tempuratures will vary with different kilns, placement of pyrometers, and whether the kiln is high temperature fiber or brick.

Squeeze Bottle Technique (First Firing) fused to stick

8 in. (20 cm) x 8 in. (20 cm) tile,
6 mm clear bottom,
colored frit in raised lines on top,

 225°F (107°C) /hr. to
1100°F (593°C)
1 min. soak

 800°F (427°C) /hr. to
1310°F (710°C)
1 min. soak (fuse until barely sticks, no venting)

ASAP to
960°F (516°C)
1 hr. soak

off

Squeeze Bottle Technique (Second Firing) full fused

8 in. (20 cm) x 8 in. (20 cm) tile,
6mm clear flipped over, now on top
fused to stick frit on the bottom, Spray A on top

 225°F (107°C) /hr. to
1100°F (593°C)
1 min. soak

 800°F (427°C) /hr. to
1500°F (816°C)
3 min. soak

ASAP to
960°F (516°C)
1 hr. soak

off

Clear Frit Overlay Technique

8 in. (20 cm) x 8 in. (20 cm) tile,
3mm clear bottom on chips
colored design & clear frit second layer

 330°F (166°C) /hr. to
1100°F (593°C)
1 min. soak

 500°F (260°C) /hr. to
1500°F (816°C)
2 min. soak

ASAP to
960°F (516°C)
1 hr. soak

off

Frit on the Shelf Technique

8 in. (20 cm) x 8 in. (20 cm) tile,
6mm clear on top,
colored frit on kiln shelf,

 225°F (107°C) /hr. to
1100°F (593°C)
1 min. soak

 800°F (427°C) /hr. to
1500°F (816°C)
4 min. soak

ASAP to
960°F (516°C)
1 hr. soak

off

Clear Frit Overlay Foil Technique

8 in. (20 cm) x 8 in. (20 cm) tile,
3mm tile on clear bottom on chips
colored design & clear frit second layer.

  330°F (166°C) /hr. to
1100°F (593°C)
1 min. soak

  500°F (260°C) /hr. to
1500°F (816°C)
2 min. soak

ASAP
960°F (516°C)
1 hr. soak

off

Slump Frit Technique

6 ½ in. (16.5 cm) x 6 ½ in. (16.5) cm tile
frit design on 3mm clear, sagged into a ring mold

  700°F (371°C) /hr. to
1100°F (593°C)
1 min. soak

ASAP to
1390°F (754°C) - 1440°F (782°C)
watch piece until desired sag achieved.

then vent down to 1050°F (566°C) then

ASAP to
960°F (516°C)
30 min. soak

off (vent after annealing to get pieces out of the
kiln fast, to take home)

Glory Hole Bundles

Bundles: cut strips ½ in. (12 mm) x 4 ¾ in.
(12 cm) long, make 3 strips wide by 12 strips
high to make a bundle 1/½ in. (4 cm) x 1 ½ in.
(4 cm) x 4 ¾ in. (12 cm), put between kiln shelf
dams

  800°F (427°C) /hr. to
1100°F (593°C)
1 min. soak

ASAP to
1385°F (752°C)
15 min. soak (check to see if the strips are stuck
together but not melted too much)

ASAP
1015°F (546°C)
hold in kiln for pick up

Annealing For Canes

1015°F (546°C)
hold in kiln for pick up, after the canes are
loaded then

ASAP to
960°F (516°C)
1 hr. soak

  50°F (10°C) to
760°F (516°C)
1 min. soak

125°F (52°C) /hr. to
150°F (66°C)
1 min. soak

off

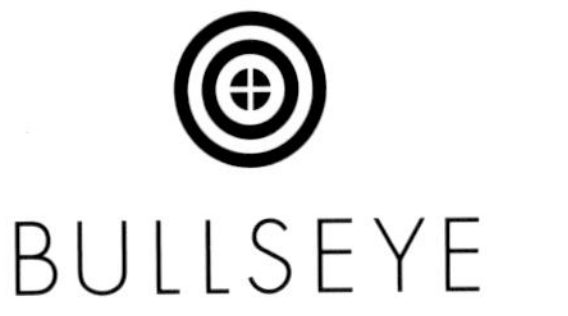

ANNEALING THICK SLABS

This annealing chart has been formulated for use with Bullseye clear glass. It is derived from Corning's method as shown in McLellan and Shand.[1] It is based on a flat slab of uniform thickness that is set up in such a fashion that it can cool equally from top and bottom.

If the piece is not set up in such a fashion that it can cool equally from top and bottom or is anything besides a flat slab of uniform thickness, select an annealing cycle for a piece that is twice the thickness of the thickest area of the piece.

Even a very conservative annealing cycle may not work if the kiln is not capable of cooling evenly.

For more Bullseye technical and product information see **www.bullseyeglass.com**

---

[1] McLellan and Shand (1984), *Glass Engineering Handbook*, 3rd Edition, New York, McGraw Hill

THICKNESS inches mm	ANNEAL SOAK TIME @ 960 °F/516 °C	INITIAL COOLING RATE °F/hr °C/hr	INITIAL COOLING RANGE °F °C	2nd COOLING RATE °F/hr °C/hr	2nd COOLING RANGE °F °C	FINAL COOLING RATE °F/hr °C/hr	FINAL COOLING RANGE °F °C	TOTAL MINIMUM TIME Hours
0.5 in	2 hr	100	960 – 800	180	800 – 700	600	700 – 70	6 hr
12 mm		55	516 – 427	99	427 – 371	330	371 – 21	
0.75 in	3 hr	45	960 – 800	81	800 – 700	270	700 – 70	10 hr
19 mm		25	516 – 427	45	427 – 371	150	371 – 21	
1.0 in	4 hr	27	960 – 800	49	800 – 700	162	700 – 70	16 hr
25 mm		15	516 – 427	27	427 – 371	90	371 – 21	
1.5 in	6 hr	12	960 – 800	22	800 – 700	72	700 – 70	33 hr
38 mm		6.7	516 – 427	12	427 – 371	40	371 – 21	
2.0 in	8 hr	6.8	960 – 800	12	800 – 700	41	700 – 70	56 hr
50 mm		3.8	516 – 427	6.8	427 – 371	22	371 – 21	
2.5 in	10 hr	4.3	960 – 800	8	800 – 700	26	700 – 70	84 hr
62 mm		2.4	516 – 427	4.3	427 – 371	14.4	371 – 21	
3.0 in	12 hr	3	960 – 800	5.4	800 – 700	18	700 – 70	119 hr
75 mm		1.7	516 – 427	3.1	427 – 371	10	371 – 21	
4.0 in	16 hr	1.7	960 – 780	3.1	780 – 680	10	680 – 70	216 hr
100 mm		0.94	516 – 416	1.7	416 – 360	5.6	360 – 21	
6.0 in	24 hr	0.75	960 – 760	1.3	760 – 660	4.5	660 – 70	499 hr
150 mm		0.42	516 – 404	0.76	404 – 349	2.5	349 – 21	
8.0 in	32 hr	0.42	960 – 740	0.76	740 – 640	2.5	640 – 70	916 hr
200 mm		0.23	516 – 393	0.42	393 – 338	1.4	338 – 21	

 Reprinted by permission from the Bullseye Glass Company, Portland, Oregon 2006

(Primary reference marked in **bold**)

index

Mr. Maglue and the Antidiscaboberator

Mr. Maglue and his dog Troby (robot dog), were walking along in
the park one day when Mr. Maglue thought of a new machine.
They rushed home and he started working on it.
After the body was made, he put the anti tubes together with the dis
tubes. He put the cabobe tube in and he connected it with the rator
and he finished the machine.
He called it the antidiscoboberator machine. He found out that it
would only do nothing. He kicked it and it started to cry.
He renamed it the human machine and he gave it to Troby to keep
company for him.

Ricky La Londe 1959 (5th grade)

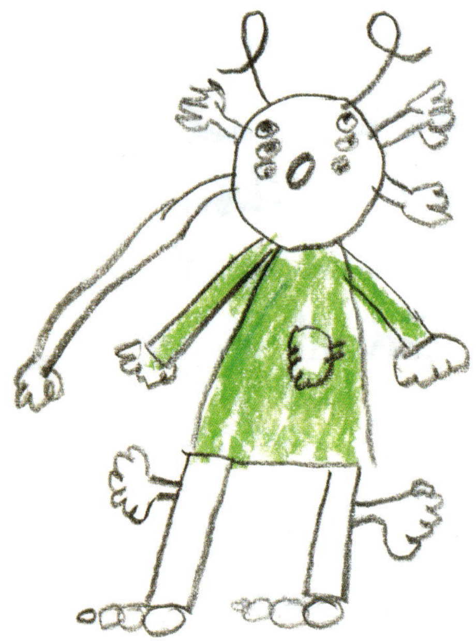

Creativity is a lifelong pursuit, aways keep it hot!

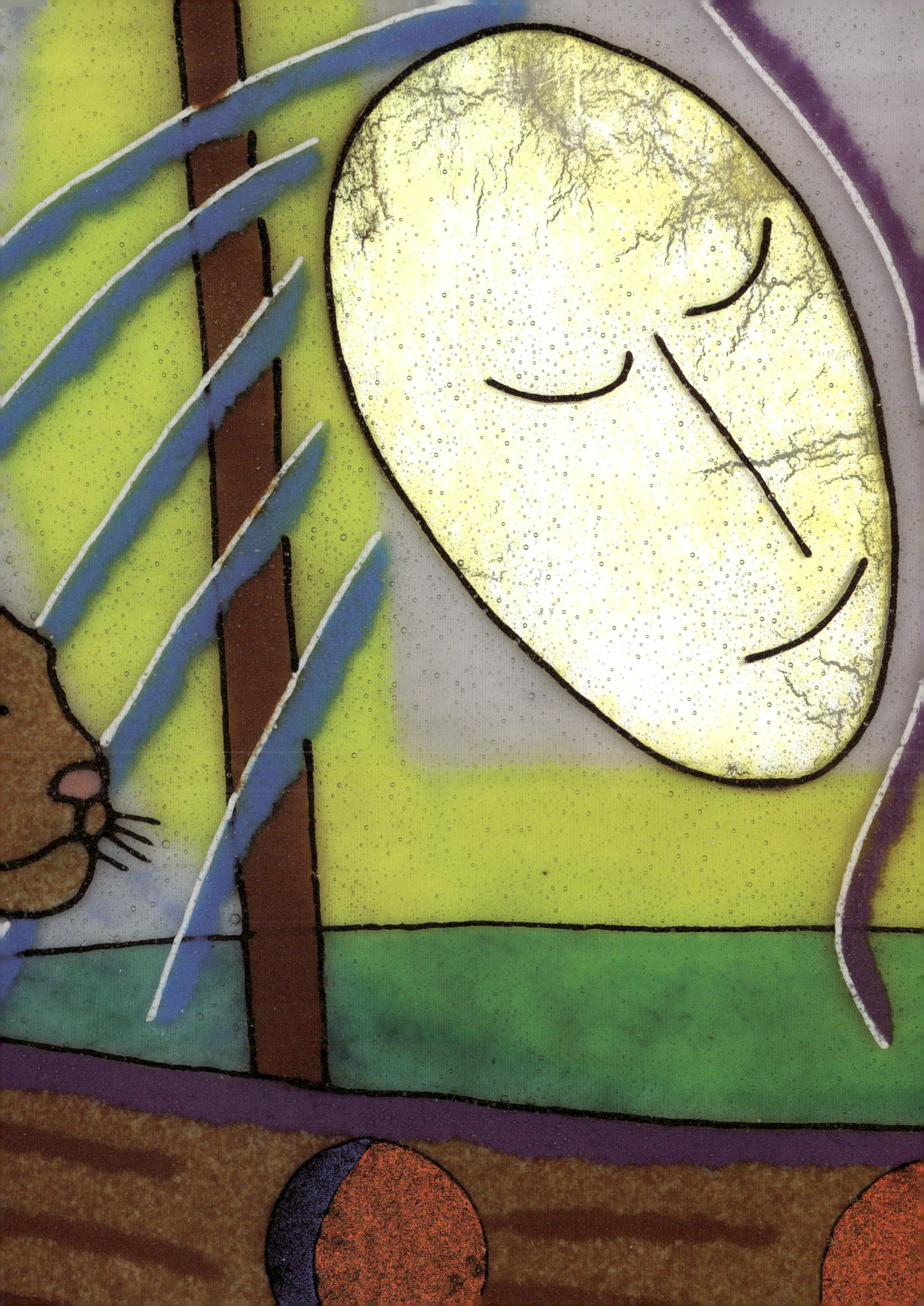

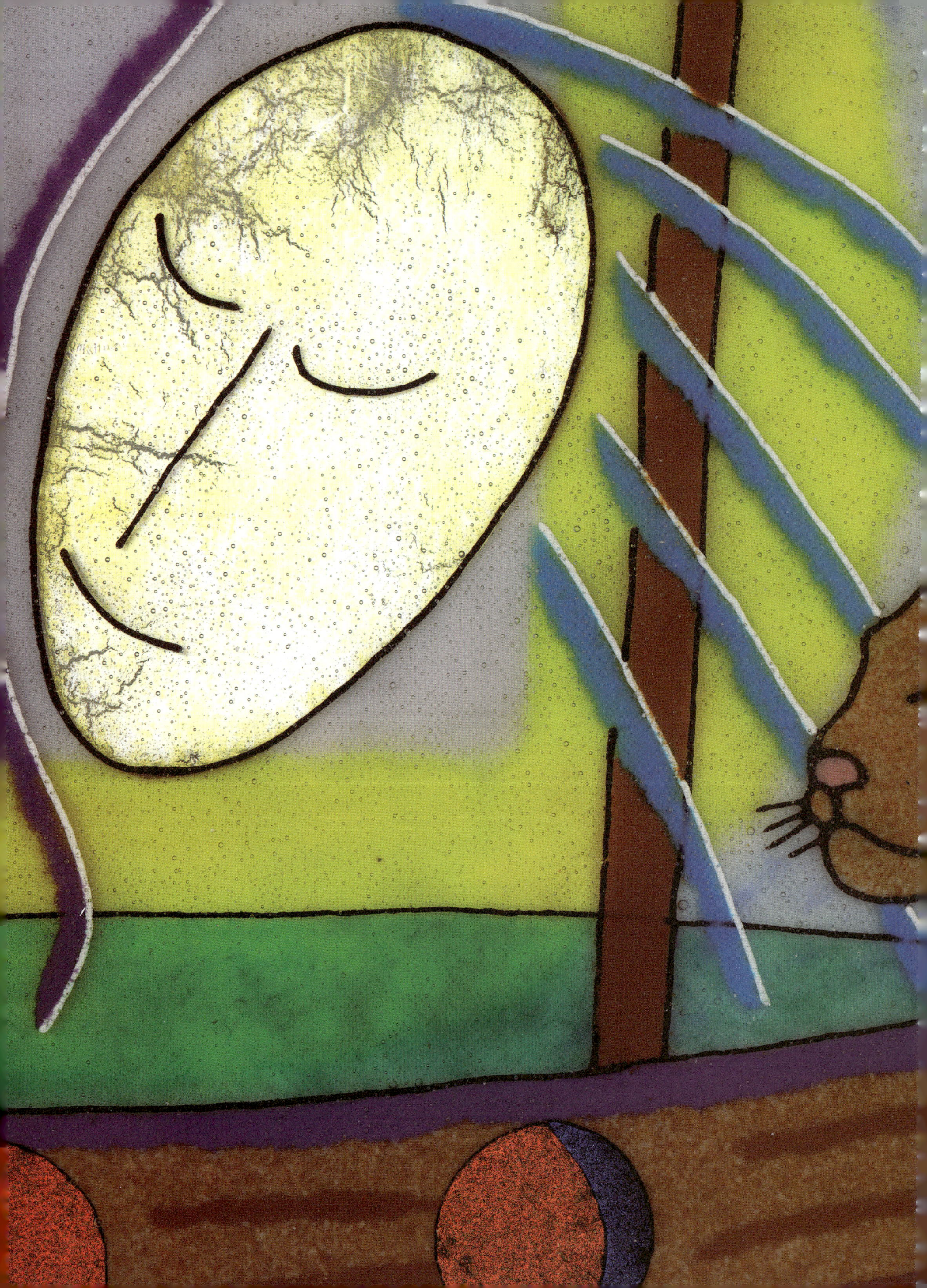